Frommer's® Washington, D.C.

My Washington, D.C.

by Elise Ford

"FOUR SCORE AND SEVEN YEARS AGO, OUR FATHERS BROUGHT FORTH on this continent, a new nation, conceived in Liberty . . ." Reading these words from Lincoln's Gettysburg Address, etched on the walls of the Lincoln Memorial, is just one of the many experiences in D.C. that evokes the inspiring idealism on which America was founded.

Grand monuments, historic structures, and memorials mark the U.S. capital like stars in a constellation. You can look up and search for the tip of the Washington Monument, point to the Capitol dome lit up at night, or spy the Washington National Cathedral's spires in the distance. From Capitol Hill to Georgetown's cobblestone streets to the stately embassies on Massachusetts Avenue, past, present, and future collide in this city. Basketball fans cheer at the MCI Center while music lovers applaud at the Kennedy Center. A jazz club is in the Smithsonian's National Museum of Natural History and an Irish pub is in Chinatown.

Tourism officials have dubbed Washington, D.C., "The American Experience," which makes it sound like a static historical diorama. Of course, the city's history is formidable, but D.C. continues to thrive and evolve, nourished by diverse communities bursting with political and cultural energy. And the photos on these pages show the city at its best.

IN THIS TEMPLE
AS IN THE HEARTS OF THE PEOPLE
FOR WHOM HE SAVED THE UNION
THE MEMORY OF ABRAHAM LINCOLN
FOREVER

© Chuck Pefley/Alamy

© Jeff Tinsley/National Museum of the American Indian

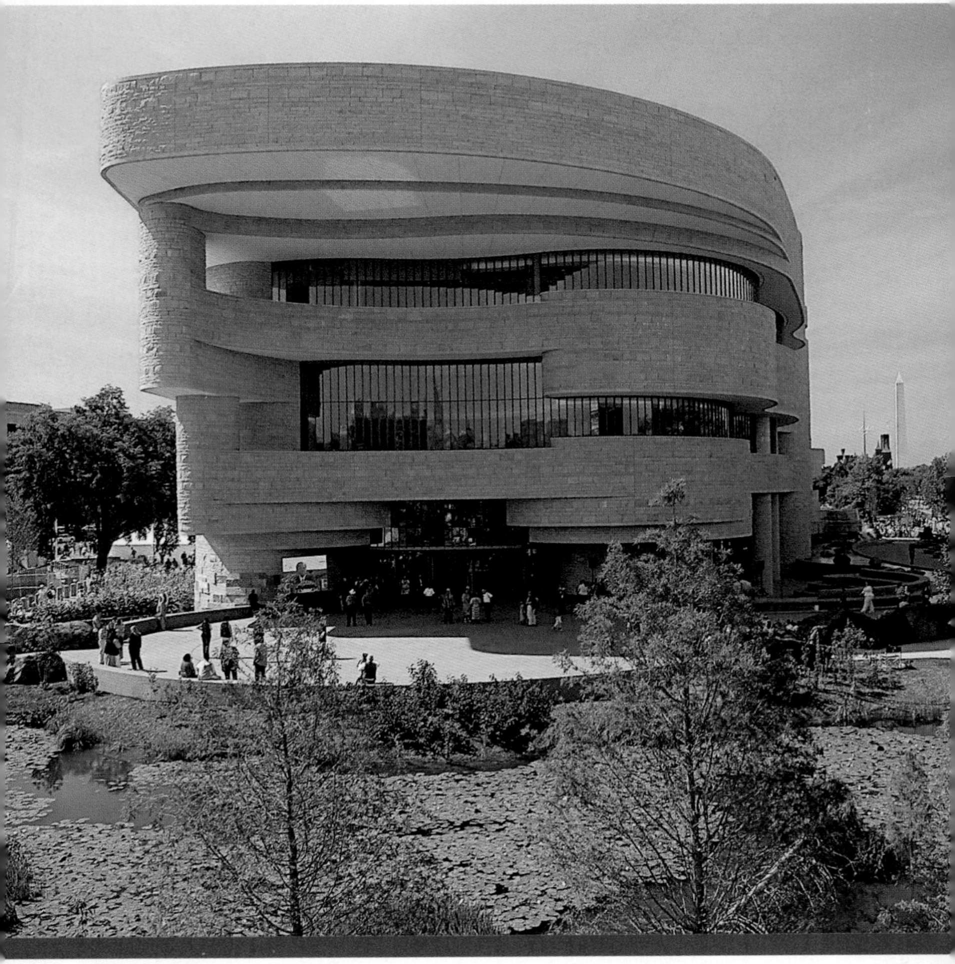

Lots of people think the best time to visit the **LINCOLN MEMORIAL (left)** is at night, when it's lit up and dramatic. Romantic, too. But I like visiting during the day—swallowed up in the crush of chattering international travelers and curious school children—and feeling oh-so-proud of being linked by nationality to this remarkable American, considered by many to be the country's greatest president.

On September 21, 2004, 25,000 Native Americans representing 400 tribes from all over the Western Hemisphere marched and danced down the National Mall—to the beat of drums and thunderous applause from more than 55,000 spectators—to herald the opening of the **NATIONAL MUSEUM OF THE AMERICAN INDIAN (above)**. When you visit, be sure to admire every detail—from the windswept-look exterior to the Indian fried bread served in the museum cafe.

First page: top, © Robert Harding Picture Library Ltd./Alamy; bottom, © David Brooks/Corbis

PAUL D CARTER • JOSEPH D ESPARZA • THOMAS W KNUCKEY
CHERRY • JOSEPH E SWEENEY • DONALD R MATHIS
MUSIL Sr • MITCHELL O BARNES • JOSE MARIA R ARREDONDO
JACKSON • GARY J SHINN • ROY M SEABROOK
PAUL G MAGERS • AUGUSTUS ADAMS • WAYNE S CRAIG
JAMES R SAXON • DENNIS L MEDUNA • JACK W BRUNSON
EDWARD A WERMAN • ANDREW C STRONG III • GEORGE H GLAWSON
GEORGE H POTTS • EDGAR D THOMAS
BOYD • JOSE ANGEL SANCHEZ
TORRES-RAMOS • LEM CLARK
WILLIAM K TAYLOR • BILLY H WYATT • EDMOND T BALLANCE
BORCHERS • MARTIN E LOVING • MICHAEL R STREET • BERNARD BARNES
ANTHONY M EILERS • JERRY L THOMAS • MAURICE H BRYANT
JOHN R MICKLE • THOMAS E EPPERSON • STEPHEN K MASDEN
JOHNNY ARTHUR • CARL W BREWSTER
LOYD E ROBINSON
CHARLES A SANCHEZ • GARY L WESTPHAL
JEFFREY D SCHUMACHER • EARL R LESTER Jr
WILLIAM T WALSH • DEE BERGERA
WAYNE A GARBER • RICHARD WILSON Jr
BILLY D PEDINGS • JAMES R VALTR
DANNY G STUDDARD • TERRY L KELLY
ERNEST D HART Jr • JOHN T DOZIER II
RAYMOND V DEBLASIO • ROGER E WITTE
BARRY A BIDWELL
JOHNSON • JOHN E LEIS
JOHNNY SOTO • CHARLES D MEIZNER
MADISON
HAROLD J RITCH
CHARLES A POPPLETON
ROBERT D BEUTEL
JAMES H SPANN
BILLY RAY COFFEY
OSCAR PAULLEY Jr
WILLIAM D THOMPSON

These are the words of my husband Jim, a veteran of the Vietnam War, to those who visit the **VIETNAM VETERANS MEMORIAL (left):** Run your fingers over the names of the lost inscribed here. Observe the reflections of others tracing a particular name. Notice the impromptu memorials left along the wall—flowers, a set of dog tags, an old photo, a faded combat badge. And listen to the murmurs of other visitors in an ongoing parade along the wall since November 13, 1982, when the memorial was dedicated.

Of all the war memorials, the **KOREAN WAR VETERANS MEMORIAL,** dedicated in 1995, moves me the most on a visceral level. The lifelike statues of 19 men, weighed down by their gear, appear to be trudging through a field. Surrounded by juniper bushes (symbolic of Korea's rugged terrain) and covered in ponchos (a reminder of the foul weather they endured), they convey in their wary poses both cold fear and courage.

© Jake Rajs/Getty Images

It can be hard to get through the doors of the **LIBRARY OF CONGRESS READING ROOM (left),** thanks to security procedures. But once you're in, patient volunteer docents treat you like you're the first one to ask how to get to the Reading Room Gallery overlook, where to find the Gutenberg Bible, and how one registers to use the Reading Room. The best-kept secret is the lineup of engaging lectures, concerts, and films the Library hosts, mostly in the evenings; see the list on www.loc.gov.

"Meet you at the elephant." Translation: Meet you in the Rotunda of the **NATIONAL MUSEUM OF NATURAL HISTORY (below).** Washingtonians and visitors alike love these hard-to-miss museum landmarks as places to rendezvous and opportunities to marvel. This natural history museum is the largest in the world, with more than 124 million artifacts—including the legendary Hope Diamond—and yet it's only one of the Smithsonian Institution's 15 museums.

© Andre Jenny/Alamy

© William S. Kuta/Alamy

I would have preferred a museum that honored our soldiers by telling their stories, the way my dad recalls his time as a POW after being captured at the Battle of the Bulge. But the still powerful **NATIONAL WORLD WAR II MEMORIAL (above)** honors those who fought and died in the war with a pavilion of 56 granite pillars (one for each state and territory); 24 bas-relief panels illustrating scenes from the Atlantic and Pacific theaters; and a wall of 4,000 gold stars—one for each 100 soldiers who perished.

At the grounds of the **WASHINGTON NATIONAL CATHEDRAL (right)**, you can pack a picnic and get comfortable on the lawn of the Bishop's Garden. Inside this sixth largest cathedral in the world, you can admire the stained glass windows, stare up at the parade of state flags arrayed high up along the walls, and listen to an organ practice (every Mon and Wed 12:30–1pm).

© Richard Cummins/Lonely Planet Images

© Jen Reilly

At **TRYST CAFÉ (above)** in Adams Morgan—an eclectic, comfy coffeehouse/lounge—patrons hook up to laptops, cellphones, and lattes during the day, and connect with each other, over cocktails, at night. Every Wednesday evening a jazz band plays for free.

Beautiful ballets grace the stage at the **KENNEDY CENTER (right),** along with the best opera, orchestra, and theater performances. You'll also find free concerts, affordable family events, and $25-per-person jazz shows. Above all, I love the center's celebratory festivals, which range from Chinese culture to American country music.

© Susana Raab/Corbis

opposite page: © William S. Helsel/Getty Images

Everyone should join the crowds on the National Mall at least once for Independence Day. Among the festivities are a parade down Constitution Avenue and a reading of the Declaration of Independence in front of the National Archives. The evening culminates in a tremendous **FOURTH OF JULY FIREWORKS DISPLAY,** set off over the Washington Monument in time to the National Symphony Orchestra's renditions of "The 1812 Overture" and "Stars and Stripes Forever."

After dining at one of **GEORGETOWN**'s **(left)** great restaurants or browsing in one of its well-known shops, I like to stroll though the neighborhood's quieter pretty parts—where dollhouse-ish dwellings and grande-dame mansions line up behind brick sidewalks. Who lives here, I wonder as I stroll by, and who lived here 200 years ago? And how ever do they fit furniture through those narrow doors?

Traveling through **ROCK CREEK PARK** **(above)**—whether on foot, bike, or by car—one can reach the National Zoo, the Kennedy Center, and neighborhoods from Foggy Bottom and Georgetown all the way to Cleveland Park and Chevy Chase. It's a haven, beautiful in every season, and it's the one place you'll see Washingtonians of all stripes, unplugged and relaxed.

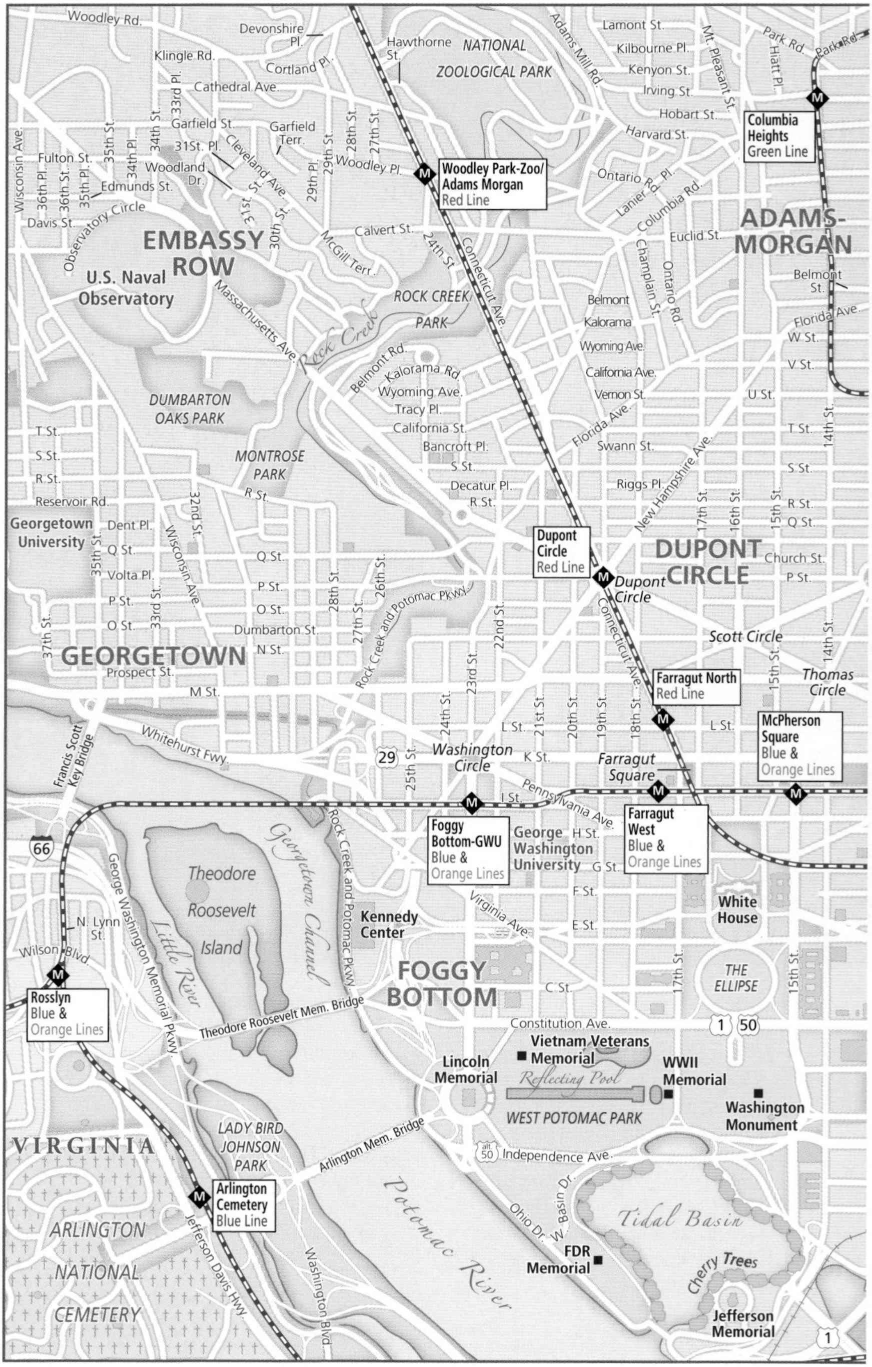

Woodley Rd.
Devonshire Pl.
Klingle Rd.
Hawthorne St.
NATIONAL ZOOLOGICAL PARK
Cortland Pl.
Cathedral Ave.
Adams Mill Rd.
Lamont St.
Kilbourne Pl.
Kenyon St.
Irving St.
Hobart St.
Harvard St.
Mt. Pleasant St.
Park Rd.
Hiatt Pl.
Columbia Heights
Green Line
Garfield St.
Garfield Terr.
31St. Pl.
Cleveland Ave.
Woodland Dr.
Woodley Pl.
Woodley Park-Zoo/
Adams Morgan
Red Line
Fulton St.
Edmunds St.
Davis St.
Observatory Circle
Wisconsin Ave.
36th Pl.
36th St.
35th Pl.
35th St.
34th Pl.
34th St.
33rd Pl.
31st. St.
30th St.
29th Pl.
29th St.
28th St.
27th St.
Ontario Rd.
Lanier Pl.
Columbia Rd.
Euclid St.
ADAMS-MORGAN
EMBASSY ROW
U.S. Naval Observatory
Calvert St.
McGill Terr.
24th St.
Connecticut Ave.
Champlain St.
Ontario Rd.
Belmont St.
Massachusetts Ave.
ROCK CREEK PARK
Rock Creek
Belmont
Kalorama
Wyoming Ave.
California Ave.
Vernon St.
Florida Ave.
W St.
V St.
U St.
Belmont Rd.
Kalorama Rd.
Wyoming Ave.
Tracy Pl.
California St.
Bancroft Pl.
S St.
Decatur Pl.
R St.
DUMBARTON OAKS PARK
MONTROSE PARK
Florida Ave.
Swann St.
Riggs Pl.
New Hampshire Ave.
T St.
S St.
R St.
Reservoir Rd.
Georgetown University
Dent Pl.
Q St.
Volta Pl.
P St.
O St.
32nd St.
Wisconsin Ave.
Q St.
P St.
O St.
Dumbarton St.
N St.
28th St.
27th St.
26th St.
Rock Creek and Potomac Pkwy.
22nd St.
Dupont Circle
Red Line
Dupont Circle
DUPONT CIRCLE
17th St.
16th St.
15th St.
14th St.
Church St.
P St.
Scott Circle
Thomas Circle
37th St.
GEORGETOWN
Prospect St.
M St.
23rd St.
Farragut North
Red Line
Francis Scott Key Bridge
Whitehurst Fwy.
24th St.
21st St.
20th St.
19th St.
18th St.
L St.
McPherson Square
Blue &
Orange Lines
29
25th St.
Washington Circle
K St.
Farragut Square
I St.
Pennsylvania Ave.
66
Foggy Bottom-GWU
Blue &
Orange Lines
George Washington University
H St.
G St.
Farragut West
Blue &
Orange Lines
Georgetown Channel
Rock Creek and Potomac Pkwy
George Washington Memorial Pkwy.
Theodore Roosevelt Island
Little River
N. Lynn St.
Wilson Blvd.
Kennedy Center
Virginia Ave.
F St.
E St.
White House
FOGGY BOTTOM
C St.
THE ELLIPSE
Rosslyn
Blue &
Orange Lines
Theodore Roosevelt Mem. Bridge
Constitution Ave.
1
50
Vietnam Veterans Memorial
Lincoln Memorial
Reflecting Pool
WWII Memorial
Washington Monument
WEST POTOMAC PARK
VIRGINIA
LADY BIRD JOHNSON PARK
Arlington Mem. Bridge
alt. 50
Independence Ave.
Arlington Cemetery
Blue Line
Potomac River
Ohio Dr.
W. Basin Dr.
Tidal Basin
ARLINGTON NATIONAL CEMETERY
Jefferson Davis Hwy.
Washington Blvd.
FDR Memorial
Cherry Trees
Jefferson Memorial
1

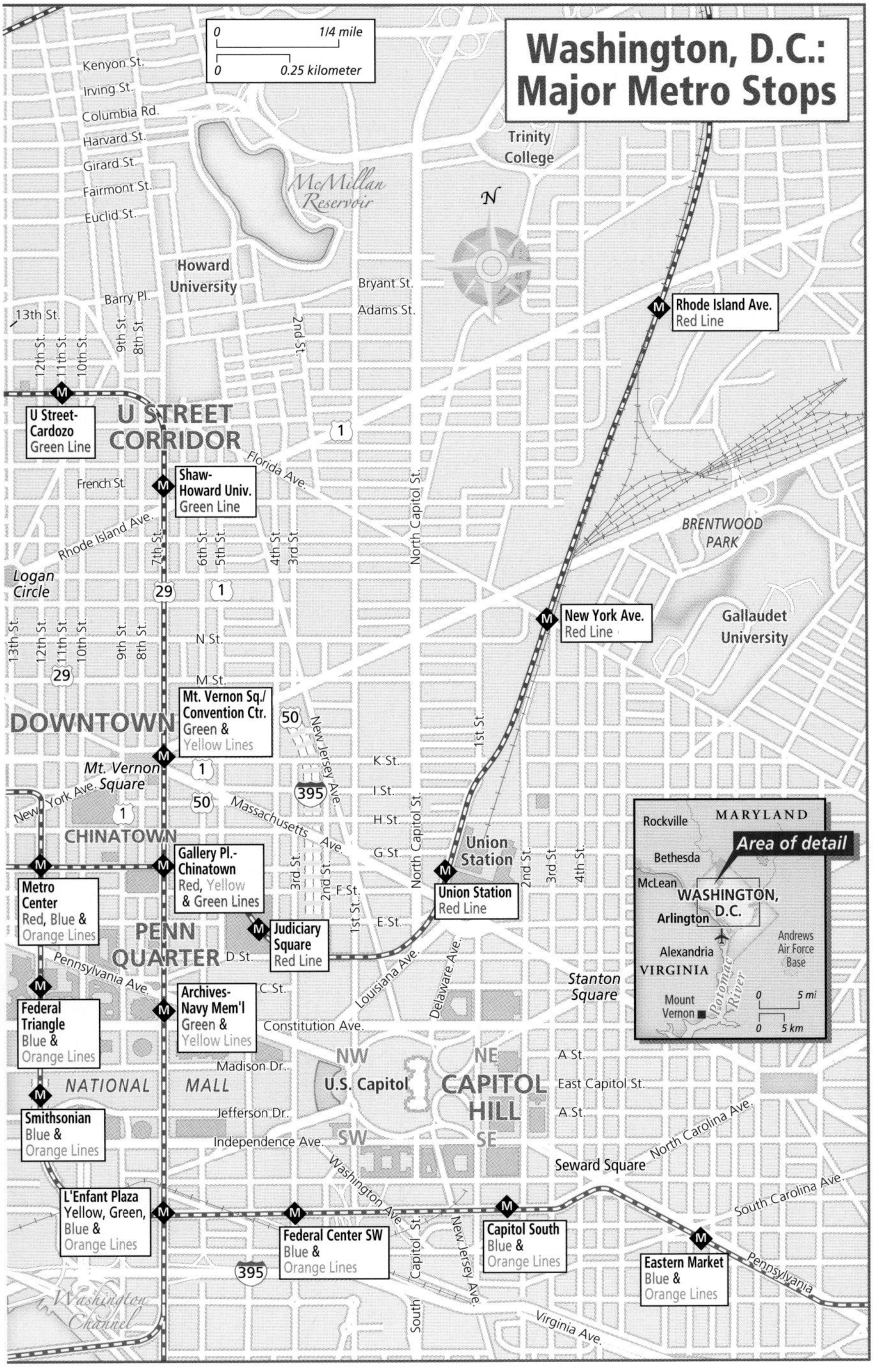

Washington, D.C.: Major Metro Stops
0 1/4 mile
0 0.25 kilometer
Kenyon St.
Irving St.
Columbia Rd.
Harvard St.
Girard St.
Fairmont St.
Euclid St.
McMillan Reservoir
Trinity College
N
Howard University
Bryant St.
Adams St.
Barry Pl.
13th St.
12th St.
11th St.
10th St.
9th St.
8th St.
2nd St.
Rhode Island Ave.
Red Line
U Street-Cardozo
Green Line
U STREET CORRIDOR
Florida Ave.
Shaw-Howard Univ.
Green Line
French St.
Rhode Island Ave.
7th St.
6th St.
5th St.
4th St.
3rd St.
North Capitol St.
BRENTWOOD PARK
Logan Circle
New York Ave.
Red Line
Gallaudet University
N St.
M St.
Mt. Vernon Sq./Convention Ctr.
Green & Yellow Lines
DOWNTOWN
New Jersey Ave.
1st St.
K St.
Mt. Vernon Square
New York Ave.
I St.
H St.
Massachusetts Ave.
CHINATOWN
Union Station
G St.
Gallery Pl.-Chinatown
Red, Yellow & Green Lines
Metro Center
Red, Blue & Orange Lines
F St.
Union Station
Red Line
Judiciary Square
Red Line
E St.
PENN QUARTER
D St.
Pennsylvania Ave.
Louisiana Ave.
Delaware Ave.
C St.
Stanton Square
Federal Triangle
Blue & Orange Lines
Archives-Navy Mem'l
Green & Yellow Lines
Constitution Ave.
Madison Dr.
NW
NE
A St.
NATIONAL MALL
U.S. Capitol
CAPITOL HILL
East Capitol St.
Smithsonian
Blue & Orange Lines
Jefferson Dr.
Independence Ave.
SW
SE
North Carolina Ave.
Seward Square
Washington Ave.
South Carolina Ave.
L'Enfant Plaza
Yellow, Green, Blue & Orange Lines
Federal Center SW
Blue & Orange Lines
Capitol South
Blue & Orange Lines
Eastern Market
Blue & Orange Lines
Pennsylvania
South Capitol St.
New Jersey Ave.
Virginia Ave.
Washington Channel
MARYLAND
Rockville
Area of detail
Bethesda
McLean
WASHINGTON, D.C.
Arlington
Andrews Air Force Base
Alexandria
VIRGINIA
Potomac River
Mount Vernon
0 5 mi
0 5 km

ATTRACTION	METRO STOP
Air and Space Museum	L'Enfant Plaza
Arena Stage	Waterfront
Arlington Cemetery	Arlington Cemetery
Bureau of Engraving & Printing	Smithsonian
Capitol Building	Capitol South
Capitol Children's Museum	Union Station
Convention Center (Old)	Metro Center
Convention Center (New)	Mount Vernon Sq-7th
Corcoran Gallery	Farragut West
Discovery Theatre	Smithsonian
Federal Bureau of Investigation	Archives
Ford's Theatre	Metro Center
Freer Gallery	Smithsonian
Hirshhorn Museum	L'Enfant Plaza
Holocaust Museum	Smithsonian
House Where Lincoln Died	Metro Center
Iwo Jima Memorial	Arlington Cemetery
Kennedy Center	Foggy Bottom-GWU
Korean War Memorial	Foggy Bottom-GWU
Library of Congress	Capitol South
Lincoln Memorial	Foggy Bottom-GWU
Mazza Gallerie/Chevy Chase Pavillion/Chevy Chase	Friendship Heights
MCI Center	Gallery Pl-Chinatown
Nat'l Aquarium	Federal Triangle
Nat'l Archives	Archives-Navy Mem'l
Nat'l Gallery of Art	Archives-Navy Mem'l
Nat'l Geographic Society	Farragut North
Nat'l Museum of African Art	Smithsonian
Nat'l Museum of Natural History	Smithsonian
Nat'l Museum of Women in Arts	Metro Center
Nat'l Postal Museum	Union Station
Nat'l Theater	Metro Center
Nat'l Zoo	Cleveland Park
Pavillion at the Old Post Office	Federal Triangle
Pentagon	Pentagon
Phillips Gallery	Dupont Circle
Ronald Reagan Nat'l Airport	Nat'l Airport
Renwick Gallery	Farragut West
Sackler Gallery	Smithsonian
Shakespeare Theater	Archives Navy Mem'l
Shops at Union Station	Union Station
Smithsonian Castle	Smithsonian
Supreme Court	Capitol South
Textile Museum	Dupont Circle
Vietnam Veterans Memorial	Foggy Bottom-GWU
Warner Theater	Metro Center
Washington Monument	Smithsonian
White House	McPherson Square
White House Visitor Center	Federal Triangle
Woodrow Wilson House	Dupont Circle

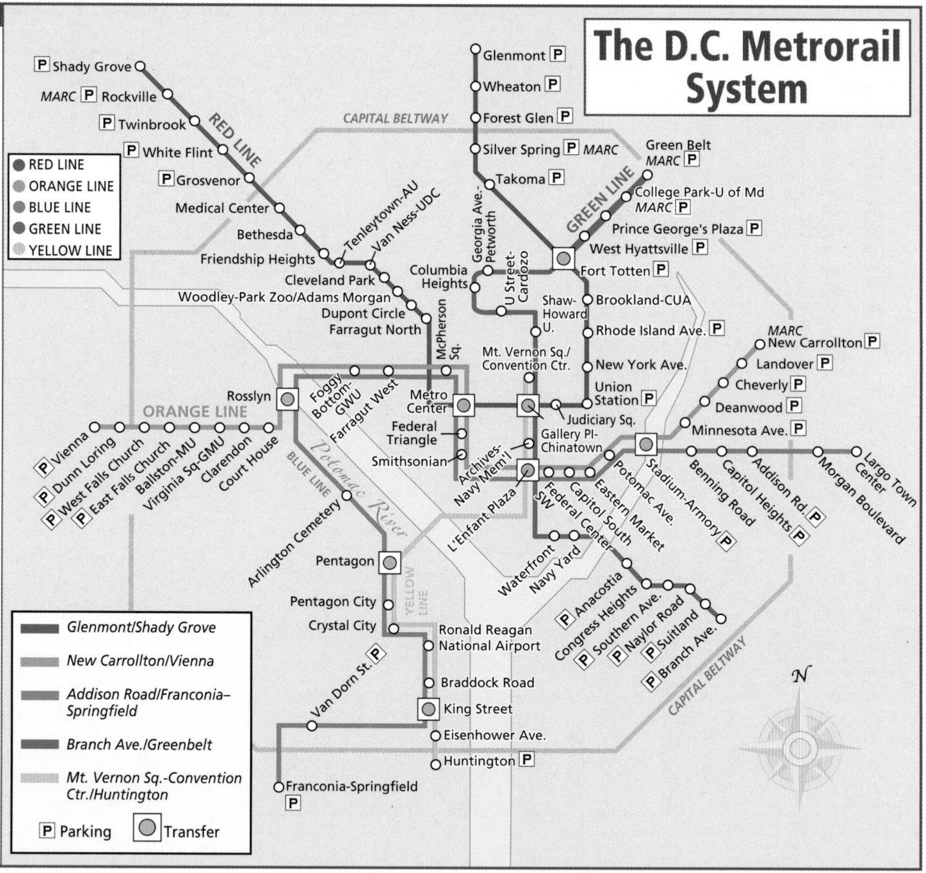

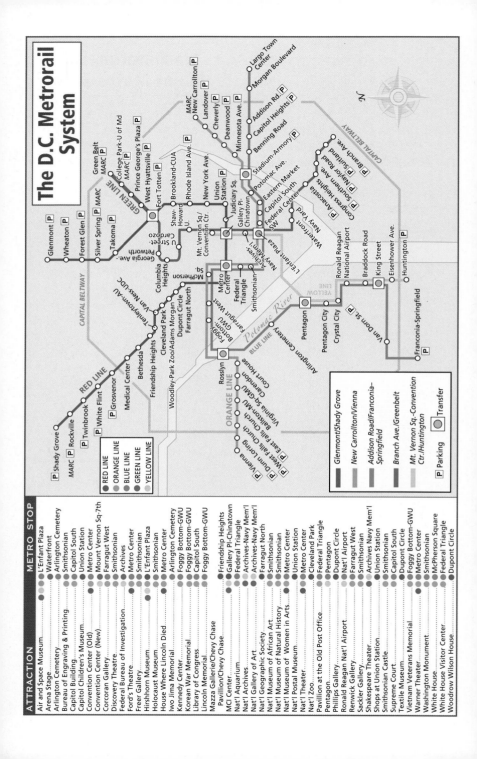

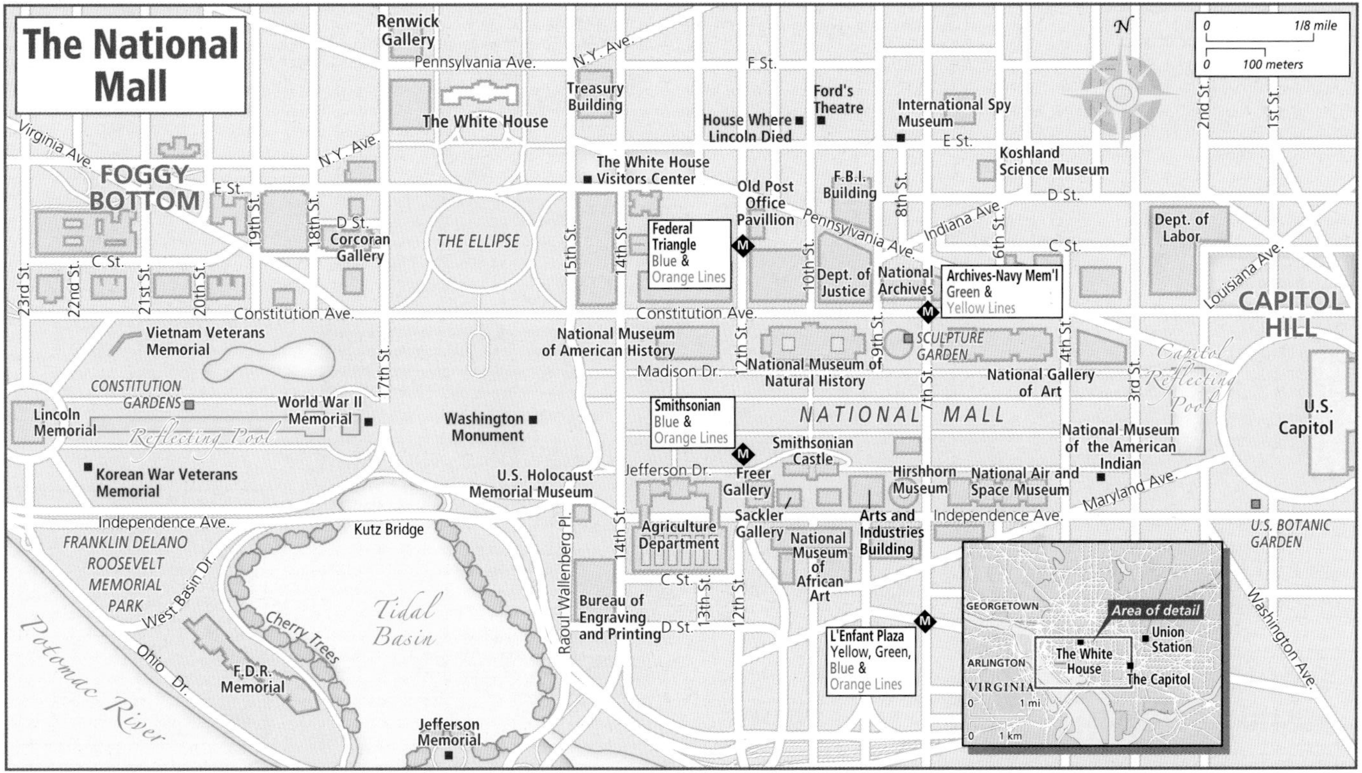
The National Mall
Renwick Gallery
Pennsylvania Ave.
N.Y. Ave.
F St.
Treasury Building
The White House
Ford's Theatre
House Where Lincoln Died
International Spy Museum
E St.
Koshland Science Museum
D St.
Virginia Ave.
FOGGY BOTTOM
E St.
19th St.
18th St.
D St.
Corcoran Gallery
THE ELLIPSE
The White House Visitors Center
15th St.
14th St.
Federal Triangle
Blue & Orange Lines
Old Post Office Pavillion
F.B.I. Building
8th St.
Pennsylvania Ave.
Indiana Ave.
6th St.
C St.
Dept. of Labor
Louisiana Ave.
CAPITOL HILL
23rd St.
22nd St.
C St.
21st St.
20th St.
10th St.
Dept. of Justice
National Archives
Archives-Navy Mem'l
Green & Yellow Lines
Constitution Ave.
Constitution Ave.
Vietnam Veterans Memorial
National Museum of American History
12th St.
National Museum of Natural History
9th St.
SCULPTURE GARDEN
4th St.
Capitol Reflecting Pool
Madison Dr.
7th St.
National Gallery of Art
3rd St.
CONSTITUTION GARDENS
17th St.
World War II Memorial
Lincoln Memorial
Reflecting Pool
Washington Monument
Smithsonian
Blue & Orange Lines
NATIONAL MALL
U.S. Capitol
National Museum of the American Indian
Korean War Veterans Memorial
U.S. Holocaust Memorial Museum
Jefferson Dr.
Smithsonian Castle
Freer Gallery
Hirshhorn Museum
National Air and Space Museum
Maryland Ave.
Independence Ave.
Kutz Bridge
Raoul Wallenberg Pl.
14th St.
Agriculture Department
Sackler Gallery
Arts and Industries Building
Independence Ave.
U.S. BOTANIC GARDEN
FRANKLIN DELANO ROOSEVELT MEMORIAL PARK
West Basin Dr.
National Museum of African Art
C St.
13th St.
12th St.
Bureau of Engraving and Printing
D St.
Tidal Basin
Cherry Trees
Potomac River
Ohio Dr.
F.D.R. Memorial
Jefferson Memorial
L'Enfant Plaza
Yellow, Green, Blue & Orange Lines
Washington Ave.
GEORGETOWN
Area of detail
Union Station
ARLINGTON
The White House
The Capitol
VIRGINIA
0 1 mi
0 1 km
0 1/8 mile
0 100 meters
N
2nd St.
1st St.

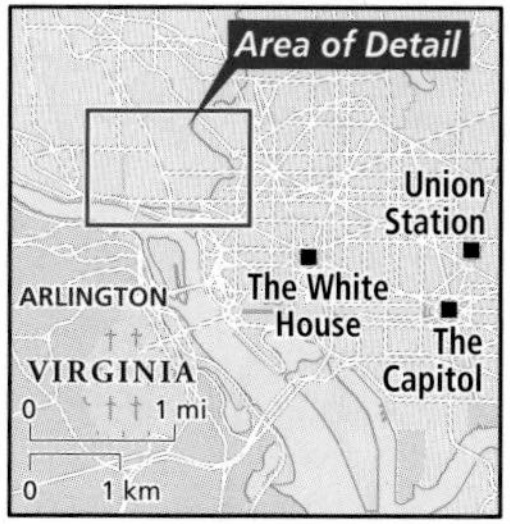

1 Dumbarton House
2 Evermay
3 Tudor Place
4 Dumbarton Oaks
5 3238 R Street NW
6 3307 N Street NW
7 Cox's Row
8 Halcyon House
9 Prospect House

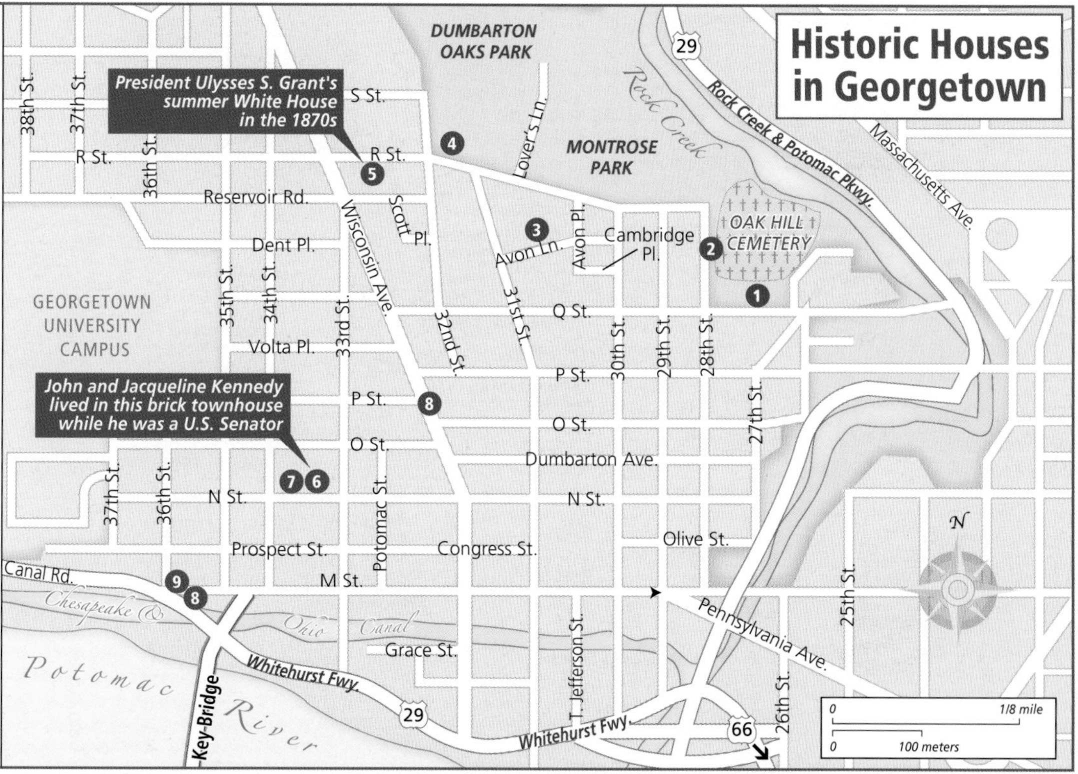

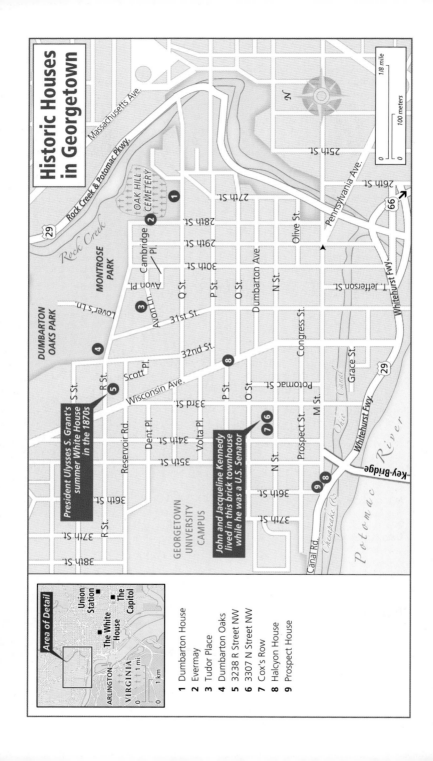

Frommer's®

Washington, D.C. 2008

by Elise Hartman Ford

Here's what the critics say about Frommer's:

"Amazingly easy to use. Very portable, very complete."

—*Booklist*

"Detailed, accurate, and easy-to-read information for all price ranges."

—*Glamour Magazine*

"Hotel information is close to encyclopedic."

—*Des Moines Sunday Register*

"Frommer's Guides have a way of giving you a real feel for a place."

—*Knight Ridder Newspapers*

Wiley Publishing, Inc.

Published by:

Wiley Publishing, Inc.
111 River St.
Hoboken, NJ 07030-5774

ISBN: 978-0-470-14434-3

Editor: Ian Skinnari
Production Editor: Katie Robinson
Cartographer: Andrew Murphy
Photo Editor: Richard Fox
Anniversary Logo Design: Richard Pacifico
Production by Wiley Indianapolis Composition Services

Front cover photo: Arlington National Cemetery: U.S. Marine Corps War Memorial
Back cover photo: Georgetown: Chesapeake and Ohio Canal

Manufactured in the United States of America

5 4 3 2 1

Contents

4 Getting to Know Washington, D.C. 56

5 Where to Stay 80

6 Where to Dine 124

7 Exploring Washington, D.C. 175

List of Maps

To Bob and Shirley
Where should we go next?

About the Author

Elise Hartman Ford has been a freelance writer in the Washington, D.C., area since 1985. Her writing has appeared in the *Washington Post, Washingtonian* magazine, the London-based *Bradman's North America Guide, The Essential Guide to Business Travel, Ladies' Home Journal,* and other national, regional, and trade publications. In addition to this guide, she is the author of *Frommer's Washington, D.C., from $80 a Day, Frommer's Memorable Walks in Washington, D.C.,* and *Unique Meeting, Wedding, and Party Places in Greater Washington.*

An Invitation to the Reader

In researching this book, we discovered many wonderful places—hotels, restaurants, shops, and more. We're sure you'll find others. Please tell us about them, so we can share the information with your fellow travelers in upcoming editions. If you were disappointed with a recommendation, we'd love to know that, too. Please write to:

Frommer's Washington, D.C. 2008
Wiley Publishing, Inc. • 111 River St. • Hoboken, NJ 07030-5774

An Additional Note

Please be advised that travel information is subject to change at any time—and this is especially true of prices. We therefore suggest that you write or call ahead for confirmation when making your travel plans. The authors, editors, and publisher cannot be held responsible for the experiences of readers while traveling. Your safety is important to us, however, so we encourage you to stay alert and be aware of your surroundings. Keep a close eye on cameras, purses, and wallets, all favorite targets of thieves and pickpockets.

Frommer's Star Ratings, Icons & Abbreviations

Every hotel, restaurant, and attraction listing in this guide has been ranked for quality, value, service, amenities, and special features using a **star-rating system.** In country, state, and regional guides, we also rate towns and regions to help you narrow down your choices and budget your time accordingly. Hotels and restaurants are rated on a scale of zero (recommended) to three stars (exceptional). Attractions, shopping, nightlife, towns, and regions are rated according to the following scale: zero stars (recommended), one star (highly recommended), two stars (very highly recommended), and three stars (must-see).

In addition to the star-rating system, we also use **seven feature icons** that point you to the great deals, in-the-know advice, and unique experiences that separate travelers from tourists. Throughout the book, look for:

Finds	Special finds—those places only insiders know about
Fun Fact	Fun facts—details that make travelers more informed and their trips more fun
Kids	Best bets for kids and advice for the whole family
Moments	Special moments—those experiences that memories are made of
Overrated	Places or experiences not worth your time or money
Tips	Insider tips—great ways to save time and money
Value	Great values—where to get the best deals

The following **abbreviations** are used for credit cards:

AE	American Express	DISC	Discover	V	Visa
DC	Diners Club	MC	MasterCard		

Frommers.com

Now that you have this guidebook to help you plan a great trip, visit our website at **www.frommers.com** for additional travel information on more than 3,600 destinations. We update features regularly to give you instant access to the most current trip-planning information available. At Frommers.com, you'll find scoops on the best airfares, lodging rates, and car rental bargains. You can even book your travel online through our reliable travel booking partners. Other popular features include:

- Online updates of our most popular guidebooks
- Vacation sweepstakes and contest giveaways
- Newsletters highlighting the hottest travel trends
- Online travel message boards with featured travel discussions

What's New in Washington, D.C.

In this 24/7 capital city, history, tradition, and long-lived establishments retain first place in importance and popularity. But it's D.C.'s big and little newness-es that signal success, and there are plenty of newness-es going on. Consider the Atlas District, a downtrodden neighborhood reinvented as a nightlife center; or the births of excellent restaurants like Central and Beck's; or the debuts of grand, fresh attractions, from the Newseum to Madame Tussaud's. Read on for the details of these and other developments in the capital.

GETTING THERE **Baltimore–Washington International Thurgood Marshall Airport**'s completed expansion includes a great new concourse to accommodate **Southwest Airline**'s (✆ 800/435-9792; www.southwest.com) many flights. At **Ronald Reagan Washington National Airport,** no news is good news. But at **Washington Dulles International Airport,** the roster of international airlines and destinations keeps on growing. Airlines recently added include **AerLingus** (✆ 800/474-7424; www.aerlingus.com), with direct flights to and from Dublin; **Iberia Airlines** (✆ 800/772-4642; www.iberia.com), traveling between Dulles and Madrid; **Copa Airlines** (✆ 800/FLY-COPA; www.copaairlines.com), flying between Panama City and Dulles; and **Qatar Airways** (✆ 877/772-2827; www.qatarairways.com), with daily service between Dulles and Dohai, Qatar.

Budget-minded domestic travelers, meanwhile, should check to see whether **Virgin America** (www.virginamerica.com) has landed at Dulles. **Virgin Atlantic** (✆ **800/862-8621;** www.virgin-atlantic.com) already operates there, and provides affordable service to and from London. Its new sidekick, Virgin America, based in and serving the U.S., is due to launch at Dulles sometime in 2008.

ACCOMMODATIONS Luxury lovers will not have the option of lodging at the marvelous **Jefferson Hotel** (1200 16th St. NW, ✆ **202/347-2200;** www.thejeffersonwashingtondc.com) until the fall of 2008, when it reopens after a massive renovation. Everything will be replaced—except those original Thomas Jefferson documents. In the meantime you might want to check out another cherished, newly renovated property: The **St. Regis Hotel, Washington, D.C.** (923 16th and K streets NW, ✆ **202/638-2626;** www.starwoodhotels.com/stregis/washingtondc), is scheduled to come back to brighter life in fall 2007 (alas, too late to be included in this edition). The St. Regis's famously ornate lobby and courtyard garden have been reappointed, but retain their European ambience. Guest rooms are sumptuous and furnished with Wi-Fi, plasma televisions with surround sound, DVD players, fax machines, Pratesi linens, and, in the bathroom, custom-designed fixtures and mosaic tiles.

DINING Washingtonians have long loved dining out—as long as they can be sure they're replete, out the door, and headed home no later than 9:30 or 10pm. Not so much anymore, though. While restaurant dining is at an all-time high, the curfew has changed. Stop in at any of the latest, hottest restaurants—**Beck's** (Belgian bistro; 1101 K St. NW, ✆ 202/408-1717; www.beckdc.com; p. 153); **Central** (French/American bistro; 1001 Pennsylvania Ave. NW, ✆ 202/626-0015; www.centralmichelrichard.com; p. 140); **Oyamel** (Mexican; 401 7th St. NW, ✆ 202/628-1005; www.oyamel.com; p. 147); **BLT Steak** (steakhouse; 1625 Eye St. NW, ✆ 202/689-8999; www.bltsteak.com; p. 149); and **Urbana** (Italian/Mediterranean; 2121 P St. NW, ✆ 202/956-6650; www.urbanadc.com; p. 160); as well as other fave, not-so-new sites, like **Zaytinya** (Greek/Turkish; 701 9th St. NW, ✆ 202/638-0800; www.zaytinya.com; p. 148)—and you will see the room's still rocking past 11pm. The social scene is a major component: The bar, comfy lounge, and inventive cocktails are de rigueur restaurant features these days, and they go a long way toward making a restaurant both a dining and nightlife destination. But perhaps Washingtonians, younger ones, anyway, are deciding that they deserve to have a great meal and a good time, too. If that's your mood, read the full reviews of the above-mentioned places to find the one that suits you best.

Of course, D.C. has many restaurants that serve up delicious meals in a quieter atmosphere. A new notable in this category is the Willard Intercontinental Hotel's **Café du Parc,** 1401 Pennsylvania Ave. NW (✆ **202/942-7000;** www.cafeduparc.com; p. 144), a two-level courtyard brasserie, whose French chef offers entrecôte (grilled steak with béarnaise sauce), among other authentic French dishes.

SIGHTSEEING The year 2008 promises to be a banner year in Washington, with the opening of the long-awaited **Capitol Visitor Center** (p. 181) beneath the U.S. Capitol Building—no more standing outside in wind-whipping cold or sweltering heat to line up for a tour—and the *re*-opening of the greatly expanded **Newseum** (✆ **888/NEWSEUM;** p. 216) in its grand new location at 6th Street and Pennsylvania Avenue NW, across the street from the National Gallery of Art. In Smithsonian news, the **National Museum of Natural History** (p. 205) christened a cool walk-through **Butterfly Pavilion** in November 2007 and is on track to pull back the curtains on its grand new **Ocean Hall** in September 2008; and the **National Museum of American History** (p. 204) reopens its doors in summer 2008, ready to show off its **Star-Spangled Banner Gallery.** A **Madame Tussaud's Wax Museum** (1025 F St. NW; p. 216) is up and running in the heart of downtown D.C., and the dedication of the National Mall's newest memorial, the **Martin Luther King National Memorial,** is scheduled to take place in December 2008.

NIGHTLIFE D.C. has a new nightlife neighborhood springing up in a rather seedy part of town, along H St. NE, between 12th and 14th streets, east of Union Station. Dubbed the "Atlas District," the street is drawing mostly 20- and 30-somethings to its live music venues and funky bars. If you like alternative music and don't mind iffy neighborhoods, you might want to trip over to the Atlas District. First, though, flip to chapter 9 to read my descriptions of two Atlas District clubs, **The Red & The Black** (1212 H St. NE, ✆ **202/399-3201;** www.redandblackbar.com; p. 272), and the **Rock and Roll Hotel** (1353 H St. NE, ✆ **202/388-7625;** www.rockandrollhoteldc.com; p. 272).

1

The Best of Washington, D.C.

Within its city limits (67 sq. miles), Washington teems with history, made and in the making; the arts; cosmopolitan culture; and magnificent parks, gardens, and architecture. Pull together a bit of the best experiences from all that D.C. offers and you've got yourself a perfect day. Here are nine categories of recommendations to get you started. Pick the ones that seem the most appealing, and then see whether you can fit them into your itinerary for an unforgettable time in the nation's capital.

1 The Most Unforgettable Travel Experiences

- **Watch the Supreme Court in Action:** Only in Washington can one watch and listen to the country's nine foremost legal experts nimbly and intensely dissect the merits of both sides of an argument, whose decisions can affect profoundly both a person and the nation. Think of the Supreme Court justices as a team representing the U.S. Constitution, and only in their chamber do you get to see them play. See p. 183.
- **View Washington Landmarks by Moonlight:** A must. There is nothing as spectacular as seeing the Lincoln Memorial illuminated at night, unless it's the sight of the White House, the Capitol, or the Washington Monument lit up after dark. Go by bus on Tourmobile or by bike via the Bike the Sites service; both operations offer narrated day- and nighttime tours. See p. 237 and p. 240.
- **Visit Your Senator or Member of Congress:** Take advantage of your constituent status and stop by your senator's and/or representative's office in the Capitol to offer your two cents on current issues. Pick up passes to the Capitol's Senate and House chambers and attend a session to observe your elected politicians at work. Try to tour the Capitol while you're here. See p. 178.
- **Bicycle past the Potomac River and Around the Tidal Basin:** Rent a bike and ride the paved bike/walking path that extends 11 miles from the Lincoln Memorial to the Maryland border (through Rock Creek Park). Or head the other direction from the Lincoln Memorial, following the combination of street, sidewalk, and pathway that encircles the cherry tree–rimmed Tidal Basin. The Potomac River, Rock Creek, and spectacular Washington sites are on either side of you as you make your way. For a really long bike ride, follow the pathway past the Lincoln Memorial, cross the Arlington Memorial Bridge to the trail on the other side, and pedal the 19 miles to Mount Vernon. See p. 232 and p. 290.
- **Order Drinks on the Sky Terrace of the Hotel Washington:** Posher bars exist, but none with this view. The experience is almost a cliché in Washington: When spring arrives, make a

date to sit on this outdoor rooftop terrace, sip a gin and tonic, and gaze at the panoramic view of the White House, the Treasury Building, the Jefferson Memorial, and more. See p. 96.

2 The Best Splurge Hotels

- **Mandarin Oriental,** 1330 Maryland Ave. SW, near National Mall (✆ **202/554-8588;** www.mandarinoriental.com/washington): This is the capital's prettiest and most luxurious hotel. You're away from it all but still within walking distance of Smithsonian museums. Its spa and restaurant are the crème de la crème, and guest room designs follow the principles of feng shui to attract good fortune. See p. 85.
- **Four Seasons Hotel,** 2800 Pennsylvania Ave. NW, Georgetown (✆ **202/342-0444;** www.fourseasons.com/washington): It's so nice to be loved, isn't it? And the Four Seasons staff make you feel that way, pampering you relentlessly and greeting you by name, remembering your likes and dislikes. Thanks to its recent multimillion-dollar renovation, the hotel guest rooms are 50% larger and twice as inviting. See p. 118.
- **Willard InterContinental,** 1401 Pennsylvania Ave. NW, Penn Quarter (✆ **202/628-9100;** www.washington.interconti.com): The Willard provided a temporary home for a president or two and continues to be a major gathering spot for capital powermongers. This homegrown, but world-class, hotel has a fine restaurant, a historic bar, a spa, and a just-opened courtyard cafe. You'd be missing something if you didn't at least step inside, even if you're not staying here. See p. 94.

3 The Best Moderately Priced Hotels

- **Capitol Hill Suites,** 200 C St. SE, Capitol Hill (✆ **202/543-6000;** www.capitolhillsuites.com): No other hotel lies closer to the Capitol . . . and the Library of Congress . . . and the Supreme Court. For rates that range from $129 to $249, this property's location and sweet suites, each equipped with a kitchenette, offer a good deal, especially with the completion of a renovation that updated decor and amenities. See p. 90.
- **Four Points by Sheraton Washington, D.C. Downtown,** 1201 K St. NW, Midtown (✆ **202/289-7600;** www.fourpoints.com/washingtondcdowntown): Plenty of attractions are within walking distance of this central downtown hotel: the Verizon Center, convention center, museums, restaurants, and clubs. But you have good reason to stay put, too: comfortable rooms, a fine fitness center, a stellar restaurant, and a rooftop pool—all for rates that can be as low as $109 (though usually start at $195). See p. 102.
- **Georgetown Suites,** 1111 30th St. NW, Georgetown (✆ **202/298-1600;** www.georgetownsuites.com): The suites are large, light-filled, and cheery and the service welcoming in this great value hotel. All sorts of lodging are available, from studio to penthouse, but all units have a full kitchen. And while hotels throughout the city increase their rates from year to year, Georgetown Suites' rates remain fairly constant, in the range of $155 for a studio to $425 for a townhouse. See p. 120.

4 The Most Unforgettable Dining Experiences

- **Michel Richard Citronelle,** in the Latham Hotel in Georgetown, 3000 M St. NW (✆ **202/625-2150**): Richard ebulliently works in his open kitchen creating sumptuous, constantly changing dishes, from fricassee of escargots to squab leg confit with macaroni gratin and black truffles. Each presentation is a work of art, with swirls of colorful sauce surrounding the main event. See p. 165.
- **Komi,** 1509 17th St. NW, Dupont Circle (✆ **202/332-9200**): A dinner at Komi restores one, thanks to creative—but not too creative—dishes (grilled asparagus with watercress and feta, squab stuffed with foie gras and figs), polished service, and a remarkably relaxed atmosphere. And then there's the chef, the unassuming Johnny Monis, who somehow has figured this all out at the tender age of 20-something. See p. 159.
- **CityZen,** 1330 Maryland Ave. SW, in the Mandarin Oriental Hotel, near National Mall (✆ **202/787-6868**): Eric Ziebold is the chef here, having previously served at the renowned French Laundry, in Napa Valley. Washingtonians don't quite know what they've done to deserve the culinary gifts he bestows upon them: North Carolina rainbow trout served with petite red Russian kale and smoked salmon roe emulsion, for example. Bring a full wallet. See p. 130.
- **1789 Restaurant,** 1226 36th St. NW, Georgetown (✆ **202/965-1789**): Isn't it romantic? Washingtonians think so, and you will too—especially if you're seated near one of the warming fireplaces on a wintry night, slurping up the restaurant's signature oyster and champagne stew with Smithfield ham and walnuts. So put on your best duds and be prepared for a relaxing meal with only your food and your dinner companion to distract you. See p. 165.
- **Restaurant Eve,** 110 S. Pitt St., Old Town Alexandria (✆ **703/706-0450**): It's as hard to book a table here as at CityZen in the District. Exotic drinks, entrees such as bouillabaisse and butter-poached halibut with lobster, and service that includes ironing tablecloths between seatings, have drawn people here from all over the area. Birthday or not, order the "birthday cake" for dessert: delicious white cake layered and iced with pink frosting and sprinkles. Yum. See p. 296.

5 The Best Things to Do for Free

- **Peruse the Constitution:** Only in Washington and only at the National Archives will you ever be able to read the original documents that so well grounded this nation in liberty. Here, you'll find the Declaration of Independence, the Constitution of the United States, and the Bill of Rights—all on display behind glass. See p. 211.
- **People-Watch at Dupont Circle:** This traffic circle is also a park, an all-weather hangout for mondo-bizarre biker-couriers, chess players, street musicians, and lovers. Sit on a bench and watch the scenes around you. See p. 55.
- **Attend a Millennium Stage Performance at the Kennedy Center:** Every evening at 6pm, the Kennedy Center presents a free 1-hour concert performed by local, up-and-coming, national, or international musicians. This is a winner. After the performance, head through the glass doors to the terrace for a view of the Potomac River. See p. 222.

- **Groove to the Sounds of Live Jazz in the Sculpture Garden:** On summer's Friday evenings at the National Gallery of Art Sculpture Garden, you can dip your toes in the fountain pool and chill, as live jazz groups serenade you from 5 to 8pm. The jazz is free; the tapas and wine and beer served in the garden's Pavilion Café are not. See p. 213.
- **Pick a Museum (Just About), Any Museum:** That's the thing about Washington—because this is the U.S. capital, many of its museums are federal institutions, which means admission is free. The National Gallery of Art, the U.S. Botanic Garden, and the Smithsonian's 16 Washington museums, from National Air and Space to the Freer Gallery, are among the many spectacular free places to visit. See chapter 7.

6 The Best Outdoor Activities

- **Ice-Skate at the National Gallery:** The National Gallery of Art Sculpture Garden pool turns into an ice-skating rink in winter. So visit the Gallery, finishing up at the Sculpture Garden, where you can rent skates and twirl around on the ice, admiring sculptures as you go. Treat yourself to hot chocolate and sandwiches at the Pavilion Café in the garden. See p. 213.
- **Attend an Event on the Mall:** Think of the National Mall as the nation's public square, where something is always going on, whether it's a book festival in the fall, the blossoming of the gorgeous cherry blossom trees in spring, or the splendid Independence Day celebration every Fourth of July. Pack a picnic and hold your own little party. See p. 15 for a calendar of annual events.
- **View Washington from the Water:** Rent a paddle boat to skim the surface of the Tidal Basin for an hour, or cruise the Potomac River aboard one of several sightseeing vessels to relax from foot-weary travels. The paddle boats give you a remarkable view of the Jefferson Memorial; river cruises offer a pleasant interval for catching a second wind, as they treat you to a marvelous perspective of the city. See chapter 7.
- **Sit at an Outdoor Café and Watch the Washington World Go By:** The capital has plenty of places that offer front-row seats, from the Penn Quarter's Les Halles, with views up and down Pennsylvania Avenue, to the Sea Catch in Georgetown, where tables overlook the C&O Canal. See chapter 6.

7 The Best Neighborhoods for Getting Lost

- **Go Behind the Scenes in Georgetown:** The truth is, you *want* to get lost in Georgetown because it's the side streets that hold the history and centuries-old houses of this one-time colonial tobacco port. And not to worry, Georgetown is so compact, you're never very far from the main drags of M Street and Wisconsin Avenue. For a back-streets tour of Georgetown, see p. 244.
- **Spend the Day in Alexandria:** Just a short distance (by Metro, car, boat, or bike) from the District is George Washington's Virginia hometown. On and off the beaten track are quaint cobblestone streets, charming boutiques and antiques stores, 18th-century houses and other historic

attractions, and fine restaurants. See p. 285.

- **Stroll Embassy Row:** Explore the neighborhood of Dupont Circle to view smaller embassies, then head northwest on Massachusetts Avenue to admire the larger ones. You'll walk along gorgeous tree-shaded streets lined with Beaux Arts mansions, many built by fabulously wealthy magnates during the Gilded Age.

8 The Best Places to Hang with the Locals

- **Shop at Eastern Market:** Capitol Hill is home to more than government buildings; it's a community of old town houses, antiques shops, and the veritable institution Eastern Market. (Although a fire in spring 2007 destroyed much of the historic interior, the market should be up and running by the time you read this.) Here, the locals barter and shop every Saturday and Sunday for fresh produce, baked goods, and flea-market bargains. See p. 253.
- **Pub- and Club-It in D.C.'s Hot Spots:** Join Washington's footloose and fancy-free any night of the week, but especially Thursday through Saturday, along U Street between 9th and 16th streets; in Adams-Morgan; and in the Penn Quarter as they start out or end up (mostly end up—clubs and bars are open late in these neighborhoods). See chapter 9 for bar and club suggestions.
- **Go for a Jog on the National Mall:** Lace up your running shoes and race down the Mall at your own pace, dodging tourists and admiring famous sites as you go. Your fellow runners will be buff military staff who've zoomed over from the Pentagon, speed-walking members of Congress, and a cross-section of downtown workers doing their best to stave off the telltale pencil pusher's paunch. Distance from the foot of the Capitol to the Lincoln Memorial: 2 miles. See p. 240.
- **Take Tea at the Top of Washington National Cathedral:** Join a certain segment of Washington society (mostly women friends and moms and daughters) for tea and a tour. Tuesday and Wednesday afternoons at 1:30pm you can tour the world's sixth-largest cathedral, then indulge in tea, scones, and lemon tarts served on the seventh floor of the West tower, whose arched windows overlook the city and beyond to Sugarloaf Mountain in Maryland. See p. 226.

9 The Best Offbeat Experiences

- **Listen to "House of the Right-Wing Son" and "When Bush Comes to Shove":** The Capitol Steps, a musical political satire troupe, performs these and other irreverent original tunes in skits that skewer politicians on both sides of the aisle. You can see them every weekend at the Ronald Reagan Building. See p. 270.
- **Salsa Up a Storm:** At Habana Village in Adams-Morgan, Lucky Bar near Dupont Circle, and other clubs and bars, you can take salsa and tango lessons, and then put your steps to the test on the dance floor. See p. 275.
- **Explore Washington from a Different Angle:** Sign up for a tour of Washington that follows a certain theme, such as Civil War landmarks,

Site Seeing: The Best Washington, D.C., Websites

- **www.bnbaccom.com:** For those who prefer to stay in a private home, guesthouse, inn, or furnished apartment, this service offers more than 30 for you to consider.
- **www.bwiairport.com:** Ground transport, terminal maps, flight status, and airport facilities for Baltimore–Washington International Airport.
- **www.culturaltourismdc.org:** Cultural Tourism DC is a grassroots, nonprofit coalition of more than 140 arts, heritage, community, and cultural organizations collaborating to promote the less known stories and attractions of Washington. The website lists tours, itineraries, calendars, and plenty of background information about historic and cultural sites that you won't find anywhere else.
- **www.dc.gov:** This is the city of Washington's website, full of details about both federal and local D.C., including history and tourism. Every day, the site lists a calendar of what's going on around town.
- **www.dcaccommodations.com:** This nicely designed site recommends hotels suited for families, women, sightseers, or business travelers.
- **www.fly2dc.com:** In addition to its extensive information about airline travel in and out of Washington (and ground transportation from each airport), this site also offers fun articles about restaurants and things to do in D.C. The monthly print magazine version, *Washington Flyer,* is available free at Washington National and Dulles airports.
- **www.washingtondchotelsonline.com:** Capitol Reservations, a 24-year-old company, represents more than 100 hotels in the Washington area, each of which has been screened for cleanliness, safety, and other factors. You can book your room online.
- **www.house.gov:** Once you're in the U.S. House of Representatives site, click on "Visiting D.C." to learn more about touring the Capitol building. The site allows you to take a virtual tour of the chamber where the House meets and to learn whether the House is in session. The site also connects you with the websites for each of the representatives; you can use this site to e-mail your representative.
- **www.kennedy-center.org:** Find out what's playing at the Kennedy Center and listen to live broadcasts through the Net.
- **www.metwashairports.com:** Ground transport, terminal maps, flight status, and airport facilities for Washington Dulles International and Ronald Reagan Washington National airports.
- **www.mountvernon.org:** Click on "Visit" for daily attractions at Mount Vernon and a calendar of events, as well as information on dining, shopping, and school programs. For a sneak preview, click on "Virtual Mansion

Tour" to see images of the master bedroom, dining room, slave memorial, and the Washingtons' tomb.

- **www.nps.gov:** This National Park Service site includes links to some dozen memorials and monuments. When you click "DC" on the map, a listing of the capital's National Park sites appears, including the National World War II Memorial, Washington Monument, Jefferson Memorial, National Mall, Ford's Theatre, FDR Memorial, Lincoln Memorial, and Vietnam Veterans Memorial.
- **www.opentable.com:** This site allows you to make reservations at some of the capital's finest restaurants.
- **www.senate.gov:** In the U.S. Senate site, click on "Visitors" for an online virtual tour of the Capitol building and information about touring the actual Senate Gallery. It takes a few seconds for the images to download, but it's worth the wait to enjoy the panoramic video tour. Also, find out when the Senate is in session. The site connects you with the websites for each of the senators; you can use this site to e-mail your senator.
- **www.si.edu:** This is the Smithsonian Institution's home page, which provides information about visiting Washington and leads you to the individual websites for each Smithsonian museum.
- **www.washington.org:** The Washington, D.C. Convention and Tourism Corporation operates this site, which gives a broad overview of what to see and do in D.C. and provides travel updates on security issues. Click on "Visitor Information" for tips on where to stay, dine, shop, and sightsee.
- **www.washingtonian.com:** The print magazine of the same name posts some of its articles here, including "What's Happening," a monthly guide to what's on at museums, theaters, and other cultural showplaces around town, and a directory of reviews of Washington restaurants. The magazine really wants you to buy the print edition, though—for sale at bookstores, drugstores, and grocery stores throughout the area.
- **www.washingtonpost.com:** The *Washington Post*'s site is an extremely helpful source for up-to-date information on restaurants, attractions, shopping, and nightlife (as well as world news).
- **www.whitehouse.gov:** Click on "History & Tours" to learn about visiting the White House and upcoming public events. You'll find all sorts of links here, from a history of the White House, to archived White House documents, to an e-mail page you can use to contact the president or vice president.
- **www.wmata.com:** Timetables, maps, fares, and more for the Metro buses and subways that serve the Washington, D.C., metro area.

theater trails, places where Dickens stopped, or scandal-laced sites, to name just a few. Several companies offer offbeat kinds of tours. See p. 236.

- **Sample Offbeat but World-Class Cuisine:** At the **minibar** inside Café Atlantico, chef José Andrés concocts whimsical little tastes—like foie gras in a cocoon of cotton candy. Thirty or more tastes make an unforgettable meal for 12 lucky people (two seatings of 6 people each) per night. See p. 139.

2

Planning Your Trip to Washington, D.C.

Sure, the devil's in the details, but so is delight. Read this chapter to confirm that you've thought of everything as you prepare for your trip, and to allow anticipation to take hold. As you find yourself thinking about attending an event that's on tap when you're in town, contemplating whether to take the Metro or taxi into the city from the airport, or imagining a stroll along the street you're looking at on the map, you might reach a natural conclusion: planning's just another way to whet your appetite to travel.

1 Visitor Information & Maps

Before you leave, contact the **Washington, D.C. Convention and Tourism Corporation (WCTC),** 901 7th St. NW, 4th Floor, Washington, DC 20001-3719 (✆ **800/422-8644** or 202/789-7000; www.washington.org), and ask for a free copy of the *Washington, D.C. Visitors Guide,* which covers hotels, restaurants, sights, shops, and more and is updated twice yearly. At the ✆ 202/789-7000 number, you can speak directly to a staff "visitor specialist" and get answers to your specific questions about the city. Be sure to consult the WCTC website, where you can read (or download) the visitors guide, along with the latest travel information, including upcoming exhibits at the museums and anticipated closings of tourist attractions. The WCTC is also the go-to place for excellent maps, which you can print from its website or order copies online or by phone, for delivery by mail.

Take a look at the D.C. government's website, **www.dc.gov**, and that of the nonprofit organization Cultural Tourism D.C., **www.culturaltourismdc.org**, for more information about the city. The Cultural Tourism D.C. site, in particular, provides helpful and interesting background knowledge of D.C.'s historic and cultural landmarks, especially in neighborhoods, or in parts of neighborhoods, not usually visited by tourists.

For additional information about Washington's most popular tourist spots, access the National Park Service website, **www.nps.gov/ncro** (the Park Service maintains Washington's monuments, memorials, and other sites), and the Smithsonian Institution's **www.si.edu**.

Also helpful is the *Washington Post* site, **www.washingtonpost.com**, which gives you up-to-the-minute news, weather, visitor information, restaurant reviews, and nightlife insights; its online City Guide, a must-read for locals and tourists alike, features a "Going Out Gurus" blog, covering daily entertainment happenings, as well as a "For Visitors" section, which you might find of use.

A final good source is *Washington Flyer* magazine, which you can obtain free at the airports, or browse online in advance (at **www.fly2dc.com**) because it often covers airport and airline news and profiles upcoming events in Washington—things

Destination Washington, D.C.: Predeparture Checklist

- Have you booked theater and restaurant reservations? If you're hoping to dine at a hot new restaurant or return to an old favorite, or if you're keen on catching a performance scheduled during your stay, why not play it safe by calling in advance? Two weeks is realistic to reserve a table, and you can't book theater tickets too early.
- Have you checked to make sure your favorite attraction is open? Some sites, such as the Pentagon, remain closed indefinitely to public tours for security reasons. Other attractions, such as the FBI Building, are closed for renovations. Call ahead for opening and closing hours, and again on the day of your visit to confirm that it's open.
- Would you like to avoid the wait of a long line or the ultimate disappointment of missing a tour altogether? A number of sightseeing attractions permit you to reserve a tour slot in advance, including the Library of Congress, the Bureau of Engraving and Printing, the National Archives, and the Kennedy Center for the Performing Arts. (Advance tickets are not necessary to tour an attraction; they just save you a long wait in a ticket line.)
- Do you have your credit card PINs? If you have a five- or six-digit PIN, did you obtain a four-digit number from your bank? Most ATMs in the Washington, D.C., area accept four-digit PINs.

you might want to know before you travel. The site also allows you to subscribe to its free weekly e-mail newsletter for the latest information. The Metropolitan Washington Airports Authority publishes the magazine, which carries comprehensive airport maps of Ronald Reagan Washington National and Washington Dulles International airports in each issue.

In addition to the Washington Post's Going Out Gurus blog (http://blog.washingtonpost.com/goingoutgurus), check out the websites and blogs of dcist.com and ontaponline.com.

2 Entry Requirements

PASSPORTS

For information on how to get a passport, go to **"Passports"** in the **"Fast Facts"** section of chapter 4—the websites listed provide downloadable passport applications as well as the current fees for processing passport applications. For an up-to-date, country-by-country listing of passport requirements around the world, go to the "Foreign Entry Requirement" website of the U.S. State Department at **http://travel.state.gov**. International visitors can obtain a visa application at the same website. ***Note:*** Children are required to present a passport when entering the United States at airports. More information on obtaining a passport for a minor can be found at http://travel.state.gov.

VISAS

For specifics on how to get a visa, go to **"Visas"** in the **"Fast Facts"** section of chapter 4.

The U.S. State Department has a **Visa Waiver Program (VWP)** allowing citizens of the following countries (at press time) to enter the United States without a visa for stays of up to 90 days: Andorra, Australia, Austria, Belgium, Brunei, Denmark, Finland, France, Germany, Iceland, Ireland, Italy, Japan, Liechtenstein, Luxembourg, Monaco, the Netherlands, New Zealand, Norway, Portugal, San Marino, Singapore, Slovenia, Spain, Sweden, Switzerland, and the United Kingdom. Canadian citizens may enter the United States without visas; they will need to show passports and proof of residence, however. ***Note:*** Any passport issued on or after October 26, 2006, by a VWP country must be an **e-Passport** for VWP travelers to be eligible to enter the U.S. without a visa. Citizens of these nations also need to present a round-trip air or cruise ticket upon arrival. E-Passports contain computer chips capable of storing biometric information, such as the required digital photograph of the holder. (You can identify an e-Passport by the symbol on the bottom center cover of your passport.) If your passport doesn't have this feature, you can still travel without a visa if it is a valid passport issued before October 26, 2005, and includes a machine-readable zone, or between October 26, 2005, and October 25, 2006, and includes a digital photograph. For more information, go to **www.travel.state.gov/visa.**

Citizens of all other countries must have (1) a valid passport that expires at least 6 months later than the scheduled end of their visit to the United States, and (2) a tourist visa, which may be obtained without charge from any U.S. consulate.

As of January 2004, many international visitors traveling on visas to the United States will be photographed and fingerprinted on arrival at Customs in airports and on cruise ships in a program created by the Department of Homeland Security called **US-VISIT.** Exempt from the extra scrutiny are visitors entering by land or those (mostly in Europe; see above) that don't require a visa for short-term visits. For more information, go to the Homeland Security website at **www.dhs.gov/dhspublic**.

MEDICAL REQUIREMENTS

Unless you're arriving from an area known to be suffering from an epidemic (particularly cholera or yellow fever), inoculations or vaccinations are not required for entry into the United States. If you have a medical condition that requires **syringe-administered medications,** carry a valid signed prescription from your physician; syringes in carry-on baggage will be inspected. Insulin in any form should have the proper pharmaceutical documentation. If you have a disease that requires treatment with **narcotics,** you should also carry documented proof with you—smuggling narcotics aboard a plane carries severe penalties in the U.S.

For **HIV-positive visitors,** requirements for entering the United States are somewhat vague and change frequently.

U.S. Entry: Passport Required

New regulations issued by the Homeland Security Department now require virtually every air traveler entering the U.S. to show a passport—and future regulations will cover land and sea entry as well. As of January 23, 2007, all persons, including U.S. citizens, traveling by air between the United States and Canada, Mexico, Central and South America, the Caribbean, and Bermuda are required to present a valid passport. Similar regulations for those traveling by land or sea (including ferries) are expected as early as January 1, 2008.

For up-to-the-minute information, contact **AIDSinfo** (© **800/448-0440** or 301/519-6616 outside the U.S.; www.aidsinfo.nih.gov) or the **Gay Men's Health Crisis** (© **212/367-1000;** www.gmhc.org).

CUSTOMS

For information on what you can bring into and take out of Washington, D.C., go to **"Customs"** in the **"Fast Facts"** section of chapter 4.

3 When to Go

The city's peak seasons generally coincide with two activities: the sessions of Congress and springtime—starting with the appearance of the cherry blossoms along the Potomac. Specifically, from about the second week in September until Thanksgiving, and again from about mid-January to June (when Congress is "in"), hotels are full with guests whose business takes them to Capitol Hill or to conferences. And mid-March through June traditionally is the most frenzied season, when families and school groups descend upon the city to see the cherry blossoms and enjoy Washington's sensational spring. This is also a popular season for protest marches. Hotel rooms are at a premium and airfares tend to be higher.

If crowds turn you off, consider visiting Washington at the end of August/early September, when Congress is still "out" and families return home to get their children back to school, or between Thanksgiving and mid-January, when Congress leaves again and many people are ensconced in their own holiday-at-home celebrations. Hotel rates are cheapest at this time, too, and many hotels offer attractive packages.

If you're thinking of visiting in July and August, be forewarned: The weather is very hot and humid. Summer is also the season for outdoor concerts, festivals, parades, and other events (see chapter 9 for details about performing arts schedules). And, of course, Independence Day (July 4th) in the capital is a spectacular celebration.

THE WEATHER

Check the *Washington Post's* website (**www.washingtonpost.com**) or the Washington, D.C. Convention and Tourism Corporation website (**www.washington.org**) for current and projected weather forecasts.

Season by season, here's what you can expect of the weather in Washington:

Fall: This is my favorite season. The weather is often warm during the day—in fact, if you're here in early fall, it may seem entirely *too* warm. But it cools off, even getting a bit crisp, at night. All the greenery that Washington is famous for dons the brilliant colors of fall foliage, and the stream of tourists tapers off.

Winter: People like to say that Washington winters are mild—and sure, if you're from Minnesota, you'll find Washington warmer, no doubt. But D.C. winters can be unpredictable: bitter cold one day, an ice storm the next, followed by a couple of days of sun and higher temperatures. Pack for all possibilities.

Spring: Early spring weather tends to be colder than most people expect. Cherry blossom season, late March to early April, can be iffy—and very often rainy. Then, as April slips into May, the weather usually mellows, and people's moods with it. Late spring is especially lovely, with mild temperatures and intermittent days of sunshine, flowers, and trees colorfully erupting in gardens and parks all over town. Washingtonians, restless after having been cooped inside for months, sweep outdoors to stroll the National Mall, sit on a park bench, or laze away an afternoon at an outdoor cafe. Spring is a great time to enjoy D.C.'s outdoor attractions. But during this season, the city is also at its most crowded with visitors and school groups.

Summer: Throngs remain in summer, and anyone who's ever spent August in D.C. will tell you how hot and steamy it can be. Though the buildings are air-conditioned, many of Washington's attractions, like the memorials, monuments, and organized tours, are outdoors and unshaded, and the heat can quickly get to you. Make sure you stop frequently for drinks (vendors are everywhere), and wear a hat, sunglasses, and sunscreen.

Average Temperatures (°F/°C) & Rainfall (in inches) in Washington, D.C.

	Jan	Feb	Mar	Apr	May	June	July	Aug	Sept	Oct	Nov	Dec
Avg. High	44/ 5	46/ 8	54/ 12	66/ 19	76/ 25	83/ 29	87/ 31	85/ 30	79/ 26	68/ 20	57/ 14	46/ 8
Avg. Low	30/ –1	29/ –1	36/ 2	46/ 8	56/ 14	65/ 19	69/ 20	68/ 20	61/ 16	50/ 10	39/ 4	32/ 0
Rainfall	3.57	2.84	3.92	3.26	4.29	3.63	4.21	3.90	4.08	3.43	3.32	3.25

WASHINGTON, D.C., CALENDAR OF EVENTS

Washington's most popular annual events are the Cherry Blossom Festival in spring, the Fourth of July celebration in summer, and the lighting of the National Christmas Tree in winter. But some sort of special event occurs almost daily. For the latest schedules, check **www.washington.org**, **www.nps.gov/ncro** (click on "Calendar of Events"), **www.culturaltourismdc.org**, **www.dc.gov**, and **www.washingtonpost.com**.

For an exhaustive list of events beyond those listed here, check http://events.frommers.com, where you'll find a searchable, up-to-the-minute roster of what's happening in Washington (and other cities all over the world).

In the calendar below, I've done my best to accurately list phone numbers for more information, but they seem to change constantly. If the number you try doesn't get you the details you need, call the **Washington, D.C. Convention and Tourism Corporation** at ✆ **202/789-7000.**

When you're in town, grab a copy of the *Washington Post,* especially the Friday "Weekend" section, or a copy of the monthly magazine, **Washingtonian,** whose "Where and When" section features recommended goings-on around town.

For annual events in Alexandria, see p. 288.

January

Martin Luther King, Jr.'s, Birthday. Events include speeches by prominent leaders and politicians, readings, dance, theater, concerts and choral performances, and prayer vigils. On the Friday preceding the national holiday (third Mon in Jan), the National Park Service holds a ceremony at the Department of Interior Building at 1849 C St. NW, attended by school children and open to the public; park rangers then transfer the wreath used during the ceremony to the Lincoln Memorial. (The entire ceremony used to take place at the Memorial but was switched indoors because of the cold.) Call ✆ **202/619-7222.** Many events take place at the Martin Luther King, Jr., Memorial Library, 901 G St. NW (✆ **202/727-0321**). Third Monday in January.

February

Black History Month. Numerous events, museum exhibits, and cultural programs celebrate the contributions of African Americans to American life, including a celebration of abolitionist Frederick Douglass's birthday. For details, check the *Washington Post* or call the National Park Service at ✆ **202/619-7222.**

Chinese New Year Celebration. A friendship archway, topped by 300 painted dragons and lighted at night, marks Chinatown's entrance at 7th and H streets NW. The celebration begins the day of the Chinese New Year and continues for 10 or more days, with traditional firecrackers, dragon dancers, and colorful street parades. Some area restaurants offer special menus. For details, call ✆ **202/789-7000.** Early February.

Abraham Lincoln's Birthday. This day is marked by a wreath laying and reading of the Gettysburg Address at noon at the Lincoln Memorial. Call ✆ **202/619-7222.** February 12.

George Washington's Birthday. Celebratory events similar to Lincoln's birthday, centered on the Washington Monument. Call ✆ **202/619-7222** for details. The Washington Monument is open, with new security barriers placed in concentric circles around the obelisk. See the review in chapter 7 of the Washington Monument for more information. Both presidents' birthdays also bring annual citywide sales. February 22. See chapter 10, "Side Trips from Washington, D.C.," for information about the bigger celebrations held at Mount Vernon and in Old Town Alexandria on the third Monday in February.

March

Women's History Month. Various institutions throughout the city stage celebrations of women's lives and achievements. For the schedule of National Park Service events, check the calendar at www.nps.gov/ncro; for Smithsonian events, call ✆ **202/357-2700;** for other events, check the websites listed in the intro to this section.

St. Patrick's Day Parade. A big parade on Constitution Avenue NW, from 7th to 17th streets, with floats, bagpipes, marching bands, and the wearin' o' the green. For parade information, call ✆ **202/789-7000** or go online at www.dcstpatsparade.com. The Sunday before March 17.

Smithsonian Kite Festival. This event is delightful if the weather cooperates—an occasion for a trip in itself. Throngs of kite enthusiasts fly their unique creations on the grounds of the Washington Monument, and compete for ribbons and prizes. Now in its 42nd year, the kite festival even has its own website: **www.kitefestival.org**. Visit the website or call ✆ **202/357-2700** or 202/357-3030 for details. To compete, just show up at the designated spot with your kite between 10am and noon and register. A Saturday in mid- or late March, or early April, but always during the Cherry Blossom Festival.

April

National Cherry Blossom Festival. Washington's best-known annual event: a 2-week festival coinciding with the blossoming of more than 3,700 Japanese cherry trees by the Tidal Basin, on Hains Point, and on the grounds of the Washington Monument. Events take place all over town, including fireworks, concerts, special art exhibits, park ranger–guided talks and tours past the cherry blossom trees, and sports competitions. A grand parade caps the festival, complete with floats, marching bands, dancers, celebrity guests, and more. For information, call ✆ **202/547-1500** or go to www.nationalcherryblossomfestival.org. Also see "Potomac Park" on p. 231 for more information about the cherry blossoms. March 29 to April 13, 2008. National and local news programs monitor the budding.

White House Easter Egg Roll. The biggie for little kids. The annual White House Easter Egg Roll continues a practice begun in 1878. Entertainment on the White House South Lawn and the Ellipse traditionally includes appearances by costumed cartoon characters, clowns, egg-decorating exhibitions, puppet and magic shows, military drill teams, an egg-rolling contest, and a hunt for 1,000 or so wooden eggs, many of them signed by celebrities, astronauts, or the president. ***Note:*** Children of all ages are welcome, as long as a child age 7 or younger, and no more than 2 adults, are in your group. You may obtain a maximum of five tickets. The hourly timed tickets are issued at the National Parks Service Ellipse Visitors Pavilion just behind the White House at 15th and E streets NW beginning at 7:30am on the Saturday before Easter and again on Easter Monday. Call ✆ **202/208-1631** for details. Easter Monday between 8am and 2pm, enter at the southeast gate on East Executive Avenue. Arrive early to make sure you get in and to allow for increased security procedures. One other precaution: Strollers are not permitted.

African-American Family Day at the National Zoo. This tradition extends back to 1889, when the zoo opened. The National Zoo, 3001 Connecticut Ave. NW, celebrates African-American families the day after Easter with music, dance, Easter egg rolls, and other activities. Free. Call ✆ **202/357-2700** for details. Easter Monday.

Thomas Jefferson's Birthday. Celebrated at the Jefferson Memorial with wreaths, speeches, and a military ceremony. Call ✆ **202/619-7222** for time and details. April 13.

White House Spring Garden Tour. These beautifully landscaped creations are open to the public for free tours, 2 days only. Tickets are required. Call ✆ **202/208-1631** for details. Two days in mid-April.

Shakespeare's Birthday Celebration. Music, theater, children's events, food, and exhibits are all part of the afternoon's hail to the bard at the Folger Shakespeare Library. Call ✆ **202/544-4600,** or go to www.folger.edu. Free admission. Mid- to late April.

Filmfest D.C. This annual film festival presents more than 100 works by filmmakers from around the globe. Screenings take place primarily in movie theaters. Tickets are usually $9 per movie and go fast; some events are free. Call ✆ **202/628-FILM** or check the website, www.filmfestdc.org. Two weeks in April.

Smithsonian Craft Show. Held in the National Building Museum, 401 F St. NW, this juried show features one-of-a-kind limited-edition crafts by more than 120 noted artists from all over the country. There's an entrance fee of about $15 per adult each day, free for children under 13. No strollers. For details, call ✆ **888/832-9554** (TDD 202/357-1729), or check the website, www.smithsoniancraftshow.com. Four days in late April.

May

Washington National Cathedral Annual Flower Mart. Now in its 69th year, the flower mart takes place on cathedral grounds, featuring displays of flowering plants and herbs, decorating demonstrations, ethnic food booths, children's rides and activities (including an antique carousel), costumed characters, puppet shows, and other entertainment. Admission is free. Call ✆ **202/537-3185** or go to www.cathedral.org for details. First Friday and Saturday in May, rain or shine.

Georgetown Garden Tour. View remarkable private gardens in one of the city's loveliest neighborhoods. Admission ($25–$30) includes light refreshments. Some years there are related events such as a flower show at a historic home. Call ✆ **202/789-7000** or browse the website www.georgetowngardentour.com for details. Early to mid-May.

Shakespeare Theatre Free for All. This free theater festival presents a different Shakespeare play each year for a 2-week run at the Carter Barron Amphitheatre in upper northwest Washington. Tickets are required, but they're free. Call ✆ **202/334-4790,** or check the website, www.shakespeare theatre.org. Evenings, end of May through early June.

Memorial Day. At 11am, a wreath-laying ceremony takes place at the Tomb of the Unknowns in Arlington National Cemetery, followed by military band music, a service, and an address by a high-ranking government official (sometimes the president); call ✆ **703/607-8000** for details. A National Memorial Day Parade marches from the Capitol, down Constitution Avenue, to the White House. Ceremonies are held at the National World War II and Vietnam Veterans Memorial (✆ **202/619-7222** for details), and other activities take place at the U.S. Navy Memorial (✆ **202/737-2300**). On the Sunday before Memorial Day, the National Symphony Orchestra performs a free concert at 8pm on the West Lawn of the Capitol to honor the sacrifices of American servicemen and women; call ✆ **202/619-7222** for details.

June

Dupont-Kalorama Museum Walk Day. This 25th annual celebration welcomes visitors to eight museums and historic houses located in several charming, off-the-Mall neighborhoods. Free food, music, tours, and crafts demonstrations are on offer. Shuttle buses travel to each location. Call ✆ **202/387-4062, ext. 12,** or access the website, www.dkmuseums.com. First full weekend in June.

Smithsonian Folklife Festival. A major event reveling in both national and international traditions in music, crafts, foods, games, concerts, and exhibits, staged the length of the National Mall. Each Folklife Festival showcases 3 or 4 cultures or themes; 2007 introduced those of the Mekong River; Northern Ireland; and the state of Virginia to festivalgoers. All events are free; most events take place outdoors. Call ✆ **202/357-2700,** or check the website, www.folklife.si.edu, or the listings in the *Washington Post,* for details. For 10 days in late June and early July, always including July 4.

July

Independence Day. There's no better place to be on the Fourth of July than in Washington, D.C. The festivities include a massive National Independence Day Parade down Constitution Avenue, complete with lavish floats, princesses, marching groups, and military bands. A morning program in front of the National Archives includes military demonstrations, period music, and a reading of the Declaration of Independence. In the evening, the National Symphony Orchestra plays on the west steps of the Capitol with guest artists (for example, Leontyne Price). And big-name entertainment precedes the fabulous fireworks display behind the Washington Monument. You can also attend a free 11am organ recital at Washington's National Cathedral. Consult the *Washington Post* or call ✆ **202/789-7000** for details. July 4, all day.

Bastille Day. This Washington tradition honors the French Independence Day with live entertainment and a

12-block race by tray-balancing waiters and waitresses, along Pennsylvania Avenue from Brasserie Les Halles to the U.S. Capitol and back. Free, *mais bien sûr.* At 12th Street and Pennsylvania Avenue NW. Call ✆ **202/347-6848.** July 14.

Capital Fringe Festival. This event debuted in 2006 and celebrates experimental theater in the tradition of the original fringe festival held annually in Edinburgh, Scotland. Five events take place at more than 20 venues daily for 10 days, adding up to about 1,000 acts in all. Local and visiting artists perform in theater, dance, music, and other disciplines. Tickets are $10 per event and the action centers on 7th Street NW in the Penn Quarter. Check the website, www.capfringe.org, for more information. The end of the month.

September

Labor Day Concert. The National Symphony Orchestra closes its summer season with a free performance at 8pm on the West Lawn of the Capitol; call ✆ **202/619-7222** for details. Sunday before Labor Day. (Rain date: Same day and time at Constitution Hall or the Kennedy Center.)

Kennedy Center Open House Arts Festival. A day-long festival of the performing arts, featuring local and national artists on the front plaza and river terrace (which overlooks the Potomac), and throughout the stage halls of the Kennedy Center. Past festivals have featured the likes of Los Lobos, Mary Chapin Carpenter, and Washington Opera soloists. Kids' activities usually include a National Symphony Orchestra "petting zoo," where children get to bow, blow, drum, or strum a favorite instrument. Admission is free, although you may have to stand in a long line for the inside performances. For details, check the *Washington Post,* call ✆ **800/444-1324** or 202/467-4600, or access the website, www.kennedy-center.org. A Saturday or Sunday in early to mid-September, 11:30am to 7:30pm.

Black Family Reunion. Performances, food, and fun are part of this 2-day celebration of the African-American family and culture, held on the Mall. Free. Check the website, www.ncnw.org/events/reunion.htm. Mid-September.

Adams-Morgan Day. Thousands turn out along 18th Street NW, Columbia Road NW, and other streets in this small neighborhood to revel in the music, art, dance, and cuisines representing the international roots of the residents. Call ✆ **202/232-1978,** or check the website, adamsmorgandayfestival.com. Second Sunday in September.

Washington National Cathedral's Open House. This sixth-largest-in-the-world cathedral celebrated its centenary in 2007. Its annual open house includes demonstrations of stone carving and other crafts utilized in building the cathedral; carillon and organ demonstrations; and performances by dancers, choirs, strolling musicians, jugglers, and puppeteers. This occasion is only one of two times annually when the Cathedral allows visitors to ascend to the top of the central bell tower for a spectacular view of the area (the Flower Mart in May is the other—see its entry, above). For details, call ✆ **202/537-6200.** A Saturday in late September or early October.

Library of Congress National Book Festival. Co-sponsored by the Library of Congress and the First Lady, this festival welcomes at least 80 established authors and their many fans to the National Mall for readings, author signings, and general hoopla surrounding the love of books. Check www.loc.gov/bookfest, or call ✆ **202/707-8000** for more information. A Saturday in late September.

October

White House Fall Garden Tour. For 2 days, visitors have an opportunity to see the famed Rose Garden and South Lawn. Admission is free, though tickets are required. A military band provides music. For details, call ✆ **202/208-1631.** Mid- to late October.

Marine Corps Marathon. More than 30,000 runners compete in this 26.2-mile race (the fifth-largest marathon in the United States). It begins at the Marine Corps Memorial (the Iwo Jima statue) and passes major monuments. Call ✆ **703/432-1159** for details. Anyone can enter; register online at www.marinemarathon.com. Fourth Sunday in October.

Halloween. There's no official celebration, but costumed shenanigans seem to get bigger every year. Giant block parties take place in the Dupont Circle and Georgetown neighborhoods. Check the *Washington Post* for special parties and activities. October 31.

November

Veterans Day. The nation's war dead are honored with a wreath-laying ceremony at 11am at the Tomb of the Unknowns in Arlington National Cemetery followed by a memorial service. The president of the United States or his stand-in officiates, as a military band performs. Wreath-laying ceremonies also take place at other war memorials in the city. Call ✆ **703/607-8000** for more information about Arlington Cemetery events and **202/619-7222** for information about events elsewhere. November 11.

December

Christmas Pageant of Peace/National Tree Lighting. At the northern end of the Ellipse, the president lights the national Christmas tree to the accompaniment of orchestral and choral music. The lighting inaugurates the 4-week Pageant of Peace, a tremendous holiday celebration full of free activities, including musical performances, mostly of local school and church choruses, nightly on the Ellipse. (Brrrr!) Call ✆ **202/208-1631,** or check the website, **www.nps.gov/whho/pageant.htm**, for details; tickets are free but required to attend the tree-lighting ceremony. The tree-lighting ceremony takes place at 5pm on a day in early December, and the Pageant of Peace continues every night throughout the month.

4 Getting There

BY PLANE

DOMESTIC AIRLINES Domestic airlines with scheduled flights into all three of Washington, D.C.'s airports—Washington Dulles International (IAD), Ronald Reagan Washington National (DCA), and Baltimore–Washington International Thurgood Marshall (BWI)—include **AirTran** (✆ 800/247-8726; www.airtran.com), **American** (✆ 800/433-7300; www.aa.com), **Continental** (✆ 800/525-0280; www.continental.com), **Delta** (✆ 800/221-1212; www.delta.com), **Northwest** (✆ 800/225-2525; www.nwa.com), **United** (✆ 800/241-6522; www.united.com), and **US Airways** (✆ 800/428-4322; www.usairways.com).

Quite a few low-fare airlines serve Washington's airports, including one, AirTran (see above for details), that serves all three. My favorite discount airline, because it is so reliable and consistently gets me the cheapest fares, is BWI's anchor, **Southwest Airlines** (✆ **800/435-9792;** www.southwest.com), whose flights to nearly 40 cities provide more than half of BWI's passenger business. **Frontier**

D.C. Metropolitan Area

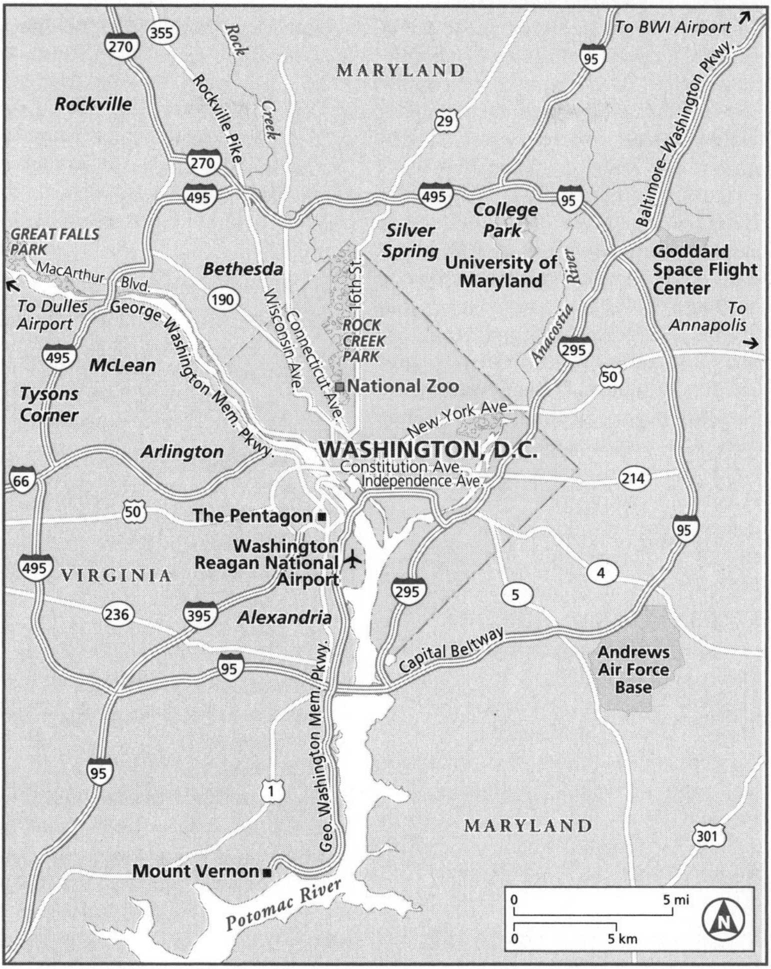

(✆ 800/432-1359; www.frontierairlines.com) and **USA 3000** (✆ **877/872-3000;** www.usa3000.com) also serve BWI.

Discount airlines, in addition to AirTran, that serve Washington Dulles Airport are United Airlines's subsidiary **Ted Airlines** (✆ 800/225-5833; www.flyted.com), **America West** (✆ 800/428-8322; www.usairways.com/awa), **JetBlue** (✆ 800/538-2583; www.jetblue.com), and, as of October 2006, Southwest. On the horizon is **Virgin America** (www.virginamerica.com), which was aiming to start up service at Dulles sometime in 2008.

Five discount airlines, including AirTran, use National Airport: Frontier, America West, **American Trans Air (ATA)** (✆ **800/435-9282;** www.ata.com), and **Spirit** (✆ **800/772-7177;** www.spiritair.com).

SHUTTLE SERVICE FROM NEW YORK, BOSTON & CHICAGO

Delta and US Airways continue to dominate the lucrative D.C.–East Coast shuttle service. Between the two of them, the airlines operate hourly or almost hourly shuttle service between Boston's Logan Airport and Washington, and New York's La Guardia Airport and Washington. The **Delta Shuttle** (✆ **800/933-5935**) travels daily between New York and Washington, while the **US Airways Shuttle** (✆ **800/428-4322**) operates daily between Boston and Washington and New York and Washington. Both airlines fly into and out of Ronald Reagan Washington National Airport. Discount airline **Southwest** (see details above) offers nearly hourly service daily between BWI and Buffalo, Chicago's Midway Airport, Providence, Hartford, Long Island, Manchester (New Hampshire), Orlando, and Nashville.

INTERNATIONAL AIRLINES The one international airline with scheduled flights into Ronald Reagan Washington National Airport is **Air Canada** (✆ 888/247-2262; www.aircanada.com).

International airlines with scheduled flights into Baltimore–Washington International Thurgood Marshall Airport include **Air Canada** (see above), **British Airways** (✆ 0870/850-9-850 in the U.K., or 800/247-9297; www.ba.com), **Mexicana** (✆ 800/531-7921; www.mexicana.com), and **Icelandair** (✆ 800/223-5500; www.icelandair.com).

Washington Dulles International Airport, with its roster of 21 international airlines and 40 international destinations, dominates the city's overseas travel market. Airlines with flights into Dulles include **Aeroflot** (✆ 888/686-4949; www.aeroflot.org), **Air Canada** (see above), **Air France** (✆ 800/321-4538; www.airfrance.com), **ANA Airways** (✆ 800/235-9262; www.anaskyweb.com), **British Airways** (see above), **Lufthansa** (✆ 800/645-3880; www.lufthansa.com), **Saudi Arabian Airlines** (✆ 800/472-8342; www.saudiairlines.com), **South African Airways** (✆ 0861/359-722 in South Africa, 800/722-9675 in the U.S.; www.flysaa.com), **MAXjet** (✆ 888/435-9629; www.maxjet.com), **Aer Lingus** (✆ 800/474-7424; www.aerlingus.com), and **Virgin Atlantic** (✆ 08705/747-747 in the U.K., or 800/862-8621 in the U.S.; www.virgin-atlantic.com).

D.C. AREA AIRPORTS

General information follows that should help you determine which airport is your best bet; for details about individual airport services, see "Visitor Information," in chapter 4.

Ronald Reagan Washington National Airport (DCA) lies across the Potomac River in Virginia, a few minutes by car, 15 to 20 minutes by Metro from downtown in non-rush-hour traffic. Its proximity to the District and its direct access to the Metro rail system are reasons why you might want to fly into National.

Approximately 13 airlines serve this airport, which has nonstop flights to 74 North American destinations, including one Caribbean and two Canadian cities. Nearly all nonstop flights are to and from cities located within 1,250 miles from Washington. The exceptions are flights between National and Phoenix, Denver, Las Vegas, Seattle, Los Angeles, and Salt Lake City.

While Washington's two other airports remain in the midst of extensive renovations, National is up-to-date with new terminals, ticket counters that provide access to passengers with disabilities, more than 100 restaurants and shops, commissioned artwork displayed throughout the terminals (go on a tour if your flight's been delayed), and climate-controlled pedestrian bridges that connect the terminal directly to the Metro station, whose Blue and Yellow lines stop here.

The Metropolitan Washington Airports Authority oversees both National and Dulles airports, so the website is the same for the two facilities: www.mwaa.com. Check there for airport information, or call ✆ **703/417-8000.** For Metro information, call ✆ **202/637-7000.**

Washington Dulles International Airport (IAD) is 26 miles outside the capital, in Chantilly, Virginia, a 35- to 45-minute ride to downtown in non-rush-hour traffic. Of the three airports, Dulles handles more daily flights, with 31 airlines flying nonstop to 120 destinations, including 39 foreign cities. And though the airport is not as convenient to the heart of Washington as National, it's more convenient than BWI, thanks to an uncongested airport access road that travels half the distance toward Washington. A decades-long expansion has so far added new concourses, a parking garage, and a pedestrian walkway between the main terminal and concourses A and B that offers travelers an option over the mobile lounges. Eventually, the airport will more than triple its annual passenger traffic to 55 million, add a runway, and add an underground airport train system that will completely replace those inconvenient and unwieldy mobile lounges that transport most travelers to and from the main and midfield terminals. The airport's website is www.mwaa.com, and its information line is ✆ **703/572-2700.**

Last but not least is **Baltimore–Washington International Thurgood Marshall Airport (BWI),** which is located about 45 minutes from downtown, a few miles outside of Baltimore. A just-completed expansion has added 11 gates to a newly improved concourse, skywalks from parking garages to terminals, and triple the amount of parking spaces. One factor especially accounts for this tremendous growth, the same that recommends BWI to travelers: the major presence of Southwest Airlines and its bargain fares. Find out whether Southwest serves your city, if you want to save some money. (A couple of other low-fare airlines operate here as well; see the "By Plane" section above.) In all, 25 airlines serve BWI, flying nonstop to 71 destinations, including 10 foreign cities. Call ✆ **800/435-9294** for airport information, or point your browser to www.bwiairport.com.

FLYING FOR LESS: TIPS FOR GETTING THE BEST AIRFARE

- Passengers who can book their ticket either **long in advance or at the last minute,** or who **fly midweek** or **at less-trafficked hours,** may pay a fraction of the full fare. If your schedule is flexible, say so, and ask if you can secure a cheaper fare by changing your flight plans.
- Search **the Internet** for cheap fares. The most popular online travel a gencies are **Travelocity.com** (www.travelocity.co.uk); **Expedia.com** (www.expedia.co.uk and www.expedia.ca); and **Orbitz.com.** In the U.K., go to **Travelsupermarket** (✆ **0845/345-5708;** www.travelsupermarket.com), a flight search engine that offers flight comparisons for the budget airlines whose seats often end up in bucket-shop sales. Other websites for booking airline tickets online include **Cheapflights.com, SmarterTravel.com, Priceline.com,** and **Opodo** (www.opodo.co.uk). Meta search sites (which find and then direct you to airline and hotel websites for booking) include **Sidestep.com** and **Kayak.com**—the latter includes fares for some budget carriers, like Jet Blue and Spirit, though not Southwest, as well as the major airlines. **Site59.com** is a great source for last-minute flights and getaways. In addition, most **airlines** offer online-only fares that even their phone agents know nothing about. British travelers should

check **Flights International** (✆ **0800/0187050;** www.flights-international.com) for deals on flights all over the world.

- Watch local newspapers for **promotional specials** or **fare wars,** when airlines lower prices on their most popular routes. Also keep an eye on price fluctuations and deals at websites such as **Airfarewatchdog.com** and **Farecast.com**.
- Try to book a ticket **in its country of origin.** If you're planning a one-way flight from Johannesburg to Washington, D.C., a South Africa–based travel agent will probably have the lowest fares. For foreign travelers on multileg trips, book in the country of the first leg; for example, book Washington–Chicago–Montréal–Washington in the U.S.
- **Consolidators,** also known as bucket shops, are wholesale brokers in the airline-ticket game. Consolidators buy deeply discounted tickets ("distressed" inventories of unsold seats) from airlines and sell them to online ticket agencies, travel agents, tour operators, corporations, and, to a lesser degree, the general public. Consolidators advertise in Sunday newspaper travel sections (often in small ads with tiny type), in both the U.S. and the U.K. They can be great sources for cheap international tickets. On the down side, bucket shop tickets are often rigged with restrictions, such as stiff cancellation penalties (as high as 50%–75% of the ticket price). And keep in mind that most of what you see advertised is of limited availability. Several reliable consolidators are worldwide and available online. **STA Travel** (www.statravel.com) has been the world's leading consolidator for students since purchasing Council Travel, but their fares are competitive for travelers of all ages. **Flights.com** (✆ **800/TRAV-800;** www.flights.com) has excellent fares worldwide, including to Washington, D.C. They also have "local" websites in 12 countries. Two other sites to consider are **FlyCheap** (✆ **800/FLY-CHEAP;** www.1800flycheap.com) and **Air Tickets Direct** (✆ **800/778-3447;** www.airticketsdirect.com).
- Join **frequent-flier clubs.** Frequent-flier membership doesn't cost a cent, but it does entitle you to free tickets or upgrades when you amass the airline's required number of frequent-flier points. You don't even have to fly to earn points; **frequent-flier credit cards** can earn you thousands of miles for doing your everyday shopping. But keep in mind that award seats are limited, seats on popular routes are hard to snag, and more and more major airlines are cutting their expiration periods for mileage points—check the details of your airline's frequent-flier program so you can avoid losing your miles before you use them. ***Inside tip:*** Award seats are offered almost a year in advance; but seats also open up at the last minute, so if your travel plans are flexible, you may strike gold. To play the frequent-flier game to your best advantage, consult the community bulletin boards on **FlyerTalk** (www.flyertalk.com) or go to Randy Petersen's **Inside Flyer** (www.insideflyer.com). Petersen and friends review all the programs in detail and post regular updates on changes in policies and trends.

ARRIVING AT THE AIRPORT

IMMIGRATION & CUSTOMS CLEARANCE Foreign visitors arriving by air, no matter what the port of entry, should cultivate patience and resignation before setting foot on U.S. soil. U.S. airports have considerably beefed up security clearances in the years since the terrorist attacks of 9/11, and clearing Customs and Immigration can take as long as 2 hours.

People traveling by air from Canada, Bermuda, and certain Caribbean countries can sometimes clear Customs and Immigration at the point of departure, which is much faster.

GETTING INTO TOWN FROM THE AIRPORT

Each of the three airports offers similar options for getting into the city. Follow the signs to "ground transportation" and look for the banners or a staff representative of the service you desire. All three airports could really use better signage, especially because their ground transportation desks always seem to be located quite a distance from the gate at which you arrive. Keep trudging, and follow baggage claim signs, too, since ground transportation operations are always situated near baggage carousels.

TAXI SERVICE For a trip to downtown D.C., you can expect a taxi to cost anywhere from $10 to $20 for the 10- to 20-minute ride from National Airport; $50 to $60 for the 30- to 45-minute ride from Dulles Airport; and $63 for the 45-minute ride from BWI.

SUPERSHUTTLE Vans (✆ **800/258-3826;** www.supershuttle.com) offer shared-ride, door-to-door service between the airport and your destination, whether in the District or in a suburban location. You can't reserve space on the van for a ride from the airport, which means that you'll probably have to wait 15 to 30 minutes before boarding (so that your driver can fill his van with enough other passengers to make his trip worthwhile). This also means that you're going to be taken to your destination in rather a roundabout way, as the driver drops off other passengers en route. If you arrive after midnight at National, Dulles, or BWI airports, you can summon a van by calling ✆ **703/416-1199.** The 24-hour service bases its fares on zip code, so to reach downtown, expect to pay about $12, plus $8 for each additional person from National; $25, plus $10 per additional person from Dulles; and $30 to $32, plus $10 per additional person from BWI. If you're calling the SuperShuttle for a ride from a D.C. area location to one of the airports, you must reserve a spot at least 24 hours in advance.

LIMOUSINES Limousine service is the most costly of all options, with prices starting at $30 at National, $65 at Dulles, and $95 at BWI, for private car transportation to downtown D.C. For pickup from BWI, reserve passage by calling ✆ **800/878-7743** or 301/912-0000; for pickup from National or Dulles, try **Red Top Executive Sedan** (✆ **800/296-3300;** www.redtopcab.com).

Free hotel/motel shuttles operate from all three airports to certain nearby properties. Best to inquire about such transportation when you book a room at your hotel.

Individual transportation options at each airport are as follows:

FROM RONALD REAGAN WASHINGTON NATIONAL AIRPORT If you are not too encumbered with luggage, you should take **Metrorail** (✆ **202/637-7000**) into the city. Metro's Yellow and Blue lines stop at the airport and connect via an enclosed walkway to level two, the concourse level, of the main terminal, adjacent to terminals B and C. If yours is one of the airlines that still uses the "old" terminal A (Spirit, AirTran, Midwest, Northwest, and ATA), you will have a longer walk to reach the Metro station. Signs pointing the way can be confusing, so ask an airport employee if you're headed in the right direction; or, better yet, head out to the curb and hop a shuttle bus to the station, but be sure to ask the driver to let you know when you've reached the Metro (it may not be obvious, and drivers don't always announce the stops). **Metrobuses** (✆ **202/637-7000**) also serve the area, should you be going somewhere off the Metro route. But Metrorail is fastest, a 15- to 20-minute non-rush-hour ride to downtown. It is safe, convenient, and cheap, costing $1.35 base fare and going up from there, depending on when (fares increase during rush hours) and where you're going.

If you're renting a car from on-site **car-rental agencies, Alamo** (✆ 703/684-0086), **Avis** (✆ 703/419-5815), **Budget** (✆ 703/419-1021), **Dollar** (✆ 703/519-8701), **Hertz** (✆ 703/419-6300), **National** (✆ 703/419-1032), or **Thrifty** (✆ 877/283-0898), go to level two, the concourse level, follow the pedestrian walkway to the parking garage, find garage A, and descend one flight. You can also take the complimentary Airport Shuttle (look for the sign posted at the curb outside the terminal) to parking garage A. If you've rented from off-premises agency **Enterprise** (✆ 703/553-7744), head outside the baggage claim area of your terminal, and catch the Enterprise shuttle bus.

To get downtown by car, follow the signs out of the airport for the George Washington Parkway. Stay on the GW Parkway until you see signs for I-395 north to Washington. Take the I-395 north exit, which takes you across the 14th Street Bridge. Stay in the left lane crossing the bridge and follow the signs for Route 1, which will put you on 14th Street Northwest. (You'll see the Washington Monument off to your left.) Ask your hotel for directions from 14th Street and Constitution Avenue Northwest. Or take the more scenic route, always staying to the left on the GW Parkway as you follow the signs for Memorial Bridge. You'll be driving alongside the Potomac River, with the monuments in view across the river; then, as you cross over Memorial Bridge, you're greeted by the Lincoln Memorial. Stay left coming over the bridge, swoop around to the left of the Memorial, take a left on 23rd Street NW, a right on Constitution Avenue, and then, if you want to be in the heart of downtown, left again on 15th Street NW (the Washington Monument will be to your right).

FROM WASHINGTON DULLES INTERNATIONAL AIRPORT The **Washington Flyer Express Bus** runs between Dulles and the West Falls Church Metro station, where you can board a train for D.C. In the airport, look for signs for the "Dulles Airport Shuttle" or ask at the information desk. Buses to the West Falls Church Metro station run daily, every 30 minutes, and cost $9 one-way. (By the way, **"Washington Flyer"** is also the name under which the taxi service operates at Dulles.)

More convenient is the **Metrobus** service (Route 5A) that runs between Dulles and the L'Enfant Plaza Metro station, located near Capitol Hill and within walking distance of the National Mall and Smithsonian museums. The bus departs hourly, daily; costs only $3; and takes about 45 to 60 minutes.

If you are renting a car at Dulles, head down the ramp near your baggage claim area, and walk outside to the curb to look for your rental car's shuttle-bus stop. The buses come by every 5 minutes or so en route to nearby rental lots. These include **Alamo** (✆ 703/260-0182), **Avis** (✆ 703/661-3505), **Budget** (✆ 703/437-9373), **Dollar** (✆ 866/434-2226), **Enterprise** (✆ 703/661-8800), **Hertz** (✆ 703/471-6020), **National** (✆ 703/260-0182), and **Thrifty** (✆ 877/283-0898).

To reach downtown Washington from Dulles by car, exit the airport and stay on the Dulles Access Road, which leads right into I-66 east. Follow I-66 east, which takes you across the Theodore Roosevelt

Tips Getting Through the Airport

- Arrive at the airport at least 1 hour before a domestic flight and 2 hours before an international flight. You can check the average wait times at your airport by going to the TSA **Security Checkpoint Wait Times** site (waittime/tsa.dhs.gov).
- Know what you can carry on and what you can't. For the latest updates on items you are prohibited to bring in carry-on luggage, go to **www.tsa.gov/travelers/airtravel**.
- Beat the ticket-counter lines by using the self-service electronic ticket kiosks at the airport or even printing out your boarding pass at home from the airline website. Using curbside check-in is also a smart way to avoid lines.
- Bring a current, government-issued photo ID such as a driver's license or passport. Children under 18 do not need government-issued photo IDs for flights within the U.S., but they do need passports for international flights to most countries.
- Help speed up security before you're screened. Remove jackets, shoes, belt buckles, heavy jewelry, and watches and place them in either your carry-on luggage or the security bins provided. Place keys, coins, cellphones, and pagers in a security bin. If you have metallic body parts, carry a note from your doctor. When possible, pack liquids in checked baggage.
- Use a TSA-approved lock for your checked luggage. Look for Travel Sentry certified locks at luggage or travel shops and Brookstone stores (there are branches of Brookstone at each of D.C.'s three airports; www.brookstone.com).

Memorial Bridge; be sure to stay in the center lane as you cross the bridge, and this will put you on Constitution Avenue. Ask your hotel for directions from this point.

FROM BALTIMORE–WASHINGTON INTERNATIONAL AIRPORT Washington's Metro service runs an Express Metro Bus ("B30") between its Metrorail Green Line Greenbelt station and BWI Airport. In the airport, head to the lower level and look for "Public Transit" signs to find the bus, which operates daily, departs every 40 minutes, takes about 30 minutes to reach the station, and costs $3. At the Greenbelt Metro station, you purchase a Metro fare card and board a Metro train, which will take you into the city. Depending on where you want to go, you can either stay on the Green Line train to your designated stop or get off at the Fort Totten Station to transfer to a Red Line train, whose stops include Union Station (near Capitol Hill) and various downtown locations. Transfers can be tricky, so you may want to ask a fellow passenger or a Metro attendant to make sure you're headed in the right direction.

You also have the choice of taking either an **Amtrak** (✆ **800/872-7245**) or a **Maryland Rural Commuter** (**MARC;** ✆ **800/325-7245**) train into the city. Both trains travel between the BWI Railway Station (✆ **410/672-6169**) and Washington's Union Station (✆ **202/484-7540**), about a 30-minute ride. Amtrak's

Tips Don't Stow It—Ship It

Though pricey, it's sometimes worthwhile to travel luggage free, particularly if you're toting sports equipment, meetings materials, or baby equipment. Specialists in door-to-door luggage delivery include **Virtual Bellhop** (www.virtualbellhop.com), **SkyCap International** (www.skycapinternational.com), **Luggage Express** (www.usxpluggageexpress.com), and **Sports Express** (www.sportsexpress.com).

service is daily (ticket prices range from $12 to $38 per person, one-way, depending on time and train type), while MARC's is weekdays only ($6 per person, one-way). A courtesy shuttle runs every 10 minutes or so between the airport and the train station; stop at the desk near the baggage-claim area to check for the next departure time of both the shuttle bus and the train. Trains depart about once per hour.

BWI operates a large offsite car-rental facility. From the ground transportation area, you board a shuttle bus that transports you to the lot. Rental agencies include **Alamo** (✆ 410/859-8092), **Avis** (✆ 410/859-1680), **Budget** (✆ 410/859-0850), **Dollar** (✆ 800/800-4000), **Hertz** (✆ 410/850-7400), **National** (✆ 410/859-8860), and **Thrifty** (✆ 410/850-7139).

Here's how you reach Washington: Look for signs for I-195 and follow I-195 west until you see signs for Washington and the Baltimore–Washington Parkway (I-295); head south on I-295. Get off I-295 when you see the signs for Route 50/New York Avenue, which leads into the District, via New York Avenue. Ask your hotel for specific directions from New York Avenue NE.

BY CAR

A full third of visitors to Washington arrive by plane, and if that's you, don't worry about renting a car. In fact, it's better if you don't, since the traffic in the city and throughout the region is absolutely abysmal, parking spaces are hard to find, garage and lot charges are exorbitant, and hotel overnight rates are even worse. And you won't even need a car: Washington is eminently walkable, subway-accessible, and taxi-abundant.

But if you are like most visitors, you're planning on driving here, traveling on one of the following major highways: I-70 and I-270, I-95, and I-295 from the north; I-95 and I-395, Route 1, and Route 301 from the south; Route 50/301 and Route 450 from the east; and Route 7, Route 50, I-66, and Route 29/211 from the west.

No matter which road you take, there's a good chance you will have to navigate some portion of the **Capital Beltway** (I-495 and I-95) to gain entry to D.C. The Beltway girds the city, about 66 miles around, with more than 56 interchanges or exits, and is nearly always congested (especially during weekday morning and evening rush hours, roughly between 5:30 to 9:30am and 3 to 7pm). Commuter traffic on the Beltway rivals, maybe surpasses, that of major L.A. freeways, and drivers can get a little crazy, weaving in and out of traffic.

Get yourself a good map before you do anything else. The **American Automobile Association (AAA; ✆ 800/763-9900** for emergency road service and for connection to the mid-Atlantic office; www.aaa.com) provides its members with maps and detailed Trip-Tiks that give precise directions to a destination, including up-to-date information about areas of construction. AAA also provides towing services should you have car trouble during your trip. If you are driving to a hotel in D.C. or its suburbs, contact the establishment to find out the best route to the hotel's address and other crucial details concerning parking availability and rates. The District is 240 miles from New York City, 40 miles from Baltimore, 700 miles from Chicago, 500 miles from Boston, and about 630 miles from Atlanta.

BY TRAIN

Amtrak (✆ **800/USA-RAIL;** www.amtrak.com) offers daily service to Washington from New York, Boston, Chicago, and Los Angeles (you change trains in Chicago). Amtrak also travels daily between Washington and points south, including Raleigh, Charlotte, Atlanta, cities in Florida, and New Orleans. Amtrak's **Acela Express** trains offer the quickest service along the "Northeast Corridor," linking Boston, New York, Philadelphia, and Washington. The trains travel as fast as 150 miles per hour, making the trip between New York and Washington in about 3 hours and 30 minutes and between Boston and Washington in about 7 hours. Amtrak runs fewer Acela trains on weekends, and honors passenger discounts, such as those for seniors and AAA members, only on weekend Acela travel.

Amtrak offers a smorgasbord of good-deal rail passes and discounted fares; although not all are based on advance purchase, you may have more discount options by reserving early. The bargain fares can be used only on certain days and hours of the day; be sure to find out exactly what restrictions apply. Tickets for children ages 2 to 15 cost half the price of a regular coach fare when the children are accompanied by a fare-paying adult. For more information, go to **www.amtrak.com** and click on the website's "Hot Deals" section, where you'll find assorted discount possibilities. Amtrak also offers tour packages through its Amtrak Vacations program (✆ **800/268-7252;** www.amtrakholidays.com).

Note: Amtrak requires reserved seating on its regional trains running between Boston and Newport News, Virginia, which means that every traveler is guaranteed a seat—in the past, during holiday and other busy travel times, passengers would cram themselves into crowded cars on this popular route, standing the whole way, if necessary.

International visitors who plan to travel to other places in the country can buy a **USA Rail Pass,** good for 5, 15, or 30 days of unlimited travel on **Amtrak** (✆ **800/USA-RAIL;** www.amtrak.com). The pass is available online or through many overseas travel agents. See Amtrak's website for the cost of travel within the western, eastern, or northwestern United States. Reservations are generally required and should be made as early as possible. Regional rail passes are also available.

Amtrak trains arrive at historic **Union Station,** 50 Massachusetts Ave. NE (✆ **202/371-9441;** www.unionstationdc.com), a short walk from the Capitol, across the circle from several hotels, and a short cab or Metro ride from downtown. Union Station is a turn-of-the-20th-century Beaux Arts masterpiece that was magnificently restored in the late 1980s. Offering a three-level marketplace of shops and restaurants, this stunning depot is conveniently located and connects with Metro service. Taxis are almost always available. (For more on Union Station, see chapters 4, 7, and 8.)

5 Money & Costs

Anyone who travels to the nation's capital expecting bargains is in for a rude awakening, especially when it comes to lodging. Less expensive than New York and London, Washington, D.C.'s hotel rates, nevertheless, average a hefty $186 per room per night, reflecting the city's popularity as a top destination among U.S. travelers. D.C.'s restaurant scene is rather more egalitarian: heavy on the fine, top-dollar establishments, where you can easily spend $100 per person, but with plenty of excellent bistros and small restaurants offering great eats at lower prices. When it comes to attractions, though, the nation's capital has the rest of the world beat, since most of its museums and tourist sites offer free admission.

ATMs

Nationwide, the easiest and best way to get cash away from home is from an ATM (automated teller machine), sometimes referred to as a "cash machine," or "cashpoint." In Washington, D.C., ATMs are ubiquitous, in locations ranging from the National Gallery of Art's gift shop, to Union Station, to grocery stores. The **Cirrus** (✆ **800/424-7787;** www.mastercard.com) and **PLUS** (✆ **800/843-7587;** www.visa.com) networks operate in D.C., as they do across the country. Go to your bank card's website or call one of your branches to find ATM locations in Washington. Be sure you know your personal identification number (PIN) and daily withdrawal limit before you depart. If your PIN is five or six digits, you should obtain a four-digit PIN from your local bank before you leave home, since the four-digit PINs are what most ATMs in Washington accept.

Note: Many banks impose a fee every time you use a card at another bank's ATM, and that fee is often higher for international transactions (up to $5 or more) than for domestic ones (where they're rarely more than $2). In addition, the bank from which you withdraw cash may charge its own fee. Visitors from outside the U.S. should also find out whether their bank assesses a 1% to 3% fee on charges incurred abroad.

CREDIT CARDS & DEBIT CARDS

Credit cards are the most widely used form of payment in the United States: **Visa** (Barclaycard in Britain), **MasterCard** (EuroCard in Europe, Access in Britain, Chargex in Canada), **American Express, Diners Club,** and **Discover.** They also provide a convenient record of all your expenses, and offer relatively good exchange rates. You can withdraw cash advances from your credit cards at banks or ATMs, but high fees make credit-card cash advances a pricey way to get cash.

It's highly recommended that you travel with at least one major credit card. You must have a credit card to rent a car, and hotels and airlines usually require a credit card imprint as a deposit against expenses.

ATM cards with major credit card backing, known as **"debit cards,"** are now a commonly acceptable form of payment in most stores and restaurants. Debit cards draw money directly from your checking account. Some stores enable you to receive cash back on your debit-card purchases as well. The same is true at most U.S. post offices.

TRAVELER'S CHECKS

Though credit cards and debit cards are more often used, traveler's checks are still widely accepted in the U.S. Foreign visitors should make sure that traveler's checks are denominated in U.S. dollars; foreign-currency checks are often difficult to exchange.

You can buy traveler's checks at most banks. Most are offered in denominations of $20, $50, $100, $500, and sometimes

What Things Cost in Washington, D.C.	US$	UK£
Cup of coffee	1.80	0.90
Movie ticket	9.75	4.90
Taxi from Dulles	55.00	28.00
Subway fare	1.35	0.68
Moderate hotel rate	200.00	100.00

$1,000. Generally, you'll pay a service charge ranging from 1% to 4%.

The most popular traveler's checks are offered by **American Express** (✆ **800/807-6233;** ✆ **800/221-7282** for card holders—this number accepts collect calls, offers service in several foreign languages, and exempts Amex gold and platinum cardholders from the 1% fee); **Visa** (✆ **800/732-1322**); and **MasterCard** (✆ **800/223-9920**). AAA members can obtain Visa checks (in denominations of $20, $50, and $100) without a fee at most **AAA offices.** AAA has a downtown Washington office, open weekdays 9am to 5:30pm, at 701 15th St. NW (✆ **202/331-3000**), not far from the White House. AAA members can also order checks online (www.aaa.com) or over the phone (✆ **866/339-3378**), for a $9.95 fee, plus a $7 shipping fee for orders under $500.

Be sure to keep a copy of the traveler's checks' serial numbers separate from your checks in the event that they are stolen or lost. You'll get a refund faster if you know the numbers.

Another option is the new **prepaid traveler's check cards,** reloadable cards that work much like debit cards but aren't linked to your checking account. The **American Express Travelers Cheque Card,** for example, requires a minimum deposit ($300), sets a maximum balance ($2,750), and has a one-time issuance fee of $15. You can withdraw money from an ATM ($2.50 per transaction, not including bank fees), and the funds can be purchased in dollars, euros, or pounds. If you lose the card, your available funds will be refunded within 24 hours.

6 Travel Insurance

The cost of travel insurance varies widely, depending on the cost and length of your trip, your age and health, and the type of trip you're taking, but expect to pay between 5% and 8% of the vacation itself. You can get estimates from various providers through **InsureMyTrip.com.** Enter your trip cost and dates, your age, and other information, for prices from more than a dozen companies.

For **U.K. citizens,** insurance is always advisable when traveling in the States. Travelers or families who make more than one trip abroad per year may find that an annual travel insurance policy works out cheaper. Check **www.moneysupermarket.com**, which compares prices across a wide range of providers for single- and multi-trip policies.

Most big travel agents offer their own insurance and will probably try to sell you their package when you book a holiday. Think before you sign. **Britain's Consumers' Association** recommends that you insist on seeing the policy and reading the fine print before buying travel insurance. **The Association of British Insurers** (✆ **020/7600-3333;** www.abi.org.uk) gives advice by phone and publishes *Holiday Insurance,* a free guide to policy provisions and prices. You might also shop around for better deals: Try **Columbus Direct** (✆ **0870/033-9988;** www.columbusdirect.net).

TRIP-CANCELLATION INSURANCE

Trip-cancellation insurance will help retrieve your money if you have to back out of a trip or depart early, or if your travel supplier goes bankrupt. Trip cancellation traditionally covers such events as sickness, natural disasters, and State Department advisories. The latest news in trip-cancellation insurance is the availability of **expanded hurricane coverage** and the **"any-reason"** cancellation coverage—which costs more but covers cancellations made for any reason. You won't get back 100% of your prepaid trip cost, but you'll be refunded a substantial portion. **TravelSafe** (✆ **888/885-7233;** www.travelsafe.com) offers both types of coverage. Expedia also offers any-reason cancellation coverage for its air-hotel packages.

For details, contact one of the following recommended insurers: **Access America** (✆ 866/807-3982; www.accessamerica.com); **Travel Guard International** (✆ 800/826-4919; www.travelguard.com); **Travel Insured International** (✆ 800/243-3174; www.travelinsured.com); and **Travelex Insurance Services** (✆ 888/457-4602; www.travelex-insurance.com).

MEDICAL INSURANCE

Although it's not required of travelers, health insurance is highly recommended. Most health insurance policies cover you if you get sick away from home—but check your coverage before you leave.

International visitors should note that unlike many European countries, the United States does not usually offer free or low-cost medical care to its citizens or visitors. Doctors and hospitals are expensive, and in most cases will require advance payment or proof of coverage before they render their services. Good policies will cover the costs of an accident, repatriation, or death. Packages such as **Europ Assistance's "Worldwide Healthcare Plan"** are sold by European automobile clubs and travel agencies at attractive rates. **Worldwide Assistance Services, Inc.** (✆ **800/777-8710;** www.worldwideassistance.com) is the agent for Europ Assistance in the United States. Worldwide Assistance Services has offices in Washington, D.C., at 1825 K St. NW, Suite 1000, Washington, DC 20006 (✆ **202/331-1609**).

Though lack of health insurance may prevent you from being admitted to a hospital in nonemergencies, don't worry about being left on a street corner to die: The American way is to fix you now and bill the living daylights out of you later.

If you're ever hospitalized more than 150 miles from home, **MedjetAssist** (✆ **800/527-7478;** www.medjetassistance.com) will pick you up and fly you to the hospital of your choice in a medically equipped and staffed aircraft 24 hours a day, 7 days a week. Annual memberships are $225 individual, $350 family; you can also purchase short-term memberships.

Canadians should check with their provincial health plan offices or call **Health Canada** (✆ **866/225-0709;** www.hc-sc.gc.ca) to find out the extent of their coverage and what documentation and receipts they must take home in case they are treated in the United States.

LOST-LUGGAGE INSURANCE

On flights within the U.S., checked baggage is covered up to $2,500 per ticketed passenger. On flights outside the U.S. (and on U.S. portions of international trips), baggage coverage is limited to approximately $9.07 per pound, up to approximately $635 per checked bag. If you plan to check items more valuable than what's covered by the standard liability, see if your homeowner's policy covers your valuables, get baggage insurance as part of your comprehensive travel-insurance package, or buy Travel Guard's "BagTrak" product.

If your luggage is lost, immediately file a lost-luggage claim at the airport, detailing the luggage contents. Most airlines require that you report delayed, damaged, or lost baggage within 4 hours of arrival. The airlines are required to deliver luggage, once found, directly to your house or destination free of charge.

7 Health

GENERAL AVAILABILITY OF HEALTHCARE

Contact the **International Association for Medical Assistance to Travelers** (IAMAT) (✆ **716/754-4883** or, in Canada, 416/652-0137; **www.iamat.org**) for tips on travel and health concerns in Washington, D.C., and elsewhere in the United States. The site provides a link that leads you to directories of health clinics and doctors located in Washington and throughout the country, as well as a link to state health departments, including D.C.'s. The United States **Centers for Disease Control and Prevention** (✆ **800/311-3435;** www.cdc.gov) provides up-to-date information on health hazards by region or country and offers tips on food safety. The website **www.tripprep.com**, sponsored by a consortium of travel medicine practitioners, Travel Health Online, offers helpful travel advice as well as a listing of reliable clinics and doctors in the D.C. area.

WHAT TO DO IF YOU GET SICK AWAY FROM HOME

We list **hospitals** and **emergency numbers** in chapter 4's "Fast Facts," p. 72.

If you suffer from a chronic illness, consult your doctor before your departure. Pack **prescription medications** in your carry-on luggage, and carry them in their original containers with the pharmacy labels—otherwise they won't make it through airport security. Visitors from outside the U.S. should carry generic names of prescription drugs. For U.S. travelers, most reliable healthcare plans provide coverage if you get sick away from home. Foreign visitors may have to pay all medical costs upfront and be reimbursed later. See "Medical Insurance," under "Travel Insurance," above.

If you get sick, consider asking your hotel concierge to recommend a local doctor. You can also try the emergency room of any D.C. hospital, all of which have walk-in clinics for emergency cases that are not life-threatening.

Avoiding "Economy Class Syndrome"

Deep vein thrombosis, or, as it's known in the world of flying, "economy-class syndrome," is a blood clot that develops in a deep vein. It's a potentially deadly condition that can be caused by sitting in cramped conditions—such as an airplane cabin—for too long. During a flight (especially a long-haul flight), get up, walk around, and stretch your legs every 60 to 90 minutes to keep your blood flowing. Other preventive measures include frequent flexing of the legs while sitting, drinking lots of water, and avoiding alcohol and sleeping pills. If you have a history of deep vein thrombosis, heart disease, or another condition that puts you at high risk, some experts recommend wearing compression stockings or taking anticoagulants when you fly; always ask your physician about the best course for you. Symptoms of deep vein thrombosis include leg pain or swelling, or even shortness of breath.

Healthy Travels to You

The following government websites offer up-to-date health-related travel advice.

- **Australia:** www.dfat.gov.au/travel/
- **Canada:** www.hc-sc.gc.ca/index_e.html
- **U.K.:** www.dh.gov.uk/PolicyAndGuidance/HealthAdviceForTravellers/fs/en
- **U.S.:** www.cdc.gov/travel/

8 Safety

STAYING SAFE

The first thing you want to do is get on the Internet and access the Washington, D.C. Convention and Tourism Corporation's website, **www.washington.org**, which publishes travel updates, sometimes on a daily basis. The travel updates alert you to the general state of affairs in D.C. and to new security and touring procedures around town, and refers you to other sections of its website for information about restaurants, hotels, and attractions.

In the years following the September 11, 2001, terrorist attack on the Pentagon, the federal and D.C. governments, along with agencies such as the National Park Service, have continued to work together to increase security, not just at airports, but around the city, including government buildings, tourist attractions, and the subway. The most noticeable and, honestly, most irksome aspect of increased security at tourist attractions can be summed up in three little words: **waiting in line.** Although visitors have always had to queue to enter the Capitol, the Supreme Court, and other federal buildings, now it takes more time to get through because of more intense scrutiny when you finally reach the door. Other federal buildings, like the Library of Congress, where you used to be able to waltz right in, now often have lines. Besides lines, you will notice vehicle barriers in place at a wider radius around the Capitol building and new vehicle barriers and better lighting installed at the Washington Monument and at the Lincoln and Jefferson memorials. Self-guided tours of the Capitol are no longer possible, and public guided tours are less comprehensive than they used to be. (A new, tightly secured underground visitors center due to open at the Capitol in 2007 should help to streamline the process.) Greater numbers of police and security officers are on duty around and inside government buildings, the monuments, and the Metro.

Just because so many police are around, you shouldn't let your guard down. Washington, like any urban area, has a criminal element, so it's important to stay alert and take normal safety precautions.

Ask your hotel front-desk staff or the city's tourist office if you're in doubt about which neighborhoods are safe. Read the section "The Neighborhoods in Brief," in chapter 4, to get a better idea of where you might feel most comfortable.

Avoid deserted areas, especially at night, and don't go into public parks at night unless there's a concert or similar occasion that will attract a crowd.

Avoid carrying valuables with you on the street, and don't display expensive cameras or electronic equipment. If you're using a map, consult it inconspicuously—or better yet, try to study it before you leave your room. In general, the more you look like a tourist, the more likely someone will try to take advantage of you. If you're walking, pay attention to who is near you as you walk. If you're attending a convention or event where you wear a name tag, remove it before venturing outside. Hold on to your purse, and place your billfold in an inside pocket. In theaters, restaurants, and other public places, keep your possessions in sight.

Remember also that hotels are open to the public, and in a large hotel, security may not be able to screen everyone entering. Always lock your room door.

Be careful crossing streets, especially in the downtown area, and be even more cautious at rush hour. Though this may seem like obvious advice, it's worth a mention here, as there's been an alarming increase lately in the number of pedestrians being hit by cars and buses. Drivers in a hurry run red lights, turn corners too quickly, and so on, so be sure to take your time and check for oncoming traffic when crossing streets, and to use the crosswalks. If you're from countries such as Great Britain or Australia, remember to look to your left first, rather than to your right, on two-way streets.

9 Specialized Travel Resources

TRAVELERS WITH DISABILITIES

Washington, D.C., is one of the most accessible cities in the world for travelers with disabilities. The best overall source of information about accessibility at specific Washington hotels, restaurants, shopping malls, and attractions is available from the nonprofit organization **Access Information.** You can read the information (including restaurant reviews) online at **www.disabilityguide.org**, or order a free copy of the *Washington, DC Access Guide* by calling ✆ **301/528-8664,** or by writing to Access Information, 21618 Slidell Rd., Boyds, MD 20841.

The **Washington Metropolitan Transit Authority** publishes accessibility information on its website **www.wmata.com**, or you can call ✆ **202/962-1245** with questions about Metro services for travelers with disabilities, including how to obtain an ID card that entitles you to discounted fares. (Make sure that you call at least 3 weeks ahead to allow enough time to obtain an ID card.) For up-to-date information about how Metro is operating on the day you're using it—to verify that the elevators are operating at the stations you'll be traveling to, for instance—call ✆ **202/962-1212.**

Each Metro station is equipped with an elevator (complete with Braille number plates) to train platforms and extrawide fare gates for wheelchair users; rail cars are fully accessible. Metro has installed punctuated rubber tiles leading up to the granite-lined platform edge to warn visually impaired Metro riders that they're nearing the tracks; barriers between rail cars prevent the blind from mistaking the gap for entry to a car. For the hearing impaired, flashing lights indicate arriving trains; for the visually impaired, door chimes let you know when the train doors are closing. Train operators make station and onboard announcements of train destinations and stops, although the noise of the train and a less-than-perfect audio system often make these announcements unintelligible. Nearly all of the District's Metrobuses have wheelchair lifts and kneel at the curb, though they aren't always operating. The TTY number for Metro information is ✆ **202/638-3780.**

Regular **Tourmobile** trams (p. 237) are accessible to visitors with disabilities. The company also operates special vans for immobile travelers, complete with wheelchair lifts. Tourmobile recommends that you call a day ahead to ensure that the van is available for you when you arrive. For information, call ✆ **703/979-0690,** or go to www.tourmobile.com.

Major Washington museums, including all **Smithsonian museum buildings,** are accessible to wheelchair visitors. A comprehensive free publication called *Smithsonian Access* lists all services available to visitors with disabilities, including parking, building access, and sign language interpreters. To obtain a copy, call ✆ **202/633-1000** or TTY 202/633-5285, or find the information online at www.si.edu/visit/visitors_with_disabilities.htm. The "633" phone numbers are the Smithsonian's main information lines, manned by well-informed volunteers, who are able to answer all of your questions about the Smithsonian museums.

Likewise, all of the memorials, including the **Lincoln, Jefferson, Franklin Delano Roosevelt, Vietnam, Korea,** and **World War II memorials** and the **Washington Monument** are each equipped to accommodate visitors with disabilities and keep wheelchairs on the premises. There's limited parking for visitors with disabilities at some of these locations. Call ahead to other sightseeing attractions for accessibility information and special services.

Washington theaters are handily equipped. Among the most accessible are the following three.

The **John F. Kennedy Center for the Performing Arts** is fully accessible. The center provides headphones to hearing-impaired patrons at no charge. A wireless, infrared listening-enhancement system is available in all theaters. Some performances offer sign language and audio description. A public TTY is located at the Information Center in the Hall of States as well as on parking lot level A. Large-print programs are available at every performance; a limited number of Braille programs are available from the house manager. All theaters in the complex are wheelchair accessible. To reserve a wheelchair, call ✆ **202/416-8340.** For other questions regarding patrons with disabilities, including information about half-price tickets (you will need to submit a letter from your doctor stating that your disability is permanent), access the center's website, www.kennedy-center.org, or call the Office for Accessibility ✆ **202/416-8727.** The TTY number is ✆ **202/416-8728.**

The **Arena Stage** (✆ **202/488-3300;** www.arenastage.org) offers audio description and sign interpretation at designated performances, as well as infrared and audio loop assisted-listening devices for the hearing impaired, plus program books in Braille and large print. The TTY box office line is ✆ **202/484-0247.** You can also call ahead to reserve handicapped parking spaces for a performance.

The **National Theatre** is wheelchair accessible and features special performances of its shows for visually and hearing-impaired theatergoers. To obtain amplified-sound earphones for narration, simply ask an usher before the performance (you'll need to provide an ID). The National also offers a limited number of half-price tickets to patrons with disabilities who have obtained a Special Patron card from the theater, or who can provide a letter from a doctor certifying disability; you may receive no more than two half-price tickets. For details, call ✆ **202/628-6161,** or go the website, www.nationaltheatre.org.

Organizations that offer a vast range of resources and assistance to travelers with disabilities include **MossRehab** (✆ **800/CALL-MOSS;** www.mossresourcenet.org); the **American Foundation for the Blind (AFB)** (✆ **800/232-5463;** www.afb.org); and **SATH (Society for Accessible Travel & Hospitality)** (✆ **212/447-7284;** www.sath.org). **AirAmbulanceCard.com** is now partnered with SATH and allows you to preselect top-notch hospitals in case of an emergency.

Access-Able Travel Source (✆ **303/232-2979;** www.access-able.com) offers a comprehensive database on travel agents from around the world with experience in accessible travel; destination-specific access information; and links to such resources as service animals, equipment rentals, and access guides.

Many travel agencies offer customized tours and itineraries for travelers with disabilities. Among them are **Flying Wheels Travel** (✆ **507/451-5005;** www.flyingwheelstravel.com) and **Accessible Journeys** (✆ **800/846-4537** or 610/521-0339; www.disabilitytravel.com).

Flying with Disability (www.flying-with-disability.org) is a comprehensive information source on airplane travel. **Avis Rent a Car** (✆ **888/879-4273**) has an "Avis Access" program that offers services for customers with special travel needs. These include specially outfitted vehicles with swivel seats, spinner knobs, and hand controls; mobility scooter rentals; and accessible bus service. Be sure to reserve well in advance.

Also check out the quarterly magazine ***Emerging Horizons*** (www.emerginghorizons.com), available by subscription ($16.95 year U.S.; $21.95 outside U.S).

The "Accessible Travel" link at **Mobility-Advisor.com** (www.mobilityadvisor.com) offers a variety of travel resources to persons with disabilities.

British travelers should contact **Holiday Care** (✆ **0845-124-9971** in the U.K. only; www.holidaycare.org.uk) to access a wide range of travel information and resources for travelers with disabilities and elderly people.

GAY & LESBIAN TRAVELERS

Washington, D.C., has a large and vibrant gay and lesbian community and clearly welcomes gay and lesbian visitors, as evidenced by the fact that the Washington, D.C. Convention and Tourism Corporation includes on its website, **www.washington.org**, a link to information for the GLBT crowd: Click on "Pride in D.C.," which appears on the site's home page. This special section covers the history of the gay rights movement in the capital; a calendar of noteworthy events, like the annual, week-long Capital Pride Celebration held in June, complete with a street fair and a parade; and favorite place recommendations made by local gays and lesbians. Better yet is the WCTC's *GLBT Traveler's Guide,* published for the first time in 2007, and covering just about every aspect of the not-straight life in D.C. You can order the 68-page guide by calling the WCTC's main number, ✆ **202/789-7000,** or download it from the website.

When in Washington, you'll want to get your hands on the *Washington Blade* (✆ **202/797-7000;** www.washingtonblade.com), a comprehensive weekly newspaper distributed free at Metro stations and hundreds of other places throughout the city, including Olsson's Books/Records, 1307 19th St. NW; Borders, 18th and L streets; and Kramerbooks, 1517 Connecticut Ave. NW. Every issue provides an extensive events calendar and a list of hundreds of resources, such as crisis centers, health facilities, switchboards, political groups, religious organizations, social clubs, and student activities; it puts you in touch with everything from groups of lesbian bird-watchers to the Asian Gay Men's Network. Gay restaurants and clubs are also listed and advertised.

Washington's gay bookstore, **Lambda Rising,** 1625 Connecticut Ave. NW (✆ **202/462-6969;** www.lambdarising.com), informally serves as an information source and gathering place for the gay community, which centers on the Dupont Circle neighborhood.

The International Gay and Lesbian Travel Association (IGLTA) (✆ **800/448-8550** or 954/776-2626; www.iglta.org) is the trade association for the gay and lesbian travel industry, and offers an online directory of gay- and lesbian-friendly travel businesses and tour operators.

Gay.com Travel (✆ **800/929-2268** or 415/644-8044; www.gay.com/travel or www.outandabout.com) is an excellent online successor to the popular ***Out & About*** print magazine. It provides regularly updated information about gay-owned, gay-oriented, and gay-friendly lodging, dining, sightseeing, nightlife, and shopping establishments in every important destination worldwide. British travelers should click on the "Travel" link at **www.uk.gay.com** for advice and gay-friendly trip ideas.

The Canadian website **GayTraveler** (**gaytraveler.ca**) offers ideas and advice for gay travel all over the world.

The following travel guides are available at many bookstores, or you can order them from any online bookseller: ***Spartacus International Gay Guide, 35th Edition*** (Bruno Gmünder Verlag; www.spartacusworld.com/gayguide); ***Odysseus: The International Gay Travel Planner, 17th Edition*** (www.odyusa.com); and the ***Damron*** guides (www.damron.com), with separate, annual books for gay men and lesbians.

SENIOR TRAVEL

Members of **AARP,** 601 E St. NW, Washington, DC 20049 (✆ **888/687-2277;** www.aarp.org), get discounts on hotels, airfares, and car rentals. AARP offers members a wide range of benefits, including *AARP: The Magazine* and a monthly newsletter. Anyone over 50 can join.

With or without AARP membership, seniors often find that discounts are available to them at hotels, especially chain hotels such as the Hilton, so be sure to inquire when you book your reservation.

Venues in Washington that grant discounts to seniors include the Metro; certain theaters, such as the Shakespeare Theatre; and those few museums, like the Phillips Collection, that charge for entry. Each place has its own eligibility rules, including designated "senior" ages: The Shakespeare Theatre's is 60 and older, the Phillips Collection's is 62 and older, and the Metro discounts seniors 65 and older. Check the websites for these and other venues to learn the specifics of individual discount programs.

Many reliable agencies and organizations target the 50-plus market. **Elderhostel** (✆ **800/454-5768;** www.elderhostel.org) arranges worldwide study programs for those age 55 and over. In 2007, Elderhostel hosted more than 17 programs in Washington, D.C., ranging from 1 to 5 days in length and covering diverse topics—from opera to architecture.

Recommended publications offering travel resources and discounts for seniors include the quarterly magazine ***Travel 50 & Beyond*** (www.travel50andbeyond.com) and the bestselling paperback ***Unbelievably Good Deals and Great Adventures That You Absolutely Can't Get Unless You're Over 50 2005–2006, 16th Edition*** (McGraw-Hill), by Joann Rattner Heilman.

FAMILY TRAVEL

To locate accommodations, restaurants, and attractions that are particularly kid-friendly, refer to the "Kids" icon throughout this guide.

Field trips during the school year and family vacations during the summer keep Washington, D.C., crawling with kids all year long. More than any other city, perhaps, Washington is crammed with historic buildings, arts and science museums, parks, and recreational sites to interest young and old alike. Some museums, like the National Museum of Natural History, have hands-on exhibits for children. Many more sponsor regular, usually free, family-oriented events, such as the Corcoran Gallery of Art's "Family Days" and the Folger Shakespeare Library's seasonal activities. It's worth calling or checking websites in advance for the schedules of the attractions you're thinking of visiting. The fact that so many attractions are free is a boon to the family budget.

Hotels, more and more, are doing their part to make family trips affordable, too.

At many lodgings, children under a certain age (usually 12) sleep free in the same room with their parents. (I've noted these policies in all the listings in chapter 5.) Hotel weekend packages often offer special family rates. See the "Family-Friendly Hotels" box on p. 93 for a rundown of the hotels that are most welcoming to young travelers.

Restaurants throughout the Washington area are growing increasingly family-friendly. Many provide kids' menus or charge less for children's portions. The best news, though, is that families are welcome at all sorts of restaurants these days and need no longer stick only to burger joints. See the "Family-Friendly Restaurants" box on p. 145 for a list of places kids will especially love.

Washington, D.C., is easy to navigate with children. The Metro covers the city, and it's safe. Children 4 and under ride free.

The *Washington Post* publishes a "Weekend" section every Friday that covers all possible happenings in the city, including family-friendly activities. If you arrive on a Friday, be sure to pick up a copy of the paper; otherwise, you can go online to www.washingtonpost.com, click on the "City Guide" section, and then click on "This Weekend" in the browsing window to read what's up, entertainment wise, in Washington.

Recommended family travel websites include **Family Travel Forum** (www.familytravelforum.com), a comprehensive site that offers customized trip planning; **Family Travel Network** (www.familytravelnetwork.com), an online magazine providing travel tips; and **TravelWithYourKids.com** (www.travelwithyourkids.com), a comprehensive site written by parents for parents offering sound advice for long-distance and international travel with children. Also look for *Frommer's Washington, D.C., with Kids,* which makes an excellent companion piece to this book, providing in-depth coverage of sightseeing with children in Washington.

AFRICAN-AMERICAN TRAVELERS

African Americans currently compose about 60% of the District's population, but have long made their home in the nation's capital, richly contributing to the District's history, culture, personality, and identity. African-American museums, monuments, memorials, musical venues, and other landmarks all over town herald their achievements, individually or as a group. Naturally, all of this makes D.C. a compelling destination for African Americans or anyone interested in their culture. From the **Smithsonian Anacostia Neighborhood Museum and Center for African American History and Culture;** to Benjamin Banneker Park; to the **jazz clubs along U Street,** where Duke Ellington and Cab Calloway once catted; to the **African-American Civil War Memorial and Museum;** to the **Mary McLeod Bethune House,** Washington's black-American heritage is here to discover. Check out the Washington Convention and Tourism Corporation's website, www.washington.org, and peruse its calendar for annual events, like the **Black Family Reunion** in September and the **Black History Month** activities in February. Browse the Cultural Tourism DC website, www.culturaltourismdc.org, to review its database of 98 sites on the **African American Heritage Trail.** (You can also order a copy of the booklet or find out where in Washington you can pick one up free.) The Cultural Tourism DC site lists guided tours that follow an African-American theme, for instance the Black Broadway tour of U Street, but you can also create your own tour with the information provided. Coming in 2008: the dedication of the **Dr. Martin Luther King, Jr., Memorial** on the National Mall.

For sources outside of Washington, you might go to **Black Travel Online** (www.blacktravelonline.com), which posts news on upcoming events and includes links to articles and travel-booking sites. **Soul of America** (www.soulofamerica.com) is a comprehensive website, with travel tips, event and family-reunion postings, and sections on historically black beach resorts and active vacations.

Agencies and organizations that provide resources for black travelers include **Rodgers Travel** (✆ **800/825-1775;** www.rodgerstravel.com) and the **African American Association of Innkeepers International** (✆ **877/422-5777;** www.africanamericaninns.com).

STUDENT TRAVEL

When it comes to admission discounts in Washington, students rule. The one caveat: You must have a valid ID, although your current school ID should be good enough. For benefits that extend beyond reduced admission to D.C. attractions, you may want to consider obtaining an **International Student Identity Card (ISIC),** from the **International Student Travel Confederation (ISTC)** (www.istc.org). ISTC was formed in 1949 to make travel around the world more affordable for students. Check out its website for comprehensive travel services information and details on how to get the ISIC, which qualifies students for substantial savings on rail passes, plane tickets, entrance fees, and more. It also provides students with basic health and life insurance and a 24-hour help line. The card is valid for a maximum of 18 months. You can apply for the card online or in person at **STA Travel** (✆ **800/781-4040** in North America; www.statravel.com), the biggest student travel agency in the world. In Washington, STA has two offices: in Georgetown, at 3301 M St. NW (✆ **202/337-6464**), and on the George Washington University campus, in the Marvin Center, at 800 21st St. NW (✆ **202/994-7800**). If you're no longer a student but are still under 26, you can get an **International Youth Travel Card (IYTC)** from the same people, which entitles you to some discounts.

Travel CUTS (✆ **800/592-2887;** www.travelcuts.com) offers similar services for both Canadians and U.S. residents. Irish students may prefer to turn to **USIT** (✆ **01/602-1904;** www.usit.ie), an Ireland-based specialist in student, youth, and independent travel.

10 Sustainable Tourism/Eco-tourism

Each time you take a flight or drive a car, CO_2 is released into the atmosphere. You can help neutralize this danger to our planet through "carbon offsetting"—paying someone to reduce your CO_2 emissions by the same amount you've added. Carbon offsets can be purchased in the U.S. from companies such as **Carbonfund.org** (www.carbonfund.org) and **TerraPass** (www.terrapass.org), and from **Climate Care** (www.climatecare.org) in the U.K.

Although one could argue that any vacation that includes an airplane flight can't be truly "green," you can go on holiday and still contribute positively to the environment. In addition to purchasing carbon offsets from the companies mentioned above, you can take other steps toward responsible travel. Choose forward-looking companies who embrace responsible development practices. An increasing number of sustainable tourism initiatives can help you plan a family trip and leave as small a "footprint" as possible on the places you visit.

Responsible Travel (www.responsibletravel.com), run by a spokesperson for responsible tourism in the travel industry, contains a great source of sustainable travel ideas and organized excursions. A review of available trips in spring 2007 revealed

Tips It's Easy Being Green

We can all help conserve fuel and energy when we travel. Here are a few simple ways you can help preserve your favorite destinations:

- Whenever possible, choose nonstop flights; they generally require less fuel than those that must stop and take off again.
- If renting a car is necessary on your vacation, ask the rental agent for the most fuel-efficient one available. Not only will you use less gas, but you'll save money at the tank.
- At hotels, request that your sheets and towels not be changed daily. You'll save water and energy by not washing them as often, and you'll prolong the life of the towels, too. (Many hotels already have programs like this in place.)
- Turn off the lights and air-conditioner (or heater) when you leave your hotel room.

none in Washington, D.C., but perhaps the company will offer one in the future, so check the website if you're interested.

The most environmentally responsible thing you can do if you're vacationing in D.C. is to leave your car at home, or, if you drive here, to park the car in the hotel lot and climb back in only when you're ready to head home. You won't need a car in the city.

D.C.'s government buildings and famous landmarks tend to get all the attention, so you may be surprised to learn that 17% of the city is national parkland, which makes the capital one of the "greenest" cities in the country. More than 230,000 acres of parkland lie within city limits; the biggest chunk is the 2,000-acre Rock Creek Park, the National Park Service's oldest urban park, founded in 1890. The city's government is committed to the environmental cause, and its City Council passed an initiative in 2006 requiring developers to follow the U.S. Green Building Council's guidelines. The Washington Nationals Ballpark will be the country's first green-certified stadium when it opens in 2008.

Additionally, a number of D.C. hotels have implemented environmentally friendly policies and initiatives. See the box "Staying Green in D.C.," in chapter 5.

11 Staying Connected

TELEPHONES

Generally, hotel surcharges on long-distance and local calls are astronomical, so you're better off using your **cellphone** or a **public pay telephone.** Many convenience groceries and packaging services sell **prepaid calling cards** in denominations up to $50; for international visitors these can be the least expensive way to call home. Many public pay phones at airports now accept American Express, MasterCard, and Visa credit cards. **Local calls** made from pay phones in most locales cost 35¢. (No pennies, please.)

Most long-distance and international calls can be dialed directly from any phone. **For calls within the United States and to Canada,** dial 1 followed by the area code and the seven-digit number. **For other international calls,** dial 011 followed by the country code, the city code, and the number you are calling.

Calls to area codes **800, 888, 877,** and **866** are toll-free. However, calls to area codes **700** and **900** (chat lines, bulletin boards, "dating" services, and so on) can be very expensive—usually a charge of 95¢ to $3 or more per minute, and they sometimes have minimum charges that can run as high as $15 or more.

For **reversed-charge or collect calls,** and for person-to-person calls, dial the number 0 and then the area code and number; an operator will come on the line, and you should specify whether you are calling collect, person-to-person, or both. If your operator-assisted call is international, ask for the overseas operator.

For **local directory assistance** ("information"), dial 411; for long-distance information, dial 1, then the appropriate area code and 555-1212.

CELLPHONES

Just because your cellphone works at home doesn't mean it'll work everywhere in the U.S. (thanks to our nation's fragmented cellphone system). It's a good bet that your phone will work in major cities, but take a look at your wireless company's coverage map on its website before heading out; T-Mobile, Sprint, and Nextel are particularly weak in rural areas. If you need to stay in touch at a destination where you know your phone won't work, **rent** a phone that does from **InTouch USA** (✆ **800/872-7626;** www.intouchglobal.com) or a rental-car location, but beware that you'll pay $1 a minute or more for airtime.

If you're not from the U.S., you'll be appalled at the poor reach of our **GSM (Global System for Mobile Communications) wireless network,** which is used by much of the rest of the world. Your phone will probably work in most major U.S. cities; it definitely won't work in many rural areas. To see where GSM phones work in the U.S., check out www.t-mobile.com/coverage/national_popup.asp. And you may or may not be able to send SMS (text messaging) home.

Washington Dulles International Airport is the only one of the three airports that offers a cellphone rental service:

Frommers.com: The Complete Travel Resource

It should go without saying, but we highly recommend **Frommers.com,** voted Best Travel Site by *PC Magazine.* We think you'll find our expert advice and tips; independent reviews of hotels, restaurants, attractions, and preferred shopping and nightlife venues; vacation giveaways; and online booking tool indispensable before, during, and after your travels. We publish the complete contents of more than 128 travel guides in our **Destinations** section covering nearly 3,600 places worldwide to help you plan your trip. Each weekday, we publish original articles reporting on **Deals and News** via our free **Frommers.com Newsletter** to help you save time and money and travel smarter. We're betting you'll find our new **Events** listings (http://events.frommers.com) an invaluable resource; it's an up-to-the-minute roster of what's happening in cities everywhere—including concerts, festivals, lectures, and more. We've also added weekly **Podcasts, interactive maps,** and hundreds of new images across the site. Check out our **Travel Talk** area, featuring **Message Boards** where you can join in conversations with thousands of fellow Frommer's travelers and post your trip report once you return.

Online Traveler's Toolbox

Veteran travelers usually carry some essential items to make their trips easier. Following is a selection of handy online tools to bookmark and use. Also see "Site Seeing: The Best Washington, D.C., Websites," in chapter 1, for a comprehensive list of helpful sites.

- **Airplane Food:** www.airlinemeals.net
- **Airplane Seating:** www.seatguru.com; and www.airlinequality.com
- **Foreign Languages for Travelers:** www.travlang.com
- **Maps:** www.mapquest.com
- **Subway Navigator:** www.subwaynavigator.com
- **Time and Date:** www.timeanddate.com
- **Travel Warnings:** http://travel.state.gov, www.fco.gov.uk/travel, www.voyage.gc.ca, www.dfat.gov.au/consular/advice
- **Universal Currency Converter:** www.xe.com/ucc
- **Visa ATM Locator:** www.visa.com; **MasterCard ATM Locator:** www.mastercard.com
- **Weather:** www.intellicast.com; and www.weather.com

Rent-a-Cellular Business Services (✆ **703/572-2558**) in Concourse B.

VOICE-OVER-INERNET PROTOCOL (VOIP)

If you have web access while traveling, you might consider a broadband-based telephone service (in technical terms, **Voice over Internet protocol,** or **VoIP**) such as Skype (www.skype.com) or Vonage (www.vonage.com), which allows you to make free international calls if you use their services from your laptop or in a cybercafe. The people you're calling must also use the service for it to work; check the sites for details.

INTERNET/E-MAIL

WITHOUT YOUR OWN COMPUTER

Increasingly, hotels provide guests computer and Internet access on one or more computers in the hotel business center, often as a complimentary service. D.C.'s **Embassy Suites Hotel Downtown** and the **Tabard Inn** (p. 110 and 112) are two such properties.

Washington doesn't offer many choices in reliable cybercafes, but if you wander the Dupont Circle neighborhood you may come upon one. The **Kramerbooks & Afterwords** bookstore, 1517 Connecticut Ave. NW (✆ **202/387-1400**), has one computer available for free Internet access, with a 15-minute time limit. Nearby is **Cyberlaptops.com,** on the second floor at 1636 R St. NW (✆ **202/462-7195**), which is mostly a laptop repair and rental shop, but also provides Internet access. For other listings, as well as the locations of **Internet kiosks** throughout the D.C. area, check the websites **www.cybercaptive.com** and **www.cybercafe.com**.

All three of Washington's airports offer some variation of Internet access, though their per-minute fee is usually higher than cybercafe prices.

WITH YOUR OWN COMPUTER

More and more hotels, resorts, airports, cafes, and retailers are going Wi-Fi (wireless fidelity), becoming "hot spots" that offer free high-speed Wi-Fi access or charge a small fee for usage. Wi-Fi is also found in campgrounds, RV parks, and even entire towns. Most laptops sold today have built-in wireless capability. To find public Wi-Fi hot spots at your destination, go to **www.jiwire.com**; its Hotspot Finder holds the world's largest directory of public wireless hot spots.

For dial-up access, most business-class hotels in the U.S. offer dataports for laptop modems, and a few thousand hotels in the U.S. and Europe now offer free high-speed Internet access.

Wherever you go, bring a **connection kit** of the right power and phone adapters, a spare phone cord, and a spare Ethernet network cable—or find out whether your hotel supplies them to guests.

For information on electrical currency conversions, see "Electricity," in the "Fast Facts" section at the end of chapter 4.

12 Packages for the Independent Traveler

Package tours are simply a way to buy the airfare, accommodations, and other elements of your trip (such as car rentals, airport transfers, and sometimes even activities) at the same time and often at discounted prices.

One good source of package deals is the airlines themselves. Most major airlines offer air/land packages, including **American Airlines Vacations** (✆ 800/321-2121; www.aavacations.com), **Continental Airlines Vacations** (✆ 800/301-3800; www.covacations.com), **Delta Vacations** (✆ 800/654-6559; www.deltavacations.com), and **United Vacations** (✆ 888/854-3899; www.unitedvacations.com). Several big **online travel agencies**—Expedia, Travelocity, Orbitz, Site59, and Lastminute.com—also do a brisk business in packages.

Travel packages are also listed in the travel section of your local Sunday newspaper. Or check ads in the national travel magazines such as *Arthur Frommer's Budget Travel Magazine, Travel & Leisure, National Geographic Traveler,* and *Condé Nast Traveler.*

13 Escorted Tours and Special-Interest Trips

Escorted tours are structured group tours, with a group leader. The price usually includes everything from airfare to hotels, meals, tours, admission costs, and local transportation.

Despite the fact that escorted tours require big deposits and predetermine hotels, restaurants, and itineraries, many people derive security and peace of mind from the structure they offer. Escorted tours—whether they're navigated by bus, motorcoach, train, or boat—let travelers sit back and enjoy the trip without having to drive or worry about details. They take you to the maximum number of sights in the minimum amount of time with the least amount of hassle. They're particularly convenient for people with limited mobility, and they can be a great way to make new friends. On the downside, you'll have little opportunity for serendipitous interactions with locals. The tours can be jampacked with activities, leaving little room for individual sightseeing, whim, or adventure—plus they often focus on the heavily touristed sites, so you miss out on many a lesser-known gem.

Often, operators and agencies offer tours embracing a special interest. For example, two organizations, **Smithsonian Journeys Travel Adventures** (✆ **800/528-8147;** www.smithsonianjourneys.com) and **Collette Vacations** (✆ **800/340-5158;** www.collettevacations.com), teamed up in 2007 to offer their "Spirit of Washington" tour, focusing on art,

Tips Ask Before You Go

Before you invest in a package deal or an escorted tour:

- Always ask about the **cancellation policy.** Can you get your money back? Is a deposit required?
- Ask about the **accommodations choices and prices** for each. Then look up the hotels' reviews in a Frommer's guide and check their rates online for your specific dates of travel. Also find out what types of rooms are offered.
- Request a complete **schedule.** (Escorted tours only)
- Ask about the **size** and demographics of the group. (Escorted tours only)
- Discuss what is included in the **price** (transportation, meals, tips, airport transfers, and so on). (Escorted tours only)
- Finally, look for **hidden expenses.** Ask whether airport departure fees and taxes, for example, are included in the total cost—they rarely are.

architecture, and American history in the nation's capital. (They offer several other packages, as well, all over the world.)

If you're interested in exploring escorted tour packages and special-interest trips, you might start by accessing the websites of two major trade organizations, the **U.S. Tour Operators Association** (✆ **212/599-6599;** www.ustoa.com) and the **National Tourism Association** (✆ **800/682-8886;** www.ntaonline.com). Tour companies and other travel professionals must satisfy certain requirements to become members, which means that you can count on finding dependable professionals in each association's roster. Both associations list their members online and offer a destination-search feature, which brings up names of companies that offer trips in that particular place.

14 Tips on Accommodations

SURFING FOR HOTELS

In addition to the online travel booking sites **Travelocity, Expedia, Orbitz, Priceline,** and **Hotwire,** you can book hotels through **Hotels.com, Quikbook** (www.quikbook.com), and **Travelaxe** (www.travelaxe.net).

HotelChatter.com is a daily webzine offering smart coverage and critiques of hotels worldwide. Go to **TripAdvisor.com** or **HotelShark.com** for helpful independent consumer reviews of hotels and resort properties.

It's a good idea to **get a confirmation number** and **make a printout** of any online booking transaction.

SAVING ON YOUR HOTEL ROOM

The **rack rate** is the maximum rate that a hotel charges for a room. Hardly anybody pays this price, however, except in high season or on holidays. To lower the cost of your room:

- **Ask about special rates or other discounts.** You may qualify for corporate, student, military, senior, frequent flier, trade union, or other discounts.
- **Dial direct.** When booking a room in a chain hotel, you'll often get a better deal by calling the individual hotel's reservation desk rather than the chain's main number.

- **Book online.** Many hotels offer Internet-only discounts, or supply rooms to Priceline, Hotwire, or Expedia at rates much lower than the ones you can get through the hotel itself.
- **Remember the law of supply and demand.** Resort hotels are most crowded and therefore most expensive on weekends, so discounts are usually available for midweek stays. Business hotels in downtown locations are busiest during the week, so you can expect big discounts over the weekend.
- **Look into group or long-stay discounts.** If you come as part of a large group, you should be able to negotiate a bargain rate. Likewise, if you're planning a long stay (at least 5 days), you might qualify for a discount. As a general rule, expect 1 night free after a 7-night stay.
- **Sidestep excess surcharges and hidden costs.** Many hotels have the unpleasant practice of nickel-and-diming its guests with opaque surcharges. When you book a room, ask what is included in the room rate, and what is extra. Avoid dialing direct from hotel phones, which can have exorbitant rates. And don't be tempted by the room's minibar offerings: Most hotels charge through the nose for water, soda, and snacks. Finally, ask about local taxes and service charges, which can increase the cost of a room by 15% or more.
- **Book an efficiency.** A room with a kitchenette allows you to shop for groceries and cook your own meals. This is a big money saver, especially for families on long stays.
- **Consider enrolling in hotel "frequent stay" programs,** which are upping the ante lately to win the loyalty of repeat customers. Frequent guests can now accumulate points or credits to earn free hotel nights, airline miles, in-room amenities, merchandise, tickets to concerts and events, discounts on sporting facilities—and even credit toward stock in the participating hotel, in the case of the Jameson Inn hotel group. Perks are awarded by not only many chain hotels and motels (Hilton HHonors, Marriott Rewards, Wyndham ByRequest, to name a few), but also individual inns and B&Bs. Many chain hotels partner with other hotel chains, car-rental firms, airlines, and credit-card companies to give consumers additional incentive to do repeat business.

LANDING THE BEST ROOM

Somebody has to get the best room in the house. It might as well be you. You can start by joining the hotel's frequent-guest program, which may make you eligible for upgrades. A hotel-branded credit card usually gives its owner "silver" or "gold" status in frequent-guest programs for free. Always ask about a corner room. They're often larger and quieter, with more windows and light, and they often cost the same as standard rooms. When you make your reservation, ask if the hotel is renovating; if it is, request a room away from the construction. If you're a light sleeper, request a quiet room away from vending or ice machines, elevators, restaurants, bars, and discos. Ask for a room that has most recently been renovated or redecorated.

If you aren't happy with your room when you arrive, ask for another one. Most lodgings will be willing to accommodate you.

3

Suggested Washington, D.C., Itineraries

Nothing is more thrilling to a traveler than that very first moment of arrival in a new place, unless it's a return to a favorite spot. When that place is Washington, D.C., both the wide-eyed ingénue and the repeat customer arrive and look about in wonder and anticipation. For Washington is a beautiful city, whose famous landmarks—the stunning Capitol, the patiently waiting Lincoln in his memorial—are living, breathing monuments to the American ideals of freedom and equality. And it's a hustling, bustling town, poised to amuse any and all with an endless menu of dining, theatrical, cultural, recreational, and shopping possibilities.

So now you've arrived, and you're standing on the threshold of an enthralling experience. How do you ensure you capture it? Simple. The following three itineraries will help guide you to it. But first, some practical advice: Read through all three itineraries to see which one most appeals to you, and to help you gauge the amount of time you'll want to allow at each site. Call ahead and make sure the places on your desired itinerary are open. Be calm and flexible: Lines to enter public buildings are longer than ever, thanks to security clearance procedures and the capital's continuing popularity. Reserve spots on tours, if the sites you're interested in offer that option, to avoid some of those waits. Most important, don't be afraid to ask questions: The police on Capitol Hill, the National Park Service rangers on duty at the memorials, and the staff at all the museums know an awful lot—take advantage of their expertise.

1 The Best of Washington in 1 Day

***Note:** For this itinerary, you need to call in advance to reserve tickets for a moonlight tour (see information below).*

The first two stops on this tour are the Capitol and the Supreme Court. If you're here on a weekend, you can cross the Supreme Court off your list, since it's open only on weekdays. If you're here on a weekday, let's be honest: When both the Supreme Court and Congress are in session, and you're hoping to attend both, and to tour the Capitol, you can expect those activities alone to take up the better part of a day. So I'm offering you some choices: Visit the Supreme Court *or* the Capitol, and continue with the itinerary as laid out; *or* hope for the best, attempt to take in both the Court *and* the Capitol, and work in other stops on this itinerary as you're able. It's possible, with everything working in your favor, to experience this itinerary in its entirety. But many factors will come into play: ebbs and flows of tourist seasons, interest in a particular case being argued in the Supreme Court, legislation up for a vote in the Senate or House, even the weather. And if you're traveling with children under age 12, that's another factor: Visit the Capitol and, if you want, do a tour of the Supreme Court, but do not try to attend a Supreme Court argument with young children. Rule of thumb: To be sure of attending a Supreme Court argument or of obtaining a ticket to tour the Capitol, line up at either place by 7:30am. ***Start:*** *Metro on the Blue Line to Capitol South, or on the Red Line to Union Station.*

---

❶ The Capitol ★★★

The story of the design and construction of the Capitol is a tumultuous one, full of strong personalities and brave compromises—kind of like the history of the United States, actually. Startling truths abound, beginning with the fact that the most important U.S. building was designed in 1792 by a Scottish-trained physician from the British West Indies. William Thornton, the first architect of the Capitol, explained himself, "I lamented not having studied architecture and resolved to attempt that grand undertaking and study at the same time." Seventy years and three architects later, the Capitol completed its most notable feature, a 287-foot-high dome, made of two enormous cast-iron shells, one inside the other, with all the exterior trim, cornices, and columns painted to look like marble. Tilt your head all the way back to see the 19-foot-statue, "Freedom," which was set in place atop the dome in December 1863, at the height of the Civil War—the same year that Abraham Lincoln issued his Emancipation Proclamation. See p. 178.

❷ Supreme Court ★★★

You don't have to be aware of the Supreme Court's schedule to know when a controversial case is up—you'll observe the line of hopeful visitors stretching across the Court's front plaza. You'll spot media types, too. The southwest corner of the plaza is a favorite location for TV correspondents to deliver on-camera reports; with the right angle, the shot captures the newsperson and the crowds of people in endless queues, framed against the backdrop of the Court's stately columned edifice and elaborate pediment inscribed with the words EQUAL JUSTICE UNDER LAW. See p. 183.

❸ Library of Congress ★★

As the world's largest library, the Library of Congress commands an inventory of some 130 million items. In an enduring effort to share its wealth, the Library reaches into its pockets, so to speak, to pull out wondrous objects from one of its particular collections, and then mounts an exhibition to show them off. One example: An ongoing exhibit titled "By Securing to Authors: Copyright, Commerce, and Creativity in America" displays an assortment of American copyrighted items, from the original Ken and Barbie dolls to Dr. Martin Luther King, Jr.'s *I Have a Dream* speech. The Library of Congress: not just for bibliophiles. See p. 223.

> **4 LE BON CAFÉ**
> Order a sandwich and try to snag a seat at one of the outside tables. Or better yet, get it to go, and proceed to your next destination, where an Elizabethan garden awaits you. ✆ **202/547-7200.** See p. 134.

❺ Folger Shakespeare Library and Garden ★

If your timing is right (try before noon or after 1pm), you'll have the garden to yourself—to sit on a bench; munch on a picnic lunch; and relax amid the English ivy, rosemary, and lavender, all plantings true to Shakespeare's day. Positioned throughout the garden are statues of characters from eight of the Bard's plays. Stop inside to see "what's on" in the

Suggested Itineraries: Day 1

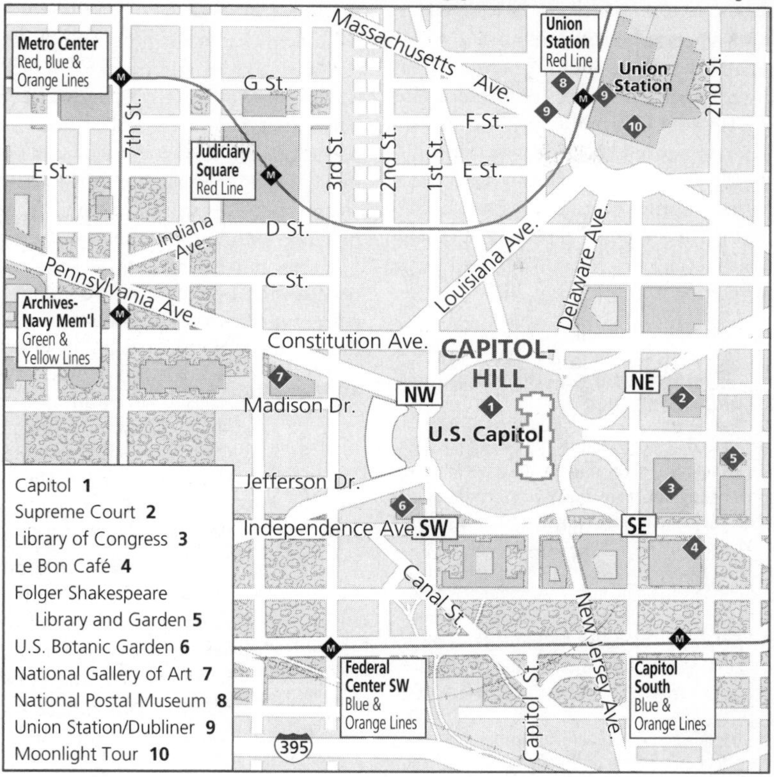

paneled, Tudor-style Great Hall, and check the calendar for plays being staged in the re-created Elizabethan Theatre. Attend an evening production, if you can; they're always a treat. See p. 216.

❻ U.S. Botanic Garden ★

Down the hill from the Capitol is this other garden—well, several gardens, in fact—contained within a large greenhouse. Not much is asked of you here—you don't have to be a gardener to appreciate the beauty of orchids or the curiosity of the "Musa Praying Hands" (it's in the banana family). Be sure to climb all the way up the stairs in the tallest part of the conservatory and look out: You'll have views of the Capitol and the neighborhood that I'll bet even most locals haven't discovered. See p. 230.

❼ National Gallery of Art ★★★

The National Gallery's special exhibits are always amazing, so if there's one being staged, go, no matter who the artist. But first, head to the East Wing and go straight to the tower at the top to take a look at the Matisse cutouts. They get less traffic than other artwork in the museum, mostly because not everyone's hip to them. Here's the tricky part, though: You should be here by 1:30pm (or 2:30pm on Sun) at the latest, for this exhibit is open only between 10am and 2pm Monday through Saturday, 11am to 3pm Sunday, to protect the pigments and paper of the cutouts. From here, you'll want to hightail it over to the West Wing, to view as much of the grand sculpture galleries and European paintings from the 13th to the 19th century as time allows. See p. 212.

Take a taxi to the National Postal Museum.

8 National Postal Museum ★

Hard to believe, but this doable-in-an-hour museum is in the Smithsonian family. Let your kids run loose—the museum is all on one level, and they won't get lost. In the meantime, you can read letters written during wartimes, learn about the history of the postal service, and develop a newfound appreciation for your postal worker back home. See p. 207.

9 UNION STATION FOOD COURT OR THE DUBLINER

The Postal Museum closes at 5:30pm, which means that you have limited time to kill before you go on to the final leg of your itinerary: the memorials by moonlight tour. If you're hungry, head right next door to the Food Court at Union Station for quick food that's less expensive than any other dining option you'll find in the neighborhood. (The local chain Burrito Brothers is worth recommending.) The added benefit is that you'll have time to admire Union Station's architecture. If you opt for The Dubliner, ✆ **202/737-3773,** p. 279 (across the street from the museum)—primarily a bar but one that offers a serviceable hamburger—you run the risk of not making it to your tour. It's your choice.

10 Union Station ★

This handsome structure is a major thoroughfare for commuters rushing for Metro and Amtrak trains, so watch out. The ticket kiosks for the various tour operations are at the front of the Main Hall, making them hard to miss; whether you've reserved space in advance (recommended) online or by phone, or you're just now purchasing your tickets, you'll need to stop by the booths to obtain the actual tour tickets. The Food Court is on the bottom level. See p. 225.

11 Moonlight Tour ★★★

Tourmobile and Old Town Trolley offer nighttime tours of the memorials and the Washington Monument. Some consider this the most dramatic way to view the historic sites. After a full day of sightseeing, it is certainly the easiest and most relaxing way to get around. Both operations offer narrated tours, with stops (for 20 min. or so) at the Lincoln, FDR, Vietnam Veterans, and Jefferson memorials. But their specific fares, routes, and schedules differ (Tourmobile's twilight tour, for instance, is a seasonal operation). Hop aboard and enjoy the ride. See p. 237.

2 The Best of Washington in 2 Days

Note: *For this itinerary, you should call in advance for restaurant and ticket reservations (see information below).*

Your second day takes you to the National Mall and the Smithsonian museums, to venture through gardens and inside some of the buildings you passed the night before on your moonlight tour. Your last stop on the Mall will be at the National Archives before crossing Pennsylvania Avenue into the heart of D.C.'s fastest growing neighborhood, the Penn Quarter, to reach the International Spy Museum. ***Suggestion:*** The National Archives and the Spy Museum accept advance tour reservations, so try to arrange for those, if you can, and you'll bypass long lines. Penn Quarter is home to so many excellent restaurants and bars that you can plan on staying here for cocktails and dinner—and nightlife, too. ***Start:*** *Metro on the Blue Line to Smithsonian or L'Enfant Plaza.*

Suggested Itineraries: Day 2

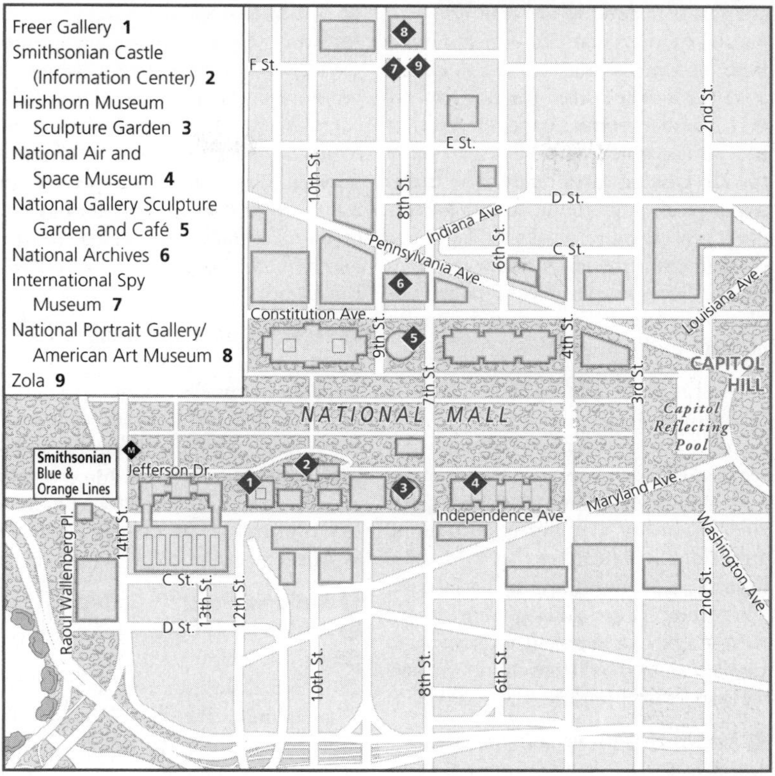

❶ Hirshhorn Museum Sculpture Garden ★

If you've gotten off to an early start, meaning 7:30am, you may find the Mall fairly deserted. Then again, Washington is a town of early risers, so there's just as good a chance that you'll find yourself scooting out of the way of joggers and suit-clad workers scurrying to offices. At 8am, the only museum site open is the Hirshhorn's Sculpture Garden, which is a sunken, green landscape displaying some 60 large-scale sculptures. Don't miss Aristide Maillol's *Action in Chains: Monument to Louis-Auguste Blanqui,* which is striking at any time of the year. See p. 199.

❷ Smithsonian Castle (Information Center)

The Smithsonian Information Center opens at 8:30am, as does its Castle Café. Stop at the information desk for brochures and information, then at the kiosk for coffee and a muffin, and sit outside in the Enid Haupt Garden to plan your moves for the day. You won't have time to tour every museum on the Mall, and at least two Smithsonians—the National Museum of American History and the Arts & Industries Building—are closed for extensive renovations. See p. 197.

❸ Freer Gallery ★

This handsome building, with its Italian Renaissance architecture and arched courtyard, is devoted to Asian art, with one major exception: its Whistler holdings. Visit the spectacular Peacock Room, so called for the golden peacock feathers that Whistler painted upon the walls of the room, which was once part of a friend's London town house. The friend was most displeased, but today's gallerygoers are generally intrigued. Continue through other chambers of the gallery to admire ancient jade objects, early Buddhist sculpture, Islamic art, and a wealth of Asian works. See p. 198.

4 National Air and Space Museum ★★

Nothing attests to human ingenuity better than this vast display of the machines we've created to fly through air and space. And yet, one of this museum's enduring attractions is something that puts those human accomplishments in perspective: The Albert Einstein Planetarium (you'll need a ticket to enter). It coaxes you to wonder about the dimensions of the universe and where it leads. See p. 200.

5 National Gallery Sculpture Garden ★

With its evening jazz in summer, ice rink in winter, and cafe all year-round, the sculpture garden is as much an urban park as a sightseeing destination. People tend to come here just to hang out. Too bad it opens so late (10am Mon–Sat, 11am Sun) and closes so early (anywhere from 5 to 9:30pm, depending on the day and time of year). See p. 213.

6 SCULPTURE GARDEN CAFE ★★

You've been on your feet since 7:30am! Treat yourself to a glass of wine, a Cuban panini (ham and roast pork), and maybe a slice of apple torte, and enjoy your feast on the terrace, with its view of the sculptures—and your next destination. ✆ **202/289-3360.** See p. 132.

7 National Archives ★★

Area residents are slow to catch on, but the National Archives has gradually been transforming itself into a multimedia complex, mounting major exhibitions, screening documentaries, and hosting talks by contemporary authors. Its finest feature, however, will always be its display of the original Declaration of Independence, U.S. Constitution, and Bill of Rights. See p. 211.

8 International Spy Museum ★

Filled to the gills with spy lore and facts—sometimes scary, sometimes silly—the best exhibits are those at the beginning, which employ interactive games to test your skills of observation and detection. At the end, you watch videos of real-life agents talk about their experiences. See p. 220.

9 National Portrait Gallery & 10 American Art Museum ★★★

Before this building was even finished, in 1867, it had already served as a Civil War hospital and as the site of Abraham Lincoln's second inaugural ball. Upon completion, the building housed patent offices, whose clerks eventually issued patents to Alexander Graham Bell, Thomas Edison, and 500,000 other inventors. The Smithsonian took over the Patent Office Building and remodeled it before opening two-museums-in-one in 1968.

By 2000, the structure was again in need of renovation, this time requiring 6 years and intense improvements. When the National Portrait Gallery and the American Art Museum reopened in July 2006, the city staged a celebration to herald this much-improved bastion of "American Originals." The museums and their vast displays do America proud, representing the nation's spirit and people at their best in every artistic genre, including presidential portraits, folk art, photographs,

Latino art, African-American art, and paintings by the masters, from Gilbert Stuart to Georgia O'Keeffe. The museums are a good last stop on this tour, since they stay open until 7pm nightly. Go. See p. 209.

11 ZOLA ★★
Zola, in the same building as the Spy Museum and across the street from the Smithsonian museums, plays upon a sleuth theme in its decor. The food's for real, though, and highly recommended. ✆ **202/654-0999.** See p. 143.

3 The Best of Washington in 3 Days

Especially if you're traveling with children younger than 11, you might start Day 3 with a lively visit to the National Zoo. Otherwise, consider visiting the U.S. Holocaust Memorial Museum in the morning and then spend the afternoon taking a restorative stroll through some of D.C.'s loveliest quarters. Obtain admission tickets ahead of time for the museum, if possible; if not, you should plan to arrive early to wait in line.
Start: *Metro on the Red Line to National Zoo to go to the zoo; Metro on the Blue Line to Smithsonian to visit the Holocaust Museum.*

---

1 National Zoological Park ★★ or 2 U.S. Holocaust Memorial Museum ★★

If you (or your children) want to get an early start on the day, the National Zoological Park, an off-the-Mall Smithsonian complex, opens at 6am, year-round. A recent development is the opening of an Asia Trail, whose winding path presents close-up sights of sloth bears sucking up termites, giant pandas frolicking in a waterfall, fishing cats caught in the act, and the assorted activities of clouded leopards and Japanese salamanders. Those three giant pandas remain the zoo's top draws. See p. 208.

Fifteen years after its debut, crowds continue to tour the U.S. Memorial Holocaust Museum, especially its heart-tearing main exhibit. Some people also come here to do research: Open to the public without appointment is a library on the 5th floor, where you can look up information on a name, a town, or any subject to do with the Holocaust. The museum, meanwhile, is expanding its mission to include special exhibits on related events—firsthand accounts and photographs depicting the persecution and torture of the people of Darfur, Sudan, for instance. See p. 214.

From the Metro's Red Line National Zoo stop, take the Metro south one stop to the Dupont Circle station. From the Metro's Blue Line Smithsonian station, take the Metro to Metro Center and switch to the Red Line, going toward Shady Grove. Debark at Dupont Circle.

3 Phillips Collection ★★

This beautiful museum-mansion was expanded in 2006 to include a sculpture garden, a new cafe, an auditorium, a gallery devoted to the works of Mark Rothko, and a larger exhibit space for postwar contemporary art. Always keep an eye out for visitors' favorite pieces: Renoir's *Luncheon of the Boating Party;* numerous Bonnards; and, on display from time to time, a painting executed by founder Duncan Phillips's wife, Marjorie Phillips: *Night Baseball.* See p. 222.

Suggested Itineraries: Day 3

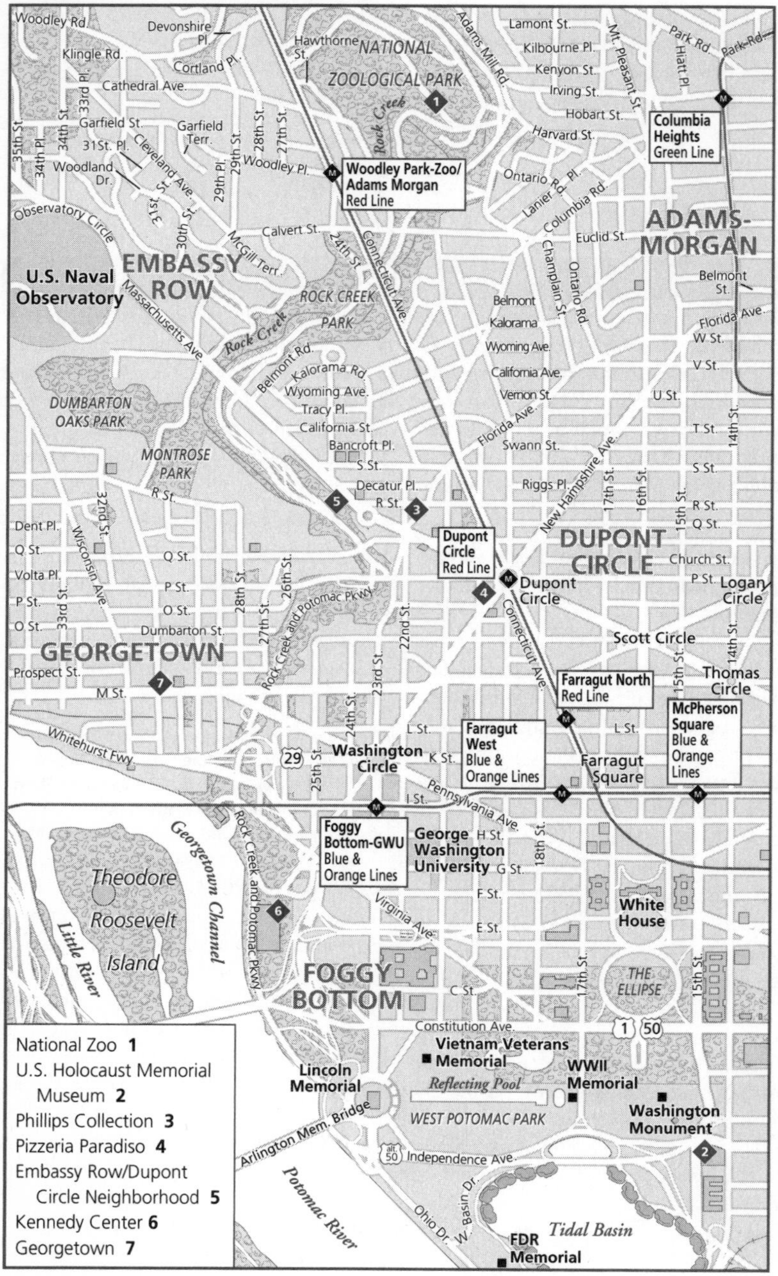

4 PIZZERIA PARADISO ★
Open daily from lunch straight through to 10pm (Sun), 11pm (Mon–Thurs), or midnight (Fri–Sat), this cherished little pizzeria serves pies that are several cuts above the average: cooked in an oak-burning oven and topped with your choice of 31 fresh ingredients, from pancetta to eggplant. ✆ **202/223-1245.** See p. 161.

5 Embassy Row and Dupont Circle ★

Stop in shops along Connecticut Avenue, and then follow side streets to discover boutiques, little art galleries, and quaint century-old town houses. If you look carefully, you'll start to notice that some of these buildings are actually embassies or historic homes. The mansion at 2340 S St. NW, for instance, is where President Woodrow Wilson lived after he left the White House. The most awesome embassies lie on Massachusetts Avenue, west of Dupont Circle. Flags and plaques clearly identify them.

Walk, if you feel up to it, or take a taxi to the Kennedy Center.

6 Kennedy Center ★

Head to the Kennedy Center for the 6pm nightly free concert in the Grand Foyer (part of the center's Millennium Stage program). At concert's end, proceed through the glass doors to the terrace overlooking Rock Creek Parkway and the Potomac River, and enjoy the view. See p. 222.

7 Georgetown ★

Finish up the day with dinner and shopping in Georgetown, where stores and restaurants tend to stay open later than those in other parts of town. See p. 165 and p. 244.

4

Getting to Know Washington, D.C.

After 23 years of living here, I am still getting to know D.C. This is a good thing. The city has so much going on in every category—from culture to commercial, transportation to neighborhood transformation—it can be hard to keep up. The capital doesn't stand still and neither should you. Read this chapter to discover what you need to know to navigate the city. Then hit the street and put your knowledge to the test, learning more along the way.

1 Orientation

On the one hand, Washington, D.C., is an easy place to get to know. It's a small city, where walking will actually get you places, but it also has a model public transportation system that travels throughout D.C.'s neighborhoods and to most tourist spots. A building height restriction creates a landscape in which the lost tourist can get his bearings from tall landmarks—the Capitol, the Washington Monument—that loom into view from different vantage points.

On the other hand, when you do need help, it's sometimes hard to find. The city lacks a single, large, comprehensive, and easy-to-find visitor's center. Signs to tourist attractions and Metro stations, even street signs, can be frustratingly inadequate. In the wake of September 11, stricter security precautions at some sightseeing attractions have made touring procedures cumbersome, and the ongoing changes can be disorienting.

The District is continually working to improve the situation. But in the meantime, you can turn to the following smaller visitor and information centers, helpful publications, and information phone lines.

VISITOR INFORMATION

INFORMATION CENTERS

At the Airports

If you're arriving by plane, you can think of your airport as a visitor information center; all three Washington-area airports offer all sorts of visitor services. See chapter 2 for specific information about each airport's location, flights, and transportation options into town.

BALTIMORE–WASHINGTON INTERNATIONAL THURGOOD MARSHALL AIRPORT (BWI; ✆ 800/435-9294; www.bwiairport.com; airport code: BWI) BWI services include five information desks (✆ **800/435-9294** for information and paging) located throughout the upper and lower levels; a customer service center (✆ **410/859-7387**) located on the upper level, between concourses B and C (the airport's Lost and Found office ✆ **410/859-7387** lies within the customer service center);

two Maryland Welcome Centers (✆ **410/691-2878**), both located on the lower level, near baggage claim carousels 3 and 13/14; three locations (✆ **410/859-4466**) for exchanging currency and providing faxing and other business services; several ATMs; plenty of public phones, many equipped with dataports and some with TDD services and voice-relay phones; many restrooms, restaurants (all equipped with high-speed wireless Internet access), shops, and bars; a playroom for kids; a small aviation museum; and even two massage services, or "relaxation destination locations," as the airport dubs them.

Other useful phone numbers: police ✆ **410/859-7040** and parking lots and garage ✆ **800/468-6294** or 410/859-9230.

RONALD REAGAN WASHINGTON NATIONAL AIRPORT ("National"; ✆ 703/417-8000; www.mwaa.com/national; airport code: DCA). You'll arrive on the second level; ticket counters are on the third level, baggage claim and ground transportation are on the first level. The second, or concourse, level is where you'll get your questions answered. Business/currency exchange centers (✆ **703/417-3201** or 703/417-3200) are located between terminals B and C. The airport has four Traveler's Aid desks, one in each of the three terminals and on the baggage claim level (✆ **703/417-1806,** 703/417-3972, or 703/417-3974). Traveler's Aid volunteers can help with all sorts of situations, from answering general travel and airport information, to providing foreign language assistance, to helping in a crisis, to paging a passenger. About 150 pay phones equipped with dataports are located throughout terminals B and C. The airport has at least seven ATMs and nearly 100 shops, restaurants, and other concessions, mostly found in "National Hall," on the second level of the main terminal.

Other useful phone numbers: lost and found ✆ **703/417-0673,** parking lots and garage ✆ **703/417-7275,** and police ✆ **703/417-8560.**

WASHINGTON DULLES INTERNATIONAL AIRPORT ("Dulles"; ✆ 703/572-2700; www.mwaa.com/Dulles; airport code: IAD). A vast expansion of Dulles continues apace, closing in on a 2009 deadline. Among improvements so far are a new concourse and a pedestrian walkway that connects the main terminal and concourses A, B, and Z. Most flights arrive at midfield terminals, where you follow the crowd, either to the pedestrian walkways or to mobile lounges, which take you to the main terminal. In time, the plan is for an underground rail system to replace the mobile lounges altogether. The satellite terminals are actually rather attractive and offer decent shopping. As at National Airport, you can count on getting help from Traveler's Aid, which operates desks at two locations in the main terminal: near the baggage claim carousels in the international arrivals area, and at the information counter near baggage claim (✆ **703/572-8296** or 703/572-2536). Phone numbers for other help desks include ✆ **703/572-2946** or 703/572-2969 for general service, foreign currency exchange, and insurance purchases. There are about 100 eateries and shops, and plentiful ATMs, restrooms, stamp vending machines, and phones.

Other useful numbers: police ✆ **703/572-2952,** lost and found ✆ **703/572-2954,** and parking lots and rates information ✆ **703/572-4500.**

Baggage claim areas are at ground level in the main terminal.

At the Train Station

Historic **Union Station** (✆ **202/371-9441;** www.unionstationdc.com), 50 Massachusetts Ave. NE, offers visitors a pleasant introduction to the capital. The building is both an architectural beauty and a useful stopping place. Here you'll find a three-level marketplace of shops and restaurants, direct access to Metro service (you'll see signs directing you to the Metro's Red Line station even before you reach the main hall of Union Station), and, when you proceed through the grand arcade straight out through the station's front doors, a stellar view of the Capitol Building.

The central information desk is in the main hall at the front of the building. You'll find ATMs in the gate area, near the side doors of the building (near the outdoor escalator to the Metro), and on the lower level, at the end of the Food Court. A Travelex Currency Exchange office (✆ **202/371-9220**) lies across from gate G and a Traveler's Aid desk (✆ **202/371-1937**) near gate D. A number of car-rental agencies operate lots here (see "Getting Around," later in this chapter, for specific names and phone numbers). For security, or for other help or information, call the main number, ✆ **202/371-9441;** for lost and found, call ✆ **202/289-8355;** for parking information, call ✆ **202/898-1950.**

Around Town

The Washington, D.C., Visitor Information Center (✆ **866/324-7386** or 202/328-4748; www.dcvisit.com) is a small visitor center inside the immense Ronald Reagan International Trade Center Building, at 1300 Pennsylvania Ave. NW. To enter the federal building, you need to show a picture ID. The visitor center lies on the ground floor of the building, a little to your right as you enter from the Wilson Plaza, near the Federal Triangle Metro. From March 15 to Labor Day, the center is open Monday through Friday, 8:30am to 5:30pm, and on Saturday from 9am to 4pm; from Labor Day to March 14, the center is open Monday through Friday 9am to 4:30pm.

Businesses have banded together in 10 D.C. neighborhoods to provide information, safety, and maintenance services for residents and visitors within their individual districts. The most established are the **Downtown D.C. Business Improvement District (Downtown D.C. BID),** 1250 H St. NW (✆ **202/638-3232;** www.downtowndc.org), which covers the territory between Union Station and the White House (Constitution to Massachusetts aves., and between 16th and First sts.); the **Golden Triangle Business Improvement District (Golden Triangle BID),** 1120 Connecticut Ave. NW (✆ **202/463-3400;** www.gtbid.com), encompassing the area between the White House and Dupont Circle (bounded by 16th and 21st sts. NW and Pennsylvania Ave. and Dupont Circle); and the **Capitol Hill Business Improvement District (Capitol Hill BID),** 30 Massachusetts Ave. NE, inside Union Station's garage (✆ **202/842-3333;** www.capitolhillbid.org), which covers the streets around the U.S. Capitol and Union Station. Look for the patrolling, red-uniformed "SAMS" (Downtown D.C. BID's safety and maintenance workers) downtown, black and gold outfitted hospitality ambassadors in the Golden Triangle area, and blue and gold attired "STARS" near Capitol Hill, if you need directions, information, or any assistance at all. From March to October the Downtown D.C. BID also has special information kiosks stationed throughout the downtown.

National Park Service information kiosks are located inside the Jefferson, Lincoln, and FDR memorials and near the Vietnam Veterans, Korean War, and World War II memorials. Park rangers are on hand at the Washington Monument at its ticket booth at the bottom of the hill, at 15th Street NW and Constitution Avenue, inside the monument, and at the Ranger Station, located at the southwest point of the monument grounds, across from the Tidal Basin (✆ **202/619-7222;** www.nps.gov/ncro).

The **White House Visitor Center,** on the first floor of the Herbert Hoover Building, Department of Commerce, 1450 Pennsylvania Ave. NW (between 14th and 15th sts.; © **202/208-1631,** or 202/456-7041 for recorded information), is open daily (except for Christmas Day, Thanksgiving, and New Year's Day) from 7:30am to 4pm.

The **Smithsonian Information Center,** in the "Castle," 1000 Jefferson Dr. SW (© **202/633-1000,** or TTY 202/357-1729; www.si.edu), is open every day but Christmas from 8:30am to 5:30pm. Call for a free copy of the Smithsonian's "Planning Your Smithsonian Visit," which is full of valuable tips, or stop at the Castle for a copy.

See chapter 7 for more information about the White House Visitor and Smithsonian Information centers.

The **American Automobile Association (AAA)** has a large central office near the White House, at 701 15th St. NW, between G Street and New York Avenue NW, Washington, DC 20005-2111 (© **202/331-3000**). Hours are 9am to 5:30pm Monday through Friday.

PUBLICATIONS

At the airport, pick up a free copy of ***Washington Flyer*** magazine (www.fly2dc.com), which is handy as a planning tool (see chapter 2).

Washington has two daily newspapers: the ***Washington Post*** (www.washington post.com) and the ***Washington Times*** (www.washingtontimes.com). The Friday "Weekend" section of the *Post* is a good source for finding out what's going on, recreation-wise. *City Paper,* published every Thursday and available free at downtown shops and restaurants, covers some of the same material, but it's a better guide to the club and art gallery scene.

HELPFUL TELEPHONE NUMBERS & WEBSITES

- **National Park Service** (© **202/619-7222;** www.nps.gov/ncro). You reach a real person when you call this phone number with questions about the monuments, the National Mall, national parklands, and any activities taking place at these locations.
- **Dial-A-Park** (© **202/619-7275**). This number provides prerecorded information about park-service events and attractions.
- **Smithsonian Museums** (© **202/633-1000;** www.si.edu). Call this main information line for the Smithsonian museums, then press "2" to listen to the recorded listing of daily events going on at each of the 19 Washington-area Smithsonian museums.

CITY LAYOUT

Washington's appearance today pays homage to the 1792 vision of French engineer Pierre Charles L'Enfant, who created the capital's grand design of sweeping avenues intersected by spacious circles, directed that the Capitol and the White House be placed on prominent hilltops at either end of a wide stretch of avenue, and superimposed this overall plan upon a traditional street grid. The city's quadrants, grand avenues named after states, alphabetically ordered streets crossed by chronologically ordered streets, and parks integrated with urban features are all ideas that started with L'Enfant. President George Washington, who had hired L'Enfant, was forced to dismiss the temperamental genius after L'Enfant apparently offended quite a number of people. But Washington recognized the brilliance of the city plan and hired surveyors Benjamin Banneker and Andrew Ellicott, who had worked with L'Enfant, to continue to implement L'Enfant's design.

The U.S. Capitol marks the center of the city, which is divided into **northwest (NW), northeast (NE), southwest (SW),** and **southeast (SE) quadrants.** Most, but

Washington, D.C., at a Glance

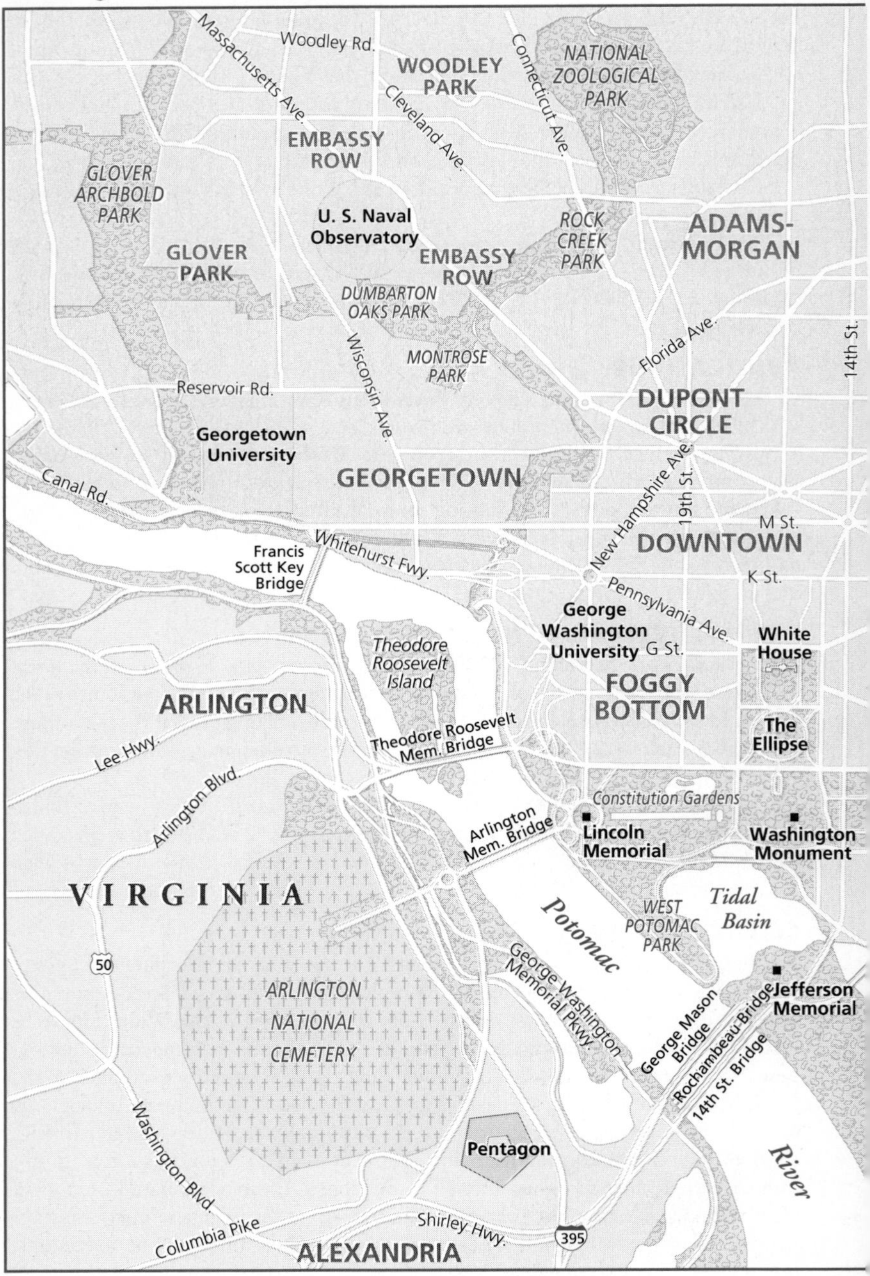

Woodley Rd.
Massachusetts Ave.
WOODLEY PARK
Connecticut Ave.
NATIONAL ZOOLOGICAL PARK
Cleveland Ave.
EMBASSY ROW
GLOVER ARCHBOLD PARK
U. S. Naval Observatory
ROCK CREEK PARK
ADAMS-MORGAN
GLOVER PARK
EMBASSY ROW
DUMBARTON OAKS PARK
Florida Ave.
14th St.
Wisconsin Ave.
MONTROSE PARK
Reservoir Rd.
DUPONT CIRCLE
Georgetown University
GEORGETOWN
New Hampshire Ave.
19th St.
Canal Rd.
M St.
DOWNTOWN
Francis Scott Key Bridge
Whitehurst Fwy.
K St.
Pennsylvania Ave.
George Washington University
G St.
White House
Theodore Roosevelt Island
FOGGY BOTTOM
ARLINGTON
The Ellipse
Theodore Roosevelt Mem. Bridge
Lee Hwy.
Arlington Blvd.
Constitution Gardens
Arlington Mem. Bridge
Lincoln Memorial
Washington Monument
VIRGINIA
Potomac
WEST POTOMAC PARK
Tidal Basin
50
George Washington Memorial Pkwy.
Jefferson Memorial
ARLINGTON NATIONAL CEMETERY
George Mason Bridge
Rochambeau Bridge
14th St. Bridge
Washington Blvd.
Pentagon
River
Columbia Pike
Shirley Hwy.
395
ALEXANDRIA

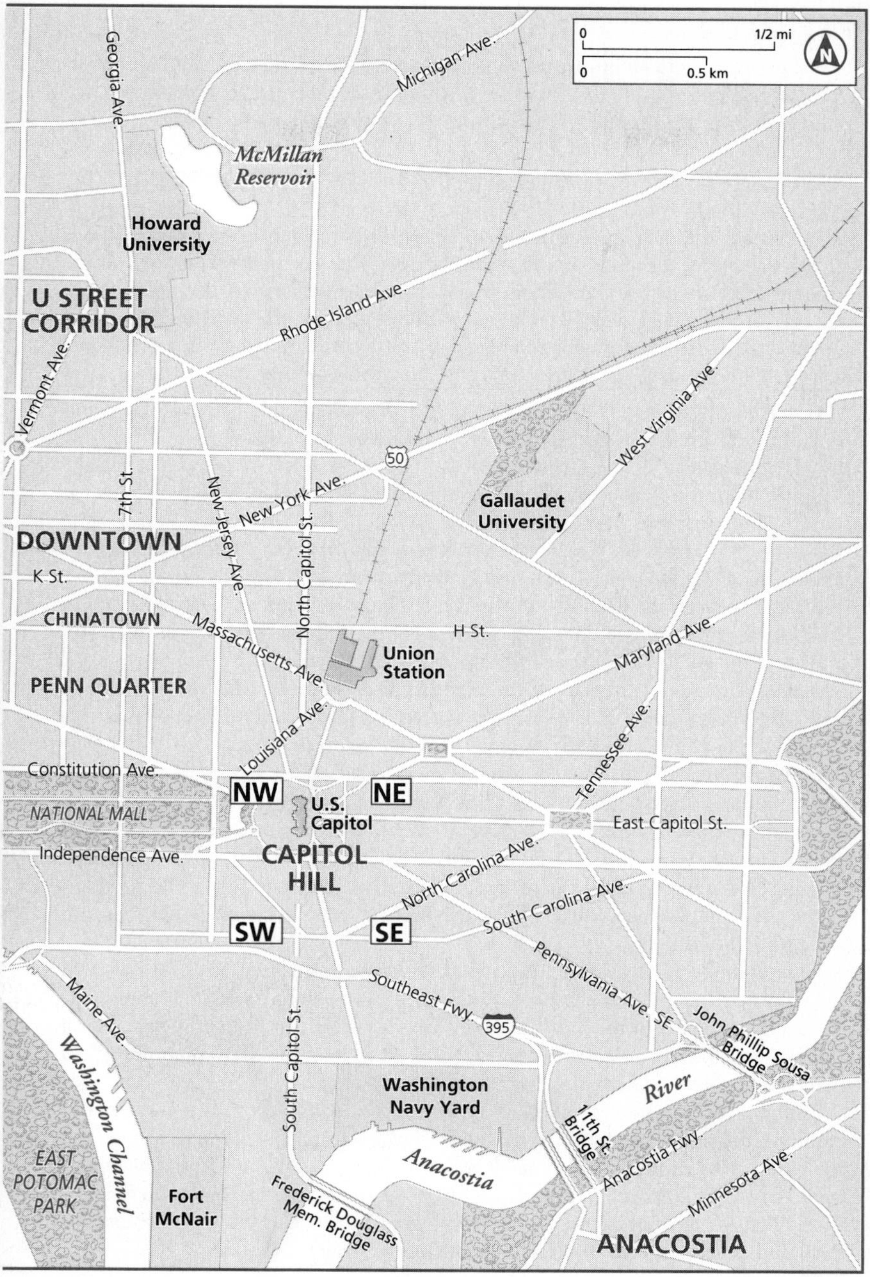
0
1/2 mi
0
0.5 km
N
Georgia Ave.
Michigan Ave.
McMillan Reservoir
Howard University
U STREET CORRIDOR
Rhode Island Ave.
Vermont Ave.
7th St.
New Jersey Ave.
North Capitol St.
New York Ave.
50
West Virginia Ave.
Gallaudet University
DOWNTOWN
K St.
CHINATOWN
Massachusetts Ave.
H St.
Union Station
Maryland Ave.
PENN QUARTER
Louisiana Ave.
Tennessee Ave.
Constitution Ave.
NW
NE
NATIONAL MALL
U.S. Capitol
East Capitol St.
Independence Ave.
CAPITOL HILL
North Carolina Ave.
South Carolina Ave.
SW
SE
Pennsylvania Ave. SE
Southeast Fwy.
395
Maine Ave.
John Phillip Sousa Bridge
South Capitol St.
Washington Navy Yard
River
Washington Channel
11th St. Bridge
Anacostia
Anacostia Fwy.
EAST POTOMAC PARK
Fort McNair
Frederick Douglass Mem. Bridge
Minnesota Ave.
ANACOSTIA

Impressions

If Washington should ever grow to be a great city, the outlook from the Capitol will be unsurpassed in the world. Now at sunset I seemed to look westward far into the heart of the continent from this commanding position.

—Ralph Waldo Emerson

not all, areas of interest to tourists are in the northwest. The boundary demarcations are often seamless; for instance, you are in the northwest quadrant when you visit the National Museum of Natural History, but by crossing the National Mall to the other side to visit, the Freer Gallery, you put yourself in the southwest quadrant. Pay attention to the quadrant's geographic suffix; as you'll notice when you look on a map, some addresses—for instance, the corner of G and 7th streets—appear in all quadrants.

MAIN ARTERIES & STREETS From the Capitol, North Capitol Street and South Capitol Street run north and south, respectively. East Capitol Street divides the city north and south. The area west of the Capitol is not a street at all, but the National Mall, which is bounded on the north by Constitution Avenue and on the south by Independence Avenue.

The primary artery of Washington is **Pennsylvania Avenue,** which is the scene of parades, inaugurations, and other splashy events. Pennsylvania runs northwest in a direct line between the Capitol and the White House—if it weren't for the Treasury Building, the president would have a clear view of the Capitol—before continuing on a northwest angle to Georgetown, where it becomes M Street.

Pennsylvania Avenue in front of the White House—between 15th and 17th streets NW—remains closed to cars for security reasons but has been remade into an attractive pedestrian plaza, lined with 88 Princeton American Elm trees.

Constitution Avenue, paralleled to the south most of the way by Independence Avenue, runs east–west, flanking the Capitol and the Mall. If you hear Washingtonians talk about the "House" side of the Hill, they're referring to the southern half of the Capitol, the side closest to Independence Avenue, and home to Congressional House offices and the House Chamber. Conversely, the Senate side is the northern half of the Capitol, where Senate offices and the Senate Chamber are found, closer to Constitution Avenue.

Washington's longest avenue, **Massachusetts Avenue,** runs parallel to Pennsylvania (a few avenues north). Along the way, you'll find Union Station and then Dupont Circle, which is central to the area known as Embassy Row. Farther out are the Naval Observatory (the vice president's residence is on the premises), Washington National Cathedral, American University, and, eventually, Maryland.

Connecticut Avenue, which runs more directly north (the other avenues run southeast to northwest), starts at Lafayette Square, intersects Dupont Circle, and eventually takes you to the National Zoo, on to the charming residential neighborhood known as Cleveland Park, and into Chevy Chase, Maryland, where you can pick up the Beltway to head out of town. Downtown Connecticut Avenue, with its posh shops and clusters of restaurants, is a good street to stroll.

Wisconsin Avenue originates in Georgetown; its intersection with M Street forms Georgetown's hub. Antiques shops, trendy boutiques, nightclubs, restaurants, and pubs all vie for attention. Wisconsin Avenue basically parallels Connecticut Avenue;

one of the few irritating things about the city's transportation system is that the Metro does not connect these two major arteries in the heart of the city. (Buses do, and, of course, you can always walk or take a taxi from one avenue to the other; read about two supplemental bus systems, the Georgetown Metro Connection shuttle and the D.C. Circulator, in the section "Getting Around," below.) Metrorail's first stop on Wisconsin Avenue is in Tenleytown, a residential area. Follow the avenue north and you land in the affluent Maryland cities of Chevy Chase and Bethesda.

FINDING AN ADDRESS If you understand the city's layout, it's easy to find your way around. As you read this, have a map handy.

Each of the four corners of the District of Columbia is exactly the same distance from the Capitol dome. The White House and most government buildings and important monuments are west of the Capitol (in the northwest and southwest quadrants), as are major hotels and tourist facilities.

Numbered streets run north–south, beginning on either side of the Capitol with 1st Street. Lettered streets run east–west and are named alphabetically, beginning with A Street. (Don't look for a B, a J, an X, a Y, or a Z St., however.) After W Street, street names of two syllables continue in alphabetical order, followed by street names of three syllables; the more syllables in a name, the farther the street is from the Capitol.

Avenues, named for U.S. states, run at angles across the grid pattern and often intersect at traffic circles. For example, New Hampshire, Connecticut, and Massachusetts avenues intersect at Dupont Circle.

With this in mind, you can easily find an address. On lettered streets, the address tells you exactly where to go. For instance, 1776 K St. NW is between 17th and 18th streets (the first two digits of 1776 tell you that) in the northwest quadrant (NW). ***Note:*** I Street is often written as "Eye" Street to prevent confusion with 1st Street.

To find an address on numbered streets, you'll probably have to use your fingers. For instance, 623 8th St. SE is between F and G streets (the 6th and 7th letters of the alphabet; the first digit of 623 tells you that) in the southeast quadrant (SE). One thing to remember: You count B as the second letter of the alphabet even though no B Street exists today (Constitution and Independence aves. were the original B sts.), but because there's no J Street, K becomes the 10th letter, L the 11th, and so on. To be honest, though, I don't know anyone who actually uses this method for figuring out an exact location.

THE NEIGHBORHOODS IN BRIEF

Capitol Hill Everyone's heard of "the Hill," the area crowned by the Capitol. When people speak of Capitol Hill, they refer to a large section of town, extending from the western side of the Capitol to the D.C. Armory going east, bounded by H Street to the north and the Southwest Freeway to the south. It contains not only the chief symbol of the nation's capital, but the Supreme Court building, the Library of Congress, the Folger Shakespeare Library, Union Station, and the U.S. Botanic Garden. Much of it is a quiet residential neighborhood of tree-lined streets and Victorian homes. There are a number of restaurants in the vicinity and a smattering of hotels, mostly close to Union Station. Keep to the well-lit, well-traveled streets at night, and don't walk alone—crime occurs more frequently in this neighborhood than in some other parts of town.

The Mall This lovely, tree-lined stretch of open space between Constitution and Independence avenues, extending for 2½ miles from the Capitol to the Lincoln Memorial, is the hub of tourist attractions. It includes most of the Smithsonian Institution museums and many other visitor attractions. The 300-foot-wide Mall is used by tourists as well as natives—joggers, food vendors, kite flyers, and picnickers among them. Most hotels and restaurants are located beyond the Mall to the north, with a few located south of the Mall, across Independence Avenue.

Downtown The area roughly between 7th and 22nd streets NW going east to west, and P Street and Pennsylvania Avenue going north to south, is a mix of the Federal Triangle's government office buildings, K Street, ground zero for the city's countless law and lobbying firms, Connecticut Avenue restaurants and shopping, historic hotels, the city's poshest small hotels, **Chinatown,** the huge new convention center, and the White House. You'll also find the historic **Penn Quarter,** now D.C.'s hottest area, which has continued to flourish ever since the 1997 opening of the Verizon Center (venue for Washington Wizards and Mystics basketball games and rock concerts). A number of off-the-Mall museums, like the International Spy Museum and the Smithsonian's National Portrait Gallery and American Art Museum, are here. You'll also find the latest hippest restaurants, boutique hotels, and art galleries. The total downtown area takes in so many blocks and attractions that I've divided discussions of accommodations (chapter 5) and dining (chapter 6) into two sections: "Midtown," roughly the area west of 15th Street to 12th Street, and north of Pennsylvania Avenue to M Street; and "Penn Quarter," roughly east of 15th Street to 8th Street, and Pennsylvania Avenue north to New York Avenue.

U Street Corridor D.C.'s avant-garde nightlife neighborhood, which runs along 14th Street and on U Street between 9th and 18th streets NW, continues to rise from the ashes of the nightclubs and theaters frequented decades ago by African Americans, when the area was known as "Black Broadway." At two renovated establishments, the Lincoln Theater and the Bohemian Caverns jazz club, where Duke Ellington, Louis Armstrong, and Cab Calloway once performed, patrons today can enjoy performances by their successors. The corridor offers many nightclubs, and more and more restaurants (see chapter 6) and little shops (see chapter 8). Go here to party, not to sleep—there are no hotels along this stretch.

Adams-Morgan Though this ever-trendy, multiethnic neighborhood is about the size of a postage stamp, it's crammed with boutiques, bars, clubs, and restaurants. Everything is located on either 18th Street NW or Columbia Road NW. You won't find any hotels here, but there are several nearby in the Dupont Circle and Woodley Park neighborhoods (see below). Parking during the day is okay, but forget it at night (although a parking garage did open recently, on 18th St., which helps things a little). Luckily, you can easily walk (be alert—the neighborhood is edgy) to Adams-Morgan from the Dupont Circle or Woodley Park Metro stops, or just taxi there. The weekend begins Thursday nights in Adams-Morgan, which is famous for its nightlife.

Dupont Circle One of my favorite parts of town, Dupont Circle is fun day or night. It takes its name from the traffic circle minipark, where Massachusetts, New Hampshire, and Connecticut avenues collide. Washington's

Impressions

My God! What have I done to be condemned to reside in such a city!

—A French diplomat in the early days

famous **Embassy Row** centers on Dupont Circle, and refers to the parade of grand embassy mansions lining Massachusetts Avenue and its side streets. The streets extending out from the circle are lively, with all-night bookstores, really good restaurants, wonderful art galleries and art museums, nightspots, movie theaters, and Washingtonians at their loosest. It is also the hub of D.C.'s gay community. There are plenty of hotels.

Foggy Bottom The area west of the White House and southeast of Georgetown, Foggy Bottom was Washington's early industrial center. Its name comes from the foul fumes emitted in those days by a coal depot and gasworks, but its original name, Funkstown (for owner Jacob Funk), is perhaps even worse. There's nothing foul (and not much funky) about the area today. This is a mixed neighborhood of town house residences, George Washington University campus buildings, small- and medium-size hotels, several fine restaurants, student bars, and the Kennedy Center, all gathered on either side of the main drag, Pennsylvania Avenue, or along its side streets.

Georgetown This historic community dates from Colonial times. It was a thriving tobacco port long before the District of Columbia was formed, and one of its attractions, the Old Stone House, dates from pre-Revolutionary days. Georgetown action centers on M Street and Wisconsin Avenue NW, where you'll find the luxury Four Seasons hotel (and less expensive digs), numerous boutiques (see chapter 8 for details), chic restaurants, and popular pubs—lots of nightlife here. But get off the main drags and see the quiet, tree-lined streets of restored Colonial row houses; stroll through the beautiful gardens of Dumbarton Oaks; and check out the C&O Canal. Georgetown is also home to Georgetown University. Note that the neighborhood gets pretty raucous on the weekends, which won't appeal to everyone.

Glover Park Mostly a residential neighborhood, this section of town, just above Georgetown and just south of the Washington National Cathedral, is worth mentioning because of the increasing number of good restaurants and bars opening along its main stretch, Wisconsin Avenue NW. Glover Park sits between the campuses of Georgetown and American Universities, so there's a large student presence here.

Woodley Park Home to Washington's largest hotel (the Marriott Wardman Park), Woodley Park boasts the National Zoo, many good restaurants, and some antiques stores. Washingtonians are used to seeing conventioneers wandering the neighborhood's pretty residential streets with their name tags still on.

2 Getting Around

Washington is one of the easiest U.S. cities to navigate, thanks to its comprehensive public transportation system of trains and buses. Ours is the second largest rail transit network and the fifth largest bus network in the country. But because Washington is of manageable size and marvelous beauty, you may find yourself shunning transportation and choosing to walk.

BY METRORAIL

If you travel Metrorail during rush hour (Mon–Fri 5–9:30am and 3–7pm), you may not be so smitten with the system, since delays can be frequent, lines at farecard machines long, trains overcrowded, and Washingtonians at their rudest. An increasing ridership is overloading the system, maintenance problems are cropping up, and the **Washington Metropolitan Area Transit Authority** (**WMATA, ✆ 202/637-7000;** www.wmata.com) is struggling just to keep pace, much less prevent future crises. Among the solutions are the addition of new trains and the installation of passenger information display boxes on station platforms reporting the number of minutes before the arrival of the next train and any delays or irregularities.

Though it's true that service has deteriorated, Washingtonians were spoiled to begin with. Stations are cool, clean, and attractive. Rides are quiet, and cars are air-conditioned and fitted with comfortable upholstered seats. You can expect to get a seat during off-peak hours (basically weekdays 10am–3pm, weeknights after 7pm, and all day weekends).

Metrorail's system of 86 stations and 106 miles of track includes locations at or near almost every sightseeing attraction; it also extends to suburban Maryland and northern Virginia. There are five lines in operation—Red, Blue, Orange, Yellow, and Green. The lines connect at several points, making transfers easy. All but Yellow and Green Line trains stop at Metro Center; all except Red Line trains stop at L'Enfant Plaza; all but Blue and Orange Line trains stop at Gallery Place/Chinatown. See the color map inside the back cover of this book.

Metro stations are indicated by discreet brown columns bearing the station's name and topped by the letter M. Below the M is a colored stripe or stripes indicating the line or lines that stop there. When entering a Metro station for the first time, go to the kiosk and ask the station manager for a free ***Metro System Pocket Guide.*** It contains a map of the system, explains how it works, and lists the closest Metro stops to points of interest. The station manager can also answer questions about routing or purchase of farecards. You can download a copy of the pocket guide and loads of information, including schedules, from Metro's website (www.wmata.com). The pocket guide is available in 11 languages, from Arabic to Vietnamese.

To enter or exit a Metro station, you need a computerized **farecard,** available at vending machines near the entrance. The machines take nickels, dimes, quarters, and bills from $1 to $20; they can return up to $4.95 in change (coins only). The vending machines labeled PASSES/FARECARDS accept both cash and credit cards. At this time, the minimum fare to enter the system is $1.35, which pays for rides to and from any point within 7 miles of boarding during nonpeak hours; during peak hours

Tips Metro Maps

D.C.'s most important Metro stops are highlighted on the "Washington, D.C. Major Metro Stops" map in the color insert at the front of this book. The insert also features a list of D.C.'s major attractions and their corresponding Metro lines. For a basic Metro map, refer to the back cover.

Tips Metro Etiquette 101

To avoid risking the ire of commuters, be sure to follow these guidelines: Stand to the right on the escalator so that people in a hurry can get past you on the left. And when you reach the train level, don't puddle at the bottom of the escalator, blocking the path of those coming behind you; move down the platform. Eating, drinking, and smoking are strictly prohibited on the Metro and in stations.

(Mon–Fri 5–9:30am and 3–7pm), $1.35 takes you only 3 miles. The maximum you will pay to the farthest destination is $3.90. Metro Authority is always contemplating a fare hike, though.

Once you're on the platform, you'll figure out your correct side of the track by finding your desired station stop on the list of upcoming stops posted on the brown pylon for trains headed in your direction. A display board overhead flashes the number of minutes anticipated before the next train pulls into the station. Lights embedded in the platform floor pulsate to alert you to the train's impending arrival. The only tricky part of traveling on Metro concerns transferring to a different line. Metro has eight transfer hubs, and probably the busiest hub is at Metro Center, where tracks crisscross on upper and lower levels and passengers can switch to a red, blue, or orange line train; read and follow the signs carefully, or ask someone for help, to make sure you get to the right track.

If you plan to take several Metrorail trips during your stay, put more value on the farecard to avoid having to purchase a new card each time you ride. For stays of more than a few days, your best value would be the **7-Day Fast Pass,** for $33 per person, which allows you unlimited travel; **1-Day Rail Passes** are available for $6.50 per person, allowing you unlimited passage for the day after 9:30am weekdays, or all day on Saturday, Sunday, and holidays. You can buy these passes online or at the Passes/Farecards machines in the stations. You can also purchase them at WMATA headquarters (weekdays only), 600 5th St. NW (© **202/637-7000;** www.wmata.com), its sales office at Metro Center (weekdays only), 12th and F streets NW, or one of the retail stores, like Giant or Safeway grocery stores, where farecards are sold.

Other passes are available—check out the website or call the main number for further information. Up to two children ages 4 and under can ride free with a paying passenger. Seniors (65 and older) and people with disabilities (with valid proof) ride Metrorail and Metrobus for a reduced fare.

When you insert your card in the entrance gate, the time and location are recorded on its magnetic tape, and your card is returned. Don't forget to snatch it up and keep it handy; ***you have to reinsert your farecard in the exit gate at your destination,*** where the fare will automatically be deducted. The card will be returned if there's any value left on it. If you arrive at a destination and your farecard doesn't have enough value, add what's necessary at the Exitfare machines near the exit gate.

Metrorail opens at 5am weekdays and 7am Saturday and Sunday, operating until midnight Sunday through Thursday, and until 3am Friday and Saturday. Call © **202/637-7000,** or visit www.wmata.com, for holiday hours and for information on Metro routes.

Tips Getting to Georgetown

Metrorail doesn't go to Georgetown, but a special shuttle bus, called the Georgetown Metro Connection, links three Metro stations (Rosslyn, Foggy Bottom, and Dupont Circle) to Georgetown. When you exit the Metro station, look for a posted blue sign with the words GEORGETOWN METRO CONNECTION stamped on it. The shuttle travels between the three stations and Georgetown, stopping at designated points along the way every 10 minutes from 7am to midnight Monday through Thursday, 7am to 2am Friday, 8am to 2am Saturday, and 8am to midnight Sunday. One-way fares cost $1.50, or 35¢ with a Metrorail transfer. See www.georgetowndc.com/shuttle.php for more information.

BY BUS

The **Metrobus** system encompasses 12,301 stops on its 335 routes (it operates on all major D.C. arteries as well as in the Virginia and Maryland suburbs). You'll know the stops by their red, white, and blue signs. However, the signs tell you only what buses pull into a given stop, not where they go. Furthermore, don't rely on the bus schedules posted at bus stops, which are sometimes out-of-date. Instead, for routing information, call ✆ **202/637-7000.** Calls are taken Monday through Thursday from 6am to 10:30pm, Friday 6am to 11:30pm, Saturday 7am to 11:30pm, and Sunday 7am to 10:30pm. Call this same number to request a free map and time schedule, and information about parking in Metrobus fringe lots, as well as for locations and hours of the places where you can purchase bus tokens.

Base fare in the District is $1.25; bus transfers are free and valid for 2 hours from boarding. There may be additional charges for travel into the Maryland and Virginia suburbs. Bus drivers are not equipped to make change, so be sure to carry exact change or tokens. If you'll be in Washington for a while and plan to use the buses a lot, consider buying a 1-week pass ($11), available online and also at the Metro Center station and other outlets. Buy tokens at the Metro Center Sales Office located at 12th and F streets. (Use the 12th St. entrance.)

Most buses operate daily almost around the clock. Service is quite frequent on weekdays, especially during peak hours. On weekends and late at night, service is less frequent.

Up to two children 4 and under ride free with a paying passenger on Metrobus, and there are reduced fares for seniors (✆ **202/637-7000**) and people with disabilities (✆ **202/962-1245** or 202/962-1100; see "Travelers with Disabilities," in chapter 2, for transit information). If you leave something on a bus, on a train, or in a station, call Lost and Found at ✆ **202/962-1195.**

BY CAR

More than half of all visitors to the District arrive by car; but when you get here, my advice is to park your car and use your own feet, Metrorail, the Georgetown Shuttle, and the D.C. Circulator to get around. If you must drive, be aware that traffic is always thick during the week, parking spaces are often hard to find, and parking lots are ruinously expensive.

Watch out for **traffic circles.** The law states that traffic already in the circle has the right of way. No one pays any attention to this rule, however, which can be frightening (cars zoom into the circle without a glance at the cars already there). The other thing you'll notice is that while some circles are easy to figure out (Dupont Circle, for example), others are nerve-wrackingly confusing (Thomas Circle, where 14th St. NW, Vermont Ave. NW, and Massachusetts Ave. NW come together, is to be avoided at all costs).

Sections of certain streets in Washington become **one-way** during rush hour: Rock Creek Parkway, Canal Road, and 17th Street NW are three examples. Other streets change the direction of some of their traffic lanes during rush hour: Connecticut Avenue NW is the main one. In the morning, traffic in four of its six lanes travels south to downtown, and in late afternoon/early evening, downtown traffic in four of its six lanes heads north; between the hours of 9am and 3:30pm, traffic in both directions keeps to the normally correct side of the yellow line. Lit-up traffic signs alert you to what's going on, but pay attention. Unless a sign is posted prohibiting it, a right-on-red law is in effect.

To keep up with street closings and construction information, go online to the *Washington Post*'s home page, at www.washingtonpost.com, and click on "Traffic," to learn about current traffic and routing problems in the District and suburban Maryland and Virginia. Another helpful source is a page on the D.C. government's website, http://dc.gov/closures, which identifies major street closures, traffic alerts, and construction in the city, though this info is not always current.

CAR RENTALS

Residents and tourists alike seem to be turning to car rental clubs that allow you more flexible car-use arrangements, whether you need a car for an hour or for a month, with parking and other services included. Two such companies operate in Washington: **Zipcars** (✆ 866/494-7227; www.zipcar.com), which has a downtown office at 717 D St. NW, entrance on 8th Street (✆ 202/737-4900); and **Flexcars,** with an office at 140 Q St. NE (✆ 202/580-7050; www.flexcar.com). They both work basically the same way: You apply and pay a membership fee or application fee ahead of time online, order the car online or by phone using a credit card, and establish exactly when and where you need a car. You receive a special card in the mail, which you use to activate the specific car you've reserved at the specific location, time, and day you've prearranged. Instructions differ slightly for Zipcar and Flexcar, but the idea is that this special card unlocks the reserved car and you climb inside to retrieve the keys, following instructions you're given ahead of time. Zipcar's rates start at $7.65 an hour, Flexcar's rates start at $8 an hour, and these fees cover gas, insurance, and parking.

All the major car-rental companies are represented in D.C., including Alamo, Avis, Budget, Dollar, Enterprise, Hertz, National, and Thrifty. Refer to the information about area airports at the beginning of this chapter for phone numbers for each company's

---

Tips **Transit Tip**

If you're on the subway and plan to continue your travel via Metrobus, pick up a free transfer at the station when you enter the system (not your destination station). Transfer machines are on the mezzanine levels of most stations. With the transfer, you pay a reduced fare, usually 35¢, when you board a bus upon exiting your Metrorail station. There are no bus-to-subway transfers.

Tips D.C. Circulator

In addition to the Georgetown Metro Connection shuttle bus, D.C. offers a second supplemental bus system that is efficient, inexpensive, and convenient. The D.C. Circulator's fleet of air-conditioned red-and-gray buses travel three circumscribed routes in the city: the north–south route between the D.C. Convention Center and the waterfront, the east–west route between upper Georgetown and Union Station, and the seasonal (late Mar to Oct) Smithsonian/National Gallery route, which simply loops around the Mall, from 4th Street to Independence Avenue, to 17th Street, to Constitution Avenue, and back around. Buses stop at designated points on their routes (look for the distinctive red and gold sign, often topping a regular Metro bus-stop sign) every 5 to 10 minutes, and operate daily between 7am and 9pm, except for the Smithsonian/National Gallery route, which operates from 10am to 4pm. In Spring 2007, the system added 9pm to midnight service Sunday to Thursday, 9pm to 2am Friday and Saturday service between upper Georgetown and the intersection of 17th and I streets NW, to provide transportation to nightlifers. The fare is $1 (35¢ with the use of a Metrorail transfer) and you can pay with exact change, use a SmarTrip Metro card, or use a D.C. Circulator bus ticket purchased at a street meter near the bus stop. For easy and fast transportation in the busiest parts of town, you can't beat it. Call © **202/962-1423** or go to www.dccirculator.com.

airport locations. All but Hertz have car rental locations within downtown D.C.: **Avis,** 1722 M St. NW (© 202/467-6585) and 4400 Connecticut Ave. NW (© 202/686-5149); **Budget,** Union Station (© 202/289-5374); **Enterprise,** 22nd Street and M Street NW (© 202/338-0015); **Alamo** and **National,** Union Station (© 202/842-7454); and **Thrifty,** inside the Verizon Center, at 7th and G streets NW (© 202/371-0485). ***Note:*** Avis and Budget rental policies require a minimum age of 25; Alamo, National, Enterprise, Hertz, and Thrifty rental policies require a minimum age of 21; Enterprise charges an additional $15 for renters 21 to 24, and Thrifty, Hertz, Alamo, and National tack on an additional $25. None of the agencies stipulates a maximum age requirement.

Car-rental rates can vary even more than airfares. Taking the time to shop around and asking a few key questions could save you hundreds of dollars:

- Are weekend rates lower than weekday rates? Ask if the rate is the same for pickup Friday morning, for instance, as it is for Thursday night.
- Is the weekly rate cheaper than the daily rate? Even if you need the car for only 4 days, it may be cheaper to keep it for 5.
- Does the agency assess a drop-off charge if you don't return the car to the same location where you picked it up? Is it cheaper to pick up the car at the airport or at a downtown location?
- Are special promotional rates available? If you see an advertised price in your local newspaper, be sure to ask for that specific rate; otherwise, you may be charged the standard cost. Terms change constantly.
- Are discounts available for members of AARP, AAA, frequent-flier programs, or trade unions?

- How much tax will be added to the rental bill? Local tax? State use tax? Local taxes and surcharges can vary from location to location, even within the same car company, which can add quite a bit to your costs.
- What is the cost of adding an additional driver's name to the contract?
- How many free miles are included in the price? Free mileage is often negotiable, depending on the length of your rental.

Some companies offer "refueling packages," in which you pay for an entire tank of gas up front. The price is usually fairly competitive with local gas prices, but you don't get credit for any gas remaining in the tank. If a stop at a gas station on the way to the airport will make you miss your plane, then by all means take advantage of the fuel purchase option. Otherwise, skip it.

For information on insurance, review your own car insurance policy and contact the **American Automobile Association (AAA)** (✆ **800/763-9900**) for advice and helpful information.

BY TAXI

District cabs continue to operate on a zone system instead of using meters, and the cabbies hope to keep it that way. By law, basic rates are posted in each cab. If you take a trip from one point to another within the same zone, the base rate is $6.50 (during non–rush hours) regardless of the distance traveled. That rate applies whether you travel a few blocks from the U.S. Capitol to the National Museum of American History, or from the Capitol all the way to Dupont Circle. Both trips traverse Zone 1, where most tourist attractions are located: the White House, most of the Smithsonian, the Washington Monument, the National Archives, the Supreme Court, the Library of Congress, the Bureau of Engraving and Printing, the Old Post Office, and Ford's Theatre. If your trip takes you into a second zone, the price goes to $8.80, $11 for a third zone, $13 for a fourth, and so on. ***Note:*** Taxis sometimes charge a $1 surcharge on top of the zone fare, to cover the high price of gasoline—check the cab's fare chart. In addition, the rates quoted above are based on the assumption that you are hailing a cab. If you telephone for a cab, you will be charged an additional $2. During rush hour—between 7 and 9:30am and 4 and 6:30pm weekdays—you pay a surcharge of $1 per trip, plus a second surcharge of $1 when you telephone for a cab, which brings the total surcharge you pay for telephoning for a cab during rush hour to $4.

Other charges might apply, as well: There's a $1.50 charge for each additional passenger after the first, so a $6.50 Zone 1 fare can become $11 for a family of four, though one child under 5 can ride free. Surcharges are also added for luggage (from 50¢ to $2 per piece, depending on size). Try **Diamond Cab Company** (✆ **202/387-6200**) or **Yellow Cab** (✆ **202/544-1212**).

The zone system is not used when your destination is an out-of-District address (such as an airport); in that case, the fare is based on mileage—$3.25 for the first half-mile or part thereof and 90¢ for each additional half-mile or part. You can call

---

Impressions

I know of no other capital in the world which stands on so wide and splendid a river. But the people and the mode of life are enough to take your hair off!

—Henry James

✆ **202/331-1671** to find out the rate between any point in D.C. and an address in Virginia or Maryland. Call ✆ **202/645-6018** to inquire about fares within the District. For more information about D.C. taxicabs than you could ever even guess was available, check out the D.C. Taxicab Commission's website, www.dctaxi.dc.gov.

It's generally easy to hail a taxi. Unique to the city is the practice of allowing drivers to pick up as many passengers as they can comfortably fit, so expect to share (unrelated parties pay the same as they would if they were not sharing). To register a complaint, note the cab driver's name and cab number and file a written complaint by either fax (✆ **202/889-3604**) or mail (Commendations/Complaints, District of Columbia Taxicab Commission, 2041 Martin Luther King Jr. Ave. SE, Room 204, Washington, DC 20020).

FAST FACTS: Washington, D.C.

American Express There's an American Express Travel Service office at 1501 K St. NW, entrance on 15th St. (✆ **202/457-1300**).

Area Codes Within the District of Columbia, it's 202. In suburban Virginia, it's 703. In suburban Maryland, it's 301. You must use the area code when dialing any number, even local calls within the District or to nearby Maryland or Virginia suburbs.

ATM Networks See "Money & Costs," p. 30.

Automobile Organizations Auto clubs will supply maps, suggested routes, guidebooks, accident and bail-bond insurance, and emergency road service. The **American Automobile Association (AAA)** is the major auto club in the United States. If you belong to an auto club in your home country, inquire about AAA reciprocity before you leave. You may be able to join AAA even if you're not a member of a reciprocal club; to inquire, call AAA (✆ **800/763-9900**). AAA is actually an organization of regional auto clubs, so look under "AAA Automobile Club" in the White Pages of the telephone directory. AAA has a nationwide emergency road service telephone number (✆ **800/AAA-HELP,** or 800/222-4357).

Business Hours Offices are usually open weekdays from 9am to 5pm. Most banks are open Monday through Thursday from 9am to 3pm, with some staying open until 5pm; 9am to 5pm on Friday, and sometimes Saturday mornings. Stores typically open between 9 and 10am and close between 5 and 6pm from Monday to Saturday. Stores in shopping complexes or malls tend to stay open late, until about 9pm on weekdays and weekends, and many malls and larger department stores are open on Sundays.

Cameras & Film Never pack film in checked bags, because the powerful scanners in U.S. airports can fog film. The film you carry with you can be damaged by scanners as well. X-ray damage is cumulative; the more times you put it through a scanner, the more likely the damage. Keep in mind that airports are not the only places where your camera may be scanned: Highly trafficked attractions are X-raying visitors' bags with increasing frequency.

Most photo supply stores sell protective pouches designed to block damaging X-rays. The pouches fit both film and loaded cameras. They should protect your film in checked baggage, but they also may raise alarms and result in a hand inspection.

You'll have little to worry about if you are traveling with digital cameras. Digital camera and storage cards are not affected by airport X-rays, according to Nikon.

Carry-on scanners will not damage videotape, but the magnetic fields emitted by the walk-through security gateways and handheld inspection wands will. Always place your loaded camcorder on the screening conveyor belt or have it hand-inspected. Be sure your batteries are charged, as you may be required to turn the device on to ensure that it's what it appears to be.

Car Rentals See "Getting Around," earlier in this chapter.

Cashpoints See "Money & Costs," in chapter 2.

Congresspersons To locate a senator or congressional representative, call the Capitol switchboard (✆ **202/225-3121**). Point your Web browser to www.senate.gov and www.house.gov to contact individual senators and congressional representatives by e-mail, find out what bills are being worked on, the calendar for the day, and more.

Currency The most common bills are the $1 (a "buck"), $5, $10, and $20 denominations. There are also $2 bills (seldom encountered), $50 bills, and $100 bills (the last two are usually not welcome as payment for small purchases).

Coins come in seven denominations: 1¢ (1 cent, or a penny); 5¢ (5 cents, or a nickel); 10¢ (10 cents, or a dime); 25¢ (25 cents, or a quarter); 50¢ (50 cents, or a half dollar); the gold-colored Sacagawea coin, worth $1; and the rare silver dollar.

For additional information see "Money & Costs," p. 30.

Customs **What You Can Bring into Washington, D.C.** Every visitor more than 21 years of age may bring in, free of duty, the following: (1) 1 liter of wine or hard liquor; (2) 200 cigarettes, 100 cigars (but not from Cuba), or 3 pounds of smoking tobacco; and (3) $100 worth of gifts. These exemptions are offered to travelers who spend at least 72 hours in the United States and who have not claimed them within the preceding 6 months. It is altogether forbidden to bring into the country foodstuffs (particularly fruit, cooked meats, and canned goods) and plants (vegetables, seeds, tropical plants, and the like). Foreign tourists may carry in or out up to $10,000 in U.S. or foreign currency with no formalities; larger sums must be declared to U.S. Customs on entering or leaving, which includes filing form CM 4790. For details regarding U.S. Customs and Border Protection, consult your nearest U.S. embassy or consulate, or **U.S. Customs** (✆ **202/927-1770;** www.customs.ustreas.gov).

What You Can Take Home from Washington, D.C.:

Canadian Citizens: For a clear summary of Canadian rules, write for the booklet *I Declare,* issued by the **Canada Border Services Agency** (✆ **800/461-9999** in Canada, or 204/983-3500; **www.cbsa-asfc.gc.ca**).

U.K. Citizens: For information, contact **HM Customs & Excise** at ✆ **0845/010-9000** (from outside the U.K., 020/8929-0152), or consult their website at **www.hmce.gov.uk**.

Australian Citizens: A helpful brochure available from Australian consulates or Customs offices is *Know Before You Go*. For more information, call the **Australian Customs Service** at ✆ **1300/363-263,** or log on to **www.customs.gov.au**.

New Zealand Citizens: Most questions are answered in a free pamphlet available at New Zealand consulates and Customs offices: *New Zealand Customs Guide for Travellers, Notice no. 4*. For more information, contact **New Zealand Customs,** The Customhouse, 17–21 Whitmore St., Box 2218, Wellington (✆ **04/473-6099** or 0800/428-786; **www.customs.govt.nz**).

Drinking Laws The legal age for purchase and consumption of alcoholic beverages is 21; proof of age is required and often requested at bars, nightclubs, and restaurants, so it's always a good idea to bring ID when you go out. Liquor stores are closed on Sunday. District gourmet grocery stores, mom-and-pop grocery stores, and 7-11 convenience stores often sell beer and wine, even on Sunday.

Bars and nightclubs serve liquor until 2am Sunday through Thursday and until 3am Friday and Saturday.

Do not carry open containers of alcohol in your car or any public area that isn't zoned for alcohol consumption. The police can fine you on the spot. And nothing will ruin your trip faster than getting a citation for DUI ("driving under the influence"), so don't even think about driving while intoxicated.

Driving Rules See "Getting Around," earlier in this chapter.

Drugstores **CVS,** Washington's major drugstore chain (with more than 40 stores), has two convenient 24-hour locations: in the West End, at 2240 M Street NW (✆ **202/296-9877**), and at 6 Dupont Circle (✆ **202/785-1466**), both with round-the-clock pharmacies. Check your phone book for other convenient locations.

Electricity Like Canada, the United States uses 110 to 120 volts AC (60 cycles), compared to 220 to 240 volts AC (50 cycles) in most of Europe, Australia, and New Zealand. Downward converters that change 220–240 volts to 110–120 volts are difficult to find in the United States, so bring one with you.

Embassies & Consulates All embassies are located in Washington, D.C. If your country isn't listed below, call for directory information in Washington, D.C. (✆ **202/555-1212**) or log on to **www.embassy.org/embassies**.

The embassy of **Australia** is at 1601 Massachusetts Ave. NW, Washington, DC 20036 (✆ **202/797-3000;** www.austemb.org). There are consulates in New York, Honolulu, Houston, Los Angeles, and San Francisco.

The embassy of **Canada** is at 501 Pennsylvania Ave. NW, Washington, DC 20001 (✆ **202/682-1740;** www.canadianembassy.org). Other Canadian consulates are in Buffalo (New York), Detroit, Los Angeles, New York, and Seattle.

The embassy of **Ireland** is at 2234 Massachusetts Ave. NW, Washington, DC 20008 (✆ **202/462-3939;** www.irelandemb.org). Irish consulates are in Boston, Chicago, New York, San Francisco, and other cities. See website for complete listing.

The embassy of **New Zealand** is at 37 Observatory Circle NW, Washington, DC 20008 (✆ **202/328-4800;** www.nzemb.org). New Zealand consulates are in Los Angeles, Salt Lake City, San Francisco, and Seattle.

The embassy of the **United Kingdom** is at 3100 Massachusetts Ave. NW, Washington, DC 20008 (✆ **202/588-6500;** www.britainusa.com). Other British consulates are in Atlanta, Boston, Chicago, Cleveland, Houston, Los Angeles, New York, San Francisco, and Seattle.

Emergencies Call ✆ **911** for police, fire, and medical emergencies. This is a toll-free call. (No coins are required at public telephones.)

If you encounter serious problems, contact the **Traveler's Aid Society International** (✆ **202/546-1127;** www.travelersaid.org), a nationwide, nonprofit, social-service organization geared to helping travelers in difficult straits, from reuniting families separated while traveling, to providing food and/or shelter to people stranded without cash, to emotional counseling. Traveler's Aid operates help desks at Washington Dulles International Airport (✆ 703/572-8296), Ronald Reagan Washington National Airport (✆ 703/417-3972), and Union Station (✆ 202/371-1937).

Gasoline (Petrol) At press time, in the U.S., the cost of gasoline (also known as gas, but never petrol), is abnormally high—over $3 a gallon. Taxes are already included in the printed price, but these vary by jurisdiction, with Northern Virginia's gas tax the lowest in the metropolitan area. One U.S. gallon equals 3.8 liters or .85 imperial gallons. Fill-up locations are known as gas or service stations.

Holidays Banks, government offices, post offices, and many stores, restaurants, and museums are closed on the following legal national holidays: January 1 (New Year's Day), the third Monday in January (Martin Luther King, Jr., Day), the third Monday in February (Presidents' Day), the last Monday in May (Memorial Day), July 4 (Independence Day), the first Monday in September (Labor Day), the second Monday in October (Columbus Day), November 11 (Veterans' Day/Armistice Day), the fourth Thursday in November (Thanksgiving Day), and December 25 (Christmas). The Tuesday after the first Monday in November is Election Day, a federal government holiday in presidential-election years (held every 4 years, this year, 2008, in fact).

For more information on holidays see "Calendar of Events," in chapter 2.

Hospitals If you don't require immediate ambulance transportation but still need emergency-room treatment, call one of the following hospitals (and be sure to get directions): **Children's Hospital National Medical Center,** 111 Michigan Ave. NW (✆ **202/884-5000**); **George Washington University Hospital,** 900 23rd St. NW at Washington Circle (✆ **202/715-4000**); **Georgetown University Medical Center,** 3800 Reservoir Rd. NW (✆ **202/444-2000**); or **Howard University Hospital,** 2042 Georgia Ave. NW (✆ **202/865-6100**).

Hot Lines To reach a 24-hour poison-control hot line, call ✆ **800/222-1222;** to reach a 24-hour crisis line, call ✆ **202/561-7000;** to reach a 24-hour rape crisis line, call ✆ **202/333-RAPE.**

Internet Access See "Staying Connected," in chapter 2.

Legal Aid If you are "pulled over" for a minor infraction (such as speeding), never attempt to pay the fine directly to a police officer; this could be construed as attempted bribery, a much more serious crime. Pay fines by mail, or directly into the hands of the clerk of the court. If accused of a more serious offense, say and do nothing before consulting a lawyer. Here the burden is on the state to prove a person's guilt beyond a reasonable doubt, and everyone has the right to remain silent, whether he or she is suspected of a crime or actually arrested. Once arrested, a person can make one telephone call to a party of his or her choice. International visitors should call their embassy or consulate.

Lost & Found Be sure to tell all of your credit card companies the minute you discover your wallet has been lost or stolen, and file a report at the nearest police precinct. Your credit card company or insurer may require a police report number or record of the loss. Most credit card companies have an emergency toll-free number to call if your card is lost or stolen; they may be able to wire you a cash advance immediately or deliver an emergency credit card in a day or two. Visa's U.S. emergency number is ✆ **800/847-2911** or 410/581-9994. American Express cardholders and traveler's check holders should call ✆ **800/221-7282.** MasterCard holders should call ✆ **800/307-7309** or 636/722-7111. For other credit cards, call the toll-free number directory at ✆ **800/555-1212.**

If you need emergency cash over the weekend when all banks and American Express offices are closed, you can have money wired to you via **Western Union** (✆ **800/325-6000;** www.westernunion.com).

Mail At press time, domestic postage rates were 26¢ for a postcard and 41¢ for a letter. For international mail, a first-class postcard costs 69¢ to Canada and Mexico and 90¢ to all other countries. For more information go to **www.usps.com** and click on "Calculate Postage."

If you aren't sure what your address will be in the United States, mail can be sent to you, in your name, c/o General Delivery at the main post office of the city or region where you expect to be. (Call ✆ **800/275-8777** for information on the nearest post office.) The addressee must pick up mail in person and must produce proof of identity (driver's license, passport, or something similar). Most post offices will hold your mail for up to 1 month, and are open Monday to Friday from 8am to 6pm, and Saturday from 9am to 3pm.

Always include zip codes when mailing items in the U.S. If you don't know your zip code, visit www.usps.com/zip4.

Maps Free city maps are often available at hotels and throughout town at tourist attractions. You can also contact the **Washington, D.C. Convention and Tourism Corporation,** 901 7th St. NW, 4th Floor, Washington, DC 20001 (✆ **202/789-7000**).

Newspapers & Magazines See "Visitor Information," earlier in this chapter.

Passports **For Residents of Australia:** You can pick up an application from your local post office or any branch of Passports Australia, but you must schedule an interview at the passport office to present your application materials. Call the **Australian Passport Information Service** at ✆ **131-232,** or visit the government website at www.passports.gov.au.

For Residents of Canada: Passport applications are available at travel agencies throughout Canada or from the central **Passport Office,** Department of Foreign Affairs and International Trade, Ottawa, ON K1A 0G3 (✆ **800/567-6868;** www.ppt.gc.ca). ***Note:*** Canadian children who travel must have their own passport. However, if you hold a valid Canadian passport issued before December 11, 2001, that bears the name of your child, the passport remains valid for you and your child until it expires.

For Residents of Ireland: You can apply for a 10-year passport at the **Passport Office,** Setanta Centre, Molesworth Street, Dublin 2 (✆ **01/671-1633;** www.irlgov.ie/iveagh). Those under age 18 and over 65 must apply for a €12 3-year passport. You can also apply at 1A South Mall, Cork (✆ **021/272-525**), or at most main post offices.

For Residents of New Zealand: You can pick up a passport application at any New Zealand Passports Office or download it from their website. Contact the **Passports Office** at ✆ **0800/225-050** in New Zealand or 04/474-8100, or log on to www.passports.govt.nz.

For Residents of the United Kingdom: To pick up an application for a standard 10-year passport (5-yr. passport for children under 16), visit your nearest passport office, major post office, or travel agency or contact the **United Kingdom Passport Service** at ✆ **0870/521-0410** or search its website at www.ukpa.gov.uk.

Police In an emergency, dial ✆ **911.** For a nonemergency, call ✆ **202/727-1010.**

Safety See "Safety," in chapter 2.

Smoking The District is smoke free, meaning that the city bans smoking in restaurants, bars, and other public buildings. Smoking is permitted outdoors, unless otherwise noted.

Taxes The United States has no value-added tax (VAT) or other indirect tax at the national level. Every state, county, and city may levy its own local tax on all purchases, including hotel and restaurant checks and airline tickets. These taxes will not appear on price tags.

The sales tax on merchandise is 5.75% in the District, 5% in Maryland, and 4.5% in Virginia. The tax on restaurant meals is 10% in the District, 5% in Maryland, and 4.5% in Virginia.

In the District, you pay 14.5% hotel tax. The hotel tax in Maryland varies by county from 5% to 8%. The hotel tax in Virginia also varies by county, averaging about 9.75%.

Telephone, Telegraph, Telex & Fax Generally, hotel surcharges on long-distance and local calls are astronomical, so you're better off using your **cellphone** or a **public pay telephone.** Most long-distance and international calls can be dialed directly from any phone. **For calls within the United States and to Canada,** dial 1 followed by the area code and the seven-digit number. **For other international calls,** dial 011 followed by the country code, city code, and the number you are calling.

Calls to area codes **800, 888, 877,** and **866** are toll-free. However, calls to area codes **700** and **900** (chat lines, bulletin boards, "dating" services, and so on) can be very expensive—usually a charge of 95¢ to $3 or more per minute, and they sometimes have minimum charges that can run as high as $15 or more.

For **reversed-charge or collect calls,** and for person-to-person calls, dial the number 0 and then the area code and number; an operator will come on the line, and you should specify whether you are calling collect, person-to-person, or both. If your operator-assisted call is international, ask for the overseas operator.

For **local directory assistance** ("information"), dial 411; for long-distance information, dial 1, then the appropriate area code and 555-1212.

Telegraph and telex services are provided primarily by Western Union. You can telegraph money, or have it telegraphed to you, very quickly over the Western Union system, but this service can cost as much as 15% to 20% of the amount sent.

Most hotels have **fax machines** available for guest use (be sure to ask about the charge to use it). Many hotel rooms are even wired for guests' fax machines. A less expensive way to send and receive faxes may be at stores such as **The UPS Store** (formerly Mail Boxes Etc.).

Time The continental United States is divided into **four time zones:** Eastern Standard Time (EST)—this is the time zone into which Washington, D.C., falls; Central Standard Time (CST); Mountain Standard Time (MST); and Pacific Standard Time (PST). Alaska and Hawaii have their own zones. For example, when it's 9am in Los Angeles (PST), it's 7am in Honolulu (HST), 10am in Denver (MST), 11am in Chicago (CST), noon in New York City (EST), 5pm in London (GMT), and 2am the next day in Sydney.

Daylight saving time takes effect at 2am the second Sunday in March until 2am the first Sunday in November, except in Arizona, Hawaii, the U.S. Virgin Islands, and Puerto Rico. Daylight savings moves the clock 1 hour ahead of standard time. For the correct time, call ✆ **202/844-2525.**

Tipping Tips are a very important part of certain workers' income, and gratuities are the standard way of showing appreciation for services provided. (Tipping is certainly not compulsory if the service is poor!) In hotels, tip **bellhops** at least $1 per bag ($2–$3 if you have a lot of luggage) and tip the **chamber staff** $1 to $2 per day (more if you've left a disaster area for him or her to clean up). Tip the **doorman** or **concierge** only if he or she has provided you with some specific service (for example, calling a cab for you or obtaining difficult-to-get theater tickets). Tip the **valet-parking attendant** $1 every time you get your car.

In restaurants, bars, and nightclubs, tip **service staff** 15% to 20% of the check, tip **bartenders** 10% to 15%, tip **checkroom attendants** $1 per garment, and tip **valet-parking attendants** $1 per vehicle.

As for other service personnel, tip **cab drivers** 15% of the fare; tip **skycaps** at airports at least $1 per bag ($2–$3 if you have a lot of luggage); and tip **hairdressers** and **barbers** 15% to 20%.

Toilets You won't find public toilets or "restrooms" on the streets in most U.S. cities but they can be found in hotel lobbies, bars, restaurants, museums, department stores, railway and bus stations, and service stations. Large hotels and fast-food restaurants are often the best bet for clean facilities. If possible, avoid the toilets at parks and beaches, which tend to be dirty; some may be unsafe. Restaurants and bars in resorts or heavily visited areas may reserve their restrooms for patrons.

Useful Phone Numbers

U.S. Dept. of State Travel Advisory: ✆ 202/663-1225

U.S. Passport Agency: ✆ 202/647-0518

U.S. Centers for Disease Control International Traveler's Hotline: ✆ 404/332-4559

Visas For information about U.S. Visas go to **http://travel.state.gov** and click on "Visas." Or go to one of the following websites:

Australian citizens can obtain up-to-date visa information from the **U.S. Embassy Canberra,** Moonah Place, Yarralumla, ACT 2600 (✆ **02/6214-5600**), or by checking the U.S. Diplomatic Mission's website at **http://usembassy-australia.state.gov/consular**.

British subjects can obtain up-to-date visa information by calling the **U.S. Embassy Visa Information Line** (✆ **0891/200-290**) or by visiting the "Visas to the U.S." section of the American Embassy London's website at **www.usembassy.org.uk**.

Irish citizens can obtain up-to-date visa information through the **Embassy of the USA Dublin,** 42 Elgin Rd., Dublin 4, Ireland (✆ **353/1-668-8777**), or by checking the "Consular Services" section of the website at **http://dublin.usembassy.gov**.

Citizens of **New Zealand** can obtain up-to-date visa information by contacting the **U.S. Embassy New Zealand,** 29 Fitzherbert Terrace, Thorndon, Wellington (✆ **644/472-2068**), or get the information directly from the "For New Zealanders" section of the website at **http://wellington.usembassy.gov**.

Weather Call ✆ **202/936-1212** or visit www.weather.com.

5

Where to Stay

Each year brings a new amenity "must" to the hotel world. In the past, we've seen hoteliers attempt to please their guests anew with in-room additions of coffeemakers, cordless phones, dataports, Internet access, CD players, and other items, and on-site access to fitness and business centers; these amenities are now considered standard at most properties. This year, it's all about the multilayered, pillow-top mattress and high-tech televisions—flatscreen or plasma. More and more of Washington's hotels offer these features, including about half of those described in this chapter. (If you don't see a mention of the special mattress or cool TV in one of my hotel write-ups, and these are important to you, be sure to ask when you book your reservation, since your desired hotel may be in the process of adding these embellishments.)

Alike in their pursuit of satisfying their customers, Washington, D.C.'s 105 hotels vary widely when it comes to individual style and level of luxury. For off-the-charts pampering, look to the city's sole winner of the Mobil Travel Guide five-star award, the Four Seasons, or to the posh Mandarin Oriental, or to either of two Ritz-Carltons. If you're seeking decent lodging at the other end of the budget scale, you might consider our good-value guesthouses and B&Bs, like the Woodley Park Guesthouse, near the National Zoo, or its just-opened sister, the Embassy Circle Inn, along Embassy Row.

Those who favor the familiarity and conveniences of chain hotels have many from which to choose: Marriotts dominate, with about 15 properties, from business-traveler favorite Courtyard by Marriotts, to the high-end traveler option, JW Marriott. The Hilton family has a strong D.C. presence in its Embassy Suites, Hampton Inn, and Hilton Garden Inn brands, all three targeted to please both business and leisure guests.

All-American Hyatt, Sheraton, and Omni chain hotels are here, as are international chain hotels, like Ireland's gracious Jurys and France's chic Sofitel. We even have an un-chainlike chain: Kimpton Group hotels, whose seven Washington properties each have their own distinct personalities, from the newest, most artful, Hotel Palomar, to the hip Hotel Helix.

And if chains, no matter how whimsical, are not for you, the capital has a slew of only-in-Washington hotels, including the Hay-Adams, across from the White House, and the River Inn, just outside Georgetown.

You'll discover descriptions of all of these hotels and inns—more than 50—within this chapter, along with tips on choosing a neighborhood, getting the best rate, landing the best room, and finding a place to stay when the whole city seems booked. So read on, to help you pick your top choices and book a reservation.

CHOOSING A NEIGHBORHOOD

Most of Washington's hotels lie downtown or near Dupont Circle, with a handful scattered in Georgetown, on Capitol Hill, and northward on Connecticut Avenue. Each of these communities has its own character, as detailed in the section "The Neighborhoods in Brief," in chapter 4.

If proximity to the capital's major attractions is most important to you, consider hotels near Capitol Hill and the National Mall. Convenient for sightseeing and in the thick of things during the day, these hotels may feel isolated at night and on weekends, when the Hill staff and office workers go home. With the exception of Capitol Hill Suites, the hotels are not near residential areas, and restaurants and shops are few.

To take the pulse of the city as it goes about its business, stay in a downtown hotel. This is also where you should bunk if you want to be able to walk to good restaurants, bars, and nightclubs. Divided into two sections here, between 6th and 15th streets NW (Penn Quarter) and between 15th and 22nd streets NW (Midtown), Washington's downtown is bustling day and night all week long. Hotels in the downtown segment east of 15th Street are close to theaters and several museums; properties on or near Pennsylvania Avenue, like the Willard and the Hotel Washington, are within walking distance of the National Mall and the White House. Downtown hotels west of 15th Street are also within a stroll of the White House, as well as some smaller museums, like Decatur House and the Renwick and Corcoran galleries.

If you prefer the feel of a residential neighborhood, look to hotels in Dupont Circle and Woodley Park. For a taste of campus life, you might choose lodging in Foggy Bottom; the accommodations near Pennsylvania Avenue and Washington Circle border George Washington University's widening campus. And if you're a serious shopper, Georgetown should be your top choice, with Dupont Circle as your second pick.

Within each neighborhood heading, this chapter further organizes hotels by rate categories, based on their lowest high-season rates for double rooms: **Very Expensive** (from about $350 and up); **Expensive** (from about $225); **Moderate** (from about $150); and **Inexpensive** (anything under $150). But these categories are intended as a general guideline only—rates can rise and fall dramatically, depending on how busy the hotel is. In 2007, the rise in D.C. hotel rates also reflected increased energy prices and property values, for which hotels were having to pay substantially higher taxes than in the past; that may still be true. Nevertheless, it's often possible to obtain a special package or a better rate than the first rate quoted, as the next section explains.

SAVING ON YOUR HOTEL ROOM

The **rack rate** is the maximum rate that a hotel charges for a room. Hardly anybody pays this price, however, except during peak season. Every hotel usually offers ways for customers to pay a lower rate than the published rate. In each hotel write-up, I mention tips for obtaining the best rate as specified by the hotel. These general guidelines also can help lower the cost of your room:

- **Ask about special rates or other discounts.** Always ask whether a room less expensive than the first one quoted is available, or whether any special rates apply to you. You may qualify for corporate, government, student, military, senior, or other discounts, and these can be substantial. Mention membership in AAA, AARP, frequent-flier programs, or trade unions, which may entitle you to special deals as well.

- **Dial direct.** When booking a room in a chain hotel, you'll often get a better deal by calling the individual hotel's reservation desk rather than the chain's main number. ***Warning:*** You'll want to confirm that you are talking to someone on-site at the hotel, even if you've dialed a local "202" phone number; increasingly, chain hotels are outsourcing the bulk of their reservation bookings to regional offices, whose staff are simply not informed enough to answer basic questions about a particular hotel. I ran into this problem at the Residence Inn Capitol, where I spoke to a regional reservations clerk (she wouldn't reveal her exact location), who didn't know whether the hotel offered views of the Capitol, and at the Omni Shoreham Hotel, where I was connected to the "concierge," who was in Nebraska!
- **Book online.** Many hotels offer Internet-only discounts, or supply rooms to Priceline, Travelocity, or Expedia at rates lower than the ones you can get through the hotel itself. (See chapter 2, "Surfing for Hotels.")
- **Remember the law of supply and demand.** Washington's downtown hotels are busiest during the week and when Congress is in session, so you can expect the best discounts over the weekend and on holidays, when Congress heads out of town. Most hotels have high-season and low-season prices, and booking the day after high season ends can mean good deals.
- **Look into group or long-stay discounts.** If you come as part of a large group, you should be able to negotiate a bargain rate, because the hotel can then guarantee occupancy in a number of rooms. Likewise, if you're planning a long stay (at least 5 days), you might qualify for a discount. As a general rule, expect 1 night free after a 7-night stay.
- **Avoid excess charges and hidden costs.** D.C. hotels charge unbelievable rates for overnight parking—usually more than $25 a night—plus tax! So if you can avoid driving to D.C., you can save yourself parking expenses, at least. Use your own cellphone, pay phones, or prepaid phone cards instead of dialing direct from hotel phones, which usually have exorbitant rates, as do the room's minibar offerings: Most hotels charge through the nose for water, soda, and snacks. Finally, ask about local taxes and service charges. The D.C. hotel sales tax is a whopping 14.5%, merchandise sales tax is 5.75%, and restaurant tax is 10%, all of which can rapidly increase the cost of a room.
- **Book an efficiency room.** A room with a kitchenette allows you to shop for groceries and cook your own meals—a big money saver, especially for families on long stays.
- **Consider enrolling in hotel "frequent-stay" programs,** which are upping the ante lately to win the loyalty of repeat customers. Frequent guests can now accumulate points or credits to earn free hotel nights, airline miles, in-room amenities, merchandise, tickets to concerts and events, and discounts on sporting facilities. Perks are awarded not only by many chain hotels and motels (Hilton HHonors, Marriott Rewards, to name two), but also by individual inns and B&Bs. Many chain hotels partner with other hotel chains, car-rental firms, airlines, and credit card companies to give consumers additional incentive to do repeat business.

LANDING THE BEST ROOM

Somebody has to get the best room in the house. It might as well be you. You can start by joining the hotel's frequent-guest program, which may make you eligible for upgrades. A hotel-branded credit card usually gives its owner "silver" or "gold" status in frequent-guest programs for free. Always ask about a corner room. They're often larger and quieter, with more windows and light, and they often cost the same as standard rooms. When you make your reservation, ask if the hotel is renovating; if it is, request a room away from the construction. Ask about nonsmoking rooms, rooms with views, rooms with twin, queen- or king-size beds. If you're a light sleeper, request a quiet room away from vending machines, elevators, restaurants, bars, and discos. Ask for one of the rooms that have been most recently renovated or redecorated. If you aren't happy with your room when you arrive, say so; most properties will try to accommodate you.

USING A LOCAL RESERVATIONS SERVICE

If you suffer from information overload and would rather someone else do the research and bargaining, you can always turn to one of the following reputable—and free!—local reservations services:

- **Capitol Reservations** (✆ **800/VISIT-DC [800/847-4832]** or 202/452-1270; www.visitdc.com) will find you a hotel that meets your specific requirements and is within your price range. The 24-year-old service works with about 100 area hotels that have been screened for cleanliness, safe locations, and other desirability factors; you can check rates and book online.
- **Washington D.C. Accommodations** (✆ **800/503-3330** or 202/289-2220; www.dcaccommodations.com) has been in business for 23 years and, in addition to finding lodgings, can advise you about transportation and general tourist information and even work out itineraries.
- **Bed & Breakfast Accommodations, Ltd.** (✆ **877/893-3233** or 413/582-9888; www.bedandbreakfastdc.com), in business since 1978, works with more than 30 homes, inns, guesthouses, and unhosted furnished apartments to find visitors lodging. Bookings accepted with American Express, Diners Club, MasterCard, Visa, and Discover.

1 Best Hotel Bets

- **Best Historic Hotel:** The **Willard InterContinental** celebrated its 100th anniversary in 2006, as the "new" 12-story Willard, replacing the original, smaller "City Hotel" that existed here between 1816 and 1906. Whether known as the City or the Willard, the hotel has hosted nearly every U.S. president since Franklin Pierce in 1853, including two presidents who lived here for a time—Lincoln in 1861 and Calvin Coolidge in 1923. President Ulysses S. Grant liked to unwind with cigar and brandy in the Willard lobby after a hard day in the Oval Office, and literary luminaries like Mark Twain and Charles Dickens used to hang out in the Round Robin bar. The hotel continues to draw political, society, business, and cultural icons today. See p. 94.
- **Best Location:** Three contenders in three different locations win this category: For a true heart-of-the-city experience, the **Hotel Monaco** (p. 92) can't be beat. The hotel lies halfway between the White House and Capitol Hill, across the street from the Verizon Center and two Smithsonian museums, and in the middle of a neighborhood known for its many restaurants, shops, and clubs. If you desire proximity to the White House, no hotel gets closer than the **Hay-Adams** (p. 98), right across Lafayette Square from the Executive Mansion. And if you'd like to be within walking distance of both Capitol Hill and the National Mall, the

Tips Staying Green in D.C.

Anyone can take steps to minimize the impact they have on the environment while traveling, regardless of where they stay. But if eco-conscious travel is your goal, and you're looking for lodgings that reflect that, you have a number of options in D.C. Here are just a few:

- **The Four Seasons** (p. 118), whose pool features a saltwater system, rather than the typical packaged chlorine chemical system, and whose dry cleaning process now uses environmentally safe products.
- **The Willard InterContinental** (p. 94), which is in the process of switching to a 100% wind-powered electrical system and to an in-house water-conservation system. The hotel has also acquired and is working to revitalize Pershing Park, a green space just across the street from the hotel, in downtown D.C.
- **Hotel Madera** (p. 111), which provides guests with free parking if they're driving a hybrid car, places recycling bins in all rooms, and stocks bathrooms with eco-friendly Aveda products. The hotel also offers overnight packages that include a selection of organic wines, chocolates, and toiletries.
- All **Marriott properties,** in D.C. and elsewhere, now have fluorescent lighting instead of standard light bulbs.

Capitol Hill Suites (p. 90) gets my vote. The only hotel truly on "the Hill," it's in a pretty neighborhood around the corner from a row of eateries and bars.

- **Best Trendy Hotel:** Without a doubt, Washington's trendiest hotels are the seven operated by the Kimpton Hotel Group, ranging from the fun and funky **Hotel Helix** (p. 102), with its platform beds, neon colors, and flatscreen TVs, to the effervescent and lovely **Hotel Monaco** (p. 92), museum-like on the outside, surprising touches on the inside, such as complimentary goldfish at check-in. Other Kimpton properties include the **Hotel Rouge** (p. 103), the **Topaz Hotel** (p. 113), the **Hotel George** (p. 89), the **Hotel Madera** (p. 111), and the **Hotel Palomar** (p. 114).
- **Best Place for a Romantic Getaway:** The posh **Ritz-Carlton Georgetown** (p. 118) is just enough off the beaten track, but still in the heart of Georgetown, to make you feel like you've really escaped; its small size, only 86 rooms, adds an air of intimacy. While the Ritz's spa, sexy bar, lovely rooms, and solicitous service may tempt you to stay put, it would be a shame to pass up the chance to stroll hand-in-hand along Georgetown's quaint streets to dine at one of the city's most romantic restaurants, 1789 (p. 165), Citronelle (p. 165), and La Chaumiere (p. 169) among them.
- **Best Washington Insider Hotel:** The **Willard** wins again. This is where the term "lobbyists" came into popular use, after all. When President Ulysses S. Grant enjoyed a brandy in the Willard lobby, he was often besieged by politicians and businessmen, clamoring for his attention—"lobbyists," Grant called them, making famous a term someone else had coined. Lobbyists still come and go here, as

do high-ranking government officials, television news anchors, and visiting heads of state. Be sure to duck your head into the Round Robin bar, as well as the Willard dining room. See p. 94.

- **Best Inexpensive Hotel:** The boutique **Jurys Normandy Inn** charges $89 to $239 for personable service and rooms that are small but charming. Extras like an exercise room, a pool, and a restaurant are available at its sister hotel around the corner. See p. 106.
- **Best Service:** The staff at **The Ritz-Carlton, Washington, D.C.** (p. 115) is engaging but not overbearing, offering quick and solicitous service, whether you've ordered a glass of wine in the lounge or room service. A technology butler is always on call to handle your high-wired needs. Likewise, the **Four Seasons** (p. 118) pampers you relentlessly and greets you by name. The hotel also offers an "I Need It Now" program that delivers any of 100 or more left-at-home essentials (tweezers, batteries, cuff links, electric hair curlers, and so on) to you in 3 minutes, at no cost. And finally, there's the **Mandarin Oriental** (see below), where staffers speak in hushed tones, almost bowing; the spa features something called an amethyst steam room; and the very design of the hotel follows the principles of feng shui, the better to attract good fortune.
- **Best Health Club:** The **Ritz-Carlton, Washington, D.C.** has the best fitness center in the city. Its two-level, 100,000-square-foot Sports Club/LA boasts state-of-the-art weight-training equipment and free weights, two regulation-size basketball courts and four squash courts, an indoor heated swimming pool and aquatics pool with sun deck, exercise classes, personal trainers, the full-service Splash Spa and Roche Salon, and its own restaurant and cafe. See p. 115.
- **Best Views:** The **Hay-Adams** has such a great, unobstructed view of the White House that the Secret Service comes over regularly to do security sweeps of the place. Ask for a room on the H Street side of the hotel, on floors six through eight. See p. 98.
- **Best for Travelers with Disabilities:** The **Omni Shoreham Hotel** has 41 specially equipped rooms for guests with disabilities, about half with roll-in showers; vibrating door knockers and pillows, TTYs, and flashing lights to alert guests when fire alarms are sounding (all of these devices are available, but you must ask for them); and the hotel carries copies of disabilityguide.org's *Access Entertainment* guide, which offers detailed information about how to travel around and enjoy D.C., if you have limited mobility. See p. 121.

2 Capitol Hill/The Mall

VERY EXPENSIVE

Mandarin Oriental, Washington, D.C. ★★★ I took the Metro to the Mandarin Oriental, but if you can afford to stay at this sumptuous hotel, you're more likely to arrive by car, limo, taxi, or perhaps yacht (the Washington waterfront is behind the hotel, across a roadway or two, but a pedestrian footbridge connects the complex with the marina and Tidal Basin). The location of this fabulously posh hotel—at the end of a concrete peninsula called the Portals complex, which plans to include offices, retail shops, and restaurants—is a bit odd. The government-building neighborhood is not attractive and at night these streets are not meant for strolling (there's nothing to do and they aren't terribly safe after dark).

Washington, D.C., Accommodations

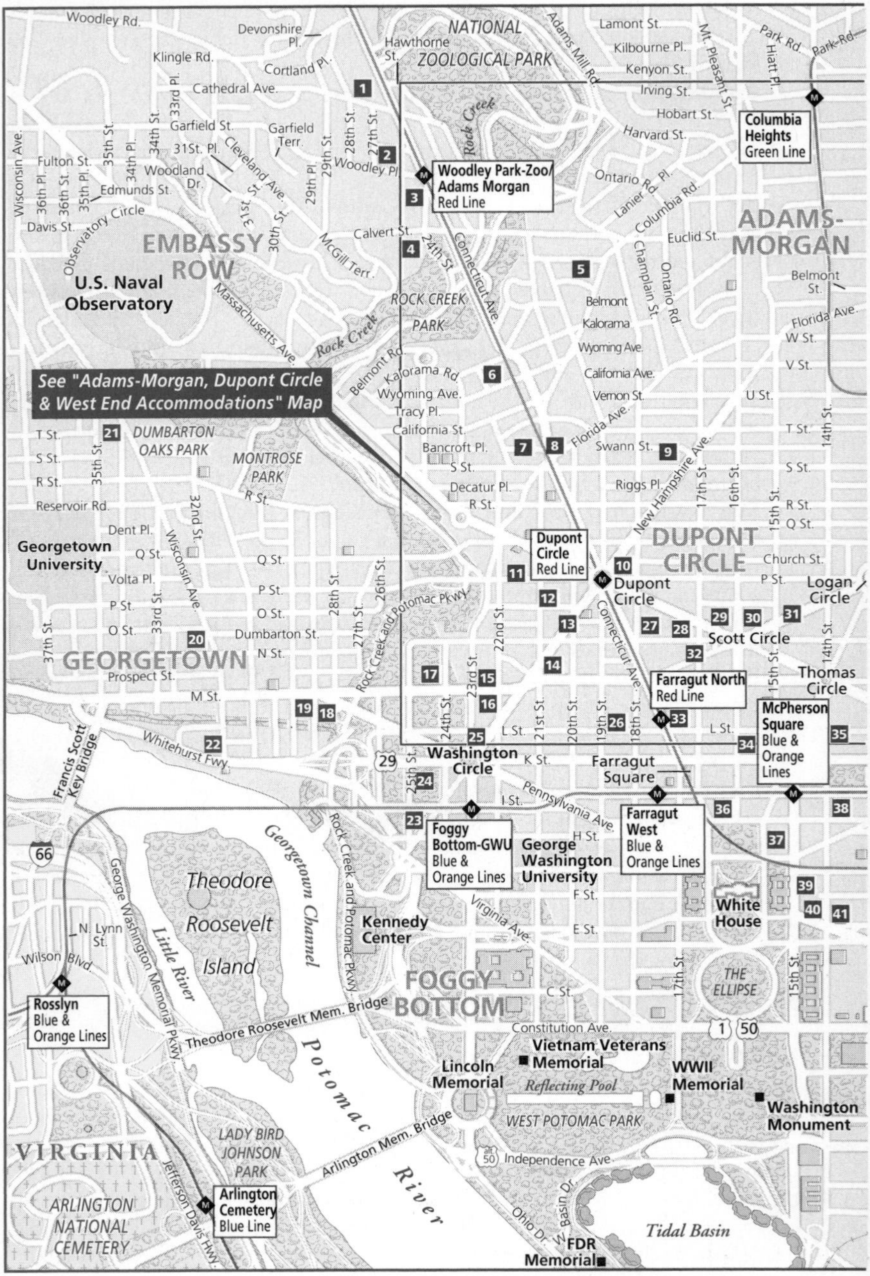

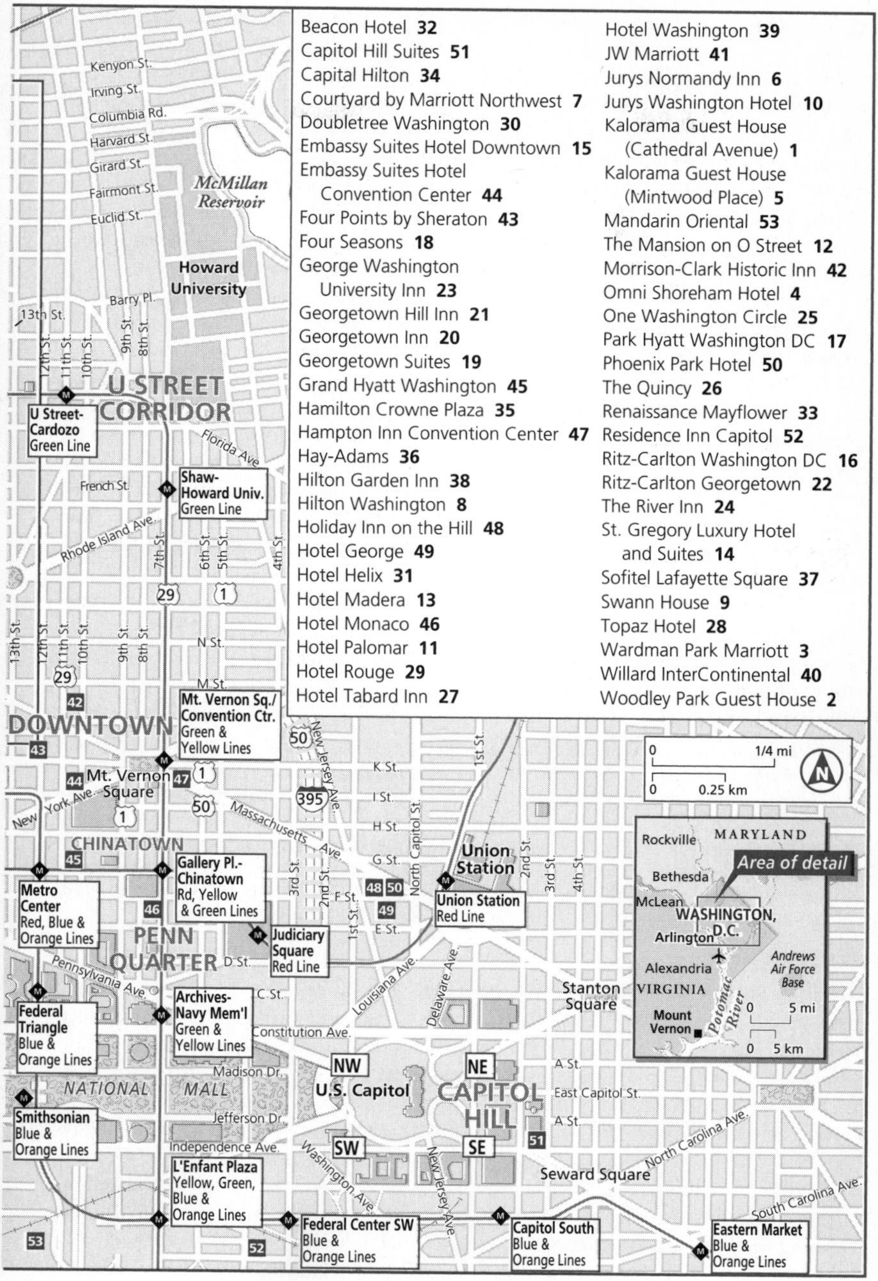
Beacon Hotel 32
Capitol Hill Suites 51
Capital Hilton 34
Courtyard by Marriott Northwest 7
Doubletree Washington 30
Embassy Suites Hotel Downtown 15
Embassy Suites Hotel Convention Center 44
Four Points by Sheraton 43
Four Seasons 18
George Washington University Inn 23
Georgetown Hill Inn 21
Georgetown Inn 20
Georgetown Suites 19
Grand Hyatt Washington 45
Hamilton Crowne Plaza 35
Hampton Inn Convention Center 47
Hay-Adams 36
Hilton Garden Inn 38
Hilton Washington 8
Holiday Inn on the Hill 48
Hotel George 49
Hotel Helix 31
Hotel Madera 13
Hotel Monaco 46
Hotel Palomar 11
Hotel Rouge 29
Hotel Tabard Inn 27
Hotel Washington 39
JW Marriott 41
Jurys Normandy Inn 6
Jurys Washington Hotel 10
Kalorama Guest House (Cathedral Avenue) 1
Kalorama Guest House (Mintwood Place) 5
Mandarin Oriental 53
The Mansion on O Street 12
Morrison-Clark Historic Inn 42
Omni Shoreham Hotel 4
One Washington Circle 25
Park Hyatt Washington DC 17
Phoenix Park Hotel 50
The Quincy 26
Renaissance Mayflower 33
Residence Inn Capitol 52
Ritz-Carlton Washington DC 16
Ritz-Carlton Georgetown 22
The River Inn 24
St. Gregory Luxury Hotel and Suites 14
Sofitel Lafayette Square 37
Swann House 9
Topaz Hotel 28
Wardman Park Marriott 3
Willard InterContinental 40
Woodley Park Guest House 2
Kenyon St.
Irving St.
Columbia Rd.
Harvard St.
Girard St.
Fairmont St.
Euclid St.
McMillan Reservoir
Howard University
Barry Pl.
13th St.
12th St.
11th St.
10th St.
9th St.
8th St.
U STREET CORRIDOR
U Street-Cardozo Green Line
Florida Ave.
French St.
Shaw-Howard Univ. Green Line
Rhode Island Ave.
7th St.
6th St.
5th St.
4th St.
N St.
M St.
DOWNTOWN
Mt. Vernon Sq./Convention Ctr. Green & Yellow Lines
Mt. Vernon Square
New York Ave.
Massachusetts Ave.
New Jersey Ave.
K St.
I St.
H St.
G St.
F St.
E St.
D St.
C St.
1st St.
2nd St.
3rd St.
North Capitol St.
CHINATOWN
Metro Center Red, Blue & Orange Lines
Gallery Pl.-Chinatown Rd, Yellow & Green Lines
Judiciary Square Red Line
Union Station
Union Station Red Line
PENN QUARTER
Pennsylvania Ave.
Louisiana Ave.
Delaware Ave.
Federal Triangle Blue & Orange Lines
Archives-Navy Mem'l Green & Yellow Lines
Constitution Ave.
Stanton Square
Madison Dr.
NATIONAL MALL
Jefferson Dr.
Independence Ave.
Smithsonian Blue & Orange Lines
NW
NE
SW
SE
U.S. Capitol
CAPITOL HILL
A St.
East Capitol St.
North Carolina Ave.
Seward Square
South Carolina Ave.
Washington Ave.
L'Enfant Plaza Yellow, Green, Blue & Orange Lines
Federal Center SW Blue & Orange Lines
Capitol South Blue & Orange Lines
Eastern Market Blue & Orange Lines
0 1/4 mi
0 0.25 km
N
Rockville
MARYLAND
Area of detail
Bethesda
McLean
WASHINGTON, D.C.
Arlington
Alexandria
VIRGINIA
Andrews Air Force Base
Mount Vernon
Potomac River
0 5 mi
0 5 km

Having said that, since it opened in March 2004, the Mandarin has been doing quite well; in fact, it has seriously upped the ante on luxury in the capital. Service is sublime. Hotel decor richly combines Asian and American traditions. The two-story lobby is a light-filled, glassed-in rotunda; the circular design used here and throughout the hotel is intended to invite good luck. Each guest room is laid out in accordance with the principles of feng shui (for example, the mirror does not face the entry door, to prevent the reflection of good fortune out of the room), and furnishings include nightstand lamps of contemporary Japanese design, replica pieces from the Smithsonian's collections, and handmade silk tapestries. On the thick-mattressed beds are sensuously beautiful Fili D'Oro linens that make you reach out your hand to touch.

Finally, the setting that separates the hotel from the rest of the city also helps create a feeling that you are away, but not away. You may not want to roam the neighborhood, but you can walk around the hotel's property, which includes terraces of landscaped gardens and views of the Tidal Basin and marina, the Jefferson Memorial, the Virginia skyline, and District buildings. Guest rooms offer these same views. And when you are on the inside, looking out from the soundproofed, elegant refuge of your room, even nearby Interstate 395 appears rather magnificent. The hotel's world-class spa, fitness center, and indoor pool offer three more reasons to stay put. The fitness center, indoor heated lap pool, and outdoor sundeck overlook the marina; the spa's Zen-like setting is the tranquil backdrop for an array of holistically luxurious treatments.

And then there's the restaurant, **CityZen** (p. 130), whose chef, Eric Ziebold, came from the West Coast's acclaimed French Laundry: If you're of the "food can be transporting" school of thought, you'll want to dine here. The Mandarin has a more casual dining room, Café MoZU, whose cuisine includes a sushi kitchen, as well as Asian-influenced American fare.

1330 Maryland Ave. SW (at 12th St.), Washington, DC 20024. ✆ **888/888-1778** or 202/554-8588. Fax 202/554-8999. www.mandarinoriental.com/washington. 400 units. $495–$695 double; $1,150–$8,000 suite. Children under 12 stay free in parent's room. For information about special packages, call the hotel directly or check the website. AE, DC, DISC, MC, V. Parking $34. Metro: Smithsonian. Dogs under 40 lb. accepted, with certain restrictions. **Amenities:** 2 restaurants (Modern American, Asian-influenced cafe cuisine); 2 bars; heated indoor pool in spa; fully equipped fitness center; 10,400-sq.-ft. full-service spa; 24-hr. concierge; business center w/full Internet access; 24-hr. room service; same-day laundry service; dry cleaning; 20 rooms for those w/limited mobility. *In room:* A/C, TV w/pay movies and HDTV, 3-line phone w/dataports, Wi-Fi ($12/day), minibar, hair dryer, iron, safe, robes, DVD/CD player.

EXPENSIVE

Holiday Inn on the Hill *Kids* Try though it might to be a very 21st-century hotel, this Holiday Inn retains a rather staid ambience, but can be counted on to provide a perfectly adequate place to spend the night. Guest rooms are done in shades of cobalt blue, with zebra wood armoires, glass-topped desks with ergonomic mesh chairs, and triple-sheeted king-size or two queen-size beds. Rooms are standard size, though bathrooms are slightly larger than hotel-normal, with a small vanity ledge just outside the bathroom for overflow counter space.

For both business and leisure travelers, the hotel's proximity to Capitol Hill and to the National Mall is its prime attraction. Several labor union headquarters are nearby, making the hotel a popular choice among the "labor" folks doing business with one of them. Families like the hotel's additional enticements, starting with the hotel's website, where kids can log on to the scrapbook page to find out what other kids have thought of their stay at the hotel, and where parents can read about family packages. For instance, a 2007 "Family Fun" deal offered a noon check-in, checkout as late as

4pm, a lunchbox prepared for four each day, breakfast for two adults, and free parking, all for a starting rate of $259 a night, when available. Other family-friendly amenities include a seasonal rooftop pool and the "kids 12 and under eat free" restaurant policy. A free 24-hour fitness center is open to those 18 and older.

To get the best deals and perks, ask about summer promotions, the "Great Rates" package, and the hotel's "Priority Club" frequent guest membership.

415 New Jersey Ave. NW (between D and E sts.), Washington, DC 20001. ✆ **800/638-1116** or 202/638-1616. Fax 202/638-0707. www.hionthehilldc.com. 343 units. Weekdays $189–$389 double (Mon and Tues are the most expensive days); weekends $99–$149 double. Extra person $20. Children under 19 stay free in parent's room. Ask about special promotions and packages. AE, DC, DISC, MC, V. Parking $30. Metro: Union Station. **Amenities:** Restaurant (American), where kids ages 12 and under eat free w/an adult; bar; outdoor (unheated) rooftop pool; 24-hr. fitness room; business center; room service (6am–11pm); same-day laundry service; dry cleaning; Wi-Fi in restaurant and part of lobby; 8 rooms for those w/limited mobility, including 4 w/roll-in showers. *In room:* A/C, TV w/pay movies and Nintendo, 2-line phone w/dataport, free Internet access, coffeemaker, hair dryer, iron.

The Hotel George ★★ Behind a facade of stainless steel, limestone, and glass is one of Washington's hippest places to stay. With a sleek white lobby, splashed with red, blue, and black furnishings; posters throughout the hotel depicting a modern-day George Washington, sans wig; and clientele tending toward celebs (everyone from singer Christina Aguilera to actor Sean Penn), the George is in every way a capital establishment. The oversize guest rooms underwent a remodeling in 2007, replacing bedding and upholstery, but the overall effect is still minimalist, all creamy white and modern, with 32-inch plasma-screen television, DVD player, and minibar hidden behind cabinet doors, and shades, not fussy drapes, nestled perfectly within the window frame. Fluffy vanilla-colored comforters rest on oversize beds; an ergonomically designed chair draws up to the black granite-topped desk. A speaker in the spacious, mirrored, marble and black-granite bathroom broadcasts TV sounds from the other room; other amenities include cordless phones, umbrellas, spa robes, and yoga essentials (mat, strap, and block, and instructional videos on a free TV channel). The newly renovated 24-hour fitness center features state-of-the-art exercise equipment, with personal TVs, and separate steam rooms for men and women. Like all Kimpton hotels, the George offers in-room spa services, which you can reserve when you book your room. The smoke-free hotel has three one-bedroom suites.

Contributing to the hotel's hipness is the presence of **Bistro Bis** (p. 131), which serves hungry lobbyists and those they are lobbying.

15 E St. NW (at N. Capitol St.), Washington, DC 20001. ✆ **800/576-8331** or 202/347-4200. Fax 202/347-4213. www.hotelgeorge.com. 139 units. Weekdays $289–$509 double; weekends $149–$349 double. Year-round $699–$950 suite. Ask about seasonal and corporate rates, and the "Hot Dates, Great Rates" deal. Extra person $25. Children under 18 stay free in parent's room. AE, DC, DISC, MC, V. Parking $34 plus tax overnight. Metro: Union Station. Pets accepted. **Amenities:** Restaurant (French bistro); small 24-hr. fitness center w/steam rooms; 24-hr. concierge; business services; room service (7am–11pm); same-day laundry service; dry cleaning; VCR rentals; 4 rooms for those w/limited mobility. *In room:* A/C, TV w/pay movies, DVD player, 2-line phone w/dataport, free high-speed Internet access, minibar, hair dryer, iron, safe, robes, umbrella.

Phoenix Park Hotel ★ The Phoenix Park is one of a cluster of hotels across from Union Station and 2 blocks from the Capitol. It's distinguished by its popular and authentic Irish pub, **The Dubliner** (p. 279), which attempts to set the tone for the entire property. Because of this well-worn, wood-paneled pub (which offers Irish fare, ale, and live Irish music nightly), and its regular hosting of Ireland-related events in its banquet rooms, the Phoenix Park attracts numerous sons and daughters of Erin and generally conveys an air of Irish hospitality. Recently renovated rooms present three color schemes—a lovely shamrock-green shade, an elegant gold, and a dusky rose—each quite attractive, decorated with pretty patterned wallpaper and drapes of the same design at the windows, enclosing a toile-printed sheer curtain. The refurbishment replaced old bedding with pillow-topped mattresses and fat old TVs with 32-inch, high-definition, flatscreen models. For the best views, ask for a room on one of the top floors (the hotel has nine), facing Massachusetts Avenue, toward the North Capitol Street end; you'll overlook the National Postal Museum, a smidgen of Union Station, and congressional buildings. Or book a one- or two-story suite, some of which have kitchenettes, working fireplaces, and spiral staircases. Irish decorative accents include linens and bathrobes, artwork, toiletries, and carpeting. Call direct to the hotel or check the website for best deals.

520 N. Capitol St. NW (at Massachusetts Ave.), Washington, DC 20001. ✆ **800/824-5419** or 202/638-6900. Fax 202/393-3236. www.phoenixparkhotel.com. 149 units. Weekdays $149–$449 double; weekends $99–$299 double; year-round $399–$1,299 suite. Extra person $30. Children under 16 stay free in parent's room. AE, DC, DISC, MC, V. Valet parking $30. Metro: Union Station. No pets. **Amenities:** Irish pub; complimentary use of small exercise room; room service (7am–11pm); same-day dry cleaning; 7 rooms for those w/limited mobility. *In room:* A/C, TV w/pay movies, 2-line phone w/dataport, wired Internet access and Wi-Fi ($9.95/day), minibar, coffeemaker, hair dryer, iron.

MODERATE

Capitol Hill Suites ★ This well-run, all-suite property comprises two buildings, located on a residential street of quaint town houses, behind the Library of Congress, and a short walk from the Capitol and Mall attractions, a food market, and more than 20 restaurants (many of which deliver to the hotel). Capitol Hill Suites is the only hotel truly *on* the Hill (on the House side of the Capitol). The term *suite* denotes the fact that every unit has a kitchenette with coffeemaker, microwave, refrigerator, plastic flatware, and glassware. Most units are efficiencies, with the kitchenette, bed, and sofa all in the same room. The best choices are one-bedroom units, in which the kitchenette and living room are separate from the bedroom. A third option is a "studio double," with two queen beds and a kitchenette, but no living room area. Some rooms in each category have pullout sofas. A $3-million renovation underway until early 2008 is adding a small fitness center, updating the air-conditioning and heating systems, and switching from somber furnishings and signature navy blue shades to more whimsical art deco designs and improved amenities, such as new flatscreen televisions. Rooms remain spacious, and include long desks, ergonomically correct desk chairs, and beds that boast pillow-top mattresses, high-thread-count sheets, and down duvets. Bathrooms are still tiny. Lobbies in both buildings feature wireless Internet access and inviting lounges; the main building's lobby is especially nice and has an enclosed fireplace, leather chairs, and an antique credenza. (Linger here long enough and you might spy a congressperson or senator—a number of members reserve suites for 100 days at a time.) The second building is home to the new fitness center and the breakfast area, where an ample continental breakfast is laid out daily: baked goods, yogurt, boiled eggs, and fruit.

200 C St. SE (at 2nd St.), Washington, DC 20003. ✆ **800/424-9165** or 202/543-6000. Fax 202/547-2608. www.capitolhillsuites.com. 152 units. $129–$249 double. Weekend and long-term rates are sometimes available. Extra person $20. Rates include continental breakfast. Children under 18 stay free in parent's room. AE, DC, DISC, MC, V. Valet parking $28 plus tax. Metro: Capitol South. Pets under 20 lb. accepted. **Amenities:** Privileges ($10 per use) at nearby Washington Sports and Health Club; small fitness center; business center; coin-op washer/dryers; same-day laundry service; dry cleaning; 8 rooms for those w/limited mobility, all w/roll-in showers. *In room:* A/C, TV w/pay movies, 2-line phone w/dataport, high-speed Internet access ($9.95/day), fridge, coffeemaker, hair dryer, iron.

Tips When All Else Fails

If your luck and time are running out and you still haven't found a place to stay, these ideas are worth a try:

- **Call one of the free reservations services** at the beginning of this chapter, including the Bed & Breakfast Accommodations service. Talk to someone "on location," who can work with you to find a place.
- **Check out the Vacation Rental by Owner website, www.vrbo.com,** and enter "Washington" as your city, to read about furnished apartments for rent around the city.
- **Consider house swapping.** Try **HomeLink International** (Homelink.org), the largest and oldest home-swapping organization, founded in 1953, with more than 13,000 listings worldwide ($90 for a yearly membership). **www.homexchangevacation.com** and **InterVac.com** are also reliable.
- **Call the Washington Convention and Tourism Corporation's local number, ✆ 202/789-7000,** and ask the tourist rep for the names and numbers of any **new or about-to-open hotels.** If the rep isn't sure, ask her to check with the marketing director. Up-and-coming hotels may have available rooms, for the simple reason that few people know about them.

Residence Inn Capitol Three blocks south of the Smithsonian's National Museum of the American Indian, this hotel made its debut in January 2005. The hotel's proximity to the American Indian museum is significant because four Native American tribes are 49% owners of the hotel, which makes this the first multitribal partnership with nontribal partners on land off a reservation. During the day, you can easily walk to the Indian and other Mall museums, as well as to Capitol Hill; at night, however, this part of town shuts down, and you'll have to travel to other neighborhoods to find restaurants and entertainment.

Hotel features mimic the look of the American Indian Museum; for instance, the Kasota limestone, which covers the museum's exterior, is used throughout the first floor of the hotel. The attractive guest rooms evince a Native American cultural motif through the use of etched wood headboards, artwork, and other design elements. The hotel's enviable site endows it with rare views from certain floors: Rooms on levels 11 through 13, at the back of the building (the side closest to the Mall), as well as some along the 3rd Street side, offer varying and somewhat distant views of the Capitol, the dome of the Indian Museum, and the Washington Monument. The best rooms survey this whole scene, which, it must be said, also includes sights of gray government buildings, construction, and railroad tracks. Metro and freight trains do rumble past here, and if you are on one of the lower floors, especially, you will probably hear them. Rooms with views of the Capitol cost an additional $40 per night.

This Residence Inn, like all Residence Inns, offers some helpful amenities for families and businesspeople who are in Washington for more than just a couple of days: The roomy suites all have fully equipped kitchens, which allows for flexible dining options. Some two-bedroom suites can connect to form a four-bedroom suite. Rates include a generous hot breakfast daily, social hours with dinner buffet Monday through Wednesday, a cookout Wednesday night (seasonally), a dessert buffet every Thursday night, and grocery shopping delivery service. The property has an indoor pool and exercise room; a gift shop, where you can purchase tour tickets; and an on-site Flexcar service, should you want to rent a car while you're here—make sure you reserve a car when you book your room reservation (see p. 69 for information about Flexcars).

333 E St. SW (at 4th St.), Washington, DC 20024. ✆ **800/331-3131** or 202/484-8280. Fax 202-554-0484. www.Marriott.com/wascp. 233 suites. $187–$329 studio; $205–$349 1-bedroom suite; $249–$389 2-bedroom suite. Add $40 per night for rooms with views of the Capitol. Weekend and long-term rates available. Rates include hot breakfast daily and "social hour" weeknights. AE, DC, DISC, MC, V. Parking $30. Metro: Federal Center Southwest. Pets accepted for a fee. **Amenities:** Indoor pool, whirlpool, and sun deck; exercise room; business center; copy/fax service; laundry valet and self-serve laundry; grocery shopping service; Wi-Fi in public space. *In room:* A/C, TV w/pay movies, 2-line phones, free Internet access, full kitchen, coffeemaker, hair dryer, iron, safe.

3 Penn Quarter

VERY EXPENSIVE

Hotel Monaco Washington D.C. ★★★ This is where I'd stay if I were a visitor to D.C. The Monaco has been winning awards and great reviews ever since it opened in the summer of 2002. Museum-like in appearance, the Monaco occupies a four-story, all marble mid-19th-century building, half of which was designed by Robert Mills, the architect for the Washington Monument, the other half designed by Thomas Walter, one of the architects for the U.S. Capitol. The two halves connect seamlessly, enclosing an interior, landscaped courtyard. Jutting into the courtyard from the F Street side of the hotel is its marvelous restaurant, **Poste** (p. 142), which has established itself as a top spot for dining. The hotel takes up an entire block, between 7th and 8th streets, and E and F streets. Superlatives are in order: The hotel is truly magnificent.

The spacious guest rooms, similarly, combine historic and hip. Their vaulted ceilings are high (12–18 ft.) and windows are long, hung with charcoal and white patterned drapes. Eclectic furnishings include neoclassic armoires and three-legged desks. (The hotel's historic status precludes it from installing closets, hence the armoires, which some guests say are too small.) A color scheme successfully marries creamy yellow walls with periwinkle blue lounge chairs and orangey-red damask pillows. (Be aware, though, that changes were being contemplated as we went to press, to refurnish guest rooms and switch to LCD flat-paneled televisions.)

Interior rooms overlook the courtyard and the restaurant; you'll see the charming, arched passageway through which horse and carriage came a century ago. Exterior rooms view city sights on floors 2 through 4; the first floor is nearly subterranean (a window close to the ceiling lets in some light), which makes these rooms a good choice if you like quiet. This is a great location: When you stay at the Monaco, you're not just downtown, you're part of the scene.

More: The Hotel Monaco gives you a complimentary goldfish at check-in (if you so request) and offers specially designed "Tall Rooms" with 18-foot-high ceilings, 96-inch-long beds, and raised showerheads. Each guest room includes yoga essentials and a free, dedicated exercise and yoga channel on TV; in-room spa services are also available.

Go to the hotel's website or call direct to the hotel to obtain lowest available rates. ***Best deal:*** On the hotel's website click on "Reservations" and then on **"Hot Dates, Great Rates"** to find dates available for rates as low as $149 a night; if you're able to book a room at the upscale Monaco at this price, you'll likely be paying less and getting more than a room at one of the "budget" chain hotels in this neighborhood.

Kids Family-Friendly Hotels

Embassy Suites Hotel Downtown (p. 110) You're close to both a Red line and a Blue line Metro station (the zoo is on the Red line; the Smithsonian museums are on the Blue line) and within walking distance of Georgetown. Your kids can sleep on the pullout sofa in the separate living room. You've got some kitchen facilities, but the complimentary breakfast in the atrium is unbelievable. There are also an indoor pool and a free game room.

Hilton Washington (p. 104) A large heated outdoor pool, three tennis courts, and a goodie bag at check-in—what more does a kid need?

Holiday Inn on the Hill (p. 88) Your children can find out what other kids have to say about the hotel by accessing the hotel's website and clicking on the "Bubbles" link, and on the "scrapbook" link from there. Meanwhile, parents can take advantage of sweet deals that provide helpful family touring tips and perks such as free parking and breakfast, for reasonable rates. The hotel has an outdoor pool, a "kids under 12 eat free" restaurant policy, Nintendo on the TV, and soap bubbles handed out to children at check-in.

Omni Shoreham Hotel (p. 121) Adjacent to Rock Creek Park, the Omni is within walking distance of the zoo and Metro and is equipped with a large outdoor pool and kiddie pool. Children receive a goodie bag at check-in, and the concierge has a supply of board games (no charge to borrow, just remember to return).

700 F St. NW (at 7th St.), Washington, DC 20004. ✆ **800/649-1202** or 202/628-7177. Fax 202/628-7277. www.monaco-dc.com. 184 units. Weekdays $309–$529 double, $409–$958 suite; weekends $189–$349 double, $289–$798 suite. Extra person $25. Children under 18 stay free in parent's room. Rates include complimentary organic coffee in morning and wine receptions in evening. AE, DC, DISC, MC, V. Parking $30 plus tax. Metro: Gallery Place. Pets welcomed—they get VIP treatment, with their own registration cards at check-in, maps of neighborhood fire hydrants and parks, gourmet puppy and kitty treats. **Amenities:** Restaurant (modern American); bar; spacious fitness center w/flatscreen TVs; 24-hr. concierge; full-service business center; 24-hr. room service; same-day laundry service; dry cleaning; 9 rooms for those w/limited mobility, 4 w/roll-in showers. *In room:* A/C, TV w/pay movies and Nintendo, Web TV access ($10/day), 2-line phones w/dataports, free Internet access, minibar, hair dryer, iron, safe, robes, CD player.

JW Marriott Hotel on Pennsylvania Avenue ★ You're in a prime location here—on Pennsylvania Avenue, adjacent to the National Theatre, 1 block from the Warner Theater, 2 blocks from the White House, and within walking distance of the Washington Monument, the Smithsonian museums, and lots of stores and restaurants. Corporate types and conventioneers make up much of the clientele, with tourists (including families) filling in the rest on weekends.

A recently completed $20-million overhaul of guest room furnishings and amenities replaced boring old bedspreads with white duvet comforters, laundered afresh after every guest. The bed itself is new, equipped with a thick mattress, and the linens include top-of-the-line 300-thread-count sheets with big pillows, and more of them. Each room has a state-of-the-art, 32-inch, LCD HDTV, able to connect with a guest's laptop or iPod. Expect a brighter, more interesting decor, too: earth-tone fabrics, cherry furnishings, and chrome-and-glass bathroom fixtures. Ask for a room on floors 3 through 15 facing Pennsylvania Avenue for views of the avenue and of the Washington Monument beyond; floors 7 and 12 on the Pennsylvania Avenue side have balconies; floors 14 and 15 are the concierge level.

For the best value, book around the Christmas holidays, any time during the summer, or on weekends. You're more likely to hear about special promotions by calling direct to the hotel or by browsing the hotel's website.

1331 Pennsylvania Ave. NW (at E St.), Washington, DC 20004. ✆ **800/228-9290** or 202/393-2000. Fax 202/626-6991. www.experiencejw.com. 772 units. Weekdays $299–$469 double; weekends $159–$259 double; year-round $479–$2,500 suites. Extra person free. AE, DC, DISC, MC, V. Valet parking $30. Metro: Metro Center. **Amenities:** 2 restaurants (both upscale American); complete health club (w/indoor swimming pool and whirlpool); concierge (morning and evening hours, weekdays only); business center; 24-hr. room service; same-day laundry service; dry cleaning; concierge-level rooms; 15 rooms for those w/limited mobility, 6 w/roll-in shower. *In room:* A/C, TV w/pay movies, 2-line phones w/dataports, high-speed Internet access ($9.95/day), minibar, coffeemaker, hair dryer, iron, safe.

Willard InterContinental Washington ★★★ A stone's throw from the White House and the Smithsonian museums, the Willard is in the heart of downtown, near plenty of excellent restaurants, 1 block from the National Theatre, and down the avenue from the Capitol. It's definitely the finest hotel in this neighborhood, among the best in the city, and also, naturally, one of the most expensive. Heads of state favor the Willard (the hotel offers one floor as "Secret Service cleared"), as do visitors from other countries and movie directors (who like to shoot scenes in the famously ornate lobby and restaurant).

The guest rooms present a handsome decor, heavy on reproduction Federal- and Edwardian-style furnishings. The rooms with the best views are the oval suites overlooking Pennsylvania Avenue to the Capitol and the rooms fronting Pennsylvania Avenue. Rooms facing the courtyard are the quietest. Best of all is the "Jenny Lind" suite, perched in the curve of the 12th floor's southeast corner; its round bull's-eye window captures glimpses of the Washington Monument.

The illustrious Willard Hotel's history is full of big moments. View the hotel's exhibit of photos and memorabilia in a wing off of Peacock Alley (the elegant corridor that leads back from the lobby), and you'll learn that the hotel has hosted nearly every U.S. president since Franklin Pierce in 1853; at least two presidents have lived here for a while—Lincoln in 1861 because of assassination threats and Calvin Coolidge in 1923 while waiting for Warren Harding's widow to pack up and move out after her husband died in office. President Ulysses S. Grant used to leave the Oval Office to unwind with cigar and brandy in the Willard lobby, where politicians and businessmen gathered around him beseeching his attention—Grant called them "lobbyists," a word that had long been around but infrequently used, and the label became a part of the capital's vernacular.

The Willard's designation as a National Historic Landmark in 1974 and magnificent restoration in the 1980s helped revitalize Pennsylvania Avenue and this part of town. Stop in at the Round Robin Bar for a mint julep (introduced here), and listen to barman Jim Hewes spin tales about all the people who have stopped or stayed here, from Mark Twain and Charles Dickens to Bill Clinton.

In late 2005, the Willard opened its state-of-the-art, 5,000-square-foot "I Spa," offering men's and women's steam and sauna rooms, cardio and weight-training equipment, and massage, facial, and body treatments. A small outdoor cafe operates seasonally, on the hotel's terrace fronting Pennsylvania Avenue. The charming **Café du Parc**

(p. 144) opened in the hotel courtyard in April 2007, providing a more casual complement to the hotel's main dining room, the grand **Willard Room** (p. 138).

Always inquire about off-season and weekend packages, when rates are sometimes halved and come with one of several complimentary options, sometimes an upgrade to a suite, valet parking, or a second room at half price.

1401 Pennsylvania Ave. NW (at 14th St.), Washington, DC 20004. ✆ **800/827-1747** or 202/628-9100. Fax 202/637-7326. www.washington.interconti.com. 332 units. Weekdays and weekends: $269–$610 double, $500–$4,200 suite. Ask about special promotions and packages. AE, DC, DISC, MC, V. Parking $28. Metro: Metro Center. Small pets accepted. **Amenities:** Restaurant (modern French-American); cafe; seasonal terrace, bar; new, thoroughly equipped fitness center and health spa; children's programs; concierge; business center; 24-hr. room service; babysitting; same-day laundry service/dry cleaning; currency exchange; airline/train ticketing. *In-room:* A/C, TV, 2-line phone w/dataport, Wi-Fi ($11/day), minibar, hair dryer, iron, safe, robes, CD player.

EXPENSIVE

Embassy Suites Hotel Convention Center ★ Business is booming in Washington and this hotel is booming along with it, thanks to its clever location a short walk from both the convention center and the heart of the Penn Quarter. Since its debut in late 2005, the hotel has often been sold out—with families during extended school breaks, and with conventioneers at other times. Like all Embassy Suites, this one provides a winning formula in its lodging layout. Every suite offers a separate living room and bedroom, with a bathroom serving as the divider. Decor is fresh and upbeat, employing light woods, earth tones, and glass accents. Each living room has a pullout sofa. Common areas in the hotel are also attractive, from the glass- and wood-paneled, six-floor atrium, to the popular Finn & Porter restaurant, in whose sunroom a stunning complimentary breakfast (waffles to custom-ordered omelets) is served daily. The hotel hosts a nightly, complimentary cocktail reception in the two-level bar at the other end of the atrium from the restaurant. While many hotels squirrel away their fitness centers on subterranean levels, this hotel's exercise room and pool are on the second floor, where wide windows overlook D.C.'s downtown. The business center offers free use of a printer and three computers, including complimentary Internet access.

900 10th St. NW (between New York Ave. and K St. NW), Washington, DC 20001. ✆ **800/EMBASSY** or 202/739-2001. Fax 202/739-2099. www.washingtonconventioncenter.embassysuites.com. 384 units. Peak weekdays $279–$399, weekends $199–$279 double; off-peak weekdays $229–$329, weekends $159–$209 double. Extra person $20. Children under 18 stay free in parent's room. Book online or call direct for best rates. AE, DC, DISC, MC, V. Valet parking $26. Metro: Metro Center. **Amenities:** Restaurant (steak, sushi, and seafood); bar; indoor pool; whirlpool; fitness center; concierge; 24-hr. business center w/free use of computers and Internet access; gift shop; room service (at lunch and dinner); coin-op laundry; same-day laundry and dry cleaning; 12 rooms for those w/limited mobility, all w/roll-in showers. *In room:* A/C, TV w/pay movies, 2-line phone w/dataports, high-speed Internet access ($9.95/day), fridge, microwave, coffeemaker, hair dryer, iron, safe.

Grand Hyatt Washington ★ Until the D.C. Convention Center's on-site, 1,500-room hotel opens (probably not until 2009), the Grand Hyatt is the largest hotel near the convention center.

The Grand Hyatt has a lot to offer besides its room count of 888. The vast lobby is in an atrium 12 stories high and enclosed by a glass, mansard-style roof. A baby grand piano floats on its own island in the 7,000-square-foot "lagoon"; waterfalls, catwalks, 22-foot-high trees, and an array of bars and restaurants on the periphery should keep you entertained. But if you get bored, head to the nearby nightspots and restaurants, or hop on the Metro, to which the Hyatt has direct access. The hotel lies between Capitol Hill and the White House, 2 blocks from the Verizon Center, and about 3 blocks from the new D.C. Convention Center, at 801 Mount Vernon Place NW.

Guest rooms feature a contemporary look of dark, hardwood furniture and hues of blue and gold. Every guest room has a "Grand Bed," a 13-inch-thick pillow-top mattress, triple-sheeted and covered with a fluffy white duvet instead of a bedspread. The Regency Club (12th) floor is the VIP level, where guests pay an extra $60 for premium services, including access to the fitness and health club and to the 12th-floor lounge, where food and beverages are available. All hotel rooms are equipped for high-speed wireless Internet access. The fitness club is state-of-the-art, offering cardio and weight equipment; spa treatment rooms; Pilates, yoga, and jazzercise classes; and massages. With total fitness in mind, this hotel is entirely smoke free, from public areas to all of its guest rooms. The Grand Hyatt honors a "Guaranteed room type on arrival" policy, which simply guarantees that you'll have a room with the specific kind of bed(s) (king, queen, or two doubles) you requested when you booked your reservation. Always ask about seasonal and special offers, and check the website for the best deals.

1000 H St. NW (at 10th St. NW), Washington, DC 20001. ✆ **800/233-1234** or 202/582-1234. Fax 202/637-4781. www.grandwashington.hyatt.com. 888 units. Weekdays $199–$429 double; weekends $129–$199 double; $450–$2,500 suite. Extra person $25. Children under 18 stay free in parent's room. Ask about special promotions and packages. AE, DC, DISC, MC, V. Valet parking $30, self-parking $20. Metro: Metro Center. **Amenities:** 4 restaurants (bistro, traditional American, contemporary American, deli); 3 bars; Starbucks; health club, lap pool, steam and sauna rooms, aerobics, and spa services (hotel guests pay $14, per room per day, for club use); concierge; business center; room service (6am–1am); in-room and health-club massage; same-day dry cleaning; concierge-level rooms; 26 rooms for those w/limited mobility, some w/roll-in showers. *In room:* A/C, TV w/pay movies, 2-line phone w/dataports, Wi-Fi ($9.95/day or $4.95/hour), minibar, coffeemaker, hair dryer, iron.

Hotel Washington ★ Built in 1918, this hotel is the oldest continuously operating hotel in Washington. Renovations throughout the years have played up the historic angle, but that may be about to change. In April 2006, new owners purchased the hotel, the first such changeover in 60 years; major renovations will certainly be underway in 2008. At this writing, it's unclear exactly what that means, but it's safe to say that reconstructed original pieces, mahogany furnishings, and an overall traditional look will be gone. Whatever its new appearance, the Hotel Washington is bound to be a hotel to consider based on its location alone, especially as the next inauguration draws near—the hotel lies directly on the parade route. From its corner perch at Pennsylvania Avenue and 15th Street, the 12-story hotel surveys the avenue, monuments, and the White House. Ask for a room facing Pennsylvania Avenue for your own private view of the Washington Monument and the White House.

With at least four theaters nearby, the Hotel Washington is often home to cast members in current shows. A mix of business and leisure travelers are attracted to the hotel for the location and views, but also for its fairly reasonable rates in this part of town. The hotel has 14 suites, all one-bedroom, most with the capability of turning into two-bedroom suites.

No other hotel in town provides the panoramic spectacle of the Hotel Washington's rooftop Sky Terrace, which is open April through October; drinks and light fare are served. The more formal Sky Room restaurant is also on the top floor.

515 15th St. NW (at Pennsylvania Ave. NW), Washington, DC 20004. ✆ **800/424-9540** or 202/638-5900. Fax 202/638-4275. www.hotelwashington.com. 345 units. Weekdays $195–$325 double; weekends $155–$285 double; $495–$800 suite. Family and other discount packages available. Extra person $20. Children under 12 stay free in parent's room. AE, DC, MC, V. Parking $28. Metro: Metro Center. Pets under 25 lb. accepted; inquire about policies when you reserve. **Amenities:** 2 restaurants (both American, one seasonal); bar; fitness center; sauna rooms; tour desk; business center; salon; room service (6:30am–11pm); same-day laundry service; dry cleaning; 12 rooms for those w/limited mobility, 2 w/roll-in showers. *In room:* A/C, TV w/pay movies, 2-line phone w/dataport, free Wi-Fi, fridge, coffeemaker, hair dryer, iron.

MODERATE

Hampton Inn Washington, D.C., Convention Center ★ This 13-story hotel opened in March 2005, 2 blocks from the convention center and the Verizon Center, and within walking distance of the many restaurants and clubs in the Penn Quarter. (Though not technically "in" the Penn Quarter, the hotel lies close enough to be included.) The Hampton Inns are a "value-priced" chain, code for "low-budget," so you may be surprised to find a more upscale version in this property. From the saltwater aquarium on display in the expansive and light-filled lobby, to guest rooms that feature a charcoal and chocolate-brown color scheme, fluffy duvets, ergonomic chairs, and lapboard bed trays, this Hampton Inn seeks to satisfy a more sophisticated traveler than usually frequents this particular Hilton brand. You can expect to pay a higher rate than is typical for a Hampton Inn, too. Other amenities include an exercise room, an indoor pool and spa, and a Hampton Inn signature perk, the "On the House Hot Breakfast Buffet," which serves up scrambled eggs, sausage, biscuits, fresh fruit, or some variation on that theme. Ask for a corner room on the Massachusetts Avenue side, high up, for the best city views, from the tip of the Capitol to the Washington Monument. In addition to standard king- and queen-bed rooms, the hotel has 10 studio suites, 12 two-room suites, and 20 king study suites (the suite holds both a king bed and a sofa bed).

901 6th St. NW (at Massachusetts Ave.), Washington, DC 20001. ✆ **800/HAMPTON** or 202/842-2500. Fax 202/842-4100. www.washingtondc.hamptoninn.com. 228 units. Weekdays $169–$299 double; weekends $129–$199 double; $249–$329 suite. Extra person $10. Children under 18 stay free in parent's room. AE, DC, DISC, MC, V. Parking $25 plus tax, in and out service. Metro: Gallery Place/Chinatown or Mount Vernon Square/Convention Center. No pets. **Amenities:** Cardio fitness center w/indoor pool and spa; 24-hr. free business center; same-day laundry service; dry cleaning; on-site washer/dryer; 20 rooms for those w/limited mobility, some w/roll-in showers. *In room:* A/C, TV w/pay movies, 2-line phone w/dataports, free Internet access, fridge, microwave, coffeemaker, hair dryer, iron, safe.

Hilton Garden Inn, Washington, D.C., Franklin Square Downtown between H and I streets, the Hilton Garden Inn is across the street from Metro's Blue Line McPherson Square station (and three stops from the Smithsonian museums station), within a short walk of the White House, and 7 blocks from the convention center and the Verizon Center. Rooms are spacious with either king-size or double beds and are designed for comfort—each room has a cushiony chair with an ottoman and a large desk with an ergonomic chair and adjustable lighting; a dial on the side of the mattress allows guests to adjust its firmness. A recently completed renovation spruced up public areas and refurbished all guest rooms with a more upscale decor, including new bed linens and drapes and 32-inch, flatscreen LCD HDTV sets, capable of connecting with a guest's personal laptop or iPod. The hotel's 24-hour pantry sells essentials; the business center allows free use of computer, faxing, and copying services. Except for guest rooms on the 14th floor, the designated smoking level, the hotel is smoke free. The hotel's location and perks make this 8-year-old hotel a good choice for both business and leisure travelers. Each of its 20 suites holds a small pullout sofa in the living room.

815 14th St. NW (between H and I sts.), Washington, DC 20005. ✆ **877/782-9444** or 202/783-7800. Fax 202/783-7801. www.washingtondcdowntown.stayhgi.com. 300 units. Weekdays $199–$399 double, $409 suite; weekends $109–$199 double, $179 suite. Extra person $10. No more than 4 people per room. Children under 18 stay free in parent's room. AE, DC, DISC, MC, V. Parking $28. Metro: McPherson Square. No pets. **Amenities:** Restaurant (American); bar w/fireplace; small fitness center w/indoor pool; business center; room service (6am–10pm); same-day laundry service; dry cleaning; on-site washer/dryer; 16 rooms for those w/limited mobility, 3 w/roll-in showers. *In room:* A/C, TV w/pay movies, 2-line phone w/dataports, free Wi-Fi, fridge, microwave, coffeemaker, hair dryer, iron.

4 Midtown

VERY EXPENSIVE

Hay-Adams ★★ This classic D.C. hotel is boutique in size and grand in sophisticated ambience. Named to *Condé Nast Traveler*'s 2007 Gold List of the "World's Top 700 Places to Stay," and winner of the magazine's 2007 "Most Excellent Hotel in North America and Canada" award, the Hay-Adams is perhaps best known for its great views and proximity to the White House. The hotel's first floor Lafayette dining room (a favorite place for a sumptuous Sunday brunch) and guest rooms on the sixth through eighth floors on the H Street side of the hotel (or as low as the second floor in winter, when the trees are bare) overlook Lafayette Square, the White House, and the Washington Monument in the background. (Expect to pay more for these guest rooms.) The sight from rooms facing 16th Street isn't bad, either: Windows overlook the yellow-painted exterior of St. John's Episcopal Church, built in 1815, and known as the "church of the presidents."

Built in the 1920s, the Hay-Adams is of Italian Renaissance–style architecture. Many of its original features, such as ornate plaster moldings, ornamental fireplaces, the walnut-paneled lobby, and high-ceilinged guest rooms, are still in place. Each guest room presents an elegant decor of sage green, off-white, beige, and gold toile fabrics; a Bose CD player; custom European linens; marble bathrooms with brass fixtures; individual thermostats; and complimentary wireless Internet access.

The hotel has about 13 one-bedroom suites (the living room and bedroom are separate) and seven junior suites (living room and bedroom are together in one space). Stop in at the Off the Record bar for casual fare at lunch and dinner and the frequent sighting of a big name in the media or administration. The hotel attracts a star-studded clientele as guests, too, so keep your eyes peeled, if you're interested.

One Lafayette Square (at 16th and H sts. NW), Washington, DC 20006. ✆ **800/853-6807** or 202/638-6600. Fax 202/638-2716. www.hayadams.com. 145 units. Weekdays $465–$900 double; weekends $389–$765 double; from $950 jr. suite; from $1,700 1-bedroom suite. Third person $30. Children under 18 stay free in parent's room. AE, DC, DISC, MC, V. Valet parking $36. Metro: Farragut West or McPherson Square. Pets under 25 lb. accepted. **Amenities:** Restaurant (American); bar; access to local health club ($15 per day); 24-hr. concierge; complimentary morning car service; secretarial and business services; complimentary 24-hr. business center; 24-hr. room service; same-day laundry service; dry cleaning; 9 rooms for those w/limited mobility, 3 w/roll-in showers. *In room:* A/C, TV w/pay movies, 2-line phone w/dataports, free Wi-Fi, minibar, hair dryer, iron, safe, robes, slippers, umbrella, CD player.

Sofitel Lafayette Square, Washington, D.C. ★★ The Sofitel, like the Hay-Adams Hotel, borders Lafayette Square and is just minutes from the White House. Although the Sofitel does not offer views of the White House, its other appealing features may make up for that, depending on your priorities.

This handsome, 12-story limestone building was erected in the early 20th century, and its distinctive facade includes decorative bronze corner panels, bas-relief sculptural panels at ground-floor level, and a 12th-floor balcony that travels the length of both the H and 15th street sides of the structure (decorative, not accessible, alas). Inside, hotel staff dressed in designer uniforms greet you with *"Bonjour!"*—a hint that the French company Accor Hotels owns the Sofitel. Noted French designer Pierre-Yves Rochon styled the interior; the hotel's restaurant, Café 15, serves French bistro fare; and the gift shop sells such specialty items as French plates and porcelain dolls. The Sofitel also has a super bar, Le Bar, which offers lunch, but not dinner. Free wireless Internet service is available throughout the hotel's public space.

Because of its corner location and exceptionally large windows, guest rooms are bright with natural light, and second- and third-floor rooms facing 15th or H street bring in even more light because their windows extend nearly from floor to ceiling. Each room sports elegantly modern decor that includes a long desk, plasma screen TV, creamy duvet with a colorful throw on a king-size bed made up with 500 thread count linens (about 17 rooms have two double beds instead of kings), a much-marbled bathroom with tub separate from the shower stall, fresh flowers, and original artwork (including dramatic photographs of Washington landmarks). In each of the 17 suites, the bedroom is separate from the living room.

806 15th St. NW (at H St.), Washington, DC 20005. ✆ **800/763-4835** or 202/737-8800. Fax 202/730-8500. www.sofitelwashingtondc.com. 237 units. Weekdays $300–$500 double; weekends $250–$400 double; from $495 suite. For lowest rates at any time, call directly to the hotel and ask about specials or packages; also check out the website. Extra person $20. Children under 12 stay free in parent's room. AE, DC, DISC, MC, V. Parking $34. Metro: McPherson Square, Farragut West, or Farragut North. Pets accepted with prior approval. **Amenities:** Restaurant (bistro chic); bar; 24-hr. state-of-the-art fitness center; 24-hr. concierge; 24-hr. business services; 24-hr. room service; same-day laundry service; dry cleaning; library w/books about D.C. and Paris; 8 rooms for those w/limited mobility, all w/roll-in showers. *In room:* A/C, TV w/pay movies, 2-line phones w/dataports, high-speed Internet access ($9.95/day), minibar, hair dryer, iron, safe, robes, slippers, CD player.

EXPENSIVE

Capital Hilton ★ This longtime Washington hotel attracts locals as well as hotel guests to its Capital City Club fitness center and full-service day spa. The club fronts on K Street, so you can work your buns off while watching the downtown Washington scene. The club doesn't have a pool but does have 60 pieces of exercise equipment, from Lifecycles to treadmills; facials, massages, and other spa services; and personal trainers. Use of the club is free to certain Hilton HHonors guests and $10 per day ($25 maximum, no matter how long your stay) for all others. The hotel's public spaces offer wireless Internet access for $11 per day.

Located just 2 blocks from the White House, the hotel has hosted 12 presidents since it opened in 1943. President Truman and his wife lived here for a time when the White House was being remodeled, and Bill Clinton interviewed his choices for vice presidential running mate here in the Ambassador Suite. Queen Elizabeth, Prince Charles, and Winston Churchill have all stayed here. The hotel often hosts political roasts, including the infamous Gridiron Club dinner.

The Hilton's central location attracts tourists and business travelers as well as presidents and royals. Nevertheless, guest rooms don't offer much in the way of character, and service is rather unremarkable. Corner rooms on the 16th Street side are the most spacious and offer the best city views. Business travelers appreciate the Tower's concierge floors (10, 11, 12, and 14) and extensive facilities. A number of suites are available, including three with outdoor patios. A recent renovation upgraded the decor and amenities in the tower rooms and suites; most of the rooms in the upgraded tower are on the high end of the price range given below. The hotel marketing director reports that "exciting" renovations are scheduled to be complete in all of the guest rooms by 2008, but he was not at liberty to reveal details, which were still being negotiated at the time of this writing; you might inquire about this when you book your reservation. Always check out the website for best deals, and AAA members, seniors, military, and families should always inquire about discounts.

1001 16th St. NW (between K and L sts.), Washington, DC 20036. ✆ **800/HILTONS** or 202/393-1000. Fax 202/639-5784. www.capital.hilton.com. 544 units. Weekdays and weekends $159–$399 double, $45 more for Tower units; $219–$459 minisuite. Extra person $30. Children 18 and under stay free in parent's room. Weekend packages and other discounts available. AE, DC, DISC, MC, V. Parking $26. Metro: Farragut West, Farragut North, or McPherson Square. **Amenities:** Restaurant (American); bar; 10,000-sq.-ft. health club and spa; concierge (6:30am–11pm); tour and ticket desk; business center; salon; room service (until 1am); massage; same-day laundry service; dry cleaning; concierge floors; ATM w/foreign currency; 13 rooms for those w/limited mobility. *In room:* A/C, TV w/pay movies, 2-line phone w/dataport, high-speed Internet access ($11/day), coffeemaker, hair dryer, iron.

Hamilton Crowne Plaza ★ This is a well-placed hotel, sort of central between the two sections of downtown: the K Street side and the revitalized Penn Quarter neighborhood surrounding the Verizon Center. The hotel's restaurant is popular with office workers at weekday lunch, thanks to a generous buffet of soups, salads, and rotisserie items, for $19. Guest rooms feature CD players, handsome royal blue robes, dark wood armoires and headboards, and comfortable accommodations like the seven-layer bed. Rooms are rather small, so those with king-size beds feel a bit tight, those with two double beds a little roomier. K Street–side rooms overlook Franklin Park, which is pleasant, and those on the upper floors offer views of the city skyline. In keeping with the times, the hotel has a designated "women's floor," accessible only to those with a special elevator key. The newly upgraded fitness center offers cardiovascular machines with built-in televisions, treadmills, and elliptical equipment.

1001 14th St. NW (at K St.), Washington, DC 20005. ✆ **800/2-CROWNE** or 202/682-0111. Fax 202/682-9525. www.hamiltonhoteldc.com. 318 units. Weekdays $119–$325 double; suites $300–$800; look for much lower rates on weekends. Extra person $20. Children under 18 stay free in parent's room. AE, DC, DISC, MC, V. Parking $28. Metro: McPherson Square. Pets accepted. **Amenities:** Restaurant (American); bar; 24-hr. fitness room; concierge; 24-hr. business center; room service (6am–midnight); same-day laundry service; dry cleaning; club level (weekdays only). *In room:* A/C, TV w/pay movies, 2-line speaker phone w/dataport, Wi-Fi ($9.95/day), coffeemaker, hair dryer, iron, safe, robes, CD player/clock radio.

Morrison-Clark Historic Inn This property is looking a bit worn and dim, but still offers a homey ambience and personable service. In addition, the inn provides hotel-like amenities, such as a fine restaurant, wireless Internet access, and a fitness center. The inn occupies twin 1864 Victorian brick town houses (with a newer wing in converted stables across an interior courtyard) and is listed on the National Register of Historic Places. Guests enter via a turn-of-the-20th-century drawing room, with Victorian furnishings and lace-curtained bay windows. Beyond this room lies a suite of lovely public spaces including the inn's restaurant. Only a couple of years ago, the Morrison-Clark's location was considered out of the way, but with the 2003 opening of the immense convention center a couple of blocks away, the inn is now in the thick of things.

The inn's high-ceilinged guest rooms are individually decorated with original artworks, sumptuous fabrics, and antique or reproduction 19th-century furnishings; all rooms are equipped with free wireless Internet access. Most popular are the grand Victorian-style rooms, with chandeliers and bedspreads. Four Victorian rooms have private porches; many others have plant-filled balconies. Guests and locals can enjoy breakfast and dinner served daily in the Victorian dining rooms. Come the warm weather, the inn hosts Big Easy cocktail receptions every Thursday, 5:30 to 7:30pm, on the veranda; come mingle with locals, sip the inn's signature "Steel Magnolia" cocktail, and munch on complimentary hors d'oeuvres, like the crab-cake puff.

1015 L St. NW (at 11th St. and Massachusetts Ave. NW), Washington, DC 20001. ✆ **800/332-7898** or 202/898-1200. Fax 202/371-0377. www.morrisonclark.com. 54 units. Weekdays $189–$379 double; weekends $129–$249 double. Extra person $20. Children under 16 stay free in parent's room. AE, DC, DISC, MC, V. Parking $26. Metro: Metro Center or Mt. Vernon Square. **Amenities:** Restaurant (American-Southern); tiny fitness center; concierge; business center; room service during restaurant hours; same-day laundry service; dry cleaning. *In room:* A/C, TV, dataport, free Wi-Fi, minibar, hair dryer, robes.

Renaissance Mayflower ★★ In the heart of downtown, the Mayflower has been the hotel of choice for guests as varied as Kurt Russell and Wynton Marsalis. The lobby, which extends an entire block from Connecticut Avenue to 17th Street, is always bustling—read "chaotic," especially at check-in/check-out times—because Washingtonians tend to use it as a shortcut in their travels.

The Mayflower is steeped in history: When it opened in 1925, it was the site of Calvin Coolidge's inaugural ball (though Coolidge didn't attend—he was mourning his son's death from blood poisoning). President-elect FDR and family lived in rooms 776 and 781 while waiting to move into the White House, and this is where he penned the words, "The only thing we have to fear is fear itself." A restoration in the 1980s uncovered large skylights and renewed the lobby's pink marble bas-relief frieze and spectacular promenade. Like the Willard Hotel, the Mayflower has mounted exhibits to showcase the hotel's long history; look for displays on the mezzanine level.

In 2004, the hotel completed a $10-million, top-to-bottom renovation that transformed the guest rooms into individual refuges of elegance: Silvery green bed coverings, embroidered drapes, silk wall coverings, pillow-topped mattresses, and sink-into armchairs are some of the finer touches. Certain gracious appointments remain: Each guest room still has its own marble foyer, high ceiling, combination of reproduction and contemporary furnishings, and Italian marble bathroom. The Mayflower now has a club level on the eighth floor, as well as 74 executive suites. In 2007, the hotel opened a new 24-hour fitness center, which measures 3,000 square feet and offers state-of-the-art equipment.

In the hotel's lovely Café Promenade, lawyers and lobbyists continue to gather for weekday power breakfasts, while hotel guests and local business folks break for high tea served every afternoon. The clubby, mahogany-paneled Town and Country Lounge is the setting for light buffet lunches and complimentary hors d'oeuvres during cocktail hour. Bartender Sambonn Lek has quite a following, as much for his conversation and magic tricks as for his mixing skills. If you like martinis, ask for the "Sam I Am" (Absolut Citron, cranberry juice, and Amaretto, with a twist of lemon); it's one of 101 martini variations in Sam's repertoire.

1127 Connecticut Ave. NW (between L and M sts.), Washington, DC 20036. ✆ **800/228-7697** or 202/347-3000. Fax 202/776-9182. www.renaissancemayflower.com. 657 units. Weekdays $199–$519 double, suites from $599; weekends $179–$299 double, suites from $599. Rates include complimentary coffee service in lobby. No charge for extra person in room. AE, DC, DISC, MC, V. Parking $32. Metro: Farragut North. **Amenities:** Restaurant (Mediterranean); lobby lounge; bar; fitness center; concierge; 24-hr. business center; 24-hr. room service; same-day laundry service; dry cleaning; club level; 15 rooms for those w/limited mobility. *In room:* A/C, TV w/pay movies, 2-line phone w/dataport, high-speed Internet access ($9.95/day), hair dryer, iron, robes.

MODERATE

Doubletree Washington Hotel ★ The Doubletree flag now waves at this property, formerly known as the Washington Terrace Hotel. By any name, it remains an urban hotel, whose beautifully landscaped terraces front and back act as buffers between the hotel and the city. The flow of the public spaces leading back to the garden courtyard, and abundant use of earth tones and sandstone in the decor, accentuate the hotel's theme of "bringing the outdoors in." This theme resonates in the guest rooms—the light golden wall coverings feature an abstract botanical pattern, and the windows are larger than the hotel norm, delivering lots of natural light. Ask for a room at the front of the hotel for a view of Scott Circle, the park across the street, and the city; request a room at the back for a view of the garden terrace. Spacious suites come with a small wet bar, a dining table, a sleeper sofa, and a larger bathroom. Guest rooms on the second through seventh floors have a Tempur-Pedic mattress (the kind that forms to your body) on the bed, while those on floors 8 and 9 have the "Sweet Dreams by Hilton" pillow-top mattress. The hotel will soon provide free wireless Internet access in all guest rooms—probably by 2008, but ask to confirm this.

Although the Doubletree Washington calls itself an "upscale boutique hotel," its large size and its practical amenities, like ergonomic chairs in the guest rooms and extensive conference and party facilities, disqualify it. But the guest rooms do have a boutiquey feel, thanks to imaginative touches such as granite-topped desks, circular nightstands, and a fanciful color scheme, like a blueberry-toned wall behind the bed (the suites feature other colors: aubergine, nectar, and sienna), contrasting with the light-toned coverings on the other walls.

1515 Rhode Island Ave. NW (at Scott Circle), Washington, DC 20005. ✆ **800/222-TREE** or 202/232-7000. Fax 202/332-8436. www.washington.doubletree.com. 220 units. Weekdays $189–$399 double; weekends $139–$189 double; rates for suites usually run $70 higher than doubles. Extra person $30. Children under 17 stay free in parent's room. AE, DC, DISC, MC, V. Parking $28. Metro: Dupont Circle, McPherson Square, or Farragut North. **Amenities:** Restaurant (contemporary American); bar; fitness center; 24-hr. concierge; business services; room service (6:30am–midnight); same-day laundry service; dry cleaning; 10 rooms for those w/limited mobility, 2 w/roll-in showers. *In room:* A/C, TV w/pay movies, 2-line phones w/dataport, free Wi-Fi, fridge, hair dryer, iron, safe, robes.

Four Points by Sheraton, Washington, D.C. Downtown ★ *Value* This contemporary property offers complimentary wired Internet access, a 650-square-foot fitness center, and an unbeatable location close to both the convention center and the Verizon Center. Add in reasonable rates and fine hotel amenities and you've got a good choice for both business and leisure visitors.

A recent refurbishment gives a stylish, retro look to the guest rooms, with the help of lots of earth tones, leather, tweeds, and modern furniture. Bedding is new, too, and now features the "Four Points," custom-designed, multilayered, pillow-top mattress. Guests have a choice of rooms with two double beds or one king bed. Corner rooms (there are only about 10) are a little more spacious than others. Be forewarned: These book first, so they are seldom available. While guest rooms offer city views, the rooftop pool and lounge present a wider vista of the city. Under separate ownership from the hotel is the recommended restaurant, **Corduroy** (p. 151).

1201 K St. NW (at 12th St.), Washington, DC 20005. ✆ **888/481-7191** or 202/289-7600. Fax 202/349-2215. www.fourpoints.com/washingtondcdowntown. 265 units. In season $195–$350 double; off-season $109–$245 double. Extra person $20. Children 12 and under stay free in parent's room. AE, DC, DISC, MC, V. Parking $28. Metro: McPherson Square or Metro Center. **Amenities**: Restaurant (seasonal American); bar; indoor heated pool on rooftop; 24-hour fitness center; complimentary Internet service in lobby; gift shop; room service (during restaurant hours); same-day laundry service; dry cleaning; executive-level rooms; 5 rooms for those w/limited mobility, 2 w/roll-in showers. *In room:* A/C, TV w/pay movies, 2-line phone w/dataport, free high-speed wired Internet access, fridge, coffeemaker, hair dryer, iron, safe, robes.

Hotel Helix ★ The Helix doesn't so much invite you in as intrigue you in. The giant, peacock-blue English lawn chairs and the Magritte-like painting out front are just the beginning. Your steps across a mosaic-tiled vestibule trigger an automatic swoosh of curtains, parting to let you inside the hotel. The small lobby is spare, its main furnishings the illuminated "pods" (podiums with flat computer screens for check-in).

The guest rooms have a minimalist quality to them, too, which is an odd thing to say about a decor that uses such startling colors: cherry red and royal blue ottomans, striped green settees, bright orange vanities in bathrooms, metallic-sheen walls, and lime green honor bar/armoires. Rooms are uncluttered and roomy, due to a design that puts the platform bed behind sheer drapes in an alcove (in the king deluxe rooms), leaving the two-person settee, a triangular desk, and the 22-inch flatscreen TV on its stainless steel stand, out in the open. Deluxe rooms, without alcoves, feel a little less spacious, but otherwise look the same. Roomiest are the 18 suites, each with a separate bedroom and, in the living room, slate blue sectional sofas. The Helix, like its sister hotels (see the Madera, Topaz, and Rouge), offers "specialty" rooms which play up particular themes, in this case, "Eats" rooms, which include Italian cafe tables and bar stools, and a fully equipped kitchenette; "Bunk" rooms, great for kids, with a separate bunk bed area where the TV has a built-in DVD player; and "Zone" rooms, equipped with a plasma-screen TV, high-tech stereo system, lava lamp, and lounge chair. The Helix is now a nonsmoking hotel. The hotel's Helix Lounge is a popular after-work spot for locals, especially from May to October, when its outdoor patio is open.

1430 Rhode Island Ave. NW (between 14th and 15th sts.), Washington, DC 20006. ✆ **866/508-0658** or 202/462-9001. Fax 202/332-3519. www.hotelhelix.com. 178 units. Weekdays and weekends $139–$319 double; specialty rooms: add $50 to double rate; suites: add $100 to double rate. Best rates usually Fri–Sun. Extra person $20. Children under 18 stay free in parent's room. Rates include "bubbly hour" (champagne) in evening. AE, DC, DISC, MC, V. Parking $26 plus tax. Metro: McPherson Square. Pets welcome. **Amenities:** Bar/cafe; exercise room; room service (during breakfast and dinner hours); same-day laundry service; dry cleaning; 9 rooms for those w/limited mobility, some w/roll-in showers. *In room:* A/C, TV w/pay movies, Web TV access (for a fee), 2-line phones w/dataports, free Wi-Fi, minibar, hair dryer, iron, CD player, Nintendo.

Hotel Rouge ★ High-energy music dances out onto the sidewalk. A red awning extends from the entrance. A guest with sleepy eyes and brilliant blue hair sits diffidently upon the white tufted leather sofa in the small lobby. Attractive, casually dressed patrons come and go, while couples roost at tables inside the adjoining Bar Rouge sipping martinis. Shades of red are everywhere: in the staff's funky shiny shirts, in the accent pillows on the retro furniture, and in the artwork. This used to be a Quality Hotel: It's come a long way, baby.

Rouge guest rooms have deep crimson drapes at the window; a floor-to-ceiling red "pleather" headboard for your comfortable, white-with-red-piping duvet-covered bed; and, in the dressing room, an Orange Crush–colored dresser, whose built-in minibar holds all sorts of red items, such as Hot Tamales candies, red wax lips, and Red Bull. Though typical boutique hotel guest rooms are notoriously cramped, that's not true here; the rooms are spacious enough to easily accommodate several armchairs and a large ottoman (in shades of red and gold), a number of funky little lamps, a huge mahogany-framed mirror leaning against a wall, and a 10-foot-long mahogany desk. The Rouge has no suites but does offer 15 specialty guest rooms, including "Chill Rooms," which have a chaise longue and a little sitting room area, DVD player, and PlayStation; "Chat Rooms," which have computer/printers; and "Chow Rooms," which have a microwave and refrigerator.

The hotel embraces the theme of adventure, inviting guests to partake of a complimentary Bloody Mary and cool pizza in the lobby on weekends, 10 to 11am. Weeknights, 5 to 6pm, the hotel serves complimentary red wine, Red Stripe Jamaican beer, and Izze Raspberry soda. The only problem with this setup is that the lobby is too tiny to accommodate more than a handful of guests. Bar Rouge to the rescue: Carry your red drink and cold pizza to the lounge, settle into one of the thronelike armchairs there, and enjoy. (Bar Rouge is open daily 7–10:30am and reopens in the evening at 5pm.) The hotel is now nonsmoking.

1315 16th St. NW (at Massachusetts Ave. NW and Scott Circle), Washington, DC 20036. ✆ **800/368-5689** or 202/232-8000. Fax 202/667-9827. www.rougehotel.com. 137 units. Weekdays and weekends $139–$339 double; add $40 to reserve a specialty room, weekdays or weekends. Best rates available on the website and by calling the 800 number and asking for promotional price. Extra person $20 (after 2 people). Rates include complimentary Bloody Marys and cold pizza weekend mornings 10–11am and complimentary wine and beer weeknights 5–6pm. Children under 18 stay free in parent's room. AE, DC, DISC, MC, V. Parking $27. Metro: Dupont Circle. Pets welcomed and pampered. **Amenities:** Bar/restaurant (American, w/a French twist); modest-size fitness center; business center; room service (7am–11pm); same-day laundry service; dry cleaning; 6 rooms for those w/limited mobility, 1 w/roll-in shower. *In room:* A/C, 27-in. flatscreen TV w/pay movies, 2-line cordless phones w/dataport, free Wi-Fi, minibar, coffeemaker, hair dryer, iron, robes, CD player.

The Quincy ★ Big changes are on display at this hotel—formerly known as the good-value property, Lincoln Suites—located in the heart of downtown, near Metro stops, restaurants, and the White House. The Quincy has gone upscale in a renovation completed in 2007, adding pillow-top mattresses, sectional sofas, flatscreen TVs, complimentary high-speed Internet access, and double-paned windows to all rooms. The top-to-bottom transformation has also altered the decor to "conservative contemporary," replacing all the furniture and carpeting so that the overall design is brighter and very 21st century. Key elements remain: Suites are large and comfortable, with about 28 offering full kitchens, while the rest have wet bars (minifridge, microwave, and coffeemaker). The Quincy has direct access to **Mackey's,** an Irish pub right next door, and to **Recessions,** a restaurant on the lower level serving American/Mediterranean cuisine.

Lots of long-term guests and repeat customers bunk here, and are often rewarded for it, with goodies in the room or complimentary room upgrades.

1823 L St. NW, Washington, DC 20036. ✆ **800/424-2970** or 202/223-4320. Fax 202/293-4977. www.quincysuites.com. 99 suites. Weekdays $169–$269; weekends $99–$189 year-round. Discounts available for long-term stays. Children under 18 stay free in parent's room. AE, DC, DISC, MC, V. Parking $28 (in adjoining garage). Metro: Farragut North or Farragut West. Pets under 25 lb. accepted, for $150 nonrefundable deposit. **Amenities:** Restaurant (American/Mediterranean); bar (Irish); free passes to the well-equipped Bally's Fitness Center nearby; 24-hr. front desk; room service (11am–11pm); coin-op washer/dryers; Mon–Sat same-day laundry service; dry cleaning; 2 rooms for those w/limited mobility, 1 w/roll-in shower. *In room:* A/C, TV w/pay movies, free hard-wired Internet access, fridge, microwave, coffeemaker, hair dryer, iron.

5 Adams-Morgan

Note: The hotels listed here are situated just north of Dupont Circle, more at the mouth of Adams-Morgan than within its actual boundaries.

EXPENSIVE

Hilton Washington ★ *Kids* This sprawling hotel, built in 1965, occupies 7 acres and calls itself a "resort"—mostly on the basis of having landscaped gardens, tennis courts, and an Olympic-style pool on its premises (unusual amenities for a D.C. hotel). From the property, you're within an easy stroll of embassies, great restaurants, museums, and the charming neighborhoods of Adams-Morgan, Woodley Park, and Dupont Circle.

The Hilton caters to corporate groups, some with families in tow (during the summer, the reception desk gives families a complimentary gift and lends them board games—ask for the "Vacation Station" perk), and is accustomed to coordinating meetings for thousands of attendees. Its vast conference facilities include one of the largest hotel ballrooms on the East Coast (it accommodates nearly 4,000). By contrast, guest

Adams-Morgan, Dupont Circle & West End Accommodations

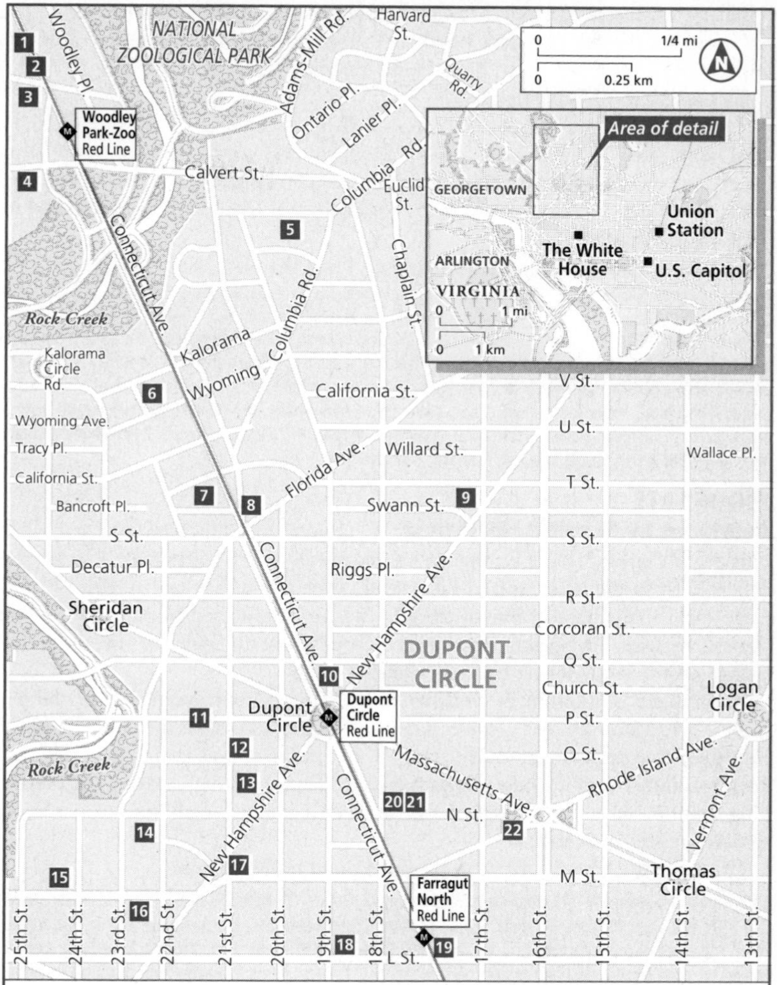

- Beacon Hotel **22**
- Courtyard by Marriott Northwest **7**
- Embassy Suites Hotel Downtown **14**
- Hilton Washington **8**
- Hotel Madera **13**
- Hotel Palomar **11**
- Hotel Tabard Inn **20**
- Jurys Normandy Inn **6**
- Jurys Washington Hotel **10**
- Kalorama Guest House (Cathedral Avenue) **1**
- Kalorama Guest House (Mintwood Place) **5**
- The Mansion on O Street **12**
- The Quincy **18**
- Omni Shoreham Hotel **4**
- Park Hyatt Washington DC **15**
- Ritz-Carlton Washington DC **16**
- Renaissance Mayflower **19**
- St. Gregory Luxury Hotel and Suites **17**
- Swann House **9**
- Topaz Hotel **21**
- Wardman Park Marriott **3**
- Woodley Park Guest House **2**

rooms are on the small side. In such a huge hotel, renovations are ongoing; a recent alteration installed elegant dark wood furnishings in every room and placed new pillow-top mattresses on every bed. From the fifth floor up, poolside, you'll have panoramic views of Washington.

The designated concierge-level rooms usually go for about $30 more than the standard room rate. The hotel has 82 suites, in all kinds of configurations, from the junior executive (in which parlor and bedroom are combined) to the huge Presidential Suite. The hotel's health club has been thoroughly renovated and expanded, and now offers extensive spa services.

1919 Connecticut Ave. NW (at T St.), Washington, DC 20009. ✆ **800/HILTONS** or 202/483-3000. Fax 202/232-0438. www.washington.hilton.com. 1,119 units. Weekdays and weekends $119–$319 double; $30 more for Towers rooms. Look for deals on the website or by calling Hilton's 800 number. Extra person $25. Children 18 and under stay free in parent's room. AE, DC, DISC, MC, V. Self-parking $23. Metro: Dupont Circle. **Amenities:** 2 restaurants (both American); deli; 2 bars (a pub, and lobby bar occasionally featuring a pianist); Olympic-style heated outdoor pool; 3 lighted tennis courts; extensive health-club facilities; concierge; transportation/sightseeing desk; comprehensive business center; lobby shops; room service (until 2am); same-day laundry service; dry cleaning; concierge-level rooms; 28 rooms for those w/limited mobility, some w/roll-in showers. *In room:* A/C, TV w/pay movies, 2-line phone w/dataport, high-speed Internet access ($12/day), coffeemaker, hair dryer, iron.

MODERATE

Courtyard by Marriott Northwest This hotel isn't much to look at from the outside, but inside it has a European feel and a well-heeled appearance. Crystal chandeliers hang in the lobby and in the restaurant, and you may hear an Irish lilt from time to time (the hotel is one of three in Washington owned by Jurys Doyle Hotel Group, an Irish management company). Guests tend to linger in the comfortable lounge off the lobby, where coffee is available all day.

A complete refurbishment in 2004 replaced just about everything in the guest rooms, which now present a comfortable and bright decor that includes cherrywood furniture, blue carpeting, and 25-inch TVs. Accommodations facing the street on the sixth to ninth floors provide panoramic views. Especially nice are the 16 "executive king" rooms, which are a little larger and are equipped with marble bathrooms, trouser presses, and robes.

For the best deals, call direct to the hotel or go to the website.

1900 Connecticut Ave. NW (at Leroy Place), Washington, DC 20009. ✆ **888/236-2427** or 202/332-9300. Fax 202/319-1793. www.marriott.com. 147 units. $99–$349 double. Extra person $15. Children under 18 stay free in parent's room. Ask about discount packages. AE, DC, DISC, MC, V. Parking $20. Metro: Dupont Circle. **Amenities:** Restaurant (American, open for breakfast and dinner); bar; outdoor pool (seasonal); small exercise room; business center; room service (5–10pm); coin-operated laundry; same-day laundry service; dry cleaning; 2 rooms for those w/limited mobility, both w/roll-in showers. *In room:* A/C, TV w/pay movies, 2-line phone w/dataport, free Internet access, coffeemaker, hair dryer, iron, safe.

INEXPENSIVE

Jurys Normandy Inn ★ *Finds* This gracious hotel is a gem—a small gem, but a gem nonetheless. Situated in a neighborhood of architecturally impressive embassies, the hotel hosts many embassy-bound guests. You may discover this for yourself on a Tuesday evening, when guests gather in the charming Tea Room to enjoy complimentary wine and cheese served from the antique oak sideboard. Here you'll also find daily continental breakfast (for about $7), complimentary coffee and tea after 10am, and cookies after 3pm. You can lounge or watch TV in the conservatory, or, in nice weather, you can move outside to the garden patio.

The six-floor Normandy has small but pretty twin and queen guest rooms, all recently remodeled and sporting a bright, contemporary look with cherrywood furnishings and fabrics in colors of light blues and greens. Rooms facing Wyoming Avenue overlook the tree-lined street, while other rooms mostly offer views of apartment buildings. The Normandy is an easy walk from the restaurants and shops in both Adams-Morgan and Dupont Circle.

2118 Wyoming Ave. NW (at Connecticut Ave.), Washington, DC 20008. ✆ **800/424-3729** or 202/483-1350. Fax 202/387-8241. www.jurysdoyle.com. 75 units. $89–$239 double. Extra person $10. Children under 12 stay free in parent's room. AE, DC, DISC, MC, V. Parking $15 plus tax. Metro: Dupont Circle. **Amenities:** Access to the neighboring Courtyard by Marriott Northwest's pool and exercise room; room service at breakfast; coin-op washer/dryers; same-day laundry service; dry cleaning (Mon–Sat); 4 rooms for those w/limited mobility, 1 w/roll-in shower. *In room:* A/C, TV, 2-line phone w/dataport, free Internet access, minifridge, coffeemaker, hair dryer, iron, safe.

Kalorama Guest House This San Francisco–style B&B has two locations: in Adams-Morgan, where a Victorian town house at 1854 Mintwood Place NW is the main dwelling, with two other houses on the same street providing additional lodging; and in nearby Woodley Park (✆ **202/328-0860;** fax 202/328-8730), where two houses at 2700 Cathedral Avenue NW offer a total of 18 guest rooms (see "Woodley Park," later in this chapter, for more information about this location). As of 2007, all of the guest rooms at both locations have new beds and, in rooms that are carpeted, new carpeting.

The cozy common areas and homey guest rooms are furnished with finds from antiques stores, flea markets, and auctions. The Mintwood Place town house has a breakfast room with plant-filled windows. There's a garden behind the house with umbrella tables.

Rooms in all the houses generally offer either double or queen-size beds, but the Mintwood Place town house offers larger units in a greater variety of configurations: There's an efficiency apartment with a kitchen, telephone, and TV; one small two-room apartment with a kitchen, cable TV, and telephone; and four suites (two 2-bedroom and two "executive" suites, in which the living room and bedroom are together). ***Note:*** The Woodley Park location has only a communal television and telephone.

Each location serves an expansive complimentary breakfast of juice, coffee, fruit, bagels, croissants, English muffins, waffles, sausage, bacon, eggs, and cereal. Guests have access to laundry and ironing facilities, a refrigerator, a seldom-used TV, and a phone (local calls are free; incoming calls are answered around the clock, so people can leave messages for you). Free Wi-Fi access is available in the common rooms of the main house. It's customary for the innkeepers to put out sherry daily, lemonade and cookies in summer, and cider and cookies in winter. Magazines, games, and current newspapers are available. All of the houses are nonsmoking. At both locations, your fellow guests are likely to be Europeans, tourists, and businesspeople.

The Mintwood Place location is near Metro stations, restaurants, nightspots, and shops. The Cathedral Avenue houses, which are even closer to the Woodley Park–Zoo Metro, offer proximity to Rock Creek Park and the National Zoo.

1854 Mintwood Place NW (between 19th St. and Columbia Rd.), Washington, DC 20009. ✆ **800/974-6450** or 202/667-6369. Fax 202/319-1262. www.kaloramaguesthouse.com. 29 units, 15 with private bathroom. $140 double with shared bathroom; $155–$185 double with private bathroom. Extra person $10. Rates include expansive breakfast. AE, DISC, MC, V. Very limited parking $15. Metro: Woodley Park–Zoo or Dupont Circle. Kids 6 and older only. **Amenities:** Washer/dryer; common fridge; common TV. *In room:* A/C.

6 Dupont Circle

EXPENSIVE

Beacon Hotel and Corporate Quarters ★ What was once the creaky Governor's House Hotel has been gutted and transformed into the Beacon, which opened in January 2005. Like its predecessor, the Beacon attracts a lively local gathering in its bar and grill, right off the lobby, which adds to the overall genial ambience of the hotel. Rooms offer every configuration imaginable: a penthouse with rooftop terrace, eight one-bedroom suites with fireplaces and great views of the city, 60 corporate quarter junior suites with pantry kitchens, and deluxe rooms. Many rooms have a sofa bed and dining area. All rooms are furnished with flatscreen TVs and contemporary touches, like wide-striped bedcovers and the large leathery-looking headboards framed in wood. The best rooms are in the "turret": the one-bedroom suites, one per floor, that perch in the corner of the building overlooking the intersection of 17th Street and Rhode Island Avenue. But the New York–style junior suites offer a great deal: Each suite's compact kitchen includes a dishwasher, fridge, stovetop, microwave, and cabinets; add the roomy living room with a sleep sofa and you've got a good home base—for both corporate folks on business and families on holiday. The hotel's 10th-floor Beacon Sky Bar, an open-air, penthouse martini bar, debuted in 2006. The seasonal bar is open Wednesday to Saturday and offers views of the Dupont Circle neighborhood and the boulevards of the city. Keep this spot in mind if you're here for the Fourth of July, since the Sky Bar's perch is prime for watching the fireworks on the Mall.

1615 Rhode Island Ave. NW (at 17th St.), Washington, DC 20036. ✆ **800/821-4367** or 202/296-2100. Fax 202/331-0227. www.beaconhotelwdc.com. 199 units. Peak season: $329–$529 weekdays, $129–$309 weekends; off-peak: $199–$289 weekdays, $109–$189 weekends. Ask for AAA or AARP discounts or check the website for best rates; always ask for promotional rates. Extra person $20, up to 3 adults maximum per room. Children under 14 stay free in parent's room. AE, DC, DISC, MC, V. Parking $25 weekdays, discounted on weekends; no oversize SUVs, buses, conversion vans. Metro: Farragut North or Dupont Circle. **Amenities:** Restaurant (modern and classic American); bar w/indoor atrium and outdoor patio; seasonal rooftop bar; in-house cardio fitness center, plus free access to nearby, fully equipped YMCA w/indoor pool; tour bus stop; 24-hr. business center; room service (6:30am–11pm); same-day laundry service; dry cleaning; 8 rooms for those w/limited mobility, 2 w/roll-in showers. *In room:* A/C, TV w/pay movies, 2-line phone w/dataport, Internet access ($11/day), coffeemaker, hair dryer, iron, robes, CD player.

The Mansion on O Street ★★ *Finds* A legend in her own time, H. H. Leonards Spero operates this Victorian property, made up of five interconnecting four- and five-story town houses, as a museum with rotating exhibits, an event space, a private club, an art gallery, an antiques emporium, and—oh, yeah—a B&B. The Mansion attracts a lot of celebrities and CEOs, mostly people who crave both luxury and privacy (H won't reveal her guests' names). If you stay here, you may find yourself buying a sweater, a painting, or maybe an antique bed. Everything's for sale.

Guest rooms are so creative they'll blow you away. Perhaps the most breathtaking is the two-level Log Cabin loft suite, with a bed whose headboard encases an aquarium, Remington bronze sculptures, and an eco-friendly bathroom outfitted with sauna, Jacuzzi, and whirlpool. The Art Deco–style penthouse takes up an entire floor, including a large living room, two bathrooms, a bedroom, and a kitchen, and has its own security cameras, elevator, 10 phones, and multiple televisions and DVD systems. The International Room (one room with a queen bed and sitting area) has a nonworking fireplace and four TVs, a combination of Victorian antiques and contemporary furnishings, a sunny sitting area, handmade prism-glass windows, and a bright bathroom with two-person Jacuzzi. The simplest of the bunch is the Country Room, decorated in blue and white, and with French doors leading to a porch overlooking O Street. Nearly all rooms have either king-size or queen-size beds, most have a whirlpool, and a few have kitchens. Elsewhere on the property, there are eight office/conference spaces, 32 far-out bathrooms, 18 fireplaces, art and antiques everywhere, and 20,000 or so books. It's possible to rent the entire mansion or a portion of it for your stay. Full business services are available. Don't miss the mansion's Sunday brunch, which is open to the public as well as guests; if you're lucky, you'll be here when an overnighting big-name musician, say Emmy Lou Harris, breaks into an impromptu jam session on a Sunday morning.

2020 O St. NW (between 20th and 21st sts.), Washington, DC 20036. ✆ **202/496-2000.** Fax 202/833-8333. www.omansion.com. 23 units, all with private bathrooms. $350–$850 double; $550–$3,000 suites. Nonprofit, group, and long-term rates available. Rates include continental breakfast. AE, DC, DISC, MC, V. Parking $25 by reservation. Metro: Dupont Circle. **Amenities:** Free passes to Sports Club/LA health club at the nearby Ritz-Carlton; concierge; state-of-the-art business center; laundry service. *In room:* A/C, TV, 2-line phone w/dataport, free Wi-Fi, iron, robes.

St. Gregory Luxury Hotel and Suites ★★ Open since June 2000, the St. Gregory is an affordable luxury property, whose ambience and decor evince a sophisticated coziness that makes one feel totally at ease. A $3-million sprucing-up in 2006–07 pushed decor toward a comfortably contemporary and sexy look, replacing furniture, linens, and carpeting with plusher versions throughout the hotel. Wingback chairs; soft benches in place of coffee tables; high-backed, boxlike sofas in red-based weave patterns; coffee-and-cream colored, textured carpeting; oversized silk-fabric-covered slipper chairs; multilayered mattresses and fluffy bedspreads are just some of the fresh appointments. Flatscreen TVs are in the rooms; flat-panel TVs are in the suites. At street level, meanwhile, the St. Gregory has pushed out the front of the building to accommodate its greenhouse-like lounge, Norma Jean's, named in honor of Marilyn Monroe, a sculpture (by J. Seward Johnson) of whom presides here. The glamorous 21 M Lounge opened in spring 2007. Situated at the corner of 21st and M streets, not far from Georgetown, Dupont Circle, Foggy Bottom, and the White House, the St. Gregory is just a stone's throw from some of the city's best restaurants.

Most of the guest rooms are one-bedroom suites, with a separate living room and bedroom, and with a pullout sofa in the living room. For privacy and views, choose one of the 16 "sky" suites on the top three floors, each with terrace and city overlooks. Of the 100 suites, 85 have pantry kitchens, including microwaves, ovens, and full-size refrigerators (the other 15 suites have no kitchens). The remaining 54 units are either king or two double beds.

Three whole floors of the hotel are reserved for club-level rooms. Crystal Waters, Denyce Graves, Dianne Reeves, Naomi Judd, and Mikhail Baryshnikov are among the many performers who gravitate to the hotel. The St. Gregory offers special rates to long-term and government guests, and to those from the diplomatic community. If you don't fall into one of those categories, check the hotel's website for great deals like the often available "One Dollar Clearance Sale": You pay a set price—this can fluctuate, sometimes $199, sometimes $289—the first night and only $1 for the second night, for Friday and Saturday, or Saturday and Sunday stays.

2033 M St. NW (at 21st St.), Washington, DC 20036. ✆ **800/829-5034** or 202/530-3600. Fax 202/466-6770. www.stgregoryhotelwdc.com. 154 units. Weekdays $329–$489 double or suite; weekends $139–$309 double or suite. Extra person $20. Children under 14 stay free in parent's room. Ask about discounts, long-term stays, AAA and AARP rates, and packages. AE, DC, DISC, MC, V. Parking $25 weekdays, discounted price on weekends (garage has maximum 6-ft. clearance). Metro: Dupont Circle or Farragut North. No pets. **Amenities:** Restaurant (contemporary American); coffee bar; bar/lounge; state-of-the-art fitness center, as well as access (for $20 fee) to the nearby and larger Sports Club/LA health club at the Ritz-Carlton; concierge; tour desk; self-serve 24-hr. business center; room service (6:30am–10:30pm); massage; babysitting; coin-op laundry room; same-day laundry service; dry cleaning; concierge-level rooms; 6 rooms for those w/limited mobility, 2 w/roll-in showers. *In room:* A/C, TV w/pay movies, 2-line phone w/dataport, Internet access ($11/day), fridge, coffeemaker, hair dryer, iron, CD player.

Swann House ★ *Finds* This stunning 1883 mansion, poised prominently on a corner 4 blocks north of Dupont Circle, has nine exquisite guest rooms. Hard to say which is the prettiest, but I do love the Blue Sky Suite, covered in blue and white toile, with the original rose-tiled working fireplace, a queen-size bed and daybed, a sitting room, and a gabled ceiling. The most romantic room might be Il Duomo, with Gothic windows, a cathedral ceiling, a working fireplace, and a turreted bathroom with angel murals, a claw-foot tub, and a rain showerhead. The Jennifer Green Room has a queen-size four-poster bed, a working fireplace, an oversize marble steam shower, and a private deck overlooking the pool area and garden. The Regent Room also has a private deck overlooking the pool, and has a whirlpool in the marble bathroom, and a king-size bed in front of a carved working fireplace. There are three suites. You'll want to spend some time on the main floor of the mansion, which has 12-foot ceilings, fluted woodwork, inlaid wood floors, a turreted living room, a columned sitting room, and a sunroom leading through three sets of French doors to the garden and pool. Check the inn's website for rate specials. No smoking.

1808 New Hampshire Ave. NW (between S and Swann sts.), Washington, DC 20009. ✆ **202/265-4414.** Fax 202/265-6755. www.swannhouse.com. 9 units, all with private bathroom (3 with shower only). $150–$365 depending on unit and season. 2-night minimum weekends, 3-night minimum holiday weekends. Extended-stay and government rates available. Extra person $35. Rates include expanded continental breakfast. AE, DISC, MC, V. Limited off-street parking $14. Metro: Dupont Circle. No children under age 12. **Amenities:** Outdoor pool; free Wi-Fi; business services; in-room massage; same-day dry cleaning. *In room:* A/C, TV, phone w/voicemail and dataport, free Wi-Fi, hair dryer, iron, robes.

MODERATE

Embassy Suites Hotel Downtown ★ *Kids* This convenient hotel—within walking distance of Foggy Bottom, Georgetown, and Dupont Circle—offers unbelievable value. You enter into a tropical and glassy eight-story atrium with two continually running waterfalls. You'll enjoy an ample complimentary breakfast—not your standard cold croissant and coffee, but stations from which you can choose omelets made to order, waffles, bacon, fresh fruit, juices, bagels, and pastries. Tables are scattered in alcoves throughout the atrium to allow for privacy. Each evening, the atrium is the setting for complimentary beverages (including cocktails) and light snacks. Parents are thrilled to discover that they can enjoy themselves at this reception on the mezzanine level while their children sit and watch that night's family video on the widescreen TV. Parents and kids both delight in the daily 9am and 6pm feedings of the schools of koi swimming in the two atrium ponds.

Thanks to a $5.8-million renovation of the entire property completed in 2005, dark marble replaces light marble, guest-room sofas are covered in maroon tapestry fabric, 32-inch plasma TVs are in every room, and wired and wireless Internet access is available throughout the hotel (guests pay $9.95 per 24 hr.). For those who've left the computer at home, there's the business center, where use of three computers and a printer is complimentary.

Every unit is a two-room suite, with a living room that closes off completely from the rest of the suite. The living room holds a queen-size sofa bed, TV, easy chair, and large table with four comfortable chairs around it. The bedroom lies at the back of the suite, overlooking a quiet courtyard of brick walkways or the street. A king-size bed or two queen beds, TV, sink, easy chair, and chest of drawers furnish this space. New bedding (triple sheets and duvets) rests on top of 12-inch thick mattresses. Between the living room and the bedroom are the bathroom, a small closet, and a kitchenette. It's worth requesting one of the eighth- or ninth floor suites with views of Georgetown and beyond, as far as Washington National Cathedral. (The hotel will note your request but won't be able to guarantee you such a suite.) For the roomiest quarters, ask for an "executive corner suite," the slightly larger, slightly more expensive suites situated in the corners of the hotel.

1250 22nd St. NW (between M and N sts.), Washington, DC 20037. ✆ **800/EMBASSY** or 202/857-3388. Fax 202/293-3173. www.washingtondc.embassysuites.com. 318 suites. $159–$339 double. Rates include full breakfast and evening reception. Ask for AAA discounts or check the website for best rates. Extra person $20 weekdays, $25 weekends. Children 18 and under stay free in parent's room. AE, DC, DISC, MC, V. Parking $24. Metro: Foggy Bottom. **Amenities:** Restaurant (northern Italian); state-of-the-art fitness center w/indoor pool, whirlpool, sauna; game room; concierge; business center; room service (11am–11pm); coin-op washer/dryers; same-day laundry service; dry cleaning; 8 rooms for those w/limited mobility, 4 w/roll-in showers. *In room:* A/C, TV w/pay movies and PlayStation, 2-line phone w/dataport, high-speed Internet access and Wi-Fi ($9.95/day), kitchenette w/fridge and microwave, coffeemaker, hair dryer, iron.

Hotel Madera ★ The Hotel Madera fancies itself as a kind of eco-conscious *pied-à-terre,* or home away from home, for travelers. Judging from the look of those I saw checking in, these tend toward the earthy, backpack-carrying kind, both international and American. The registration line of four people stretched almost to the door in the afterthought of a lobby. Tiny though it is, the lobby is worth admiring: The registration desk is covered in leather; a hammered copper mobile of abstract leaflike shapes dangles overhead.

Guest rooms are large (this used to be an apartment building), measuring an average 430 square feet. Those on the New Hampshire Avenue side have balconies that offer city views; if you have trouble sleeping, ask for a higher-up room on this side, because you're directly over the restaurant entrance and, in pleasant weather, its popular outdoor cafe. Or you could request a room at the back of the house; those on floors 6 through 10 have pretty good views of Rock Creek Park, Georgetown, and the Washington National Cathedral. All rooms are comfortable and furnished with beds whose wild-looking headboards are giant dark wood panels inset with a patch of vibrant blue padded mohair. Other distinct touches: pillows covered in animal print or satiny fabrics, grass-clothlike wall coverings, and black granite with chrome bathroom vanities. Like many Kimpton Hotels, the Madera offers "specialty" rooms, which here include "Nosh" rooms (studio with kitchenette and grocery shopping service), "Flash" rooms (with personal computer, printer), "Strength" (has a Nautilus machine) and "Cardio" (has a treadmill, or an exercise bike, or elliptical steps) rooms, and "Screening" rooms (equipped with a second TV, DVD player, and a library of DVDs).

The Madera has an excellent restaurant, **Firefly** (p. 159).

1310 New Hampshire Ave. NW (between N and O sts.), Washington, DC 20036. ✆ **800/368-5691** or 202/296-7600. Fax 202/293-2476. www.hotelmadera.com. 82 units. Weekdays and weekends $169–$409 double; add $40 to the going rate for a specialty room. For best rates, call direct to the hotel or go to its website. Extra person $20. Children under 16 stay free in parent's room. Rates include evening wine hour. AE, DC, DISC, MC, V. Parking: $28 plus tax. Metro: Dupont Circle. Pets welcome. **Amenities:** Bar/restaurant (American bistro); access to the posh Sports Club/LA health club at the nearby Ritz-Carlton ($15 per guest per day); 24-hr. concierge; business center; room service (during restaurant hours); same-day laundry service; dry cleaning; 6 rooms for those w/limited mobility, all w/roll-in showers. *In room:* A/C, TV w/pay movies, 2-line cordless phones w/dataports, free Wi-Fi, minibar, coffeemaker w/organic coffee, hair dryer, iron, safe, robes, umbrella, CD player.

Moments All That Jazz

For a pleasurable evening's entertainment, you might need look no farther than the lobby lounge of your own or a nearby hotel. The genre is usually jazz, the performers are top-notch, and the admission is free. So if it's a Sunday night, you might want to plant yourself in the paneled parlor of the **Hotel Tabard Inn** (p. 112) to listen to bassist Victor Dvoskin, often accompanied by a guitarist, play world-class jazz. In the Garden Terrace of the **Four Seasons** (p. 118), Saturday's the best night to catch some cool jazz, performed by the Marshall Keyes trio or another of D.C.'s top musicians with regular gigs at the hotel. In the West End, the **Ritz-Carlton Hotel** (p. 115) features mellow tunes by the likes of the Bertram McLeish Trio Monday through Saturday nights. Order a drink and perhaps a bite to eat, then settle into a comfy lounge chair to enjoy the show.

Hotel Tabard Inn If you favor the offbeat and the personal over brand names and cookie-cutter chains, this might be the place for you. The Tabard Inn, named for the hostelry in Chaucer's *Canterbury Tales,* is actually three Victorian town houses that were joined in 1914 and have operated as an inn ever since. Situated on a quiet street of similarly old dwellings, the Tabard is a well-worn, funky hotel that's looked after by a congenial staff who clearly cherish the place.

The heart of the ground floor is the dark-paneled lounge, with worn furniture, a wood-burning fireplace, the original beamed ceiling, and bookcases. Washingtonians like to come here for a drink, especially in winter, or to linger before or after dining in the charming **Tabard Inn** restaurant (p. 160).

From the lounge, the inn leads you up and down stairs, along dim corridors, and through nooks and crannies to guest rooms. Do you like chartreuse? (Ask for room no. 3.) How about aubergine? (Ask for room no. 11.) Each is different, but those facing N Street are largest and brightest, and some have bay windows. Furnishings are a mix of antiques and flea-market finds. Perhaps the most eccentric room is the spacious top-floor "penthouse," which has skylights, exposed brick walls, an ample living room, and the overall feel of a New York City loft. The inn is not easily accessible to guests with disabilities. Free wireless Internet access is available in most rooms and in the public areas (the inn warns, however, that service is mostly reliable but not guaranteed). Guests have free access to a computer in the lobby.

1739 N St. NW (between 17th and 18th sts.), Washington, DC 20036. ✆ **202/785-1277.** Fax 202/785-6173. www.tabardinn.com. 40 units, 27 with private bathroom (6 with shower only). $107–$137 double with shared bathroom; $158–$218 double with private bathroom. Extra person $15. Rates include continental breakfast. AE, DC, DISC, MC, V. Limited street parking, plus 2 parking garages on N St. Metro: Dupont Circle. Small and confined pets accepted for a $20 fee. **Amenities:** Restaurant (regional American) w/lounge (free live jazz Sun evenings); free access to nearby YMCA (w/extensive facilities that include indoor pool, indoor track, and racquetball/basketball courts); laundry service; fax, iron, hair dryer, and safe available at front desk. *In room:* A/C, dataport, free Wi-Fi.

Jurys Washington Hotel ★ *Value* This hotel gets high marks for convenience (it's right on Dupont Circle), service, and comfort. Open since 2000, the hotel is favored by business groups especially, who like its reasonable rates. A thorough renovation continues into 2008, putting an urban chic spin on guest room appearance and amenities. Among the changes are spa-style bathrooms, with heated marble floors and Kohler rain showerheads equipped with body massage features; luxurious pillow-top mattresses with down comforters, duvet covers, and bolster pillows; and LG flatscreen televisions. Each of the large rooms is furnished with two double beds with firm mattresses, a desk, and a wet-bar alcove. Despite its prime location in a sometimes raucous neighborhood, the hotel's rooms are insulated from the noise. Rooms on higher floors offer the best views of the city and of Dupont Circle. An Irish management company owns this hotel (along with two other properties in Washington, D.C.), and the comfortable and attractive hotel pub, Biddy Mulligan's, proudly features a bar imported from the Emerald Isle. Its American restaurant, Dupont Grille, provides a perfect spot to slurp a cosmo and dine on macadamia nut crusted rack of lamb, while watching an entertaining cast of Dupont Circle characters pass by. Check the hotel's website for lowest rates.

1500 New Hampshire Ave. NW (across from Dupont Circle), Washington, DC 20036. ✆ **877/587-9787** or 202/483-6000. Fax 202/328-3265. www.jurysdoyle.com. 314 units. $99–$349 double; from $600 suite (there are only 5). Extra person $15. Children 17 and under stay free in parent's room. AE, DC, DISC, MC, V. Parking $20. Metro: Dupont Circle. **Amenities:** Restaurant (American); bar; exercise room; 24-hr. concierge; business center; room service (6:30am–midnight); same-day laundry service; dry cleaning; 11 rooms for those w/limited mobility, 4 w/roll-in showers. *In room:* A/C, TV w/pay movies, 2-line phone w/dataport, free Wi-Fi, minibar, coffeemaker, hair dryer, iron, safe.

Topaz Hotel ★ Like the Hotel Rouge, the Topaz is an upscale boutique hotel for those who think young. This hotel seems tamer than the Rouge, but it still has a buzz about it, a pleasant, interesting sort of buzz. The reception area, lobby, and bar flow together, which makes for a party atmosphere in the evenings when the Topaz Bar is awash with an after-work crowd. The bar's worth a look at least, for the decor of velvety settees, zebra-patterned ottomans, and a lighting system that fades in and out.

A whimsical decor rules in the guest rooms, where a refurbishment completed in 2007 transformed rooms with splashes of emerald, sapphire, ruby, and other jewel tones, on wallpaper, down comforter, armoire, and armchair. The rooms are unusually large (in its former life as the Canterbury Hotel, these were "junior suites" and held kitchenettes), and each has an alcove where the desk is placed, and a separate dressing room that holds a dressing table and cube-shaped ottoman. The Topaz pursues a sort of New Age wellness motif; do note the smooth "energy" stones and horoscope placed upon your pillow. You also have the option to book a specialty room: either a "fitness" guest room, which includes a piece of exercise equipment (either a treadmill or a stationary bike) and fitness magazines; or a "yoga" room, which comes with an exercise mat, an instructional tape, padded pillows, special towels, and yoga magazines. Smoking is not permitted in any of the guest rooms.

The Topaz lies on a quiet residential street, whose front-of-the-house windows overlook picturesque town houses.

1733 N St. NW (right next to the Tabard Inn [see above] between 17th and 18th sts.), Washington, DC 20036. ✆ **800/424-2950** or 202/393-3000. Fax 202/785-9581. www.topazhotel.com. 99 units. Weekdays and weekends $139–$409 double; add $40 to rate for specialty rooms. It is very likely that you can get a much lower rate by calling direct to the hotel or by booking a reservation online. Extra person $20. Children under 16 stay free in parent's room. Rates include complimentary morning energy potions. AE, DC, DISC, MC, V. Parking $26 plus tax. Metro: Dupont Circle. Pets welcome. **Amenities:** Bar/restaurant (innovative American w/an Asian influence); access to nearby health club ($5 per guest); 24-hr. concierge; 24-hr. business center; room service (7am–11pm); same-day laundry service; dry cleaning; 5 rooms for those w/limited mobility, 2 w/roll-in showers. *In room:* A/C, TV w/pay movies, 2-line cordless phones w/dataports, free Wi-Fi, minibar, hair dryer, iron, safe, robes, CD player, teapot w/exotic teas.

7 Foggy Bottom/West End

VERY EXPENSIVE

Hotel Palomar ★★ If you like a hotel to be more than simply a place to turn in for the night, you will love the 2-year-old Palomar. This Kimpton Hotel offers a rocking scene nightly in the restaurant's bar/lounge **Urbana** (p. 160), a complimentary wine reception each evening in the lobby, and a warmly whimsical decor in the guest rooms. The hotel lies in the throbbing heart of the fun Dupont Circle neighborhood, full of art galleries, boutiques, and excellent restaurants, and it regularly invites local artists to pop in for the evening wine hour. In fact, the Palomar fancies itself a kind of art gallery, with its creative use of color and design, from the creamy Murano glass chandeliers and displays of handcrafted decorative arts in the lobby, to the splashes of mulberry and magenta, zebrawood, and faux leather finishes in the guest rooms. These are spacious rooms, averaging 520 square feet, and comfortably appointed, with a maneuverable, oversized elliptical desk, an ergonomic mesh chair, and an undulating chaise longue. The bathrooms hold granite-topped vanities and L'Occitane bath products. And even if your only concern is that good night's sleep, you'll be happy here, for soft white Frette linen sheets and duvets make up the plush feather beds. When you do turn in, you'll find on your pillow a card displaying an original artwork, this hotel's signature nightly turndown practice. As at most other Kimpton properties, the Palomar also offers a variety of specialty rooms, which include 18 "Tall" rooms (the beds are 90-in. kings) and 8 "Motion" rooms (each comes with your choice of available in-room exercise equipment).

2121 P St. NW (at 21st St.), Washington, DC 20037. ✆ **877/866-3070** or 202/448-1800. Fax 202/448-1801. www.hotelpalomar-dc.com. 335 units. $189–$469 double; from $500 suite. Book online for best rates. Extra person $30. Children under 16 stay free in parent's room. Rates include evening wine reception and morning coffee (in lobby). AE, DC, DISC, MC, V. Parking $32. Metro: Dupont Circle. Pets welcome. **Amenities:** Restaurant (Italian/Mediterranean); bar/lounge; outdoor (seasonal) lap pool with sun deck and private cabanas; 24-hour fitness center; 24-hour concierge; 24-hour business center; 24-hour room service; same-day laundry and dry cleaning; 16 rooms for those w/limited mobility, 6 with roll-in showers; *In room:* A/C, flatscreen TV with pay movies, multiline cordless phone w/dataports, free Wi-Fi, minibar, hair dryer, iron, safe, robes, umbrella, CD/DVD players.

Park Hyatt, Washington, D.C. ★★ Hotels are always undergoing some form of renewal, though most changes tend not to be all that noticeable to the public. But if you've stayed at the Park Hyatt, Washington, D.C., prior to 2006, you are certainly going to notice the difference now. This luxury brand of the Hyatt family has been reinvented to the tune of $24 million, top-to-bottom, guest rooms to restaurant. Guest rooms first: Still generously sized (the smallest is the "Park" room, at 408 sq. ft.; most are "Park Deluxe" rooms, which measure 618 sq. ft.), these overnight quarters are both homey and handsome. Wood-slat blinds are on the windows, puffy down duvets cover the beds, and decorative features include coffee table books on American culture, like the one in my room full of Annie Leibowitz photo portraits of American musicians. (Here's an idea for a grand, all-American cultural experience: Bunk at this hotel, dine in the hotel's **Blue Duck Tavern** (p. 162), and visit the Smithsonian American Art Museum and National Portrait Gallery (p. 209).) The flatscreen television in the Park Deluxe rooms pivots in the wall to present an antique chessboard on its reverse side (decorative, not functional). Adding pretty color are creamy yellow leather chairs, including one that rocks. Bathrooms are spa-like, with floor, ceiling, and walls of dark gray limestone. Everything is out in the open, from the deep soaking marble tub to its adjoining shower—which is not a stall, but a large corner of the room outfitted with a rain showerhead—to the toilet, situated behind a doorless partition. Shaker-designed wooden trays hold toiletries on the long marble vanity. Parisian parfumeur Blaise Mautin created a fragrance and bathroom amenities specifically for this hotel. American designer Tony Chi is behind the overall new look and feel of this Park Hyatt.

First floor common rooms are equally remarkable, starting with the high-ceilinged lobby, where the lit-up reception area appears like an altar in front of you. To the right of reception are two places you must make time for: first, the tea cellar, complete with a tea humidor for storing the cellar's collection of rare and single estate teas from remote regions of China, Japan, Sri Lanka, and the Himalayas (even if you're not a tea drinker, the cellar is intriguing), and second, the hotel's restaurant, the Blue Duck Tavern, which serves food that's simply out of this world.

2400 M St. NW (at 24th St.), Washington, DC 20037. ✆ **800/778-7477** or 202/789-1234. Fax 202/419-6795. www.parkhyattwashington.com. 215 units. From $350 Park Room double, from $450 Park Deluxe double; from $750 suites. For best rates, go to the hotel's website or call the main reservation number. Extra person $60. Children under 18 stay free in parent's room. Families should ask about the family plan. AE, DC, DISC, MC, V. Parking $35. Metro: Foggy Bottom or Dupont Circle. Pets welcome, with $100 fee per stay. **Amenities:** Restaurant (regional American); lounge; tea cellar; indoor pool (daytime hours); 24-hour fitness center; 24-hour concierge; complimentary Audi sedan service upon availability, Mon–Fri 7–11am; 24-hour business center; 24-hour room service; in-room massage; same day laundry and dry cleaning, with pressing; children's welcome gifts at check-in; 12 rooms for those w/limited mobility, all with roll-in showers. *In room:* A/C, flatscreen HDTV, cordless phone with 2 lines and dataports, complimentary wired Internet access, Wi-Fi ($9.95/day), minibar/fridge, hair dryer, safe, robes.

The Ritz-Carlton, Washington, D.C. ★★★ From the cadre of doormen and valet parking attendants who greet you effusively when you arrive, to the graceful young women in long dresses who swan around you serving cocktails in the bar and lounge, the Ritz staff always looks after you.

The hotel is built around a multitiered Japanese garden and courtyard with reflecting pools and cascading waterfall; guest rooms on the inside of the complex overlook the waterfall or terraced garden, while guest rooms on the outside perimeter view landmarks and cityscapes. Even standard rooms are very large, and richly furnished with a firm king-size bed covered in both a duvet and a bedspread, decorative inlaid wooden furniture, a comfy armchair and ottoman, and very pretty artwork. The marble bathroom is immense, with long counter space, separate bathtub and shower stall, and the toilet in its own room behind a louvered door. The clock radio doubles as a CD player, and the phone features a button for summoning the "technology butler" (a complimentary, 24/7 service for guests with computer questions). Other nice touches in the rooms include an umbrella, windows that open, and an outlet for recharging laptops. Among the different versions of suites available, most are "executives," which include a sitting room and separate bedroom.

Guests enjoy free use of the hotel's fitness center, the two-level, 100,000-square-foot **Sports Club/LA,** which leaves all other hotel health clubs in the dust with its state-of-the-art weight-training equipment and free weights, two regulation-size basketball courts and four squash courts, an indoor heated swimming pool and an aquatics pool with a sun deck, exercise classes, personal trainers, the full-service Splash Spa and Roche Salon, and a restaurant and cafe.

The Ritz's bar and lounge are also exceptionally inviting, with lots of plush upholstered couches and armchairs, a fire blazing in the fireplace in winter, and a pianist playing nightly. The lobby lounge is the setting for daily afternoon tea, jazz trio performances Monday through Saturday evenings, and occasional events, such as the chocolate decadence buffet staged the first Friday of every month.

1150 22nd St. NW (at M St.), Washington, DC 20037. ✆ **800/241-3333** or 202/835-0500. Fax 202/835-1588. www.ritzcarlton.com/hotels/washington_dc. 300 units. $499 double; from $649 suite. No charge for extra person in the room. Ask about discount packages. AE, DC, DISC, MC, V. Valet parking $28. Metro: Foggy Bottom or Dupont Circle. Pets accepted and pampered (no fee). **Amenities:** Restaurant (American); lounge; health club and spa (the best in the city; see above); 24-hr. concierge; business center (open weekdays); 24-hr. fax and currency-exchange services; salon; 24-hr. room service; in-room massage; same-day laundry; dry cleaning w/1-hr. pressing; club level w/5 complimentary food presentations throughout the day (including a chef station each morning to prepare individual requests); 10 rooms for those w/limited mobility, 6 w/roll-in showers. *In room:* A/C, TV w/pay movies, 2-line phone, Wi-Fi ($10/day), minibar/fridge, hair dryer, iron, safe, robes, umbrella, CD player.

MODERATE

George Washington University Inn Rumor has it that this whitewashed brick inn used to be a favorite spot for clandestine trysts for high-society types. These days you're more likely to see Kennedy Center performers, corporate folks, visiting professors, and parents of GW students. The university purchased the hotel (formerly known as the Inn at Foggy Bottom) in 1994 and renovated it. The most recent refurbishment, in 2006, replaced linens and carpeting, wallpaper, and drapes, all in keeping with the guest rooms' traditional greens and blues decor.

Rooms are a little larger and corridors are a tad narrower than those in a typical hotel, and each room includes a roomy dressing chamber. More than one-third of the units are one-bedroom suites. These are especially spacious, with living rooms that hold a sleeper sofa and a TV hidden in an armoire (there's another in the bedroom). The suites, plus the 16 efficiencies, have kitchens. The spaciousness and the kitchen facilities make this a popular choice for families and for long-term guests.

A fairly safe and lovely neighborhood, it's within easy walking distance to Georgetown, the Kennedy Center, and downtown. But keep an eye peeled—you have to pass through wrought-iron gates into a kind of cul-de-sac to find the inn.

Off the lobby is the excellent restaurant, **Notti Bianche,** which opened in spring 2005.

If it's not full, the inn may be willing to offer reduced rates. Mention your affiliation with George Washington University, if you have one, to receive a special "GWU" rate.

824 New Hampshire Ave. NW (between H and I sts.), Washington, DC 20037. ✆ **800/426-4455** or 202/337-6620. Fax 202/298-7499. www.gwuinn.com. 95 units. Weekdays $159–$269 double, $179–$289 efficiency, $199–$309 1-bedroom suite; weekends $139–$209 double, $159–$229 efficiency, $179–$249 1-bedroom suite. Children under 12 stay free in parent's room. AE, DC, DISC, MC, V. Limited parking $22. Metro: Foggy Bottom. **Amenities:** Restaurant (Italian trattoria); complimentary passes to nearby fitness center; room service; coin-op washer/dryers; same-day laundry service; dry cleaning; 5 rooms for those w/limited mobility, 1 w/roll-in shower. *In room:* A/C, TV w/pay movies and Nintendo, 2-line phone w/dataport, free Internet access, fridge, microwave, coffeemaker, hair dryer, iron, safe, robes, slippers, umbrella, CD player.

One Washington Circle Hotel Built in 1960, this building was converted into a hotel in 1976, making it the city's first all-suite hotel property. The George Washington University purchased the hotel in 2001, closed the place down and totally renovated it, reopening in 2002. Five types of suites are available, ranging in size from 390 to 710 square feet. The one-bedroom suites have a sofa bed and dining area; all rooms are spacious, evince a contemporary look, and have walkout balconies, some overlooking the Circle and its centerpiece, the statue of George Washington. But keep in mind that across the Circle is George Washington University Hospital's emergency room entrance, which is busy with ambulance traffic; even with the installation of double-paned windows, you may still hear sirens, so ask for a suite on the L Street side if you desire a quieter room. Ninety percent of the suites have full kitchens, each with an oven, a microwave, and a refrigerator; the rest have kitchenettes.

Clientele is mostly corporate, but families like the outdoor pool, in-house restaurant, prime location near Georgetown and the Metro, and that full kitchen. Call the hotel directly for best rates. And mention a GWU affiliation if you have one and you may receive a reduced rate. The well-reviewed **Circle Bistro** serves contemporary bistro food.

One Washington Circle NW (between 22nd and 23rd sts. NW), Washington, DC 20037. ✆ **800/424-9671** or 202/872-1680. Fax 202/887-4989. www.thecirclehotel.com. 151 units. Smallest suites: weekdays $159–$299, weekends $139–$199; largest suites: weekdays $199–$339, weekends $179–$239. Call hotel to get best rates. Extra person: $20. Children under 12 stay free in parent's room. AE, DC, MC, V. Parking $25. Metro: Foggy Bottom. **Amenities:** Restaurant (traditional bistro w/Mediterranean flair); bar; outdoor pool; on-site fitness center; concierge; room service (7am–midnight weekends, 7am–11pm weekdays); coin-op washer/dryers; same-day laundry service; dry cleaning; 5 rooms for those w/limited mobility, 1 w/roll-in shower. *In room:* A/C, TV w/pay movies and Nintendo, 2-line cordless phones, free Internet access, full kitchens (in 90% of suites, w/oven, fridge, microwave), coffeemaker, hair dryer, iron, robes, CD player.

The River Inn ★ The River Inn lies on a quiet residential street of old town houses, a 5-minute walk from the Kennedy Center, and a 10-minute walk from Georgetown. The inn has always been a sweet little secret, all the more so since a 2003 redesign. In the guest rooms, tall, milk-chocolate–brown leather headboards crown the beds; comfortable armchairs have soft leather footstools; the armoire is ebony; the general color scheme is coppery gold, rust, and brown; and the cool chaise longue unfolds into a sofa bed. (The architectural design team, Adamstein and Demetriou, is a married couple famous in D.C. for the many restaurant interiors the two have fashioned, from Zengo to Zaytinya.) Suites are spacious and all hold both a bed and the sleeper lounge, a large dressing room, and a separate kitchen equipped with the works, from gas stovetop to pots and pans. Free Internet access is available in every guest room. All but 31 suites combine the bedroom and living room areas, and include a 6-foot desk that doubles as work space and dining table in a corner off the kitchen. Those 31 suites are roomy one-bedrooms, with an expansive living room (with sleep sofa) and a separate bedroom that holds a king-size bed and a second TV. Best are the one-bedroom suites on the upper floors that have views of the Potomac River. You can even spy the Washington Monument from some of the rooms, like no. 804, for example.

Many corporate and government guests book long-term stays and benefit from special rates and amenities. The River Inn has a modest exercise room and a tiny (50-seat) and rather nice and moderately priced restaurant, **Dish+Drinks.** A complimentary *Washington Post* is delivered to your door daily. Check the hotel's website or call directly to the hotel for best rates. Try to call between the hours of 8am and 7pm to reach one of the hotel's personable and helpful reservations staff; only two people answer those calls, so you may have to wait, but it's worth it. (At nighttime, a remote call center books reservations.)

924 25th St. NW (between K and I sts.), Washington, DC 20037. ✆ **800/424-2741** or 202/337-7600. Fax 202/337-6520. www.theriverinn.com. 125 units. Peak season weekdays $219–$299 double, $269–$349 1-bedroom suite; off-peak season weekday $159–$199 double, $209–$249 1-bedroom suite. Peak-season weekends $149–$199 double, $199–$249 1-bedroom suite; off-peak-season weekends $99–$149 double, $149–$199 1-bedroom suite. Extra person $20. Children under 18 stay free in parent's room. AE, DC, DISC, MC, V. Parking $20. Metro: Foggy Bottom. **Amenities:** Restaurant (American); bar; small fitness center w/treadmill, stair climber, stationary bike, and other equipment; room service during restaurant hours; coin-op laundry; same-day laundry/dry cleaning; 2 rooms for those w/limited mobility. *In room:* A/C, TV w/pay movies, 2-line phone w/dataport, free Internet access, fridge, microwave, coffeemaker, hair dryer, iron, safe, robes, slippers, umbrella.

8 Georgetown

VERY EXPENSIVE

Four Seasons ★★★ An immense renovation completed in autumn 2005 brought big changes to this Four Seasons, starting with the gutting and redesign of all of the guest rooms in the hotel's main building. Guest rooms are fewer now, but much larger, measuring between 500 and 700 square feet. They feature the handiwork of world-famous interior designer Pierre-Yves Rochon, who transformed the landmark Four Seasons Georges V Hotel in Paris and created the distinctive look of the Sofitel Lafayette Square Hotel, right here in Washington. No sooner was the renovation complete than the Mobil Travel Guide awarded its coveted five stars to the Four Seasons, the only hotel so recognized in the city. The new decor includes custom-crafted furniture and color schemes of either celadon or purple. Most rooms have sleeper sofas, and all have 32-inch plasma-screen televisions. Bathrooms are more spacious, too, and very prettily turned out in pear- and maple-wood accents, with a deep soaking tub separate from the shower. The hotel's lobby and lower levels, which hold the restaurant, conference room, spa, and exercise center, stayed open during the renovation, and remain untouched.

The hotel's auxiliary wing, which debuted in 1999, encompasses 25 guest rooms and 35 suites, each offering soundproof accommodations, an office equipped with a fax machine, at least three telephones with two-line speakers, portable telephones, and headsets for private TV listening.

Despite all that's new, certain Four Seasons characteristics hold true: The hotel continues to attract the rich, the famous, and the powerful—people used to being catered to. Staff members are trained to know the names, preferences, and even allergies of guests, and repeat clientele rely on this discreet attention.

The hotel sits at the mouth of Georgetown, backing up against Rock Creek Park and the C&O Canal. Original avant-garde artwork from the personal collection of former owner William Louis-Dreyfus (yes, Julia's dad) continues to hang in every room and public space, thanks to an agreement negotiated by the new owner. Transmitters installed throughout the hotel allow you wireless connection to the Internet on your laptop wherever you go in the hotel. The Four Seasons is always devising fresh ways to pamper its guests, like the popular "On the Road to Room Service," which allows guests who have been picked up by the hotel's car service to place a room-service order from the limo, and have the meal delivered to their guest room moments after they arrive.

2800 Pennsylvania Ave. NW (which becomes M St. a block farther along), Washington, DC 20007. ✆ **800/332-3442** or 202/342-0444. Fax 202/944-2076. www.fourseasons.com/washington. 211 units. Weekdays $595–$725 double, $895–$6,500 suite; weekends from $395 double, from $495 suite. Extra person $40. Children under 18 stay free in parent's room. AE, DC, DISC, MC, V. Parking $39. Metro: Foggy Bottom. Pets accepted, up to 15 lb. **Amenities:** Formal restaurant (regional American); lounge (for afternoon tea, cocktails); extensive state-of-the-art fitness club and spa w/personal trainers, lap pool, Vichy shower, hydrotherapy, facials, and synchronized massage (2 people work on you at the same time); children's program (various goodies provided but no organized activities); 24-hr. concierge; complimentary sedan service daily within the District; 24-hr. business center; salon; 24-hr. room service; in-room massage; babysitting; same-day laundry service; dry cleaning; 7 rooms for those w/limited mobility, some of which have roll-in showers. *In room:* A/C, TV w/pay movies and Web access, Wi-Fi ($10/day), minibar, coffeemaker, hair dryer, iron, safe, robes, high-tech CD player.

The Ritz-Carlton Georgetown ★★ Staff at area hotels have taken to calling this hotel the "Baby Ritz," to distinguish it from the other, larger Ritz on 22nd Street. The moniker is the only cute thing about the hotel, however. The Georgetown Ritz is a sophisticated property, exclusively small (only 86 rooms), and designed to feel like a refuge in the middle of wild and woolly Georgetown. The hotel opened in April 2003, after years of construction. Look for the 130-foot-high smokestack to guide you to the hotel, which is built on the site of a historic incinerator and incorporates the smokestack into the design. In fact, you can have a meeting at the bottom of the smokestack, which, obviously, is inoperative. The lobby, whose brick walls are original to the incinerator, always smells of a recently lit fire, even on a summer day. (There's a large fireplace at one end of the lobby.) The restaurant is called "Fahrenheit," the bar is called "Degrees," and the signature drink is the "Fahrenheit 5 Martini." To get to your room, you have to go down one level from the lobby, and travel along a wide, cavelike corridor with vaulted brick ceiling, to a special elevator. You must have a key card to operate the elevator, so anyone visiting you at the hotel must either be escorted by a staff person or be met by you. Rooms are very large, decorated in serious colors of moss green, gold, and a burnt red, with lots of dark wood furniture and accents. Ritz-Carlton hotels have the best bathrooms, and this property is no exception: spacious, marble vanities, separate tub and shower, fancy wood shelving.

3100 South St. NW (at 31st St., between K and M sts.), Washington, DC 20007. ✆ **800/241-3333** or 202/912-4100. Fax 202/912-4199. www.ritzcarlton.com/hotels/georgetown. 86 units. From $499 double; suites start at $749. No charge for extra person in the room. Check website or 800 number for weekend packages and specials. AE, DC, DISC, MC, V. Valet parking $32. Metro: Foggy Bottom, with Georgetown shuttle bus connection. Small (under 30 lb.) pets accepted (no fee). **Amenities:** Restaurant (seasonal American); bar; lobby lounge; fitness room (complimentary) and spa; 24-hr. concierge; fax and some currency-exchange services; 24-hr. room service; in-room massage; same-day laundry service; dry cleaning; 1-hr. pressing; 3 rooms for those w/limited mobility, all w/roll-in showers. *In room:* A/C, TV w/pay movies and Web access, 2-line phone, Wi-Fi ($10/day), minibar, hair dryer, iron, safe, robes, umbrella, CD player.

EXPENSIVE

Georgetown Inn This hotel is in the thick of Georgetown. Come the third weekend in May, the hotel is full of the proud parents of students graduating from blocks-away Georgetown University. (The hotel books up 2 years in advance for graduation weekend.) Its location is what best recommends the hotel, so if you're a shopper, visiting the university, or conducting business in Georgetown, this is a good pick.

A million-dollar renovation completed in 2006 refurbished the lobby, corridors, and guest rooms. Guest rooms now have new upholstery, beds with thick mattresses, and drapes. The hotel's general style remains traditional American, heavy on the dark woods with pretty sage green accents in fabrics. About one-third of the rooms hold two beds, the others have a king or queen bed; some rooms connect with the 10 suites, helpful to families traveling with children. Ask for an "executive room" if you'd like a sitting area with pullout sofa, and extra conveniences like a reading lamp over the bed. Best are those 10 one-bedroom suites, in which bedroom and large living room are separate. The bathrooms have only showers (some also have bidets), no tub.

The Daily Grill has an outpost here, offering the same generous portions of American food served at its original D.C. location, at 1200 18th St. NW.

1310 Wisconsin Ave. NW (between N and O sts.), Washington, DC 20007. ✆ **800/368-5922** or 202/333-8900. Fax 202/333-8308. www.georgetowncollection.com. 96 units. Peak season $239–$399 double weekdays, $189–$339 weekends; off-peak season from $159 double weekdays, from $129 double weekends; suites from $345. Ask about promotional rates. Extra person $20. Children under 12 stay free in parent's room. AE, DC, DISC, MC, V. Valet parking $28 plus tax. Metro: Foggy Bottom, with Georgetown shuttle bus connection. **Amenities:** Restaurant (American); bar; access to an outdoor pool; exercise room, plus free access to nearby health club and spa; room service during restaurant hours; same-day laundry service; dry cleaning; 4 rooms for those w/limited mobility, all w/roll-in showers. *In room:* A/C, TV w/pay movies and Nintendo, 2-line phones w/dataport, Wi-Fi ($9.95/day), hair dryer, iron.

MODERATE

Georgetown Suites ★ This hotel was designed to meet the needs of business travelers on extended visits, but its casual atmosphere and kitchen suites work well for families, too. The hotel offers quite a good deal for your money: friendly service; clean, bright, and spacious lodging; and up-to-date amenities. It has two locations, each within a block of the other.

The main building, which I prefer, is the one on 30th Street (a quiet residential street that's only steps away from Georgetown's action). This building offers a large lobby for hanging out; it almost feels like a student lounge, with the TV going; games, books, magazines, and daily newspapers scattered across tabletops in front of love seats and chairs; and a cappuccino machine on the counter. In the morning, an extensive breakfast, featuring everything from waffles to fresh pastries, is laid out here. By contrast, the property on 29th Street (known as the "Harbor Building"), situated right next to the Whitehurst Freeway, is much noisier, and has a very small lobby (although you can linger outside in the brick courtyard, where there are flowering plants and Victorian white wooden benches). Continental breakfast is served there, too, in the lobby.

Accommodations at both locations have living rooms, dining areas, and fully equipped kitchens. In 2006, the hotel replaced the bedding in every room with big mattresses and fluffy duvets covering down comforters. An upgrade in 2007 replaced all televisions with flatscreen models. About half of the units are studios and half are one-bedroom suites. Glass-topped tables, chrome-framed chairs, and pastel-striped fabrics figure prominently in the decor. The biggest and best suites are the three two-level, two-bedroom town houses attached to the main building. These feature modern furnishings, sunken Jacuzzi tubs and double sinks in the bathrooms, TVs with VCRs, CD players, and other deluxe amenities. The town houses have their own doors on 29th Street, through which you may exit; to enter a town house, you must go through the hotel, as your key will not unlock the 29th Street door. This building also has two penthouse suites, which have their own terraces overlooking the rooftops of Georgetown.

1111 30th St. NW (just below M St.) and 1000 29th St. NW (at K St.), Washington, DC 20007. ✆ **800/348-7203** or 202/298-1600. Fax 202/333-2019. www.georgetownsuites.com. 220 units. Weekdays $155 studio, $215 1-bedroom suite; weekends $155 studio, $185 1-bedroom suite. Penthouse suites from $350, town houses from $425. Rollaway or sleeper sofa $10 extra. Rates include continental breakfast. AE, DC, DISC, MC, V. Limited parking $15. Metro: Foggy Bottom, with a 15-min. walk. **Amenities:** Small exercise room; business center w/computers and free Wi-Fi; coin-op laundry; same-day laundry service; dry cleaning; 2 rooms for those w/limited mobility, both w/roll-in showers. *In room:* A/C, TV, 2-line phone w/dataport, free Wi-Fi, full kitchen (w/fridge, coffeemaker, microwave, and dishwasher), hair dryer, iron, safe.

9 Woodley Park

VERY EXPENSIVE

Wardman Park Marriott Hotel ★ This is Washington's biggest hotel, resting on 16 acres just down the street from the National Zoo and several good restaurants. Its size and location (the Woodley Park–Zoo Metro station is literally at its doorstep) make it a good choice for conventions, tour groups, and individual travelers.

From the outside, the hotel resembles a college campus: There's an old part, built in 1918, whose entrance is draped by stately trees, and a new part, preceded by a great

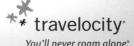

green lawn. The oldest section is the nicest, though it houses only a fraction of the hotel's rooms: about 100, each with high ceilings, ornate crown moldings, and an assortment of antique French and English furnishings. This was once an apartment building whose residents included presidents Hoover, Eisenhower, and Johnson (before they were presidents), as well as actors Marlene Dietrich and Douglas Fairbanks, Jr., and author Gore Vidal. The hotel, at year's end 2007, was just putting the final touches on a major renovation of all guest rooms and public spaces. Expect a fresh look and up-to-date amenities: multilayered Marriott brand bedding; flatscreen TVs; long desks with high-backed chairs; new carpeting, wall-coverings, and bathrooms fixtures—the works. The Wardman Park now has one fine restaurant, the Stone's Throw, which includes four separate dining areas, a chef's table, and a bar. Harry's Bar and Starbucks remain, but now both offer outdoor seating in the center of beds of blooming flowers—especially pleasant in spring. Also brand new is the state-of-the-art fitness center. Wireless Internet access is available in the Lobby Lounge, Starbucks, and the atrium.

2660 Woodley Rd. NW (at Connecticut Ave. NW), Washington, DC 20008. ✆ **800/228-9290** or 202/328-2000. Fax 202/234-0015. www.marriotthotels.com/wasdt. About 1,300 units. Weekdays $309 double; weekends $119–$289 double; $350–$2,500 suite. Children under 18 stay free in parent's room. AE, DC, DISC, MC, V. Valet parking $24, self-parking $19. Metro: Woodley Park–Zoo. Pets under 20 lb. accepted, but charges may apply; call for details. **Amenities:** Restaurant (American); pub (serves meals); deli/pastry shop; lobby bar; Starbucks; outdoor heated pool w/sun deck; well-equipped fitness center; concierge; business center; salon; room service (6am–1am); in-room massage; babysitting; coin-op washer/dryers; same-day laundry service; dry cleaning; concierge-level rooms; 32 rooms for those w/limited mobility, 10 w/roll-in showers. *In room:* A/C, TV w/pay movies, 2-line phone w/dataport, Internet access ($9.95/day), coffeemaker, hair dryer, iron, safe.

EXPENSIVE

Omni Shoreham Hotel ★ *Kids* This is Woodley Park's *other* really big hotel, although with 834 rooms, the Omni Shoreham is still about 500 short of the behemoth Marriott Wardman Park. And it's all the more appealing for it, since it's not quite so overwhelming as the Marriott. Its design—wide corridors, vaulted ceilings and archways, and arrangements of pretty sofas and armchairs in the lobby and public spaces—endows the Shoreham with the air of a grand hotel. The Omni rightfully boasts its status as the city's largest AAA four-diamond hotel, as well as its membership in Historic Hotels of America. Guest rooms evince a certain elegance and they remain twice the size of your average hotel room. A summer 2007 renovation replaced bedding in every guest room with thick pillow-top mattresses and old model televisions with flatscreen versions. The hotel sits on 11 acres overlooking Rock Creek Park and beyond. Its location and the gorgeous landscaping heighten a resort ambience. Insist on a parkside room, if one is available, and the higher up and more central, the better. Though a trifle smaller, these lodgings are quieter and offer those spectacular views—you can even spot the Washington Monument from some rooms.

With its 22 meeting rooms and seven ballrooms (some of which open to terraces overlooking the park!), the hotel is popular as a meeting and convention venue. Leisure travelers, especially families, appreciate the Shoreham for its large outdoor swimming pool; its proximity to the National Zoo, excellent restaurants, and the Woodley Park–Zoo Metro station; and the immediate access to biking, hiking, and jogging paths through Rock Creek Park. The Omni offers rental bikes, jogging trail maps, a wildlife observation deck, bird charts, hammocks, and assorted other amenities to help you enjoy its park location.

Children receive a goodie bag at check-in that includes coloring books, puzzles, playing cards, postcards, and candy. You can walk to the more hip neighborhoods of Adams-Morgan and Dupont Circle from the hotel; the stroll to Dupont Circle, taking you over the bridge that spans Rock Creek Park, is especially nice (and safe at night, too).

Built in 1930, the Shoreham has been the scene of inaugural balls for every president since FDR. Do you believe in ghosts? Ask about Room no. 870, the haunted suite (available for $3,000 a night).

2500 Calvert St. NW (near Connecticut Ave.), Washington, DC 20008. ✆ **800/843-6664** or 202/234-0700. Fax 202/265-7972. www.omnishorehamhotel.com. 834 units. $199–$359 double; suites from $350 and way up. Call the hotel directly for best rates. Extra person $30. Children under 18 stay free in parent's room. AE, DC, DISC, MC, V. Valet parking $30, self-parking $23. Metro: Woodley Park–Zoo. Pets allowed, $50 cleaning fee. **Amenities:** Restaurant (continental; terrace overlooks Rock Creek Park); gourmet carryout; bar/lounge (serves light fare); fitness center and spa w/heated outdoor pool, separate kids' pool, and whirlpool; concierge; travel/sightseeing desk; ATM; business center; shops; 24-hr. room service; massage; same-day laundry service; dry cleaning; children's gifts; 41 rooms for those w/limited mobility, half w/roll-in showers. *In room:* A/C, TV w/pay movies and Nintendo, 2-line phone w/dataport, Wi-Fi ($9.95/day), coffeemaker, hair dryer, iron, robes.

INEXPENSIVE

In addition to the Woodley Park Guest House, listed below, you might consider the Woodley Park location of the **Kalorama Guest House,** at 2700 Cathedral Ave. NW (entrance on 27th St.; ✆ **800/974-9101** or 202/328-0860; fax 202/328-8730; www.kaloramaguesthouse.com), which has 18 units, 12 with private bathrooms. Rates are $140 for a double with a shared bathroom, $155 to $185 for a double with private bathroom, and include an expansive breakfast. A communal television and telephone are available in the parlor; individual guest rooms do not provide TV or telephone at this location. Free Wi-Fi access is available in the common rooms of the main house. Very limited parking (only two spots) is available for $15, and the Woodley Park–Zoo Metro stop is nearby. See p. 107 for the full listing for the main location of the Kalorama Guest House in Adams-Morgan for more information.

Woodley Park Guest House This charming, 18-room B&B offers clean, comfortable, and cozy lodging; inexpensive rates; a super location; and a personable staff. How's that for a recommendation? Four local couples bought the 100-year-old property in 2000, gutted it, and made the place over. Guests hail from around the globe, a fact which inspired the owners to add an actual globe to the breakfast room; it's common practice for people sitting across the table from each other in the morning to go over to the globe and point out exactly where they live: the Arctic Circle, Brazil, Seattle—visitors come from all over, says co-owner Courtney Lodico.

Special features of the guesthouse include a wicker-furnished, tree-shaded front porch; exposed, century-old brick walls; beautiful antiques (mostly purchased from Antique Row in Kensington, Maryland; see chapter 8 for information about these shops); and breathtaking original art. (The innkeepers buy works only from artists who have stayed at the guesthouse, so the art is diffuse rather than profuse, and each piece quite different.) Rooms have either one or two twins, one double, or one queen bed, each covered with a pretty chenille spread or quilt. An intimate alternative to the grand 1,200-room Marriott Wardman Park hotel directly across the street, the guesthouse nevertheless benefits from its proximity to the big hotel, because it's able to offer lodgers quick access to airport shuttles and taxis and views of the Wardman Park's beautifully landscaped gardens. Meanwhile, the Woodley Park–Zoo Metro

Finds A Cool Inn in a Hot Neighborhood

Spring 2005 witnessed the opening of the sophisticated **Georgetown Hill Inn** (1832 Wisconsin Ave. NW, ✆ **202/298-6021**; www.georgetownhillinn.com), whose eight suites reside above the popular Café Divan, at the northern tip of Georgetown. (Cafe owner Cavit Ozturk also owns the inn.) These one- and two-bedroom suites are sveltely angled into the unusual contours of the triangularly shaped building and furnished with Italian, German, and French designs: Think suede sofas and cool light fixtures. Bathrooms are marble; televisions are plasma; kitchens are stainless steel, compact, and well equipped. The feel of the place is at once homey and haute. Rates run from $250 to $380 per night. This part of Georgetown is quieter and less crowded, yet full of excellent restaurants, beginning with Café Divan. You're only a 5- or 10-minute walk from the heart of Georgetown, but oh what a happy difference that little distance makes!

stop is literally catty-cornered to the inn, Connecticut Avenue and its good restaurants 1 block away, and Rock Creek Park and the National Zoo only a few minutes farther than that.

Note: If this inn is booked, ask about the innkeepers' newest location, a spectacular, turn-of-the-20th-century mansion at 2224 R St. NW, along Embassy Row, 3 blocks from the Dupont Circle Metro station. After completely renovating the mansion, the owners opened the **Embassy Circle Inn** (✆ **877/232-7744** or 202/232-7744; www.embassycircle.com) in spring 2007. Access the website to get a sense of the elegant accommodations, including 10 spacious guest rooms, each with private bathroom, and magnificent common rooms. Rates run $200 to $260.

2647 Woodley Rd. NW (at Connecticut Ave. NW), Washington, DC 20008. ✆ **866/667-0218** or 202/667-0218. Fax 202/667-1080. www.woodleyparkguesthouse.com. 18 units, 11 with private bathroom (shower only), 7 (6 single rooms, 1 double) with shared bathroom. $95 single; $110 double with shared bathroom; $140–$195 double with private bathroom. Rates include continental breakfast. AE, MC, V. On-site parking $16. Metro: Woodley Park–Zoo. (Well-behaved) children over 12. **Amenities:** Laundry and ironing service. *In room:* A/C, phone w/voicemail and dataports, free high-speed Internet access.

6

Where to Dine

Each year brings an explosion of promising new restaurants to the capital, but this year's crop seems especially noteworthy. The chef/owner of what I consider the city's best restaurant, Michel Richard of **Citronelle,** in Georgetown, has opened **Central,** an American/French brasserie on Pennsylvania Avenue. Robert Wiedmaier, whose high-end, West End dining room, **Marcel's,** always gets high marks for its elegant Belgian/French cuisine, is doing a brisk business at his more casual, most delicious, **Beck's,** on K St. And superman Jose Andres, he of **Jaleo, Café Atlantico, Zaytinya,** and **minibar,** has moved his Mexican **Oyamel** from suburban Virginia to the heart of the Penn Quarter neighborhood, which means that D.C. finally has an authentic Mexican restaurant (even if Andres is a Spaniard).

In all, Washington has about 2,000 restaurants, offering irresistible tastes of world cuisines for every budget. Space constraints limit me to review a mere fraction—about 100. I've included all the above mentioned restaurants, as well as old faithfuls, little sandwich places, neighborhood joints, special occasion destinations, intimate eateries, and party-hearty spots, to cover every type of dining experience you might desire.

If a place beckons, call ahead for **reservations,** especially for Saturday night. More and more restaurants are affiliated with an online reservation service called **www.opentable.com**, so you can also reserve your table online.

If you wait until the last minute to make a reservation, expect to dine really early, say 5:30 or 6pm, or after 9:30pm. Or you can sit at the bar and eat, which can be more of a culinary treat than you might imagine: Some of the best restaurants, including Palena, Citronelle, and PS7's, offer a reasonably priced bar menu. See "A Seat at the Bar," p. 172.

Better yet, consider a restaurant that doesn't take reservations. This practice seems to be on the upswing and works for places like Pesce and Lauriol Plaza, where the atmosphere is casual, the wait can become part of the experience, and the food is worth standing in line for.

Few places require men to wear a jacket and tie; I've made a special note in the listings for those places that do. If you're driving, call ahead to inquire about valet parking, complimentary or otherwise—on Washington's crowded streets, this service can be a true bonus.

I've listed the closest Metro station to each restaurant only when it's within walking distance of that restaurant. The closest Metro stop to Georgetown is the Blue Line's Foggy Bottom station, where you can hop on the Georgetown Metro Connection shuttle bus for a short ride to Georgetown.

ABOUT THE PRICES

I've selected a range of menus and prices in the major "restaurant" neighborhoods of Washington. Restaurant groupings are first by location, then alphabetically in each price category. Keep in mind that the price categories refer to dinner prices, but some very expensive restaurants offer affordable lunches, early-bird dinners, tapas, or bar meals. The prices within each review refer to the cost of individual entrees, not the entire meal. I've used the following price categories: **Very Expensive** (main courses at dinner average more than $30); **Expensive** ($20 to $30); **Moderate** ($10 to $19); and **Inexpensive** ($10 and under).

1 Best Dining Bets

- **Best for Romance:** The **1789** (p. 165) is renowned for its romantic ambience—this is where Nicole Kidman brought beau Keith Urban on his 38th birthday. The five dining rooms are cozy dens—complete with historical prints on the walls, silk-shaded brass oil lamps on tables, and, come winter, fires crackling in the fireplaces. You'll want to dress up, but don't worry, the 1789 isn't at all stuffy. And if the oyster and champagne stew with Smithfield ham and walnuts doesn't put your date in the mood for love, nothing will. Other worthy contenders: **Taberna del Alabardero** (p. 150) and **Palena** (p. 172).
- **Best for Business: Charlie Palmer Steak** (p. 129), conveniently located within a walk of the Capitol, is a favorite spot for expense-account lobbyists and lawyers, who enjoy its great bar, private rooms, cleverly laid out seating that allows for discreet conversations, and fine cuts of steak. And then there's **The Caucus Room** (p. 135), where there's always a whole lot of handshaking going on.
- **Best for Regional Cuisine:** The **Blue Duck Tavern** (p. 162) pays homage to the tastes of various American regional cuisines by stating the provenance of each dish right there on the menu: the seasonal farm vegetables are from the Tuscarora Co-op, in Pennsylvania; the duck is from Crescent Farms, in New York. **Johnny's Half Shell** (p. 131), meanwhile, is the place to go for superb Eastern Shore delicacies: crab cakes, crab imperial, soft-shell crab. While Washington doesn't have its own cuisine, per se, its central location within the Mid-Atlantic/Chesapeake Bay region gives it license to lay claim to these local favorite foods. And nobody does 'em better than Johnny's.
- **Best Decor:** The **Willard Room,** in the historic Willard Hotel, stands out for its elegance. Its expansive dining room has a two-story-high ceiling, oak-paneled walls, enormous windows hung with shimmery drapes, green marble columns, beautifully upholstered chairs, and tables placed well apart from each other. The service and the food match the decor. See p. 138.
- **Best Haute Cuisine:** Two restaurants vie for this title: **CityZen** (p. 130) and **Michel Richard Citronelle** (p. 165). Chef Eric Ziebold came to CityZen from the renowned French Laundry, in Napa Valley; his culinary skills can take a simple mushroom and transform it (fry it, add truffles) into a spiritual experience. Likewise, Michel Richard is an artist in the kitchen, creating heavenly foods using cuttlefish, pig's feet, foie gras—or really, any ingredient he so chooses.

- **Best Mexican Restaurant:** Jose Andres has added another top draw to his restaurant fiefdom: **Oyamel,** where the tableside-churned guacamole is made to your specifications of spiciness and the menu features items you won't see on offer at any other of D.C.'s Mexican cantinas, like the *"cochinita pibil con cebolla en escabeche"* (Yucatan-style pit-barbecued pork with pickled red onion and Mexican sour orange), hmmmmm. See p. 147.
- **Best French Cuisine:** You can go in two directions here. For exquisite, upscale French cuisine, consider Michel Richard's **Citronelle** (p. 165), **Marcel's** (p. 164), **Palena** (p. 172), and **Gerard's Place** (p. 152). Not only are these the best French restaurants, but they are among the top 10 restaurants in the city, period. For French classics, with Moulin Rouge ambience, check out **La Chaumiere** (p. 169), whose nightly specials and rustic decor have been attracting regulars for more than 30 years, and two charming new bistros, the **Café du Parc** (p. 144), and Michel Richard's **Central** (p. 140).
- **Best Italian Cuisine: Tosca** (p. 138) is a winner, serving fine and unusual dishes derived from the chef's northern Italian upbringing. At **Obelisk** (p. 158), chef/owner Peter Pastan crafts elegantly simple and delicious food in a pleasantly sparse room.
- **Best Pizza:** At **Pizzeria Paradiso,** peerless chewy-crusted pies are baked in an oak-burning oven and crowned with delicious toppings; you'll find great salads and sandwiches on fresh-baked focaccia here, too. See p. 161.
- **Best for "Taste of Washington" Experience:** Eat lunch at **The Monocle** (p. 132) and you're bound to see a Supreme Court justice, congressman, or senator dining here, too. For some down-home and delicious Washington fun, sit at the counter at **Ben's Chili Bowl** (p. 155), and chat with the owners and your neighbor over a chili dog or plate of blueberry pancakes; the place is an institution, and you can stop by anytime—it's open for breakfast, lunch, and dinner.

2 Restaurants by Cuisine

AMERICAN/NEW AMERICAN

Acadiana ★ (Penn Quarter, $$$, p. 138)
Ben's Chili Bowl (U Street Corridor, $, p. 155)
Blue Duck Tavern ★★ (West End, $$$$, p. 162)
Butterfield 9 ★★ (Penn Quarter, $$$$, p. 135)
Café Saint-Ex ★ (U St. Corridor, $$, p. 155)
Cashion's Eat Place ★★ (Adams-Morgan, $$$, p. 156)
Central ★★ (Penn Quarter, $$$, p. 140)
CityZen ★★★ (Capitol Hill, $$$$, p. 130)
Clyde's of Georgetown (Georgetown, $$, p. 169)
Corduroy ★★ (Midtown, $$$, p. 151)
Creme Café ★ (U St. Corridor, $$, p. 155)
DC Coast ★ (Midtown, $$$, p. 152)
Equinox ★★ (Midtown, $$$$, p. 149)
Firefly ★ (Dupont Circle, $$$, p. 159)
Hank's Oyster Bar ★ (Dupont Circle, $$, p. 161)
Hook ★ (Georgetown, $$$, p. 167)
Johnny's Half Shell ★★ (Capitol Hill, $$$, p. 131)

Key to Abbreviations: $$$$ = Very Expensive $$$ = Expensive $$ = Moderate $ = Inexpensive

Kinkead's ★★ (Foggy Bottom, $$$$, p. 163)
Komi ★★★ (Dupont Circle, $$$, p. 159)
Le Bon Café (Capitol Hill, $, p. 134)
Mendocino Grille and Wine Bar ★ (Georgetown, $$$, p. 168)
The Monocle (Capitol Hill, $$$, p. 132)
Old Ebbitt Grill (Penn Quarter, $$, p. 147)
Oval Room ★ (Midtown, $$$, p. 153)
Palena ★★★ (Cleveland Park, $$$$, p. 172)
Poste ★ (Penn Quarter, $$$, p. 142)
PS7's ★★ (Penn Quarter, $$$, p. 142)
1789 ★★★ (Georgetown, $$$$, p. 165)
Sonoma ★ (Capitol Hill, $$, p. 134)
Tabard Inn ★★ (Dupont Circle, $$$, p. 160)
Vidalia ★★ (Midtown, $$$$, p. 151)
Willard Room ★ (Penn Quarter, $$$$, p. 138)
Zola ★★ (Penn Quarter, $$$, p. 143)

ASIAN FUSION
Café Asia (Midtown, $, p. 154)
Teaism (Dupont Circle, $, p. 162)
TenPenh ★ (Penn Quarter, $$$, p. 143)
Zengo ★ (Penn Quarter, $$$, p. 143)

AUSTRIAN
Leopold's Kafe & Konditorei ★ (Georgetown, $$, p. 170)

BARBECUE
Old Glory Barbecue (Georgetown, $$, p. 170)

BELGIAN
Brasserie Beck ★★ (Midtown, $$, p. 153)
Belga Café ★ (Capitol Hill, $$$, p. 130)

CHINESE
Ching Ching Cha (Georgetown, $, p. 170)
City Lights of China (Dupont Circle, $$, p. 161)
Tony Cheng's Seafood Restaurant ★ (Penn Quarter, $, p. 148)

ETHIOPIAN
Meskerem (Adams-Morgan, $, p. 158)
Zed's (Georgetown, $, p. 170)

FRENCH
Bistro Bis ★★ (Capitol Hill, $$$, p. 131)
Bistro D'Oc ★ (Penn Quarter, $$, p. 144)
Bistrot du Coin (Dupont Circle, $$, p. 160)
Bistrot Lepic ★ (Georgetown, $$$, p. 166)
Café du Parc ★ (Penn Quarter, $$, p. 144)
Central ★★ (Penn Quarter, $$$, p. 140)
Gerard's Place ★★ (Midtown, $$$, p. 152)
IndeBleu ★ (Penn Quarter, $$$, p. 141)
La Chaumiere ★★ (Georgetown, $$, p. 169)
Les Halles ★ (Penn Quarter, $$, p. 146)
Marcel's ★★ (Foggy Bottom, $$$$, p. 164)
Michel Richard Citronelle ★★★ (Georgetown, $$$$, p. 165)
Montmartre ★ (Capitol Hill, $$, p. 134)
Palena ★★★ (Cleveland Park, $$$$, p. 172)
Urbana ★ (Dupont Circle, $$$, p. 160)
Willard Room ★ (Penn Quarter, $$$$, p. 138)

GREEK

Komi ★★★ (Dupont Circle, $$$, p. 159)
Zaytinya ★★ (Penn Quarter, $$, p. 148)

INDIAN

Bombay Club ★ (Midtown, $$, p. 153)
IndeBleu ★ (Penn Quarter, $$$, p. 141)
Indique ★ (Cleveland Park, $$, p. 173)
Heritage India ★ (Glover Park, Dupont Circle, $$, p. 171)
Rasika ★★ (Penn Quarter, $$, p. 148)

ITALIAN

Cafe Milano ★ (Georgetown, $$$, p. 166)
D'Acqua ★ (Penn Quarter, $$$, p. 140)
Matchbox ★ (Penn Quarter, $$, p. 147)
Obelisk ★★★ (Dupont Circle, $$$$, p. 158)
Palena ★★★ (Cleveland Park, $$$$, p. 172)
Pizzeria Paradiso ★ (Dupont Circle, $, p. 161)
Teatro Goldoni ★★ (Midtown, $$$$, p. 151)
Tosca ★★★ (Penn Quarter, $$$$, p. 138)
Urbana ★ (Dupont Circle, $$$, p. 160)

JAPANESE

Ching Ching Cha (Georgetown, $, p. 170)
Kaz Sushi Bistro ★ (Foggy Bottom, $$$, p. 164)
Sushi-Ko ★ (Glover Park, $$, p. 171)

LATIN AMERICAN

Café Atlantico ★★ (Penn Quarter, $$$, p. 139)
Ceiba ★ (Penn Quarter, $$$, p. 140)
Las Canteras ★ (Adams-Morgan, $$, p. 156)
Lauriol Plaza ★ (Adams-Morgan, $$, p. 156)
Oyamel ★★★ (Penn Quarter, $$, p. 147)
Zengo ★ (Penn Quarter, $$$, p. 143)

MEXICAN

Lauriol Plaza ★ (Adams-Morgan, $$, p. 156)
Oyamel ★★★ (Penn Quarter, $$, p. 147)
Rosa Mexicano ★ (Penn Quarter, $$$, p. 142)

MIDDLE EASTERN

Bistro Tabaq ★ (U St. Corridor, $$, p. 154)
Lebanese Taverna (Woodley Park, $$, p. 174)
Zaytinya ★★ (Penn Quarter, $$, p. 148)

PERUVIAN

Las Canteras ★ (Adams- Morgan, $$, p. 156)

PIZZA

Matchbox ★ (Penn Quarter, $$, p. 147)
Pizzeria Paradiso ★ (Dupont Circle, $, p. 161)

SEAFOOD

D'Acqua ★ (Penn Quarter, $$$, p. 140)
Johnny's Half Shell ★★ (Capitol Hill, $$$, p. 131)
Hank's Oyster Bar ★ (Dupont Circle, $$, p. 161)
Hook ★ (Georgetown, $$$, p. 167)
Legal Sea Foods ★ (Midtown, $$, p. 146)
Kinkead's ★★ (Foggy Bottom, $$$$, p. 163)
Oceanaire Seafood Room ★ (Penn Quarter, $$$, p. 141)
Pesce ★ (Dupont Circle, $$$, p. 159)

The Prime Rib ★★ (Midtown, $$$$, p. 150)
Sea Catch (Georgetown, $$$, p. 168)
Tony Cheng's Seafood Restaurant ★ (Penn Quarter, $, p. 148)

SOUTHERN/SOUTHWESTERN
Acadiana ★ (Penn Quarter, $$$, p. 138)
Creme Café ★ (U St. Corridor, $$, p. 155)
Vidalia ★★ (Midtown, $$$$, p. 151)

SPANISH
Jaleo ★ (Penn Quarter, $$, p. 144)
Lauriol Plaza ★ (Adams-Morgan, $$, p. 156)
Taberna del Alabardero ★★ (Midtown, $$$$, p. 150)

STEAK
BLT Steak ★ (Midtown, $$$$, p. 149)
The Caucus Room ★★ (Penn Quarter, $$$$, p. 135)
Charlie Palmer Steak ★ (Capitol Hill, $$$$, p. 129)
Les Halles ★ (Penn Quarter, $$, p. 146)
The Palm ★ (Midtown, $$$$, p. 150)
The Prime Rib ★★ (Midtown, $$$$, p. 150)

THAI
Sala Thai (Dupont Circle, $, p. 162)

TURKISH
Zaytinya ★★ (Penn Quarter, $$, p. 148)

3 Capitol Hill

For information on eating at the Capitol and other government buildings, see the box titled "Views with a Meal," on p. 132.

VERY EXPENSIVE

Charlie Palmer Steak ★ STEAK Washington restaurant critics continue to give Charlie Palmer Steak (or "CP Steak," if you want to be cool) high marks, both for its seafood entrees, like the Maine lobster poached in butter fondue, and for its steaks. Beef predominates, from the excellent wagyu sirloin to the rib-eye "cowboy cut," with "progressive American" veal, pork, fish, and fowl dishes splitting the rest of the list. The only steakhouse on Capitol Hill, CP Steak is more elegant than one might expect. Its dining room has three fireplaces, deep-cushioned couches, and intimate seating areas. The ceilings are high, the rooms expansive. It's a place to see and be seen—in big groups, preferably. The bar and lounge are made for circulating. The most provocative feature is the glass-walled wine storage "cube," which appears to float upon a shallow pool of water; the inventory stocks 10,000 bottles of exclusively American wines, representing every state. Guests survey the wine list via the eWinebook, a kind of Palm Pilot that allows you to scroll through the selections, while a sommelier is on hand for consultation. The restaurant advertises that it overlooks the Capitol, but views are seasonal: In winter, you'll see more of the Capitol than you do in summer, when only the Capitol dome and the grounds are visible. CP Steak also offers a Sunday brunch, when it serves the most decadent steak and eggs in town.

101 Constitution Ave. NW (at Louisiana Ave.). ✆ **202/547-8100.** www.charliepalmer.com. Reservations recommended. Lunch main courses $13–$36; dinner main courses $23–$85; Sun brunch $36. AE, DC, DISC, MC, V. Mon–Fri 11:30am–2:30pm and 5:30–10pm; Sat 5–10:30pm; Sun 11am–2:30pm and 5–10pm. Metro: Union Station.

CityZen ★★★ MODERN AMERICAN Chef Eric Ziebold's previous gig was as chef de cuisine at Napa Valley's The French Laundry, one of the most celebrated restaurants in the country. With that pedigree, it's no wonder that CityZen, opened in 2004, continues to fill tables nightly and chalk up awards, like its AAA five-diamond rating in 2007. Located in the deluxe Mandarin Oriental Hotel, CityZen's dining room is temple-like: cathedral ceiling, dimly lit, with a coterie of acolytes flitting back and forth between tables and kitchen. You choose among three prix-fixe menus: three courses for $75, a six-course vegetarian tasting menu for $90, or a six-course $105 tasting menu. Starting with an *amuse bouche* of fried mushroom with truffle butter; moving on to a grilled pork jowl with marinated French green lentils, micro watercress, and shaved foie gras confit; and further on to the crispy skin filet of Atlantic black bass served with Rancho Gordo shelling beans, CityZen chorizo, and baby leeks—every taste is exquisite and out of the ordinary. Waitstaff bring intermission refreshments, such as olive oil custard topped with infused butter or ginger sorbet in homemade root beer. Only a food artist would think to create sensations like the cardamom-dusted orange cruller with kumquat marmalade and African amber tea sorbet. The restaurant's 800-bottle wine selection concentrates on bordeaux, burgundy, and California cabernet.

As mentioned in the review of the Mandarin Oriental Hotel (p. 85), the hotel is in an odd neighborhood, off by itself in a sea of government buildings and construction. But it's worth finding your way here. Enjoy a drink first in the hotel lounge overlooking a landscaped terrace or in CityZen's handsome lounge and bar (with its amazing "wall of fire"). Dress nicely (no denim, shorts, or sneakers).

In the Mandarin Oriental Hotel, 1330 Maryland Ave. SW (at 12th St.). ✆ **202/787-6868.** www.mandarinoriental.com/washington (then click on "Dining"). Reservations recommended. Open for dinner only: prix-fixe $75 for 3-course menu; 6-course tasting menus $90 (vegetarian) and $105. AE, DC, DISC, MC, V. Tues–Thurs 6–9:30pm; Fri–Sat 5:30–9:30pm. Metro: Smithsonian.

EXPENSIVE

Belga Café ★ BELGIAN Belga Café is located on a street called "Barracks Row," named for the Marine Corps barracks bordering the street to the east. This is one of those D.C. neighborhoods that's been here forever—the Marine Barracks and the Navy Yard, just blocks away, sprouted 200 years ago—but now is being revitalized by merchants and the city. New bars, restaurants, and shops are opening all the time along 8th Street, and this trend will continue as construction of the somewhat-nearby Washington Nationals baseball stadium approaches completion.

But back to the Belga: When it opened in late 2004, the cafe was almost too popular for its own good. Things have quieted down somewhat, service has improved, and you can probably now snag a table without a wait. Enjoy sitting at the outdoor cafe on a fine spring day or inside the bustling, noisy, European-ish dining room. Everything's a waffle at brunch and lunch, meaning many of the sandwiches—croque-monsieur to hamburger—are served on *wafel* (waffled) bread. The menu might look gimmicky, since every item gets its Flemish name first, followed by the translation: *dagsoep* (soup of the day), *waterzooi* (free-range chicken with vegetables). I recommend the Belgian fries; the Belgian beers (7 on tap, another 30 or so in bottles); the mussels, accompanied by one of five sauces; and the *eendenborst,* which is duck breast à l'orange with duck confit, salsify, and orange cacao sauce. Order the Belgian waffles, not the French toast, at brunch.

514 Eighth St. SE (at Pennsylvania Ave.). ✆ **202/544-0100.** www.belgacafe.com. Reservations accepted. Main courses $7.75–$17 at brunch, $8.50–$28 at lunch, $17–$28 at dinner. AE, DC, DISC, MC, V. Lunch daily 11:30am–3pm; brunch Sat–Sun 11am–3:30pm; dinner Sun 5–9:30pm, Mon–Thurs 5:30–10pm, Fri–Sat 5:30–11pm. Metro: Eastern Market.

Bistro Bis ★★ FRENCH BISTRO The chic Hotel George is the home of this excellent French restaurant, whose chef/owner, Jeff Buben, and his wife, Sallie, also run Vidalia (p. 151). You can sit at tables in the bar area (which always seems loud, even when it's not that crowded), on the balcony overlooking the bar, or at leather banquettes in the main dining room. In warm weather, there's a sidewalk cafe. The menu covers French classics like bouillabaisse, boeuf bourguignon, and steak frites. But Buben gives the traditional his own twist: Seared scallops Provençal comes with the anticipated tomatoes, garlic, and olives, but also an eggplant custard. A spring appetizer might be a crab fritter Provençal: soft-shell crab tempura lightly fried with olives and roasted garlic. The beet salad arrives with goat cheese, walnuts, and arugula and is dressed with a citron olive oil vinaigrette. Many items, including the sea scallops and the steak frites, appear on both the lunch and dinner menus but are considerably cheaper at lunch. The wine list is mostly French and American. Look around the dining room for nightly news types, since Bis's proximity to the Capitol, lovely setting, and scrumptious cuisine make it a must-stop for movers and shakers.

15 E St. NW. ✆ **202/661-2700.** www.bistrobis.com. Reservations recommended. Breakfast $9–$14; brunch main courses $12–$18 or prix-fixe $30 menu; lunch main courses $14–$24; dinner main courses $20–$32. AE, DC, DISC, MC, V. Daily 7–10:30am, 11:30am–2:30pm, and 5:30–10:30pm. Metro: Union Station.

Johnny's Half Shell ★★ *Finds* AMERICAN/SEAFOOD Until September 2006, Johnny's was a neighborhood joint in Dupont Circle. Having outgrown its small space, Johnny's moved into this much larger Capitol Hill location, but maintains the same warm vibes and welcoming atmosphere, with the help of many of its faithful P Street staff. This Johnny's also mimics the decor of the original, by featuring an aquarium behind the long bar, booths along one paneled wall, a tile floor, and a partly open kitchen. One thing's for sure: The regional cuisine remains unbeatable.

The menu continues to offer its reliably good, farm-raised chicken with old-fashioned Eastern Shore slippery dumplings, garden peas, and button mushrooms; the crabmeat imperial with a salad of *haricots verts* (young green beans), tomatoes, and shallots; the delicious fried oyster po' boy sandwich (at lunch only); and Maryland crab cakes with coleslaw and french fries. If the sautéed soft-shell crabs with Old Bay and basil beurre blanc and corn pudding are on the menu, get them: This is the best place in town to enjoy them. Oysters and Wellfleet clams on the half shell are always available, of course. The short wine list includes a few selections by the glass; there are four beers on tap. Desserts are simply perfect, including homemade ice cream; a choice of apple or Meyer lemon tart; chocolate angel food cake with caramel sauce, and coconut passion fruit layer cake.

In May 2007, Johnny's opened a *taqueria,* which serves breakfast tacos, scrambled eggs, and waffles until 10am, and five varieties of soft tacos priced at no more than $2.50 each, plus a daily special at $5.50, 10am to 3pm. The *taqueria* is a takeout operation, open weekdays only, and is located just behind Johnny's main entrance.

400 N. Capitol St. NW (at E St.). ✆ **202/737-0400.** www.johnnyshalfshell.net. Reservations recommended. Breakfast main courses $7–$11, lunch main courses $6.95–$28, dinner main courses $16–$28; taqueria: breakfast and lunch items $1.50–$5.50. AE, MC, V. Mon–Fri 7–9:30am and 11:30am–2:30pm; Mon–Thurs 5–10:30pm; Fri–Sat 5–11pm; taqueria: Mon–Fri 7am–3pm. Metro: Union Station.

Views with a Meal

Is there anything more wonderful than discovering that the attraction you are currently visiting also offers an excellent repast? Most tourist sites provide sustenance of some sort, generally humdrum in taste and high in price. A very few establishments proffer a delightful setting and food that's a real pleasure to eat. At the pinnacle of my list in Washington are the **National Gallery of Art**'s restaurants, and in particular the **Sculpture Garden Pavilion Café (✆ 202/289-3360)**, where you can sip a glass of wine and savor Cuban panini (mo-jo roasted pork with crinkle-cut pickles, mustard, ham, cheese, and onions on Cuban bread), sitting inside in the glass pavilion in winter or on the terrace in warm weather, in view of sculpture, the landscaped garden, and grand sights of Washington. The gallery's **Cascades** and the **Garden Café** (**✆ 202/712-7460**) are worthy second choices, offering a wide range of appetite pleasers and really lovely surroundings.

Four other eateries are worth special mention: The **National Museum of the American Indian's Mitsitam Café** (**✆ 202/633-7044**) seeks to educate as well as please the palate, since its menu represents traditional dishes from various Native American regions—for example, cedar-planked juniper salmon from the Pacific Northwest, buffalo burgers from the Great Plains, and, a favorite, fry bread from all over. The **International Spy Museum's Spy City Café** (**✆ 202/654-0995**) is one of the rare museum eateries to open early—8am weekdays and 9am weekends—and is rightly famous for its cleverly named hot dogs, like the Red Square Dog. The newly opened **Vradenburg Café** (**✆ 202/387-2151**), in the **Phillips Collection,** is operated by a local bakery chain, Firehook Bakery, which Washingtonians love for its sandwiches on thick breads and for its selection of delicious desserts. **Union Station's Food Court** is exceptional in its variety; individual purveyors from around the world sell their own national specialty: Italian, Greek, Mexican, Chinese, Indian, Japanese, Middle Eastern, and American in all its forms.

Finally, you just can't beat the atmosphere (political) and value (cheap) of the all-American food served in certain dining rooms on Capitol Hill. While touring the Hill, keep these places in mind:

For a most exclusive experience, try to dine in either the **House of Representatives Restaurant** (also called the "Members' Dining Room") in Room H118, at the south end of the Capitol (**✆ 202/225-6300**), or the **Senate Dining Room** in Room S110 at the north end of the Capitol (**✆ 202/224-4100**); to do so,

The Monocle *Finds* AMERICAN A Capitol Hill institution, The Monocle has been around since 1960. At this men-in-suits place, the litter of briefcases resting against the too-close-together tables can make for treacherous navigating. But you might want to take a look at whose briefcase it is you're stumbling over, for its proximity to both the Supreme Court and the Capitol guarantees that The Monocle is the haunt of Supreme Court justices and members of Congress. The Monocle updated its menu (for the first time?) in April 2007, but certain favorites remain: At lunch you'll want you must contact your representative's or senator's office and follow the proper procedure to obtain official permission.

You are always welcome (after you've gone through security, of course) in the eateries located in the Capitol office buildings across the street from the Capitol. These are quite affordable—your meal isn't taxed, for one thing—and you'll be surrounded by Hill staffers, who head to places like the immense, full-service **Rayburn House Office Building Cafeteria** (✆ **202/225-7109**), which is in Room B357, in the basement of the building, at First Street and Independence Avenue SW. Adjoining the cafeteria is a carryout that sells pizza and sandwiches. In the basement-level **Longworth Building Cafeteria,** Independence Avenue and South Capitol Street SE (✆ **202/225-0878**), you can grab a bite from a fairly nice food court. By far the best value for visitors is the **Dirksen Senate Office Building South Buffet Room,** First and C streets NE (✆ **202/224-4249**). For just $13 per adult, $8.75 per child under 10, you can choose from a buffet that includes a carving station and eight other hot entrees; the price covers a nonalcoholic drink and dessert, too. The dining room is often crowded but accepts reservations for parties of more than five. Other options include the Russell Carryout and the Cannon Carryout, both in the basement of the Cannon Building. All of these eateries are open weekdays only. The carryouts stay open until late afternoon, while the other dining rooms close at 2:30pm.

When the **Capitol Visitors Center** debuts in 2008, you'll find a large dining hall—accommodating 600 people—within it. Can't tell you more than that at this time, but check it out if you're planning to tour the Capitol in 2008.

Right across the street from the Capitol are two other institutions offering inexpensive dining and fair views (of famous sights or people) at weekday breakfast and lunch: the **Library of Congress's Cafeteria** and its more formal **Montpelier Room** (✆ **202/707-8300**), where the options usually cost under $10 per person and the views are of Capitol Hill; and the **Supreme Court's Cafeteria** (✆ **202/479-3246**), where you may spy a famous lawyer or member of the press, but not any of the justices, who have their own dining room.

to order the hamburger, which is excellent, the tasty federal salad (field greens and tomatoes tossed with balsamic vinaigrette), or the white-bean soup, when it's on the menu. At dinner, consider the roasted oysters, the pork-rib chop with Pommery mustard sauce, or "Crab Conrad," a lump crab dish that owner John Valanos created to honor his father, Conrad Valanos, who opened The Monocle in 1960.

107 D St. NE. ✆ **202/546-4488.** www.themonocle.com. Reservations recommended. Lunch main courses $13–$26; dinner main courses $17–$35. AE, DC, DISC, MC, V. Mon–Fri 11:30am–10:30pm. Closed 2 weeks preceding Labor Day. Metro: Union Station.

MODERATE

Montmartre ★ FRENCH Montmartre's ambience is warmed by its decor—pale yellow-orange walls, exposed wood ceiling, cozy bar, and old wooden tables, all fronted by a sidewalk cafe, open in warm weather. The owners here are French, and Montmartre is their little French restaurant offering big French pleasures: chicory salad tossed with goat cheese and croutons; chestnut soup; pistou; potato gratin; flat iron beef with Jerusalem artichokes; seared monkfish wrapped in smoked bacon; and calves' liver sautéed with smothered onions, bok choy, potato purée, and a balsamic vinegar sauce. Desserts, like the Alsatian apple tart, don't disappoint.

327 7th St. SE. ✆ **202/544-1244.** www.montmartre.us/index.htm. Reservations recommended. Lunch main courses $13–$19; brunch main courses $8.95–$17; dinner main courses $16–$20. AE, DC, DISC, MC, V. Tues–Sun 11:30am–2:30pm; Sun 5:30–9pm; Tues–Thurs 5:30–10pm; Fri–Sat 5:30–10:30pm. Metro: Eastern Market.

Sonoma ★ AMERICAN Oenophiles and lounge lovers have equal reason to visit Sonoma, since the restaurant offers 40 wines by the glass from its inventory of 200 Californian wines, and a lively lounge scene on the second floor. And though 20- and 30-something Hill staffers quickly made this place their own after Sonoma opened in summer 2005, lots of people are happy to meet up here. (Families with small children should look elsewhere.) Plates of charcuterie and cheeses are for sharing, while a menu of "firsts" offers pastas and "seconds" lists meat and seafood dishes. Do try a small plate of the charcuterie, then follow it up with a house-made goat cheese ravioli and the coffee-glazed Duroc baby back ribs. A variety of salads and pizzas are also available. The smart-looking Sonoma stands out on this stretch of Pennsylvania Avenue, where most of its neighbors are coffeehouses and bars. The long narrow dining room often fills up with a drinking crowd waiting for a table in the evening, and that's when you'll want to head upstairs and check out the lounge, which has a fireplace and overlooks Pennsylvania Avenue. As the night progresses, the tables turn and the second floor gets crowded; at that point, it's time to move on.

223 Pennsylvania Ave. SE (at 2nd St. SE). ✆ **202/544-8088.** www.sonomadc.com. Reservations recommended. Lunch and dinner main courses $12–$27. AE, DC, DISC, MC, V. Mon–Fri 11:30am–2:30pm; Sun–Thurs 5:30–10pm; Fri–Sat 5:30–11pm. Metro: Capitol South.

INEXPENSIVE

Le Bon Café *Finds* AMERICAN Pennsylvania Avenue on Capitol Hill is a stretch of been-around-a-while pubs, as well as newer coffeehouses, bakeries, and the occasional fine dining establishment. The Capitol looms over the neighborhood, whose other big buildings hold the Library of Congress and Senate and House offices. Government edifices aside, this part of town is actually mostly residential. Pennsylvania Avenue and its town-house lined side streets compose a village, enlivened by the presence of young staffers who swarm here for lunch, dinner, coffee, or a drink. The local chains Firehook Bakery and Burrito Brothers have outposts here, as do national chains Starbucks and Cosi. Those are all fine places, but my favorite is the tiny Le Bon Café, whose menu is short but sweet: homemade pumpkin gingerbread and scones, smoked turkey club sandwich on farm bread, grilled salmon Niçoise salad, and the like. And it's cheap: The most expensive single item is that salmon salad, for $8.95. Seating inside is minimal, with most people grabbing food to go; in pleasant weather, you can sit at outdoor tables. ***FYI:*** Pete's Diner and Carryout, right next door, also attracts a loyal Hill following with its low prices and burgers-and-fried-chicken menu, so stop there, if you've got a greasy spoon kind of appetite.

210 2nd St. SE (at Pennsylvania Ave. SE). ✆ **202/547-7200.** Breakfast items $2.25–$5; salads/sandwiches/soups $3.85–$8.95. Mon–Fri 7am–3:30pm; Sat–Sun 8am–3:30pm. Metro: Capitol South.

4 Downtown, Penn Quarter

VERY EXPENSIVE

Butterfield 9 ★★ NEW AMERICAN This restaurant offers menus to please everyone, including a bar menu that pairs small plates individually priced at $4 to $6, with a complementary 3-ounce glass of wine, each priced from $4.50 to $6; a $4.50 glass of Vouvray accompanies the $5 dish of ricotta gnocchi, for example. Butterfield also offers a good-value $38 pre/post-theater menu, which gives you three delicious courses for the price of the average dinner entree, and a $70 vegetarian tasting menu. On the regular menu, popular dinner dishes include a roasted pheasant appetizer, roasted ostrich filet, and yellowfin tuna and tiger shrimp served in a black currant and pink peppercorn sauce.

You're sure to spot owner Amarjeet (Umbi) Singh as he circulates through the restaurant. Singh opened Butterfield 9 in 2001 to instant acclaim—for the food, but also for the sophisticated decor, which features large, stylized black-and-white prints of handsome men and women dressed in 1930s, '40s, and '50s fashions. The overall ambience is of a dinner club from a different era, specifically the one that Nick and Nora Charles inhabited in the *Thin Man* movies. (Butterfield 9 refers to a phone exchange used in the films.) This is a good choice if you're in the mood for romance, and you should let the staff know that, too, since certain tables provide added intimacy.

600 14th St. NW. ✆ **202/289-8810.** www.butterfield9.com. Reservations recommended. Lunch main courses $10–$19 and $25 prix-fixe menu; dinner main courses $22–$39; $38 pre/post-theater menu. AE, DC, DISC, MC, V. Mon–Fri 11:30am–2:30pm; Sun–Thurs 5:30–9pm; Fri–Sat 5:30–11pm. Metro: Metro Center.

The Caucus Room ★★ STEAK Washington's powerful people like steakhouses. Since the Caucus Room is owned by a bipartisan bunch of heavy-hitting politicos and entrepreneurs (Democratic lobbyist Tommy Boggs and former Republican National Committee chairman Haley Barbour, to name but 2 of the 70 investors), the Caucus Room was almost a guaranteed success even before it opened in August 2000. At lunch and dinner, it's a true Washington scene, with all that that entails: a sprinkling of congressmen and -women, television newscasters, and corporate VIPs throughout the main dining room; lots of backslapping and shaking of hands; and private meetings taking place behind closed doors (the restaurant has a number of private dining rooms).

But they wouldn't keep coming back if the food weren't so good. Enduring favorites are the steaks, natch, and certain nonmeat entrees, such as the crab cakes (the pass/fail test for a D.C. restaurant) and seared fish, like a recent preparation of seared rockfish, sesame crusted and served with Asian vegetables. Even side dishes, like the creamed spinach and the horseradish-spiked mashed potatoes, are winners.

After you finish your main course, lean back against the leather banquette and discreetly search for famous faces as you enjoy dessert, maybe a chocolate mousse or

Capitol Hill, Downtown & Foggy Bottom Dining

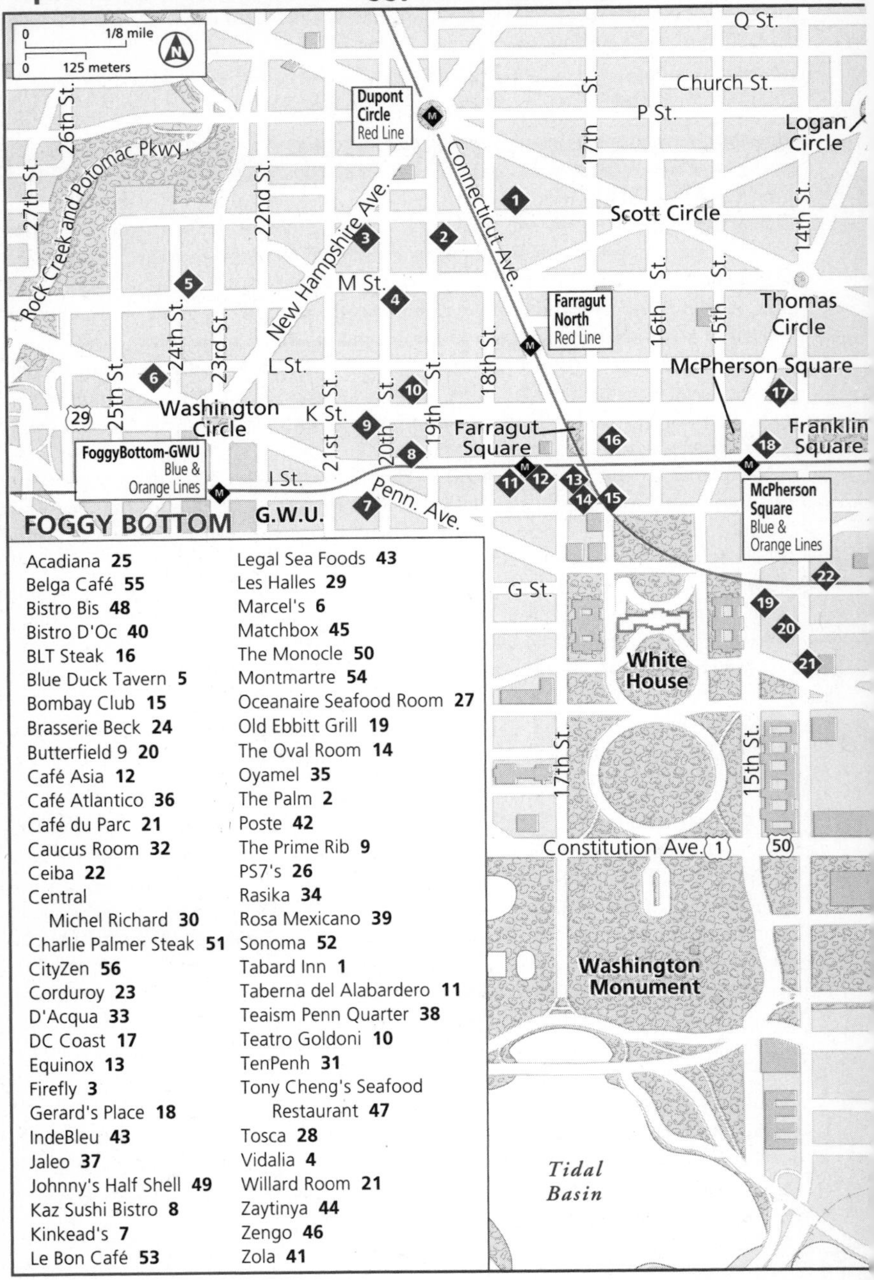

Acadiana **25**
Belga Café **55**
Bistro Bis **48**
Bistro D'Oc **40**
BLT Steak **16**
Blue Duck Tavern **5**
Bombay Club **15**
Brasserie Beck **24**
Butterfield 9 **20**
Café Asia **12**
Café Atlantico **36**
Café du Parc **21**
Caucus Room **32**
Ceiba **22**
Central Michel Richard **30**
Charlie Palmer Steak **51**
CityZen **56**
Corduroy **23**
D'Acqua **33**
DC Coast **17**
Equinox **13**
Firefly **3**
Gerard's Place **18**
IndeBleu **43**
Jaleo **37**
Johnny's Half Shell **49**
Kaz Sushi Bistro **8**
Kinkead's **7**
Le Bon Café **53**
Legal Sea Foods **43**
Les Halles **29**
Marcel's **6**
Matchbox **45**
The Monocle **50**
Montmartre **54**
Oceanaire Seafood Room **27**
Old Ebbitt Grill **19**
The Oval Room **14**
Oyamel **35**
The Palm **2**
Poste **42**
The Prime Rib **9**
PS7's **26**
Rasika **34**
Rosa Mexicano **39**
Sonoma **52**
Tabard Inn **1**
Taberna del Alabardero **11**
Teaism Penn Quarter **38**
Teatro Goldoni **10**
TenPenh **31**
Tony Cheng's Seafood Restaurant **47**
Tosca **28**
Vidalia **4**
Willard Room **21**
Zaytinya **44**
Zengo **46**
Zola **41**

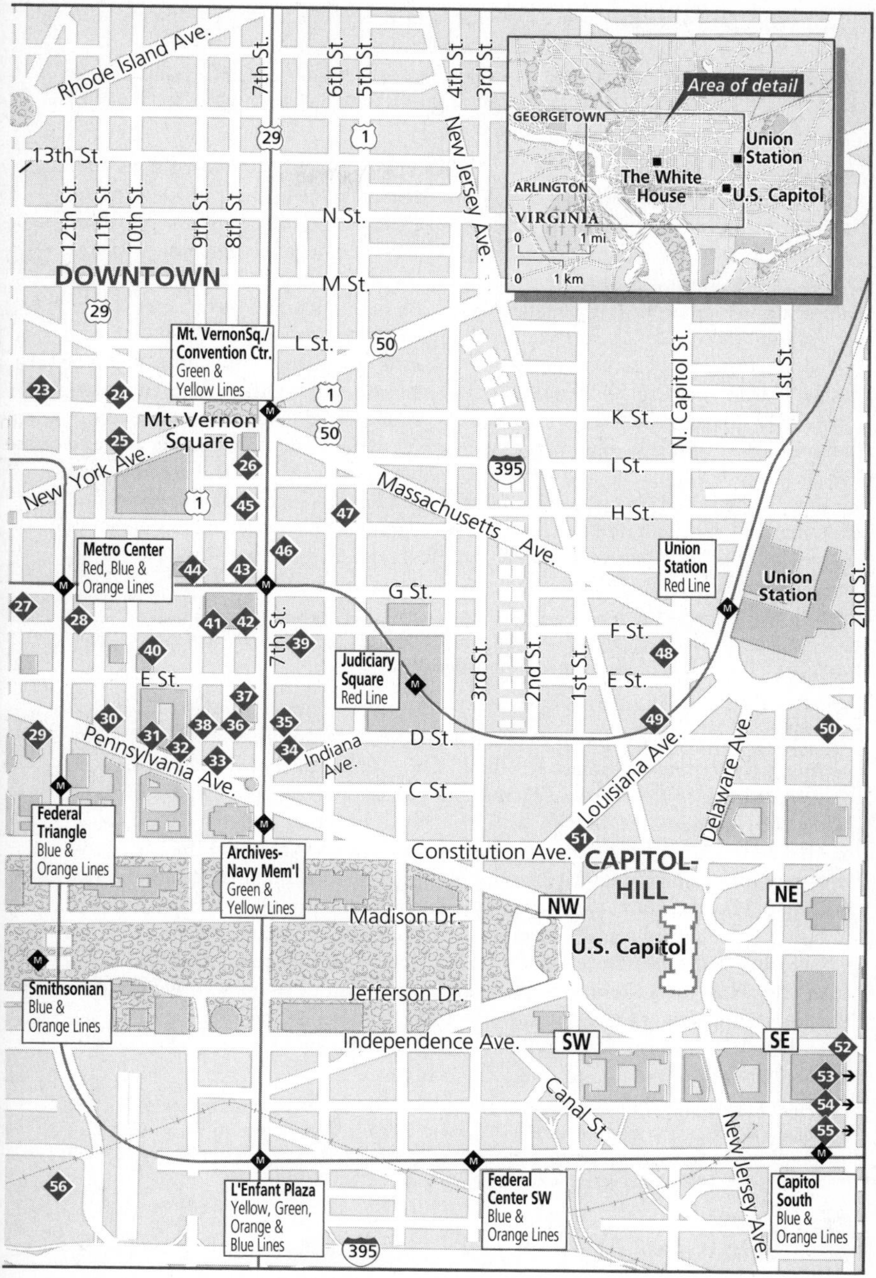
Rhode Island Ave.
7th St.
6th St.
5th St.
4th St.
3rd St.
Area of detail
GEORGETOWN
Union Station
The White House
ARLINGTON
U.S. Capitol
VIRGINIA
0
1 mi
0
1 km
29
1
13th St.
12th St.
11th St.
10th St.
9th St.
8th St.
N St.
New Jersey Ave.
DOWNTOWN
M St.
29
Mt. VernonSq./ Convention Ctr.
Green & Yellow Lines
L St.
50
1
50
23
24
25
Mt. Vernon Square
K St.
N. Capitol St.
1st St.
I St.
395
New York Ave.
26
Massachusetts Ave.
1
45
47
H St.
Metro Center
Red, Blue & Orange Lines
46
44
43
Union Station
Red Line
Union Station
2nd St.
G St.
27
28
41
42
7th St.
39
40
F St.
48
Judiciary Square
Red Line
3rd St.
2nd St.
1st St.
E St.
E St.
37
30
38
36
35
49
50
29
31
32
Pennsylvania Ave.
34
Indiana Ave.
D St.
33
Louisiana Ave.
Delaware Ave.
C St.
Federal Triangle
Blue & Orange Lines
Archives-Navy Mem'l
Green & Yellow Lines
51
Constitution Ave.
CAPITOL-HILL
NW
NE
Madison Dr.
U.S. Capitol
Smithsonian
Blue & Orange Lines
Jefferson Dr.
Independence Ave.
SW
SE
52
53
54
55
Canal St.
New Jersey Ave.
56
L'Enfant Plaza
Yellow, Green, Orange & Blue Lines
395
Federal Center SW
Blue & Orange Lines
Capitol South
Blue & Orange Lines

pecan pie. ***Tip:*** Make sure you sit in the main dining room when Congress is in session; otherwise, you'll find the Caucus Room fairly deserted.

401 9th St. NW (at D St.). ✆ **202/393-1300.** www.thecaucusroom.com. Reservations recommended. Lunch items $17–$40; dinner main courses $27–$60. AE, DISC, MC, V. Mon–Fri 11:30am–2pm; Mon–Sat 5:30–10pm. Metro: Navy/Archives or Gallery Place.

Tosca ★★★ NORTHERN ITALIAN Washington, which probably has more Italian restaurants than any other kind of ethnic eatery, saw the opening of several more in 2007, including the excellent Il Mulino and D'Acqua (p. 140). Nevertheless, Tosca has nothing to worry about. Tosca remains the city's standout fine *ristorante italiano.*

Tosca's interior design of pale pastels in the thick carpeting and heavy drapes creates a hushed atmosphere, a suitable foil to the rich food. The menu, meanwhile, emphasizes the cooking of the Lake Como region of Italy. A good example of a traditional pasta dish is the *scapinasch,* a ravioli of aged ricotta and raisins (or sometimes it's made with amaretto cookies) with butter and sage sauce. Other dishes to recommend are a grilled rack of veal with a mix of wild mushrooms and a roasted Mediterranean sea bass with balsamic vinegar sabayon and sautéed spinach with pine nuts and raisins. Tosca has something for everyone, including simply grilled fish accompanied by organic vegetables for the health conscious, and desserts such as tiramisu or ricotta and goat cheese fritters for those with a sweet tooth. No wonder the restaurant is always full. But even when there's a crowd, Tosca doesn't get too noisy—the restaurant's designers kept acoustics in mind.

1112 F St. NW. ✆ **202/367-1990.** www.toscadc.com. Reservations recommended. Lunch main courses $12–$24; dinner main courses $14–$42; pretheater menu $35; tasting menus $65–$95. AE, DC, MC, V. Mon–Fri 11:30am–2:30pm; Mon–Thurs 5:30–10:30pm; Fri–Sat 5:30–11pm. Metro: Metro Center.

Willard Room ★ AMERICAN/FRENCH For the ultimate Washington experience: Take a taxi (better yet, a limo) to the Willard Hotel, and stroll through the lobby, heading right, to find the Round Robin bar. Enjoy a mint julep, old-fashioned, or gin rickey and listen to the tales told by the seasoned bartenders about Charles Dickens, Nathaniel Hawthorne, and others who frequented this hotel in earlier days. Proceed to the Willard Room, which has to be the most elegant dining room in the capital: two-story-high ceiling, walnut-paneled walls, green marble columns, sumptuous fabrics, tables placed far from each other throughout the room. Enjoy an exquisite repast of classic dishes: Caesar salad, Maine lobster poached with onion ginger ravioli, or rack of lamb with herbs Provençal. Discreetly observe the presence of the royal family from Denmark, or the former prime minister from Israel. Ask for your bill, add a healthy tip, and then wander out to Peacock Alley and peruse the information on display about the history of the Willard (2006 marked the centenary of the "new" Willard). Return to the Round Robin for a nightcap.

1401 Pennsylvania Ave. NW. ✆ **202/637-7440.** Reservations recommended. Breakfast main courses $9–$25; lunch main courses $23–$28; dinner main courses $26–$36; Sun brunch $65; pretheater dinner $47. AE, DC, DISC, MC, V. Mon–Fri 7:30–10am and 11:30am–2pm; Sat 8am–noon; Sun 11am–2pm; Sun 5:30–9:30pm; Mon–Thurs 6–10pm; Fri–Sat 5:30–10pm. Metro: Metro Center.

EXPENSIVE

Acadiana ★ AMERICAN/SOUTHERN This glass-walled triangle-shaped restaurant lies close to the convention center, which might interest you if you're in need of a Sazerac or mint julep pick-me-up in the middle of your meetings, especially since the bar stays open straight through from lunch to dinner and offers a menu of appetizers. The restaurant's high ceilings, ornate chandeliers, and oversized urns and other features fit with the over-the-top atmosphere that prevails. This is New Orleans central, right here, and New Orleanians say the cuisine's the real thing, starting with the biscuits, served with a pepper jelly and cream cheese condiment; continuing on to deviled eggs, charbroiled oysters, and crabmeat and artichoke gratin starters; and even further to jambalaya, étouffée, red snapper in an almondine sauce, and barbecue shrimp. Service is excellent.

901 New York Ave. NW (at 9th St.). ✆ **202/408-8848.** www.acadianarestaurant.com. Reservations recommended. Lunch main courses $15–$20; dinner main courses $25–$30. AE, DC, MC, V. Mon–Fri 11:30am–2:30pm; Mon–Thurs 5:30–10:30pm; Fri–Sat 5:30–11pm; Sun 5:30–9:30pm. Metro: Mount Vernon Sq./7th St. Convention Center.

Café Atlantico ★★ *Finds* LATIN AMERICAN Chef José Andrés is associated with seven restaurants in the Washington area; was inducted in 2007 into the James Beard Foundation's Who's Who of Food and Beverage in America (one of only 191 members); has been called the "boy wonder of culinary Washington" by the *New York Times;* hosts a daily television show about food that airs in Spain; is set to launch a 26-episode national cooking show here in the U.S. in 2008; serves on the board of D.C.'s largest food-for-the-homeless operation, D.C. Central Kitchen; and has authored two cookbooks, the latest of which, *Passport to Spain,* has just been published—all before his 40th birthday.

It all started here. Well no, it all started in the farm town of Mieres, in northern Spain, where Andrés was born. But his success in America began 15 years ago when he was hired as the chef at nearby Jaleo, and then at Café Atlantico. Though he wears several toques now—he remains connected to Jaleo and is the chef behind one of the city's newest sensations, Oyamel, as well as the ever-popular Zaytinya, too—you will find Andrés in residence at the **minibar** ★★★, upstairs at Café Atlantico, working with Café Atlantico chef Katsuya Fukushima to create 30 to 40 small concoctions, from foie gras in a cocoon of cotton candy to pineapple raviolis, for six people per seating, Tuesday to Saturday, at 6 and 8:30pm. The gourmet adventure costs $120 per person, not including wine, tax, and tip, and requires a reservation that's best made a month in advance.

The main restaurant of Café Atlantico, meanwhile, rocks on. All week long, but especially on weekend nights, this is a favorite hot spot in Washington's hottest neighborhood. The colorful three-tiered restaurant throbs with Latin, calypso, and reggae music, and everyone is having a fiesta—including, it seems, the waiters. If the place is packed, try to snag a seat at the second-level bar, where you can watch the genial bartender mix the potent drinks for which Café Atlantico is famous: the *caipirinha,* made of limes, sugar, and *Cachaçha* (sugar-cane liqueur); or the *mojito,* a rum and crushed-mint cocktail.

Seated at the bar or table, you'll watch as your waiter makes fresh guacamole to your specified degree of spicy. As for the main dishes, you can't get a more elaborate meal for the price. Check out the ceviche, Cornish hen wrapped in bacon served with deconstructed mole sauce, and seared scallops with coconut crispy rice and ginger, squid, and squid ink oil (though the menu changes, you're sure to find these or their equivalent listed); and tropical side dishes and pungent sauces produce a burst of color on the plate. Feel free to ask your friendly waiter for guidance.

405 8th St. NW (at D St. NW). ✆ **202/393-0812.** www.cafeatlantico.com. Reservations recommended. Lunch main courses $8–$16; dinner main courses $18–$28; pretheater menu $30 (nightly 5–6:30pm); Latino dim sum brunch (Sat–Sun): you can choose a la carte ($2–$9 each) items, pay $25 for a vegetarian all-you-can-eat meal, or $35 for a deluxe version. AE, DC, DISC, MC, V. Mon–Fri 11:30am–2:30pm; Sat–Sun brunch 11:30am–2:30pm; Sun–Thurs 5–10pm; Fri–Sat 5–11pm; bar stays open late on weekends. Metro: Archives–Navy Memorial or Gallery Place/Verizon Center.

Ceiba ★ CONTEMPORARY LATIN AMERICAN Ceiba is the creation of Jeff Tunks, the chef maestro behind TenPenh, DC Coast, and Acadiana (p. 143, 152, and 138). Here at Ceiba, Tunks works his magic on seviches, offering four variations—grouper, shrimp, tuna, and striped bass—which you may order individually or as a sampler; and on other authentic Latin dishes, like the Veracruz-style red snapper, topped with tomatoes, capers, olives, and jalapeños. As is true at all Tunks establishments, fulsome drinks are integral to the experience and the ones offered here go down nicely: mojitos, mango margaritas, and pisco sours, as well as fine wines from Argentina and Chile. If you're stopping in for a quick fix, the bar menu complements those cocktails with tastes of octopus salad, beef empanadas, seviches, and assorted others; each item is reasonably priced from $9 to $16. If you like to be where the action is, try for a table in the main dining room, to your right as you walk in, rather than the room to your left.

701 14th St. NW. ✆ **202/393-3983.** www.ceibarestaurant.com. Reservations recommended. Lunch main courses $11–$17; dinner main courses $11–$29; pretheater menu $29. AE, DC, DISC, MC, V. Mon–Fri 11:30am–2:30pm; Mon–Thurs 5:30–10:30pm; Fri–Sat 5:30–11pm; bar stays open weekdays from 2:30pm to closing and Sat from 5:30pm to closing. Metro: Metro Center.

Central Michel Richard ★★ FRENCH BISTRO This place makes you feel good as soon as you walk through the door. It's a French-American brasserie with a *joie de vivre* ambience and a menu full of precociously re-created American and French classics: A lobster burger is layered with scallop mousse, macaroni and cheese is creamy with sour cream as well as cheeses, the fried chicken is an ungreasy version lightly dusted with bread crumbs, and on and on, the names of French dishes ping-ponging with American, hanger steak and onion soup to apple pan dowdy and banana split. The French fries, a country unto themselves, are perfection. Michel Richard is the chef of Citronelle (p. 165), the city's best restaurant, and he opened Central in early 2007 to entice younger diners with smaller budgets. The Frenchman, who has lived in the U.S. for 30 years, has a special fondness for his adopted country and it shows—and not just in the menu. The bistro is half dining room, half bar and exhibition kitchen, and there's an actual television in the bar. Richard wants you to have fun and, from all appearances, Central's succeeding on that score.

1001 Pennsylvania Ave. NW (at 11th St.). ✆ **202/626-0015.** www.centralmichelrichard.com. Reservations recommended. Main courses $12–$29 at lunch, $18–$32 at dinner. AE, DC, DISC, MC, V. Mon–Fri 11:45 am–2:30pm and 5:30–10:30pm, Fri–Sat 5:30–11pm. Metro: Metro Center.

D'Acqua ★ ITALIAN/SEAFOOD D'Acqua's window-fronted dining room overlooks the Navy Memorial and courtyard, as well as a slice of Pennsylvania Avenue; its seasonal sidewalk seating allows one to feel a part of the capital's bustling scene—during the day, especially. On display inside are decorative elements meant to convey an Italian coastal feel: Murano glass wallpaper insets, glazed walls and stucco columns, and a colorful palette of Tuscan gold and Mediterranean blue. The expansive L-shaped bar terminates at one end in a display of that day's fresh fish options, usually a dozen, presenting a wide range. You can select your fish and then request it be grilled, oven roasted, or salt-crust baked; but the menu also offers a variety of its own meat, fish, and pasta preparations, like the delicious *triangoli di pesce,* which is seafood and porcini ravioli with lemon and marjoram sauce. D'Acqua's opening in late 2006 means the nearby, inestimable Tosca (p. 138) now has some competition for excellent Italian cuisine in this part of town; Tosca's is still best, but D'Acqua might be a better fit for you if the combination of an Italian accent, fresh fish, and a less formal atmosphere seem more appealing.

801 Pennsylvania Ave. NW (at 8th St.). ✆ **202/783-7717.** www.dacqua.com. Reservations accepted. Main courses $11–$24 at lunch, $20–$36 at dinner. AE, DC, DISC, MC, V. Mon–Thurs 11am–11pm, Fri 11am–midnight, Sat 5pm–midnight, Sun 5–11pm. Metro: Gallery Place/Chinatown or Archives/Navy Memorial.

IndeBleu ★ FRENCH/INDIAN IndeBleu's opening in December 2004 brought out fashion models, members of the press, and photographers clicking away at the scene. Everyone was curious to see whether what they'd heard was true: that the lounge was furnished with swinging sofas, orange chaise longues, padded walls, and tons of cushions, and that the dining room offered a catwalk and a chef's table that pivoted into the kitchen. The crowd came, confirmed, and continues to return. In the meantime, though, IndeBleu has established the club and dining room as two separate destinations. The first-level lounge still features a bar with disappearing bottle shelves, white granite, and stone floors, and that hipper-than-thou sunken cocktail den and pod-shaped DJ booth, but it goes by the name "Tantra" now and opens nightly at 5pm, catering to 20- and 30-something singles. Upstairs is the dining room and that catwalk connecting one section to another, floor-to-ceiling windows overlooking the National Portrait Gallery and the Penn Quarter neighborhood, and serious diners ready to perk up their taste buds. IndeBleu's cooking continues on its exotic track. Menu highlights include appetizers of lobster and lump crab stacked with marinated mango, pine nuts, and curry oil; and a duck and foie gras confit; and an entree of tandoori rack of lamb with green lentil ragout, grilled portobello, and mojito sauce.

707 G St. NW. ✆ **202/333-2538.** www.bleu.com. Reservations recommended. Lunch main courses $15–$24; dinner main courses $26–$39. AE, DC, DISC, MC, V. Mon–Fri 11:30am–1:30pm; Sun–Wed 5:30–9:30pm; Thurs–Sat 5:30–10:30pm; lounge Sun–Thurs 5pm–1:30am, Fri–Sat 5pm–2:30am. Metro: Gallery Place/Chinatown.

Oceanaire Seafood Room ★ SEAFOOD The Oceanaire is a good spot for a lively party, with its red-leather booths, Art Deco decor, long bar, and festive atmosphere. It would be hard to get romantic or serious about business here—there's just too much to distract you, like the sight of mile-high desserts en route to another table. Oceanaire serves big portions of everything (including cocktails, another reason to bring a bunch of friends here). On a menu that proclaims, "Fresh fish flown in daily from around the world!" you'll read intriguing names of fish on offer that day: grilled Hawaiian opah moonfish, Tasmanian steelhead trout, Ecuadorian mahimahi, and so on. These are usually served simply grilled or broiled. The waitstaff excel at explaining the tastes and textures of everything on the menu, so don't hesitate to ask. Two of the best entrees are the crab cakes, which are almost all lump crabmeat, and the fisherman's platter, a fresh, fried selection of oysters, scallops, shrimp, and other seafood, with hot matchstick fries alongside it all. The dozen varieties of oysters are fresh and plump, but if you want to start with a salad, consider the BLT, which is exactly as it sounds, like eating a bacon-lettuce-tomato sandwich without the toast.

1201 F St. NW. ✆ **202/347-2277.** www.theoceanaire.com. Reservations recommended. Lunch main courses $19–$28; dinner main courses $20–$36. AE, DISC, MC, V. Mon–Thurs 11:30am–10pm; Fri 11:30am–11pm; Sat 5–11pm; Sun 5–9pm. Metro: Metro Center.

Poste ★ MODERN AMERICAN This lovely brasserie lies within one of Washington's coolest hotels, the Monaco. You find its separate entrance via an arched carriageway that leads to a stone-paved courtyard, where the restaurant sets up tables in warm weather. Inside, past a small bar-lounge, is the dining area, which includes an exhibition kitchen, banquettes, and a quieter back room. Poste finally seems to have settled into a pleasant culinary groove, thanks to chef Robert Weland, who arrived in May 2004. Weland uses seasonal local ingredients to create modern American fare heavily influenced by traditional French cuisine. At lunch that means a croque-monsieur is made with Virginia ham and Gruyère on brioche; at dinner, your selections may include French onion soup, herbed fresh ricotta ravioli, red wine–braised rabbit, steak frites, and cassoulet. Desserts, too, blend French and American tastes; try the chocolate *pot de crème* (custard), which lists chili(!) as an ingredient. A wine list of 100 California and French bottles offers nearly 30 wines by the glass.

555 8th St. NW, in the Hotel Monaco. ✆ **202/783-6060.** www.postebrasserie.com. Reservations recommended. Breakfast main courses $6.75–$14; brunch main courses $10–$22; lunch main courses $10–$18; dinner main courses $19–$28; pretheater menu $30. AE, DISC, MC, V. Mon–Fri 7–10am and 11:30am–2:30pm; Sat–Sun 9am–2pm and noon–4pm; Mon–Thurs 5–10pm; Fri–Sat 5–10:30pm; Sun 5–9pm; bar open daily 11:30am to closing. Metro: Gallery Place/Verizon Center.

PS7's ★★ MODERN AMERICAN Chef Peter Smith opened PS7's in 2006 after many years working the kitchen at the award-winning Vidalia (p. 151). His culinary artistry is on excellent display here, but first one must navigate the tricky menu, which presents foods in five price categories, rather than in traditional appetizer, entree, dessert order. For example, among the offerings for $10, you might find a salad, a soup, and a vegetable carpaccio; for $13, a tuna tartare or poached mussels; for $15 a cider-braised pork belly or the ham-wrapped monkfish; for $18 red wine–braised beef short ribs or pan-seared sea scallops; and for $23 pan-roasted rockfish or trio of veal. Each price category offers three to five varied choices, encouraging you to think outside the box, ordering as many as you want in a single price category or choosing a couple from each. And though the portions are small, the food is rich . . . and delicious. We liked the short ribs, tuna sliders (bites of tuna tartare on Parker dinner rolls), fried oysters, and spring rolls. The dining room is elegantly modern, with floor-to-ceiling windows, lots of dark wood, and hues of charcoal, brown, and blue. The restaurant also has an expansive bar/lounge, whose menu features several items from the main menu, including those tuna sliders and fried oysters, each priced at $7 during the popular happy hour. But the lounge seating can make noshing problematic, so stand for a drink and then head to the dining room for a proper tuck-in.

777 I St. NW (at 8th St.). ✆ **202/742-8550.** www.ps7restaurant.com. Reservations accepted. Main courses $7–$15 at lunch, $10–$23 at dinner, $77 5-course tasting menu ($107 w/wine). AE, DC, DISC, MC, V. Mon–Fri 11:30am–2:30pm; Mon–Thurs 5:30–9:45pm; Fri–Sat 5:30–10:45pm; lounge menu available Mon–Fri all day, Fri–Sat 5:30pm–closing. Metro: Gallery Place/Chinatown.

Rosa Mexicano ★ MEXICAN It's a chain, but hey, so what? Most of its other locations are in the Big Apple, and this one stands out in the nation's capital for its sensational decor, if nothing else: a beautiful blue glass-tiled wall, over which flows a veil of water; 14-foot-high ceilings; and full-wall windows overlooking the hottest crossroads in town, at 7th and F streets, across from the Verizon Center. The place is popular. *Washington Flyer* magazine reports that Rosa serves "13,000 margaritas and 4,500 orders of guacamole every month." Trust those numbers, because both the guacamole and the margs are super. Other tasty items include quesadillas, grilled beef short ribs, and the *queso fundido* (melted cheese). Like a growing number of restaurants throughout the city, Rosa Mexicano's bar stays open from lunch until closing, even when the dining room shuts down. So if you're hungry or thirsty between lunch and dinner, stop in at the bar to consume your share of this month's quota of 13,000 margaritas and 4,500 orders of guacamole.

575 7th St. NW (at F St.). ✆ **202/783-5522.** rosamexicano.com. Reservations recommended. Lunch main courses $10–$19; dinner main courses $17–$28. AE, DC, DISC, MC, V. Mon–Fri 11:30am–3pm; Sat–Sun noon–3pm; Sun–Thurs 5–10:30pm; Fri–Sat 5–11:30pm; bar open daily from 11:30am to closing. Metro: Gallery Place/Verizon Center.

TenPenh ★ ASIAN FUSION The atmosphere is lively, and the food here stellar. TenPenh has a separate, loungey, hard-to-leave bar, but the dining room itself is inviting, with soft lighting, comfortable booths, and an open kitchen. Jeff Tunks, the man also behind DC Coast, Ceiba, and Acadiana, presents translations of dishes he's discovered in travels throughout Asia: crispy whole fish; five-spice chili tea rubbed beef tenderloin; Chinese-style smoked lobster (also available at DC Coast); wok-seared calamari; and dumplings filled with steamed shrimp and chive. In spring, look for soft-shell crab on the menu. Spring is when the sidewalk tables open up, too, and you can sit outside on a warm day and take in the sights of the capital as you finish your meal with ginger citrus crème brûlée.

1001 Pennsylvania Ave. NW (at 10th St.). ✆ **202/393-4500.** www.tenpenh.com. Reservations recommended. Lunch main courses $13–$18; dinner main courses $15–$28. AE, DISC, MC, V. Mon–Fri 11:30am–2:30pm; Mon–Thurs 5:30–10:30pm; Fri–Sat 5:30–11pm; bar stays open weekdays from 2:30pm to closing and Sat from 5:30pm to closing. Metro: Archives–Navy Memorial.

Zengo ★ LATIN/ASIAN FUSION Downstairs is the lounge, a pulsing after-work destination for a multiethnic cross-section of Washington professionals. Men and women in suits balance small plates of tapas on their laps, or lean back upon the puffy, low-slung sofas and ottomans to drink Zengo's signature mojitos and margaritas. Up two intimidating flights of wide, marble steps lies the dining room, which is just as popular and features a ceviche bar, a glass-enclosed private dining room, and tables scattered throughout the large room, with some overlooking 7th Street. Latin-Asian cuisine might be a new concept, but D.C. diners are nothing if not intrepid. And it turns out that bravery is not needed anyway, since seviches, sushi rolls, and dim sum appetizers marry Asian and Latin tastes quite nicely, whether in a Thai chicken empanada or a won ton taco. Entrees, like the adobo grilled mahimahi, prove the same.

781 7th St. NW (at H St.). ✆ **202/393-2929.** www.modernmexican.com. Reservations recommended. Lunch main courses $17–$24; dinner main courses $19–$29. AE, MC, V. Mon–Fri 11:30am–2:30pm; Sun–Thurs 5–11pm; Fri–Sat 5–11:30pm. Metro: Gallery Place/Verizon Center.

Zola ★★ AMERICAN Zola acquired a new chef in spring 2007, Bryan Moscatello, who is committed to continuing his predecessor's bent for "straight ahead American" cuisine, while adding his own creative twists. Not sure how that translates exactly, but count on deliciousness: a simple ham and Gouda sandwich at lunch, delicately roasted sea scallops with creamy parsnip purée, preceded by an artichoke and goat cheese tart or lobster "mac and cheese" at dinner, followed by such sweet desserts as the trio of butterscotch puddings, each incorporating a different single-malt Scotch whiskey into the custard: a 12-year-old Balvenie, a 15-year-old Aberlour, and a 21-year-old Dalmore. Zola is a cleverly designed restaurant, trading on its location next to the International Spy Museum for a decor that includes red velvet booths, backlit panels of coded KGB documents, and a center-pivoted swinging wall/door that's like something straight out of the TV show *Get Smart.* Zola, in its superb downtown location, has become a popular place for the young and single to hang. Servers are friendly. A $30 pretheater menu, available nightly 5 to 7pm, offers great value.

800 F St. NW (at 8th St.). ✆ **202/654-0999.** www.zoladc.com. Reservations recommended. Lunch main courses $10–$23; dinner main courses $16–$25; pretheater prix-fixe menu $30. AE, DC, DISC, MC, V. Mon–Thurs 11:30am–11pm; Fri 11:30am–midnight; Sat 5pm–midnight; Sun 5–9pm. Metro: Gallery Place/Chinatown.

MODERATE

Bistro D'Oc ★ FRENCH Grab your best girl or guy and duck in here at lunch to sit at a table set against the storefront window. Watch busloads of tourists waiting in line to enter Ford's Theater across the street, before turning your attention to the meal: croque-monsieur, the *potage parisien* (potato and leek soup with Gruyère and croutons), or perhaps a salad of avocado, beets, and celeriac rémoulade. As you sup, the chef might emerge from the kitchen to chat French with regulars, or to greet friends stopping in to say hello. From time to time, the place may erupt in more French, much commotion, and many kisses. The bartender will go out for a smoke and you'll watch him from your window perch, as you and your companion continue to sit there, enjoying each other's company and the Frenchness of the restaurant, with its orangey red-washed walls and Provençal tablecloths. If you're here at dinner, choose the hanger steak and pommes frites, mussels in cream sauce, bouillabaisse, or just about anything on this menu representing the tastes of Languedoc, in southwestern France. An extensive wine list includes selections from the Languedoc region.

518 10th St. NW (between E and F sts. NW). ✆ **202/393-5444.** www.bistrodoc.com. Reservations recommended. Lunch and brunch main courses $12–$19, dinner main courses $13–$22, daily pretheater (5:30–7pm) and post-theater (9–10pm) menu $22. AE, DC, DISC, MC, V. Mon–Sat 11:30am–2:30pm; Sun 11:30am–4pm (brunch); Mon–Thurs 5:30–10pm; Fri–Sat 5:30–11pm; Sun 4–8:30pm. Metro: Metro Center.

Café du Parc ★ FRENCH BRASSERIE Although Washington has only recently come into its own as a great restaurant destination, the city has always been known for its excellent French establishments, from Le Lion D'Or 25 years ago to Citronelle today. This year has added several more French eateries, including the delightful Café du Parc, situated next to the Willard Hotel. The sunny two-level bistro overlooks Pershing Park and offers courtyard seating during clement weather. Renowned Michelin-starred chef Antoine Westermann oversees the menu and has dispatched his own assistants to staff the cafe (you can watch them at work in the open kitchen on the second floor). Café du Parc, with its dishes redolent of Paris—*les tomates farcies aux legumes* (tomatoes stuffed with vegetables) and *choucroute alsacienne* (sauerkraut with pork and sausages)—is a must for any francophile, though most dine here at lunch, when the ambience is decidedly livelier than later in the day. (The lunch menu is a shortened version of the dinner menu.). If the 96-seat cafe is booked, you can carry out certain items daily until 5pm.

1401 Pennsylvania Ave. NW, part of the Willard InterContinental Washington Hotel (at 14th St.). ✆ **202/942-7000.** www.cafeduparc.com. Reservations accepted. Main courses $9.95–$18 at breakfast, $16–$18 at lunch, $17–$24 at dinner. AE, DC, DISC, MC, V. Mon–Fri 6:30–10:30am and 11:30am–2:30pm; Sat–Sun 7–11am and noon–2:30pm; Sun–Thurs 6–10pm; Fri–Sat 6–11pm; limited menu daily 2:30–6pm; carryout daily until 5pm. Metro: Metro Center or Federal Triangle.

Jaleo ★ *Finds* SPANISH In theater season, Jaleo's dining room fills and empties each evening according to the performance schedule of the Shakespeare Theater, right next door. Lunchtime always draws a crowd from nearby office buildings and the Hill. This restaurant and executive chef/partner José Andrés (see Café Atlantico for more

Kids Family-Friendly Restaurants

Nearly every restaurant welcomes families these days, starting, most likely, with the one in your hotel. What you need to know, mom and dad, is that many Washington restaurants are playgrounds for the city's vast population of young professionals. For example, I would love to recommend Matchbox, which serves an excellent pizza and other items kids love, but its reservations-only-for-six-or-more policy means that you and your little darlings are going to be waiting for your table (and there's almost always a wait) either in the jumping-all-day bar or out on the street in the middle of Chinatown. So read over this chapter and choose a place that sounds like its food, fun, and flexibility factors suit your family, but also consider dining early and getting a table away from the bar scene. Chinese restaurants and museum cafes are always a safe bet, and so are these:

Lebanese Taverna (p. 174) Its location down the hill from the National Zoo and its voluminous menu (including items marked for "the little ones") make the taverna attractive to mom, dad, and the whole caboodle. Around for nearly 2 decades, the taverna has fallen off the radar of food critics pursuing the latest greatest craze. But locals continue to favor the place and the result is that the owners keep opening new locations—there are five now.

Legal Sea Foods (p. 146) Believe it or not, this seafood restaurant has won awards for its kids' menu. It features the usual macaroni and cheese and hot dogs, but it also offers kids' portions of steamed lobster; fried popcorn shrimp; a small fisherman's platter of shrimp, scallops, and clams; and other items, each of which comes with fresh fruit, fresh vegetables, and a choice of rice, mashed potatoes, or french fries. Prices range from $1.95 to $17.

Old Glory Barbecue (p. 170) A boisterous, laid-back place where the waiters are friendly without being patronizing. Go early, since this is one of those restaurants that become more of a bar as the evening progresses. There is a children's menu, but you may not need it—the barbecue, burgers, muffins, fries, and desserts are so good that everyone can order from the main menu.

about Andrés) may be credited with initiating the tapas craze in Washington, where it remains popular 15 years after Jaleo debuted. Though the menu offers a handful of entrees (available only after 5pm), you really want to consider those tapas—60 at last count, but more are always being added. These include a very simple but not-to-be-missed grilled bread layered with a paste of fresh tomatoes and topped with anchovies, date and bacon fritters, *torta es pagnola* (a layered omelet), savory warm goat cheese served with toast points, a skewer of grilled chorizo sausage atop garlic mashed potatoes, a delicious mushroom tart served with roasted red-pepper sauce, and gazpacho. Paella is among the few heartier entrees (it feeds two to four). Spanish wines, sangrias, and sherries are available by the glass. Finish with a rum-and-butter–soaked apple charlotte in bread pastry or a plate of Spanish cheeses. The casual-chic interior focuses on a large mural of a flamenco dancer inspired by John Singer Sargent's painting *Jaleo*.

Jaleo has two suburban locations, at 7271 Woodmont Ave., Bethesda, Maryland (✆ **301/913-0003**), and 2250-A Crystal Drive, Arlington, Virginia (✆ **703/413-8181**).

480 7th St. NW (at E St.). ✆ **202/628-7949.** www.jaleo.com. Reservations accepted at lunch and for dinner until 6:30pm. Dinner main courses $16–$18; tapas $3.95–$9.95. AE, DC, DISC, MC, V. Sun–Mon 11:30am–10pm; Tues–Thurs 11:30am–11:30pm; Fri–Sat 11:30am–midnight. Metro: Archives or Gallery Place.

Legal Sea Foods ★ *Kids* SEAFOOD This famous family-run Boston-based seafood empire, whose motto is "If it's not fresh, it's not Legal," made its Washington debut in 1995. This location's expansive dining room features exposed brick and beams, booths, and an oyster bar. Sporting events, especially Boston games, are aired on a TV over the handsome bar. You're right across the street from the Verizon Center, where the city's basketball and hockey teams play. As for the food, not only is everything fresh, but it's all from certified-safe waters.

Legal's buttery-rich clam chowder is a classic. Other worthy appetizers include garlicky golden-brown farm-raised mussels and fluffy pan-fried Maryland lump crab cakes served with mustard sauce and salad. You can have one of eight or so varieties of fresh fish grilled or opt for one of Legal's specialty dishes, like the baked Boston scrod or the New England fried clams. Top it off with a slice of Boston cream pie. Diners with celiac disease, that is, an allergy to wheat and gluten, will be happy to know that Legal has a special gluten-free menu; parents will be glad that Legal's award-winning kid's menu offers not just macaroni and cheese, but steamed lobster, popcorn shrimp, and other items, each of which comes with fresh fruit and vegetable, plus a choice of rice, mashed potatoes, or french fries. At lunch, the lobster roll is a real treat.

You'll find another Legal Sea Foods at National Airport (✆ **703/413-9810**).

704 7th St. NW (between G and H sts.). ✆ **202/347-0007.** www.legalseafoods.com. Reservations recommended, especially at lunch. Lunch main courses $9.95–$16; sandwiches $7.95–$18; dinner main courses $14–$35. AE, DC, DISC, MC, V. Mon–Thurs 11am–10pm; Fri–Sat 11am–11pm; Sun noon–10pm. Metro: Gallery Place/Chinatown.

Les Halles ★ FRENCH/STEAK You will be happiest here ordering something steakish, whether *onglet,* a boneless French cut hanger steak, steak au poivre, steak tartare, New York sirloin, or some other cut; all come with frites, which are a must. The menu isn't all beef, but it is classic French, featuring cassoulet, *confit de canard* (duck leg slow-cooked in its own fat to crispness), escargots, onion soup, *choucroute garnie* (melange of smoked pork, sausages, and sauerkraut), and an irresistible *frisée aux lardons* (a savory salad of chicory studded with hunks of bacon and toast, smeared thickly with Roquefort). If you spy something on the menu that's not Gallic, ignore it. Les Halles, bowing to Washingtonians' ghastly work schedules, started serving breakfast Monday through Friday, opening at 7am; choices range from a simple French croissant to a big American plate of steak and eggs and home fries.

Les Halles is big but charmingly French. The banquettes, pressed-tin ceiling, mirrors, wooden floor, and side bar capture the feel of a brasserie. A vast window front overlooks Pennsylvania Avenue and the awning-covered sidewalk cafe. Every July, from the 4th to the 14th, Les Halles hosts its Liberty Festival, to celebrate America's Independence Day and France's Bastille Day (July 14). The celebration culminates in the annual Bastille Day races, for which the city actually closes a stretch of Pennsylvania Avenue that serves as the racetrack. The event turns into a wild block party.

1201 Pennsylvania Ave. NW. ✆ **202/347-6848.** www.leshalles.net. Reservations recommended. Breakfast main courses $2.50–$13; lunch and dinner main courses $9.50–$26; pretheater menu Mon–Sat $18. AE, DC, DISC, MC, V. Mon–Fri 7:30–11:30am; daily 11:30am–midnight. Metro: Metro Center or Federal Triangle.

Matchbox ★ PIZZA/ITALIAN This restaurant started out in 2003 as a skinny, three-level town house in Chinatown, an odd place to find a pizzeria, maybe, but welcome, nonetheless. By 2006, Matchbox had grown so popular that it expanded into an L-shaped structure that nearly triples its capacity and includes a patio. The key things here are the wood-fired brick ovens, which bake the thin pizza crust at temperatures as high as 900°F. You can choose a regularly featured pizza, like the "prosciutto white," which is topped with prosciutto, kalamata olives, fresh garlic, ricotta cheese, fresh mozzarella, and extra-virgin olive oil; or you can request your own set of toppings, from smoked bacon to artichoke hearts. Matchbox is actually a cut above a pizzeria, for it also serves super salads (the chopped salad is my favorite: diced tomatoes, crispy bacon, hair-thin "pasta ringlets," and greens in a creamy herb vinaigrette), appetizers, sandwiches, and entrees (the honey-glazed pecan crusted chicken is a keeper); its full bar on the first floor is quite the social scene.

713 H St. NW. ✆ **202/289-4441**. www.matchboxdc.com. Pizzas and sandwiches $10–$21; main courses at lunch and dinner $16–$26. AE, DC, DISC, MC, V. Sun 11:30am–11pm, Mon–Fri 11am–midnight; Sat noon–1am. Metro: Gallery Place/Chinatown.

Old Ebbitt Grill AMERICAN You won't find this place listed among the city's best culinary establishments, but you can bet it's included in every tour book. It's an institution. The original Old Ebbitt was established in 1856, at 14th and F streets, around the corner. The Grill moved to this location in 1980, bringing much of the old place with it. Among its artifacts are animal trophies bagged by Teddy Roosevelt, and Alexander Hamilton's wooden bears—one with a secret compartment in which it's said he hid whiskey bottles from his wife. The Old Ebbitt is attractive in a fusty sort of way, with Persian rugs strewn upon worn oak floors, beveled mirrors, flickering gaslights, etched-glass panels, and paintings of Washington scenes. The long, dark mahogany Old Bar area emphasizes the men's saloon ambience.

Tourists and office people fill the Ebbitt during the day, but flirting singles take it over at night. You'll generally have to wait for a table if you don't reserve ahead. The waiters are friendly and professional in a programmed sort of way; service could be faster. Menus change daily but always include certain favorites: burgers, trout Parmesan (Virginia trout dipped in egg batter and Parmesan cheese, flash fried), crab cakes, and oysters—Old Ebbitt's raw bar is its saving grace when all else fails; the *Washington Post* food critic has claimed that this is the best raw bar in town, and that's saying something. Aside from the fresh oysters, the tastiest dishes are usually the seasonal ones; fresh ingredients make all the difference.

675 15th St. NW (between F and G sts.). ✆ **202/347-4801**. www.ebbitt.com. Reservations recommended. Breakfast $8.95–$14; brunch $4.95–$25; lunch and dinner main courses $12–$26; raw bar $8.95–$21. AE, DC, DISC, MC, V. Mon–Fri 7:30am–1am; Sat–Sun 8:30am–1am; bar open until 2am Sun–Thurs, 3am Fri–Sat. Metro: McPherson Square or Metro Center.

Oyamel ★★★ MEXICAN Jose Andres, the 30-something Spaniard who has wowed us repeatedly as chef at Jaleo, Café Atlantico, Zaytinya, and minibar, does it again, even better, at Oyamel. With its limited reservations policy, meant to encourage passersby and spontaneous walk-ins; open-all-day hours; menu of antojitos priced below $10 each (the menu lists a few entrees, but it's these small plates that you'll want to order); hearty cocktails; and exuberant atmosphere, Oyamel serves as the ultimate chill pill for the capital's hungry and stressed-out wonks at their most wound-up. See for yourself, and when you do, order the Oyamel margarita, which is topped with salt-air foam; the table-made guacamole (ask for the spiciest version, which is still not that spicy); something from the specials, like the beer-battered soft-shell crab (only $10!) served with a mango-roasted corn salsa that I gobbled up; or, from the main menu, the *cochinita pibil con cebolla en escabeche* taco (only $3.50!), which is a tortilla wrapped around Yucatan-style pit-barbecued pork. With its lively bar scene and prime corner location in the heart of the Penn Quarter, Oyamel is always hopping.

401 7th St. NW (at D St.). ✆ **202/628-1005.** www.oyamel.com. Limited reservations. Small plates and tacos $3.50–$10, entrees $19–$25 at both lunch and dinner. AE, DC, DISC, MC, V. Sun–Mon 11:30am–10pm; Tues–Thurs 11:30am–11:30pm; Fri–Sat 11:30am–midnight. Metro: Gallery Place/Chinatown or Archives/Navy Memorial.

Rasika ★★ INDIAN This sexy-cool restaurant opened in December 2005 and immediately started to attract the Washington glitterati, including not only Bill and Hil Clinton, but also daughter Chelsea and her pals. Soft lighting, cinnamon and spice tones, silk panels, and dangling glass beads contribute a rich and sensuously attractive feeling to the dining room and its adjoining lounge. Everyone's drinking martinis, the clove or the pomegranate, usually. As for the food, it's divine: Try the crispy spinach, ginger scallops, tandoori salmon, black cod, or lobster masala.

633 D St. NW (at 7th St.). ✆ **202/637-1222.** www.rasikarestaurant.com. Reservations recommended. Lunch main courses $7–$20; dinner main courses $15–$28; pretheater menu $28. AE, DC, DISC, MC, V. Mon–Fri 11:30am–2:30pm; Mon–Thurs 5:30–10:30pm; Fri–Sat 5:30–11:30pm; lounge stays open throughout the day serving light meals. Metro: Archives/Navy Memorial or Gallery Place/Verizon Center.

Zaytinya ★★ GREEK/TURKISH/MIDDLE EASTERN How popular is Zaytinya? Well, the restaurant serves, on average, 750 people per night during the week and 1,000 per night on weekends. It's big and it's busy and it always has been. Executive Chef José Andrés is behind it all (see reviews of Jaleo, where he continues as the executive chef/partner, and of Café Atlantico, where he is the creative director).

The place takes reservations only at lunch and for pretheater dinners, 5 to 6:30pm, so if you have to wait for a table, join the rollicking bar scene, where 20- and 30-somethings can be counted on to provide nightly entertainment. Once seated, you receive a basket of hot and billowy-thin shells of pita bread, along with a saucer of olive oil swirled with pomegranate syrup. Your waiter will guide you through the menu; explain that the wine list, like the meze dishes, are a mixture of Greek, Turkish, and Lebanese specialties; and inform you that the word "Zaytinya" is Turkish for "olive oil." Although the dinner menu lists several entrees, what you want to do here is order lots of little dishes: zucchini-cheese cakes, which come with a caper and yogurt sauce; the carrot-apricot–pine nut fritters, served with pistachio sauce; sardines; a marinated salmon; *fattoush,* or salad of tomatoes and cucumbers mixed with pomegranate reduction, sumac, and olive oil, with crispy pita-bread croutons; and shrimp with tomatoes, onions, ouzo, and kefalograviera cheese. For dessert, try a Turkish coffee chocolate cake, or the seductive apples in saffron cream.

701 9th St. NW (at G St.). ✆ **202/638-0800.** www.zaytinya.com. Reservations at lunch and pretheater dinner 5–6:30pm. Meze items $3.75–$9.75; dinner main courses $13–$25. AE, DC, DISC, MC, V. Sun–Mon 11:30am–10pm; Tues–Thurs 11:30am–11:30pm; Fri–Sat 11:30am–midnight. Metro: Gallery Place/Chinatown (9th St. exit).

INEXPENSIVE

Tony Cheng's Seafood Restaurant ★ CHINESE/SEAFOOD Most of the restaurants in Chinatown look seedy, no matter how good the food might be. Tony Cheng's is the most presentable of Chinatown's eateries, and it's also a good choice if you like Cantonese specialties and spicy Szechuan and Hunan cuisine. Downstairs is the Mongolian Barbecue eatery, where you have a choice of dipping your own vegetables, seafood, and meats in a "hot pot" of boiling broth; or a $16-per-person, all-you-can-eat spread of foods you select for the chef to barbecue over a huge grill. The second-floor Tony Cheng's Seafood Restaurant has been here for decades and has earned a reputation for its Cantonese roast duck (see it for yourself before ordering, since it is displayed in a case at the back of the restaurant); lobster or Dungeness crab, stir-fried and served with either ginger and scallions or black bean sauce; and Szechuan crispy beef, to name just a few. Dim sum is available at lunch daily, but during the week you order items off the menu, rather than from rolling carts.

619 H St. NW (between 6th and 7th sts.). ✆ **202/842-8669** (Mongolian Barbecue) and **202/371-8669** (Seafood Restaurant). Reservations recommended. Mongolian Barbecue main courses $16 all-you-can-eat, or $11–$20. Seafood restaurant lunch main courses $10–$15; dinner main courses $13–$19. AE, MC, V. Sun–Thurs 11am–11pm; Fri–Sat 11am–midnight. Metro: Gallery Place/Chinatown.

5 Midtown

VERY EXPENSIVE

BLT Steak ★ STEAK Does D.C. really need another steakhouse? The arrival of BLT Steak in late 2006 has convinced us that, yes, we do. The BLT stands not for bacon, lettuce, and tomato, but for Bistro Laurent Tourondel, the chef, whose other BLTs are located in New York City and San Juan. The capital's BLT lies on a street between the White House and the K Street corridor of law firm and lobbyist offices, and attracts a steady stream of power brokers. The restaurant, with its expansive bar, suede seats, large and airy room, and soul-music sound system (no Frank Sinatra here) is also a popular stomping ground for young professionals on weeknights. A meal begins with a basket of enormous, complimentary Gruyère popovers and a little pot of country pâté. Menu recommendations include the raw bar offerings, hanger steak, the American wagyu rib-eye (if you don't mind paying $92 for your entree!), blue cheese Tater Tots, onion rings, any of the salads, and the souffléd crepe with ricotta cheese for dessert.

1625 I St. NW (at 17th St.). ✆ **202/689-8999.** www.bltsteak.com. Reservations accepted. Main courses $16–$45 at lunch, $24–$45 at dinner. (Prices go as high as $92 for wagyu beef.) AE, DC, DISC, MC, V. Mon–Fri 11:30am–2:30pm; Mon–Thurs 5:30–11pm; Fri–Sat 5:30–11:30pm. Metro: Farragut West or Farragut North.

Equinox ★★ NEW AMERICAN Everyone seems to love Equinox, whose proximity to the White House guarantees a high-and-mighty clientele. Regulars appreciate that Equinox is not splashy in any way—it's just a pretty, comfortable restaurant serving creatively delicious American food. Even if you aren't vegetarian, you'll eat all your vegetables here, because as much care is taken with these garnishes as with the entree itself. And every entree comes with a garnish or two, like the creamed spinach or the forest mushrooms with applewood bacon, or the white bean ragout. You can order additional side dishes; consider the macaroni and cheese: Vermont cheddar, Gruyère, and black truffle reduction. The home runs, of course, are the entrees. You order a la carte for lunch, and both a la carte or one of three tasting menus for dinner: $57 for three courses, $70 for four courses, and $85 for six courses. Standouts have included pan-roasted Alaska halibut with artichoke ragout; crab cakes made with lump crab mixed with capers, brioche bread crumbs, mayonnaise, and lemon-butter sauce; and grilled rib back of natural pork with horseradish-potato purée. The menu identifies dishes made from animals raised in accordance with Humane Farm Animal Care guidelines.

818 Connecticut Ave. NW. ✆ **202/331-8118.** www.equinoxrestaurant.com. Reservations recommended. Lunch main courses $19–$28; dinner main courses $30–$35. Dinner tasting menus: $57, $70, and $85. AE, DC, DISC, MC, V. Mon–Fri 11:30am–2pm; Mon–Thurs 5:30–10pm; Fri–Sat 5:30–10:30pm; Sun 5–9pm. Metro: Farragut West.

The Palm ★ *Finds* STEAK The Palm is one in a chain of 29 locations that started nearly 80 years ago in New York—but here in D.C., it feels like an original. The Washington Palm is 36 years old and though recently renovated and expanded to include a glass-enclosed veranda, its walls, like those in all Palms, are still covered with the caricatures of regulars, the famous, and the not-so-famous. If you think you see Tim Russert or Larry King at a table, you're probably right. You can't go wrong with steak, whether it's the 36-ounce dry-aged New York strip, or sliced in a steak salad. Oversize lobsters are a specialty, and certain side dishes are a must: creamed spinach, onion rings, palm fries (something akin to deep-fried potato chips), and hash browns. You can order half-portions of these, so you have no excuse but to order at least one. Several of the longtime waiters like to kid with you a bit, but the service is always fast.

1225 19th St. NW. ✆ **202/293-9091.** www.thepalm.com. Reservations recommended. Lunch main courses $13–$20; dinner main courses $15–$64 (most items are in the neighborhood of $30–$39). AE, DC, MC, V. Mon–Fri 11:45am–10:30pm; Sat 5:30–10:30pm; Sun 5:30–9:30pm. Metro: Dupont Circle.

The Prime Rib ★★ STEAK/SEAFOOD The Prime Rib has plenty of competition in D.C., but it makes no difference. Beef lovers still consider this The Place. It's got a definite men's club feel about it, with brass-trimmed black walls, leopard-skin carpeting, and comfortable black-leather chairs and banquettes. Waiters are in black tie, and a pianist at the baby grand plays show tunes and Irving Berlin classics at lunch; at dinner, a bass player joins the pianist.

The meat is from the best grain-fed steers and has been aged for 4 to 5 weeks. Steaks and cuts of roast beef are thick, tender, and juicy. In case you had any doubt, The Prime Rib's prime rib is the best item on the menu—juicy, thick, top-quality meat. For less carnivorous diners, there are about a dozen seafood entrees, including an excellent crab imperial. Mashed potatoes are done right, as are the fried potato skins, but I recommend the hot cottage fries.

2020 K St. NW. ✆ **202/466-8811.** www.theprimerib.com. Reservations recommended. Jacket and tie required for men. Lunch main courses $12–$25; dinner main courses $27–$49. AE, DC, MC, V. Mon–Thurs 11:30am–3pm and 5–11pm; Fri 11:30am–3pm and 5–11:30pm; Sat 5–11:30pm. Metro: Farragut West.

Taberna del Alabardero ★★ *Finds* SPANISH Dress up to visit this truly elegant restaurant, where you receive royal treatment from the Spanish staff, who are accustomed to attending to the real thing—Spain's King Juan Carlos and Queen Sofia have dined here. The taberna is also a favorite of dignitaries attending meetings at the nearby World Bank and International Monetary Fund.

The dining room is ornate, with red tufted banquettes, green satin stretched across chairs, and gilded cherubs placed at ceiling corners. Order a plate of tapas to start: lightly fried calamari, shrimp in garlic and olive oil, artichokes sautéed with thin smoky serrano ham, and marinated mushrooms. Although the a la carte menu changes with the seasons (look for the duck breast with sweet vinegar sauce in spring), several paellas are always available, including the rich and flavorful seafood paella served on saffron rice. Other signature dishes are the stuffed squid sauced in its own ink and the traditional salted cod *(bacalao)*. The wine list features a healthy selection of American wines, along with some 250 Spanish wines. Good deal: Weekdays 3 to 7pm, tapas are half-price and sangria is $3 per glass or $12 for a pitcher.

1776 I St. NW (entrance on 18th St. NW). ✆ **202/429-2200.** www.alabardero.com. Reservations recommended. Jacket and tie for men suggested. Tapas $6–$16. Lunch main courses $18–$26; dinner main courses $29–$37. AE, DC, DISC, MC, V. Mon–Fri 11:30am–2:30pm; Mon–Sat 5:30–10:30pm. Metro: Farragut West.

Teatro Goldoni ★★ VENETIAN ITALIAN Teatro's dining room is dramatic, displaying Venetian masks, immense murals, and harlequin colored glass panels. Chef/owner Fabrizio Aielli is on view, performing as if on stage, inside his elevated glass-enclosed kitchen. And the food, served with a flourish, is as dramatic as the decor. The lobster risotto and the *fritto misto,* both always on the menu, are recommended, but just about any choice is sensational: risotto with porcini and truffle oil, the seared tuna topped with foie gras, the stewed beef in Barolo wine, or the ravioli stuffed with truffle-oil flavored potatoes and leeks. Classic tiramisu is a specialty, but the warm chocolate and almond cake is also very good. Bring a party of people; in true Goldoni tradition, the Teatro is a good spot for a celebration, especially Friday and Saturday nights, when there's live jazz. A weekday bar lunch deal draws the office crowd: $13 for a Venetian specialty, like a bowl of *rigatoni alla matriciana* (pasta in a light tomato sauce with onions and pancetta), plus a glass of wine.

1909 K St. NW. ✆ **202/955-9494.** www.teatrogoldoni.com. Reservations recommended. Lunch main courses $19–$25; dinner main courses $19–$40. AE, DC, DISC, MC, V. Mon–Fri 11:30am–2pm; Mon–Thurs 5:30–10pm; Fri–Sat 5–11pm. Metro: Farragut North or Farragut West.

Vidalia ★★ REGIONAL AMERICAN/SOUTHERN Chef R.J. Cooper tied with Palena (p. 172) chef Frank Ruta for the James Beard Foundation's 2007 award as the best chef for the Mid-Atlantic region. You'll understand why when you dine here. Vidalia's cuisine marries tastes of various regions of the South, with an emphasis on New Orleans. Featured dishes might include a roasted young pig with braised savoy cabbage or rockfish filé with succotash and turnip greens. A signature entree is scrumptious sautéed shrimp on a mound of creamed grits and caramelized onions with tasso ham in a cilantro butter sauce. Corn bread and biscuits with apple butter are served at every meal. Vidalia is known for its lemon chess pie and pecan pie, but always check out alternatives, which might be an apple napoleon or caramel cake. Vidalia offers an extensive wine list, at least 30 of which are offered by the glass, in both 3-ounce and 6-ounce pours.

If you're hesitant to dine at a restaurant that's down a flight of steps from the street, your doubts will vanish as soon as you enter Vidalia's tiered dining room. There's a party going on down here. In fact, arrive between 5 and 7pm weeknights and you'll get in on the extremely popular wine tastings in the cozy wine bar. The chef sends out little canapés, like miniature BLTs, and both the wine tastings and the hors d'oeuvres are complimentary!

1990 M St. NW. ✆ **202/659-1990.** www.vidaliadc.com. Reservations recommended. Lunch main courses $16–$24; dinner main courses $27–$39. AE, DC, DISC, MC, V. Mon–Fri 11:30am–2:30pm; Mon–Thurs 5:30–10pm; Fri–Sat 5:30–10:30pm; Sun 5–9:30pm. Metro: Dupont Circle.

EXPENSIVE

Corduroy ★★ AMERICAN No matter how exceptional the hotel, its hotel restaurant doesn't always meet the same standards. And when you're talking about a hotel like the Four Points Sheraton, aimed at the convention crowd, let's face it, you're not expecting culinary creativity in the kitchen. Corduroy, with chef Tom Power at the helm, proves the exception. In residence here since 2000, Power has steadily built a following in this food-mad city, where diners can tell you exactly how many stars the best restaurants have been awarded by local food critics: Corduroy received three stars and came in at #16 out of the *Washingtonian* magazine's 2007 ranking of the city's top 100 restaurants. Pretty amazing. So, better call for a reservation. The dining room is finely decorated in earth tones and mahogany accents, the atmosphere is relaxed, and the dishes are simple but superb: crispy striped bass with sherry vinegar, Copper Ridge Farm Prime rib-eye with rutabaga gratin, parsnip soup, lobster salad, seared sea scallops with seasonal mushrooms, and vanilla bean crème brûlée.

1201 K St. NW, inside the Four Points Sheraton Hotel. ✆ **202/589-0699.** www.corduroydc.com. Reservations recommended. Breakfast main courses $9–$13; lunch main courses $10–$17; dinner main courses $18–$32. AE, DC, DISC, MC, V. Mon–Fri 6:30–10:30am and noon–2:30pm; Sat–Sun 7–11am; Mon–Thurs 5:30–10:30pm; Fri–Sat 5:30–11pm. Metro: McPherson Square or Metro Center.

DC Coast ★ AMERICAN The dining room is sensational: two stories high, with glass-walled balcony, immense oval mirrors hanging over the bar, and a full-bodied stone mermaid poised to greet you at the entrance. Gather at the bar first to feel a part of the loud and trendy scene; while you're there, why not nosh on something from the bar menu, perhaps the crispy fried calamari or maybe a luscious flat-bread pizza? This continues to be one of the city's most popular restaurants, so call ahead to book a reservation. Chef Jeff Tunks, the chef behind **TenPenh, Ceiba,** and **Acadiana** (p. 143, 140, and 138), started his dynasty with DC Coast, which opened in 1998. Here, Tunks fuses the coastal cuisines of the Mid-Atlantic, Gulf, and West Coast. Almost always on the menu are his Chinese-style smoked lobster with crispy fried spinach, pan-roasted sea scallops, and the crispy whole striped bass, and the fish filet encrusted with portobello paste and served with truffled potatoes and porcini broth. Seafood is a big part of the menu, but there are a handful of meat dishes too; try the pork chop with sweet potato purée.

1401 K St. NW. ✆ **202/216-5988.** www.dccoast.com. Reservations recommended. Lunch main courses $14–$19; dinner main courses $19–$29. AE, DC, DISC, MC, V. Mon–Fri 11:30am–2:30pm; Mon–Thurs 5:30–10:30pm; Fri–Sat 5:30–11pm; bar stays open weekdays from 2:30pm to closing and Sat from 5:30pm to closing. Metro: McPherson Square.

Gerard's Place ★★ FRENCH Gerard Pangaud departed his restaurant in 2006 to head up a local cooking school, leaving others in charge of his kitchen. But he missed his original métier. So foodies can breathe a sigh of relief, for Gerard is back to supervise the kitchen goings-on and create new dishes, even as he continues his work at the cooking school. Dine at Gerard's Place for elegant French cuisine that's among the best in the city. The dish that made the restaurant famous, poached lobster with Sauternes sauce, still appears on both the lunch and dinner menus ($62!), though slightly reinvented: fresh mango, lime, piquillo peppers, and spinach are its sidekicks now. Diners may order a la carte or choose a $30 prix-fixe menu at lunch or the $87 chef's tasting menu at dinner. Besides the lobster, look for an appetizer of seared sea scallops with parsley mousse and garlic flan, or an entree of roasted duck breast served in a red-wine sauce with roasted rhubarb, or an organic hanger steak with Parmesan herb gnocchi, or whatever the season inspires Pangaud to invent. All desserts are made to order, whether the trio of house-made fruit sorbets or the Tarte Tatin of mango, so you must specify your dessert at the same time you order your entree. The dining room itself is small, seating only 50 at a time, and somewhat modest in design. And this is a quiet restaurant, not a place to get rowdy. You're here for the food and quiet conversation.

915 15th St. NW. ✆ **202/737-4445.** www.gerardsplacedc.net. Reservations recommended. Lunch main courses $23–$62, prix-fixe menu $30; dinner main courses $25–$62; chef's tasting menu $87. AE, MC, V. Mon–Fri 11:30am–2pm; Mon–Thurs 5:30–9pm; Fri–Sat 5:30–9:30pm. Metro: McPherson Square.

The Oval Room ★ MODERN AMERICAN The Oval Room is a local favorite, another winner for owner Ashok Bajaj, who also owns the Bombay Club (see below), right across the street, and Rasika (p. 148), in the Penn Quarter. The restaurant was in transition for a while there, as chefs came and went. Chef Tony Conti, who previously served as executive sous chef for Jean-Georges Vongerichten in New York, happily seems to be staying put. His reasonably priced modern American cuisine offers ricotta gnocchi, caramelized beef tenderloin, crispy snapper, and the like. The Oval Room is a handsome restaurant, with contemporary art hanging on its pale green walls. Its atmosphere is congenial, not stuffy, no doubt because the bar area separating the restaurant into two distinct rooms sends cheerful sounds in either direction. In case you haven't made the connection, the Oval Room is a short walk from the White House.

800 Connecticut Ave. NW (at Lafayette Square). ✆ **202/463-8700.** www.ovalroom.com. Reservations recommended. Lunch main courses $7–$24; dinner main courses $16–$30; pretheater dinner (5:30–6:30pm) $29. AE, DISC, MC, V. Mon–Thurs 11:30am–10:15pm; Fri 11:30am–10:30pm; Sat 5–10:30pm. Metro: Farragut West.

MODERATE

Bombay Club ★ *Finds* INDIAN The delightful Bombay Club pleases patrons who know their Indian food as well as those who've never tried it: Dishes present an easy introduction to Indian food for the uninitiated, and are sensitive to varying tolerances for spiciness. I'm a wimp in the "heat" department, my husband's the opposite, and we're both happy here.

The spiciest item on the menu is the fiery green chile chicken ("not for the faint-hearted," the menu warns). You can't go wrong ordering a tandoori entree, that is, a food that has been marinated, then grilled and baked in a clay oven. Most popular are the tandoori salmon; the chicken tandoori, which is marinated in an almond, cashew, yogurt, ginger, and garlic dressing; and the delicately prepared lobster Malabar. The Bombay Club is known for its vegetarian offerings (try the black lentils cooked overnight on a slow fire) and for its Sunday champagne brunch, which offers a buffet of fresh juices, fresh baked breads, and assorted Indian dishes. Patrons are as fond of the service as the cuisine: Waiters seem straight out of *Jewel in the Crown,* attending to your every whim. This is one place where you can linger over a meal as long as you like. Slow-moving ceiling fans and wicker furniture accentuate the colonial British ambience. A pianist plays nightly.

815 Connecticut Ave. NW. ✆ **202/659-3727.** www.bombayclubdc.com. Reservations recommended. Main courses $7.50–$24; Sun brunch $20. AE, DC, MC, V. Mon–Fri and Sun brunch 11:30am–2:30pm; Mon–Thurs 6–10:30pm; Fri–Sat 6–11pm; Sun 5:30–9pm. Metro: Farragut West.

Brasserie Beck ★★ BELGIAN The doors opened in April 2007, the place started rocking, and it hasn't stopped. Chef Robert Wiedmaier's West End restaurant, Marcel's (p. 164), is one of the best fine-dining establishments in the District. Beck's, which, like Marcel's, is named for one of Wiedmaier's young sons, has immediately taken off as one of the city's best bistros and hot spots. Like other new restaurants—for instance BLT Steak, Urbana, and Central—the bar scene is a crucial element of both ambience and popularity, and Beck's beckons, seating 21 people at its huge marble-and-walnut bar, and handling many more beyond that. Restaurant design also plays its part: Beck's features an attractive open kitchen of glass, steel, and cobalt blue tiles, and the overall feel of a large train station, with large round clocks on display beneath 22-foot-high ceilings. But in the end it comes down to the food, and here, Beck's pegs it: Belgian tastes of in-house cured salmon, beef carbonnade, steamed mussels served three ways, frites, duck confit, lamb sausage, and the list goes on. Beer lover's bonus: a large assortment of Belgian beers on tap and by the bottle.

1101 K St. NW (at 11th St.). ✆ **202/408-1717.** www.beckdc.com. Reservations recommended. Main courses $16–$23 at lunch and dinner. AE, MC, V. Mon–Sat 11am–midnight. Metro: McPherson Sq.

INEXPENSIVE

Café Asia ASIAN FUSION It's easy to miss Café Asia, nestled as it is between hair salons and offices on I Street right near the White House. Inside is a different story. The decor and menu both stand out in really interesting ways. The restaurant has three levels to it, set within an atrium. From street level, walk downstairs to the main dining room—the furniture here looks like it was made for child's play; it comes in circular and rectangular shapes and colors of orange, yellow, and white, and these pieces are set closer to the ground than normal. Upstairs is more of a lounge area, overlooking the lower level; one more flight up is reserved mostly for private parties.

The menu here is pan-Asian: Chinese, Indonesian, Japanese, Thai. If your waitress steers you to something "interesting," you can take that to mean "spicy," like the Indonesian fried rice, which is "more interesting than Chinese." (Yeah—it's got chiles in it, for one thing.) So if you like Americanized, or tamed down, Asian food, you might be happy with the teriyaki and satays. You have many more choices if you want to sample exotic food. Have a glass of water handy, but do try the *nasi uduk,* which is a tasty Indonesian coconut rice platter with spicy beef, crispy anchovies, pickled vegetables, *emping* (acorn chips), chicken satay, and spicy prawn sauce. Another winner is the *ikan pepes,* which is Indonesian grilled fish filet with spicy turmeric sauce, fresh basil, and lemon grass, wrapped in banana leaves. Café Asia also serves delicious sushi. Young professionals throng Café Asia's happy hour, Monday through Saturday, 4:30 to 7:30pm, when nigiri sushi is available for $1 per piece and select draft beers are sold for $2.

1720 I St. NW. ✆ **202/659-2696.** www.cafeasia.com. Reservations accepted. Lunch and dinner main courses $7–$14. AE, DC, DISC, MC, V. Mon–Thurs 11:30am–11pm; Fri 11:30am–midnight; Sat noon–midnight; Sun noon–11pm. Metro: Farragut West.

6 U Street Corridor

MODERATE

Bistro Tabaq ★ MIDDLE EASTERN Tabaq resides in a four-story building, but its restaurant levels are on the first and fourth floor. The fourth floor is where you want to be, since this puts you on the roof, with a glorious view of the city, including the far-off Capitol and Washington Monument. A glass ceiling and glass doors open and close to accommodate the weather, so you can dine here year-round. The terrace is very dimly lit, which makes this a favorite spot for couples, but a frustrating experience for anyone trying to decipher the menu in the almost-dark. And a word about those four flights to the top: Women might want to don longer skirts, so as not to reveal too much to the ones following in their wake, and to opt for lower heels, rather than trying to teeter their way up. Tabaq does try to keep to a dress code, though, so forget the athletic look. It's all about tapas here, with about 40 from which to choose.

Winners include hummus, the tabaq salad, and something called *manti,* which is a Turkish-style beef ravioli, served with red pepper, garlic, and yogurt. From the small list of entrees, the Mediterranean sea bass, served with almond and currant rice, is your best choice. If the wait's too long for the terrace, you can always dine in the first-floor Red Room, quite nice actually and romantic in its own way.

1336 U St. NW (at 13th St.). ✆ **202/265-0965.** www.tabaqdc.com. Reservations accepted. Main courses $11–$20. AE, DC, DISC, MC, V. Sun–Thurs 5–11pm; Fri–Sat 5pm–midnight; Sat–Sun 11am–4pm. Metro: U St.–Cardozo.

Café Saint-Ex ★ AMERICAN There goes the neighborhood, some say, only we're talking gentrification here. Some longtime residents are not so crazy about the fact that this precious restaurant/bar is attracting legions, including food critics, who are awarding the place several stars. And you know what that means: double-parked cars, lines out the door, and rowdy customers into the wee hours. This part of D.C. is changing, no doubt about it, and if you're intrigued, Café Saint-Ex is worth investigating. Named for author/aviator Antoine de Saint-Exupéry, the dining room builds on the flight idea with black and white photos of pilots and aviation memorabilia. The critics are crowing about the charming atmosphere and certain items on the menu, like the roast chicken; the grilled mahimahi; and the beets, orange, and goat cheese salad. Personally, I love the fried green tomato BLT. D.C. hipsters stay on or arrive later to get in on Saint's nightlife scene, which features a DJ spinning tunes downstairs at Gate 54: usually hip-hop or indie, depending on the night.

1847 14th St. NW, between S and T sts. ✆ **202/265-7839.** www.saint-ex.com. Reservations recommended. Lunch and brunch main courses $9–$19; dinner main courses $10–$23; pretheater menu $28. AE, MC, V. Lunch Tues–Fri 11am–5pm; Brunch Sat–Sun 11am–4pm; Dinner daily 5pm–1:30am (until 2:30am Fri–Sat). Metro: U St.–Cardozo.

Creme Café and Lounge ★ AMERICAN/SOUTHERN All sorts of restaurants are opening in this U Street neighborhood, and all sorts of people are flocking to dine here. But the streets remain urban and edgy in appearance and in fact, no matter how upscale their eateries, crime occurs more often here than in most other parts of town. Crème, meanwhile, is a cross between upscale and down-home. First off, it's Creme, as in *cream,* not crème, as in *them.* On the menu are shrimp and grits, pork and beans, things like that, but these are a twist on your grandmother's versions, hearty and delicious, but more sophisticated: The beans are no ordinary canned baked beans but a mélange of cannellini and fava beans. Like everyplace else on U Street, Creme gets noisy and crowded as the night goes on, but try to stick around long enough for dessert: The coconut cake's my favorite—and everyone else's, too, it seems.

1322 U St. NW (at 14th St.). ✆ **202/234-1884.** No reservations. Dinner main courses $14–$18. AE, DC, DISC, MC, V. Sun–Thurs 6–10:30pm; Fri–Sat 6–11:30pm; Sat 11am–3pm; Sun 11am–4pm. Metro: U St.–Cardozo.

INEXPENSIVE

Ben's Chili Bowl *Finds* AMERICAN Ben's is a veritable institution, a mom-and-pop place, where everything looks, tastes, and probably even costs the same as when the restaurant opened in 1958. Ben's has won national recognition, too, most recently when it was chosen by the 2004 James Beard Foundation Awards as an "America's Classic," one of four restaurants in the country so named for being "renowned for their timeless appeal."

The most expensive item on the menu is the veggie-burger sub, for $7.75. Formica counters, red bar stools, and a jukebox that plays Motown and reggae tunes—that's Ben's. Ben's continues as a gathering place for black Washington and visitors like Bill Cosby, who's a longtime customer (a chili dog is named after him). Everyone's welcome, though, even the late-nighters who come streaming out of nearby nightclubs at 2 or 3 in the morning on the weekend. Of course, the chili, cheese fries, and half-smokes are great, but so are the breakfast items. Try the salmon cakes, grits, scrapple, or blueberry pancakes (available during breakfast hours only).

1213 U St. NW. ✆ **202/667-0909.** www.benschilibowl.com. Reservations not accepted. Main courses $2.50–$7.40. No credit cards. Mon–Thurs 6am–2am; Fri–Sat 6am–4am; Sun noon–8pm. Metro: U St.–Cardozo.

7 Adams-Morgan

EXPENSIVE

Cashion's Eat Place ★★ *Finds* AMERICAN Cashion's has all the pleasures of a neighborhood restaurant—easy, warm, comfortable—combined with out-of-this-world cuisine. Chef/Owner Ann Cashion continues to rack up culinary awards as easily as she pleases her patrons. Her menu changes daily, always featuring about eight entrees, split between seafood and meat: rabbit stuffed with ham and truffles; fritto misto of whole jumbo shrimp and black sea bass filet, served with onion rings and house-made tartar sauce; or pork loin with garlic sauce. The side dishes that accompany each entree, such as lemon cannelloni bean purée or radish and sprout salad, are equally appealing. Desserts, like coconut layer cake with huckleberries, or chocolate cinnamon mousse, are worth saving room for. Sunday brunch is popular, too; you can choose from breakfast fare (challah French toast, spinach and Gruyère omelets) or heartier items (grilled rainbow trout, croque-monsieurs).

The charming dining room curves around a slightly raised bar. In warm weather, the glass-fronted Cashion's opens invitingly to the sidewalk, where you can also dine. Tables at the back offer a view of the small kitchen, where Cashion and her staff work away. In winter, ask for a table away from the front door, which lets in a blast of cold air with each new arrival.

1819 Columbia Rd. NW. ✆ **202/797-1819.** www.cashionseatplace.com. Reservations recommended. Brunch $8.95–$12; dinner main courses $19–$30. MC, V. Tues 5:30–10:30pm; Wed–Sat 5:30–11pm; Sun 11:30am–2:30pm and 5:30–10:30pm.

MODERATE

Las Canteras ★ PERUVIAN Traditional and contemporary Peruvian dishes are on the menu at this affordable new restaurant in the heart of Adams-Morgan, including three versions of *cebiche* (fish marinated in lime juice); *causa* (a dish made with mashed potatoes stuffed with chicken); and quinoa salad, which tosses the quinoa (grain) with chickpeas, tahini, and lime juice. Las Canteras is a pretty restaurant, decorated with colorful Peruvian fabrics, handcrafted wrought-iron chandeliers, and photographs on the walls of Machu Pichu and other Andean landmarks. Head here Tuesday through Thursday night at 5pm to receive the early bird special, a three-course meal for $20.

2307 18th St. NW (at Kalorama St.). ✆ **202/265-1780.** www.lascanterasdc.com. Main courses $11–$18 at lunch and dinner. AE, DISC, MC, V. Tues–Sun 11am–3pm and 5–11pm.

Lauriol Plaza ★ MEXICAN/SPANISH/LATIN AMERICAN This place is large (it seats 330) but immensely popular, so despite its size, you may still have to wait for a table. Lauriol Plaza looks like a factory from the outside, but inside it's stunning. You have a choice of sitting at sidewalk tables, on the rooftop deck, or in the two-tiered

Adams-Morgan & Dupont Circle Dining

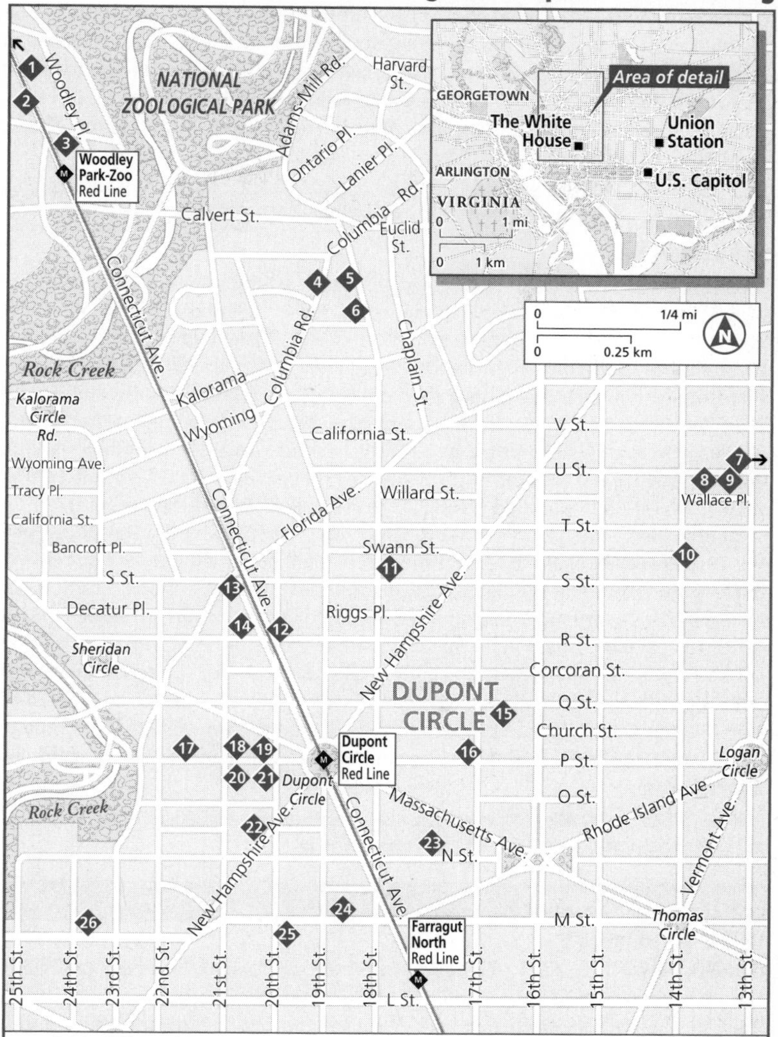

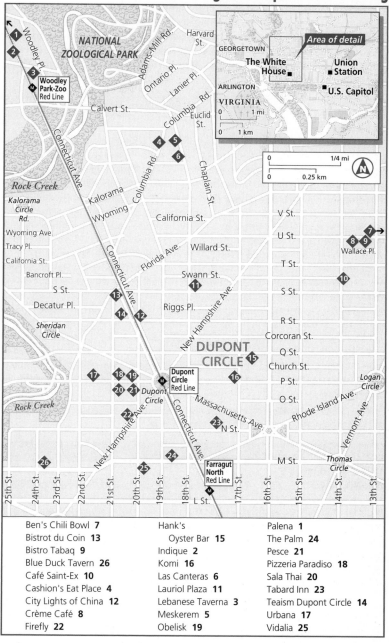

Ben's Chili Bowl **7**
Bistrot du Coin **13**
Bistro Tabaq **9**
Blue Duck Tavern **26**
Café Saint-Ex **10**
Cashion's Eat Place **4**
City Lights of China **12**
Crème Café **8**
Firefly **22**
Hank's Oyster Bar **15**
Indique **2**
Komi **16**
Las Canteras **6**
Lauriol Plaza **11**
Lebanese Taverna **3**
Meskerem **5**
Obelisk **19**
Palena **1**
The Palm **24**
Pesce **21**
Pizzeria Paradiso **18**
Sala Thai **20**
Tabard Inn **23**
Teaism Dupont Circle **14**
Urbana **17**
Vidalia **25**

dining room with its large mural of a Spanish fiesta on one wall and windows covering another. Try the margaritas, *carne asada* (grilled meat) fajitas, and tasty *camarones diablo* (six broiled jumbo shrimp seasoned with spices). Anything mesquite grilled is sure to please. Servings seem as large as the restaurant. Sunday brunch, also recommended, is served from 11am to 3pm. With so many diners here, Lauriol Plaza is a good place to people-watch.

1835 18th St. NW. ✆ **202/387-0035.** www.lauriolplaza.com. Reservations not accepted. Main courses $6.50–$18. AE, DC, DISC, MC, V. Sun–Thurs 11:30am–11pm; Fri–Sat 11:30am–midnight. Metro: Dupont Circle.

INEXPENSIVE

Meskerem ETHIOPIAN In the past few years, Washington has seen an explosion of Ethiopian restaurants, notably in the Ninth and U streets area, where you will find at least 10 cafes offering authentic Ethiopian cuisine, backed up by traditional or contemporary musical entertainment. But Meskerem in Adams-Morgan was one of the first Ethiopian restaurants to open in Washington and remains among the best, especially for newcomers to the food. It's attractive; the three-level high-ceilinged dining room has an oval skylight girded by a painted sunburst and yellow-washed walls hung with African art and musical instruments. On the mezzanine level, you sit at *messobs* (basket tables) on low, carved Ethiopian chairs or upholstered leather poufs.

Diners share large platters of food, which they scoop up with a sourdough crepe-like pancake called *injera* (no silverware here). You'll notice a lot of *watt* dishes, which refers to the traditional Ethiopian stew, made with your choice of beef, chicken, lamb, or vegetables, in varying degrees of hot and spicy; the *alicha watts* are milder and more delicately flavored. You might share an entree—perhaps *yegeb kay watt* (succulent lamb in thick, hot *berbere* sauce)—along with a platter of five vegetarian dishes served with tomato and potato salads. Some combination platters comprise an array of beef, chicken, lamb, and vegetables. There's a full bar, and the wine list includes Ethiopian honey wine and beer. Ethiopian singers perform Friday and Saturday nights from 11pm to 3am.

2434 18th St. NW. ✆ **202/462-4100.** Reservations recommended. Lunch and dinner main courses $9–$13. AE, DC, MC, V. Daily noon–midnight, with bar staying open until 3am Fri–Sat.

8 Dupont Circle

VERY EXPENSIVE

Obelisk ★★★ ITALIAN Obelisk is the most consistently excellent restaurant in the city. Service and food are simply the best. In this pleasantly spare room that seats only 36, the walls are decorated with 19th-century French botanical prints and Italian lithographs. Here, owner Peter Pastan and chef Jerry Corso present small fixed-price menus of sophisticated Italian cuisine, using the freshest possible ingredients. Each night, diners are offered two or three choices for each of five courses. Dinner might begin with an antipasti misti of zucchini fritters, deep-fried risotto croquettes, and garbanzo beans with tuna in olive oil; followed by sweetbread and porcini ravioli with sage butter; and then an artfully arranged dish of grilled stuffed quail and duck sausage with spinach, or black bass with peppers, fennel and green sauce . . . or whatever the chef has been inspired to create. A cheese course is next and the meal concludes with dessert, perhaps pear spice cake, rose-petal panna cotta, or some other heavenly concoction. Divine breads and desserts are all baked in-house. Pastan's carefully crafted wine list represents varied regions of Italy, as well as California vintages.

The fixed-price menu is a good value, but the cost of wine and coffees can easily double the price per person.

2029 P St. NW. ✆ **202/872-1180.** Reservations recommended. Fixed-price 5-course dinner $65. DC, MC, V. Tues–Sat 6–9:30pm. Metro: Dupont Circle.

EXPENSIVE

Firefly ★ CONTEMPORARY AMERICAN This is a small but popular restaurant, which can make you feel a bit squeezed in. The floor-to-ceiling "firefly tree" hung with lanterns heightens this feeling. But the food is quite good. We enjoyed the roasted chicken with green garlic rice, and the grilled New York steak with horseradish twice-baked potatoes. If fries don't come with your meal, it's worth ordering them as a side; they arrive hot and salty in a paper cone set in its own stand. At lunch, consider the Firefly hoagie or the chicken Cobb salad. Desserts remain the restaurant's one weak area. Firefly lies within the Hotel Madera (see review, chapter 5) but has a separate entrance.

In the Hotel Madera, 1310 New Hampshire Ave. NW. ✆ **202/861-1310.** www.firefly-dc.com. Reservations recommended. Brunch main courses $9–$16; lunch main courses $10–$23; dinner main courses $18–$28. AE, DC, DISC, MC, V. Mon–Fri 7–10am; Sat 8–10am; Mon–Fri 11:30am–2:30pm; Sun 10am–2:30pm; Sun–Thurs 5:30–10pm; Fri–Sat 5:30–10:30pm. Metro: Dupont Circle.

Komi ★★★ *Finds* NEW AMERICAN/GREEK Chef/owner Johnny Monis, at 29, looks like Johnny Depp and cooks like nobody's business. You may see him at the back of the restaurant in the half-exposed kitchen. As young as he is, Monis knows what he wants and continues to fiddle with his menu and dining room to achieve it. A slight renovation in 2006 created a Mediterranean feel, removed tables to make more room, and added tablecloths to buffer the sounds of the nightly full house. In 2007, Monis went completely to a five-course prix-fixe menu. Komi remains a comfortably attractive shotgun-length dining room where one can enjoy really superb, Greek-influenced dishes. These include the *mezethakia* first course (crispy artichoke, smoked prosciutto, fava beans, and aged pecorino cheese); the *macaronia* second course, which offers a choice of six or so pasta dishes, like the Gorgonzola raviolini with pears and almonds; and the third-course entrees, which might include a *bronzini* (Mediterranean sea bass) roasted in the oven in parchment paper, or the roasted quail stuffed with foie gras and figs. Greek-style doughnuts are always an option for dessert. Servers are some of the most efficient but charming staff in the city.

1509 17th St. NW (near P St.). ✆ **202/332-9200.** www.komirestaurant.com. Reservations recommended. Tues–Sat $78 prix-fixe dinner, or $145 with wine pairings. AE, MC, V. Tues–Sat from 5:30pm. Metro: Dupont Circle.

Pesce ★ SEAFOOD Tables are close together and every table is full—that's Pesce, where a no-reservations policy and a reliably pleasing menu means that there's usually a line. A large blackboard displays a long list of daily specials: Smoked trout and fusilli, *brandade* (a pounded combination of fish, olive oil, garlic, milk, and cream), grilled whole flounder, scallops, and soft-shell crabs were among recent options. Pesce draws a wide swath of Washingtonians, from the secretary of state to NPR correspondents to locals from the neighborhood, everyone ready for a convivial time and good eats.

2016 P St. NW (near 20th St.). ✆ **202/466-3474.** www.pescebistro.com. Reservations accepted at lunch and for parties of 6 or more at dinner. Lunch $13–$19, dinner main courses $19–$29. AE, DC, DISC, MC, V. Mon–Fri 11:30am–2:30pm; Mon–Thurs 5:30–10pm; Fri–Sat 5:30–10:30pm; Sun 5–9:30pm. Metro: Dupont Circle.

Tabard Inn ★★ AMERICAN In spite of the fact that this restaurant lies inside the Hotel Tabard Inn (see description in chapter 5), the Tabard Inn is largely a beloved local spot. Saturday and Sunday brunch is a tradition for bunches of friends and families, weekday lunch pulls in the staff from surrounding embassies and association offices, and dinner seats couples, business partners, and Washingtonians meeting pals in town for meetings. The fetchingly homey main dining room holds wooden tables, hanging plants, a black and white tile floor, and windows overlooking a brick-walled garden. The kitchen smokes its own salmon (as it has for 25 years); cures its own pastrami, tasso ham, and prosciutto; and bakes its own bread and pastries, so these items are awfully good. Everything's good, though, and everything's fresh, from the oysters delivered straight from the coast of Maine to the grilled Hereford rib-eye steak, served with fingerling potatoes and baby carrots. Desserts, with names like peach Linzer crusted cobbler and chocolate mousse pudding cake, are as delicious as they sound.

1739 N St. NW (at 17th St., in the Hotel Tabard Inn). ✆ **202/331-8528.** www.tabardinn.com. Reservations recommended. Lunch and brunch main courses $10–$15; dinner main courses $18–$30. AE, DC, DISC, MC, V. Mon–Fri 7–9:30am and 11am–2:30pm; Sat 8–10am; Sun 8–9:30am; Sat brunch 11am–2:30pm; Sun brunch 10:30am–2:30pm; Sun–Thurs 6–9:30pm; Fri–Sat 6–10pm. Metro: Dupont Circle.

Urbana Restaurant and Wine Bar ★ FRENCH/ITALIAN Northern Italy and Southern France are the menu influences, but the ambience is all Dupont Circle's, meaning that Urbana's clientele draws from the fun and artsy neighborhood in which the restaurant lies. This is one of those places where the cocktails are as important as the meal—try the English Summer, a mix of Pimm's, Kettle One Citroen, and ginger beer. Thin-crust pizzas are a must at lunch or in the adjoining rowdy lounge in the evening. From the dinner menu, an awesome *osso buco* and a thyme-scented wild king salmon are among the winning options.

2121 P St. NW (at 21st St.), in the Hotel Palomar. ✆ **202/956-6650.** www.urbanadc.com. Reservations accepted. Main courses $7.95–$15 at breakfast and brunch; $10–$16 at lunch; $20–$31 at dinner. AE, DC, DISC, MC, V. Mon–Fri 7–10:30am and 11am–3pm; Sat–Sun 8am–3pm; Sun–Thurs 5–10pm; Fri–Sat 5–11pm. (Lounge stays open later.) Metro: Dupont Circle.

MODERATE

Bistrot du Coin FRENCH Michel Richard, acclaimed chef of Michel Richard Citronelle and Central (p. 165 and 140), once said that when he's homesick, he visits this restaurant, because it feels like France to him. The wooden facade that draws your attention from the street, the way the whole glass front of the dining room opens right to the sidewalk, the zinc bar, the moody waiters—everything speaks of a Paris bistro, most of all the food.

The Bistrot has remained very much the same as when it opened in 2000: the noise, the inconsistent service, the menu. Twenty-somethings love to party here, especially on weekends. Mussels, curried and creamed, or hiding in a thick gratin of leeks, are the favorite dish. Others to recommend are the cassoulet, which is delicious, and not too hearty; the *tartine baltique,* which turns out to be an open-faced sandwich with smoked salmon, tamara onions, capers, and olive oil; the comforting onion soup; and the tasty steak frites. The menu presents a limited number of wines, or select an aperitif from a list of 16, very reasonably priced.

1738 Connecticut Ave. NW. ✆ **202/234-6969.** www.bistrotducoin.com. Main courses $13–$24. AE, DISC, MC, V. Sun–Wed 11:30am–11pm; Thurs–Sat 11:30am–1am; also Sat–Sun brunch 11am–4pm. Metro: Dupont Circle.

City Lights of China CHINESE The best of the Washington area's Chinese restaurants are not in the city at all, but in the suburbs. Chinatown, of course, still has several, including Tony Cheng's (p. 148). City Lights, meanwhile, has done quite well for itself in its Dupont Circle location since 1987, feeding the office and after-work crowd hungry for dumplings and fried rice. You can join the fray and dine in, if you like, but if you are staying at a nearby hotel, you might consider ordering food to go, as well; takeout prices are cheaper for some items. Some of the most popular dishes include crisp fried Cornish hen prepared in a cinnamon-soy marinade and served with a tasty dipping sauce (this is an appetizer), Chinese eggplant in garlic sauce, stir-fried spinach, crisp fried shredded beef, and Peking duck. The setting, a three-tiered dining room with much of the seating in comfortable leather booths and banquettes, is unpretentious. Neat white-linen tablecloths, cloth flower arrangements in lighted niches, and green neon track lighting complete the picture. There's a full bar.

1731 Connecticut Ave. NW (between R and S sts.). ✆ **202/265-6688.** www.citylightsofchina.com. Reservations recommended. Lunch main courses $12–$24 (most are about $13); dinner main courses $11–$27 (most are about $15). AE, DC, DISC, MC, V. Mon–Fri 11:30am–10:30pm; Sat noon–11pm; Sun noon–10:30pm; dinner from 3pm daily. Metro: Dupont Circle.

Hank's Oyster Bar ★ AMERICAN/SEAFOOD Deep in the heart of Dupont Circle is this lively, laid-back hangout, fronted by a sidewalk cafe in warm weather. Decor inside is cozy and casual, with exposed brick walls and pipes and a mix of seating at the bar, tall round tables, and the usual wooden rectangles. You want to order the specials at Hank's, which on a recent night included a sautéed soft-shell crab in citrus butter and pan-roasted halibut with tomato-lemon relish. Signature dishes feature classics like popcorn shrimp and calamari, and, of course, fresh oysters served on the half shell, fried, or in a po' boy. Hank's easy atmosphere puts you in a good mood and gives you a merry send-off, when you've got a fun night on the town planned.

1624 Q St. NW (at 17th St.). ✆ **202/462-4265.** www.hanksdc.com. Dinner main courses $14–$22; brunch main courses $7–$17. AE, MC, V. Sun–Tues 5:30–10pm; Wed–Sat 5:30–11pm; Sat–Sun 11am–3pm. Metro: Dupont Circle.

INEXPENSIVE

Pizzeria Paradiso ★ PIZZA/ITALIAN No contest, this is still the best pizza place in the city. Peter Pastan, master chef/owner of Obelisk (located right next door and reviewed above), owns this classy, often crowded, 10-table-plus-counter-seating pizzeria. An oak-burning oven at one end of the charming room produces exceptionally doughy but light pizza crusts. The no-reservations policy means you'll have a wait, if you arrive at peak times. It's worth the wait, though. Pizzas range from the plain Paradiso, which offers chunks of tomatoes covered in melted mozzarella, to the robust Siciliana, a blend of nine ingredients including eggplant and red onion. Or you can choose your own toppings from a list of 31. As popular as the pizzas are the panini (sandwiches) of homemade focaccia stuffed with marinated roasted lamb and vegetables and other fillings, and the salads, such as the panzanella (thick crusts of bread with chopped zucchini and peppers tossed with balsamic vinegar and olive oil). Paradiso serves beer and wine and good desserts. Pizzeria Paradiso has another location, at 3282 M St. NW (✆ **202/337-1245**), in Georgetown, right next door to Dean & Deluca. This location is larger, and has a full bar and a private party room.

2029 P St. NW. ✆ **202/223-1245.** www.eatyourpizza.com. Pizzas $9.50–$17; sandwiches and salads $4.95–$7.95. DC, MC, V. Mon–Thurs 11:30am–11pm; Fri–Sat 11:30am–midnight; Sun noon–10pm. Metro: Dupont Circle.

Sala Thai THAI At lunch, you'll see a lot of diners sitting alone and reading newspapers, happy to escape the office. At dinner, the restaurant is filled with groups and couples, plus the occasional family. Among the 82 items on the menu, look for *nua kra ting tone,* which is spicy beef with onion, garlic, and parsley sauce, and *ka prow,* which is an even spicier dish of either beef, chicken, or pork sautéed with basil leaves and chile. The restaurant is downstairs from the street, with no windows to watch what's happening on P Street; but you're really here for the food, which is excellent and cheap. Even conventional Pad Thai doesn't disappoint. Pay attention if your waiter cautions you about the level of spiciness of a dish you order—for some dishes (like the stir-fried sliced pork in red curry sauce with peppers), you'll need an asbestos tongue. Sala Thai has several locations throughout the D.C. area, including one at 1301 U St. (© **202/462-1333**); if you like jazz, make sure you dine at this location Thursday to Saturday 7 to 10:30pm, when a trio or quartet performs.

2016 P St. NW. © **202/872-1144.** www.salathaidc.com. Reservations accepted for 5 or more. Lunch main courses $6.95–$11; dinner main courses $7.95–$17. AE, DC, DISC, MC, V. Mon–Thurs 11:30am–10:30pm; Fri 11:30am–11pm; Sat noon–11pm; Sun noon–10:30pm. Metro: Dupont Circle.

Teaism Dupont Circle *Finds* ASIAN FUSION Occupying a turn-of-the-20th-century neoclassical building on a tree-lined street, Teaism has a lovely rustic interior. A display kitchen and tandoor oven dominate the sunny downstairs room, which offers counter seating along a wall of French windows, open in warm weather. Upstairs seating is on banquettes and small Asian stools at handcrafted mahogany tables.

The impressive tea list comprises close to 30 aromatic blends, most of them from India, China, and Japan. On the menu is light Asian fare served on stainless steel plates or in lacquer lunchboxes (Japanese "bento boxes," which hold a delicious meal of, for example, teriyaki salmon, cucumber-ginger salad, a scoop of rice with seasoning, and fresh fruit—all $8.75). Dishes include Thai chicken curry with sticky rice, buffalo burger with Asian slaw, and a portobello and goat cheese sandwich. Baked jasmine crème brûlée and salty oat cookies are among desserts. At breakfast, you might try ginger scones or cilantro eggs and sausage with fresh tandoor-baked onion naan bread. Everything's available for takeout. Teapots, cups, and other gift items are for sale. ***Note:*** Teaism has two other locations, both convenient for sightseeing. **Teaism Lafayette Square,** 800 Connecticut Ave. NW (© **202/835-2233**), is across from the White House; it's open weekdays from 7:30am to 5:30pm and serves afternoon tea. **Teaism Penn Quarter** ★, 400 8th St. NW (© **202/638-6010**), which is near the Verizon Center, the National Gallery, and nightspots, is the only branch that serves beer, wine, and cocktails. Teaism Penn Quarter is open daily, serving all three meals and afternoon tea, and brunch on Saturday and Sunday.

2009 R St. NW (between Connecticut and 21st sts.). © **202/667-3827.** www.teaism.com. All menu items $1.50–$10. AE, MC, V. Mon–Thurs 8am–10pm; Fri 8am–11pm; Sat 9am–11pm; Sun 9am–10pm. Metro: Dupont Circle.

9 Foggy Bottom/West End

VERY EXPENSIVE

Blue Duck Tavern ★★ CONTEMPORARY AMERICAN And now for something completely different. The Park Hyatt Washington hotel's (p. 114) major renovation in 2006 extended to its in-house restaurant, formerly known as Melrose. The only holdover from that establishment is the award-winning chef, Brian McBride, who now presides over the Blue Duck Tavern's open kitchen. Forget any preconceptions of "open kitchen." Here, no walls separate the cooking area from the dining room. McBride and his crew dance in and around counters, the wood burning oven, and the immense Molteni commercial oven range, in full view. Designer Tony Chi, who transformed the look of the entire hotel, also molded this light-filled space, which mixes modern American materials, like stainless steel and polished glass, with classic features, like dark oak and blue burlap. McBride does the same in his cuisine, choosing the freshest produce, meats, and seafood from local and regional artisans and purveyors and using a combination of traditional and state-of-the-art cooking methods and equipment to prepare exquisite, one-of-a-kind dishes—right in front of you. The menu identifies the farm or other source of the prime ingredients for each dish. Then it's up to you to choose from three columns of categories that cover nearly every food grouping, from soup and salad, to meat and charcuterie, to fish and shellfish. Among the home runs so far are the baked Rhode Island clams with smoked bacon, peppers, and garlic; the galantine of duck and mushrooms with cherry preserve; jumbo lump crab cakes with rémoulade sauce; and the barbecued casserole of rice beans. The house-made steak fries are in a class of their own, so be sure to order those. And absolutely save room for dessert, like the chocolate cake flamed in bourbon, accompanied by a scoop of ice cream that you'll see hand-cranked minutes before it's delivered to your table. The wine list features 60 American wines and 300 from around the world. The Blue Duck Tavern was the only D.C. restaurant to make *Conde Nast Traveler*'s 2007 "Hot List" of the world's 95 top restaurants.

24th and M sts. NW, in the Park Hyatt Washington Hotel. ✆ **202/419-6755.** www.blueducktavern.com. Reservations recommended. Breakfast main courses $5–$16; brunch main courses $12–$26; lunch main courses $8–$26; dinner main courses $17–$35. AE, DC, DISC, MC, V. Daily 6:30–10:30am, 11:30am–2:30pm, and 5:30–10:30pm. Metro: Foggy Bottom or Dupont Circle.

Kinkead's ★★ AMERICAN/SEAFOOD Award-winning chef/owner Bob Kinkead is the star at this three-tier, 220-seat restaurant. He orchestrates his kitchen staff in full view of the upstairs dining room, where booths and tables neatly fill the nooks and alcoves of the town house. At street level is a scattering of tables overlooking the restaurant's lower level, the more casual bar and cafe, where a jazz group or pianist performs Tuesday through Sunday evenings, 6:30 to 10pm. ***Beware:*** If the waiter tries to seat you in the "atrium," you'll be stuck at a table mall-side just outside the doors of the restaurant.

Kinkead's menu (which changes daily) features primarily seafood, but always includes at least one beef and one poultry entree. Among the favorite dishes are the fried Ipswich clams; cod topped with crab imperial; clam chowder; and pepita-crusted salmon with shrimp, crab, and chiles. Chef Kinkead piles on appetizing garnishes—that crab-crowned cod, for instance, comes with sweet potato purée and ham-laced spoon bread. The wine list comprises more than 300 selections, and you can trust expert sommelier Michael Flynn to lead you to one you'll enjoy. You can't go wrong with the desserts either, like the chocolate dacquoise with cappuccino sauce. If you're hungry but not ravenous on a late weekday afternoon, stop in for some delicious light fare: fish and chips, lobster roll, soups, and salads.

2000 Pennsylvania Ave. NW. ✆ **202/296-7700.** www.kinkead.com. Reservations recommended. Lunch and dinner main courses $22–$37; light fare $6–$25. AE, DC, DISC, MC, V. Sun–Fri 11:30am–2:30pm; Sun–Thurs 5:30–10pm; Fri–Sat 5:30–10:30pm (light fare served weekdays 2:30–5:30pm). Metro: Foggy Bottom.

Value Pretheater Dinners = Great Deals

Some of Washington's finest restaurants make you an offer you shouldn't refuse: a three-course dinner for just a little bit more than the cost of a typical entree. It's the pretheater dinner, available in the early evening on certain nights at certain restaurants; and while your choices may be limited, your meal will undoubtedly be delicious.

At one end of the spectrum is **Marcel's** ★★ (p. 164), whose $48 fixed-price includes a starter, such as an arugula salad with caramelized shallots; an entree, like pan-seared Norwegian salmon; and a dessert of either crème brûlée or chocolate terrine. Marcel's offers this menu nightly from 5:30 to 7pm and throws in complimentary limo service to get you to the Kennedy Center, returning you to the restaurant after the show for the dessert portion, if you haven't already consumed it.

Café Atlantico's ★★ (p. 139) pretheater menu allows you three courses for $30; sample dishes are foie gras terrine as a first course, duck confit with candied pumpkin seeds or chicken with a Veracruz sauce for the main course, and sorbet or warm chocolate cake to finish. The restaurant's pretheater menu is available nightly between 5 and 6:30pm.

Other restaurants in this chapter that offer a pretheater menu are **Zola** ★★ (p. 143), **Rasika** ★★ (p. 148), **1789** ★★★ (p. 165), and **Café Saint-Ex** ★ (p. 155).

Marcel's ★★ FRENCH When you walk through the front door, look straight ahead into the exhibition kitchen—chances are you'll be staring directly into the eyes of chef Robert Wiedmaier (or his chef de cuisine, if Wiedmaier should be performing in his exhibition kitchen at Beck's—keep reading). In any case, Wiedmaier's vivid style and cuisine are firmly on display here, with French dishes that include nods to his Belgian training: duck breast with baby turnips, rose lentils, and Calvados sauce; or venison with ragout of winter mushrooms and Madeira sauce. Wiedmaier's *boudin blanc* sausage is said to be out of this world, if you like that sort of thing. Desserts usually include seasonal tarts such as spring pear tart with raspberry coulis.

Marcel's, named after Wiedmaier's young son, hews to a country French decor that includes panels of rough stone framed by rustic shutters and antique hutches displaying Provençal pottery. Drapes and carpeting help buffer the conversational buzz that otherwise would ricochet off the stone walls and floors. To the right of the exhibition kitchen is a spacious wine bar, with its own menu (the full dinner menu is also available at some tables), and lovely live jazz nightly year-round. Marcel's offers seating on the patio—right on Pennsylvania Avenue—in warm weather. Widely successful from the start is Marcel's sibling, **Brasserie Beck** (p. 153), which opened in 2007; you guessed it: Beck's is named after Wiedmaier's second-born son.

2401 Pennsylvania Ave. NW. ✆ **202/296-1166.** www.marcelsdc.com. Reservations recommended. Dinner main courses $29–$42; pretheater dinner 5:30–7pm (including round-trip limo to/from Kennedy Center) $48. AE, MC, V. Sun 5:30–9:30pm; Mon–Thurs 5:30–10pm; Fri–Sat 5:30–11pm. Metro: Foggy Bottom.

EXPENSIVE

Kaz Sushi Bistro ★ JAPANESE Amiable chef/owner Kazuhiro ("Kaz") Okochi opened his own place in this handsome town house, after having worked at Sushi-Ko (p. 171) for many years. Kaz's is said to be the best place for sushi in the Washington area, and aficionados vie for one of the six chairs at the bar to watch Kaz and his staff do their thing, especially at lunch, when fellow diners are likely to be Japanese men in Washington on business and young Washingtonians. Besides sushi, Kaz is known for his briny lobster with wasabi mayo and grilled baby octopus, and for his bento boxes, offering exquisite tastings of pan-seared salmon, spicy broiled mussels, and the like. Kaz is one of few chefs in the area trained to handle torafugu, the blowfish, which can be poisonous if not cleaned properly. The blowfish, if available, is served in winter. This is also the place to come for premium sakes and a large selection of teas.

1915 I St. NW. ✆ **202/530-5500.** Reservations recommended. www.kazsushi.com. Sushi a la carte $4–$9; lunch main courses $13–$20; dinner main courses $19–$27. AE, DC, DISC, MC, V. Mon–Fri 11:30am–2pm; Mon–Sat 6–10pm. Metro: Farragut West.

10 Georgetown

VERY EXPENSIVE

Michel Richard Citronelle ★★★ INNOVATIVE FRENCH If Citronelle's ebullient chef/owner Michel Richard is in the kitchen (and you know when he is, since the dining room views the open kitchen), diners in the know decline the menu and ask simply for whatever it is he wants to make. Whether you go that route, or choose from the fixed-price or tasting menus, you're in for a (very expensive) treat. Emerging from the bustling kitchen are appetizers like the fricassee of escargots, an eggshell filled with caviar, sweetbreads, porcinis, and crunchy pistachios, and entrees like the crispy lentil-coated salmon or squab leg confit with macaroni gratin and black truffles. Each presentation is a work of art, with swirls of colorful sauce surrounding the main event. If you're passionate about food, you may want to consider dining at the chef's table, which is in the kitchen, so you can watch Richard at work. This will cost you: $285 per person, with a minimum of six people, is the stated price, but that's to give you a ballpark idea; call for more exact information. One less expensive option is available at Citronelle: You can dine in the restaurant's bar and lounge (see "A Seat at the Bar," p. 172).

Citronelle's decor is also breathtaking and includes a wall that changes colors, a state-of-the-art wine cellar (a glass-enclosed room that encircles the dining room, displaying its 8,000 bottles and a collection of 18th- and 19th-century corkscrews), and a Provençal color scheme of mellow yellow and raspberry red.

Michel Richard's richly layered chocolate "bar" with sauce noisette (hazelnut sauce) is recommended for dessert, if available. Citronelle's extensive wine list offers about 20 premium by-the-glass selections, but with all those bottles staring out at you from the wine cellar, you may want to spring for one. Also consider dining at Richard's new French/American bistro, **Central** (p. 140), for a less expensive, less elaborate, but every bit as delicious meal.

In the Latham Hotel, 3000 M St. NW. ✆ **202/625-2150.** www.citronelledc.com. Reservations required. Jacket required, tie optional for men at dinner. Open for dinner only. Fixed-price 3-course dinner $95; fixed-price tasting menu $155. Bar/lounge main courses $12–$38. AE, DC, MC, V. Daily 6–10pm.

1789 ★★★ AMERICAN Esteemed executive chef Ris Lacoste has departed 1789, ensconced in plans to open her own restaurant in the capital (stay tuned). Successor Nathan Beauchamp is the latest chef in the restaurant's 46-year history to take command, and the reviews are all good. Beauchamp's hits include a grilled wild salmon with local oysters and brioche pudding, and a thick pork chop served with pomegranate-braised onions and rapini. The menu changes daily but at least two dishes for which Lacoste became famous are often available (their recipes are posted on the restaurant's website): the oyster and champagne stew with Smithfield ham and walnuts, and the roast rack of Colorado lamb with creamy feta potatoes au gratin in red-pepper-purée-infused merlot sauce.

Locals, like journalist and D.C. socialite Sally Quinn, and visiting celebrities, like Nicole Kidman and beau Keith Urban, love the 1789 for its romantic ambience; the five dining rooms, especially those on the first floor, are cozy dens, with a homey decor that includes historical prints on the walls, silk-shaded brass oil lamps on tables, and, come winter, fires crackling in the fireplaces. So put on your best duds and be prepared for a relaxing meal with only the food and your dinner companion to distract you. The formal but cozy restaurant occupies two floors (three, if you count the room reserved for private parties) of a Federal town house near Georgetown University.

The nightly pretheater menu, 6 to 6:45pm Monday to Friday, includes appetizer, entree, dessert, and coffee for $35. The same deal is available after 9pm Sunday through Thursday and after 10pm Friday and Saturday nights.

1226 36th St. NW. ✆ **202/965-1789.** www.1789restaurant.com. Reservations recommended. Jacket required for men. Main courses $29–$38; fixed-price pretheater menu $35. AE, DC, DISC, MC, V. Mon–Thurs 6–10pm; Fri 6–11pm; Sat 5:30–11pm; Sun 5:30–10pm.

EXPENSIVE

Bistrot Lepic & Wine Bar ★ FRENCH Bistrot Lepic is the real thing—a charming French restaurant that seems plucked right off a Parisian side street. The atmosphere is bustling and cheery, and you hear a lot of French spoken—not just by the waiters, but also by customers. The Bistrot is a neighborhood place, and you'll often see diners waving hellos across the room to each other or even table-hopping. In its 13 years, the restaurant has made some changes to accommodate its popularity, most recently turning the upstairs into an Asian-accented wine bar and lounge; so if you arrive early for your reservation, you now have a place to wait. (In the past, one had to hover, hungry-eyed, at the door.) Or you can come just to hang out, sip a glass of wine, and munch on delicious little somethings from the wine bar menu, where the most expensive item is the $14 terrine of homemade foie gras, or specialties of the house, like the cassoulet, from the regular menu. The wine bar hosts complimentary wine tastings every Tuesday 6 to 8pm. No need to make a reservation at the wine bar unless you plan to order dinner from the regular menu.

This is traditional French cooking, updated. The seasonal menu offers such entrees as grilled rainbow trout with tomatoes, capers, and olives; beef medallions with polenta and shiitake mushroom sauce; and sautéed sea scallops with ginger broccoli mousse. Depending on the season, specials might turn up rare tuna served on fennel with citrus vinaigrette or perhaps grouper with a mildly spicy lobster sauce upon a bed of spinach.

1736 Wisconsin Ave. NW. ✆ **202/333-0111.** www.bistrotlepic.com. Reservations recommended. Lunch main courses $14–$19; dinner main courses $17–$26. AE, DC, DISC, MC, V. Daily 11:30am–2:30pm; Sun–Thurs 5:30–9:30pm; Fri–Sat 5:30–10:30pm; wine bar daily 5:30pm–midnight.

Cafe Milano ★ ITALIAN The beautiful-people factor rises exponentially here as the night wears on. Cafe Milano has long been a magnet for Washington's famous, attractive, and powerful—so much so that the restaurant was named "Power Spot of the Year" in 2005 by the Restaurant Association of Metropolitan Washington. But this restaurant/nightclub/bar also serves good food. Salads are big, pasta servings are small, and fish and meat entrees are just the right size. We had the endive, radicchio, and

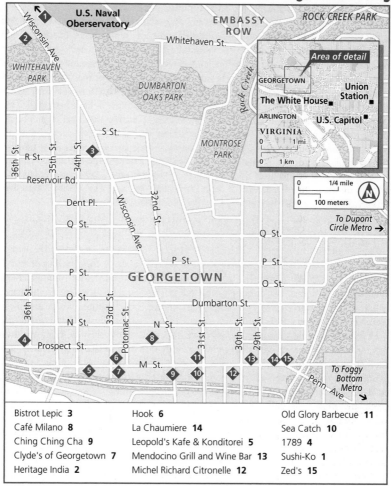

Georgetown Dining

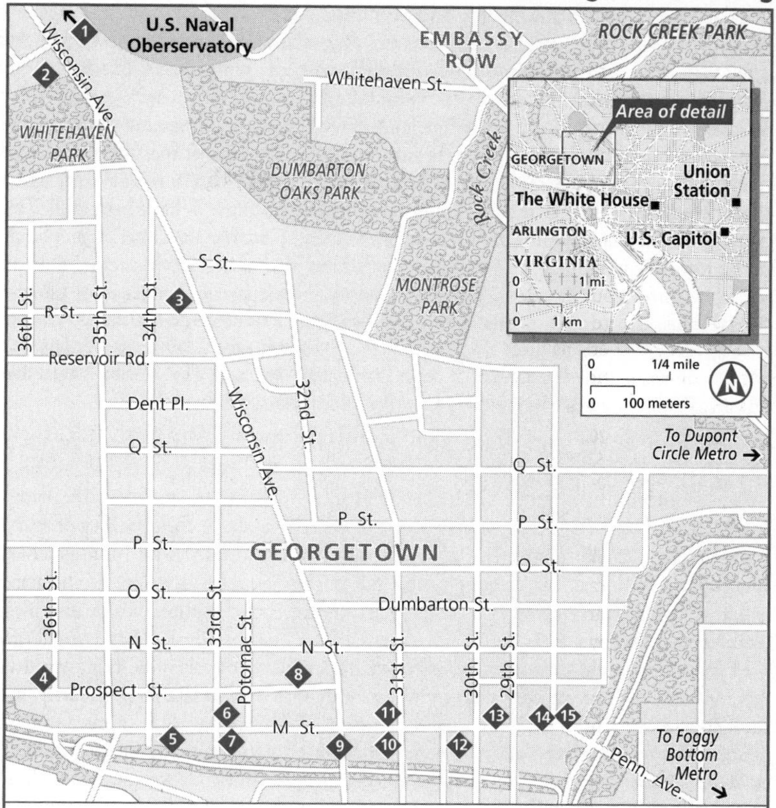

Bistrot Lepic **3**	Hook **6**	Old Glory Barbecue **11**
Café Milano **8**	La Chaumiere **14**	Sea Catch **10**
Ching Ching Cha **9**	Leopold's Kafe & Konditorei **5**	1789 **4**
Clyde's of Georgetown **7**	Mendocino Grill and Wine Bar **13**	Sushi-Ko **1**
Heritage India **2**	Michel Richard Citronelle **12**	Zed's **15**

arugula salad topped with thin sheets of Parmesan cheese; a *panzanella* salad of tomatoes, potatoes, red onion, celery, and cucumber basking in basil and olive oil; *cappellacci* (round ravioli) pockets of spinach and ricotta in cream sauce; sautéed sea bass on a bed of vegetables with lemon chive sauce; and the Santa Babila pizza, which has tomatoes, fresh mozzarella, oregano, and basil on a light pizza crust. All were delicious. Cafe Milano opens to a sidewalk cafe during the warm months. A bevy of good-humored waiters takes care of you.

3251 Prospect St. NW. ✆ **202/333-6183.** www.cafemilano.net. Reservations recommended. Lunch main courses $14–$32 (most entrees are under $20); dinner main courses $15–$42. Sun–Tues 11:30am–11pm (bar menu served until midnight); Wed–Sat 11:30am–midnight (bar menu served until 1am).

Hook ★ AMERICAN/SEAFOOD Georgetown can always use another good restaurant (as opposed to another busy bar or boutique store), so the fairly new Hook (opened mid-2007) is a welcome addition. Situated in the thick of it, near the intersection of M Street and Wisconsin Avenue, the restaurant's bar wisely lies at the front, the spare, all-white dining room beyond that, with the semi-open kitchen pulling up the rear. Hook is committed to the "sustainable" movement, which means that the chef shops for locally farmed produce and that the menus are printed on 100% post-consumer recycled paper, to give just two examples. But Hook's real "hook" is sustainable, in-season and available, seafood, so you can expect that the blackfin tuna that arrives with the crème fraîche and potato purée on your plate to have been pulled from the water sometime within the preceding 24 hours. Get this: The chef receives a daily text message from Tobago island fishermen telling him of that day's catch, and the fish arrive within 18 to 24 hours. Be sure to order one of pastry chef Heather Chittum's lovely desserts, from warm madeleine cookies to an inventive carrot cake.

3241 M St. NW (between Wisconsin Ave. and 33rd St.). ✆ **202/625-4488.** www.hookdc.com. Main courses $12–$17 at brunch and lunch, $22–$28 at dinner. AE, DC, DISC, MC, V. Sat–Sun 10:30am–2:30pm; Wed–Fri 11:30am–2:30pm; Sun–Tues 5–10pm; Wed–Thurs 5–11pm; Fri–Sat 5pm–midnight.

Mendocino Grille and Wine Bar ★ AMERICAN As its name suggests, you should come here to enjoy West Coast wine, along with contemporary American cuisine and a California-casual ambience. Most of the 200-or-so bottles on the wine list are California vintages, and waiters are knowledgeable about the specifics of each, so don't hesitate to ask questions. California-casual doesn't mean cheap, though: Bottles range from $20 to $500, although most fall in the $50 to $60 range. The restaurant offers 35 wines by the glass, in different sizes, the better for tastings, and many of these run between $6 and $10 each.

Fresh ingredients predominate, whether it's an entree of crispy-skin branzino with cockles and chorizo, or baby Pennsylvania lamb with Northern Neck spinach, olives, and sunchokes.

Rough-textured slate walls alternate with painted patches of Big Sur sky to suggest a West Coast winery in California's wine-growing region. The wall sconces resemble rectangles of sea glass and the dangling light fixtures look like turned-over wineglasses. It's a very pleasant place, where Georgetown neighbors tend to congregate nightly down the length of the handcrafted cherrywood bar. Also read about Mendocino's sister restaurant, **Sonoma** (p. 134).

2917 M St. NW. ✆ **202/333-2912.** www.mendocinodc.com. Reservations recommended. Open for dinner only. Dinner main courses $27–$32. AE, DC, DISC, MC, V. Sun–Thurs 6–10pm; Fri–Sat 5:30–11pm.

Sea Catch Restaurant and Raw Bar SEAFOOD If you're walking around Georgetown and the crowds are starting to get to you, duck into the brick passageway that lies to the right of a little coffee bar and Mr. Smith's bar on M Street (at 31st St.) and follow it back to the little plaza, where you will find the entrance to the Sea Catch, a true refuge. (Or else you can walk south on 31st St. from M St., and turn right, into the plaza.) Since 1988, the Sea Catch has perched on the bank of the C&O Canal, with an awning-covered wooden deck where you can watch ducks, punters, and mule-drawn barges glide by while you dine. The innlike main dining room has a working fireplace and rough-hewn fieldstone walls from Georgetown quarries. There's also a handsome white Carrara-marble raw bar and a deluxe brasserie. Classic jazz recordings play in the background.

Nothing at the Sea Catch is fried or breaded. For openers, plump farm-raised oysters, clams, house-smoked fish, and other raw-bar offerings merit consideration. Daily fresh fish and seafood specials may include big, fluffy jumbo lump crab cakes served with julienne vegetables in a rémoulade sauce or grilled marinated squid with fennel and basil aioli. The kitchen will prepare dishes to your specifications, including live lobster from the tanks. An extensive wine list highlights French, Italian, and American selections. Fresh-baked desserts usually include a signature Key lime tart.

1054 31st St. NW. ✆ **202/337-8855.** www.seacatchrestaurant.com. Reservations recommended. Lunch main courses $9–$32; dinner main courses $19–$49 (most items are $25–$29). AE, DC, DISC, MC, V. Mon–Sat noon–3pm and 5:30–10pm.

MODERATE

Clyde's of Georgetown AMERICAN Clyde's has been a favorite watering hole for an eclectic mix of Washingtonians since 1963. You'll see university students, Capitol Hill types, affluent professionals, Washington Redskins, romantic duos, and well-heeled ladies who lunch. Theme park–ish in decor, its dining areas include a cherry-paneled front room with oil paintings of sport scenes, and an atrium with vintage model planes dangling from the glass ceiling and a 16th-century French limestone chimney piece in the large fireplace.

Clyde's is known for its burgers, chili, and crab cake sandwiches. Appetizers are a safe bet, and Clyde's take on the classic Niçoise (chilled grilled salmon with greens, oven-roasted roma tomatoes, green beans, and grilled new potatoes in a tasty vinaigrette) is also recommended. Sunday brunch is a tradition, so popular that the brunch is offered on Saturday as well. The menu is reassuringly familiar—steak and eggs, omelets, waffles—with an assortment of sandwiches, burgers, and salads thrown in. Among bar selections are about 10 draft beers. Wines are half-price on Sundays until 10:30pm.

Note: You can park in the underground Georgetown Park garage for $1 per hour for the first 2 hours (a deal in Georgetown!). Just show your meal receipt and ask the mall concierge to validate your parking ticket.

Clyde's inaugurated its second D.C. location (the restaurant has suburban locations, too) in late summer 2006, **Clyde's of Gallery Place,** at 707 7th St. NW (✆ **202/349-3700**) in the Gallery Place complex across from the Verizon Center, Penn Quarter neighborhood. See its listing in the nightlife chapter, p. 279.

3236 M St. NW. ✆ **202/333-9180.** www.clydes.com. Reservations recommended. Lunch/brunch $7.95–$18; dinner main courses $11–$26 (most under $12); burgers and sandwiches (except for crab cake sandwich) $10 or less. AE, DC, DISC, MC, V. Mon–Thurs 11:30am–midnight; Fri 11:30am–1am; Sat 10am–1am; Sun 9am–midnight (Sat–Sun brunch until 4pm).

La Chaumiere ★★ FRENCH After 31 years, La Chaumiere is still going strong. This rustically handsome dining room centers on a large hearth, which makes it an especially welcoming place in winter. Year-round, the restaurant fills up with locals who know the specials by heart, as in, if it's Tuesday, that means "crabe en chemise" is on the menu: crepes filled with crabmeat, mushrooms, and champagne sauce. La Chaumiere prepares the full range of French classics just right, whether it's cassoulet or a chocolate soufflé. The service is warm but professional, and the diners who gather here are a motley bunch, alike at least in their love of this kitchen's authentic French cooking.

2813 M St. NW (at 28th St.). ✆ **202/338-1784.** www.lachaumieredc.com. Reservations accepted. Lunch main courses $13–$18; dinner main courses $15–$30 (most are under $20). AE, DC, MC, V. Mon–Fri 11:30am–2:30pm; Mon–Sat 5:30–10:30pm.

Leopold's Kafe & Konditorei ★ *Finds* AUSTRIAN If you find yourself at the western end of Georgetown, caught in the maze of high-end shops collectively known as Cady's Alley, you owe it to yourself to track down Leopold's and treat yourself to a delicious taste of Sachertorte or veal schnitzel. This may be the only place in Washington that serves Austrian food; it is certainly one of the most adorable eateries, with its whimsically modern furniture and bright whites punched up with orange. The customers represent a cross section of Washington, from chic to bohemian, and offer an intriguing picture to contemplate as you sip your Viennese coffee and enjoy your *apfelstrudel.* The cafe offers a full bar.

3315 Cady's Alley, #213 (off of M St. NW). (Find the passageway at 3318 M St., between 33rd and 34th sts., and walk back to Leopold's.) ✆ **202/965-6005.** www.kafeleopolds.com. Reservations recommended. Breakfast items $1.75–$10; lunch and dinner main courses $13–$22. AE, DISC, MC, V. Sun 8am–9pm; Tues–Thurs 8am–10pm; Fri–Sat 8am–11pm.

Old Glory Barbecue *Kids* BARBECUE Raised wooden booths flank one side of the restaurant; an imposing, old-fashioned dark wood bar with saddle seat stools extends down the other. Recorded swing music during the day, more mainstream music into the night, plays in the background. Old Glory boasts the city's "largest selection of single-barrel and boutique bourbons" and a rooftop deck with outdoor seating and views of Georgetown.

After 9pm or so, the two-story restaurant becomes packed with the hard-drinkin' young and restless. In early evening, though, Old Glory is prime for anyone—singles, families, or an older crowd—although it's almost always noisy. Come for the messy, tangy, delicious spareribs; hickory-smoked chicken; tender, smoked beef brisket; or marinated, wood-fired shrimp. Six sauces are on the table, the spiciest being the vinegar-based East Carolina and Lexington. The complimentary corn muffins and biscuits; side dishes of collard greens, succotash, and potato salad; and desserts like apple crisp and coconut cherry cobbler all hit the spot.

3139 M St. NW. ✆ **202/337-3406.** www.oldglorybbq.com. Reservations accepted Sun–Thurs; reservations not accepted Fri–Sat. Main courses $7.95–$25. AE, DC, DISC, MC, V. Sun 11am–2am (brunch from 11am–3pm); Mon–Thurs 11:30am–2am; Fri–Sat 11:30am–3am.

INEXPENSIVE

Ching Ching Cha *Finds* CHINESE/JAPANESE Located just below M Street, this sky-lit tearoom offers a pleasant respite from the crowds. You can sit on pillows at low tables or on chairs set at rosewood tables. Choices are simple: individual items like a tea-and-spice boiled egg, puff pastry stuffed with lotus-seed paste, or five-spice peanuts. Most typical is the $12 "tea meal," which consists of miso soup, your choice of three marinated cold vegetables, rice, and your choice of the featured meal, whether curry chicken, salmon with mustard-miso sauce, or steamed teriyaki-sauced tofu. Emphasis is really on the tea, of which there are 70 choices, including several different green, black, medicinal, and oolong teas, plus a Fujian white tea and a ginseng brew.

1063 Wisconsin Ave. NW. ✆ **202/333-8288.** www.chingchingcha.com. Reservations not accepted. All food items $4–$12; pot of tea $5–$20. AE, DISC, MC, V. Tues–Sat 11:30am–9pm; Sun 11:30am–7pm.

Zed's ETHIOPIAN Like **Meskerem** (p. 158) in Adams-Morgan, Zed's was one of the first Ethiopian restaurants to open in D.C. And like Meskerem, its menu offers a good introduction to Ethiopian cuisine. Just ask Sen. Hillary Clinton or actor Clint Eastwood, two of the many celebrities who've sampled Zed's over the years.

Zed's is a pretty, charming little place, easy to find in Georgetown on its corner right across the street from the Four Seasons hotel. Indigenous paintings, posters, and artifacts adorn pine-paneled walls, fresh flowers grace the tables, and Ethiopian music plays in the background.

Highly recommended are the *doro watt* (chicken stewed in a tangy, hot red chile–pepper sauce), the *infillay* (strips of tender chicken breast flavored with seasoned butter and honey wine served with a delicious chopped spinach and rice side dish), flavorful lamb dishes, and the deep-fried whole fish—all scooped up with the sourdough crepelike pancake called *injera,* of course. Consider ordering more of the garlicky chopped collard greens; red lentil purée in spicy red-pepper sauce; or a chilled purée of roasted yellow split peas mixed with onions, peppers, and garlic. There's a full bar, and, should you have the inclination, try the Italian pastries for dessert.

1201 28th St. NW (at M St.). ✆ **202/333-4710.** www.zeds.net. Reservations accepted for 5 or more. Main courses $9–$35 (most are under $20). AE, DC, MC, V. Daily 11am–11pm.

11 Glover Park

The blue-painted Georgetown Metro Connection shuttles (see information in chapter 4, "Getting to Know Washington, D.C.") travel as far as R Street and Wisconsin Avenue, and the D.C. Circulator buses travel as far as Whitehaven Street, both just a little bit short (south) of Glover Park; you can walk it easily, but it is all uphill. Regular Metro buses (the no. 30 series) travel to Glover Park. Perhaps the easiest thing to do is take a taxi.

MODERATE

Heritage India ★ INDIAN This elegant two-story dining room caters to those with sophisticated tastes for Indian food. You'll find all the standards here: tandoori dishes, lamb vindaloo, and vegetarian entrees, such as the *palak makai* (herbed spinach), and vegetable fritters, each dish carefully prepared and seasoned. Service could be better, but the overall experience is rewarding. A second Heritage India is located in the Dupont Circle neighborhood, 1337 Connecticut Ave. NW (✆ **202/331-1414**), but this one is a "brasserie and lounge," whose menu includes contemporary Indian cuisine. Small plates of samosas, pakoras, and kebabs go down nicely with a cocktail, and that's what the younger crowd comes here for, along with the dishes served at the original location and some more intriguing dishes, such as the hummus made with roasted garlic and black beans, and the tandoori-smoked mozzarella.

2400 Wisconsin Ave. NW (near Calvert St.). ✆ **202/333-3120.** www.heritageindiaofgeorgetown.com. Reservations accepted. Lunch main courses $7.95–$13; dinner main courses $11–$24. AE, DC, DISC, MC, V. Daily 11:30am–2:30pm and 5:30–10:30pm.

Sushi-Ko ★ JAPANESE Sushi-Ko was Washington's first sushi bar when it opened 32 years ago, and it remains the best. The sushi chefs are fun to watch—try to sit at the sushi bar, and if you do, ask chef Koji Terano to serve you his choice selections. You can expect superb sushi and sashimi standards, as well as daily specials, like a sea trout napoleon (diced sea trout layered between rice crackers), flounder sashimi with a black truffle sauce, and the delicately fried soft-shell crab (in season, spring and

A Seat at the Bar

Dining out in Washington can be many things: a culinary adventure, a happy pastime, a chance to transact business, a romantic interlude . . . and a competitive sport. Most restaurants require reservations, and in this cut-throat town, all the best seem always to be booked. Oh pooh! What's a hungry, reservation-less, good-food lover to do? Head to the bar, of course. In an effort to please those who haven't managed to reserve a table in their main dining rooms, but who nevertheless hope to sample some of their food, glorious food, a number of the city's top restaurants have started serving modified versions of their regular menus at the bar. The experience often proves more intimate and convivial than that in the main dining room, and here's the kicker: it's always less expensive. Consider these:

At **Palena,** 3529 Connecticut Ave. NW (✆ **202/537-9250**), you sit on comfy stools at the bar and enjoy chef Frank Ruta's exquisitely prepared Kobe beef cheeseburger with brioche bun and *sottocenere* (a creamy Italian cheese with black truffles), Caesar salad, pastas, roasted chicken, a charcuterie plate, fried lemons (don't knock 'em til you try 'em) and onion rings, all perfectly done—and everything costing less than $14. On Monday nights, the main dining room is closed and this bar area at the front of the house becomes **Palena's Café,** serving just the bar menu (this is a favorite 20-something gathering space and time).

At **Michel Richard Citronelle,** in the Latham Hotel, 3000 M St. NW (✆ **202/625-2150**), the bar/lounge is located on a level just above the main dining

summer). Another option to capture the full range of tastes here: Order a bunch of the "small dishes," like the grilled baby octopus with mango sauce, or asparagus with smoked salmon and mustard dashi sauce. The tempuras and teriyakis are also excellent. And there's a long list of sakes, as well as burgundy wines and Japanese beer. 2309 Wisconsin Ave. NW. ✆ **202/333-4187.** www.sushiko.us. Reservations recommended. Main courses $14–$24. AE, MC, V. Tues–Fri noon–2:30pm; Mon–Thurs 6–10:30pm; Fri 6–11pm; Sat 5:30–11pm; Sun 5:30–10pm.

12 Woodley Park & Cleveland Park

VERY EXPENSIVE

Palena ★★★ CONTEMPORARY AMERICAN/FRENCH/ITALIAN One Metro stop past the Woodley Park–Zoo station takes you to the residential neighborhood of Cleveland Park, which is exploding with good restaurants. Palena is one that's worth the trip.

Palena is the creation of two former White House chefs, Executive Chef Frank Ruta and Pastry Chef Ann Amernick, who worked together at the White House in the 1980s. Ruta received his most recent culinary recognition from the 2007 James Beard Foundation, winning, along with Vidalia chef R.J. Cooper (p. 151), its Mid-Atlantic chef award. Ruta turns out French- and Italian-inspired dishes, such as Portuguese sardines in puff pastry, cod roasted in lavender-infused olive oil, and Dover sole filet room. There are bar stools, but also a collection of tables. The a la carte menu offers a range of items, from $12 mushroom cigars (fried mushroom duxelles with ginger sauce) to $38 duck, served medium rare, with duck leg confit. So many people have raved about the lobster burger ($28) that Richard includes it on the menu at his new restaurant, Central (p. 140). This is Richard's award-winning cuisine, at a fraction of the cost of his tasting menus.

CityZen, in the Mandarin Oriental Hotel, 1330 Maryland Ave. SW (✆ **202/787-6868**), offers perhaps the most jaw-dropping bar meal: Chef Eric Ziebold's three-course tasting menu in his main dining room costs $75; at the bar, Ziebold's edited version goes for $45. The chef does not present a set bar menu but pulls one or two choices from each course on offer that night, so you can be sure you're dining on the same heavenly fare as those seated at tables: maybe a pickled shad with braised celery and potato crisps, or braised shoat shoulder with English peas. And the service is sublime.

Other bar scenes to recommend: **Marcel's** (p. 164), whose wine bar menu ranges from a gratin of endive for $13 to beef carbonade, in $15 and $28 portions (Marcel's also features live jazz in the wine bar nightly); **Bistrot Lepic** (p. 166), another wine bar, offering both bar item menus and specialties of the house; and **PS7's** (p. 142), whose lounge is a cool scene and its menu even cooler—try the risotto balls, tuna sliders, and house-made half-smokes.

stuffed with porcini and pan roasted with artichokes and endive. Amernick's contributions range from complimentary caramels at dinner's conclusion, to the fresh sorbets, cheesecake, bread pudding, and other offerings on the dessert menu. This is an elegant restaurant, with an old-world feel. Because of its immediate and sustained success, it's sometimes hard to get a reservation, but worth trying for. Or you can dine at the bar (see "A Seat at the Bar," above). Palena's Café, which is the name for the front of the house, is open on Monday nights, serving just that bar/cafe menu. Reservations are not accepted and the place is standing room only.

3529 Connecticut Ave. NW. ✆ **202/537-9250.** www.palenarestaurant.com. Reservations recommended. Jacket and tie preferred for men. Fixed-price menus $57 (3-course), $66 (4-course), and $75 (5- to 6-course). AE, DC, DISC, MC, V. Mon (cafe only) and Tues–Sat 5:30–10pm. Metro: Cleveland Park.

MODERATE

Indique ★ INDIAN Cleveland Park is an upscale residential community of old streets lined with towering trees and Victorian houses. A preponderance of wonks, intellects, and journalists live here with their families. It's an unlikely mecca for the wild-and-crazy 20-something crowd, but thanks to a stretch of Connecticut Avenue between Porter and Macomb streets, where a number of hot bars and restaurants lie, that's what it's become—a mini-mecca, let's say. In the middle of this designated hot zone lies Indique, a two-story, glass-fronted Indian restaurant that's quite the scene.

Partiers on the weekend pack the downstairs bar area, drinking pomegranate martinis. Diners without reservations, and even sometimes those with reservations, wait for tables to become available upstairs, downstairs, wherever. Indian cuisine happens to be in vogue at the moment, but regardless, Indique's is very good. Come here for the Cornish hen curry, vegetable samosas, and tandoori shrimp.

3512–14 Connecticut Ave. NW (between Porter and Ordway sts.). ✆ **202/244-6600.** www.indique.com. Reservations accepted. Lunch main courses $9–$11; dinner main courses $11–$21. AE, DC, DISC, MC, V. Daily noon–3pm; Sun–Thurs 5:30–10:30pm; Fri–Sat 5:30–11pm. Metro: Cleveland Park.

Lebanese Taverna *Kids* MIDDLE EASTERN This family-owned restaurant, which opened in 1990, gives you a taste of Lebanese culture—its cuisine, decor, and music. It's very popular, especially on weekends, so expect to stand in line. (Reservations are accepted only for seating before 6:30pm.) Diners, once seated in the courtyard-like dining room, where music plays and prayer rugs hang on the walls, hate to leave. The wood-burning oven in the back bakes the pita breads and several appetizers. Order meze dishes for the table: hummus, tabbouleh, baba ghanouj, stuffed grape leaves, cheese pastries, couscous, and pastry-wrapped spinach pies *(fatayer bi sabanikh),* enough for dinner for a couple or as hors d'oeuvres for more. Also consider entrees, such as the roasted half chicken wrapped in bread and served with garlic purée. The wealth of meatless dishes will delight vegetarians, while rotisserie items, especially the chicken and the chargrilled kabobs of chicken and shrimp, will please all others.

2641 Connecticut Ave. NW. ✆ **202/265-8681.** www.lebanesetaverna.com. Reservations accepted before 6:30pm. Lunch main courses $5.95–$18; dinner main courses $8.50–$20. AE, DC, DISC, MC, V. Mon–Fri 11:30am–2:30pm; Sat noon–3pm; Mon 5:30–10pm; Tues–Thurs 5–10:30pm; Fri–Sat 5:30–11pm; Sun 4:30–9:30pm. Metro: Woodley Park–Zoo.

7

Exploring Washington, D.C.

Big things are happening in Washington: The long-awaited **Capitol Visitor Center** beneath the U.S. Capitol Building finally, finally is scheduled to debut in fall of 2008, just in time for the 2009 inauguration; the enormous **Newseum** has opened in its new downtown location on Pennsylvania Avenue, at 6th Street NW, and is drawing great crowds; the **National Museum of Natural History** christened a cool walk-through **Butterfly Pavilion** in November 2007 and is on track to pull back the curtains on its grand new **Ocean Hall** in September 2008; a **Madame Tussaud's Wax Museum** is up and running in the heart of downtown D.C.; the **National Museum of American History** reopens its doors in summer 2008, ready to show off its **Star-Spangled Banner Gallery;** and dedication of the National Mall's newest memorial, the **Martin Luther King National Memorial,** takes place December 2008. Wow.

But for all its changes, the capital stays wonderfully the same, offering visitors a menu that includes the three houses of government, scores of museums, more than 100 memorials, an abundance of historic houses and federal buildings, acres and acres of gorgeous parkland, and numerous outdoor activities.

Whether new, old, or tried and true, there's much to do and celebrate in the nation's capital. Now comes the hard part: figuring out where you want to go and what to see first. If you'd like some help, flip back to chapter 3, "Suggested Washington, D.C., Itineraries," which offers 1-, 2-, and 3-day scenarios for tackling the town. Otherwise, peruse this chapter, see what strikes your fancy, put on some good walking shoes, and head out.

Heads Up

Seven years after September 11, 2001, Washington, D.C., has a firm handle on workable security precautions, and for visitors that means standing in line at attractions—security clearances, no matter how efficient, do take time. At many tourist sites, like the Smithsonian's National Air and Space Museum and National Museum of Natural History, and at most government buildings, staff search handbags, briefcases, and backpacks, and you must walk past metal detectors, which means that during the busy spring and summer seasons, you may be queuing outside as you wait your turn to pass through security. So pack your patience, but otherwise carry as little as possible, and certainly no sharp objects. Museums and public buildings rarely offer the use of lockers.

Washington, D.C., Attractions

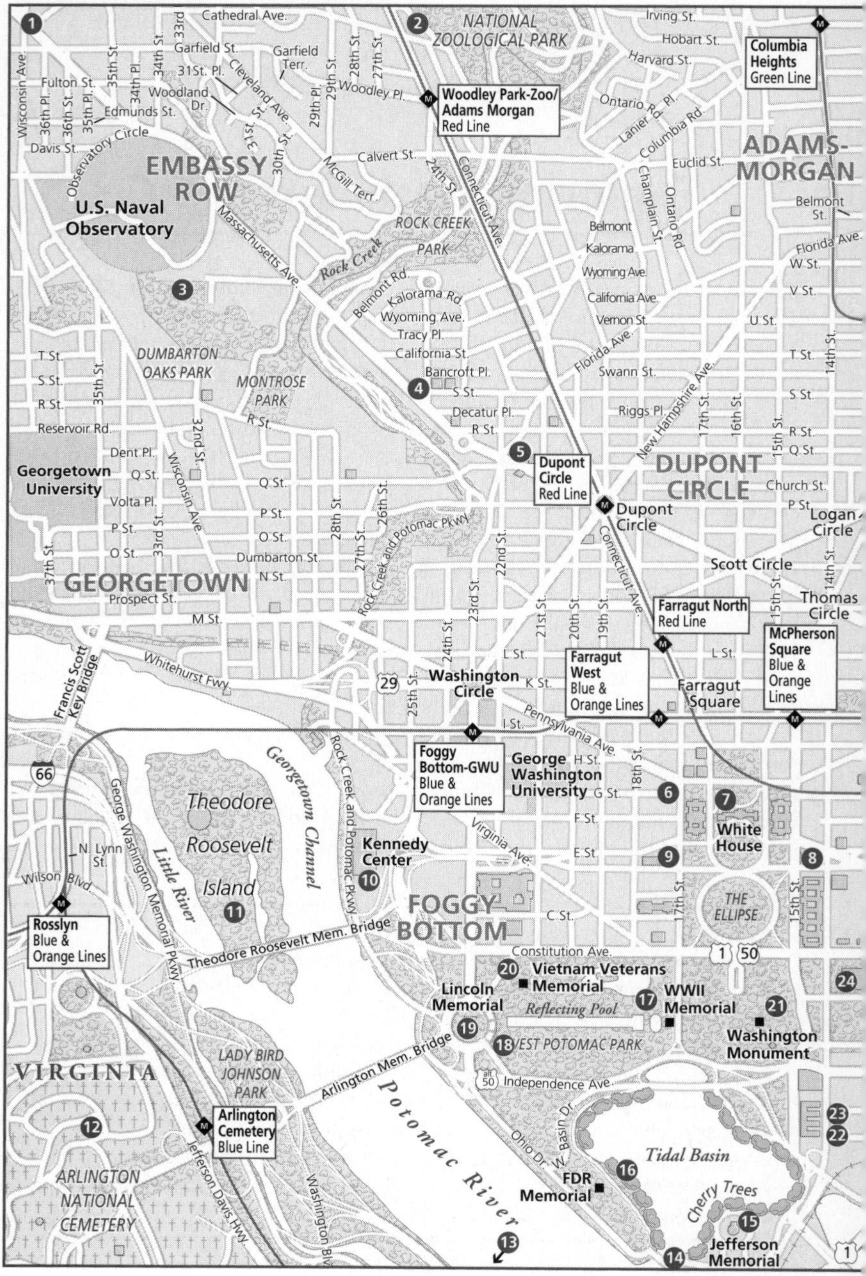

Anacostia Community Museum **51**
Arlington National Cemetery **12**
Arthur M. Sackler Gallery **28**
Arts and Industries Building **30**
Bureau of Engraving and Printing **22**
Capitol **45**
Corcoran Gallery of Art **9**
Dumbarton Oaks **3**
Enid A. Haupt Garden **29**
Folger Shakespeare Library **48**
FDR Memorial **16**
Freer Gallery of Art **27**
George Mason Memorial **14**
Hirshhorn Museum **31**
International Spy Museum **40**
Jefferson Memorial **15**
John F. Kennedy Center **10**
Korean War Veterans Memorial **18**
Marian Koshland Science Museum **42**
Library of Congress **47**
Lincoln Memorial **19**
Madame Tussauds **39**
National Air and Space Museum **32**
National Archives **36**
National Gallery of Art **34**
National Gallery of Art Sculpture Garden **35**
National Museum of African Art **29**
National Museum of American History **24**
National Museum of the American Indian **33**
National Museum of Natural History **25**
National Museum of Women in the Arts **38**
National Postal Museum **43**
National Zoological Park **2**
Newseum **37**
Pentagon **13**
Phillips Collection **5**
Renwick Gallery **6**
Sewall-Belmont House **50**
Smithsonian Information Center **26**
Smithsonian American Art Museum and National Portrait Gallery **41**
Supreme Court **49**
Theodore Roosevelt Island **11**
Union Station **44**
U.S. Botanic Garden **46**
U.S. Holocaust Memorial Museum **23**
Vietnam Veterans Memorial **20**
Washington Monument **21**
Washington National Cathedral **1**
White House **7**
White House Visitor Center **8**
Woodrow Wilson House **4**
World War II Memorial **17**

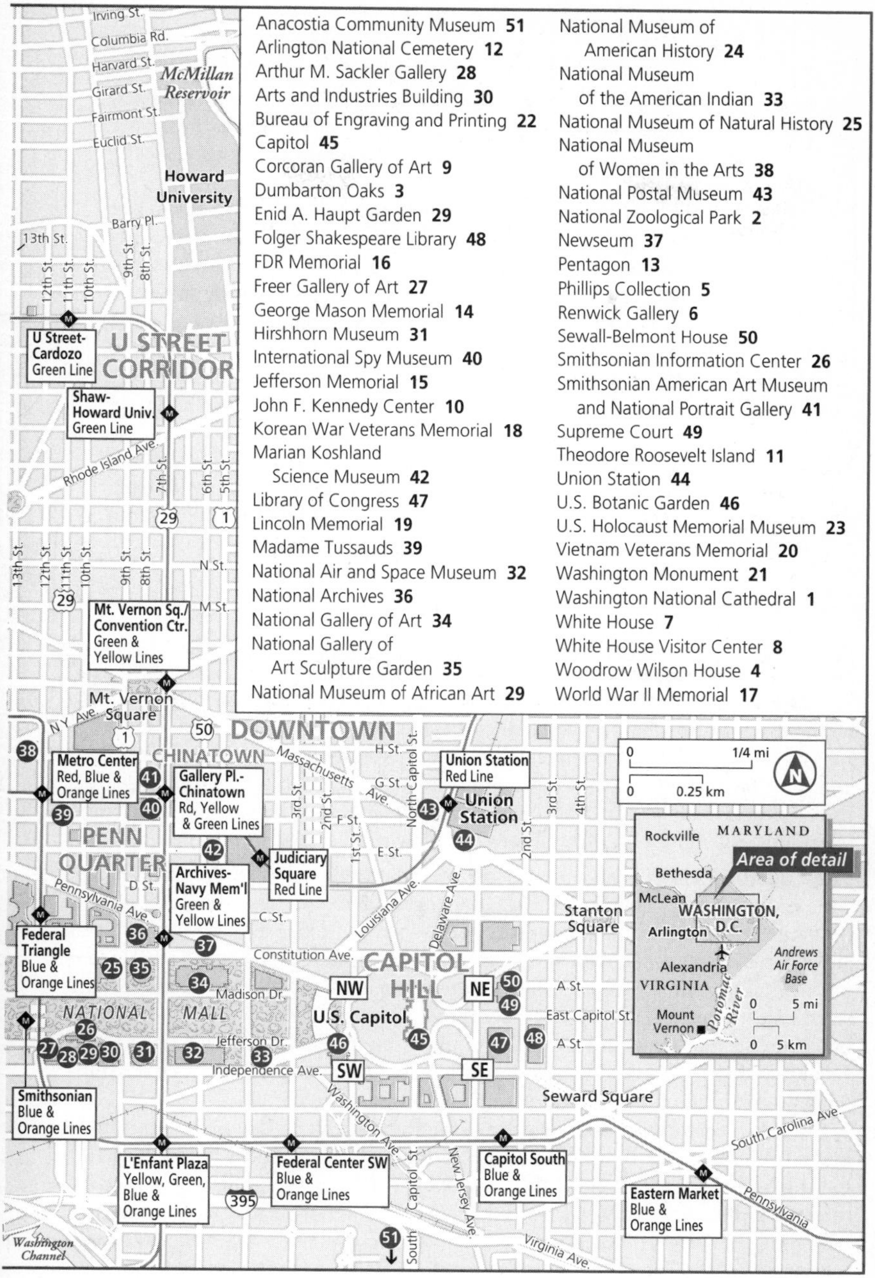

Call Ahead

Here's a crucial piece of advice: **Call the places you plan to tour each day before you set out.** Many of Washington's government buildings, museums, memorials, and monuments are open to the general public nearly all the time—except when they're not.

Because buildings like the Capitol, the Supreme Court, and the White House are offices as well as tourist destinations, the business of the day always poses the potential for closing one of those sites, or at least sections, to sightseers. There's also the matter of maintenance. The steady stream of visitors to Washington's attractions necessitates ongoing caretaking, which may require closing an entire landmark, or part of it, to the public, or put in place new hours of operation or procedures for visiting. (Construction of the Capitol's visitor center is one such example.) Finally, Washington's famous museums, grand halls, and public gardens double as settings for press conferences, galas, special exhibits, festivals, and other events, so you might arrive at, say, the National Air and Space Museum on a Sunday afternoon, only to find some of its galleries off-limits because caterers are setting up for an event. Want to avoid frustration and disappointment? Call ahead.

1 The 3 Houses of Government

The buildings housing the executive, legislative, and judicial branches of the U.S. government remain among the most visited sites in Washington. All three—the White House, the Capitol, and the Supreme Court—are stunning to behold and experience, and offer fascinating lessons in American history and government. Although these three landmarks are not as freely open to the public as they were before the terrorist attacks of September 11, 2001, all three do allow tours.

The Capitol ★★★ The Capitol is as majestic up close as it is from afar. For 135 years it sheltered not only both houses of Congress, but also the Supreme Court and, for 97 years, the Library of Congress as well. When you tour the Capitol, you'll learn about America's history as you admire the place in which it unfolded. Classical architecture, interior embellishments, and hundreds of paintings, sculptures, and other artworks are integral elements of the Capitol. The 30-minute tour (see detailed procedures below) takes you to the Crypt, the Rotunda, and National Statuary Hall. (For an in-depth description and information about the history and art of the Capitol, go to www.aoc.gov and click on the link "Visiting the Capitol.")

On the massive bronze doors leading to the **Rotunda** are portrayals of events in the life of Columbus. The Rotunda—a huge 96-foot-wide circular hall capped by a 180-foot-high dome—is the hub of the Capitol. The dome was completed, at Lincoln's direction, while the Civil War was being fought. Ten presidents have lain in state here, with former President Ronald Reagan being the most recent; when Kennedy's casket was displayed, the line of mourners stretched 40 blocks. On rare occasions, someone other than a president, military hero, or member of Congress receives this posthumous recognition. In October 2005, Congress paid tribute to Rosa Parks by allowing her body to lie in state here, the first woman to be so honored. (Parks was the black

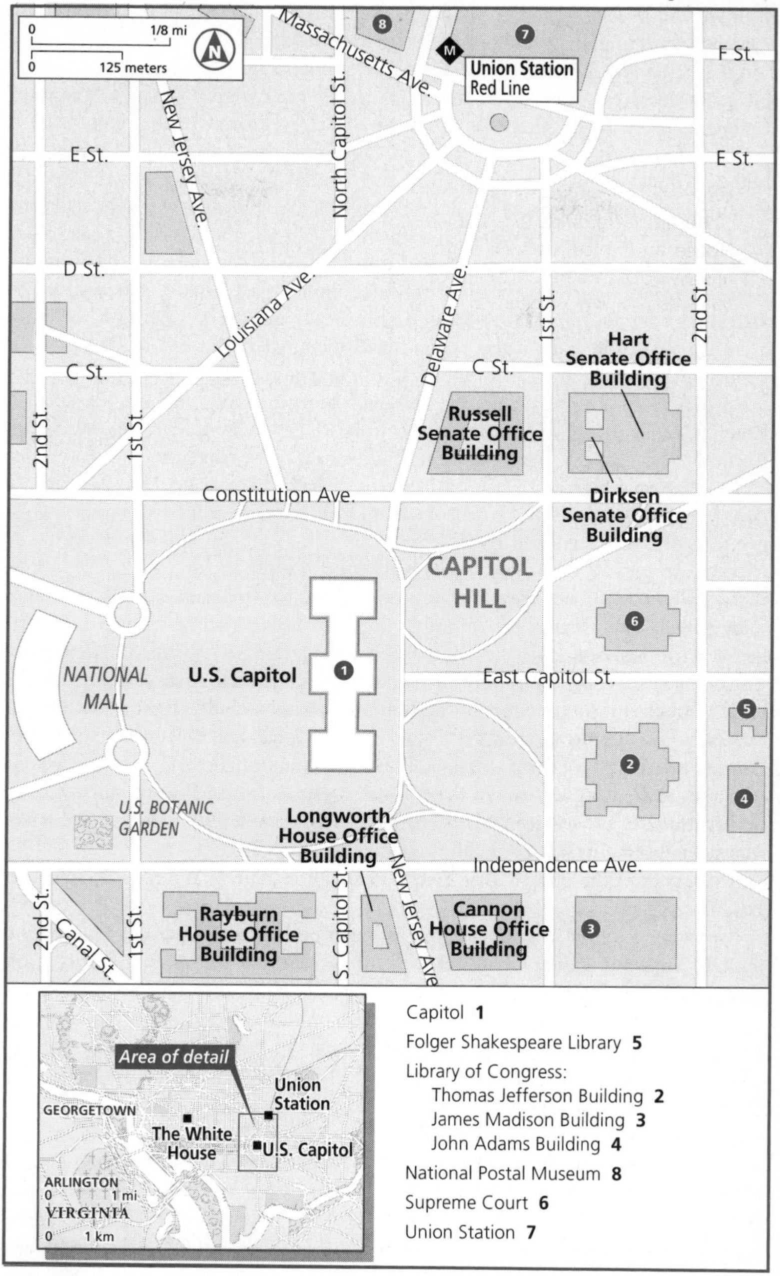
0
1/8 mi
0
125 meters
N
Massachusetts Ave.
Union Station
Red Line
M
F St.
E St.
E St.
New Jersey Ave.
North Capitol St.
D St.
Louisiana Ave.
Delaware Ave.
1st St.
2nd St.
Hart
Senate Office
Building
C St.
C St.
Russell
Senate Office
Building
2nd St.
1st St.
Constitution Ave.
Dirksen
Senate Office
Building
CAPITOL
HILL
NATIONAL
MALL
U.S. Capitol
East Capitol St.
U.S. BOTANIC
GARDEN
Longworth
House Office
Building
Independence Ave.
2nd St.
Canal St.
1st St.
Rayburn
House Office
Building
S. Capitol St.
New Jersey Ave.
Cannon
House Office
Building
Area of detail
Union
Station
GEORGETOWN
The White
House
U.S. Capitol
ARLINGTON
0
1 mi
VIRGINIA
0
1 km
Capitol 1
Folger Shakespeare Library 5
Library of Congress:
Thomas Jefferson Building 2
James Madison Building 3
John Adams Building 4
National Postal Museum 8
Supreme Court 6
Union Station 7

woman who in 1955 refused to relinquish her seat to a white man on a Montgomery, Alabama, bus, thereby sparking a civil rights movement.)

Embracing the Rotunda walls are eight immense oil paintings commemorating great moments in American history, such as the presentation of the Declaration of Independence and the surrender of Cornwallis at Yorktown. In the dome is an allegorical fresco masterpiece by Constantino Brumidi, *Apotheosis of Washington,* a symbolic portrayal of George Washington surrounded by Roman gods and goddesses watching over the progress of the nation. Brumidi was known as the "Michelangelo of the Capitol" for the many works he created throughout the building. (Take another look at the dome and find the woman directly below Washington; the triumphant *Armed Freedom* figure is said to be modeled after Lola Germon, a beautiful young actress with whom the 60-year-old Brumidi conceived a child.) Beneath the dome is a *trompe l'oeil* frieze depicting major developments in the life of America, from Columbus's landing in 1492 to the birth of the aviation age in 1903. Don't miss the sculptures in the Rotunda: a pensive Abraham Lincoln, a dignified Dr. Martin Luther King, Jr., and a ponderous trinity of suffragists Elizabeth Cady Stanton, Susan B. Anthony, and Lucretia Mott—these and others are represented here.

The **National Statuary Hall** was originally the chamber of the House of Representatives. In 1864, it became Statuary Hall, and the states were invited to send two statues each of native sons and daughters to the hall. There are 100 statues in all, New Mexico completing the collection with its contribution in 2005 of Po'Pay, a Pueblo Indian, who in 1680 led a revolt against the Spanish that helped to save Pueblo culture. (Stay tuned: The District of Columbia hopes to honor two of its own homegrown heroes with statues, despite the fact that Congress refuses to recognize D.C. as a state.) Because of space constraints, only 38 statues reside in the Hall, with the remaining scattered throughout the corridors of the Capitol. Statues include Ethan Allen, the Revolutionary War hero who founded the state of Vermont, and Missouri's Thomas Hart Benton, not the 20th-century artist famous for his rambunctious murals, but his namesake and uncle, who was one of the first two senators from Missouri and whose antislavery stance in 1850 cost him his Senate seat. Eight women are represented, including Montana's Jeannette Rankin, the first woman to serve in Congress.

The **Crypt** of the Capitol lies directly below the Rotunda and is used mainly as an exhibit space.

Following the tour, you are allowed to linger on the first floor, and to wander past the **Old Supreme Court Chamber,** which has been restored to its mid-19th-century appearance. The Supreme Court met here from 1810 to 1860; busts of the first four chief justices are on display—John Marshall, John Rutledge, John Jay, and Oliver Ellsworth—and so are some of their desks, believed to have been purchased in the 1830s. The justices handed down a number of noteworthy decisions here, including that of Dred Scott v. Sandford, which denied the citizenship of blacks, whether slaves or free, and in so doing precipitated the nation's Civil War.

You will not see them on your tour, but the **south and north wings** of the Capitol hold the House and Senate chambers, respectively. The House of Representatives chamber is the largest legislative chamber in the world, and the setting for the president's annual State of the Union addresses. (See the information below about watching Senate and House activity.)

Procedures for Touring the Capitol: All tours of the Capitol are guided, led by a Capitol Guide Service guide. You'll need to obtain a pass to go on the tour, which is free and lasts about 30 minutes. The Capitol has quite a list of items it prohibits, and

The Opening of the Capitol Visitor Center

Under construction since mid-2002, a comprehensive, underground Capitol Visitor Center is scheduled to open in fall 2008, years behind schedule. If it has opened by the time you visit, you should enter at the East Front of the Capitol (along 1st St., across from the Library of Congress) to line up for your tour. You should still arrive early to receive a timed pass, but you will no longer have to wait outside. The visitor center has 26 restrooms (compared to the 5 public restrooms the Capitol has had until now), a dining facility that seats 600, and an orientation film shown in two theaters. If the center has not opened, you'll want to follow the touring procedures outlined in excruciating detail below. No matter what, call ✆ **202/225-6827** in advance of your visit; that way you'll know for sure whether the Capitol is open to the public the day you wish to visit, whether the new center is open, and the latest procedures for touring.

the recording that you listen to on the ✆ **202/225-6827** number recites them for you, everything from large bags of any kind to food and drink. Leave everything possible back at the hotel.

You have two options: If you are part of a group of no more than 40, you may arrange a tour in advance by contacting your congressional office at least 1 month ahead, and following the procedures that office outlines for you. If you are on your own, or with family or friends, get to the Capitol early (by 7:30am during the cherry-blossom season and spring break) to stand in line for one of a limited number of timed tickets the Capitol distributes daily, starting at 9am. Head to the ticket kiosk at the southwest corner of the Capitol grounds, near the intersection of 1st Street and Independence Avenue SW, across 1st Street from the U.S. Botanic Garden (Metro: Federal Center Southwest, on the Blue and Orange lines). Tickets are first come, first served. Each person gets only one ticket (so no sending dad to get tickets for the whole family) and every person, including children of any age, must have a ticket. Once you receive your ticket, you're free to wander or get a snack while you wait for your turn to tour the Capitol. Again, call the recorded information line (✆ **202/225-6827**) on the morning of your visit to confirm exactly where and how to obtain your ticket.

Procedures for Visiting the House Gallery or Senate Gallery: Try to visit when both the Senate and House are **in session** ★★★. In fact, the Senate Gallery is open to visitors only when it is in session, but the House Gallery is open to visitors whether or not it is in session. (Children under 6 are not allowed in the Senate gallery.) You must have a separate pass, one for each gallery. Once obtained, the passes are good through the remainder of the Congress. You can obtain visitor passes in advance by contacting the offices of your representative and senator and requesting that they mail a House pass and a Senate gallery pass (Capitol switchboard is ✆ **202/224-3121**). District of Columbia and Puerto Rico residents should contact their delegate to Congress.

If you don't receive advance passes, you'll have to pick them up yourself at your members' offices. If you've obtained your tour-of-the-Capitol pass and have some time to kill, this works out perfectly: Off to the side of the ticket kiosk is a directory that tells you the office locations for your senator and representative. Since Congressional representatives and delegates have offices on the south side, or Independence Avenue side, of the Capitol, and since the ticket kiosk is quite near Independence Avenue, it makes sense for you to drop in on your representative's or delegate's office, rather than

Tips In Your Extra Time

What to do when you've snagged a timed pass for a tour that's hours from now? A few suggestions on Capitol Hill: Visit your senator's or representative's office; wander around the Capitol Grounds and discover fine statuary, like the Garfield Monument, and private garden spots; tour the U.S. Botanic Garden (p. 230) or the National Museum of the American Indian (p. 203); or get a bite to eat, either at the American Indian museum's eatery, which everyone seems to love, or up the hill, at Le Bon Café (210 2nd St. SE, ✆ **202/547-7200**), a good little sandwich place. (If you listen up when you stand in line, you're bound to overhear some juicy Capitol Hill scuttlebutt.)

visit your senator. As a courtesy, your representative's office should give you passes to both the Senate and House galleries. (***Note:*** International visitors can obtain both House and Senate gallery passes by presenting a passport or a valid driver's license with photo ID to the Capitol Guide Service staff in the House of Representative's Gallery line, in the Capitol's South Screening Facility.)

Passes in hand, this is what you do: To visit the Senate gallery, go to the public door on the north side, or the Constitution Avenue side of the Capitol; you'll have to pass through security clearance, but here, at least, the Capitol does allow you to check certain items, like cameras.

A visit to the House chamber tends to take more time—as much as 2 hours sometimes. You pass through security clearance (again, you should be able to check certain items) in the same area as those who are going on the guided tours, that is, up the path to the public entrance to the Capitol on the Independence Avenue side of the building. Instead of proceeding directly to the gallery, however, you (usually) are handed a secondary pass and sent back out through a separate door to wait outside until the crowds thin inside enough for you to reenter and walk through the halls to the House chamber. This convoluted procedure is more about traffic flow than security: You're visiting Congress, after all, where your representatives are trying to work hard on your behalf.

Confused? Unsure about where to go, or what to do? Just look around: Capitol Hill policemen are everywhere and happy to point you in the right direction.

You'll know that the House and/or the Senate is in session if you see flags flying over their respective wings of the Capitol (**remember:** House, south side; Senate, north side), or you can check the weekday "Today in Congress" column in the *Washington Post* for details on times of the House and Senate sessions and committee hearings. This column also tells you which sessions are open to the public. Or access the Capitol's website, **www.aoc.gov**, which helpfully provides information about the history, art, and construction of the Capitol building; an in-depth education on the legislative process; schedules of bill debates in the House and Senate, committee markups, and meetings; and lots of other good stuff. The aoc.gov page has links to the individual Senate (www.senate.gov) and House (www.house.gov) pages, or you can go directly to those sites to connect to your senate or house representative's page.

Capitol and Capitol Visitor Center: On East Capitol St. (at 1st St. NW); Temporary tour ticket kiosk: at the bottom of the hill from the Capitol (near the intersection of 1st St. and Independence Ave. SW). ✆ **202/225-6827.** www.aoc.gov, www.house.gov, www.senate.gov. Free admission. Year-round 9am–4:30pm Mon–Sat, with first tour starting at 9:30am and last tour starting at 3:30pm. Closed for tours Sun and Jan 1, Thanksgiving, and Dec 25. Parking at Union Station or on neighborhood streets. Metro: Union Station or Capitol South (to walk to the Capitol Visitor Center and the East Front of the Capitol); Federal Center Southwest (to find the ticket kiosk for tours, if the Visitor Center has not yet opened).

The Supreme Court of the United States ★★★ The highest tribunal in the nation, the Supreme Court is charged with the power of "judicial review": deciding whether actions of Congress, the president, the states, and lower courts, in other words, of all branches of government and government officials, are in accordance with the Constitution, and with applying the Constitution's enduring principles to novel situations and a changing country. Arguably the most powerful people in the nation, the Court's chief justice and eight associate justices hear only about 75 to 100 of the most vital cases of the 8,000 to 9,000 petitions for writ certiorari submitted to the Court each year. The Court's rulings are final, reversible only by an Act of Congress.

Hard to believe, but the Supreme Court—in existence since 1789—did not have its own building until 1935. The justices met in New York, Philadelphia, and assorted nooks of the Capitol (see the Capitol's write-up above) until they finally got their own place. Architect Cass Gilbert designed the stately Corinthian marble palace that houses the Court today. Best known for his skyscrapers, like New York's 761-foot-high Woolworth Building, completed in 1913, Gilbert was an interesting choice for the Supreme Court commission in a city where Congress restricts building height to 160 feet.

You'll have plenty of time to admire the exterior of this magnificent structure if you're in town when the Court is in session and decide to try **seeing a case being argued** ★★★ because—yup, you guessed it—you have to wait in line (sometimes for hours) on the front plaza of the building. But do try! The experience is totally worth the wait. People queue in every city for tickets to concerts and sports events. But only in Washington does a wait in line grant one the privilege of watching and listening to the country's nine foremost legal experts nimbly and intensely dissect the merits of both sides of an argument, whose decisions can affect profoundly both the person and the nation. The standing-in-line itself brings with it the same sort of thrill that builds in collective anticipation of a great performance.

Here's what you need to know: Starting the first Monday in October, continuing through late April, the Court "sits" for 2 weeks out of every month to hear two to four arguments each day, Monday through Wednesday, from 10am to noon, and from 1 to 2pm or 3pm. You can find out the specific dates and names of arguments in advance by calling the Supreme Court (✆ **202/479-3211**) or, better yet, by going to the website, **www.supremecourtus.gov**, where the argument calendar and the "Merits Briefs" (case descriptions) are posted.

Plan on arriving at the Supreme Court at least 90 minutes in advance of a scheduled argument during the fall and winter, and as early as 3 hours ahead in March and April, when schools are often on spring break and students lengthen the line. (Dress warmly; the stone plaza is exposed and can be witheringly cold.) Controversial cases also attract crowds; if you're not sure whether a particular case has created a stir, call the Court information line to reach someone who can tell you. The Court allots only about 150 first-come, first-served seats to the general public, but that number fluctuates from case to case, depending on the number of seats that have been reserved by the lawyers arguing the case and by the press. The Court police officers direct you into one line initially; when the doors finally open, you form a second line if you want to attend only 3 to 5 minutes of the argument.

The justices release opinions on an ongoing basis throughout the term, on every third Monday and, if any are ready, on argument days—the opinions are delivered before the arguments begin. Then, mid-May to late June, you can attend brief sessions (about 15 min.) at 10am on Monday, when the justices release remaining orders and opinions for the term. Again, you must stand in line on the front plaza to enter the building.

Leave your cameras, recording devices, and notebooks at your hotel; they're not allowed in the Courtroom. ***Note:*** But *do* bring quarters. Security procedures require you to leave all your belongings, including outerwear, purses, books, sunglasses, and so on, in a lower-level checkroom where there are coin-operated lockers that accept only quarters.

Once inside, pay close attention to the many rituals. At 10am, the marshal announces the entrance of the justices, and all present rise and remain standing while the justices take their seats (in high-backed, cushioned swivel chairs, by the way) following the chant: "The Honorable, the Chief Justice and Associate Justices of the Supreme Court of the United States. Oyez! Oyez! Oyez! All persons having business before the Honorable, the Supreme Court of the United States, are admonished to draw near and give their attention, for the Court is now sitting. God save the United States and this Honorable Court!" Unseen by the gallery is the "conference handshake"; following a 19th-century tradition symbolizing a "harmony of aims if not views," each justice shakes hands with each of the other eight when they assemble to go to the bench. The Court has a record before it of prior proceedings and relevant briefs, so each side is allowed only a 30-minute argument.

When the Court is not in session, you can tour the building and attend a **free lecture** in the courtroom about Court procedure and the building's architecture. Lectures are given every hour on the half-hour from 9:30am to 3:30pm. After the talk, explore the Great Hall and go down a flight of steps to see the **24-minute film** on the workings of the Court. On the same floor is an exhibit highlighting the "History of High Courts Around the World," on display indefinitely. Allow about an hour to tour. A gift shop and a public cafeteria are open to the public.

One 1st St. NE (between E. Capitol St. and Maryland Ave. NE). ✆ **202/479-3000.** www.supremecourtus.gov. Free admission. Mon–Fri 9am–4:30pm. Closed all federal holidays. Metro: Capitol South or Union Station.

The White House ★★ It's amazing when you think about it: This house has served as residence, office, reception site, and world embassy for every U.S. president since John Adams. The White House is the only private residence of a head of state that has opened its doors to the public for tours, free of charge. It was Thomas Jefferson who started this practice, which is stopped only during wartime. The war on terrorism caused the administration in 2002 to close the White House for public tours for about 2 years. Thankfully, the White House is once again open for public tours, though not walk-up tours. See the box "How to Arrange a White House Tour," below.

An Act of Congress in 1790 established the city, now known as Washington, District of Columbia, as the seat of the federal government. George Washington and city planner Pierre L'Enfant chose the site for the White House (or "President's House," as it was called before whitewashing brought the name "White House" into use) and staged a contest to find a builder. Although Washington picked the winner—Irishman James Hoban—he was the only president never to live in the White House. The structure took 8 years to build, starting in 1792, when its cornerstone was laid, and its facade is made of the same stone that was used to construct the Capitol. In 1814, during the War of 1812, the British set fire to the White House, gutting the interior; the exterior managed to endure only because a rainstorm extinguished the fire. What you

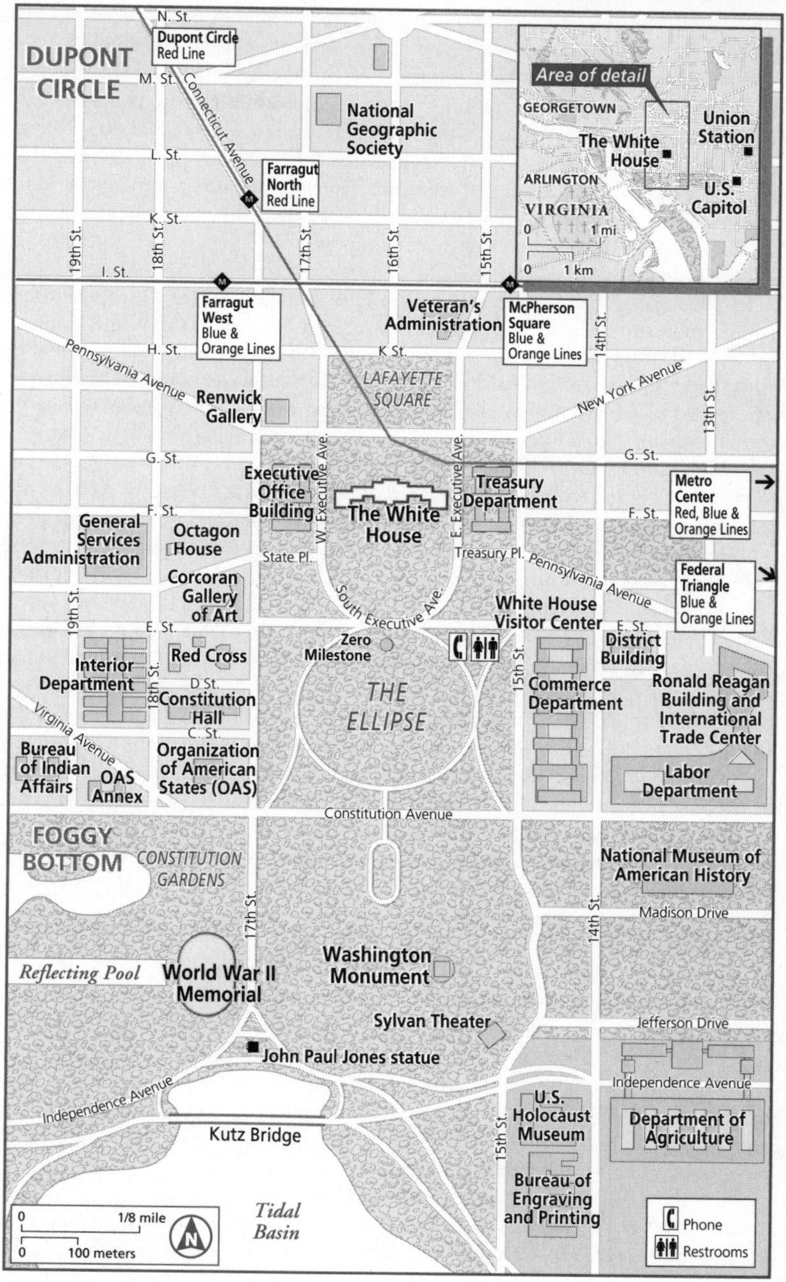
N. St.
Dupont Circle Red Line
DUPONT CIRCLE
M. St.
Connecticut Avenue
National Geographic Society
L. St.
Farragut North Red Line
K. St.
19th St.
18th St.
17th St.
16th St.
15th St.
I. St.
Area of detail
GEORGETOWN
The White House
Union Station
ARLINGTON
U.S. Capitol
VIRGINIA
0 1 mi
0 1 km
Farragut West Blue & Orange Lines
Veteran's Administration
McPherson Square Blue & Orange Lines
14th St.
Pennsylvania Avenue
H. St.
K St.
LAFAYETTE SQUARE
New York Avenue
Renwick Gallery
13th St.
G. St.
W. Executive Ave.
E. Executive Ave.
Executive Office Building
Treasury Department
The White House
Metro Center Red, Blue & Orange Lines
F. St.
General Services Administration
Octagon House
State Pl.
Treasury Pl.
Corcoran Gallery of Art
South Executive Ave.
Federal Triangle Blue & Orange Lines
White House Visitor Center
E. St.
Zero Milestone
District Building
Interior Department
Red Cross
D St.
Constitution Hall
C. St.
THE ELLIPSE
Commerce Department
Ronald Reagan Building and International Trade Center
Virginia Avenue
Bureau of Indian Affairs
OAS Annex
Organization of American States (OAS)
Labor Department
Constitution Avenue
FOGGY BOTTOM
CONSTITUTION GARDENS
National Museum of American History
Madison Drive
Reflecting Pool
World War II Memorial
Washington Monument
Sylvan Theater
Jefferson Drive
John Paul Jones statue
Independence Avenue
Independence Avenue
U.S. Holocaust Museum
Department of Agriculture
Kutz Bridge
Bureau of Engraving and Printing
Tidal Basin
0 1/8 mile
0 100 meters
N
Phone
Restrooms

see today is Hoban's basic creation: a building modeled after an Irish country house (in fact, Hoban had in mind the house of the Duke of Leinster in Dublin).

Alterations over the years have incorporated the South Portico in 1824, the North Portico in 1829, and electricity in 1891, during Benjamin Harrison's presidency. In 1902, repairs and refurnishings of the White House cost nearly $500,000. No other great change took place until Harry Truman's presidency, when the interior was completely renovated, after the leg of Margaret Truman's piano cut through the dining room ceiling. The Trumans lived at Blair House across the street for nearly 4 years while the White House interior was shored up with steel girders and concrete. It's as solid as Gibraltar now.

In 1961, Jacqueline Kennedy formed a Fine Arts Committee to help restore the famous rooms to their original grandeur, ensuring treatment of the White House as a museum of American history and decorative arts. "It just seemed to me such a shame when we came here to find hardly anything of the past in the house, hardly anything before 1902," Mrs. Kennedy observed. Presidents through the years have put their own stamp on the White House, one recent example being President George W. Bush's addition of the T-ball field to the South Lawn.

Highlights of the tour include the **Gold-and-White East Room,** the scene of presidential receptions, weddings (Lynda Bird Johnson, for one), and other dazzling events. This is where the president entertains visiting heads of state and the place where seven of the eight presidents who died in office (all but Garfield) laid in state. It was also where Nixon resigned. The room's early-18th-century style was adopted during the Theodore Roosevelt renovation of 1902; it has parquet Fontainebleau oak floors and white-painted wood walls with fluted pilasters and classical relief inserts. Note the famous Gilbert Stuart portrait of George Washington that Dolley Madison saved from the British torch during the War of 1812. The portrait is the only object to have remained continuously in the White House since 1800 (except during times of reconstruction).

You'll visit the **Green Room,** which was Thomas Jefferson's dining room but today is used as a sitting room. Mrs. Kennedy chose the green watered-silk-fabric wall covering. In the **Oval Blue Room,** decorated in the French Empire style chosen by James Monroe in 1817, presidents and first ladies have officially received guests since the Jefferson administration. It was, however, Van Buren's decor that began the "blue room" tradition. The walls, on which hang portraits of five presidents (including Rembrandt Peale's portrait of Thomas Jefferson and G. P. A. Healy's of Tyler), are covered in reproductions of early-19th-century French and American wallpaper. Grover Cleveland, the only president to wed in the White House, was married in the Blue Room. This room was also where the Reagans greeted the 52 Americans liberated after being held hostage in Iran for 444 days, and every year it's the setting for the White House Christmas tree.

The **Red Room,** whose satin-covered walls and Empire furnishings are red, is used as a reception room, usually for afternoon teas. Several portraits of past presidents and a Gilbert Stuart portrait of Dolley Madison hang here. Dolley Madison used the Red Room for her famous Wednesday-night receptions.

From the Red Room, you enter the **State Dining Room.** Modeled after late-18th-century neoclassical English houses, this room is a superb setting for state dinners and luncheons. Below G. P. A. Healy's portrait of Lincoln is an inscription written by John Adams on his second night in the White House (FDR had it carved into the mantel): "I Pray Heaven to Bestow The Best of Blessings on THIS HOUSE and on All that shall here-after Inhabit it. May none but Honest and Wise Men ever rule under this Roof."

Tips How to Arrange a White House Tour

The White House allows groups of 10 or more to tour the White House, Tuesday through Saturday, from 7:30am to 12:30pm. Tours are self-guided and most people take no more than an hour to go through. You must have a reservation to tour the White House. At least 2 months and as far as 6 months in advance of your trip, call your senator's or representative's office with the names of the people in your group, and ask for a specific tour date. The tour coordinator consults with White House on availability and, if your date is available, contacts you to obtain the names, birth dates, Social Security numbers (for those 14 and older), and other information for each of the people in your party. The Secret Service reviews the information and clears you for the tour, putting the names of the people in your group on a confirmed reservation list; you'll receive a confirmation number and the date and time of your tour usually about 1 month in advance of your trip. On the day of your tour, call ✆ **202/456-7041** to make sure that the White House is still open that day to the public. Then off you go, to the south side of East Executive Avenue, near the Southeast Gate of the White House, with photo IDs for everyone in your party who is 15 or older.

Do not bring the following prohibited items: backpacks, book bags, handbags, or purses; food and beverages; strollers; cameras; video recorders or any type of recording device; tobacco products; personal grooming items, from cosmetics to hairbrush; any pointed objects, whether a pen or a knitting needle; aerosol containers; guns; ammunition; fireworks; electric stun guns; maces; martial arts weapons/devices; or knives of any description. Cellphones are okay, but not the kind that are also cameras. The White House does not have a coat-check facility, so there is no place for you to leave your belongings while you go on the tour. There are no public restrooms or telephones in the White House, and picture taking and videotaping are prohibited. ***Best advice:*** Leave everything but your wallet back at the hotel.

If your party numbers fewer than 10 people, I'm afraid you're probably out of luck; though congressional offices used to try putting strangers together to make a group of 10, most congressional staff found the process unworkable. Your senator's or representative's office might be the exception, however, so go ahead and call.

Note: Even if you have successfully reserved a White House tour for your group, you should still call ✆ **202/456-7041** before setting out in the morning, in case the White House is closed on short notice because of unforeseen events. If this should happen to you, you should make a point of walking by the White House anyway, since its exterior is still pretty awe-inspiring. Stroll past it on Pennsylvania Avenue, down 15th Street past the Treasury Building, and along the backside and South Lawn, on E Street.

1600 Pennsylvania Ave. NW (visitor entrance gate at E St. and E. Executive Ave.). ✆ **202/456-7041** or 202/208-1631. www.whitehouse.gov. Free admission. Tours for groups of 10 or more who have arranged the tour through their congressional offices. Metro: Federal Triangle.

The White House Visitor Center The Visitor Center opened in 1995 to provide extensive interpretive data about the White House and to serve as a ticket-distribution center (though that function is suspended indefinitely). It is run under the auspices of the National Park Service and the staff is well informed. The 30-minute video about the White House, *Where History Lives,* provides interior views of the presidential precincts (it runs continuously throughout the day). Pick up a copy of the National Park Service's brochure on the White House, which tells you a little about what you'll see in the eight or so rooms you tour and a bit about the history of the White House. The White House Historic Association runs a small shop here. Before you leave the Visitor Center, take a look at the exhibits, which include information about the architectural history of the White House; portrayals by photographers, artists, journalists, and political cartoonists; anecdotes about first families (such as the time prankster Tad Lincoln stood in a window above his father and waved a Confederate flag at a military review); details about what goes on behind the scenes, focusing on the vast staff of servants, chefs, gardeners, Secret Service people, and others who maintain this institution; highlights of notable White House ceremonies and celebrations, from a Wright Brothers' aviation demonstration in 1911 to a ballet performance by Baryshnikov during the Carter administration; and photographs of the ever-changing Oval Office as decorated by administrations from Taft to Bush.

1450 Pennsylvania Ave. NW (in the Dept. of Commerce Building, between 14th and 15th sts.). ✆ **202/208-1631.** Free admission. Daily 7:30am–4pm. Closed Jan 1, Thanksgiving, and Dec 25. Metro: Federal Triangle.

2 The Major Memorials

The National Park Service has a new name for the national parkland that extends from the Capitol to the Potomac River, encompassing the memorials, Washington Monument, National Mall, and West and East Potomac parks: **National Mall and Memorial Parks.** Not only that, but the Park Service now operates a radio station, **1670 AM,** that broadcasts prerecorded information regarding visiting hours at park sites and news items about this area; only those within 3 miles of the Mall can access the 10-watt signal, so maybe it will be most useful to all those drivers circling the Mall in search of a parking space.

The National Mall and Memorial Parks' major memorials honor esteemed presidents, war veterans, founding fathers, and, coming at the end of 2008, a civil rights leader. On November 13, 2006, thousands attended the official groundbreaking for the National Mall's newest memorial, the **Martin Luther King, Jr., National Memorial,** with many more anticipated for the memorial's dedication in December 2008. Located on a 4-acre parcel at the intersection of West Basin Drive and Independence Avenue, adjoining the Tidal Basin and adjacent to the FDR Memorial, and positioned in a direct line with the Lincoln and Jefferson memorials, the King Memorial pays tribute to the Baptist minister, who advocated nonviolence and direct action to force social change, and whose efforts and compelling speeches profoundly moved the country toward that achievement—before he was assassinated at the age of 39 on April 4, 1968.

All of these memorials are located in picturesque **West Potomac Park** (p. 231 for full details on the park and its famous **cherry blossoms**), which lies at the western end of the Mall, where it borders the Potomac River and encircles the Tidal Basin. Unfortunately, none of the memorials lies directly on a Metro line, so you can expect a bit of a walk from the specified station.

The easiest thing to do, if you're up to it, is to walk from one monument or memorial to the next. Dress for the weather: light clothing, shades, and sunscreen in summer; a hat, gloves, and warm jacket in winter—these monuments are set in wide open spaces, with little to no protection from the elements. But when the weather is lovely, so is the experience of sauntering around West Potomac Park.

Or, you can go by **Tourmobile** (p. 237), which continually picks up and discharges passengers at each of these sites throughout the day. Tourmobile, in fact, might be the best way to get around, since parking spaces, which have always been scarce, are even more so now that security barriers have overtaken some of the lots. The National Park Service manages all of these properties and maintains information about each of them, including upcoming events, at **www.nps.gov**; click on "DC," then scroll down the page to click on the names of individual parks.

Some believe the best time to visit the memorials is at night, when they're illuminated in all their imposing white-stone glory and the crowds have thinned. Try it—all of the memorials are safe to visit after dark, with park rangers on hand until 11:30pm year-round, except for the Washington Monument, which closes at 5pm now. You may view the exteriors anytime.

Washington Monument ★★★ *Kids* The idea of a tribute to George Washington first arose 16 years before his death, at the Continental Congress of 1783. But the new nation had more pressing problems and funds were not readily available. It wasn't until the early 1830s, with the 100th anniversary of Washington's birth approaching, that any action was taken.

Then there were several fiascoes. A mausoleum was provided for Washington's remains under the Capitol Rotunda, but a grandnephew, citing Washington's will, refused to allow the body to be moved from Mount Vernon. In 1830, Horatio Greenough was commissioned to create a memorial statue for the Rotunda. He came up with a bare-chested Washington, draped in classical Greek garb; a shocked public claimed he looked as if he were "entering or leaving a bath," and so the statue was relegated to the Smithsonian. Finally, in 1833, prominent citizens organized the Washington National Monument Society. Treasury Building architect Robert Mills's design was accepted.

The cornerstone was laid on July 4, 1848, and for the next 37 years, watching the monument grow, or not grow, was a local pastime. Declining contributions and the Civil War brought construction to a halt at an awkward 150 feet (you can still see a change in the color of the stone about halfway up). The unsightly stump remained until 1876, when President Grant approved federal monies to complete the project. Dedicated in 1885, it was opened to the public in 1888.

Visiting the Washington Monument: A series of security walls encircles the Washington Monument grounds, a barrier to vehicles but not people; the National Park

---

Finds Rise Above the Crowds

When the line is too long at the Washington Monument, walk over to the **Old Post Office Pavilion** at 1100 Pennsylvania Ave. NW (© **202/606-8691**), to ride two sets of elevators 270 feet up to the 12th-floor clock tower, for a fabulous, 360-degree view of the city. No, it's not quite the same vista as that of the Monument, which stands at a little over 555 feet high and surveys the Mall and beyond. But this is the second highest view of the capital, putting Pennsylvania Avenue, the Capitol, and other landmarks in your sights. The National Park Service operates the service, which is free and available daily. Enter the pavilion and look for the glass elevator.

Service has gone to a good bit of trouble to incorporate these 33-inch-high walls into a pleasing landscape design. Please be aware that large backpacks and open containers of food or drink are not allowed inside the monument; small sealed containers are okay. You'll need a ticket (see information below), and then you pass through a small screening facility before entering the monument's large elevator, which whisks you upward for 70 seconds.

Reaching the top, you'll be standing in the highest tip of the world's tallest free-standing work of masonry. The Washington Monument lies at the very heart of Washington, D.C., landmarks, and its 360-degree views are spectacular. Due east are the Capitol and Smithsonian buildings; due north is the White House; due west are the World War II and Lincoln memorials (with Arlington National Cemetery beyond); due south is the Jefferson Memorial, overlooking the Tidal Basin and the Potomac River. "On a clear day, you can see west probably 60 miles, as far as the Shenandoah Mountains," says National Park Service spokesperson Bill Line. Like being at the center of a compass, the monument provides a marvelous orientation to the city.

The glass-walled elevator slows down in its descent, to allow passengers a view of some of the 192 carved stones inserted into the interior walls that are gifts from foreign countries, all 50 states, organizations, and individuals. One stone you usually get to see is the one given by the state of Alaska in 1982—it's pure jade and worth millions. There are stones from Siam (now Thailand), the Cherokee Nation, the Vatican, and the Sons of Temperance, to name just a few.

Allow half an hour here, plus time spent waiting in line. A concession stand is open at the corner of 15th Street and Madison Drive NW.

Ticket Information: Admission to the Washington Monument is free, but you still have to get a ticket. The ticket booth is located in the Monument Lodge, at the bottom of the hill from the monument, on 15th Street NW, between Madison and Jefferson drives. It opens daily at 8:30am. Tickets are usually gone by 9am, so plan to get there by 7:30 or 8am, especially in peak season. The tickets grant admission at half-hour intervals between the stated hours, on the day you visit. If you want to get them in advance, call the National Park Reservation Service (© **877/444-6777**) or go to www.recreation.gov. The tickets themselves are free, but you'll pay $1.50 per ticket, plus $2.85 for shipping and handling, if you're ordering 10 or more days in advance; otherwise, you'll pick up the tickets at the "will call" window at the ticket kiosk. To make sure that you get tickets for your desired date, reserve these tickets at least 2 weeks in advance.

Directly south of the White House, on 15th St. (between Madison Dr. and Constitution Ave. NW). © **202/426-6841.** www.nps.gov/wamo. Free admission. Daily 9am–4:45pm. Last elevators depart 15 min. before closing (arrive earlier). Closed Dec 25, open until noon July 4th. Limited parking. Metro: Smithsonian, then a 10-min. walk, or take Tourmobile or the D.C. Circulator (takes you close though not directly to it).

National World War II Memorial ★★ When this memorial was dedicated on May 29, 2004, 150,000 people attended: President Bush; members of Congress; Marine Corps General (retired) P. X. Kelley, who chaired the American Battle Monuments

---

Impressions

May the spirit which animated the great founder of this city descend to future generations.

—John Adams

D.C. Circulator

Meet your new best friends. This fleet of large red-and-gray buses travels three routes, chauffeuring office workers and tourists alike to the busiest spots in town, including Georgetown, the National Mall, the convention center, and the Penn Quarter. A ride costs only $1, well worth it when you want to quickly and easily travel, say, from the Washington Monument at one end of the Mall to the National Museum of the American Indian at the other end, and you're too tired to walk. The city's subway system is fantastic, but this air-conditioned bus, which arrives at each stop every 10 minutes, helps fill in Metro's gaps. So look for the posted signs on the Mall and around the city and keep an eye out for the brightly colored buses. See "Getting Around," in chapter 4, for more details.

Commission, the group that spearheaded construction of the memorial; actor Tom Hanks and now-retired news anchor Tom Brokaw, both of whom had been active in eliciting support for the memorial; and last, but most important, thousands of World War II veterans and their families. These legions of veterans, some dressed in uniform, many wearing a cap identifying the name of the veteran's division, turned out with pride, happy to receive the nation's gratitude, 60 years in the making, expressed profoundly in this memorial.

Designed by Friedrich St. Florian and funded mostly by private donations, the memorial fits nicely into the landscape between the Washington Monument grounds to the east, and the Lincoln Memorial and its reflecting pool to the west. St. Florian purposely situated the 7½-acre memorial so as not to obstruct this long view down the Mall: Fifty-six 17-foot-high granite pillars representing each state and territory stand to either side of a central plaza and the Rainbow Pool. Likewise, 24 bas-relief panels divide down the middle so that 12 line each side of the walkway leading from the entrance at 17th Street. The panels to the left, as you walk toward the center of the memorial, illustrate seminal scenes from the war years as they relate to the Pacific theater: Pearl Harbor, amphibious landing, jungle warfare, a field burial, and so on; the panels to the right are sculptured scenes of war moments related to the Atlantic theater: Rosie the Riveter, Normandy Beach landing, the Battle of the Bulge, the Russians meeting the Americans at the Elbe River. A man named Raymond Kaskey, an architect and sculptor, sculpted these panels based on archival photographs.

Large open pavilions stake out the north and south axes of the memorial, and semicircular fountains create waterfalls on either side. Inscriptions at the base of each pavilion fountain mark key battles. Beyond the center Rainbow Pool is a wall of 4,000 gold stars, one star for every 100 soldiers who died in World War II. People often leave photos and mementos around the memorial, which the National Park Service gathers up daily (the NPS is currently deciding how best to maintain an archive of these mementos). If you are lucky, you will see World War II veterans when you visit this memorial. For compelling, firsthand accounts of World War II experiences, combine your tour here with an online visit to the Library of Congress's Veterans History Project, at www.loc.gov/vets; see the Library of Congress entry later in this chapter for more information.

From the 17th Street entrance walk south around the perimeter of the memorial to reach a ranger station, where there are brochures and registry kiosks, the latter for

Tips Memorial Day

It's most fitting to honor America's veterans on Memorial Day by heading to Washington to visit the war memorials on the National Mall, but if you're contemplating such a trip there's something you should know: You'll be in the company of hundreds of thousands of motorcyclists. Every year, legions of bikers from across the country roar into town to pay tribute to America's war veterans, prisoners of war, and those missing in action. The event is known as "Rolling Thunder," and it's taken place for 21 years. Bikers start arriving on the Friday preceding Memorial Day and park their motorcycles all over the grounds and streets near the Vietnam, Lincoln, and World War II memorials. A tour of the National Mall anytime during this weekend is a noisy affair, culminating in the earsplitting finale on Sunday, as the official Rolling Thunder parade vrooms from the starting point at the Pentagon, around the Mall, winding up at the Vietnam Veterans Memorial. If you're a biker, by all means, join the parade. Otherwise, stand back and salute. By the way, some of the tour bus services, like Tourmobile, suspend their tours on the day of the parade.

looking up names of veterans. Better information and faster service is available online at www.wwiimemorial.com.

On 17th St., near Constitution Ave. NW. ✆ **800/639-4WW2** or 202/426-6841. www.nps.gov/wwii. Free admission. Ranger on duty daily 9:30am–11:30pm, except Dec 25. Limited parking. Metro: Farragut West, Federal Triangle, or Smithsonian, with 20–25 min. walk, or take Tourmobile, or catch the D.C. Circulator.

Lincoln Memorial ★★★ *Kids* This beautiful and moving tribute to the nation's 16th president attracts millions of visitors annually. Like its fellow presidential memorials, the Lincoln was a long time in the making. Although it was planned as early as 1867—2 years after Lincoln's death—Henry Bacon's design was not completed until 1912, and the memorial was dedicated in 1922.

The neoclassical temple-like structure, similar in architectural design to the Parthenon in Greece, has 36 fluted Doric columns representing the states of the Union at the time of Lincoln's death, plus two at the entrance. On the attic parapet are 48 festoons symbolizing the number of states in 1922, when the monument was erected. Hawaii and Alaska are noted in an inscription on the terrace. Due east is the Reflecting Pool, lined with American elms and stretching 2,000 feet toward the Washington Monument and the Capitol beyond.

The memorial chamber has limestone walls inscribed with the Gettysburg Address and Lincoln's Second Inaugural Address. Two 60-foot-high murals by Jules Guerin on the north and south walls depict, allegorically, Lincoln's principles and achievements. On the south wall, an Angel of Truth freeing a slave is flanked by groups of figures representing Justice and Immortality. The north-wall mural portrays the unity of North and South and is flanked by groups of figures symbolizing Fraternity and Charity. Most powerful, however, is Daniel Chester French's 19-foot-high seated statue of Lincoln, which disappears from your sightline as you get close to the base of the memorial, then emerges slowly into view as you ascend the stairs.

Lincoln's legacy has made his memorial the site of numerous demonstrations by those seeking justice. Most notable was a peaceful demonstration of 200,000 people on August 28, 1963, at which the Rev. Dr. Martin Luther King, Jr., proclaimed, "I have a dream." Look for the words "I have a dream. Martin Luther King, Jr., The March on Washington for Jobs and Freedom, August 28, 1963," inscribed and centered on the granite step, 18 steps down from the chamber. The inscription, which the National Park Service added in July 2003, marks the precise spot where King stood to deliver his famous speech.

Rangers present 20- to 30-minute programs as time permits throughout the day. Thirty minutes is sufficient time for viewing this memorial.

On the western end of the Mall, at 23rd St. NW (between Constitution and Independence aves.). ✆ **202/426-6842.** www.nps.gov/linc. Free admission. Ranger on duty daily 9:30am–11:30pm except Dec 25. Limited parking. Metro: Foggy Bottom, then a 30-min. walk, or take Tourmobile, or catch the D.C. Circulator to 17th and Constitution and walk from there.

Korean War Veterans Memorial ★ This privately funded memorial, founded in 1995, honors those who served in Korea, a 3-year conflict (1950–53) that produced almost as many casualties as Vietnam. It consists of a circular "Pool of Remembrance" in a grove of trees and a triangular "Field of Service," highlighted by lifelike statues of 19 infantrymen, who appear to be trudging across fields. A 164-foot-long black-granite wall depicts the array of combat and support troops that served in Korea (nurses, chaplains, airmen, gunners, mechanics, cooks, and others); a raised granite curb lists the 22 nations that contributed to the U.N.'s effort there; and a commemorative area honors KIAs, MIAs, and POWs. Plan to spend 15 minutes for viewing.

Southeast of the Lincoln Memorial, on the Independence Ave. SW side of the Mall. ✆ **202/426-6841.** www.nps.gov/kowa. Free admission. Ranger on duty daily 9:30am–11:30pm except Dec 25. Limited parking. Metro: Foggy Bottom, with 30-min. walk, or take Tourmobile.

Vietnam Veterans Memorial ★★ The Vietnam Veterans Memorial is possibly the most poignant sight in Washington: two long, black-granite walls in the shape of a V, each inscribed with the names of the men and women who gave their lives, or remain missing, in the longest war in American history. Even if no one close to you died in Vietnam, it's wrenching to watch visitors grimly studying the directories to find out where their loved ones are listed, or rubbing pencil on paper held against a name etched into the wall. The walls list close to 60,000 people, most of whom died very young.

Because of the raging conflict over U.S. involvement in the war, Vietnam veterans had received almost no recognition of their service before the memorial was conceived by Vietnam veteran Jan Scruggs. The nonprofit Vietnam Veterans Memorial Fund raised $7 million and secured a 2-acre site in tranquil Constitution Gardens to erect a memorial that would make no political statement about the war and would harmonize with neighboring memorials. By separating the issue of the wartime service of individuals from the issue of U.S. policy in Vietnam, the VVMF hoped to begin a process of national reconciliation.

Yale senior Maya Lin's design was chosen in a national competition open to all citizens over 18 years of age. The two walls are angled at 125° to point to the Washington Monument and the Lincoln Memorial. The wall's mirror-like surface reflects surrounding trees, lawns, and monuments. The names are inscribed in chronological order, documenting an epoch in American history as a series of individual sacrifices from the date of the first casualty in 1959. The National Park Service continues to add names over the years, of those Vietnam veterans who die eventually of injuries sustained during the war.

The wall was erected in 1982. In 1984, a life-size sculpture of three Vietnam soldiers by Frederick Hart was installed at the entrance plaza. Near the statue, a flag flies from a 60-foot staff. Another sculpture, the *Vietnam Veterans Women's Memorial,* which depicts three servicewomen tending a wounded soldier, was installed on Veterans Day 1993. You should allow about 20 to 30 minutes here.

Be sure to seek out the knowledgeable park rangers if you have any questions.

Northeast of the Lincoln Memorial, east of Henry Bacon Dr. (between 21st and 22nd sts. NW, on the Constitution Ave. NW side of the Mall). © **202/426-6841.** www.nps.gov/vive. Free admission. Ranger on duty daily 9:30am–11:30pm except Dec 25. Limited parking. Metro: Foggy Bottom, with 25-min. walk, or take Tourmobile, or catch the D.C. Circulator to 17th and Constitution and walk from there.

Franklin Delano Roosevelt Memorial ★★★ The FDR Memorial has proven to be one of the most popular of the presidential memorials since it opened in 1997. Its popularity has to do as much with its design as the man it honors. This 7½-acre outdoor memorial stretches out, rather than rising up, across the stone-paved floor. Granite walls define the four "galleries," each representing a different term in FDR's presidency from 1933 to 1945. Architect Lawrence Halprin's design includes waterfalls, sculptures (by Leonard Baskin, John Benson, Neil Estern, Robert Graham, Thomas Hardy, and George Segal), and Roosevelt's own words carved into the stone.

One drawback of the FDR Memorial is the noise. Planes on their way to or from nearby Reagan National Airport zoom overhead, and the many displays of cascading water can sound thunderous. When the memorial first opened, adults and children alike arrived in bathing suits and splashed around on warm days. Park rangers don't allow that anymore, but they do allow you to dip your feet in the various pools. A favorite time to visit is at night, when dramatic lighting reveals the waterfalls and statues against the dark parkland.

Conceived in 1946, the FDR Memorial had been in the works for 50 years. Part of the delay in its construction can be attributed to the president himself. FDR had told his friend Supreme Court Justice Felix Frankfurter, "If they are to put up any memorial to me, I should like it to be placed in the center of that green plot in front of the Archives Building. I should like it to consist of a block about the size [of this desk]." In fact, such a plaque sits in front of the National Archives Building. Friends and relatives struggled to honor Roosevelt's request to leave it at that, but Congress and national sentiment overrode them.

As with other presidential memorials, this one opened to some controversy. Advocates for people with disabilities were incensed that the memorial sculptures did not show the president in a wheelchair, which he used after he contracted polio. President Clinton asked Congress to allocate funding for an additional statue portraying a wheelchair-bound FDR. You will now see a small statue of FDR in a wheelchair, placed at the very front of the memorial, to the right as you approach the first gallery. Step inside the gift shop to view a replica of Roosevelt's wheelchair, as well as one of the rare photographs of the president sitting in a wheelchair. The memorial is probably the most accessible tourist attraction in the city; as at most of the National Park Service locations, wheelchairs are available for free use on-site.

If you don't see a posting of tour times, look for a ranger and request a tour; the rangers are happy to oblige. Thirty minutes is sufficient time to allot here.

On West Basin Dr., alongside the Tidal Basin in West Potomac Park (across Independence Ave. SW from the Mall). © **202/426-6841.** www.nps.gov/frde. Free admission. Ranger on duty daily 9:30am–11:30pm, except for Dec 25. Limited parking. Metro: Smithsonian, with a 30-min. walk, or take Tourmobile.

George Mason Memorial ★ This memorial honors George Mason, author of the Virginia Declaration of Rights, which had much to do with the establishment of the United States Bill of Rights. Dedicated on April 9, 2002, the memorial consists of a bronze statue of Mason, set back in a landscaped grove of trees and flower beds (lots and lots of pansies), arranged in concentric circles around a pool and fountain. Mason appears in 18th-century garb, from buckled shoes to tricorn hat, seated on a marble bench, but leaning backward on one arm and gazing off in the general direction of the Washington Monument. Two stone slabs are inscribed with some of Mason's words, like these, referring to Mason's rejection of slavery, "that slow Poison, which is daily contaminating the Minds & Morals of our People." Wooden benches at the site present a pleasant opportunity to learn about Mason, and take a break, before moving on. ***Note:*** The memorial is easy to miss, since it does not lie on the Tidal Basin path. As you approach the Jefferson Memorial from the direction of the FDR Memorial, or as you approach the FDR Memorial from the direction of the Jefferson, you'll come to the bridge that arches over the inlet leading from the Tidal Basin to the Potomac River; look straight across from the bridge, and there you'll see it.

At East Basin and Ohio Dr. SW (between the Jefferson and FDR memorials). ✆ **202/426-6841.** www.nps.gov/gemm. Free admission. Always open, though rangers generally are not posted here. To find out more about George Mason, visit the Jefferson Memorial, a 5-min. walk away, across the street, on the Tidal Basin, where a park ranger is on duty 9:30am–11:30pm. Limited parking. Metro: Smithsonian, with a 25-min. walk, or take Tourmobile.

Jefferson Memorial ★★ President John F. Kennedy, at a 1962 dinner honoring 29 Nobel Prize winners, told his guests that they were "the most extraordinary collection of talent, of human knowledge, that has ever been gathered together at the White House, with the possible exception of when Thomas Jefferson dined alone." Jefferson penned the Declaration of Independence and served as George Washington's secretary of state, John Adams's vice president, and America's third president. He spoke out against slavery, although, like many of his countrymen, he kept slaves himself. He also established the University of Virginia and pursued wide-ranging interests, including architecture, astronomy, anthropology, music, and farming.

Franklin Delano Roosevelt, a great admirer of Jefferson, spearheaded the effort to build him a memorial, although the site choice was problematic. The Capitol, the White House, and the Mall were already located in accordance with architect Pierre L'Enfant's master plan for the city, and there was no spot for such a project that would maintain L'Enfant's symmetry. So the memorial was built on land reclaimed from the Potomac River, now known as the Tidal Basin. Roosevelt laid the cornerstone in 1939 and had all the trees between the Jefferson Memorial and the White House cut down so that he could see the memorial every morning.

The memorial is a columned rotunda in the style of the Pantheon in Rome, whose classical architecture Jefferson himself introduced to this country (he designed his home, Monticello, and the earliest University of Virginia buildings in Charlottesville). On the Tidal Basin side, the sculptural group above the entrance depicts Jefferson with Benjamin Franklin, John Adams, Roger Sherman, and Robert Livingston, all of whom worked on drafting the Declaration of Independence. The domed interior of the memorial contains the 19-foot bronze statue of Jefferson standing on a 6-foot pedestal of black Minnesota granite. The sculpture is the work of Rudolph Evans, who was chosen from more than 100 artists in a nationwide competition. Jefferson is depicted wearing a fur-collared coat given to him by his close friend, the Polish general Tadeusz

Kosciuszko. If you follow Jefferson's gaze, you see that, sure enough, the Jefferson Memorial and the White House have an unimpeded view of each other.

Rangers present 20- to 30-minute programs throughout the day as time permits. Twenty to thirty minutes is sufficient time to spend here.

Preservation and security improvements may still be underway in 2007. Parking lots are nearby, just around the bend on Ohio Drive.

On Ohio Dr. SW, at the south shore of the Tidal Basin (in West Potomac Park). ✆ **202/426-6841.** www.nps.gov/thje. Free admission. Ranger on duty daily 9:30am–11:30pm, except Dec 25. Limited parking. Metro: Smithsonian, with a 20- to 30-min. walk, or take Tourmobile.

3 The Smithsonian Museums

Wealthy English scientist James Smithson (1765–1829), the illegitimate son of the duke of Northumberland, never explained why he willed his vast fortune to the United States, a country he had never visited. Speculation is that he felt the new nation, lacking established cultural institutions, most needed his bequest. Smithson died in Genoa, Italy, in 1829. Congress accepted his gift in 1836; 2 years later, half a million dollars' worth of gold sovereigns (a considerable sum in the 19th century) arrived at the U.S. Mint in Philadelphia. For the next 8 years, Congress debated the best possible use for these funds. Finally, in 1846, James Polk signed an act into law establishing the Smithsonian Institution and authorizing a board to receive "all objects of art and of foreign and curious research, and all objects of natural history, plants, and geological and mineralogical specimens . . . for research and museum purposes."

Since then, private donations have swelled Smithson's original legacy many times over. Although the Smithsonian acquires approximately 70% of its yearly budget from congressional allocations, the institution depends quite heavily on these monies from private donors, especially since many of the museums are in need of renovation. In a sign of the times, and due to the need of the Smithsonian for larger contributions, the institution has imposed an admission fee for the first time ever (for one museum's exhibit only): $5 to enter the Butterfly Pavilion at the National Museum of Natural History (p. 205). General admission to the rest of the museum, and to all other Smithsonian museums, remains free. Of the 16 Smithsonian museums in the Washington, D.C., area, 10 are on the Mall (see map on p. 176). The National Zoological Park is also a Smithsonian property, as are two additional museums in New York City. The institution is planning to open at least one more Smithsonian museum, the National Museum of African American History and Culture, adjacent to the Washington Monument, bounded by Constitution Avenue NW, Madison Drive NW, and 14th and 15th streets NW; completion of the museum is a long way off.

The Smithsonian's collection of nearly 137 million objects spans the entire world and all of its history, its peoples and animals (past and present), and our attempts to probe into the future. So vast is the collection that Smithsonian museums display only about 1% or 2% of the collection's holdings at any given time. Its holdings, in every area of human interest, range from a 3.5-billion-year-old fossil to inaugural gowns worn by the first ladies. Thousands of scientific expeditions sponsored by the Smithsonian have pushed into remote frontiers in the deserts, mountains, polar regions, and jungles.

To find out information about any of the Smithsonian museums, call ✆ **202/633-1000** or TTY 202/357-1729. The information specialists who answer are very professional and always helpful. The Smithsonian museums also share a website, **www.si.edu**, which helps get you to their individual home pages.

Tips **Information, Please**

If you want to know what's happening at any of the Smithsonian museums, just get on the phone. Dial ✆ **202/633-1000** to reach a recorded information line that lists daily activities and special events; this number also directs you to press "0" to speak directly to a Smithsonian information specialist if you have specific questions.

Smithsonian Information Center (the "Castle") Make this your first stop, and enter through the Enid A. Haupt Garden (see the "Parks & Gardens" section, later in this chapter) for a pleasurable experience. Built in 1855, this Norman-style red-sandstone building, popularly known as the "Castle," is the oldest building on the Mall.

The main information area here is the Great Hall, where a 24-minute video overview of the institution runs throughout the day in two theaters. There are two large schematic models of the Mall (as well as a third in Braille), which allow visitors to locate nearly 100 popular attractions and Metro and Tourmobile stops.

The entire facility is accessible to persons with disabilities, and information is available in a number of foreign languages. The information desk's volunteer staff can answer questions and help you plan a Smithsonian sightseeing itinerary. Most of the museums are within easy walking distance of the facility.

While you're here, notice the charming vestibule, which has been restored to its turn-of-the-20th-century appearance. It was originally designed to display exhibits at a child's eye level. The gold-trimmed ceiling is decorated to represent a grape arbor with brightly plumed birds and blue sky peeking through the trellis. This is also where the Castle Cafe is located, and though the items are awfully pricey, you can't beat the convenience and the fact that it's open at 8:30am. So why not grab a cup of joe and a muffin, then settle yourself outside on a bench in the Enid A. Haupt Garden with your guidebook and maps to plan your day.

1000 Jefferson Dr. SW. ✆ **202/633-1000.** Daily 8:30am–5:30pm, info desk 9am–4pm. Closed Dec 25. Metro: Smithsonian.

Anacostia Community Museum This museum is inconveniently located, but that's because it was initially created in 1967 as a neighborhood museum (which makes it unique among the Smithsonian branches). It's devoted to the African-American experience, focusing on Washington, D.C., and the Upper South. The permanent collection includes about 7,000 items, ranging from videotapes of African-American church services to art, sheet music, historic documents, textiles, glassware, and anthropological objects. In addition, the Anacostia produces a number of shows each year and offers a comprehensive schedule of free educational programs and activities in conjunction with exhibit themes. Allow about an hour here.

1901 Fort Place SE (off Martin Luther King Jr. Ave.). ✆ **202/633-4820.** www.si.edu/anacostia. Free admission. Daily 10am–5pm. Closed Dec 25. Metro: Grab a bus transfer when you enter the station and take a Green line train traveling in the direction of Anacostia; get off at the Anacostia station and head to the exit marked "Local," turn left after exiting, then take a W2 or W3 bus, on Howard Rd., directly to the museum.

Arthur M. Sackler Gallery ★ Asian art is the focus of this museum and the neighboring Freer (together, they form the National Museum of Asian Art in the United States). The Sackler opened in 1987, thanks to Arthur M. Sackler's gift of 1,000 priceless works. Since then, the museum has received 11th- to 19th-century Persian and Indian paintings, manuscripts, calligraphies, miniatures, and book bindings from the collection of Henri Vever. In spring 2003, art collector Robert O. Muller bequeathed the museum his entire collection of 4,000 Japanese prints and archival materials.

Your visit begins in the entrance pavilion, where a series of rotating installations, collectively titled "Perspectives," showcases the works of contemporary artists from Asia and the Asian Diaspora. The Sackler is coaxing you to appreciate the less familiar aspects of Asian art and culture.

The Sackler's permanent collection displays Khmer ceramics; ancient Chinese jades, bronzes, paintings, and lacquerware; 20th-century Japanese ceramics and works on paper; ancient Near Eastern works in silver, gold, bronze, and clay; and stone and bronze sculptures from South and Southeast Asia. With the addition of Muller's bequest, the Sackler now has a sumptuous graphic arts inventory, covering a century of work by Japanese master printmakers. Supplementing the permanent collection are traveling exhibitions from major cultural institutions in Asia, Europe, and the United States. In the past, these have included such wide-ranging areas as 15th-century Persian art and culture, photographs of Asia, and art highlighting personal devotion in India. A visit here is an education in Asian decorative arts, but also in antiquities.

To learn more, arrive in time for a highlights tour, offered daily, except Wednesday, at 12:15pm. Also enlightening, and more fun, are the public programs that both the Sackler and the Freer Gallery frequently stage, such as performances of contemporary Asian music, tea ceremony demonstrations, and Iranian film screenings. All are free, but you might need tickets; for details, call the main information number or check out the website. Allow at least an hour to tour the Sackler.

The Sackler is part of a museum complex that houses the National Museum of African Art. It shares its staff and research facilities with the adjacent Freer Gallery, to which it is connected via an underground exhibition space.

1050 Independence Ave. SW. ✆ **202/633-4880.** www.asia.si.edu. Free admission. Daily 10am–5:30pm; in summer, museum often stays open Thurs until 8pm, but call to confirm. Closed Dec 25. Metro: Smithsonian.

Arts and Industries Building The building is closed for an extensive renovation. Completed in 1881 as the first U.S. National Museum, this redbrick and sandstone structure was the scene of President Garfield's Inaugural Ball. (It looks quite similar to the Castle, so don't be confused; from the Mall, the Arts and Industries Building is the one on the left.) From 1976 to the mid-1990s it housed exhibits from the 1876 U.S. International Exposition in Philadelphia—a celebration of America's centennial that featured the latest advances in technology.

Weather permitting, a 19th-century **carousel** operates across the street, on the Mall.

900 Jefferson Dr. SW (on the south side of the Mall).

Freer Gallery of Art ★ Charles Lang Freer, a collector of Asian and American art from the 19th and early 20th centuries, gave the nation 9,000 of these works for his namesake gallery's 1923 opening. Freer's original interest was American art, but his good friend James McNeill Whistler encouraged him to collect Asian works as well. Eventually the latter became predominant. Freer's gift included funds to construct a museum and an endowment to add to the Asian collection, which now numbers more than 26,000 objects. It includes Chinese and Japanese sculpture, lacquer, metalwork, and ceramics; early Christian illuminated manuscripts; Iranian manuscripts, metalwork, and miniatures; ancient Near Eastern metalware; and South Asian sculpture and paintings.

The Freer is mostly about Asian art, but it also displays some of the more than 1,200 American works (the world's largest collection) by **Whistler.** Most remarkable and always on view is the famous **Peacock Room.** Originally a dining room designed for the London mansion of F. R. Leyland, the Peacock Room displayed a Whistler painting called *The Princess from the Land of Porcelain.* But after his painting was installed, Whistler was dissatisfied with the room as a setting for his work. When Leyland was away from home, Whistler painted over the very expensive leather interior and embellished it with paintings of golden peacock feathers. Not surprisingly, a rift ensued between Whistler and Leyland. After Leyland's death, Freer purchased the room, painting and all, and had it shipped to his home in Detroit. It is now permanently installed here. Other American painters represented in the collections are Thomas Wilmer Dewing, Dwight William Tryon, Abbott Henderson Thayer, John Singer Sargent, and Childe Hassam. You could spend a happy 1 to 2 hours here.

The Freer Gallery is an oasis on the Mall, especially if you arrive here after visiting its voluminous and crowded sisters, the Natural History and Air and Space museums. Housed in a grand granite-and-marble building that evokes the Italian Renaissance, the pristine Freer has lovely sky-lit galleries. The main exhibit floor galleries encircle a beautiful landscaped courtyard, complete with loggia and central fountain. If the weather's right, it's a pleasure to sit out here and take a break from touring. An underground exhibit space connects the Freer to the neighboring Sackler Gallery, and both museums share the **Meyer Auditorium,** which is used for free chamber music concerts, dance performances, Asian feature films, and other programs. Inquire about these, as well as children's activities and free tours given daily, at the information desk.

Jefferson Dr. SW at 12th St. SW (on the south side of the Mall). ✆ **202/633-4880.** www.asia.si.edu. Free admission. Daily 10am–5:30pm; in summer, gallery often stays open Thurs until 8pm, but call to confirm. Closed Dec 25. Metro: Smithsonian.

Hirshhorn Museum and Sculpture Garden ★ This museum of modern and contemporary art is named after Latvian-born Joseph H. Hirshhorn, who, in 1966, donated his vast collection—more than 4,000 drawings and paintings and 2,000 pieces of sculpture—to the United States "as a small repayment for what this nation has done for me and others like me who arrived here as immigrants." The Hirshhorn opened in 1974 to display these works, adding 5,500 more bequeathed by Hirshhorn in 1981, upon his death.

Constructed 14 feet above ground on sculptured supports, the doughnut-shaped concrete-and-granite building stands 82 feet high and measures 231 feet in diameter. The cylindrically shaped building encloses a hollow core, where a fountain spouts water five stories high. The building's light and airy interior holds three levels of galleries, each following a circular route that makes it easy to see every exhibit without getting lost in a honeycomb of galleries. Natural light from floor-to-ceiling windows makes the inner galleries the perfect venue for regarding sculpture—second only to the beautiful tree-shaded sunken **Sculpture Garden** ★ across the street (don't miss it). Make your way to the third-floor oculus and you'll be rewarded with a dramatic view of the National Mall.

Don't miss the Hirshhorn's "Ways of Seeing" project on the lower-level galleries, which displays innovative groupings of different works focusing on a particular theme, as chosen by an invited artist. For instance, a 2007 grouping conceived by contemporary artist John Baldessari included paintings by Milton Avery, Thomas Eakins, and

Phillip Guston and sculpture by Emily Kaufman, the differences in time, technique and subject granting viewers a different "way of seeing" these individual pieces of art.

A rotating show of about 600 pieces is on view at all times. The collection features just about every well-known 20th-century artist and touches on most of the major trends in Western art since the late 19th century, with particular emphasis on our contemporary period. Among the best-known pieces are Rodin's *Monument to the Burghers of Calais* (in the Sculpture Garden), Hopper's *First Row Orchestra,* de Kooning's *Two Women in the Country,* and Warhol's *Marilyn Monroe's Lips.*

Pick up a free calendar when you enter to find out about free films, lectures, concerts, and temporary exhibits. Free tours of the collection are given daily, and of the Sculpture Garden, weather permitting, in summer; call for information about them.

Independence Ave. at 7th St. SW (on the south side of the Mall). ✆ **202/633-4674.** www.hirshhorn.si.edu. Free admission. Museum daily 10am–5:30pm; in summer museum often stays open Thurs until 8pm, but call to confirm. Sculpture Garden daily 7:30am–dusk. Closed Dec 25. Metro: L'Enfant Plaza (Smithsonian Museums/Maryland Ave. or Smithsonian exit).

National Air and Space Museum ★★ Kids With the opening of the Steven F. Udvar-Hazy Center in December 2003, the National Air and Space Museum now bills itself as "One museum, two locations." It's not realistic, however, to visit both museums in 1 day. The flagship museum on the National Mall consumes 2 or 3 hours—longer, if you attend an IMAX film or planetarium show; the round-trip to the satellite Udvar-Hazy Center, located on the grounds of Washington-Dulles International Airport, takes about 2 hours (space fans might say 2 weeks), and the touring of that museum another 2 or 3 hours. You could do it, but you'd be frantic.

So start with this one, the original, ever-popular Air and Space Museum on the Mall. The museum, now in its 32nd year, chronicles the story of the mastery of flight, from Kitty Hawk to outer space. It holds the largest collection of historic aircraft and spacecraft in the world—so many, in fact, that the museum is able to display only about 10% of its artifacts at any one time, hence the opening of the Udvar-Hazy Center.

During the tourist season and on holidays, arrive before 10am to make a beeline for the film ticket line when the doors open. The not-to-be-missed **IMAX films** ★ shown here are immensely popular, and tickets to most shows sell out quickly. You can purchase same-day tickets by phone or in person at the Lockheed Martin IMAX Theater box office on the first floor, or in advance, online, up to 24 hours before showtime. Surcharges apply to phone and online orders. Two or more films play each day, most with aeronautical or space-exploration themes; *To Fly* and *Roving Mars* are two that were running in 2007. Tickets cost $8.50 for adults, $7 for ages 2 to 12, $7.50 for ages 60 or older; they're free for children under 2. You can also see IMAX films most evenings after the museum's closing; call for details (✆ **877/932-4629**).

You'll also need tickets to attend a show at the **Albert Einstein Planetarium** ★, which creates "an astronomical adventure" as projectors display space imagery upon a 70-foot-diameter dome, making you feel as if you're traveling in 3-D through the cosmos. The planetarium's newest feature is the 23-minute **Cosmic Collisions,** which takes you on a trip through time and space, where you encounter cosmic collisions and hypersonic impacts, as narrated by Robert Redford. Shown less frequently is the planetarium's longtime feature, called "Infinity Express: A 20-Minute Tour of the Universe," which gives you the sensation that you are zooming through the solar system, as it explores such questions as "How big is the universe?" and "Where does it end?" Tickets are $8.50 for adults, $7 for ages 2 to 12, $7.50 for ages 60 or older.

Among the 22 exhibitions on display throughout the museum is one that children especially love: **How Things Fly,** which includes wind and smoke tunnels, a boardable Cessna 150 airplane, and dozens of interactive exhibits that demonstrate principles of flight, aerodynamics, and propulsion. All the aircraft are originals. Kids also flock to the walk-through **Skylab orbital workshop,** part of the Space Race exhibition on the first floor. Both children and adults stand in line to take their turn on the museum's **Flight Simulators.** (The Udvar-Hazy Center has several, too.) You'll be strapped in and given a joystick, and for about 5 minutes you'll truly feel as if you are in the cockpit and airborne, maneuvering your craft up, down, and upside-down on a wild adventure, thanks to virtual reality images and high-tech sounds. You must pay $7 ($7.50 at the Udvar-Hazy Center) to enjoy the ride and measure at least 48 inches to go it alone. (Children under 48 in. must measure at least 42 in. and be accompanied by an adult.)

Other galleries highlight the solar system, U.S. manned space flights, sea-air operations, and aviation during both world wars. An important exhibit is **Beyond the Limits: Flight Enters the Computer Age,** illustrating the primary applications of computer technology to aerospace. **Explore the Universe** presents the major discoveries that have shaped the current scientific view of the universe; it illustrates how the universe is taking shape, and probes the mysteries that remain. Hundreds of space and aircraft artifacts dangle before your eyes everywhere you look, but don't miss the Wright Brothers **1903 Flyer,** which hangs from the ceiling in the exhibit, **Milestones of Flight.** In late 2007, the museum debuted **America by Air,** an exhibit that covers an expanded history of commercial air travel.

The museum's cafeteria, The Wright Place, offers food from three popular American chains: McDonald's, Boston Chicken, and Donato's Pizza; its three-level, 12,000-square-foot shop is the largest Smithsonian store.

At the Udvar-Hazy Center you'll find two hangars, one for aviation artifacts, the other for space artifacts, and a 164-foot-tall observation tower for watching planes leave and arrive at Dulles Airport. The center's James S. McDonnell Space Hangar stretches the length of three football fields and stands 10 stories high, the better to house the enormous *Enterprise,* NASA's first space shuttle; the tiny "Anita," a spider carried on Skylab for web formation experiments; the manned maneuvering unit used for the first untethered spacewalk; a full-scale prototype of the Mars Pathfinder Lander; and Pegasus, the first aircraft-launched rocket booster to carry satellites into space. Eventually, the gallery will hold more than 200 aircraft and 135 spacecraft. The center will also serve as the Air and Space Museum's primary restoration facility, and the public will be able to watch specialists at work. This location also shows IMAX films.

On Independence Ave. SW, between 4th and 7th sts. (on the south side of the Mall, with entrances on Jefferson Dr. or Independence Ave.). ✆ **202/633-1000** (for both locations), or 877/932-4629 for IMAX ticket information. www.nasm.si.edu. Free admission. Both locations daily 10am–5:30pm. The mall museum often opens at 9am in summer, but call to confirm. Free 1½-hr. highlight tours daily at 10:30am and 1pm. Closed Dec 25. Metro: L'Enfant Plaza (Smithsonian Museums/Maryland Ave. exit) or Smithsonian. The Udvar-Hazy Center is located at 14390 Air and Space Museum Pkwy., Chantilly, VA.

National Museum of African Art ★ Founded in 1964, and part of the Smithsonian since 1979, the National Museum of African Art moved to the Mall in 1987 to share a subterranean space with the Sackler Gallery (see above) and the Ripley Center. Its aboveground domed pavilions reflect the arch motif of the neighboring Freer Gallery of Art (see above).

The museum collects and exhibits ancient and contemporary art from the entire African continent, and rotates displays of its 8,500-piece permanent collection. The

Museum Exhibits Scheduled for 2008

The following listings, though hardly comprehensive, should give you an idea about 2008's upcoming or current shows at major Washington museums. Because schedules sometimes change, it's always a good idea to call ahead. See individual entries in this chapter for phone numbers and addresses.

Anacostia Community Museum "Separate but Unequal: Local Negro Baseball Teams" (May 18–Oct 5). Oral remembrances, historical photographs, and memorabilia tell the story of Washington's Negro hometown team, the Grays, who delivered a near-unbeatable record from 1937 to 1947.

Hirshhorn Museum and Sculpture Garden "The Cinematic Effect: Illusion, Reality and the Moving Image," Part I: Dreams (Feb 14–May 11); Part II: Realisms (June 19–Sept 7). This exhibit explores the ways contemporary art and film reflect our ideas of fact and fiction. "Dreams" looks at the experience of film viewing as the transition between waking and a dreamlike state; "Realisms" focuses on the question of reality versus illusion.

National Air and Space Museum "In Plane View: Abstractions of Flight" (Nov 17, 2007, to Jan 27, 2008). Museum photographer Carolyn Russo's exhibit of 55 color photographs reveal the simple beauty of aircraft and spacecraft design.

National Gallery of Art "In the Forest of Fontainebleau: Painters and Photographers from Corot to Manet" (Mar 2–June 8). Reveals the role of the Forest of Fontainebleau in the development of 19th-century landscape painting.

National Museum of Natural History "Written in Bone" (Nov 17, 2007, to Oct 2008). In recognition of the 400th anniversary of Jamestown, the first

museum's contemporary African art collection comprises the largest public holding in the United States. Among the museum's holdings are the **Eliot Elisofon Photographic Archives,** encompassing 300,000 photographic prints and transparencies and 120,000 feet of film on African arts and culture. A small, ongoing permanent exhibit of ceramic arts displays 14 traditional and contemporary pieces from the museum's 140-works collection. Most exciting is the new Walt Disney–Tishman African Art collection. In September 2005, the Walt Disney World Company donated to the museum its Tishman collection of 525 objects representing every area of Africa. The collection spans art forms, from textiles to jewelry, and centuries, from ancient to contemporary times. An inaugural exhibit highlighting 80 works from the collection is on view through September 2008, with a rotating selection of at least 60 works permanently on display.

Inquire at the desk about special exhibits, workshops (including excellent children's programs), storytelling, lectures, docent-led tours, films, and demonstrations. A comprehensive events schedule provides a unique opportunity to learn about the diverse cultures and visual traditions of Africa. Plan on spending a minimum of 30 minutes here.

950 Independence Ave. SW. ✆ **202/633-4600.** www.nmafa.si.edu. Free admission. Daily 10am–5:30pm. Closed Dec 25. Metro: Smithsonian.

permanent English settlement in the New World, the museum presents archaeological discoveries that connect the significance of Jamestown's history with the American way of life.

National Postal Museum "Postal Inspectors: The Silent Service" (Feb 2007 to Feb 2009). Spotlights the oldest federal law enforcement agency and its role in fighting crime throughout American history.

Phillips Collection "Jacob Lawrence's Migration Series: Selections from the Phillips Collection" (May 3–Oct 26). A presentation of 30 panels from Lawrence's 60-panel *Migration* series depicting the 20th-century movement of more than six million African Americans from the rural South to the urban North during and after World War I.

Renwick Gallery of the Smithsonian American Art Museum "Going West! Quilts and Community along the Great Platte River Road" (Oct 5, 2007, to Jan 21, 2008). This display of 50 quilts reveals the role played by quilts and quilt making in frontier women's lives as America expanded westward in the 19th century.

Sackler Gallery "Garden and Cosmos: The Royal Paintings of Jodhpur" (June 7–Sept 7). Newly discovered paintings form the core of this exhibit of 17th- to 19th-century works, encompassing 61 paintings and a silk embroidered tent.

Smithsonian American Art Museum "Aaron Douglas: African American Modernist" (May 9–Aug 3). Presents the first nationally touring retrospective of the work of Aaron Douglas (1899–1979), one of the foremost visual artists from the Harlem Renaissance.

National Museum of the American Indian ★ *Kids* The National Museum of the American Indian officially opened on September 21, 2004, taking 5 years and $219 million to construct. Outside and in, this museum is strikingly handsome. Consider its exterior: Its burnt-sand-colored exterior of Kasota limestone wraps around the undulating walls of the museum, making the five-story building a standout among the many white-stone structures on the National Mall. Its interior design incorporates themes of nature and astronomy. For instance, the Potomac (a Piscataway word meaning "where the goods are brought in") is a rotunda that serves as the museum's main gathering place; it is also "the heart of the museum, the sun of its universe" (as noted in the museum's literature). Measuring 120 feet in diameter, with an atrium rising 120 feet to the top of the dome overhead, the Potomac is the central entryway into the museum, a venue for performances, and a hall filled with celestial references, from the equinoxes and solstices mapped on the floor beneath your feet to the sights of sky visible through the oculus in the dome above your head.

A gift shop, a theater, and the museum's excellent restaurant, Mitsitam, occupy most of the remaining space on the first floor. A second shop and the museum's main galleries lie upstairs on the second and third levels. Three permanent exhibits, "Our

Universes: Traditional Knowledge Shapes Our World," "Our Peoples: Giving Voice to Our Histories," and "Our Lives: Contemporary Life and Identities," use videos, interactive technology, and displays of artifacts to help you learn about Native cosmologies, history, and contemporary cultural identity, of Native Americans as an overall group of people, but also within certain individual tribes. An exhibit called "Window on the Collections: Many Hands, Many Voices" displays 3,500 objects behind glass; a computer kiosk in front of each case allows a museumgoer to zoom in and learn more about a particular item on view. These precious wood and stone carvings, masks, pottery, feather bonnets, and so on are a fraction of the 800,000 objets d'art amassed by a wealthy New Yorker named George Gustav Heye (1874–1957). Heye founded the New York Museum of the American Indian, this museum's predecessor.

The National Museum of the American Indian does not provide much direction to self-guided touring, which tends to leave visitors at a loss as to how to proceed through the museum. Faced with the vast display of objects and with galleries that have no obvious beginning or end, tourists wander around, adopting a scattershot approach to the information, emerging eventually with more of an impression than with a coherent understanding of the Indian experience, and overwhelmed by the variety and number of artifacts and details. Perhaps that's intentional. Best advice? Stop at the Welcome Desk when you enter to sign up for a highlights tour.

4th St. and Independence Ave. SW. ✆ **202/633-1000.** www.nmai.si.edu. Free admission. Daily 10am–5:30pm. Closed Dec 25. Metro: Federal Center Southwest or L'Enfant Plaza.

National Museum of American History ★★★ *Kids* If you are planning a trip to Washington before July 2008, this museum will still be closed for renovation. You'll be able to see some 150 objects of the museum's favorite items, like Dorothy's ruby slippers and Abraham Lincoln's top hat, in a special temporary exhibit at the National Air and Space Museum (p. 200); and another 60 items, including sports memorabilia and a grand piano, at the Smithsonian's American Art Museum (p. 208). The museum's press office assured me that the American History museum is on track to reopen in summer of 2008, though the exact date was not certain at press time. If you arrive after the reopening, you've got a lot to see.

As a bastion of U.S. culture and history, this museum tells America's story in terms of everyday life, at its most varied and evolving. Its objects can evoke feelings of awe: the desk on which Thomas Jefferson wrote the Declaration of Independence; affection: Dorothy's ruby slippers; or connection: Julia Child's kitchen. And some things here—the museum's ultimate possession, the huge **original Star-Spangled Banner** ★★★, for example—evoke all three emotions at once.

So prized is the flag that the museum's renovation showcases the 30-by-34-foot wool and cotton flag in a multistory gallery with floor-to-ceiling glass windows designed to give visitors a sense of the same "dawn's early light" that Francis Scott Key observed the morning of September 14, 1814, when he spied the flag—this very flag—waving above Fort McHenry in Baltimore's harbor, at the height of the War of 1812. Key's emotion at the sight moved him to pen the poem that, when put to music, eventually became the U.S. national anthem.

You'll notice another renovation improvement on the museum's first and second floors: the 10-foot-high "artifact walls" displaying assorted pieces from the museum's three-million-object collection.

Best to start your tour at the new Welcome Center on the second floor, to figure out how you'd like to proceed. In spite of the many and much-needed architectural enhancements, like the new skylight and grand staircase, you'll find that quite a bit of the prerenovation museum's attractions remain.

On the third floor lies the exhibit **The American Presidency: A Glorious Burden,** which explores the power and meaning of the presidency by studying those who have held the position. (There's a gift shop just for this exhibit on this floor.) Continue on this floor to the exhibit **The Price of Freedom: Americans at War,** which examines major American military events and explores the idea that America's armed forces reflect American society. Among the items on display here are George Washington's commission from Congress as commander-in-chief of the Continental Army, and the uniform jacket that Andrew Jackson wore during the Battle of New Orleans in the War of 1812.

One of the most popular exhibits on the second floor is **First Ladies: Political Role and Public Image,** which displays the first ladies' gowns and tells you a bit about each of these women. Following that, find the exhibit called **Within These Walls . . . ,** which interprets the rich history of America by tracing the lives of the people who lived in this 200-year-old house, transplanted from Ipswich, Massachusetts. If this personal approach to history appeals to you, continue on to **Field to Factory,** which tells the story of African-American migration from the South between 1915 and 1940.

First-floor exhibits explore the development of farm and power machinery. A temporary exhibit whose popularity may make it a permanent display is ***Bon Appétit!* Julia Child's Kitchen at the Smithsonian,** a presentation of the famous chef's actual kitchen from her home in Cambridge, Massachusetts. When she moved to California in late 2001, Child donated her kitchen and all that it contained (1,200 items in all) to the museum. Most of these are on display, vegetable peeler to kitchen sink. Also look here for **America on the Move,** which details the story of transportation in America since 1876: 300 artifacts displayed within period settings.

Inquire at the information desk about highlight tours, films, lectures, concerts, and hands-on activities for children and adults, and be sure to visit the museum's gift shops and dining options, also revamped during the remodeling.

On Constitution Ave. NW, between 12th and 14th sts. NW (on the north side of the Mall, with entrances on Constitution Ave. and Madison Dr.). ✆ **202/633-1000.** www.americanhistory.si.edu. Free admission. Daily 10am–5:30pm. Closed Dec 25. Metro: Smithsonian or Federal Triangle.

National Museum of Natural History ★★ *Kids* Before you step inside the museum, stop outside first, on the 9th Street side of the building, to visit the **butterfly garden.** Four habitats—wetland, meadow, wood's edge, and urban garden—are on view, designed to beckon butterflies and visitors alike. The garden is at its best in warm weather, but it's open year-round. (And if you like that, you're going to love the museum's new Butterflies and Plants exhibit, which includes a Butterfly Pavilion—keep reading!)

Now go inside. Children refer to this Smithsonian showcase as "the dinosaur museum," since there's a dinosaur hall, or as "the elephant museum," since a huge **African bush elephant** is the first thing you see in the Rotunda, if you enter from the Mall. Whatever you call it, the National Museum of Natural History is the largest of its kind in the world, and one of the most visited museums in Washington. It contains more than 126 million artifacts and specimens, everything from Ice Age mammoths to the legendary Hope Diamond.

Note: The museum is in the middle of an extensive renovation, including the creation of a brand new, 22,000-square-foot **Ocean Hall** (scheduled to open Sept 2008 and designed by the same firm that created the exhibits and spaces of the highly interactive

International Spy Museum; see review later in this chapter). The following information is therefore subject to change.

If you have children, you might want to make your first stop the first-floor **Discovery Room,** which is filled with creative hands-on exhibits "for children of all ages." Call ahead or inquire at the information desk about hours. Also on this floor is the **Kenneth E. Behring Hall of Mammals.** This exhibit represents the "new" face of the museum: set in the restored west wing, with up-to-date lighting and sound, the Hall of Mammals features interactive dioramas that explain how mammals evolved and adapted to changes in habitat and climate over the course of millions of years. At least 274 taxidermied mammals, from polar bear to tiger, are on display, along with a dozen mammal fossils. From time to time, the hall erupts with animal sounds, all part of exhibit wizardry that helps make this a lifelike experience.

Other Rotunda-level displays include the **fossil collection,** which traces evolution back billions of years and includes a 3.5-billion-year-old stromatolite (blue-green algae clump) fossil—one of the earliest signs of life on Earth—and a 70-million-year-old dinosaur egg. **Ancient Seas and Ice Age** features a 100-foot-long mural depicting primitive whales, a life-size walk-around diorama of a 230-million-year-old coral reef, and more than 2,000 fossils that chronicle the evolution of marine life. The **Dinosaur Hall** displays giant skeletons of creatures that dominated the earth for 140 million years before their extinction about 65 million years ago. Mounted throughout the Dinosaur Hall are replicas of ancient birds, including a life-size model of the *Quetzalcoatlus northropi,* which lived 70 million years ago, had a 40-foot wingspan, and was the largest flying animal ever. Also residing above this hall is the jaw of an ancient shark, the *Carcharodon megalodon,* which lived in the oceans 5 million years ago. A monstrous 40-foot-long predator, with teeth 5 to 6 inches long, it could have consumed a Volkswagen Bug in one gulp. Elsewhere on this floor is the **African Voices Hall,** which presents the people, cultures, and lives of Africa, through photos, videos, and more than 400 objects.

Upstairs lies another exhibit popular among the under-10 crowd: the **O. Orkin Insect Zoo** ★, where kids enjoy looking at tarantulas, centipedes, and the like, and crawling through a model of an African termite mound. Right next door is the museum's newest offering, **Butterflies and Plants: Partners in Evolution,** a 4,000-square-foot exhibit that illustrates the evolving relationship between butterflies and plants over millions of years. The exhibit includes a walk-through, 1,400-square-foot Butterfly Pavilion featuring live butterflies and plants. ***Note:*** The museum charges a $5 fee for admission to the pavilion portion of the exhibit.

Ever a big draw is the **Janet Annenberg Hooker Hall of Geology, Gems, and Minerals** ★★, which showcases the Hope Diamond; the 23.1-carat Burmese Carmen Lucia ruby, one of the largest and finest rubies in the world; and other treasures of the National Gem Collection. Besides staring spellbound at priceless jewelry, you can learn all you want about earth science, from volcanology to the importance of mining. Interactive computers, animated graphics, and a multimedia presentation of the "big picture" story of the earth are some of the things that have moved the exhibit and the museum a bit further into the 21st century.

Don't miss the **Discovery Center,** funded by the Discovery Channel, featuring the Johnson **IMAX theater** with a six-story-high screen for 2-D and 3-D movies (*Lions 3D, Roar of the Kalahari* was among those shown in 2007), a six-story Atrium Cafe with a food court, and expanded museum shops. The museum also offers the small **Fossil Café,** located within the Fossil Plants Hall on the first floor. In this 50-seat cafe,

Fun Fact **Museum with the Mostest**

Of the 136 million objects in the Smithsonian's total collections, 126 million belong to the National Museum of Natural History.

the tables' clear plastic tops are actually fossil cases that present fossilized plants and insects for your inspection as you munch away on smoked turkey sandwiches, goat-cheese quiche, and the like.

The theater box office is on the first floor of the museum; you can purchase tickets by phone (✆ **202/633-4629** or 877/932-4629), online, or at the box office, at least 30 minutes before the screening. The box office is open daily from 9:45am to the last show. Films are shown continuously throughout the day. Ticket prices are $8.50 for adults and $7 for children (2–12), and $7.50 for seniors 60 or older. On Friday nights from 6 to 10pm, the theater stages live jazz, starring excellent local musicians ($10 cover for the music, or free with same-night IMAX ticket stub). This is really a supper club, since a cash bar and an extensive dinner buffet are also on hand.

On Constitution Ave. NW., between 9th and 12th sts. (on the north side of the Mall, with entrances on Madison Dr. and Constitution Ave.). ✆ **202/633-1000**, or 202/633-4629 for information about IMAX films. www.mnh.si.edu. Free admission. Daily 10am–5:30pm. In summer the museum often stays open until 7:30pm, but call to confirm. Closed Dec 25. Free highlight tours Feb–July Tues–Fri 10:30am and 1:30pm. Metro: Smithsonian or Federal Triangle.

National Postal Museum ★ This museum is, somewhat surprisingly, a hit, and a pleasant hour spent for the whole family. Bring your address book, and you can send postcards to the folks back home through an interactive exhibit that issues a cool postcard and stamps it. That's just one feature that makes this museum visitor-friendly. Many of its exhibits involve easy-to-understand activities, like postal-themed video games.

The museum documents America's postal history from 1673 (about 170 years before the advent of stamps, envelopes, and mailboxes) to the present. (Did you know that a dog sled was used to carry mail in Alaska until 1963, when it was replaced by an airplane?) In the central gallery, suspended from the 90-foot-high atrium ceiling, are three planes that carried mail in the early decades of the 20th century. These, along with a railway mail car, an 1851 mail/passenger coach, and a replica of an airmail beacon tower, are all part of the **Moving the Mail** exhibit, recently amplified by a new exhibit, **On the Road,** which explores the history of city mail vehicles, like the 1931 Ford Model A mail truck on display. **Customers and Communities** traces the evolution of mail delivery as it expanded to reach growing populations in both rural areas and the cities. In **Binding the Nation,** historic correspondence illustrates how mail kept families together in the developing nation. Several exhibits deal with the famed Pony Express, a service that lasted less than 2 years but was romanticized to legendary proportions by Buffalo Bill and others. In the Civil War section you'll learn about Henry "Box" Brown, a slave who had himself "mailed" from Richmond to a Pennsylvania abolitionist in 1856. A more telling exhibit for our times is **In the Line of Duty, Dangerous Disasters and Good Deeds,** which reveals the stories of postal workers as everyday heroes.

The Art of Cards and Letters gallery displays rotating exhibits of personal (sometimes wrenching, always interesting) correspondence taken from different periods in history, as well as greeting cards and postcards; "War Letters Lost and Found" was the theme of the letters most recently on display. In addition, the museum houses a vast research library for philatelic researchers and scholars, a stamp store, and a museum shop. Inquire about free walk-in tours at the information desk.

Opened in 1993, this off-the-Mall Smithsonian museum occupies the lower level of the palatial Beaux Arts quarters of the Old City Post Office Building, which was designed by architect Daniel Burnham and is situated next to Union Station.

2 Massachusetts Ave. NE (at 1st St.). ✆ **202/633-5555.** www.si.edu/postal. Free admission. Daily 10am–5:30pm. Closed Dec 25. Metro: Union Station.

National Zoological Park ★★ *Kids* The **giant pandas** are the zoo's biggest draw, and though Mei Xiang and Tian Tian now have an adorable cub, Tai Shan, born July 9, 2005, don't stop with them; continue on.

Established in 1889, the National Zoo is home to about 400 species—some 2,400 animals—many of them rare and/or endangered. A leader in the care, breeding, and exhibition of animals, it occupies 163 beautifully landscaped and wooded acres and is one of the country's most delightful zoos. You'll see cheetahs, zebras, camels, elephants, tapirs, antelopes, brown pelicans, kangaroos, hippos, rhinos, giraffes, apes, and, of course, lions, tigers, and bears.

Enter the zoo at the Connecticut Avenue entrance; you'll be right by the Education Building, where you can pick up a map and find out about feeding times and any special activities. Note that from this main entrance, you're headed downhill; the return uphill walk can prove trying if you have young children and/or it's a hot day. But the zoo rents strollers, and snack bars and ice-cream kiosks are scattered throughout the park.

The zoo animals live in large, open enclosures—simulations of their natural habitats—along two easy-to-follow numbered paths: **Olmsted Walk** and the **Valley Trail.** You can't get lost and it's hard to miss a thing. Be sure to catch **Amazonia,** where you can hang out for an hour peering up into the trees and still not spy the sloth. (Do yourself a favor and ask the attendant where it is.)

If your children are ages 3 to 8, don't miss the **Kids' Farm** at the very bottom of the zoo, to give the kids a chance to observe farm animals up close. Ducks, chickens, goats, cows, and miniature donkeys are among the animals milling around. Children might also enjoy the vegetable garden and pizza sculpture. In September 2006, a new permanent exhibit opened, the **Asia Trail,** whose winding path presents close-up sights of sloth bears, frolicking giant pandas, fishing cats, and the assorted activities of clouded leopards and Japanese salamanders.

The zoo offers several dining options, including the Mane Restaurant, the Panda Café, and a number of snack stands. Other facilities include stroller-rental stations, a number of gift shops, a bookstore, and several paid-parking lots. The lots fill up quickly, especially on weekends, so arrive early or take the Metro.

3001 Connecticut Ave. NW (adjacent to Rock Creek Park). ✆ **202/633-4800.** www.si.edu/natzoo. Free admission. Apr–Oct (weather permitting) grounds daily 6am–8pm, animal buildings daily 10am–6pm; Nov–Mar grounds daily 6am–6pm, animal buildings daily 10am–4:30pm. Closed Dec 25. Metro: Woodley Park–Zoo or Cleveland Park.

Renwick Gallery of the Smithsonian American Art Museum ★ *Finds* A department of the Smithsonian American Art Museum (though located nowhere near it), the Renwick Gallery is a showcase for American creativity in crafts and decorative arts, housed in a historic mid-1800s landmark building of the French Second Empire style. It's located on the same block as the White House, just across Pennsylvania Avenue. The original home of the Corcoran Gallery, which now lies a short walk away, down 17th Street, it was saved from demolition by First Lady Jacqueline Kennedy in 1963, when she recommended that it be renovated as part of the Lafayette Square restoration. In 1965, it became part of the Smithsonian and was renamed for its architect, James W. Renwick, Jr., who also designed the Smithsonian Castle.

On view on the first floor are temporary exhibits of American crafts and decorative arts. On the second floor, the museum's rich and diverse displays boast changing crafts exhibits and contemporary works from the museum's permanent collection, such as Larry Fuente's *Game Fish,* or Wendell Castle's *Ghost Clock.* Also on the second floor is the **Victorian Grand Salon,** styled in 19th-century opulence, and worth a visit on its own merits: Its wainscoted rose walls and 40-foot-high laylight (a skylight unexposed to the outside) evoke another era. On display indefinitely are hundreds of portraits, landscapes, and scenes of Indian life, all painted by George Catlin, who traveled west of the Mississippi in the 1830s, visiting 50 Native American tribes and recording what he saw in paint. Tour the entire gallery for about an hour, rest for a minute, and then go on to your next destination.

The Renwick offers a comprehensive schedule of crafts demonstrations, lectures, and musical performances. Also check out the museum shop near the entrance for books on crafts, design, and decorative arts, as well as craft items, many of them for children. ***Note:*** The main branch of the Smithsonian American Art Museum (below) is located at 8th and F streets NW, in the Penn Quarter neighborhood.

1661 Pennsylvania Ave. NW (at 17th St. NW). ✆ **202/633-2850.** http://americanart.si.edu. Free admission. Daily 10am–5:30pm. Closed Dec 25. Metro: Farragut West or Farragut North.

Smithsonian American Art Museum and National Portrait Gallery ★★★

On July 1, 2006, the historic landmark building that houses both the Smithsonian American Art Museum and the National Portrait Gallery reopened after a 6-year renovation, proving to all who visit that it was well worth the wait. The structure itself is magnificent. Begun in 1836 and completed in 1868 to serve as the nation's Patent Office, it is the third oldest federal building in the capital. With immense porticoes and columns on the outside, and colonnades, double staircases, vaulted galleries, and skylights inside, the museum captures your attention, no matter how or where you stand to look at it. The building occupies an entire city block, from 7th to 9th streets and from F to G streets.

As for the art presented throughout these three levels: It's like a shot in the arm for America. You will see here the faces of America's founding fathers and mothers, great American heroes and cultural icons, and scenes from American history and way of life,

---

Fun Fact **Early Risers?**

Zoo grounds open daily at 6am, which might be too early for a lot of tourists, but not for families whose young children like to rise at the crack of dawn. You know who you are. If you find yourselves trapped and restless in the hotel room, hop on the Red Line Metro, which opens at 5am weekdays, 7am Saturday and Sunday (or drive—no problem parking at that hour), get off at the Woodley Park–Zoo station, and walk up the hill to the zoo. Lots of animals are outdoors and on view. A Starbucks, which opens at 6am Monday to Saturday and 6:30am Sunday, is directly across from the zoo's entrance on Connecticut Avenue. Good morning.

---

from the moment this country's story began, 400 years ago. Inscribed on the walls intermittently throughout the galleries are quotes from writers like William Faulkner and Eudora Welty and lyrics from musicians like Bob Dylan, which add poignancy and a certain context for this grand American experience. For that is what is going on here, as you poke along, viewing here an Edward Hopper, there a Gilbert Stuart, now a portrait of Samuel Clemens (Mark Twain), and on to contemporary art by Sean Scully.

Together, the Portrait Gallery and the American Art Museum display nearly 2,000 works from their permanent collections. The galleries flow one into another, so you may not always realize that you have stepped from an American Art wing into the Portrait Gallery wing—nor is it necessary to notice. Just wander and enjoy: the folk art, introductory "American Experience" landscapes and photographs, special exhibits, American Origins portraits, and other works on the first floor; portraits of America's presidents, an exhibit on "The Presidency and the Cold War," graphic arts, and American art through 1940 on the second floor; and art since 1945 and portraits of 20th-century Americans on the third floor. Expect to be dazzled by the creations of such American masters as Winslow Homer, Georgia O'Keeffe, David Hockney, Robert Rauschenberg, Thomas Cole, Andrew Wyeth, Mary Cassatt, and so many others. In addition, don't miss the two-level Lunder Conservation Center, where you'll be able to watch conservators working to preserve art pieces, and the Luce Foundation Center for American Art, which stores another 3,300 objects in such a way that they remain on view to the public. Finally, the museum offers a fine cafe on the third floor, sensational seating seasonally outdoors within the frame of the second level's portico, and a wonderful year-round enclosed courtyard cafe. ***Please note:*** The Smithsonian American Art Museum and National Portrait Gallery are located near the National Mall, but not on it; they're across from the Verizon Center in the heart of the Penn Quarter neighborhood.

8th and F sts. NW. ✆ **202/633-1000.** http://ReynoldsCenter.org. Free admission. Daily 11:30am–7pm. Closed Dec. 25. Metro: Gallery Place/Chinatown.

4 Other Attractions on or near the Mall

Bureau of Engraving & Printing This is where they will literally show you the money. A staff of 2,600 works around the clock churning it out at the rate of about $700 million a day. Everyone's eyes pop as they walk past rooms overflowing with new greenbacks. But the money's not the whole story. The bureau prints many other products, including 25 billion postage stamps a year, presidential portraits, and White House invitations.

Note: The Bureau of Engraving and Printing responds to Department of Homeland Security "Code Orange" warnings by halting its public tours. Call ahead to confirm that tours are on a normal schedule when you're here.

Many people line up each day to get a peek at all the moola, so arrive early, especially during the peak tourist season.

To save time and avoid a line, consider securing VIP, also called "congressional," tour tickets from your senator or congressperson; write or call at least 3 months in advance for tickets.

Tickets for general-public tours are generally not required from September to February; simply find the visitors entrance at 14th and C streets. March through August, however, every person taking the tour must have a ticket. To obtain a ticket, go to the ticket booth on the Raoul Wallenberg (formerly 15th St.) side of the building and show a valid photo ID. You will receive a ticket specifying a tour time for that same day, and be directed to the 14th Street entrance of the bureau; you are allowed as many as eight tickets per person. The ticket booth opens at 8am and closes when tickets sell out for the day.

The 45-minute guided tour begins with a short introductory film. Then you'll see, through large windows, the processes that go into the making of paper money: the inking, stacking of bills, cutting, and examination for defects. Most printing here is done from engraved steel plates in a process known as intaglio, the hardest to counterfeit, because the slightest alteration will cause a noticeable change in the portrait in use. Additional exhibits include bills no longer in use, counterfeit money, and a $100,000 bill designed for official transactions. (Since 1969, the largest denomination printed for the general public is $100.)

After you finish the tour, allow time to explore the **Visitor Center,** open from 8:30am to 3pm (until 7:30pm in summer), where exhibits include informative videos, money-related electronic games, and a display of $1 million. Here, too, you can buy gifts ranging from bags of shredded money—no, you can't tape it back together—to copies of documents such as the Gettysburg Address.

14th and C sts. SW. ✆ **800/874-2330.** www.moneyfactory.com. Free admission. Mon–Fri 9–10:45am and 12:30–2pm (last tour begins at 1:40pm); in summer, extended hours 5–6:40pm. Closed Dec 25–Jan 1 and federal holidays. Metro: Smithsonian (Independence Ave. exit).

National Archives The Rotunda of the National Archives displays the country's most important original documents: the Declaration of Independence, the Constitution of the United States, and the Bill of Rights (collectively known as the Charters of Freedom). Until recently, however, it wasn't possible to get a very good look at these documents, and when you did, you had to view the Constitution one page at a time. A superb renovation showcases the exhibit, known as "The National Archives Experience," whose display cases allow all visitors, but especially children and those in wheelchairs, much better viewing of the Charters. And, for the first time, you are able to see all four pages of the Constitution in one visit. Fourteen document cases trace the story of the creation of the Charters and the ongoing influence of these fundamental documents on the nation and the world. A restoration of Barry Faulkner's two larger-than-life murals brings the scenes to vivid life. One mural, titled *The Declaration of Independence,* shows Thomas Jefferson presenting a draft of the Declaration to John Hancock, the presiding officer of the Continental Congress; the other, titled *The Constitution,* shows James Madison submitting the Constitution to George Washington and the Constitutional Convention. Be sure not to miss viewing the original 1297 Magna Carta, on display as you enter the Rotunda; the document is one of only three or four known to exist, and the only original version residing permanently in the United States.

In late 2004, the National Archives debuted **Public Vaults,** an exhibit that features interactive technology and displays of documents and artifacts to explain the country's development in the use of records, from Indian treaties to presidential websites. You can listen to recorded voices of past presidents as they deliberated over pressing issues of the time, and you can scour newly declassified documents. During the day, the William C. McGowan Theater continually runs dramatic films illustrating the relationship between records and democracy in the lives of real people, and at night it serves as a premier documentary film venue for the city. The Lawrence F. O'Brien Gallery rotates exhibitions of Archives documents.

As a federal institution, the National Archives is charged with sifting through the accumulated papers of a nation's official life—billions of pieces a year—and determining what to save and what to destroy. The Archives' vast accumulation of census figures, military records, naturalization papers, immigrant passenger lists, federal documents, passport applications, ship manifests, maps, charts, photographs, and motion picture film (and that's not the half of it) spans 2 centuries. Anyone age 16 and over is welcome to use the National Archives center for genealogical research—this is where Alex Haley began his work on *Roots.* Call for details.

The National Archives building itself is worth an admiring glance. The neoclassical structure, designed by John Russell Pope (also the architect of the National Gallery of Art and the Jefferson Memorial) in the 1930s, is an impressive example of the Beaux Arts style. Seventy-two columns create a Corinthian colonnade on each of the four facades. Great bronze doors mark the Constitution Avenue entrance and four large sculptures representing the Future, the Past, Heritage, and Guardianship sit on pedestals near the entrances. Huge pediments crown both the Pennsylvania Avenue and Connecticut Avenue entrances to the building. Allow about 90 minutes to view everything.

700 Pennsylvania Ave. NW (between 7th and 9th sts. NW; tourists enter on Constitution Ave., researchers on Pennsylvania Ave.). ✆ **202/357-5000.** www.archives.gov. Free admission. March 15 to Labor Day daily 10am–7pm; day after Labor Day to Mar 14 daily 10am–5:30pm. Call for research hours. Closed Dec 25. Metro: Archives–Navy Memorial.

National Gallery of Art ★★★ This museum is such a treasure. Housing one of the world's foremost collections of Western paintings, sculpture, and graphic arts, from the Middle Ages into the 21st century, the National Gallery has a dual personality. The original West Building, designed by John Russell Pope (architect of the Jefferson Memorial and the National Archives), is a neoclassic marble masterpiece with a domed rotunda over a colonnaded fountain and high-ceilinged corridors leading to delightful garden courts. At its completion in 1941, the building was the largest marble structure in the world. It was a gift to the nation from financier/philanthropist Andrew W. Mellon, who also contributed the nucleus of the collection, including 21 masterpieces from the Hermitage, two Raphaels among them. The modern East Building, designed by I. M. Pei and opened in 1978, is composed of two adjoining triangles with glass walls and lofty tetrahedron skylights. The pink Tennessee marble from which both buildings were constructed was taken from the same quarry; it forms an architectural link between the two structures. Only a small percentage of the National Gallery's collection of 109,000 works is on display at one time. The Gallery's permanent collection offers reason enough to visit, but its mounted exhibitions make this museum a further must—they're always fantastic; see the box "Museum Exhibits Scheduled for 2008," earlier in this chapter, for a taste of what's happening at the Gallery.

The West Building: From the Mall entrance, you can stop first at the **Art Information Room** to design your own tour on a computer, if you like. But don't spend too much time here. Step into the gorgeous Rotunda, which leads right and left of you

---

Tips Avoiding the Lines at the National Archives

You'll still have to pass through a security clearance line, but you can avoid the general admission line by contacting visitorservices@nara.gov to reserve a space on a self-guided tour, or call ✆ **202/357-5450** for a slot on a guided tour of the National Archives.

---

to light-filled halls punctuated with sculpture; off these long corridors stem intimate **painting galleries** organized by age and nationality. To your left, as you face away from the Mall, are works by the older Masters, from 13th-century Italians to 16th-century Germans. To your right are their younger counterparts, from 18th- and 19th-century French and Spanish artists to later works by British and American artists. These are creations by El Greco, Bruegel, Poussin, Vermeer, Van Dyck, Rubens, Fra Angelico, Gilbert Stuart, Winslow Homer, Constable, Turner, Mary Cassatt, you name it. The only Leonardo da Vinci painting in the Western Hemisphere hangs here, his *Ginevra de' Benci,* just another masterpiece among this bevy of masterpieces.

Descend the grand marble staircase to the ground floor, where the museum's **newly renovated sculpture galleries** are columned, vaulted, and filled with light. Highlights here range from Chinese porcelain, to Renaissance decorative arts, to 46 wax statuettes by Degas, to Honoré Daumier's entire series of bronze sculptures, including all 36 of his caricatured portrait busts of French government officials.

The **National Gallery Sculpture Garden** ★, just across 7th Street from the West Wing, opened to the public in May 1999. The park takes up 2 city blocks and features open lawns; a central pool with a spouting fountain (the pool turns into an ice rink in winter); an exquisite glassed-in pavilion housing an excellent cafe; 17 sculptures by renowned artists like Roy Lichtenstein and Ellsworth Kelly (and Scott Burton, whose *Six-Part Seating* you're welcome to sit upon) and, the latest installment, a Paris Metro sign; and informally landscaped shrubs, trees, and plants. It continues to be a hit, especially in warm weather, when people sit on the wide rim of the pool and dangle their feet in the water while they eat their lunch. Friday evenings in summer, the gallery stages live jazz performances here.

The East Building: This wing is a showcase for the museum's collection of 20th-century art, including works by Picasso, Miró, Matisse, Pollock, and Rothko; for an exhibit called **Small French Paintings,** which I love; and for the gallery's special exhibitions. But chances are, the first thing you'll notice in this wing is the famous, massive aluminum **Alexander Calder mobile** dangling in the seven-story sky-lit atrium. And here's a tip that lots of people don't know: If you make your way to the tippy-top of the East Wing, whether by elevator or stairs, you reach a level that's actually named the "Tower," where you are rewarded with the sight of four Matisse cutouts, swirls of colorful paper creations framed against a background of white.

Altogether, you should allow a leisurely 2 hours to see everything here.

Pick up a floor plan and calendar of events at an information desk to find out about National Gallery exhibits, films, tours, lectures, and concerts. Immensely popular is the gallery's Sunday concert series, now in its 66th year, with concerts performed most Sunday evenings, October through June, at 6:30pm in the beautiful garden court of the West Building. Admission is free and seating is on a first-come basis; my suggestion is to tour the gallery in late afternoon, lingering until 6pm, when the galleries close and the queuing begins, in the Rotunda. The concerts feature chamber music, string quartets, pianists, and other forms of classical music performances. Call ✆ **202/842-6941.**

The gallery offers school tours, wide-ranging introductory tours, and tours in several languages. The gift shop is a favorite. You'll also find several pleasing dining options—among them the concourse-level Cascade Café, which has multiple food stations; the Garden Café, on the ground floor of the West Building; and the sculpture garden's Pavilion Café.

On Constitution Ave. NW between 3rd and 7th sts. NW (on the north side of the Mall). ✆ **202/737-4215.** www.nga.gov. Free admission. Gallery: Mon–Sat 10am–5pm; Sun 11am–6pm. Sculpture Garden: late May to mid-Sept

Mon–Thurs and Sat 10am–7pm, Fri 10am–9:30pm, Sun 11am–7pm; mid-Sept to late May Mon–Sat 10am–5pm, Sun 11am–6pm. Closed Jan 1 and Dec 25. Metro: Archives, Judiciary Square, or Smithsonian.

United States Holocaust Memorial Museum ★★ Twenty-four million people have visited this museum since it opened in 1993, and the museum continues to be a top draw. If you arrive without a reserved ticket specifying an admission time, you'll have to join the line of folks seeking to get one of the 1,575 day-of-sale tickets the museum makes available each day (see "Holocaust Museum Touring Tips," below). The museum opens its doors at 10am and the tickets are usually gone by 10:30am. In peak season, it's recommended that you get in line early in the morning (around 8am).

The noise and bustle of so many visitors can be disconcerting, and it's certainly at odds with the experience that follows. But things settle down as you begin your tour. When you enter, you will be issued an identity card of an actual victim of the Holocaust; at several points in the tour, you can find out the location and status of the person on your card—by 1945, 66% of those whose lives are documented on these cards were dead.

From its collection of more than 12,435 artifacts, the museum has organized some 900 items and 70 video monitors to reveal the Jewish experience in three parts: Nazi Assault, Final Solution, and Last Chapter. The tour begins on the fourth floor, where exhibits portray the events of 1933 to 1939, the years of the Nazi rise to power. On the third floor (documenting 1940–44), exhibits illustrate the narrowing choices of people caught up in the Nazi machine. You board a Polish freight car of the type used to transport Jews from the Warsaw ghetto to Treblinka and hear recordings of survivors telling what life in the camps was like.

The second floor recounts a more heartening story: It depicts how non-Jews throughout Europe, by exercising individual action and responsibility, saved Jews at great personal risk. Denmark—led by a king who swore that if any of his subjects wore a yellow star, so would he—managed to hide and save 90% of its Jews. Exhibits follow on the liberation of the camps, life in Displaced Persons camps, emigration to Israel and America, and the Nuremberg trials. At the end of the permanent exhibition is a most compelling and heartbreaking hour-long film called *Testimony,* in which Holocaust survivors tell their stories. The tour concludes in the hexagonal Hall of Remembrance, where you can meditate and light a candle for the victims. The museum notes that most people take 2 to 3 hours on their first visit; many people take longer.

In addition to its permanent and temporary exhibitions, the museum has a Resource Center for educators, which provides materials and services to Holocaust educators and students; an interactive computer learning center; and a registry of Holocaust survivors, a library, and archives, which researchers may use to retrieve historic documents, photographs, oral histories, films, and videos.

The museum recommends not bringing children under 11; for older children, it's advisable to prepare them for what they'll see. You can see some parts of the museum without tickets, including two special areas on the first floor and concourse: **Daniel's Story: Remember the Children** and the **Wall of Remembrance** (Children's Tile Wall), which commemorates the 1.5 million children killed in the Holocaust, and the **Wexner Learning Center.** There's a cafeteria and museum shop on the premises.

100 Raoul Wallenberg Place SW (formerly 15th St. SW; near Independence Ave., just off the Mall). ✆ **202/488-0400.** www.ushmm.org. Free admission. Daily 10am–5:30pm, staying open until 8pm Tues and Thurs mid-Apr to mid-June. Closed Yom Kippur and Dec 25. Metro: Smithsonian.

Tips Holocaust Museum Touring Tips

Because so many people want to visit the museum (it has hosted as many as 10,000 visitors in a single day), tickets specifying a visit time (in 15-min. intervals) are required. Reserve as many as 10 tickets in advance via Tickets.com (✆ **800/400-9373;** www.tickets.com) for a small fee. If you order well in advance, you can have tickets mailed to you at home. You can also get same-day tickets at the museum beginning at 10am daily (lines form earlier, usually around 8am). Note that same-day tickets are limited, and one person may obtain a maximum of four.

5 More Museums

The Corcoran Gallery of Art ★★ This elegant art museum, a stone's throw from the White House, is a favorite party site in the city, hosting everything from inaugural balls to wedding receptions.

The first art museum in Washington, the Corcoran Gallery was housed from 1869 to 1896 in the redbrick and brownstone building that is now the Renwick. The collection outgrew its quarters and was transferred in 1897 to its present Beaux Arts building, designed by Ernest Flagg.

The collection, shown in rotating exhibits, focuses chiefly on American art. A prominent Washington banker, William Wilson Corcoran was among the first wealthy American collectors to realize the importance of encouraging and supporting this country's artists. Enhanced by further gifts and bequests, the collection comprehensively spans American art from 18th-century portraiture to 20th-century moderns like Nevelson, Warhol, and Rothko. Nineteenth-century works include Bierstadt's and Remington's imagery of the American West; Hudson River School artists; expatriates like Whistler, Sargent, and Mary Cassatt; and two giants of the late 19th century, Homer and Eakins.

The Corcoran is not exclusively an American art museum. On the first floor is the collection from the estate of Sen. William Andrews Clark, an eclectic grouping of Dutch and Flemish masters, European painters, French Impressionists, Barbizon landscapes, Delft porcelains, a Louis XVI *salon dore* (an extravagant room with gilded ornaments and paneling) transported in toto from Paris, and more. Clark's will stated that his diverse collection, which any curator would undoubtedly want to disperse among various museum departments, must be shown as a unit. He left money for a wing to house it and the new building opened in 1928. Don't miss the small walnut-paneled room known as "Clark Landing," which showcases 19th-century French Impressionist and American art; a room of exquisite Corot landscapes; another of medieval Renaissance tapestries; and numerous Daumier lithographs donated by Dr. Armand Hammer. Allow an hour for touring the collection.

Pick up a schedule of events or check the website for information about temporary exhibits, gallery talks, concerts, art auctions, and more. There is some street parking.

The charming Café des Artistes is open for lunch daily (except Tues) from 11am to 3pm, for dinner on Thursday from 5 to 8pm, and for Sunday brunch from 10:30am to 2pm (reservations accepted for parties of six or more); call ✆ **202/639-1786** for more information. The Corcoran has a nice gift shop.

Not to Miss!

October 2007 saw the opening of two grand attractions in downtown Washington: the **Newseum,** at 555 Pennsylvania Ave. NW, and **Madame Tussauds Washington,** at 1025 F St. NW. While their debuts came too late to be given firsthand descriptions in this edition, they arrived just in time for anyone who plans to visit the capital in 2008. Here are some details:

Newseum: This is an immense museum, whose focus is the news. The 250,000-square-foot, seven-level building holds 14 galleries, 15 theaters, two broadcast studios, and a dozen interactive and hands-on exhibits. It traces the history of the news business for the past 5 centuries, and covers individual themes—from photojournalism, to First Amendment rights, to the emergence and further developments of electronic news. Located just off the National Mall, the Newseum also encompasses a two-level conference center and a three-level restaurant, The Source by Wolfgang Puck. 555 Pennsylvania Ave. NW (between 5th and 6th sts.). ✆ **888/NEWSEUM** (639-7386). www.newseum.org. Admission: Adults $17.91 (on Dec. 15, 1791, the first 10 amendments, the Bill of Rights, became part of the U.S. Constitution), seniors $16, children ages 7 to 12 $13, children under 7 admitted free with an adult. Daily 9am to 5pm; closed Thanksgiving, Christmas Day, and Jan. 1. Metro: Archives/Navy Memorial or Gallery Place/Verizon Center.

Madame Tussauds Washington: Only six other Madame Tussauds exist, only two others are located in the U.S., and only one allows you the pleasure of sizing up George Washington, mingling with Beyonce, or helping Tiger Woods line up his putt. Madame Tussauds is a wax museum whose life-size wax figure replicas of famous Americans and historic icons appear in one of four sections: The Spirit of Washington, D.C.; Behind the Scenes; Glamour; and Sports. Interactive displays allow visitors to step into the pictures of historic, celebrity, and sports events, whether to attend George Washington's inauguration or to hang with Julia Roberts. 1025 F St. NW (between 10th and 11th sts.). ✆ **202/942-7300.** www.madametussaudsdc.com. Daily 10am–5pm. Metro: Metro Center.

500 17th St. NW (between E St. and New York Ave.). ✆ **202/639-1700.** www.corcoran.org. $14 adults, $12 seniors, $10 students, children under 6 free. Sun–Mon and Wed 10am–6pm; Thurs 10am–9pm; Fri–Sat 10am–5pm. Closed Jan 1 and Dec 25. Metro: Farragut West or Farragut North.

Folger Shakespeare Library *Finds* "Shakespeare taught us that the little world of the heart is vaster, deeper, and richer than the spaces of astronomy," wrote Ralph Waldo Emerson in 1864. A decade later, Amherst student Henry Clay Folger was profoundly affected by a lecture Emerson gave similarly extolling the bard. Folger purchased an inexpensive set of Shakespeare's plays and went on to amass the world's largest (by far) collection of the bard's works, today housed in the Folger Shakespeare Library. By 1930, when Folger and his wife, Emily, laid the cornerstone of a building to house the collection, it comprised 93,000 books, 50,000 prints and engravings, and thousands of manuscripts. The Folgers gave it all as a gift to the American people. The library opened in 1932 and celebrated its 75th anniversary in 2007.

The building itself has a marble facade decorated with nine bas-relief scenes from Shakespeare's plays; it is a striking example of Art Deco classicism. A statue of Puck stands in the west garden. An **Elizabethan garden** on the east side of the building is planted with flowers and herbs of the period. Most remarkable here are eight sculptures each depicting figures from a particular scene in a Shakespeare play. Each work is welded onto the top of a pedestal, on which are inscribed the play's lines that inspired the sculptor, Greg Wyatt. These statues are half the size of those that Wyatt created for the Great Garden at New Place in Stratford-upon-Avon, England. Inquire about guided tours scheduled at 10 and 11am on every third Saturday from April to October. The garden is also a quiet place to have a picnic.

The facility, which houses some 256,000 books, 116,000 of which are rare (pre-1801), is an important research center not only for Shakespearean scholars, but also for those studying any aspect of the English and continental Renaissance. A multimedia computer exhibition called *The Shakespeare Gallery* offers users a close-up look at some of the Folgers' treasures, as well as Shakespeare's life and works. And the oak-paneled **Great Hall,** reminiscent of a Tudor long gallery, is a popular attraction for the general public. On display are rotating exhibits from the permanent collection: books, paintings, playbills, Renaissance musical instruments, and more. Plan on spending at least 30 minutes here.

At the end of the Great Hall is a theater designed to suggest an Elizabethan innyard where plays, concerts, readings, and Shakespeare-related events take place (see chapter 9 for details).

201 E. Capitol St. SE. ✆ **202/544-4600.** www.folger.edu. Free admission. Mon–Sat 10am–4pm. Free walk-in tours daily at 11am, with an extra tour added Sat at 1pm. Closed federal holidays. Metro: Capitol South or Union Station.

Ford's Theatre and Lincoln Museum *Kids* ***Note:*** The theater and its tiny museum are closed for renovation until late 2008, but the Petersen House across the street remains open. For background purposes, here's what you'll want to know:

On April 14, 1865, President Abraham Lincoln was in the audience at Ford's Theatre, one of the most popular playhouses in Washington. Everyone was laughing at a funny line from Tom Taylor's celebrated comedy, *Our American Cousin,* when John Wilkes Booth crept into the president's box, shot the president, and leapt to the stage, shouting, *"Sic semper tyrannis!"* ("Thus ever to tyrants!"). With his left leg broken from the vault, Booth mounted his horse in the alley and galloped off. Doctors carried Lincoln across the street to the house of William Petersen, where the president died the next morning.

The theater was closed after Lincoln's assassination and used as an office by the War Department. In 1893, 22 clerks were killed when three floors of the building collapsed. It remained in disuse until the 1960s, when it was remodeled and restored to its appearance on the night of the tragedy.

517 10th St. NW (between E and F sts.). ✆ **202/426-6925.** www.nps.gov/foth. Closed until late 2008. Metro: Metro Center.

The House Where Lincoln Died (the Petersen House) *Kids* After Lincoln was mortally wounded at Ford's Theatre, the doctors attending him had him carried out into the street, where boarder Henry Safford, standing in the open doorway of his rooming house, gestured for them to bring the president inside. So Lincoln died in

Museums of Special Interest

To the right person, with a specific interest, these lesser-known museums can be more than fascinating. Don't try to drop in without calling because most are not open daily, and some require appointments.

Anderson House, 2118 Massachusetts Ave. NW (✆ **202/785-2040**): A century-old, 50-room mansion of amazing design and impressive art and furnishings. The mansion is headquarters for the Society of the Cincinnati, which was founded in 1783 by Continental officers (including George Washington) who had served in the American Revolution. Metro: Dupont Circle.

Art Museum of the Americas, 201 18th St. NW, within the Organization of American States (✆ **202/458-6016;** www.museum.oas.org): From 80 to 200 works by contemporary Latin and Caribbean artists, on display from the museum's permanent collection. An Aztec garden and a second gallery in adjoining OAS building. Metro: Farragut West, then walk south about 6 blocks.

Daughters of the American Revolution (DAR) Museum, 1776 D St. NW (✆ **202/879-3241;** www.dar.org/museum): Early American furnishings and decorative arts. Metro: Farragut West, then walk south about 5 blocks.

Decatur House ★, 1610 H St. NW at Lafayette Park (✆ **202/842-0920;** www.decaturhouse.org): Historic house museum with permanent collection of Federalist and Victorian furnishings. Metro: Farragut West or McPherson Square.

Dumbarton House, 2715 Q St. NW (✆ **202/337-2288;** www.dumbartonhouse.org): Another historic house museum, with a permanent collection of 18th- and 19th-century English and American furniture and decorative arts. Metro: Dupont Circle, with a 20-minute walk along Q Street. See box "The Roads Less Traveled," p. 244.

Frederick Douglass National Historic Site, 1411 W St. SE (✆ **202/426-5961;** www.nps.gov/frdo): Last residence of the famous African-American 19th-century abolitionist. Metro: Anacostia, then catch bus no. B2, which stops by the house.

Hillwood Museum and Gardens, 4155 Linnean Ave. NW (✆ **202/686-8500;** www.hillwoodmuseum.org): Magnificent estate of Marjorie Merriweather Post, who collected art and artifacts of 18th-century France and Imperial Russia. Formal gardens, grand rooms, high tea. Metro: Van Ness or Cleveland Park.

Hillyer Art Space, 9 Hillyer Court NW (✆ **202/338-0680;** www.artsandartists.org/artspace.php): This new, hip little two-room gallery is an arm of International Arts & Artists, and displays works of both regional and international artists in its mission to "increase cross-cultural understanding and exposure to the arts internationally." Metro: Dupont Circle.

Interior Department Museum, 1849 C St. NW (✆ **202/208-4743;** www.doi.gov/interiormuseum): Permanent exhibits relating to the work of agencies that fall within the Interior Department's jurisdiction: national parks, land management, Indian affairs, fish and wildlife services, environmental protection. Metro: Farragut West, then walk about 6 blocks south.

Kreeger Museum, 2401 Foxhall Rd. NW (✆ **202/338-3552;** www.kreeger museum.org): This museum in a residential neighborhood is a treasure trove of art from the 1850s to the 1970s, including Impressionist paintings and the works of many American artists. No Metro; take a cab.

Mary McLeod Bethune Council House National Historic Site, 1318 Vermont Ave. NW (✆ **202/673-2402;** www.nps.gov/mamc): Last residence of African-American activist/educator Bethune, who was a leading champion of black and women's rights during FDR's administration. Metro: McPherson Square.

National Building Museum, 401 F St. NW (✆ **202/272-2448;** www.nbm.org): Housed within a historic building is this fine museum devoted to architecture, building, and historic preservation. Metro: Judiciary Square.

National Geographic Museum, 17th and M streets NW. (✆ **202/857-7588;** www.nationalgeographic.com/museum): Rotating exhibits related to exploration, adventure, and earth sciences, using interactive programs and artifacts. Metro: Farragut North (Connecticut Ave. and L St. exit).

Old Stone House, 3051 M St. NW (✆ **202/426-6851;** www.nps.gov/olst): A 1765 structure said to be the oldest in D.C. still standing on its original foundations. Colonial appearance, English garden. Metro: Foggy Bottom, with a 15-minute walk.

Sewall-Belmont House, 144 Constitution Ave. NE (✆ **202/546-3989;** www. sewallbelmont.org): A must for those interested in women's history, the historic house displays memorabilia of the women's suffrage movement, which got its start here. Metro: Union Station.

Textile Museum, 2320 S St. NW (✆ **202/667-0441;** www.textilemuseum.org): Historic and contemporary handmade textile arts, housed in historic John Russell Pope mansion. Metro: Dupont Circle, Q Street exit, then walk a couple of blocks up Massachusetts Avenue until you see S Street.

Tudor Place, 1644 31st St. NW (✆ **202/965-0400;** www.tudorplace.org): An 1816 mansion with gardens, home to Martha Washington's descendants until 1984. Metro: Dupont Circle, with a 25-minute walk along Q Street. See box "The Roads Less Traveled," p. 244.

United States Navy Memorial and Naval Heritage Center, 701 Pennsylvania Ave. NW (✆ **202/737-2300;** www.lonesailor.org): Plaza honors men and women of the U.S. Navy; museum features interactive video kiosks used to learn about Navy ships, aircraft, and history. Metro: Archives–Navy Memorial.

Woodrow Wilson House, 2340 S St. NW (✆ **202/387-4062;** www.woodrow wilsonhouse.org): The former home of this president, preserved the way it was when he lived here in the 1920s. Docents guide visitors on hour-long tours, pointing out noteworthy objects and telling stories about the 28th president. Metro: Dupont Circle, Q Street exit, then walk a couple of blocks up Massachusetts Avenue until you reach S Street.

the home of William Petersen, a German-born tailor. Now furnished with period pieces, the dark, narrow town house looks much as it did on that fateful April night. It takes about 5 minutes to troop through the building. You'll see the front parlor where an anguished Mary Todd Lincoln spent the night with her son, Robert. In the back parlor, Secretary of War Edwin M. Stanton held a cabinet meeting and questioned witnesses. From this room, Stanton announced at 7:22am on April 15, 1865, "Now he belongs to the ages." Lincoln died, lying diagonally because he was so tall, on a bed the size of the one in the room. (The Chicago Historical Society owns the actual bed and other items from the room.) In 1896, the government bought the house for $30,000, and it is now maintained by the National Park Service.

516 10th St. NW. ✆ **202/426-6924.** Free admission. Daily 9am–5pm. Closed Dec 25. Metro: Metro Center.

International Spy Museum ★★ *Kids* A visit here begins with a 5-minute briefing film, followed by a fun indoctrination into "Tricks of the Trade." Interactive monitors test one's powers of observation and teach you what to look for when it comes to suspicious activity. In addition to surveillance games, this first section displays trick equipment (such as a shoe transmitter used by Soviets as a listening device and a single-shot pistol disguised as a lipstick tube) and runs film in which spies talk about bugging devices and locks and picks. You can watch a video that shows individuals being made up for disguise, from start to finish, and you can crawl on your belly through ductwork in the ceiling overhead. (The conversations you hear are taped, not floating up from the room of tourists below.)

Try to pace yourself, though, because there's still so much to see, and you can easily reach your limit before you get through the 68,000-square-foot museum. The next section covers the history of spying (the second oldest profession) and tells about famous spy masters over time, from Moses; to Sun Tzu, the Chinese general, who wrote *The Art of War* in 400 B.C.; to George Washington, whose Revolutionary War letter of 1777 setting up a network of spies in New York is on view. Learn about the use of codes and code-breaking in spying, with one room of the museum devoted to the Enigma cipher machine used by the Germans (whose "unbreakable" codes the Allied cryptanalysts succeeded in deciphering) in World War II. An actual Enigma machine is displayed, and interactive monitors allow you to simulate the experience of using an Enigma machine, while learning more about its invention and inventor.

Much more follows: artifacts from all over (this is the largest collection of international espionage artifacts ever put on public display); a re-created tunnel beneath the divided city of Berlin during the Cold War; the intelligence-gathering stories of those behind enemy lines and of those involved in planning D-day in World War II; an exhibit on escape and evasion techniques in wartime; the tales of spies of recent times, told by the CIA and FBI agents involved in identifying them; and a mock-up of an intelligence agency's 21st-century operations center.

In June 2007, the museum debuted its **Operation Spy** experience, a 1-hour interactive immersion into espionage activities. Participants pretend to be intelligence officers and work in small teams as they conduct video surveillance of clandestine meetings, decrypt secret audio conversations, conduct polygraph tests, and so on, all in a day's work for a real-life spy. (You pay to play: a hefty $14 for those 12 and older, or $24 for combined admission to both the museum and this special feature; not recommended for children under 12.)

You exit the museum directly to its gift shop, which leads to the Spy City Café.

While you may look with suspicion on everyone around you when you leave the museum, you can trust that what you've just learned at the museum is authoritative: The Spy Museum's executive director was with the CIA for 36 years, and his advisory board includes two former CIA directors, two former CIA disguise chiefs, and a retired KGB general.

Consider ordering advance tickets for next-day or future date tours through Ticketmaster (✆ **800/551-SEAT**), which you can pick up at the Will Call desk inside the museum. You can also purchase advance tickets, including those for tours later in the day, at the box office.

800 F St. NW (at 8th St. NW). ✆ **866/779-6873** or 202/393-7798. www.spymuseum.org. Admission $16 adults (ages 12–65), $15 for seniors, $13 for children ages 5–11. Operation Spy: $14 for ages 12 and up. Combined admission fee: $24. Open daily, but hours vary; generally, 9am–8pm Apr 1–Aug 11, 10am–8pm Aug 12–Sept 2, 10am–6pm Sept 3–Feb 28, 9am–6pm Mar 1–31. Check website for details. Closed Thanksgiving, Dec 25, and Jan 1. Metro: Gallery Place/Chinatown or National Archive/Navy Memorial.

Marian Koshland Science Museum ★ The National Academy of Sciences operates this small museum, which was conceived of by molecular biologist Daniel Koshland, in memory of his wife, the immunologist and molecular biologist Marian Koshland, who died in 1997. The museum opened in April 2004 in the heart of downtown D.C. Recommended for children over 13, and especially for those with a scientific bent, the museum presents state-of-the-art exhibits that explore the complexities of science. (Do pay attention to the museum's age recommendation; I had a hard time wrapping my brain around the various exhibits, interesting though they were, and I'm a little bit older than 13.) Three exhibits currently on show are the Wonders of Science, which includes animations of groundbreaking research and an introductory film about the nature of science; Global Warming Facts and Our Future; and Infectious Disease, which covers the challenges to human health.

6th and E sts. NW. ✆ **202/334-1201.** www.koshlandsciencemuseum.org. Admission $5 adults, $3 ages 5–18 and seniors (65+). Wed–Mon 10am–6pm. Closed Thanksgiving, Christmas, and New Year's Day. Metro: Gallery Place/Chinatown or Judiciary Square.

National Museum of Women in the Arts This museum marked its 20th anniversary in 2007, its stunning collection still the foremost museum in the world dedicated to celebrating "the contribution of women to the history of art." Founders Wilhelmina and Wallace Holladay, who donated the core of the permanent collection—more than 250 works by women from the 16th to the 20th century—became interested in women's art in the 1960s. After discovering that no women were included in H. W. Janson's *History of Art,* a standard text (which did not address this oversight until 1986!), the Holladays began collecting art by women, and the concept of a women's art museum soon evolved.

Since its opening, the collection has grown to more than 3,000 works by more than 800 artists, including Rosa Bonheur, Frida Kahlo, Helen Frankenthaler, Barbara Hepworth, Georgia O'Keeffe, Camille Claudel, Lila Cabot Perry, Mary Cassatt, Elaine de Kooning, Käthe Kollwitz, and many other lesser-known artists from earlier centuries. You will discover here, for instance, that the famed Peale family of 19th-century portrait painters included a very talented sister, Sarah Miriam Peale. The collection is complemented by an ongoing series of changing exhibits. You should allow an hour for touring.

The museum is housed in a magnificent Renaissance Revival landmark building designed in 1907 as a Masonic temple by noted architect Waddy Wood. Its sweeping marble staircase and splendid interior make it a popular choice for wedding receptions. Lunch (weekdays only) in the Mezzanine Café (✆ **202/628-1068**), and you'll be surrounded by works from the museum's permanent collection.

1250 New York Ave. NW (at 13th St.). ✆ **800/222-7270** or 202/783-5000. www.nmwa.org. $8 adults, $6 students over 18 with ID and seniors over 60, free for youth 18 and under. (These are general admission rates; special exhibition prices may be higher.) Mon–Sat 10am–5pm; Sun noon–5pm. Closed Jan 1, Thanksgiving, and Dec 25. Metro: Metro Center (13th St. exit).

Phillips Collection ★★ This charming museum is even more alluring now that its expansion is complete. Its elegant 1890s Georgian Revival mansion anchors the Phillips, as it has since the gallery opened in 1921 (America's first museum of modern art). Founders Duncan and Marjorie Phillips, avid collectors and proselytizers of modernism, once lived here, where now reside Impressionist, modernist, and American master gems from the 2,500-work permanent collection. Intimate galleries retain homey features: leaded- and stained-glass windows, oak paneling, plush chairs and sofas, and individually designed fireplaces. The new wing houses the main entrance, as well as galleries devoted to special exhibits; a cafe run by a local favorite, Firehook Bakery (see "Gourmet Goodies to Go," in chapter 8, for details); a sculpture garden in the courtyard; and, most wonderfully, the Rothko Room, the small room devoted to four large, color-intense paintings by abstract expressionist Mark Rothko.

Best known for its Renoir masterpiece, *Luncheon of the Boating Party,* the Phillips boasts works by Daumier, Bonnard, Vuillard, van Gogh, Cézanne, Picasso, Degas, Klee, and Matisse. Ingres, Delacroix, Manet, El Greco, Goya, Corot, Constable, Courbet, Giorgione, and Chardin are among the premodernists represented. American notables, besides Rothko, include Dove, Hopper, Marin, Eakins, Homer, Lawrence, and O'Keeffe. You'll enjoy viewing the collection for an hour or so.

A full schedule of events includes temporary shows with loans from other museums and private collections, gallery talks, and concerts in the ornate music room. Concerts take place October to May on Sunday at 4pm; arrive early. On Thursday, the museum stays open until 8:30pm for **Artful Evenings,** usually a lecture or film screening.

Note: The Phillips Collection's admission structure is a little confusing: You may tour the permanent collection for free on weekdays. To tour the permanent collection on weekends, and to tour whatever special exhibit is currently running, whatever day of the week you are there, you pay the admission fee established for that special exhibition. This fee can vary, anywhere from $8 to $14 per person. The Phillips almost always has a special exhibition on view. You may order tickets in advance at the Phillips, or through Ticketmaster, online at www.ticketmaster.com, or by phone at ✆ **800/551-SEAT.**

1600 21st St. NW (at Q St.). ✆ **202/387-2151.** www.phillipscollection.org. Admission: See information in the note, above. Tues–Sat 10am–5pm year-round (Thurs until 8:30pm); Sun 11am–6pm. Closed federal holidays. Metro: Dupont Circle (Q St. exit).

6 Other Attractions

John F. Kennedy Center for the Performing Arts ★ Opened in 1971, the Kennedy Center is both the national performing arts center and a memorial to John F. Kennedy. Set on 17 acres overlooking the Potomac, the striking facility, designed by noted architect Edward Durell Stone, encompasses an opera house, a concert hall, two stage theaters, a theater lab, and a theater devoted exclusively to family productions.

The best way to experience the Kennedy Center is to attend a performance. (Check the website or call the toll-free number below and request the current issue of *Kennedy Center News Magazine,* a free publication that describes all Kennedy Center happenings and prices. See chapter 9 for specifics on theater, concert, and dance offerings, including highlights of the 2007–08 season.) But the Center also offers free 50-minute guided tours, which include some restricted areas.

Tours depart from the parking plaza, Level A, at the Tour desk, located across from the lower-level gift shops. You tour the **Hall of Nations,** which displays the flags of all nations diplomatically recognized by the United States. Throughout the center you'll see gifts from more than 40 nations, including all the marble used in the building (3,700 tons), which Italy donated. First stop is the **Grand Foyer,** scene of many free concerts and programs and the reception area for all three theaters on the main level; the 18 crystal chandeliers are a gift from Sweden. You'll also visit the **Israeli Lounge** (where 40 painted and gilded panels depict scenes from the Old Testament); the **Concert Hall,** home of the National Symphony Orchestra; the newly remodeled **Opera House;** the **African Room** (decorated with beautiful tapestries from African nations); the **Eisenhower Theater;** the **Hall of States,** where flags of the 50 states and four territories are hung in the order in which they joined the Union; the **Performing Arts Library;** and the **Terrace Theater,** a bicentennial gift from Japan. If there's a rehearsal going on, the tour skips the visits to the theaters.

Tours are offered in English, French, German, Spanish, and Japanese. You can beat the crowds by writing in advance to a senator or congressperson for passes for a free congressional ("VIP") tour, given year-round Monday through Friday at 9:30am and 4:30pm, and at 9:30am on Saturday and Sunday. Call ✆ **202/416-8340** for details.

Add another 15 minutes after the tour to walk around the building's terrace for a panoramic view of Washington.

2700 F St. NW (at New Hampshire Ave. NW and Rock Creek Pkwy.). ✆ **800/444-1324,** or 202/467-4600 for information or tickets. www.kennedy-center.org. Free admission. Daily 10am–midnight. Free guided tours Mon–Fri 10am–5pm; Sat–Sun 10am–1pm. Metro: Foggy Bottom (free shuttle service between the station and the center, running every 15 min. 9:45am–midnight weekdays, 10am–midnight Sat, and noon–midnight Sun). Bus: 80 from Metro Center. Parking $15.

Library of Congress ★ The question most frequently asked by visitors to the Library of Congress is "Where are the books?" They are on the 532 miles of shelves located throughout the library's three buildings: the **Thomas Jefferson, James Madison Memorial,** and **John Adams** buildings. Established in 1800, "for the purchase of such books as may be necessary for the use of Congress," the library today serves the nation, with holdings for the visually impaired (for whom books are recorded on cassette and/or translated into Braille), research scholars, college students—and tourists. Its first collection of books was destroyed in 1814 when the British burned the Capitol (where the library was then housed) during the War of 1812. Thomas Jefferson then sold the institution his personal library of 6,487 books as a replacement, and this became the foundation of what would grow to become the world's largest library.

Today, the collection contains a mind-boggling 134 million items. Its buildings house more than 20 million cataloged books, 59 million manuscripts, 14 million prints and photographs, 2.8 million audio holdings (discs, tapes, talking books, and so on), about a million movies and videotapes, musical instruments from the 1700s, and the letters and papers of everyone from George Washington to Groucho Marx. Its archives also include the letters, oral histories, photographs, and other documents of war veterans from World War I to the present, all part of its **Veterans History Project;** go to www.loc.gov/vets to listen to or read some of these stories, especially if you plan on visiting the National World War II Memorial.

Just as impressive as the library's holdings is its architecture. Most magnificent is the ornate Italian Renaissance–style **Thomas Jefferson Building,** which was erected between 1888 and 1897 to hold the burgeoning collection and establish America as a cultured nation with magnificent institutions equal to anything in Europe. Fifty-two painters and sculptors worked for 8 years on its interior. There are floor mosaics of Italian marble, allegorical paintings on the overhead vaults, more than 100 murals, and numerous ornamental cornucopias, ribbons, vines, and garlands. The building's exterior has 42 granite sculptures and yards of bas-reliefs. Especially impressive are the exquisite marble **Great Hall** and the **Main Reading Room,** the latter under a 160-foot dome. Originally intended to hold the fruits of at least 150 years of collecting, the Jefferson Building was, in fact, filled up in a mere 13 years. It is now supplemented by the James Madison Memorial Building and the John Adams Building.

On permanent display in the Jefferson Building's Great Hall are several exhibits: The **American Treasures of the Library of Congress** rotates a selection of more than 300 of the rarest and most interesting items from the library's collection—like Thomas Jefferson's rough draft of the Declaration of Independence with notations by Benjamin Franklin and John Adams in the margins, and the contents of Lincoln's pockets when he was assassinated. Be sure to obtain a free audio wand before you view the American Treasures exhibit so that you can listen to audio treasures: a Duke Ellington recording, an excerpt of Martin Luther King's delivery of his "I have a dream" speech, and so on.

Across the Great Hall from the American Treasures exhibit is one that showcases the **World Treasures of the Library of Congress.** Its multimedia display of books, maps, videos, and illustrations invites visitors to examine artifacts from the library's vast international collections. Tucked away in a corner of the Jefferson Building is another permanent exhibit, the **Bob Hope Gallery of American Entertainment,** which presents, on a rotating basis, film clips, memorabilia, and manuscript pages from a collection that the comedian donated to the library in 2000. The **Gershwin Room** houses George and Ira Gershwin memorabilia, including a piano, a desk, music manuscripts, and other of the American jazz composers' prized possessions.

If you are waiting for your tour to start (see schedule below), take in the 12-minute orientation film in the Jefferson's visitors' theater or browse in its gift shop.

Also, be sure to pick up a calendar of events when you visit. Concerts take place in the Jefferson Building's elegant **Coolidge Auditorium.** The concerts are free but require tickets, which you can obtain through Ticketmaster (✆ **800/551-7328**). Across Independence Avenue from the Jefferson Building is the **Madison Building,** which houses the Copyright Office, the **Mary Pickford Theater,** a venue for classic film screenings, a cafeteria, and the more formal Montpelier Room restaurant (the latter is open to small groups only, and sometimes requires reservations; call ✆ **202/707-8300**), which are open for lunch weekdays. Find out more about the library's free film and concert series by accessing the LOC website, and clicking "Resources for Visitors" and then "Calendar of Events."

Anyone over 18 may use the library's collections, but first you must obtain a user card with your photo on it. Go to Reader Registration in Room LM 140 (street level of the Madison Building) and present a driver's license or passport. Then head to the Information Desk in either the Jefferson or Madison buildings to find out about the research resources available to you and how to use them. Most likely, you will be directed to the Main Reading Room. All books must be used on-site.

101 Independence Ave. SE (at 1st St. SE). ✆ **202/707-8000.** www.loc.gov. Free admission. Madison Building Mon–Fri 8:30am–9:30pm; Sat 8:30am–6:30pm. Jefferson Building Mon–Sat 10am–5pm. Closed federal holidays. Stop at the information desk inside the Jefferson Building's west entrance on 1st St. to obtain same-day free tickets to tour the Library. Tours of the Great Hall: Mon–Fri 10:30 and 11:30am, and 1:30, 2:30, and 3:30pm; Sat 10:30 and 11:30am, and 1:30 and 2:30pm. Contact your congressional representatives to obtain tickets for congressional, or "VIP," tours, a slightly more personal tour given weekdays at 8:30am and 2pm. Metro: Capitol South.

Union Station ★ When you visit Union Station, you're stepping into the heart (or at least into a major artery) of everyday Washington life. Located within walking distance and full view of the Capitol, the station is a vital crossroads for locals, including Hill staffers who debark the Metro's Red Line at its stop here ("Union Station" is the station name, naturally); commuters, who ride MARC and Amtrak trains from more distant locales, like Baltimore; residents who walk or Metro here to shop, work, dine, or dawdle; and travelers from all over who arrive and depart by train all day long. Paths collide, quite literally sometimes, as ambling visitors and people running to catch a train crisscross the same ground.

When it opened in 1907, this was the largest train station in the world. It was designed by noted architect Daniel H. Burnham, who modeled it after the Baths of Diocletian and Arch of Constantine in Rome. Its facade includes Ionic colonnades fashioned from white granite and 100 sculptured eagles. Graceful 50-foot Constantine arches mark the entranceways, above which are poised six carved fixtures representing Fire, Electricity, Freedom, Imagination, Agriculture, and Mechanics. Inside is the **Main Hall,** a massive rectangular room with a 96-foot barrel-vaulted ceiling, an expanse of white-marble flooring, and a balcony adorned with 36 Augustus Saint-Gaudens sculptures of Roman legionnaires. Off the Main Hall is the **East Hall,** shimmering with scagliola marble walls and columns, a gorgeous hand-stenciled skylight ceiling, and stunning murals of classical scenes inspired by ancient Pompeian art. (Today this is the station's most pleasant shopping venue: less crowded and noisy, with small vendors selling pretty jewelry and other accessories.)

In its time, this "temple of transport" has witnessed many important events. President Wilson welcomed General Pershing here in 1918 on his return from France. South Pole explorer Rear Admiral Richard Byrd was also feted at Union Station on his homecoming. And Franklin D. Roosevelt's funeral train, bearing his casket, was met here in 1945 by thousands of mourners.

But after the 1960s, with the decline of rail travel, the station fell on hard times. Rain caused parts of the roof to cave in, and the entire building—with floors buckling, rats running about, and mushrooms sprouting in damp rooms—was sealed in 1981. That same year, Congress enacted legislation to preserve and restore this national treasure, to the tune of $160 million. The remarkable restoration involved hundreds of European and American artisans who were meticulous in returning the station to its original design.

At least 25 million people come through Union Station's doors yearly. About 120 retail and food shops on three levels offer a wide array of merchandise. And you'll be happy to find that most of the offerings in the Food Court are not fast-food joints but an eclectic mix of excellent, mostly homegrown, restaurants. The sky-lit **Main Concourse,** which extends the entire length of the station, is the primary shopping area as well as a ticketing and baggage facility. A nine-screen **cinema complex** lies on the lower level, across from the Food Court. You could spend half a day here shopping, or about 20 minutes touring. Stop by the visitor kiosk in the Main Hall. See chapter 8 for information about Union Station **shops.**

50 Massachusetts Ave. NE. © **202/371-9441.** www.unionstationdc.com. Free admission. Daily 24 hr. Shops Mon–Sat 10am–9pm; Sun noon–6pm. Parking $1 for 2 hr. with store's or restaurant's stamped validation; $7 for 2–3 hr. with validated ticket. Without validation, parking rates start at $5 for the 1st hr., and go up from there. Metro: Union Station.

Washington National Cathedral ★ Pierre L'Enfant's 1791 plan for the capital city included "a great church for national purposes," but possibly because of early America's fear of mingling church and state, more than a century elapsed before the foundation for Washington National Cathedral was laid. Its actual name is the Cathedral Church of St. Peter and St. Paul. The church is Episcopal, but it has no local congregation and seeks to serve the entire nation as a house of prayer for all people. It has been the setting for every kind of religious observance, from Jewish to Serbian Orthodox.

A church of this magnitude—it's the sixth largest cathedral in the world, and the second largest in the U.S.—took a long time to build. Its principal (but not original) architect, Philip Hubert Frohman, worked on the project from 1921 until his death in 1972. The foundation stone was laid in 1907 using the mallet with which George Washington set the Capitol cornerstone. Construction was interrupted by both world wars and by periods of financial difficulty. The cathedral was completed with the placement of the final stone on the west front towers on September 29, 1990, 83 years (to the day) after it was begun.

English Gothic in style (with several distinctly 20th-century innovations, such as a stained-glass window commemorating the flight of *Apollo 11* and containing a piece of moon rock), the cathedral is built in the shape of a cross, complete with flying buttresses and 110 gargoyles. It is, along with the Capitol and the Washington Monument, one of the dominant structures on the Washington skyline. Its 57-acre landscaped grounds have two lovely gardens (the lawn is ideal for picnicking), four schools, a greenhouse, and two gift shops.

Over the years, the cathedral has been, and continues to be, a truly historic place. Services to celebrate the end of World Wars I and II were held here. It was the scene of President Wilson's funeral (he and his wife are buried here), as well as President Eisenhower's. Helen Keller and her companion, Anne Sullivan, were buried in the cathedral at her request. And during the Iranian crisis, a round-the-clock prayer vigil was held in the Holy Spirit Chapel throughout the hostages' captivity. When they were released, the hostages came to a service here. President Bush's National Prayer and Remembrance service on September 14, 2001, following the cataclysm of September 11, was held here.

The best way to explore the cathedral is to take a 30-minute **guided tour;** the tours leave continually from the west end of the nave. You can also walk through on your own, using a self-guiding brochure available in several languages. Call about group and special-interest tours, both of which require reservations and fees (© **202/537-5700**). Allow additional time to tour the grounds or "close" and to visit the **Observation Gallery** ★, where 70 windows provide panoramic views. Tuesday and Wednesday afternoon tours are followed by a high tea in the Observation Gallery for $25 per person; reservations required. Call © **202/537-8993** or book online at www.visit.cathedral.org/tea.

cathedral hosts numerous events: organ recitals; choir performances; an annual flower mart; calligraphy workshops; jazz, folk, and classical concerts; and the playing of the 53-bell carillon. Check the cathedral's website for schedules.

Massachusetts and Wisconsin aves. NW (entrance on Wisconsin Ave.). ✆ **202/537-6200.** www.nationalcathedral.org. Donation $3 adults, $2 seniors, $1 children. Cathedral Mon–Fri 10am–5:30pm; Sat 10am–4:30pm; Sun 8am–6:30pm; May 1 to Labor Day, the nave level stays open Mon–Fri until 8pm. Gardens daily until dusk. Regular tours Mon–Sat 10–11:30am and 12:45–4pm (Sat 3:30pm); Sun 12:45–2:30pm. No tours on Palm Sunday, Easter, Thanksgiving, Dec 25, or during services. Services vary throughout the year, but you can count on a weekday Evensong service at 5:30pm, a weekday noon service, and an 11am service every Sun; call for other service times. Metro: Tenleytown, with a 20-min. walk. Bus: Any N bus up Massachusetts Ave. from Dupont Circle or any 30-series bus along Wisconsin Ave. This is a stop on the Old Town Trolley Tour.

7 Just Across the Potomac: Arlington National Cemetery

The land that today comprises Arlington County originally was carved out of Virginia as part of the nation's new capital district. In 1847, the land was returned to the state of Virginia, although it was known as Alexandria County until 1920, when the name was changed to avoid confusion with the city of Alexandria.

The county got its name from its famous estate, Arlington House, built by a descendant of Martha Washington, George Washington Parke Custis, whose daughter married Robert E. Lee. The Lees lived in Arlington House on and off until the onset of the Civil War in 1861. After the first Battle of Bull Run, at Manassas, several Union soldiers were buried here; the beginnings of Arlington National Cemetery date from that time. The Arlington Memorial Bridge leads directly from the Lincoln Memorial to the Robert E. Lee Memorial at Arlington House, symbolically joining these two figures into one Union after the Civil War.

Arlington has long been a residential community, with most people commuting into Washington to work and play. In recent years, however, the suburb has come into its own, booming with business, restaurants, and nightlife, giving residents reasons to stay put and tourists more incentive to visit (see "Electric Avenues for Live-Music Lovers," in chapter 9). Here are some sites worth seeing:

Arlington National Cemetery ★★ Upon arrival, head over to the **Visitor Center,** where you can view exhibits, pick up a detailed map, use the restrooms (there are no others until you get to Arlington House), and purchase a **Tourmobile ticket** ($7 per adult, $3.50 for children 3–11), which allows you to stop at all major sites in the cemetery and then reboard whenever you like. Service is continuous and the narrated commentary is informative; this is the only guided tour of the cemetery offered. If you've got plenty of stamina, consider doing part or all of the tour on foot. Remember as you go that this is a memorial frequented not just by tourists but also by those attending burial services or visiting the graves of beloved relatives and friends who are buried here.

This shrine occupies approximately 612 acres on the high hills overlooking the capital from the west side of the Memorial Bridge. It honors many national heroes and more than 260,000 war dead, veterans, and dependents. Many graves of the famous at Arlington bear nothing more than simple markers. Five-star General John J. Pershing's is one of those. Secretary of State John Foster Dulles is buried here. So are President William Howard Taft and Supreme Court Justices Thurgood Marshall and William Brennan. Cemetery highlights include:

The Tomb of the Unknowns, containing the unidentified remains of service members from both world wars, the Korean War, and, until 1997, the Vietnam War. In 1997, the remains of the unknown soldier from Vietnam were identified as those of

Air Force 1st Lt. Michael Blassie, whose A-37 was shot down in South Vietnam in 1962. Blassie's family, who had reason to believe that the body was their son's, had besought the Pentagon to exhume the soldier's remains and conduct DNA testing to determine if what the family suspected was true. Upon confirmation, the Blassies buried Michael in his hometown of St. Louis. The crypt honoring the dead but unidentified Vietnam War soldiers will remain empty. The entire tomb is an unembellished, massive white-marble block, moving in its simplicity. A 24-hour honor guard watches over the tomb, with the changing of the guard taking place every half-hour April to September, every hour on the hour October to March, and every hour at night year-round.

Within a 20-minute walk, all uphill, from the Visitor Center is **Arlington House** (**© 703/235-1530;** www.nps.gov/arho), whose structure was begun in 1802, by Martha and George Washington's grandson, George Washington Parke Custis (actually, Custis was George Washington's adopted grandson). Custis's daughter, Mary Anna Randolph, inherited the estate, and she and her husband, Robert E. Lee, lived here between 1831 and 1861. When Lee headed up Virginia's army, Mary fled, and federal troops confiscated the property. A fine melding of the styles of the Greek Revival and the grand plantation houses of the early 1800s, the house has been administered by the National Park Service since 1933.

You tour the house on your own; park rangers are on-site to answer your questions. The house remains open but is likely to be unfurnished until 2010, as a renovation gets underway. Slave quarters and a small museum adjoin. Admission is free. It's open daily from 9:30am to 4:30pm (closed Jan 1 and Dec 25).

Pierre Charles L'Enfant's grave was placed near Arlington House at a spot that is believed to offer the best view of Washington, the city he designed.

Below Arlington House is the **Gravesite of John Fitzgerald Kennedy.** John Carl Warnecke designed a low crescent wall embracing a marble terrace, inscribed with the 35th president's most famous utterance: "And so, my fellow Americans, ask not what your country can do for you; ask what you can do for your country." Jacqueline Kennedy Onassis rests next to her husband, and Robert Kennedy is buried close by. The Kennedy graves attract streams of visitors. Arrive close to 8am to contemplate the site quietly; otherwise, it's often crowded. Looking north, there's a spectacular view of Washington.

In 1997, the **Women in Military Service for America Memorial** (**© 800/222-2294** or 703/533-1155; www.womensmemorial.org) was added to Arlington Cemetery to honor the more than two million women who have served in the armed forces from the American Revolution to the present. The impressive memorial lies just beyond the gated entrance to the cemetery, a 3-minute walk from the Visitor Center. As you approach the memorial, you see a large, circular reflecting pool, perfectly placed within the curve of the granite wall rising behind it. Arched passages within the 226-foot-long wall lead to an upper terrace and dramatic views of Arlington National Cemetery and the monuments of Washington; an arc of large glass panels (which form the roof of the memorial hall) contains etched quotations from famous people about contributions made by servicewomen. Behind the wall and completely underground is the **Education Center,** housing a **Hall of Honor,** a gallery of exhibits tracing the history of women in the military, a theater, and a computer register of servicewomen, which visitors may access for the stories and information about 250,000 individual military women, past and present. Hours are 8am to 5pm (until 7pm Apr–Sept). Stop

Arlington National Cemetery

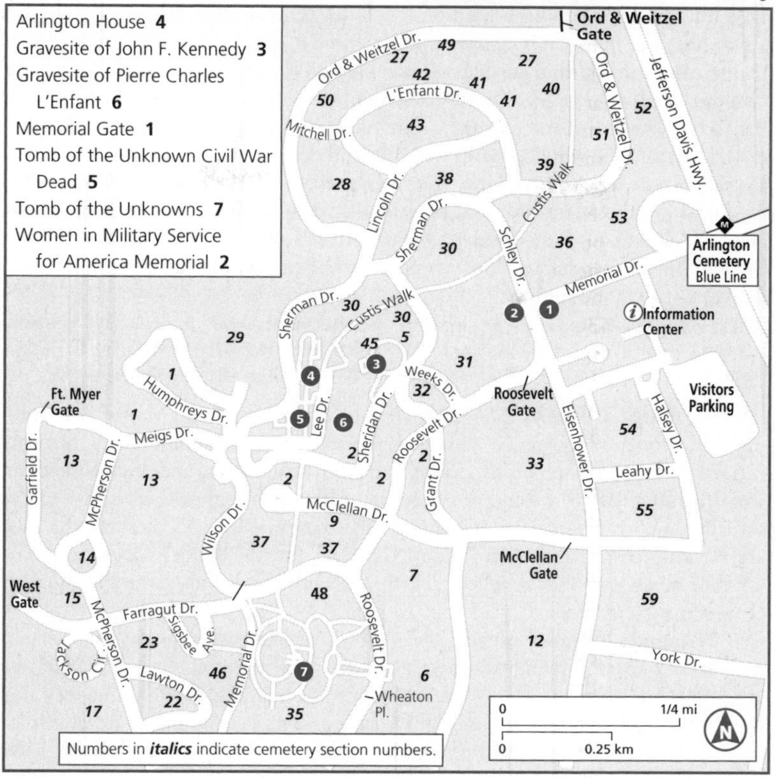

at the reception desk for a brochure that details a self-guided tour through the memorial. The memorial is open every day but Christmas.

Plan to spend half a day at Arlington Cemetery and the Women in Military Service Memorial.

Just across the Memorial Bridge from the base of the Lincoln Memorial. ✆ **703/607-8000.** www.arlingtoncemetery.org. Free admission. Apr–Sept daily 8am–7pm; Oct–Mar daily 8am–5pm. Metro: Arlington National Cemetery. If you come by car, parking is $1.25 an hr. for the 1st 3 hr., $2 an hr. thereafter. The cemetery is also accessible via Tourmobile.

8 Parks & Gardens

Washington is extensively endowed with vast natural areas, all centrally located within the District. Included in all this greenery are thousands of parkland acres, two rivers, the mouth of a 185-mile-long tree-lined canalside trail, an untamed wilderness area, and a few thousand cherry trees. And there's much more just a stone's throw away.

GARDENS

Dumbarton Oaks *Finds* This 19th-century Georgetown mansion named for a Scottish castle is a research center for studies in Byzantine and pre-Columbian art and history, as well as landscape architecture. Its magical yards, which wind gently down to Rock Creek Ravine, are modeled after European gardens. The pre-Columbian museum, designed by Philip Johnson, is a small gem, and the Byzantine collection is a rich one. The mansion is closed until sometime in 2008 for renovation, but its staggeringly beautiful **formal gardens** remain open to the public. The gardens include an Orangery, a Rose Garden, wisteria-covered arbors, groves of cherry trees, and magnolias. You're likely to spend as much as an hour here when everything is in bloom, but expect to share the winding paths with like-minded wanderers. You can't picnic here; instead, exit at R Street, turn left, cross an honest-to-goodness Lovers' Lane, and proceed next door to Montrose Park, to hold your picnic. There is parking on the street. See box "The Roads Less Traveled: A Back-Street Tour of Historic Georgetown, with Stops at Shops," in chapter 8, which points you here and to other nearby attractions, including shops and dining.

1703 32nd St. NW (garden entrance at 31st and R sts.). ✆ **202/339-6401.** www.doaks.org. Gardens Tues–Sun, year-round, weather-permitting: 2–6pm Mar 15–Oct 31; 2–5pm Nov 1–Mar 14. Admission Mar 15–Oct 31 $8 adults, $5 children under 12 and seniors; Nov–Mar 14 free. Gardens are closed national holidays and Dec 24.

Enid A. Haupt Garden Named for its donor, a noted supporter of horticultural projects, this stunning garden presents elaborate flower beds and borders, plant-filled turn-of-the-20th-century urns, 1870s cast-iron furnishings, and lush baskets hung from reproduction 19th-century lampposts. Although on ground level, the garden is actually on a 4¼-acre rooftop above the subterranean Ripley Center and the Sackler and African Art museums. An **"Island Garden"** near the Sackler Gallery, entered via a 9-foot moon gate, has benches backed by English boxwoods set under the canopy of weeping cherry trees.

A **"Fountain Garden"** outside the African Art Museum provides granite seating with walls overhung by hawthorn trees. Three small terraces, shaded by black sourgum trees, are located near the Arts and Industries Building. And five majestic linden trees shade a seating area around the **Downing Urn,** a memorial to American landscapist Andrew Jackson Downing, who designed the National Mall. Downing's words are inscribed on the base of the urn: "Build halls where knowledge shall be freely diffused among men, and not shut up within the narrow walls of narrower institutions. Plant spacious parks in your cities and unclose their gates as wide as the gates of morning to the whole people." Elaborate cast-iron carriage gates made according to a 19th-century design by James Renwick, flanked by four red sandstone pillars, are placed at the Independence Avenue entrance to the garden.

10th St. and Independence Ave. SW. ✆ **202/633-1000.** Free admission. Late May to Aug daily 7am–9:15pm; Sept to mid-May daily 7am–5:45pm. Closed Dec 25. Metro: Smithsonian.

United States Botanic Garden ★ For the feel of summer in the middle of winter, for the sight of lush, breathtakingly beautiful greenery and flowers all year round, stop in at the Botanic Garden, located at the foot of the Capitol, next door to the National

---

Tips **Closed for Now**

The Smithsonian's National Museum of American History is closed until the summer of 2008, the Ford's Theatre and Lincoln Museum is closed until late 2008, and the Smithsonian's Arts and Industries Building is closed indefinitely, as all three museums undergo extensive renovations. The FBI Building remains closed for public tours indefinitely. The Dumbarton Oaks Museum (not the gardens!) are closed for renovation work until sometime in 2008.

Museum of the American Indian. The grand conservatory devotes half of its space to exhibits that focus on the importance of plants to people, and half to exhibits that focus on ecology and the evolutionary biology of plants. But those finer points may escape you as you wander through the various chambers, outdoors and indoors, upstairs and down, gazing in stupefaction at so much fauna and flora. The conservatory holds 4,000 living species (about 26,000 plants); a high-walled enclosure, called "The Jungle," of palms, ferns, and vines; an Orchid Room; a meditation garden; a primeval garden; and gardens created especially with children in mind. And there are sounds—I swear I heard a frog or two. Just outside the conservatory is the newly debuted National Garden, which includes the First Ladies Water Garden, a formal rose garden, a butterfly garden, and a lawn terrace. Ask at the front desk about tours. The USBG sometimes offers entertainment and periodically publishes calendars of events.

Also visit the garden annex across the street, **Bartholdi Park.** The park is about the size of a city block, with a stunning cast-iron classical fountain created by Frédéric Auguste Bartholdi, designer of the Statue of Liberty. Charming flower gardens bloom amid tall ornamental grasses, benches are sheltered by vine-covered bowers, and a touch and fragrance garden contains such herbs as pineapple-scented sage.

100 Maryland Ave. SW (between 1st and 3rd sts. SW, at the foot of the Capitol on the National Mall). ✆ **202/225-8333.** www.usbg.gov. Free admission. Daily 10am–5pm. Metro: Federal Center SW.

PARKS

POTOMAC PARK

West and East Potomac parks, their 720 riverside acres divided by the Tidal Basin, are most famous for their spring display of **cherry blossoms** and all the hoopla that goes with it. So much attention is lavished on Washington's cherry blossoms that the National Park Service devotes a home page to the subject: www.nps.gov/nama/planyourvisit/cherry-blossom-bloom.htm. (Also go to www.nationalcherryblossomfestival.org.) You can access this site to find out forecasts for the blooms and assorted other details. You can also call the National Park Service (✆ **202/485-9880**) for information. In all, there are more than 3,700 cherry trees planted along the Tidal Basin in West Potomac Park, East Potomac Park, the Washington Monument grounds, and other pockets of the city.

To get to the Tidal Basin by car (*not* recommended in cherry-blossom season—actually, let me be clear: *impossible* in cherry blossom season), you want to get on Independence Avenue and follow the signs posted near the Lincoln Memorial that show you where to turn to find parking and the FDR Memorial. If you're walking, you'll want to cross Independence Avenue where it intersects with West Basin Drive (there's a stoplight and crosswalk), and follow the path to the Tidal Basin. There is no convenient Metro stop near here.

West Potomac Park encompasses Constitution Gardens; the Vietnam, Korean, Lincoln, Jefferson, World War II, and FDR memorials; a small island where ducks live; and the Reflecting Pool (see "The Major Memorials," p. 188, for full listings of the memorials). It has 1,678 cherry trees bordering the Tidal Basin, some of them Akebonos with delicate pink blossoms, but most Yoshinos with white, cloudlike flower clusters. The blossoming of the cherry trees is the focal point of a 2-week-long celebration, including the lighting of the 300-year-old Japanese Stone Lantern near Kutz Bridge, presented to the city by the governor of Tokyo in 1954. (This year's Cherry Blossom Festival is scheduled to run Mar 29–Apr 13, 2008.) The trees bloom for a little less than 2 weeks beginning sometime between March 20 and April 17; April 4 is the average date. Planning your trip around the blooming of the cherry blossoms is an iffy proposition, and

Tips **Cherry Night**

The National Park Service offers several kinds of cherry blossom tours, but the best is the lantern walk, which takes place at night. You bring your own flashlight and a park ranger guides you beneath the canopy of cherry blossoms for 1½ miles around the Tidal Basin.

I wouldn't advise it. All it takes is one good rain and those cherry blossoms are gone. The cherry blossoms are not illuminated at night.

East Potomac Park has 1,681 cherry trees in 10 varieties. The park also has picnic grounds, tennis courts, three golf courses, a large swimming pool, and biking and hiking paths by the water.

ROCK CREEK PARK

Created in 1890, **Rock Creek Park** ★ (**www.nps.gov/rocr**) was purchased by Congress for its "pleasant valleys and ravines, primeval forests and open fields, its running waters, its rocks clothed with rich ferns and mosses, its repose and tranquillity, its light and shade, its ever-varying shrubbery, its beautiful and extensive views." A 1,750-acre valley within the District of Columbia, extending 12 miles from the Potomac River to the Maryland border, it's one of the biggest and finest city parks in the nation. Parts of it are still wild; coyotes have been sighted here, joining the red and grey foxes, raccoons, and beavers already resident.

The park's offerings include the Old Stone House in Georgetown, Carter Barron Amphitheater (see chapter 9), playgrounds, an extensive system of beautiful hiking and biking trails, sports facilities, remains of Civil War fortifications, and acres and acres of wooded parklands. See also p. 229 for a description of the formal gardens at **Dumbarton Oaks,** which border Rock Creek Park in upper Georgetown.

For full information on the wide range of park programs and activities, visit the **Rock Creek Nature Center and Planetarium,** 5200 Glover Rd. NW (✆ **202/895-6070**), Wednesday through Sunday from 9am to 5pm. To get to the Nature Center by public transportation, take the Metro to Friendship Heights and transfer to bus no. E2 to Military Road and Oregon Avenue/Glover Road, then walk up the hill about 100 yards to the Nature Center. Call ✆ **202/895-6070** to request a brochure that provides details on picnic locations.

The Nature Center and Planetarium is the scene of numerous activities, including weekend planetarium shows for kids (minimum age 4) and adults; nature films; crafts demonstrations; live animal demonstrations; guided nature walks; plus a daily mix of lectures, films, and other events. Self-guided nature trails begin here. All activities are free, but for planetarium shows you need to pick up tickets a half-hour in advance. There are also nature exhibits on the premises. The Nature Center is closed on federal holidays.

Not far from the Nature Center is **Fort DeRussey,** one of 68 fortifications erected to defend the city of Washington during the Civil War. From the intersection of Military Road and Oregon Avenue, you walk a short trail through the woods to reach the fort, whose remains include high earth mounds with openings where guns were mounted, surrounded by a deep ditch/moat.

At Tilden Street and Beach Drive, you can see a water-powered 19th-century gristmill, used until not so long ago to grind corn and wheat into flour. It's called **Peirce Mill** (a man named Isaac Peirce built it), but it's currently closed for repairs.

Northern Rock Creek Park Area

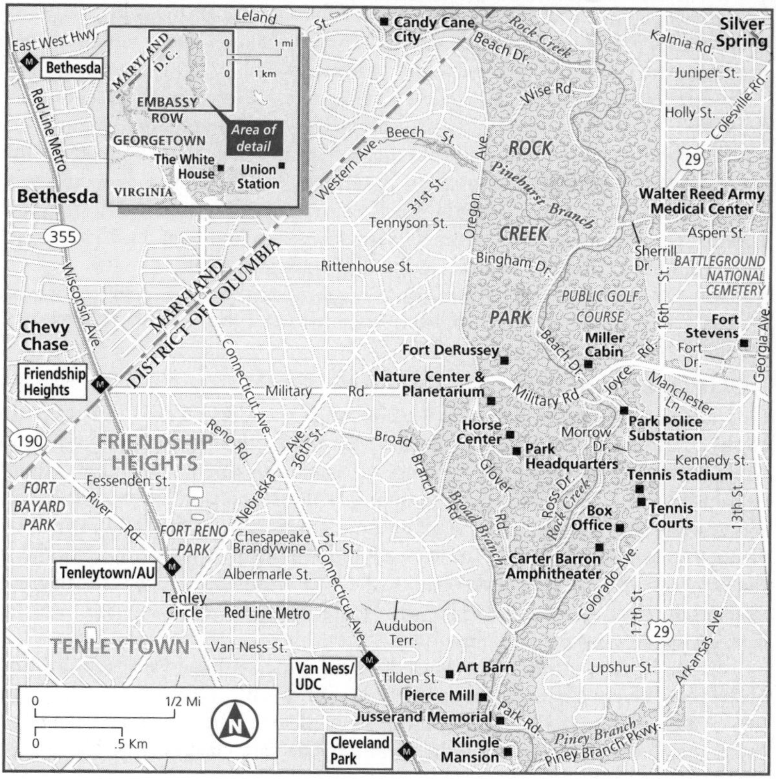

Poetry readings and workshops are held during the summer at **Miller's Cabin,** the one-time residence of High Sierra poet Joaquin Miller, Beach Drive north of Military Road. Call ✆ **202/895-6070** for information.

You'll find convenient free **parking** throughout the park.

THEODORE ROOSEVELT ISLAND PARK ★★

A serene 91-acre wilderness preserve, Theodore Roosevelt Island is a memorial to the nation's 26th president, in recognition of his contributions to conservation. During his administration, Roosevelt, an outdoor enthusiast and expert field naturalist, set aside a total of 234 million acres of public lands for forests, national parks, wildlife and bird refuges, and monuments.

Native American tribes were here first, inhabiting the island for centuries, until the arrival of English explorers in the 1600s. Over the years, the island passed through many owners before becoming what it is today—an island preserve of swamp, marsh, and upland forest that's a haven for rabbits, chipmunks, great owls, foxes, muskrats, turtles, and groundhogs. It's a complex ecosystem in which cattails, arrow arum, and pickerel-weed grow in the marshes, and willow, ash, and maple trees root on the mud flats. You can observe these flora and fauna in their natural environs on 2.5 miles of foot trails.

In the northern center of the island, overlooking a terrace encircled by a water-filled moat, stands a 17-foot bronze statue of Roosevelt. Four 21-foot granite tablets are inscribed with tenets of his conservation philosophy.

To drive to the island, take the George Washington Memorial Parkway exit north from the Theodore Roosevelt Bridge. The parking area is accessible only from the northbound lane; park there and cross the pedestrian bridge that connects the lot to the island. You can also rent a canoe at Thompson's Boat Center (p. 240) and paddle over, or take the pedestrian bridge at Rosslyn Circle, 2 blocks from the Rosslyn Metro station. You can picnic on the grounds near the memorial; if you do, allow about an hour here. Expect bugs in summer and muddy trails after a rain.

In the Potomac River, between Washington and Rosslyn, VA. See access information above. ✆ **703/289-2550.** www.nps.gov/this. Free admission. Daily dawn–dusk. Metro: Rosslyn, then walk 2 blocks to Rosslyn Circle and cross the pedestrian bridge to the island.

ACTIVITIES ON THE C&O CANAL

One of the great joys of living in Washington is the **C&O Canal** (**www.nps.gov/choh**) and its unspoiled 185-mile towpath. You leave urban cares and stresses behind while hiking, strolling, jogging, cycling, or boating in this lush, natural setting of ancient oaks and red maples, giant sycamores, willows, and wildflowers. But the canal wasn't always just a leisure spot for city people. It was built in the 1800s, when water routes were considered vital to transportation. Even before it was completed, though, the canal was being rendered obsolete by the B&O Railroad, which was constructed at about the same time and along the same route. Today, its role as an oasis from unrelenting urbanity is even more important.

A good source of information about the canal is the National Park Service office at **Great Falls Tavern Visitor Center,** 11710 MacArthur Blvd., Potomac, MD (✆ **301/767-3714**). At this 1831 tavern, you can see museum exhibits and a film about the canal; there's also a bookstore on the premises. The park charges an entrance fee, $5 per car, $3 per walker or cyclist.

In Georgetown, the **Georgetown Information Center,** 1057 Thomas Jefferson St. NW (✆ **202/653-5190**), can also provide maps and information.

Hiking any section of the flat dirt towpath or its more rugged side paths is a pleasure (and it's free). There are picnic tables, some with barbecue grills, about every 5 miles on the way to Cumberland, beginning at **the Boat House at Fletcher's Cove** (✆ **202/244-0461**), which is about 3¼ miles out of Georgetown and is a good place to rent bikes or boats or to purchase bait, tackle, and a fishing license. Enter the towpath in Georgetown below M Street via Thomas Jefferson Street. If you hike 14 miles, you'll reach **Great Falls,** a point where the Potomac becomes a stunning waterfall plunging 76 feet. Or drive to Great Falls Park on the Virginia side of the Potomac.

Much less strenuous than hiking is a **mule-drawn 19th-century canal boat trip** led by Park Service rangers in period dress. They regale passengers with canal legend and lore and sing period songs. These boats depart from mid-April to mid-October. Both the Georgetown and Great Falls barge rides last about 1 hour and 10 minutes and cost $7 for adults, $5 for seniors over 61, and $5 for children ages 4 to 14. Check the website, www.nps.gov/choh, for the latest schedules.

Call any of the above information numbers for details on riding, rock climbing, fishing, bird-watching, concerts, ranger-guided tours, ice skating, camping, and other canal activities.

Finds Albert Einstein Memorial, 22nd Street and Constitution Avenue Northwest

In a grove of holly and elm trees, at the southwest corner of the National Academy of Science grounds, you'll find this dear memorial displaying the slouching figure of brilliant scientist, great thinker, and peace activist Albert Einstein. He sits slightly bent and sideways, upon a granite bench, leaning on one hand and holding in the other a bronze sheet of paper on which are written mathematical equations for which he is famous. At his feet is a celestial map. His gaze looks worn and warm. The statue measures 12 feet in height and weighs 4 tons, yet children cannot resist crawling upon it, and leaning up against this man.

9 Especially for Kids

As far as I know, Pierre L'Enfant and his successors were not thinking of children when they incorporated the long, open stretch of the Mall into their design for the city. But they may as well have. This 2-mile expanse of lawn running from the Lincoln Memorial to the Capitol is a playground, really, and a backyard to the Smithsonian museums, National Gallery, and memorials that border it. You can visit any of these sites assured that if one of your little darlings starts to misbehave, you'll be able to head right out the door to the National Mall, where numerous distractions await. The Mall is always busy with walkers, joggers, and bikers. Vendors sell ice cream, soft pretzels, and sodas. Festivals of all sorts take place on a regular basis, whether it's the grand Smithsonian Folklife Festival for 10 days at the end of June into July (see calendar, chapter 2), or the Kite Festival in spring. Weather permitting, a 19th-century carousel operates in front of the Arts and Industries Building on the south side of the Mall. Right across the Mall from the carousel is the children-friendly National Gallery Sculpture Garden, whose shallow pool is good for splashing one's feet in summer and for ice skating in winter, when it turns into an ice rink.

You don't need the excuse of recalcitrant children to enjoy the Mall, of course, though it's always good to have an escape route. The truth is, many of Washington's attractions hold various enchantments for children of all ages. It might be easier to point out which ones are not recommended for your youngest: the Supreme Court, the chambers of Congress, the U.S. Holocaust Memorial Museum, and the Marian Koshland Science Museum. Generally speaking, the bigger and busier the museum, the better it is for kids. On the Mall, these would be the two top draws: the National Museum of Natural History and the National Air and Space Museum, each of which has special areas and exhibits aimed specifically at children. (The National Museum of American History, when it reopens in summer of 2008, will be another contender.)

I have two daughters, ages 15 and 20; their favorite Washington activities over the years have included paddle-boating on the Tidal Basin (p. 241); shopping in Georgetown; attending plays at the Folger Theatre, the National Theatre, and the Kennedy Center; Wizards and Mystics basketball games at the Verizon Center (p. 267); ice skating at the National Gallery; and visiting the National Zoo, the International Spy Museum, the National Postal Museum, the Albert Einstein Memorial (above), and special exhibits at the National Gallery of Art, as long as we had something to eat at one of the cafes. (Parents, you will be happy to note that many of the museums offer food of some sort, or vendor carts at the curb.)

Kids Favorite Children's Attractions

Check for special children's events at museum information desks when you enter. As noted within the listings for individual museums, some children's programs are also great fun for adults. I recommend the programs at the **Corcoran Gallery of Art,** the **Folger Shakespeare Library,** the **Phillips,** and the **Sackler Gallery** in particular. (The gift shops in most of these museums have wonderful toys and children's books.) Call ahead to find out which programs are running. Here's a rundown of big kid-pleasers in town (for details, see the full entries earlier in this chapter):

- **International Spy Museum** (p. 220): Both kids and adults enjoy pretending to be spies, testing their powers of observation, and trying to figure out how the Enigma machine works. Sleuths over 12 will love the museum's new Operation Spy.
- **Lincoln Memorial** (p. 192): Kids know a lot about Lincoln and enjoy visiting his memorial. A special treat is visiting after dark.
- **National Air and Space Museum** (p. 200): Spectacular IMAX films (don't miss), thrilling flight simulators, planetarium shows, missiles, rockets, a walk-through orbital workshop, and flight simulators.
- **National Museum of the American Indian** (p. 203): Pick up a copy of the Family Guide for tips on enjoying this treasury of Native American history and culture with kids. Interesting multimedia and hands-on activities.
- **National Museum of Natural History** (p. 205): A Discovery Room just for youngsters, the new Butterfly Pavilion and exhibit, as well as the outdoor butterfly garden, an insect zoo, shrunken heads, dinosaurs, and the IMAX theater showing 2-D and 3-D films.
- **National Zoological Park** (p. 208): Pandas! Cheetahs! Kids always love a zoo, and this is an especially good one, with a Kids Farm added in 2005.
- **Washington Monument** (p. 189): Spectacular 360-degree views from the center of Washington, D.C.

For more ideas, consult the Friday "Weekend" section of the *Washington Post,* which lists numerous activities (mostly free) for kids: special museum events, children's theater, storytelling programs, puppet shows, video game competitions, and so forth. Call the Kennedy Center and the National Theatre to find out about children's shows; see chapter 9 for details.

I've noted "Family-Friendly Hotels" in chapter 5; a few, though not many, hotels have pools, and some offer little goodie packages at check-in. The "Organized Tours" and "Outdoor Activities" sections below may also be your saving grace when you've run out of steam or need a jump-start to your day.

10 Organized Tours

Enterprising individuals and organizations keep coming up with new ways to introduce the city. Go to the Cultural Tourism D.C. website, www.culturaltourismdc.org, and click on "Tours and Trails" for a longer list of organized tours. Here's a sampling of what's available.

ON FOOT

A Tour de Force (✆ **703/525-2948;** www.atourdeforce.com) is historian and raconteur Jeanne Fogel's 24-year-old company. She offers various modes of transport, from walking to bus, SUV, and limo tours. Fogel custom designs the route around the city per your request and size of group, from a romantic tour for a couple to a traditional sightseeing excursion for a convention crowd. Fogel (or her stand-in) peppers her narration with little-known anecdotes and facts about neighborhoods, historic figures, and the most visited sites. Call for rates.

Spies of Washington Tour (✆ **703/569-1875;** www.spiesofwashingtontour.com) offers four walking tours that focus on espionage-related sites in Georgetown and around the White House, Pennsylvania Avenue, Capitol Hill, and the Russian Embassy areas. Carol Bessette, a retired Air Force intelligence officer, conducts the tours, which cost $12 per person. Private tours and bus tours are also available.

Guided Walking Tours of Washington ★ (✆ **301/294-9514;** www.dcsightseeing.com) offers 2-hour walks through the streets of Georgetown, Adams-Morgan, and other locations, guided by author/historian Anthony S. Pitch. Inquire about private tours. Rates are $15 per person.

Segway Tours (✆ **877/SEG-TOUR;** www.citysegwaytours.com/washington) are available March through November, and though technically they are "on foot," Segways are self-propelling scooters that operate based on "dynamic stabilization" technology, which uses your body movements. Tours last 4 hours, cost $70 per person, and include training; age 16 and up.

BY BUS

TOURMOBILE Best-known and least expensive, **Tourmobile Sightseeing** (✆ **888/868-7707** or 202/554-5100; www.tourmobile.com) is a good choice if you're looking for an easy-on/easy-off tour of major sites, especially since security concerns have made the already limited parking nearly nonexistent. The comfortable red, white, and blue sightseeing trams travel to as many as 24 attractions (the company changes its schedule and number of stops, depending on whether sites are open for public tours), including Arlington National Cemetery. Tourmobile is the only narrated sightseeing shuttle tour authorized by the National Park Service.

The company offers a number of different tours, but the most popular is the **American Heritage Tour,** which stops at 21 sites on or near the National Mall and at three sites in Arlington Cemetery. (Again, the number of stops may be fewer than 21, if regularly scheduled stops, like the White House, are not open for public tours due to increased security.) Normally, stops include the memorials and Washington Monument, Union Station, the National Gallery, most of the Smithsonian museums (National Air and Space, National Museum of Natural History, and the Arts and Industries Building/Hirshhorn Museum), the Capitol, and several other locations. In Arlington Cemetery, the bus stops at the Kennedy grave sites, the Tomb of the Unknowns, and Arlington House. You simply hop on a Tourmobile at any of the designated locations, pay the driver when you first board the bus (you can also purchase tickets at the Union Station and Washington Monument booths, or inside the Arlington National Cemetery Visitor Center, or, for a small surcharge, order your ticket in advance from Ticketmaster at ✆ **800/551-SEAT** or www.ticketmaster.com). Along the route, get off at any stop to visit monuments or buildings. When you finish exploring each area, just show your ticket and climb aboard the next Tourmobile that comes along. The buses travel in a loop, serving each stop about every 15 to 30 minutes. One fare allows you to use the buses all day. The charge for the American Heritage Tour is $25 for anyone 12 and older, $12 for children 3 to 11. For Arlington Cemetery only, those 12 and older pay $7, children $3.50. Children under 3 ride free. Buses follow circuits from the Capitol to Arlington Cemetery and back. Well-trained and personable narrators give commentaries about sights along the route and answer questions.

The trams are heated in winter, but they're not air-conditioned in summer; and though the windows stay open, they can get hot and uncomfortable. Readers also report that Tourmobiles, being the largest trams, take a long time to load and unload passengers, which can be frustrating to those anxious to see the sights.

Tourmobiles operate 9:30am to 4:30pm, daily year-round, except Christmas. (In the busy tourist season, Tourmobile sometimes extends its hours.) Call Tourmobile or visit the website for further information and rates for other tours.

OLD TOWN TROLLEY **Old Town Trolley tours** (© **202/832-9800;** www.historictours.com) offer fixed-price, on-off service as you travel in three loops around the city, with a transfer point at the Lincoln Memorial stop to go on to Arlington Cemetery, and a second transfer point at Ford's Theatre to get to Georgetown and to Washington National Cathedral. Many hotels sell tickets (see chapter 5); otherwise, you can purchase tickets online or at the Old Town Trolley Tour booths at Union Station, the D.C. Visitor Center in the Ronald Reagan Building, and many other places around town. Buses operate daily from 9am to 4:30pm, extended to 5:30pm in summer. The cost is $32 for adults, $16 for children 4 to 12, free for children under 4. You can buy tickets online in advance and at a discount, and use those e-tickets to board at any of the stops on the route. The full tour, which is narrated, takes 2 hours (if you don't get off and tour the sites, obviously), and trolleys come by every 30 minutes or so. Old Town Trolley tours cost more than Tourmobile tours, perhaps because the buses travel to neighborhoods and attractions away from the Mall.

BY BOAT

Since Washington is a river city, why not see it by boat? Potomac cruises allow sweeping vistas of the monuments and memorials, Georgetown, the Kennedy Center, and other Washington sights. Read the information below carefully, since not all boat cruises offer guided tours. Some of the following boats leave from the Washington waterfront and some from Old Town Alexandria:

Spirit of Washington Cruises, Pier 4 at 6th and Water streets SW (© **866/302-2469** or 202/554-8000; www.spiritcruises.com; Metro: Waterfront), offers a variety of trips daily, including evening dinner, lunch, brunch, and moonlight dance cruises, as well as a half-day excursion to Mount Vernon and back. Lunch and dinner cruises include a 40-minute musical revue. Prices start at $45 for a lunch excursion and $69 for a dinner cruise. Call to make reservations.

The *Spirit of Washington* is a luxury climate-controlled harbor cruise ship with carpeted decks and huge panoramic windows designed for sightseeing. There are three well-stocked bars onboard. Mount Vernon cruises are aboard an equally luxurious sister ship, the *Spirit of Washington II.*

Potomac Party Cruises (© **703/683-6076;** www.dandydinnerboat.com) operates *The Dandy* and *Nina's Dandy,* both climate-controlled, all-weather, glassed-in floating restaurants that run year-round. Lunch, evening dinner/dance, and special charter cruises are available daily. You board both vessels in Old Town Alexandria, at the Prince Street pier, between Duke and King streets. Trips range from $41 for a 2½-hour weekday lunch cruise to $89 for a 3-hour Saturday dinner cruise (not including gratuity, tax, and bar charges).

Odyssey III (✆ **866/306-2469;** www.odysseycruises.com) was designed specifically to glide under the bridges that cross the Potomac. The boat looks like a glass bullet, with its snub-nosed port and its streamlined 240-foot-long glass body. The wraparound see-through walls and ceiling allow for great views. You board the *Odyssey* at the Gangplank Marina, on Washington's waterfront, at 6th and Water streets SW (Metro: Waterfront). Cruises available include lunch, Sunday brunch, and dinner excursions, with live entertainment provided during each cruise. It costs $42 for a 2-hour weekday lunch cruise and $102 for a 3-hour Saturday dinner cruise (not including tax, gratuity, and bar charges).

The **Potomac Riverboat Company** ★ (✆ **877/511-2628** or 703/684-0580; www.potomacriverboatco.com) offers three narrated tours April through October aboard the *Matthew Hayes* or the *Miss Mallory,* on a 90-minute round-trip tour past Washington monuments and memorials; the *Admiral Tilp,* on an 80-minute round-trip tour of Old Town Alexandria's waterfront; and the *Miss Christin,* which cruises to Mount Vernon, where you hop off and reboard after you've toured the estate. You board the boats at the pier behind the Torpedo Factory in Old Town Alexandria, at the foot of King Street; or, for the Washington monuments and memorials tour, Georgetown's Washington Harbour. *Matthew Hayes/Miss Mallory* tickets are $24 for adults, $12 for children ages 2 to 12; *Admiral Tilp* tickets are $12 for adults, $6 for children ages 2 to 12; and *Miss Christin* round-trip tickets are $34 for adults, $17 for children ages 6 to 11, and include admission to Mount Vernon. A concession stand selling light refreshments and beverages is open during the cruises.

The **Capitol River Cruise**'s *Nightingale I* and *Nightingale II* (✆ **800/405-5511** or 301/460-7447; www.capitolrivercruises.com) are historic 65-foot steel riverboats that can accommodate 90 people. The *Nightingale*'s narrated jaunts depart Georgetown's Washington Harbour every hour on the hour, from noon to 9pm, April through October (the 9pm outing is offered in summer months only). The 45-minute narrated tour travels past the monuments and memorials to National Airport and back. A snack bar onboard sells light refreshments, beer, wine, and sodas; you're welcome to bring your own picnic aboard. The price is $12 per adult, $6 per child ages 3 to 12 (tickets are less if you purchase them online). To get here, take Metro to Foggy Bottom and then the Georgetown Metro Connection Shuttle or walk into Georgetown, following Pennsylvania Avenue, which becomes M Street. Turn left on 31st Street NW and follow to the Washington Harbour complex, on the water.

A BOAT ON WHEELS Old Town Trolley also operates **DC Ducks** (✆ **202/832-9800;** www.dcducks.com), which feature unique land and water tours of Washington aboard the *DUKW,* an amphibious army vehicle (boat with wheels) from World War II that accommodates 30 passengers. Ninety-minute guided tours aboard the open-air canopied craft include a land portion taking in major sights—the Capitol, Lincoln Memorial, Washington Monument, White House, and Smithsonian museums—and a 30-minute Potomac cruise. Purchase tickets inside Union Station at the information desk; board the vehicle just outside the main entrance to Union Station. Hours vary, but departures usually follow a daily 11am, 1pm, and 3pm schedule (Mar–Oct). Tickets cost $29 for adults, $14 for children 4 to 12, free for children under 4. Tickets cost less online.

BY BIKE

Bike the Sites, Inc. ★ (✆ **202/842-2453;** www.bikethesites.com) offers a more active way to see Washington, in season, from March 1 to November. The company has designed several different biking tours of the city, including the popular Capital Sites Ride, which takes you past museums, memorials, the White House, Capitol, and Supreme Court. The ride takes 3 hours, covers 7 to 8 miles, and costs $40 per adult, $30 per child 12 and under. Bike the Sites provides you with a comfort mountain bicycle fitted to your size, bike helmet, water bottle, light snack, and two guides to lead the ride. All tours start from the rear plaza, 12th Street NW side of the Old Post Office Pavilion, which is located at 1100 Pennsylvania Ave. NW (Metro: Federal Triangle, on the Blue and Orange Line). Guides impart historical and anecdotal information as you go. The company rents bikes to those who want to go their own, unnarrated way, for $7 an hour ($15 minimum) or $35 a day, including helmet, bike, lock, and pump. It also customizes guided bike rides to suit your tour specifications.

11 Outdoor Activities

For information about spectator sports venues, including how to buy tickets and where to go to watch **Washington Wizards** (men's) and **Mystics** (women's) basketball games, the **Capitals** ice hockey meets, and **Nationals** baseball games, see "Indoor Arenas & Outdoor Pavilions," in chapter 9.

But if you prefer to work up your own honest sweat, Washington offers plenty of pleasant opportunities in many lush surroundings. See "Parks & Gardens," earlier in this chapter, for complete coverage of the city's loveliest green spaces.

Joggers can enjoy a run on the Mall or along the path in Rock Creek Park.

As mentioned above, you can rent bikes from **Bike the Sites,** or from the **Boat House at Fletcher's Cove,** Reservoir and Canal roads (✆ **202/244-0461;** www.fletcherscove.com), or **Thompson's Boat Center,** 2900 Virginia Ave. at Rock Creek Parkway NW (✆ **202/333-4861** or 202/333-9543; www.thompsonboatcenter.com; Metro: Foggy Bottom, with a 10-min. walk); both Fletcher's and Thompson's rent bikes, weather permitting, from about mid-March to mid-October. At **Big Wheel Bikes,** 1034 33rd St. NW, right near the C&O Canal just below M Street (✆ **202/337-0254;** www.bigwheelbikes.com), you can rent a bike year-round, Wednesday through Sunday. If you need suggested routes or want company, check out Friday's *Washington Post* "Weekend" section, which lists cycling trips. Rock Creek Park has an **11-mile paved bike route** ★ from the Lincoln Memorial through the park into Maryland. Or you can follow the bike path from the Lincoln Memorial and go over the Memorial Bridge to pedal to Old Town Alexandria and to Mount Vernon (see chapter 10). On weekends and holidays, a large part of Rock Creek Parkway is closed to vehicular traffic. The C&O Canal and the Potomac parks, described earlier in "Parks & Gardens," also have extended bike paths. A new 7-mile path, the **Capital Crescent Trail,** takes you from Georgetown to the suburb of Bethesda, Maryland, following a former railroad track that parallels the Potomac River for part of the way and passes by old trestle bridges and pleasant residential neighborhoods.

Thompson's Boat Center and the **Boat House at Fletcher's Cove** (see above for both) rent boats following the same schedule as their bike rental season, basically March to November. Thompson's has canoes, kayaks, and rowing shells (recreational and racing), and is open for boat and bike rentals daily in season from 8am to 5pm.

Fletcher's is right on the C&O Canal, about 3¼ miles from Georgetown. In addition to renting bikes, canoes, and kayaks, Fletcher's also sells fishing licenses, bait, and tackle. Open 7am to 7pm daily in season, Fletcher's is accessible by car (west on M St. to Canal Rd.) and has plenty of free parking.

From mid-March to mid-October, weather permitting, you can rent **paddle boats** ★ on the north end of the Tidal Basin off Independence Avenue (✆ **202/479-2426;** www.tidalbasinpeddleboats.com). Four-seaters are $16 an hour; two-seaters are $8 an hour, daily from 10am to 6pm.

Washington has numerous **hiking paths.** The C&O Canal offers 185 miles stretching from D.C. to Cumberland, Maryland; Theodore Roosevelt Island has more than 88 wilderness acres to explore; and Rock Creek Park boasts 20 miles of hiking trails (maps are available at the Visitor Information Center or Park Headquarters).

If you're coming to Washington in winter, you can go **ice skating** on the C&O Canal (call ✆ **301/299-3613** for information on ice conditions), as long as you bring your own skates. For a really fun experience, head to the **National Gallery Sculpture Garden Ice Rink** ★, on the Mall at 7th Street and Constitution Avenue NW (✆ **202/289-3360**), where you can rent skates, twirl in view of the sculptures, and enjoy hot chocolate and a sandwich in the Pavilion Café, right next to the rink. Another outdoor rink where you can rent skates is **Pershing Park,** at 14th Street and Pennsylvania Avenue NW (✆ **202/737-6938**).

If it's summer and your hotel doesn't have a pool, you might consider one of the neighborhood pools, including a large outdoor pool at 25th and N streets NW (✆ **202/727-3285**) and the Georgetown outdoor pool at 34th Street and Volta Place NW (✆ **202/282-2366**). Keep in mind that these are likely to be crowded.

Tennis lovers will have a hard time finding public courts in Washington. **East Potomac Park** (✆ **202/554-5962**) has 24 tennis courts (10 clay, 14 hard courts), 3 illuminated at night, and 5 indoor courts; the park rents rackets, as well. Fees vary with court surface and time of play. **Montrose Park,** right next to Dumbarton Oaks (p. 229) in Georgetown, has several courts available free on a first-come, first-served basis; but they're often in use.

8

Shopping

Nothing reveals the personality of a city better than a survey of its shopping scene. A handy little search tool on the *Washington Post* website's City Guide page, www.washingtonpost.com/cityguide, allows one to browse its list of some 600 D.C. stores, then sort them into categories, from beauty to shoe stores. The guide, though not comprehensive, is sufficiently extensive and up-to-date to reveal some rather interesting facts: that women's clothing stores score the highest number (127), with home and garden furnishings shops coming in second (125), gift stores third (100), beauty shops (including spas and hair salons) fourth (96), and bookstores in fifth place (60).

What does that tell you? Washington women are successful and understand that fashionable dress, coiffure, and makeup are all part of that package; that Washingtonians take care to decorate their house and garden, which is in line with the idea that we entertain a lot; that gift giving is a part of the culture, for those who live here as well as for the city's many visitors buying take-home purchases; and, last but not least, that we are a wonky and well-read bunch. All true.

(And what must one make of the fact that men's clothing stores number only 50? The obvious, I'm afraid: that Washington men, successful though they may be, are not quite hip to the concept of looking the part.)

This chapter should enlighten you further. Not only do we have many women's clothing stores, but they are of every type, haute couture to preppie. Our furnishings stores represent global designs. Best of all, perhaps, are the beloved homegrown shops of resident entrepreneurs, from the Zenith art gallery in the Penn Quarter, to Alex, a contemporary clothing store featuring creations of international and local designers and some vintage fashions, in Foggy Bottom.

Note: Most of the stores listed are located within the District, although I do include some suburban suggestions, for malls, department stores, and other notable shops, that lie outside the city.

1 The Shopping Scene

Most Washington-area stores are open from 10am to 5 or 6pm Monday through Saturday. Sunday hours tend to vary, with some stores opting not to open at all and others with shorter hours of noon to 5 or 6pm. Two neighborhoods prove the exception to these rules: Many stores in the Penn Quarter and in Georgetown keep later hours and are also open on Sunday. One example is the downtown Macy's department store (p. 260), in the heart of Penn Quarter, whose hours are noon to 6pm Sunday; 10am to 8pm Monday, Thursday, and Friday; 9am to 9pm Tuesday; and 9am to 10pm Wednesday and Saturday. Other exceptions include suburban shopping malls, which are open late nightly, and antiques stores and art galleries, which tend to keep their own hours. Be safe and call ahead if there's a store you really want to get to.

Sales tax on merchandise is 5.75% in the District, 5% in Maryland, and 4.5% in Virginia. Most gift, arts, and crafts stores, including those at the Smithsonian museums, will handle shipping for you; clothing stores generally do not.

2 Great Shopping Areas

UNION STATION It's a railroad station, a historic landmark, an architectural marvel, a Metro stop, and a shopping mall. Yes, the beauteous Union Station offers some fine shopping opportunities; it's certainly the best on Capitol Hill, with more than 100 clothes and specialty shops, and more than 40 eateries. Metro: Union Station.

PENN QUARTER The area bounded east and west by 7th and 14th streets NW, and north and south by New York and Pennsylvania avenues NW, is in a frenzy of development. The latest buzz comes from the opening of a multiuse complex, **Gallery Place,** at 7th and H streets, in the heart of Chinatown, backing up to the Verizon Center and overtopping the Chinatown/Gallery Place Metro stop. Gallery Place combines condominiums, offices, a bowling alley/bar, a 14-screen theater, stores that range from Urban Outfitters to Aveda, and several restaurants. Elsewhere in the neighborhood you'll find a long list of "name" stores, such as Banana Republic, Ann Taylor, H&M, Jos. A. Bank Clothiers, and Filene's Basement; and one-of-a-kind places, such as Apartment Zero and Olsson's Books. Look for the huge Borders bookstore at 14th and F streets NW, in the grand old Garfinckel's Building. Macy's (formerly known as "Hecht's"), at 12th and G streets, continues as the sole department store downtown. Metro: Metro Center, Chinatown/Gallery Place, or Archives/Navy Memorial.

ADAMS-MORGAN Centered on 18th Street and Columbia Road NW, Adams-Morgan is a neighborhood of ethnic eateries and nightclubs interspersed with the odd secondhand bookshop and eclectic collectibles stores. It's a fun area for walking and shopping. Parking is possible during the day but impossible at night. For the closest Metro, you have a few choices: Woodley Park–Zoo/Adams-Morgan, then walk south on Connecticut Avenue NW until you reach Calvert Street, cross Connecticut Avenue, and follow Calvert Street across the Duke Ellington Memorial Bridge until you reach the junction of Columbia Road NW and 18th Street NW. Sunday through Friday evenings and all day Saturday, you can catch the no. 98 Adams-Morgan–U Street Link shuttle bus, which loops between the Woodley Park and the African-American Civil War Memorial/Cardozo (at 13th and U sts. NW) Metro stations, departing every 15 minutes from each location, traveling along 18th Street in the heart of Adams-Morgan, where you can hop off; it costs only 25¢. Second choice: Dupont Circle; exit at Q Street NW and walk up Connecticut Avenue NW to Columbia Road NW.

CONNECTICUT AVENUE/DUPONT CIRCLE Running from the mini–Wall Street that is K Street north to S Street, Connecticut Avenue NW is a main thoroughfare, where you'll find traditional clothing at Brooks Brothers, Talbots, Ann Taylor, and Burberry's; casual duds at the Gap; discount items at Filene's Basement and the Ann Taylor Loft; and haute couture at Rizik's. Closer to Dupont Circle are coffee bars and neighborhood restaurants, as well as art galleries; funky boutiques; gift, stationery, book, and record shops; and stores with a gay and lesbian slant. Metro: Farragut North at one end, Dupont Circle at the other.

U STREET CORRIDOR/14TH STREET Urbanistas have been promoting this neighborhood for years, but now the number of cool shops, restaurants, and bars has

Finds The Roads Less Traveled: A Back-Street Tour of Historic Georgetown, with Stops at Shops

Most people who visit Georgetown never get off the beaten track of the M Street/lower Wisconsin Avenue axis. Too bad for them, but good for you: While they bump into each other in the crowded bottom of Georgetown, you can tour the lovely, quiet streets in upper Georgetown, where a number of historic houses and beautiful gardens lie close to fun boutiques and delectable cafes. Consider this less-traveled route. (See the color map on the last page of the color insert at the front of the book.)

Tudor Place, Dumbarton House, and the garden at Dumbarton Oaks are open for tours, but not every day, so call for hours if you want to incorporate house and garden tours in your back-street stroll; please note that all other houses on the tour are privately owned and not open to the public.

From the corner of Q Street and Wisconsin Avenue (a stop on the Metro Connection Shuttle's Wisconsin Avenue line), walk east along Q Street to 31st Street and take a left on 31st Street to **Tudor Place** (**✆ 202/965-0400**), an 1816 mansion and gardens where Martha Washington's descendants lived until 1984. From Tudor Place, return to Q Street and walk farther east to no. 2715, **Dumbarton House** (**✆ 202/337-2288**), a Federal-style mansion built in 1805 and filled with 18th- and 19th-century furnishings and decorative arts.

Retrace your steps as far as 28th Street and proceed north on 28th Street, stopping to admire the 18th-century estate **Evermay,** built by a Scottish merchant, as you continue on your way to **Dumbarton Oaks Garden** (p. 229; **✆ 202/339-6401**) at 31st and R streets. From the garden, walk westward on R Street to Wisconsin Avenue, passing en route **3238 R St. NW,** an early-19th-century Federal brick building once used as a summer White House by President Ulysses S. Grant—its high elevation made it cooler than 1600 Pennsylvania Ave.

You have now reached Wisconsin Avenue, just a little farther north of the hustle-bustle, but a sweet spot for shopping at one-of-a-kind shops and for enjoying a scrumptious repast. Turn south on Wisconsin Avenue to find Italian

hit the critical mass mark, winning the area widespread notice. If you shun brand names and box stores, you'll love the boutiques along U and 14th streets. Look for provocative handles, like Go Mama Go! and Pulp, then step inside to inspect their equally intriguing merchandise. Metro: U St./African-American Civil War Memorial/Cardozo.

GEORGETOWN Georgetown is the city's main shopping area. In the heart of the neighborhood, stores line Wisconsin Avenue and M Street NW, and they also fan out along side streets. (For a tour of Georgetown that combines historic houses, shopping, and dining, see "The Roads Less Traveled," above.) You'll find both chain and one-of-a-kind shops, chic as well as thrift. Sidewalks and streets are almost always crowded, and parking can be tough. Weekends, especially, bring out all kinds of yahoos, who and French home and garden accessories at **Amano** (no. 1677, ✆ **202/298-7200**), beautiful stationery at **Rooms with a View** (no. 1661, ✆ **202/625-0610**), and a variety of women's trendy clothing boutiques at **Sugar** (no. 1633, ✆ **202/333-5331**), **Sassanova** (no. 1641, ✆ **202/471-4400**), **Sherman Pickey** (no. 1647, ✆ **202/333-4212**), and **Urban Chic** (no. 1626, ✆ **202/338-5398**). In the middle of the block is **Patisserie Poupon** (✆ **202/342-3248**)—I highly recommend that you pause for a ham-and-cheese sandwich and, *absolument,* for a pastry dessert: Choose from tarts, éclairs, individual little cakes, and chocolate in all its forms.

Cross Wisconsin Avenue to continue your tour on the other side. Walk south on Wisconsin Avenue to N Street and turn right, following the street to **no. 3307,** the brick town house where John and Jacqueline Kennedy lived when Kennedy was a U.S. senator. In the same block, a few houses up at **nos. 3327–3339,** are five charming houses known collectively as **"Cox's Row,"** for owner John Cox, who built the dwellings in 1817. Cox, who was the first elected mayor of Georgetown, lived at no. 3339; Revolutionary War hero the Marquis de Lafayette stayed at no. 3337 on a visit in 1824. Follow N Street to 36th Street, and turn left and again left on Prospect Street to reach **Prospect House,** at no. 3508. This restored Georgian-style house was built in 1788 by Revolutionary War hero and wealthy tobacco merchant James McCubbin Lingan; the house, like the street, was named for the views one once had here of the Potomac River. From here, it's a short stroll to **Halcyon House,** at 3400 Prospect St., whose original owner, Benjamin Stoddert, was a Revolutionary War cavalry officer and first secretary of the navy. Two hundred years ago, the Potomac River lapped right up to Stoddert's terraced garden, designed by Pierre L'Enfant.

If you still have some energy left, finish the tour by visiting a Washington hot spot, the **Café Milano,** 3251 Prospect St. NW (✆ **202/333-6183**). Then go home knowing that you've seen more of the "real" Georgetown than most Washingtonians.

are mainly here to drink. Visit Georgetown on a weekday morning, if you can. Weeknights are another good time to visit, for dinner and strolling afterward. Metro: Foggy Bottom, then catch the bright blue Georgetown Metro Connection bus, which runs every 10 minutes, takes only a few minutes to reach Georgetown, and costs 35¢ with a Metrorail transfer, or $1.50 without a transfer. Metro buses (the no. 30 series: 30, 32, 34, 35, 36) travel through Georgetown from different parts of the city. Or catch the D.C. Circulator bus (see chapter 4 for more information), which costs just $1 to board. Otherwise, consider taking a taxi. If you drive, you'll find parking lots expensive and tickets even more so, so be careful where you plant your car.

UPPER WISCONSIN AVENUE NORTHWEST In a residential section of town known as Friendship Heights on the D.C. side and Chevy Chase on the Maryland side (7 miles north of Georgetown, straight up Wisconsin Ave.) is a quarter-mile shopping district that extends from Saks Fifth Avenue at one end to Sur La Table at the other. In between are Lord & Taylor, Neiman Marcus, Bloomingdale's, Banana Republic, Jimmy Choo, Christian Dior, Barney's Co-Op, Polo, Tiffany's, Versace, and two malls (the Mazza Gallerie and the Chevy Chase Pavilion). The street is too wide and traffic always too snarled to make this a pleasant place to stroll, although teenagers do love to loiter here. Drive if you want and park in the garages beneath the Mazza Gallerie or the Chevy Chase Pavilion. Or take the Metro; the strip is right on the Red Line, with the "Friendship Heights" exits leading directly into each of the malls and into Bloomingdale's.

OLD TOWN ALEXANDRIA Old Town, a Virginia neighborhood beyond National Airport, resembles Georgetown in its picturesque location on the Potomac, historic-home lined streets, and plentiful shops and restaurants, as well as in its less desirable aspects: heavy traffic, crowded sidewalks, difficult parking. Old Town extends from the Potomac River in the east to the King Street Metro station in the west, and from about 1st Street in the north to Green Street in the south, but the best shopping is in the center, where King and Washington streets intersect. Weekdays are a lot tamer than weekends. It's always a nice place to visit, though; the drive alone is worth the trip. See chapter 10 for full coverage of Alexandria. Metro: King Street, then take a blue and gold DASH bus (free weekends, otherwise the fare is $1) to reach the heart of Old Town.

3 Shopping A to Z

ANTIQUES

A few miles north of the city is not too far to go for the good deal or true bonanza you're likely to discover on **Antique Row.** Some 40 antiques and collectible shops line Howard Avenue, on either side of Connecticut Avenue, in Kensington, Maryland, offering every sort of item in a wide variety of styles, periods, and prices. If you don't drive or taxi, you'll have to take the Metro and two buses. From Dupont Circle, board an L2 bus and get a transfer from the driver. Ask him to tell you when you reach the transfer point for the L8 bus. Once there, board the L8 bus and ask to be let off at Connecticut and Knowles avenues. Howard Avenue is 1 block north of Knowles. For antiques in D.C. and Alexandria, try these:

Brass Knob Architectural Antiques When old homes and office buildings are demolished in the name of progress, these savvy salvage merchants spirit away salable treasures, from lots and lots of light fixtures and chandelier glass to wrought-iron fencing. 2311 18th St. NW. ✆ **202/332-3370.** www.thebrassknob.com. Metro: Woodley Park or Dupont Circle. A second location near Capitol Hill stocks old house parts: the **Brass Knob's Back Doors Warehouse,** 57 N St. NW (at First St. NW) (✆ **202/265-0587**).

Cherry This is an antiques store, all right, but as its name suggests, a little offbeat. Expect affordable eclectic furnishings and decorative arts, and lots of mirrors and sconces. 1526 Wisconsin Ave. NW. ✆ **202/342-3600.** www.cherryantiques.com. Metro: Foggy Bottom, then walk or take the Georgetown Metro Connection shuttle or the D.C. Circulator.

Cherub Antiques Gallery The Cherub Antiques Gallery specializes in Art Nouveau and Art Deco; signed Tiffany, Steuben, Lalique, and Gallé pieces; Liberty arts and crafts; and Louis Icart etchings. 2918 M St. NW. ✆ **202/337-2224.** www.trocadero.com/cherubgallery. Metro: Foggy Bottom, then take the Georgetown Metro Connection shuttle or the D.C. Circulator.

Gore-Dean This store grows ever bigger, the better to accommodate an expanding inventory that runs from furnishings and fabrics (some American pieces, but mostly 18th- and 19th-century European furnishings) to decorative accessories, paintings, prints, and porcelains. Includes a lampshade shop, garden shop, and framing studio. 3338 M St. NW. ✆ **202/625-9199.** www.goredean.com. Metro: Foggy Bottom, then take the Georgetown Metro Connection or D.C. Circulator.

Marston-Luce Stop in here at least to admire, if not buy, a beautiful 18th- or 19th-century French furnishing or two. 1651 Wisconsin Ave. NW. ✆ **202/333-6800.** Metro: Foggy Bottom, then take the Georgetown Metro Connection or D.C. Circulator.

Millennium Decorative Arts This is antiques shopping for the TV generation, where anything made between the 1930s and the 1970s is considered collectible. The shop works with nearly a score or so of dealers; stock changes weekly. Funky wares run from Bakelite to Heywood-Wakefield blond-wood beauties to toasters to used drinking glasses. Call for hours, since the shop tends to be open only on weekends. 1528 U St. NW. ✆ **202/483-1218.** www.millenniumdecorativearts.com. Metro: U St.–Cardozo.

Old Print Gallery Open since 1971, this gallery carries original American and European prints from the 17th to the 19th century, including political cartoons, maps, and historical documents. It's one of the largest antique print and map shops in the United States. Prices range from $45 to $10,000. 1220 31st St. NW. ✆ **202/965-1818.** www.oldprintgallery.com. Metro: Foggy Bottom, then take the Georgetown Metro Connection or D.C. Circulator.

Susquehanna Antiques This is Georgetown's largest collection of fine American, English, and European furniture, paintings, and garden items of the late 18th and early 19th centuries. The shop is nearly 100 years old. 3216 O St. NW. ✆ **202/333-1511.** www.susquehannaantiques.com. Metro: Foggy Bottom, then take the Georgetown Metro Connection or D.C. Circulator.

ART GALLERIES

Art galleries abound in Washington, but especially in the Dupont Circle, Georgetown, and Penn Quarter neighborhoods.

DUPONT CIRCLE

For all galleries listed below, the closest Metro stop is Dupont Circle. If you're in town the first Friday of the month, don't miss the Dupont Circle gallery walk, free and open to the public, 6 to 8pm.

David Adamson Gallery This gallery showcases digital printmaking and photography and the works of contemporary artists, like local Kevin MacDonald, as well as national and international artists Jim Dine, Chuck Close, and William Wegman. ***Note:*** Three other galleries are located in this same building, including **Hemphill** (✆ **202/234-5601;** www.hemphillfinearts.com), devoted to contemporary art and exhibits of socially relevant, historically significant import. The location is actually on the very outskirts of Dupont Circle; follow P Street east about 5 blocks until you reach 14th Street. 1515 14th St. NW. ✆ **202/232-0707.** www.adamsongallery.com.

Spectrum Gallery Spectrum moved from Georgetown to this new location in June 2006. A cooperative venture since 1966, the gallery's 30 professional Washington-area artists include painters, potters, sculptors, photographers, collagists, and printmakers, all of whom share in shaping gallery policy, maintenance, and operation. The art is reasonably priced. 1421 22nd St. NW (at P St.). ✆ **202/833-1616.** www.spectrumgallery.org.

Studio Gallery This artist-owned gallery—the longest-running of its kind in the area—shows the works of some 37 local and professional artists, fine arts in all media. Don't miss the sculpture garden. 2108 R St. NW. ✆ **202/232-8734.** www.studiogallerydc.com.

GEORGETOWN

For all the galleries listed below, the closest Metro stop is Foggy Bottom; from there, you can walk, hop on the D.C. Circulator bus, or transfer to the Georgetown Metro Connection bus to get you the rest of the way.

Addison/Ripley Fine Art This gallery represents both nationally and regionally recognized artists, from the 19th century to the present; works include paintings, sculpture, photography, and fine arts. 1670 Wisconsin Ave. NW. ✆ **202/338-5180.** www.addisonripleyfineart.com.

Govinda Gallery This place, a block from the campus of Georgetown University, generates a lot of media coverage, since it often shows artwork created by famous names and features photographs of celebrities. 1227 34th St. NW. ✆ **202/333-1180.** www.govindagallery.com.

Guarisco Gallery, Ltd. Its display of 19th- and early-20th-century paintings, watercolors, and sculptures by the likes of Camille Pissarro, T. Robinson, and H. Lebasque make this gallery as much a museum as a shop. 2828 Pennsylvania Ave. NW (in the courtyard of the Four Seasons Hotel). ✆ **202/333-8533.** www.guariscogallery.com.

7TH STREET ARTS CORRIDOR

A couple of these galleries predate the renaissance taking place in this downtown neighborhood. To get here, take the Metro to either Archives/Navy Memorial (Blue–Orange Line) or Gallery Place/Chinatown/Verizon Center (Red–Yellow Line).

Flashpoint Flashpoint is a dance studio, theater lab, office space, and art gallery all in one. Its art gallery is dedicated to nurturing emerging local artists, who tend to use a variety of media, including video, sculpture, photography, and drawings to tell their personal stories. 916 G St. NW. ✆ **202/315-1305.** www.flashpointdc.org.

Touchstone Gallery The first floor of this historic building houses Apartment Zero, a stylish contemporary furniture and design store, well worth a visit on its own merits. Then head upstairs to the second floor to find **Touchstone,** whose 16-foot-high ceilings and spacious rooms form the backdrop for a self-run co-op studio for 35 to 40 contemporary artists, each of whom has at least one work on display at all times. 406 7th St. NW (between D and E sts.). ✆ **202/347-2787;** www.touchstonegallery.com.

Zenith Gallery Across the street from Touchstone is the 30-year-old Zenith, which exhibits diverse works by contemporary artists, most American, about half of whom are local. You can get a good deal here, paying anywhere from $50 to $50,000 for a piece. Among the things you'll find are annual humor shows, neon exhibits, realism, abstract expressionism, and landscapes. Browse the gift shop for artistic housewares and clever jewelry. 413 7th St. NW. ✆ **202/783-2963.** www.zenithgallery.com.

BEAUTY

Georgetown is the hot spot for the best hair salons and cosmetic stores, while spas are more evenly scattered throughout the city. Here's a sampling of some of the best places to go for beauty treatments and products.

Blue Mercury Half "apothecary," half spa, this chain's two D.C. locations offer a full selection of facial, massage, waxing, and makeup treatments, as well as a smorgasbord of high-end beauty products, from Acqua di Parma fragrances to Kiehl's skincare line. Very popular, so you might want to call in advance of your trip. Georgetown: 3059 M St. NW. ✆ **202/965-1300.** www.bluemercury.com. Metro: Foggy Bottom, then take the Georgetown Metro Connection shuttle. Dupont Circle: 1619 Connecticut Ave. NW ✆ **202/462-1300.** Metro: Dupont Circle.

The Grooming Lounge Not your father's barber shop. Famous for its 30-minute "hot lather shave," The Grooming Lounge also dispenses treatments with names like "The Commander in Chief" and sells beauty accessories, um, I mean, grooming tools, from nail clippers to special shaving brushes. Or you can just get a haircut. 1745 L St. NW. ✆ **202/466-8900.** www.groominglounge.com. Metro: Farragut North or Farragut West.

Okyo Beauty Salon This is probably D.C.'s most popular hair salon, known as much for its celebrity clientele as for its fantastic cuts and coloring. Expect high prices and a tight schedule. 2903 M St. NW. ✆ **202/342-2675.** www.okyosalon.com. Metro: Foggy Bottom, then take the Georgetown Metro Connection shuttle.

SomaFit If your hotel doesn't have a fitness center or spa, visit this ultracool, one-stop-spot for a workout, massage, yoga class, pedicure, facial—whatever your little body needs or desires. This is not a membership facility, so all you have to do is call or check online for a class schedule, and just show up (only a handful of classes require that you reserve a space in advance); or call to schedule a spa treatment. 2121 Wisconsin Ave. NW. ✆ **202/965-2121.** www.somafit.com. Metro: Foggy Bottom, then take the Georgetown Metro Connection shuttle; or hop on the D.C. Circulator bus.

BOOKS

Washingtonians are readers, so bookstores constantly pop up throughout the city. An increasingly competitive market means that chain bookstores do a brisk business, even though D.C. can claim more general-interest, independent bookstores than any other city. Here are some favorite bookstores in general, used, and special-interest categories.

GENERAL

Barnes & Noble This three-story shop in Georgetown is well-stocked in all genres, including sizable software, travel-book, children's-title, and music sections. The store has a cafe on the second level. 3040 M St. NW. ✆ **202/965-9880.** www.barnesandnoble.com. Metro: Foggy Bottom, then take the Georgetown Metro Connection shuttle. Other area locations include 555 12th St. NW (✆ **202/347-0176**) and 4801 Bethesda Ave., in Bethesda, MD (✆ **301/986-1761**).

B. Dalton This all-purpose bookstore is heavy on the bestsellers and carries magazines, too. Union Station. ✆ **202/289-1724.** www.barnesandnoble.com. Metro: Union Station.

Borders With its overwhelming array of books, records, videos, and magazines, Borders competes neck and neck with Barnes & Noble. Many hardcover bestsellers are 30% off. 1800 L St. NW. ✆ **202/466-4999.** www.borders.com. Metro: Farragut North. Other Borders stores in the District include 600 14th St. NW (✆ **202/737-1385**) and 5333 Wisconsin Ave. NW (✆ **202/686-8270**), in upper northwest D.C.

Bridge Street Books A small, serious shop specializing in politics, poetry, literature, history, philosophy, and publications you won't find elsewhere. Bestsellers and discounted books are not its specialty. 2814 Pennsylvania Ave. NW (next to the Four Seasons Hotel). ✆ **202/965-5200.** Metro: Foggy Bottom, then take the Georgetown Metro Connection shuttle.

Chapters: A Literary Bookstore Chapters celebrates its 23rd anniversary in 2008 and continues to concentrate on selling new and backlisted fiction. The store hosts regular events, such as its "Dejeuner du Mercredi" gatherings of Francophiles every Wednesday at noon for French chitchat, and author readings by the likes of Michael Cunningham and Ann Hood. Tea is always available, and on Friday afternoons they break out the sherry and cookies. 445 11th St. NW (inside building at 1001 Pennsylvania Ave.). ✆ **202/737-5553.** www.chaptersliterary.com. Metro: Archives/Navy Memorial, or Metro Center, 11th St. exit.

Kramerbooks & Afterwords Café *Finds* Opened in 1976, Kramer's was the first bookstore/cafe in Washington, maybe in this country, and has launched countless romances. It's jammed, is often noisy, stages live music Wednesday through Saturday evenings, and is open all night weekends. Paperback fiction takes up most of its inventory, but the store carries a little of everything. 1517 Connecticut Ave. NW. ✆ **202/387-1400.** www.kramers.com. Metro: Dupont Circle, Q St. exit.

Olsson's Books and Records This 36-year-old independent, quality bookstore chain tends toward literary tomes rather than the trashy stuff, and employs helpful staff who know what they're talking about and will order books they don't have in stock. Some discounts are given on books, tapes, and CDs, and their regular prices are pretty good, too.

Besides this 7th Street NW store, there is one other Olsson's bookstore in the District at 1307 19th St. NW (✆ 202/785-1133). In the suburbs are four other Olsson's: in Old Town Alexandria, Virginia, at 106 S. Union St. (✆ 703/684-0077); in Arlington, Virginia, at 2111 Wilson Blvd. (✆ 703/525-4227) and at 2200-G Crystal Dr. (✆ 703/413-8121); and at National Airport (✆ 703/417-1087). The stores on 7th Street and in Alexandria each have a creditable cafe, known for its loungy atmosphere, made-in-house selections, and artistic crowd. 418 7th St. NW. (✆ **202/638-7610**). www.olssons.com. Metro: Gallery Place or Archives/Navy Memorial.

Politics and Prose Bookstore Located a few miles north of downtown in a residential area, this much-cherished two-story shop may be worth going out of your way for. It has vast offerings in literary fiction and nonfiction alike and an excellent children's department. The store has expanded again and again over the years to accommodate its clientele's love of books; its most recent enlargement added to the travel and children's sections. The shop hosts author readings nearly every night of the year. A warm, knowledgeable staff will help you find what you need. Downstairs is a cozy coffeehouse. Staff-recommended books are 20% off; otherwise, discounts are available only to members. 5015 Connecticut Ave. NW. ✆ **202/364-1919.** www.politics-prose.com. Metro: Van Ness–UDC, and walk, or transfer to an "L" bus to take you the ¾ mile from there.

Trover Shop This family-owned and -operated shop is close to 50 years old and is the only general-interest bookstore on Capitol Hill; specializations include Capitol Hill treatises (where else can you find the Directory to Congress?), political selections, magazines, and Washington Nationals merchandise. The store discounts 30% on the *Washington Post* hardcover fiction and nonfiction bestsellers. 221 Pennsylvania Ave. SE. ✆ **202/547-BOOK.** www.trover.com. Metro: Capitol South.

OLD & USED BOOKS

Second Story Books If it's old, out of print, custom bound, or a small-press publication, this is where to find it. The store also specializes in used CDs and vinyl and has an interesting collection of antique French and American advertising posters. 2000 P St. NW. ✆ **202/659-8884.** www.secondstorybooks.com. Metro: Dupont Circle.

SPECIAL-INTEREST BOOKS

American Institute of Architects Bookstore This store is geared toward architects, selling mostly theory and history books, although it does carry some coffee-table architectural photograph books and some gifts. 1735 New York Ave. NW. ✆ **202/626-7475.** www.aia.org. Metro: Farragut West.

Back Stage Books and Costumes Back Stage is headquarters for Washington's theatrical community, which buys its books, scripts, trades, and sheet music here. It's also a favorite costume-rental shop. 545 8th St. SE. ✆ **202/544-5744.** www.backstagebooks.com. Metro: Eastern Market.

Candida's World of Books Here you'll find books, language learning materials, and travel guides, in 15 languages, catering to D.C.'s international population and those who visit. 1541 14th St. NW. ✆ **202/667-4811.** www.candidasworldofbooks.com. Metro: Dupont Circle or U St. Cardozo, with a 4- or 5-block walk from either station. (Call for more exact info or check the website.)

Franz Bader Bookstore This store stocks books on art, art history, architecture, and photography, as well as exhibition catalogs. 1911 I St. NW. ✆ **202/337-5440.** Metro: Farragut West or Farragut North.

Lambda Rising This gay and lesbian bookstore in the heart of the Dupont Circle neighborhood is the unofficial headquarters for the gay/lesbian/bisexual community, carrying every gay, lesbian, bisexual, and transgender book in print, as well as videos, music, and gifts. 1625 Connecticut Ave. NW. ✆ **202/462-6969.** www.lambdarising.com. Metro: Dupont Circle, Q St. exit.

Reiter's Bookstore This independent bookstore in the middle of the George Washington University campus is one of the leading scientific, technical, medical, and professional bookshops in the area. It's a great place to stumble into, even if you're not scientifically inclined, because it also has a fine children's science section, some amusing mathematical and scientific toys, and humorous T-shirts ("Hey You, Get Out of the Gene Pool!"). 2021 K St. NW. ✆ **202/223-3327.** www.reiters.com. Metro: Foggy Bottom.

CAMERAS & FILM DEVELOPING

Penn Camera Exchange Penn Camera has been owned and operated by the Zweig family since 1953; its staff is quite knowledgeable, and its inventory wide-ranging. Their specialty is quality equipment and archival paper processing—not cheap, but worth it. 840 E St. NW. ✆ **202/347-5777.** www.penncamera.com. Metro: Gallery Place or Metro Center. Also at 1015 18th St. NW (✆ **202/785-7366**).

Ritz Camera Centers Ritz sells camera equipment for the average photographer and offers 1-hour film processing. Call for other locations; there are many throughout the area. 1029 Connecticut Ave. NW. ✆ **202/659-8430.** www.ritzcamera.com. Metro: Dupont Circle.

CRAFTS

A mano Owner Adam Mahr frequently forages in Europe and returns with the unique handmade, imported French and Italian ceramics, linens, and other decorative accessories for home and garden that you'll covet here. 1677 Wisconsin Ave. NW. ✆ **202/298-7200.** www.amano.bz. Metro: Foggy Bottom, then take the Georgetown Metro Connection shuttle or board the D.C. Circulator.

Appalachian Spring Country comes to Georgetown. This store sells pottery, jewelry, newly made pieced and appliqué quilts, stuffed dolls and animals, candles, rag rugs, handblown glassware, an incredible collection of kaleidoscopes, glorious weavings, and wooden kitchenware. Everything is made by hand in the United States. 1415 Wisconsin Ave. NW (at P St.). ✆ **202/337-5780.** Metro: Foggy Bottom, then take the Georgetown Metro Connection shuttle or D.C. Circulator. There's another branch in Union Station (✆ **202/682-0505**).

Go Mama Go! *Finds* Owner and globe trekker Noi Chudnoff brings pieces of the world home to sell in her shop (things like Italian glassware, Dutch art, Pennsylvania tableware, and Czech crystal). 1809 14th St. NW (at S St.). ✆ **202/299-0850.** www.gomamago.com. Metro: U St.–Cardozo.

Indian Craft Shop *Finds* The Indian Craft Shop has represented authentic Native American artisans since 1938, selling their hand-woven rugs and handcrafted baskets, jewelry, figurines, paintings, pottery, and other items. Since the shop is situated inside a federal government building, you must pass through security and show a photo ID to enter. Use the C Street entrance, which is the only one open to the public. The shop is open weekdays and the third Saturday of each month. Department of the Interior, 1849 C St. NW, Room 1043. ✆ **202/208-4056.** www.indiancraftshop.com. Metro: Farragut West, with a bit of a walk from the station.

The Phoenix Around since 1955, the Phoenix still sells those embroidered Mexican peasant blouses popular in hippie days; high-end Mexican folk and fine art; handcrafted sterling silver jewelry from Mexico and all over the world; clothing in natural fibers from Mexican and American designers like Eileen Fisher and Flax; collectors' quality masks; and decorative doodads in tin, brass, copper, and wood. 1514 Wisconsin Ave. NW. ✆ **202/338-4404.** www.thephoenixdc.com. Metro: Foggy Bottom, then take the Georgetown Metro Connection shuttle or D.C. Circulator.

Torpedo Factory Art Center Once a munitions factory, this three-story building built in 1918 now houses more than 84 working studios and the works of about 165 artists, who tend to their crafts before your very eyes, pausing to explain their techniques or to sell their pieces. Artworks include paintings, sculpture, ceramics, glasswork, and textiles. 105 N. Union St., Alexandria. ✆ **703/838-4565.** www.torpedofactory.org. Metro: King St., then take the DASH bus (AT2, AT5) eastbound to the waterfront.

DISCOUNT SHOPPING

Discount shops in Washington are few and far between, with a few notable exceptions listed below. Also check out the listing of flea markets, later in this section.

Filene's Basement *Value* Its reign might be over in Boston, but Filene's is still going strong in Washington, selling designer and famous-name clothes and accessories, as well as home furnishings. 1133 Connecticut Ave. NW, Midtown. ✆ **202/872-8430.** www.filenesbasement.com. Metro: Farragut North. Also at 529 14th St. NW, in the National Press Bldg. (✆ **202/638-4110**), and in the Mazza Gallerie in upper northwest Washington, 5300 Wisconsin Ave. NW (✆ **202/966-0208**).

Potomac Mills Mall *Value* When you're stuck in the traffic that always clogs this section of I-95, you may wonder if a trip to Potomac Mills is worth it. Believe it or not, this is one of the most popular tourist attractions in the Washington area; it's one of the largest indoor outlet malls around, with more than 220 shops such as Old Navy Outlet, Nordstrom RACK, and Polo Ralph Lauren. A huge IKEA store, which used to anchor the mall, has seceded, moving to its separate location across the street from Potomac Mills. 30 miles south on I-95 in Prince William, VA. Call ✆ **703/496-9301** for information about Potomac Mills. www.potomacmills.com. Accessible by car, or by shuttle bus (weekdays only) from the Franconia/Springfield Metro station, at the end of the Blue line in Northern Virginia.

THRIFT/CONSIGNMENT/SECONDHAND SHOPS

Christ Child Opportunity Shop *Value* Proceeds from sales go to children's charities. Here you'll find the usual thrift-shop jumble of jewelry, antiques, and collectibles—odds and ends. Most merchandise is left on consignment; if you know antiques, you might find bargains in jewelry, silver, china, quilts, and other items. 1427 Wisconsin Ave. NW (at P St.). ✆ **202/333-6635.** Metro: Foggy Bottom, then take the Georgetown Metro Connection shuttle or D.C. Circulator.

Secondhand Rose *Value* This upscale second-floor consignment shop specializes in designer merchandise. Creations by Chanel, Armani, Donna Karan, Calvin Klein, Yves Saint-Laurent, Ungaro, Ralph Lauren, and others are sold at about a third of the original price. A stunning Scaasi black-velvet and yellow-satin ball gown might go for $400 (from $1,200 new); Yves Saint-Laurent pumps in perfect condition can be had for as little as $45. Everything is in style, in season, and in excellent condition. Secondhand Rose is also a great place to shop for gorgeous furs, designer shoes and bags, and costume jewelry. 1516 Wisconsin Ave. NW (between P St. and Volta Place). ✆ **202/337-3378.** Metro: Foggy Bottom, then take the Georgetown Metro Connection shuttle.

Secondi Inc. On the second floor of a building right above Starbucks is this high-style consignment shop that sells women's clothing and accessories, including designer suits, evening wear, and more casual items—everything from Kate Spade to Chanel. 1702 Connecticut Ave. NW (between R St. and Florida Ave.). ✆ **202/667-1122.** www.secondi.com. Metro: Dupont Circle.

FARMER'S & FLEA MARKETS

Alexandria Farmers' Market The oldest continuously operating farmers' market in the country (since 1752), this market offers locally grown fruits and vegetables, along with delectable baked goods, cut flowers, and plants. Open year-round, Saturday mornings from 5 to 10am. 301 King St. (at Market Square in front of the city hall), in Alexandria. ✆ **703/838-4770.** Metro: King St., then take the free-on-weekends DASH bus (AT2, AT5) eastbound to Market Square.

Dupont Circle FreshFarm Market *Kids* At least 30 local farmers sell their flowers, produce, eggs, and cheeses here. The market also features kids' activities and guest appearances by chefs and owners of some of Washington's best restaurants: Bis, Montmartre, and 1789. Held Sundays rain or shine, year-round, from 10am to 1pm January through March and 9am to 1pm, the rest of the year. The FreshFarm Market organization stages other farmers markets on other days around town; go to the website for locations, dates, and times. On 20th St. NW (between Q St. and Massachusetts Ave.), and in the adjacent Riggs Bank parking lot. ✆ **202/362-8889.** www.freshfarmmarkets.org. Metro: Dupont Circle, Q St. exit.

Eastern Market *Value* A devastating fire in April 2007 gutted this Capitol Hill institution, a market that had been in continuous operation since 1873. But some vendors are operating in temporary stalls outside the market, and soon they will move across the street to a new, but temporary, building. Meanwhile, renovation continues on the historic market building, which is slated to re-open in late 2008 or early 2009, thanks to an intense effort by the surrounding community and the D.C. government, led by D.C. Mayor Adrian Fenty, to rebuild this essential and beloved neighborhood emporium. In fact, the outdoor farmers market stalls have remained open throughout, selling fresh produce and other goods on Saturdays and flea market items on Sundays. If Eastern Market's South Hall has been restored, you can expect to see an inside bazaar Tuesday through Sunday, where greengrocers, butchers, bakers, farmers, artists, craftspeople, florists, and other merchants sell their wares. And if all is well, Saturday morning will once again be the best time to go to experience a D.C. tradition: blueberry pancakes at the Market Lunch counter. Saturday 7am to 6pm, Sunday 9am to 4pm (call for other days and time of operations). 225 7th St. SE (between North Carolina Ave. and C St. SE). ✆ **202/544-0083.** www.easternmarket.net. Metro: Eastern Market.

Montgomery County Farm Woman's Cooperative Market Vendors set up inside every Saturday year-round from 7am to about 3:30pm to sell preserves, home-grown veggies, cut flowers, slabs of bacon and sausages, and mouthwatering pies, cookies, and breads; there's an abbreviated version on Wednesday. Outside, on Saturday, Sunday, and Wednesday, you'll find flea market vendors selling everything from rugs to tablecloths to furniture to sunglasses. 7155 Wisconsin Ave., in Bethesda. ✆ **301/652-2291.** Metro: Bethesda.

FASHION

See also "Discount Shopping," above, and "Shoes," later in this section.

CHILDREN'S CLOTHING

If your youngster has spilled grape juice all over his favorite outfit and you need a replacement, you can always head to the downtown **Macy's** (p. 260) or **H&M** (p. 255), or to the nearest **Gap Kids:** in Georgetown at 1267 Wisconsin Ave. NW (✆ **202/333-2411**). Chic moms undeterred by expense shop at the Georgetown store, while practical moms shop at the midtown Kid's Closet.

Kid's Closet *Kids* Now in its 26th year, Kid's Closet has seen numerous chichi children's clothing stores come and go in D.C. The secret to its staying power lies in full view: Its storefront display of affordable and practical kids' clothes are cute enough for you to imagine your child in them, but not so precious as to make you worry in advance about how you're going to remove the inevitable stains. The store is easy to find, since it stands out among the bank and restaurant facades in this downtown block. 1226 Connecticut Ave. NW. ✆ **202/429-9247.** www.kidsclosetdc.com. Metro: Dupont Circle or Farragut North.

Piccolo Piggies *Kids* Here you'll love the cutie-pie children's garb, Petit Bateau to Lilly Pulitzer, for newborns up to age 14 for girls and up to age 10 for boys, as well as shoes, furniture, toys, and accessories. 1533 Wisconsin Ave. NW. ✆ **202/333-0123.** www.piccolo-piggies.com. Metro: Foggy Bottom, then take the Georgetown Metro Connection shuttle or the D.C. Circulator.

MEN'S CLOTHING

Local branches of **Banana Republic** are at Wisconsin and M streets in Georgetown (✆ **202/333-2554**) and F and 13th streets NW (✆ **202/638-2724**); **The Gap** has several locations in Washington, including 1120 Connecticut Ave. NW (✆ **202/429-0691**) and 1258 Wisconsin Ave. NW (✆ **202/333-2657**).

Brooks Brothers Brooks sells traditional men's clothes, as well as the fine line of Peal & Company Collection shoes. This store made the news as the place where Monica Lewinsky bought a tie for President Clinton. It also sells an extensive line of women's clothes. 1201 Connecticut Ave. NW. ✆ **202/659-4650.** www.brooksbrothers.com. Metro: Dupont Circle or Farragut North. Other locations are at Potomac Mills (p. 252), at National Airport (✆ **703/417-1071**), and at 5504 Wisconsin Ave., in Chevy Chase, MD (✆ **301/654-8202**).

Burberry's Here you'll find those plaid-lined trench coats, of course, along with well-tailored English clothing for men and women. Hot items include cashmere sweaters and camel's hair duffel coats for men. 1155 Connecticut Ave. NW. ✆ **202/463-3000.** www.burberry.com. Metro: Farragut North.

Daddy & Son Camiceria Italiana This is the Italian men's store sole retail location in the U.S. Expect to find exquisite Italian designs with fine touches, like mother-of-pearl buttons, hand-finished ties, shirts, and sweaters for boys and men. 1704 Connecticut Ave. NW. ✆ **202/462-1324.** www.daddyesonusa.com. Metro: Dupont Circle.

H&M This Swedish-based store sells trendy clothes for the whole family at reasonable prices. Some designer knockoffs. 1025 F St. NW. ✆ **202/347-3306.** www.hm.com. Metro: Metro Center. A second location, in the Shops at Georgetown Park Mall, 3222 M St. NW (✆ **202/298-6792**), sells only women's and youth lines.

Jos. A. Bank Clothiers If you admire the Brooks Brothers line, but only wish it were more affordable, look here. This century-old clothier sells suits, corporate casual, weekend casual, and formal attire at prices "20% to 30% lower than competitors." Union Station. ✆ **202/289-9087.** www.josbank.com. Metro: Union Station. Two other locations: Lincoln Square, 555 11th St. NW (✆ **202/393-5590**) and 1200 19th St. NW (✆ **202/466-2282**).

Sherman Pickey Prep to the max is this store but also a little fey: Think red corduroys. Both men and women's clothes are on sale here, including Bill's Khakis and Barbour Outerwear for men, embroidered capris, and ribbon belts for women. It's not a chain, though, so it's different in that respect. 1647 Wisconsin Ave. NW. ✆ **202/333-4212.** www.shermanpickey.com. Metro: Foggy Bottom, then take the Georgetown Metro Connection Shuttle or the D.C. Circulator.

Thomas Pink For those who like beautifully made, bright-colored shirts, this branch of the London-based high-end establishment should please. The store also sells ties, boxer shorts, women's shirts, cuff links, and other accessories. 1127 Connecticut Ave. NW (inside the Mayflower Hotel). ✆ **202/223-5390.** www.thomaspink.com. Metro: Farragut North.

Urban Outfitters For the latest in casual attire, from fatigue pants to tube tops. The shop has a floor of women's clothes and a floor of men's clothes, as well as apartment wares, travel books and accessories, cards, and candles. 3111 M St. NW. ✆ **202/342-1012.** www.urbn.com. Metro: Foggy Bottom, then take the Georgetown Metro Connection shuttle or D.C. Circulator. Second location: Gallery Place, 737 7th St. NW ✆ **202/737-0259.** Metro: Gallery Place.

WOMEN'S CLOTHING

Washington women have many more clothing stores to choose from than men. Stores selling classic designs dominate, including **Ann Taylor,** at Union Station (✆ **202/371-8010**), 1140 Connecticut Ave. NW (✆ **202/659-0120**), 600 13th St. NW (✆ **202/737-0325**), and Georgetown Park, 3222 M St. NW (✆ **202/337-0843**); and **Talbots,** at 1122 Connecticut Ave. NW (✆ **202/887-6973**), and Georgetown Park, 3222 M St. NW (✆ **202/338-3510**). Beneath their modest apparel, however, Washington women like to wear racy **Victoria's Secret** lingerie—you'll find stores in Union Station (✆ **202/682-0686**) and Georgetown Park (✆ **202/965-5457**), as well as at Connecticut and L streets NW (✆ **202/293-7530**).

See "Men's Clothing," immediately above, for locations of Banana Republic, Gap, Sherman Pickey, H&M, Brooks Brothers, and Urban Outfitters, all of which also sell women's clothes.

Hip boutiques and upscale shops proliferate as well:

Alex Located near George Washington University, not your typical retail area, Alex sells contemporary clothes and accessories for men and women. It often features fashions by international designers, from Canada's Dubuc to Serbia's Dragana, as well as the creations (especially jewelry) of young local designers, with some vintage couture and consignment pieces thrown in. 1919 Pennsylvania Ave. NW. ✆ **202/296-2610.** (Website under reconstruction at press time.) Metro: Foggy Bottom.

Betsey Johnson New York's flamboyant flower-child designer personally decorated the bubble-gum-pink walls in her Georgetown shop. Her sexy, offbeat, play-dress-up styles are great party and club clothes for the young and the still-skinny young at heart. This is the only Betsey Johnson store in D.C. 1319 Wisconsin Ave. NW. ✆ **202/338-4090.** www.betseyjohnson.com. Metro: Foggy Bottom, then take the Georgetown Metro Connection shuttle or D.C. Circulator.

Betsy Fisher A walk past the store is all it takes to know that this shop is a tad different. Its windows and racks show off whimsically feminine fashions by new American, French, and Italian designers. 1224 Connecticut Ave. NW. ✆ **202/785-1975.** www.betsyfisher.com. Metro: Dupont Circle.

French Connection This outpost of the London-based chain features clothes that are slouchy and hip, but not outrageous, for both men and women. 1229 Wisconsin Ave. NW. ✆ **202/965-4690.** www.frenchconnection.com. Metro: Foggy Bottom, then take the Georgetown Metro Connection shuttle or D.C. Circulator.

Meeps Vintage Fashionette This pioneer shop recently moved from its U Street corridor neighborhood around the corner to lower Adams Morgan, but its clientele and inventory remain the same: men and women urbanistas attracted to vintage clothes, 1930s gabardine suits to 1950s cocktail dresses to satiny lingerie; local designer ware also sold. 2104 18th St. NW ✆ **202/265-6546.** www.meepsdc.com. Metro: U St.–Cardozo or Woodley Park–Zoo, with a bit of a walk from either station.

Nana's Owner Jackie Flanagan left the world of advertising and publishing to open this store a couple of years ago, naming it after her fashion-wise grandmother. The shop sells new creations from independent U.S. and Canadian designs, and vintage styles of work and play clothes, the idea being to mix old and new for a fresh look. Handbags, gifts, and bath products also on sale. 1528 U St. NW (between 15th and 16th sts.). ✆ **202/667-6955.** www.nanadc.com. Metro: U St.-Cardozo.

Rizik Brothers The year 2008 marks Rizik's centennial anniversary. This downtown high-fashion store sells bridal dresses and other high-toned fashions by European and American designers such as Christian LaCroix, Brioni, and Escada Sport. 1100 Connecticut Ave. NW. ✆ **202/223-4050.** www.riziks.com. Metro: Farragut North.

Wink Look for Wink beneath the Steve Madden store, and you'll discover Seven jeans and clothes by Diane von Furstenberg, Miguelina, Blue Cult, and happy women of all ages sorting through the mix. 3109 M St. NW. ✆ **202/338-9465.** www.shopwinkdc.com. Metro: Foggy Bottom, then take the Georgetown Metro Connection Shuttle or D.C. Circulator.

Zara This cheery store is an outpost of a popular chain started in Spain. Clothes are both dressy and casual, but all trendy. A sprinkling of coats is also found here, when the season calls for it. 1234-44 Wisconsin Ave. NW. ✆ **202/944-9797.** www.zara.com. Metro: Foggy Bottom, then take the Georgetown Metro Connection Shuttle or D.C. Circulator.

GIFTS/SOUVENIRS

See also "Crafts," earlier in this section. Museum gift shops are also full of possibilities.

America! Stop here if you want to pick up a baseball cap with COMMANDER IN CHIEF printed across its bill, a T-shirt proclaiming I LOVE MY COUNTRY, IT'S THE GOVERNMENT I'M AFRAID OF, White House guest towels, or other impress-the-folks-back-home items. Union Station. ✆ **202/842-0540.** www.americastore.com. Metro: Union Station. Or save your shopping for the airport; America! has at least one location at National (✆ 703/417-1782) and several at Dulles (Terminal B: ✆ 703/572-2543; Terminal C: ✆ 703/572-6033; Terminal D: ✆ 703/572-6070).

Chocolate Moose *Finds* Its website welcomes browsers with the words "Serving weirdly sophisticated Washingtonians since 1978, but now attempting to reach out to the rest of you." I guess my family qualifies as weirdly sophisticated, since we're long-time fans. My husband endears himself to me and our daughters when he brings home gifts from this shop: a Wonder Woman daybook; chunky, transparent, red heart-shaped earrings; wacky cards; paperweight snow globes with figurines inside; candies; eccentric clothing; and other funny, lovely, and useful presents. 1743 L St. NW. ✆ **202/463-0992.** www.chocolatemoosedc.com. Metro: Farragut North.

Pulp Gifts *Finds* You'll find must-have items here that you never even knew existed: a deck of slang flashcards, "Dancin' in the Streets" T-shirts, and crazy greeting cards. 1803 14th St. NW. ✆ **202/462-7857.** www.pulpdc.com. Metro: U St.–Cardozo.

GOURMET GOODIES TO GO

Demanding jobs and hectic schedules leave Washingtonians less and less time to prepare their own meals. Or so they say. At any rate, a number of fine-food shops and bakeries are happy to come to the rescue. Even the busiest bureaucrat can find the time to pop into one of these gourmet shops for a movable feast.

See also "Farmer's & Flea Markets," above.

Bread Line *Finds* Bread Line is wildly popular and attracts the White House crowd for lunch, with favorite sandwiches like the roast pork bun or the muffuletta; tasty soups; and desserts such as bread puddings, pear tarts, and delicious cookies. Seating is available, but most people buy carryout. The shop also sells freshly baked loaves of wheat bread, flat breads, baguettes, and more. Open weekdays 7:30am to 3:30pm. 1751 Pennsylvania Ave. NW. ✆ **202/822-8900.** www.breadlinedc.com. Metro: Farragut West or Farragut North.

Dean & Deluca This famed New York store operates this fabulous emporium in a historic Georgetown building that was once an open-air market. Though it is now closed in, this huge space still feels airy, with its high ceiling and windows on all sides. You'll pay top prices, but the quality is impressive—charcuterie, fresh fish, produce, cheeses, prepared sandwiches and cold pasta salads, hot-ticket desserts, like crème brûlée and tiramisu, and California wines. Also on sale are housewares; on-site is an espresso bar/cafe. 3276 M St. NW. ✆ **202/342-2500.** www.deandeluca.com. Metro: Foggy Bottom, then take the Georgetown Metro Connection shuttle or the D.C. Circulator.

Firehook Bakery Known for its sourdough baguettes, apple-walnut bread, fresh fruit tarts, red-iced elephant and blue-iced donkey cookies, and sandwiches like smoked chicken on sesame semolina bread. Firehook now runs the Vradenburg Café at the Phillips Collection (see "Views with a Meal," in chapter 6), as well as the cafe at the National Building Museum (see "Museums of Special Interest," chapter 7). 1909 Q St. NW. ✆ **202/588-9296.** www.firehook.com. Metro: Dupont Circle. Also at 912 17th St. NW (✆ 202/429-2253), 3411 Connecticut Ave. NW (✆ 202/362-2253), 215 Pennsylvania Ave. SE (✆ 202/544-7003), 555 13th St. NW (✆ 202/393-0952), 441 4th St. NW (✆ 202/347-1760), and at 2 locations in Alexandria, VA.

Marvelous Market First there were the breads: sourdough, baguettes, olive, rosemary, croissants, scones. Now, there are things to spread on the bread, including smoked salmon mousse and tapenade; pastries to die for, from gingerbread to flourless chocolate cake; and prepared foods, such as soups, empanadas, and pasta salads. The breakfast spread on Sunday mornings is sinful, and individual items, like the croissants, are tastier and less expensive here than at other bakeries. The location is grand, with 18th-century chandeliers, an antique cedar bar, and a small number of tables. 1511 Connecticut Ave. NW. ✆ **202/332-3690.** www.marvelousmarket.com. Metro: Dupont Circle. Also at 3217 P St. NW (✆ 202/333-2591), 5035 Connecticut Ave. NW (✆ 202/686-4040), 1800 K St. NW (✆ 202/828-0944), 303 7th St. SE (✆ 202/544-7127).

HOME FURNISHINGS

You may not have come to Washington to shop for furniture, but step inside these beguiling shops and you may change your mind.

Apartment Zero Located on the first floor of a historic building in the delicious Penn Quarter, this sophisticated store sells hot-off-the-design-floor furnishings: Eames sofas, Zanzibar stools, "orange slice" chairs, and "petits fours" benches. The clever designers are from around the world; the prices are out of this world. Besides furniture, Apartment Zero sells everything else you need for the home, from light fixtures to bed linens. 406 7th St. NW. ✆ **202/628-4067.** www.apartmentzero.com. Metro: Gallery Place/Verizon Center or Archives/Navy Memorial.

Cady's Alley Cady's Alley refers not to a single store, but to the southwest pocket of Georgetown, where about 20 stores reside, in and around said alley, which dangles south of M Street. These are tony, big-name places, and include Waterworks, Thos. Moser Cabinetmakers, Baker Furniture, and European outposts, such as the high-concept designs of Ligne Roset and the hip kitchen furnishings of Bulthaup. 3318 M St. NW (between 33rd and 34th sts.). www.cadysalley.com. Metro: Foggy Bottom, then take the Georgetown Metro Connection Shuttle or D.C. Circulator.

Home Rule *Value* Unique housewares; bath, kitchen, and office supplies; and gifts cram this tiny store. You'll see everything from French milled soap to martini glasses. 1807 14th St. NW (at S St.). ✆ **202/797-5544.** www.homerule.com. Metro: U St.–Cardozo (call for specific directions from the station).

JEWELRY

Beadazzled The friendly staff helps you assemble your own affordable jewelry from an eye-boggling array of beads and artifacts. The store also sells textiles, woodcarvings, and other crafts from around the world. 1507 Connecticut Ave. NW. ✆ **202/265-BEAD.** www.beadazzled.net. Metro: Dupont Circle.

Chas Schwartz & Son In business since 1888, Chas Schwartz specializes in diamonds and sapphires, rubies and emeralds, and is one of the few distributors of Hidalgo jewelry (enameled rings and bracelets). The professional staff also repairs watches and jewelry. 1400 F St. NW, or enter through the Willard Hotel, at 1401 Pennsylvania Ave.

NW. ✆ **202/737-4757.** www.chasschwartzjewelers.com. Metro: Metro Center. There's another branch at the Mazza Gallerie (✆ **202/363-5432**); Metro: Friendship Heights.

Keith Lipert Gallery This decorative-arts gallery suffered a tremendous fire in January 2006 but reopened in July, to resume selling Venetian glassware, high-end costume jewelry by designers such as Oscar de la Renta, and cute little old things, like Art Deco–styled handbags. The owner shops in Europe for fashion jewelry and for exquisite gifts suitable for giving to diplomats and international business executives. 2922 M St. NW. ✆ **202/965-9736.** www.keithlipertgallery.com. Metro: Foggy Bottom, then take the Georgetown Metro Connection.

Tiffany & Co. Tiffany is known for exquisite diamonds and other jewelry that can cost hundreds of thousands of dollars. But you may not know that the store carries less expensive items as well, like $35 candlesticks. Tiffany will engrave, too. Other items include tabletop gifts and fancy glitz: china, crystal, flatware, and a bridal registry service. 5481 Wisconsin Ave., Chevy Chase, MD. ✆ **301/657-8777.** www.tiffany.com. Metro: Friendship Heights.

Tiny Jewel Box The first place Washingtonians go for estate and antique jewelry, but this six-story store next to the Mayflower Hotel also sells the pieces of many designers, from Links of London to Christian Tse, as well as crystal and other house gifts. In the month leading up to Mother's Day, the Tiny Jewel Box holds its Top-to-Bottom Sale, where you can save anywhere from 10% to 75% on most merchandise, including jewelry, handbags, and home accessories. 1147 Connecticut Ave. NW. ✆ **202/393-2747.** www.tinyjewelbox.com. Metro: Farragut North.

MALLS

If malls are your thing, D.C. has plenty for you to choose from: **Chevy Chase Pavilion,** 5335 Wisconsin Ave. NW (✆ **202/686-5335;** www.ccpavilion.com; Metro: Friendship Heights); **Gallery Place,** 7th and H sts. NW (✆ **202/338-5200;** www.galleryplace.com; Metro: Gallery Place/Verizon Center); **Mazza Gallerie,** 5300 Wisconsin Ave. NW (✆ **202/966-6114;** www.mazzagallerie.com; Metro: Friendship Heights); the **Shops at Georgetown Park,** 3222 M St. NW (✆ **202/342-8190;** www.shopsatgeorgetownpark.com; Metro: Foggy Bottom, then take the Georgetown Metro Connection shuttle or D.C. Circulator); **Tysons Corner Center,** 1961 Chain Bridge Rd., McLean, VA (✆ **703/893-9400;** www.shoptysons.com); and **Tysons Corner II, The Galleria,** 2001 International Dr., McLean, VA (✆ **703/827-7700;** www.shoptysonsgalleria.com). **Ronald Reagan Washington National Airport,** Arlington, VA (✆ **703/417-8600;** www.mwaa.com/National), has 100 stores to choose from, too, if you want to do some souvenir shopping on your way out of town. Also see the listing for **Potomac Mills** on p. 252.

Even if you aren't a mall rat, you might want to check out the following two establishments, which do double duty as both shopping centers and attractions:

Pavilion at the Old Post Office Not so much a mall as a tourist trap with souvenir shops and a food court. But you can ride a pair of elevators to the clock tower for a stunning view of the city (p. 189). 1100 Pennsylvania Ave. NW. ✆ **202/289-4224.** www.oldpostofficedc.com. Metro: Federal Triangle.

Union Station One of the most popular tourist stops in Washington, Union Station boasts magnificent architecture and more than 100 shops, including Pendleton's and Appalachian Spring (p. 251). Among the places to eat are America, B. Smith, and an impressive food court. There's also a nine-screen movie-theater complex here. 50 Massachusetts Ave. NE. ✆ **202/371-9441** or 202/289-1908. www.unionstationdc.com. Metro: Union Station.

MISCELLANEOUS

Fahrneys Pens, Inc. People come from all over to purchase the finest fountain pens, or to have them engraved or repaired. In business since 1929, Fahrneys is an institution, selling the best pens in the business, such as Montblanc, Cross, and Waterman. 1317 F St. NW (between 13th and 14th sts.). ✆ **800/624-7367** or 202/628-9525. www.fahrneyspens.com. Metro: Metro Center.

Emergency Shopping

You've just arrived in town, but your luggage hasn't—the airline lost it. Or you're about to depart for home or another destination and you notice that the zipper to your suitcase is broken. Or you've arrived at your hotel all in one piece, only to discover you've forgotten something essential: underwear, allergy medicine, an umbrella. What's a lonesome traveler to do? One of these suggestions might prove your salvation.

CVS: This is Washington's main pharmacy and essentials chain. Among the items sold at CVS stores are pantyhose, over-the-counter and prescription medicines, toys, greeting cards, wrapping paper and ribbon, magazines, film and 1-hour photo developing, batteries, candy, some refrigerated food such as milk and orange juice, and office supplies. The stores are ubiquitous, so chances are you'll find one near you. Two conveniently located 24-hour branches are at 2240 M St. NW (✆ **202/296-9877;** Metro: Gallery Place/Verizon Center) and at 6 Dupont Circle NW (✆ **202/785-1466;** Metro: Dupont Circle); www.cvs.com.

Cobbler's Bench Shoe Repair: This shop on the lower (food court) level of Union Station is open daily, Monday to Friday from 7am to 8pm, Saturday 9am to 6pm, and Sunday noon to 6pm, to come to the rescue of travelers whose shoes or luggage need mending. The cobbler also cuts keys and sells repair items. Union Station, lower level. (✆ **202/898-9009**). Metro: Union Station.

Macy's: This former Hecht's remains an old reliable and the only department store located downtown. But though it's been around a while, the store continually updates its merchandise to keep up with the times. Run here if you need cosmetics, clothes (for men, women, and children), shoes (but not for children), electronics, appliances, lingerie, luggage, raincoats, and countless other need-immediately goods. Open daily: noon to 6pm Sunday; 10am to 8pm Monday, Thursday, and Friday; 9am to 9pm Tuesday; and 9am to 10pm Wednesday and Saturday. 1201 G St. NW. (✆ **202/628-6661**). www.macys.com. Metro: Metro Center.

Metro Stations: If it starts raining and you're scrambling to find an umbrella, look no farther than your closest Metro station, where vendors are at the ready selling umbrellas and other handy things.

Ginza, "for Things Japanese" In business since 1955, Ginza sells everything Japanese, from incense to kimonos to futons to Zen rock gardens. 1721 Connecticut Ave. NW. ✆ **202/332-7000.** www.ginzaonline.com. Metro: Dupont Circle.

Paper Source If you're a stationery freak like I am, you'll have to stop here to revel in the beautiful writing and wrapping papers, supplies of notebooks, journals, albums, ribbons, folders, containers, and other essentials. This store is the chain's only mid-Atlantic location. I believe it's the best stationery store in D.C. 3019 M St. NW. ✆ **202/298-5545.** www.paper-source.com. Metro: Foggy Bottom, with a 25-min. walk.

MUSIC

See also the listings for **Olsson's Books and Records,** p. 250, **Barnes & Noble,** p. 249, and **Borders,** p. 249.

DJ Hut Everything for lovers of hip-hop, reggae, R&B, and go-go. 2010 P St. NW, 2nd floor. ✆ **202/659-2010.** www.djhut.com. Metro: Dupont Circle.

Melody Record Shop CDs, cassettes, and tapes, including new releases, are discounted here, plus the shop always has a table of unused but not newly released CDs that sell for about $10 each. Melody offers a wide variety of rock, classical, jazz, pop, show, and folk music, as well as a vast number of international selections. This is also a good place to shop for discounted portable electronic equipment, blank tapes, and cassettes. Its knowledgeable staff is a plus. 1623 Connecticut Ave. NW. ✆ **202/232-4002.** www.melodyrecords.com. Metro: Dupont Circle, Q St. exit.

SHOES

For men's dress shoes, try **Brooks Brothers** (p. 254). There are local outlets of **Foot Locker** at Union Station (✆ **202/289-8364**) and 1934 14th St. NW (✆ **202/319-8934**). **Nine West** sells women's shoes from locations at Union Station (✆ **202/216-9490**), 1001 Connecticut Ave. NW (✆ **202/452-9163**), and 1227 Wisconsin Ave. NW (✆ **202/337-7256**).

Carbon "Changing D.C. from federal to funky" is this store's self-proclaimed purpose, and its merchandise is persuasive in this regard: Blackstones, Pikolinos, and Bronx are some of the names it carries in men's footwear. Carbon also carries women's shoes, and accessories and some clothes and furnishings for both sexes. 2643 Connecticut Ave. NW. ✆ **202/232-6645.** www.carbondc.com. Metro: Woodley Park–Zoo.

Comfort One Shoes Despite its unhip name, this store sells a great selection of popular styles for both men and women, including Doc Martens, Birkenstocks, and Ecco. You can always find something that looks good and actually feels comfortable. 1630 Connecticut Ave. NW. ✆ **202/328-3141.** www.comfortoneshoes.com. Metro: Dupont Circle. Also at 1607 Connecticut Ave. NW (✆ **202/667-5300**), 3222 M St. NW (✆ **202/333-3399**), and other locations.

Fleet Feet Though part of a national chain, this store feels decidedly part of the community, an Adams-Morgan neighborhood fixture since 1984. The couple who owns the shop, Phil and Jan Fenty, are the parents of D.C. mayor Adrian Fenty, whom you might find racing next to you during the weekly Sunday morning 5-mile fun run that Fleet Feet launches from its doorstep at 9am. (Just show up, if you're interested.) Merchandise-wise, the store sells sports and running shoes, apparel, and accessories, and is known for its friendly staff. 1841 Columbia Rd. NW. ✆ **202/387-3888.** www.fleetfeetdc.com. Metro: U St.–Cardozo or Woodley Park–Zoo, with a bit of a walk from either station.

Wild Women Wear Red Mostly funky but comfy shoes, including Mary Janes and Lisa Nadings, but also accessories, like handmade crocheted handbags and jewelry crafted by local artists, are on sale in this boutique, whose walls are hung with images of Indira Ghandi and Rosie the Riveter. 1512 U St. NW. ✆ **202/387-5700.** www.wildwomenwearred.com. Metro: U Street-Cardozo.

WINE & SPIRITS

Barmy Wine and Liquor Located near the White House, this store sells it all, but with special emphasis on fine wines and rare cordials. 1912 L St. NW. ✆ **202/833-8730.** Metro: Farragut North.

Central Liquor *Value* This is like a clearinghouse for liquor: Its great volume allows the store to offer the best prices in town on wines and liquor. The store carries more than 250 single-malt scotches. 917 F St. NW. ✆ **800/835-7928** or 202/737-2800. www.centralliquors.com. Metro: Gallery Place.

Schneider's of Capitol Hill Two blocks south of Union Station is this family-run liquor store, in business for half a century. With a knowledgeable and enthusiastic staff, a 12,000-bottle inventory of wine, and a fine selection of spirits and beer, this shop is a find on Capitol Hill. 300 Massachusetts Ave. NE. ✆ **202/543-9300.** www.cellar.com. Metro: Union Station.

9

Washington, D.C., After Dark

Washington by day is a city so full of things to do that you'll never get to them all. Washington by night is no different. And the options get better and more extensive by the hour.

D.C.'s hip neighborhood repertoire now goes way beyond Georgetown to include the U and 14th street corridors, Penn Quarter, Adams-Morgan, Barracks Row on Capitol Hill, the "Atlas District's" H Street NE (just east of Union Station), Dupont Circle, and even the upper-northwest upscale residential Cleveland Park. Restaurants are destinations in themselves, serving up a sexy lounge alongside the dining room. Bars are as much about making the scene as having a drink.

Locals have always loved their live music venues and these strongholds continue to thrive. But if you prefer DJ-driven beats, you'll find all the best in the latest, hottest clubs. Spoken-word joints? Got 'em. Bowling alley for the drinking crowd? Got it. Classic fare, like Shakespeare, comedy, Broadway musicals, symphonies, opera, ballet? Whatever you want, Washington's got it.

Read over the listings that follow to see what most appeals to you. For up-to-date schedules of events, from live music and theater, to children's programs and flower shows, check the Friday "Weekend" section of the ***Washington Post,*** or go online, and browse the *Post's* nightlife information at **www.washingtonpost.com**. Also visit www.washingtonpost.com's "Going Out Gurus" blog, accessible from its City Guide link; the "GOGs" answer questions about nightlife live online every Thursday at 1pm, and transcripts stay posted for a time. The ***City Paper,*** available free at restaurants, bookstores, and other places around town, and online at **www.washingtoncitypaper.com**, is another excellent source. Finally, check out the blog **www.dcist.com** for an irreverent inside look at what's going on around town.

TICKETS

TICKETplace, Washington's only discount day-of-show ticket outlet, has one location: at 407 7th St. NW, between D and E streets (Metro: Gallery Place/Verizon Center or Archives/Navy Memorial). Call © **202/TIC-KETS** (842-5387) for information. You can purchase tickets at the booth or online at www.ticketplace.org. On the day of performance only (except Sun and Mon; see below), you can buy half-price tickets (with select debit and credit cards: Visa, MasterCard, American Express, and Discover; but cash, personal checks, and traveler's checks are not accepted) to performances with tickets still available at most major Washington-area theaters and concert halls, as well as for performances of the opera, ballet, and other events. TICKETplace is open Tuesday through Friday from 11am to 6pm and Saturday from 10am to 5pm; half-price tickets for Sunday and Monday shows are sold on Saturday. Though tickets are half-price, you have to pay a per-ticket service charge of 12% of the full face value of the ticket.

Tickets are available online Tuesday through Friday, between noon and 4pm. Again, the tickets sold are for same-day performances, at half-price, plus the per-ticket service charge, which for online sales is 17% of the full face value of the ticket. You must pay by credit card, using MasterCard or Visa, and then pick up the tickets at the "Will Call" booth of the theater you're attending; bring your credit card and a photo ID. TICKETplace is a service of the Cultural Alliance of Washington, in partnership with the Kennedy Center, the *Washington Post,* and Ticketmaster.

You can buy full-price tickets for most performances in town through **Ticketmaster** (✆ **800/551-7328;** www.ticketmaster.com); expect to pay taxes, plus a service charge, an order processing fee, and a facility fee (if a particular venue tacks on that charge). Or you can visit one of Ticketmaster's numerous locations throughout the city, including Macy's Department Store, 12th and G streets NW (Metro: Metro Center), and the D.C. Visitor Center in the Ronald Reagan Building, at 1300 Pennsylvania Ave. NW (Metro: Federal Triangle); you usually will not have to pay a convenience or order processing fee when you purchase tickets in person. When you pay by credit card at TICKETplace and Ticketmaster, you have to show an ID to prove you are the credit card holder.

Another ticket outlet worth checking out is **Tickets.com** (formerly Protix). While Ticketmaster has a wider selection, Tickets.com offers some performances Ticketmaster doesn't. Call ✆ **800/955-5566,** access its website at www.tickets.com, or visit one of its D.C. outlets, including one inside the Olsson's Bookstore at 418 7th St. NW, directly across from the TICKETplace office, in the Penn Quarter.

1 The Performing Arts

Washington's performing arts scene has an international reputation. Almost anything on Broadway has either been previewed here or will eventually come here. Better yet, D.C. is home to truly excellent and renowned repertory theater troupes, and to fine ballet, opera, and symphony companies. Rock bands, headliner comedians, and jazz/folk/gospel/R&B/alternative and other musical groups make Washington a must-stop on their tours.

THE TOP THEATERS

Arena Stage This outpost on the unhandsome Washington waterfront is worth seeking out, despite its poor location. (Dine at a downtown restaurant, then drive or take a taxi here; you can take the Metro, but be especially careful walking the block or so to the theater, as this area isn't heavily trafficked or well lit.)

Founded by the brilliant Zelda Fichandler in 1950, the Arena Stage is home to one of the oldest acting ensembles in the nation. Several works nurtured here have moved to Broadway, and many graduates have gone on to commercial stardom, including Ned Beatty, James Earl Jones, Robert Prosky, and Jane Alexander. The excellence of Arena productions has brought the theater much success, to the extent that a major expansion is underway, with 2008 the target year for opening.

Arena presents eight productions annually on two stages: the **Fichandler** (a theater-in-the-round) and the smaller, fan-shaped **Kreeger.** In addition, the Arena houses the **Old Vat,** a space used for new play readings and special productions.

The 2007–08 September-to-June season includes a tribute to Arthur Miller, with the staging of his *Death of a Salesman* and *A View from the Bridge;* a musical, *Ella,* celebrating

Ella Fitzgerald; and the regional premiere of Lisa Kron's Tony-award-winning comedy, *Well.*

The Arena Stage has always championed new plays and playwrights and is committed to producing works from America's diverse cultures, as well as to reintroducing the works of past masters. 1101 6th St. SW (at Maine Ave.). ✆ **202/488-3300.** www.arenastage.org. Tickets $47–$74; discounts available for students, people with disabilities, groups, and seniors. Metro: Waterfront.

John F. Kennedy Center for the Performing Arts This 37-year-old theater complex strives to be not just the hub of Washington's cultural and entertainment scene, but a performing arts theater for the nation. The center lies between the Potomac River and a crisscross of major roadways, which makes it sound like it's easily accessible when, in fact, its location has tended to isolate it from the rest of town. Congress has rejected the Center's bid for funding that would have allowed the complex to expand and connect to the rest of the city, including the National Mall. The Kennedy Center will certainly plead its case again, but for now, the center remains just a bit west of the city's main action.

The Kennedy Center stages top-rated performances by the best ballet, opera, jazz, modern dance, musical, and theater companies in the world. Ticket prices vary from $18 for a children's play to as much as $600 for a night at the opera, although most fall in the $30 to $75 range.

The Kennedy Center is committed to being a theater for the people, and toward that end, it continues to stage its **free concert series,** known as "Millennium Stage," which features daily performances by area musicians and sometimes national artists each evening at 6pm in the center's Grand Foyer. (You can check out broadcasts of the nightly performances on the Internet at www.kennedy-center.org/millennium.) The Friday "Weekend" section of the *Washington Post* lists the free performances scheduled for the coming week.

The Kennedy Center is actually made up of six different national theaters: the Opera House, the Concert Hall, the Terrace Theater, the Eisenhower Theater, the Theater Lab, and the Family Theater.

The Kennedy Center's 2007–08 season includes a February-long festival that salutes Japan, **Japan! Culture + Hyperculture;** and a tribute throughout March to playwright August Wilson, presenting staged readings in the intimate Terrace Theatre, of all 10 of his works, including *Gem of the Ocean* and *Fences.* For more information, check out the Kennedy Center's online information at www.kennedy-center.org. Highlights of the Kennedy Center's 2007–08 season include the following:

- **Washington National Opera** (www.dc-opera.org) performances of Puccini's *La Boheme* and Verdi's *Rigoletto,* with artistic director Placido Domingo (tickets often sell out before the season begins);
- **National Symphony Orchestra** concerts, under the direction of Leonard Slatkin, presented in the Concert Hall from September to June;
- Performances by the **New York City Ballet, the American Ballet Theatre, the Suzanne Farrell Ballet, and the Kirov Ballet;**
- **Broadway musicals** *My Fair Lady* and *The Lion King;*
- **Kennedy Center Jazz series** performances by assorted masters, from Dianne Reeves to Dave Brubeck and Ramsey Lewis;

Fun Fact Longer Than the Washington Monument Is Tall

Most Kennedy Center performances take place in theaters that lie off the Grand Foyer. But even if the one you're attending is on the Roof Terrace Level, one floor up, make sure you visit the Foyer anyway. The Grand Foyer is one of the largest rooms in the world. Measuring 630 feet long, 40 feet wide, and 60 feet high, the foyer is longer than the Washington Monument is tall (at 555⅝ ft.). Millennium Stage hosts free performances here nightly at 6pm, the famous Robert Berks sculpture of President John F. Kennedy is here, and just beyond the foyer's glass doors is the expansive terrace, which runs the length of the building and overlooks the Potomac River.

- **Family Theater** productions, like the **National Symphony Orchestra's Teddy Bear Concerts;** and
- Continuing performances of the comedy whodunit *Shear Madness,* now in its 21st year at the Kennedy Center.

2700 F St. NW (at New Hampshire Ave. NW and Rock Creek Pkwy.). ✆ **800/444-1324** or 202/467-4600 for tickets and information. www.kennedy-center.org. 50% discounts are offered (for select performances) to students, seniors 65 and over, people with permanent disabilities, enlisted military personnel, and persons with fixed low incomes (✆ **202/416-8340** for details). Garage parking $15. Metro: Foggy Bottom (though it's a fairly short walk, there's a free shuttle between the station and the Kennedy Center, departing every 15 min. 9:45am–midnight Mon–Fri, 10am–midnight Sat, noon–midnight Sun). Bus: 80 from Metro Center.

National Theatre The splendid Federal-style National Theatre is the oldest continuously operating theater in Washington (since 1835) and the third-oldest in the nation. It's exciting just to see the stage on which Sarah Bernhardt, John Barrymore, Helen Hayes, and so many other notables have performed. The 1,672-seat National is the closest thing Washington has to a Broadway-style playhouse. The 2007–08 season includes the musicals *Avenue Q* and *Spamalot.*

One thing that has never flagged at The National is its commitment to offering free public-service programs: Saturday-morning children's theater (puppets, clowns, magicians, dancers, and singers) and Monday-night showcases of local groups and performers September through May, plus free summer films. Call ✆ **202/783-3372** for details. 1321 Pennsylvania Ave. NW. ✆ **800/447-7400** or 202/628-6161 to charge tickets. www.nationaltheatre.org. Tickets $40–$150 (most are in the $70–$80 range); discounts available for students, seniors, military personnel, and people with disabilities. Metro: Metro Center.

Shakespeare Theatre Company: at the Lansburgh Theatre and Sidney Harman Hall This is top-level Shakespeare, with superb acting. Try your best to get tickets; the productions are reliably outstanding. Season subscriptions claim many of the seats, and the plays almost always sell out; so if you're interested in attending a play here, buy your tickets now. The Shakespeare Theatre Company's productions at the Lansburgh Theatre have long been so popular that the production company has opened a second theater, the Sidney Harman Hall, at 650 F St. NW, across the street from the Verizon Center and just around the corner from the Lansburgh on 7th St. NW. The 2007–08 season will see the Lansburgh stage three plays in its 451-seat theater and Harman Hall present five plays in its 776-seat theater; with eight productions,

1,227 seats, and two locations, Bard lovers should have a greater chance of scoring tickets. Among the classical ensemble company's 2007–08 season promised presentations are *The Taming of the Shrew, Antony and Cleopatra,* and *Julius Caesar,* as well as two plays by Christopher Marlowe, *Tamburlaine* and *Edward II.* As always, the company is staging its annual, free-admission, 2-week run of a Shakespeare production at the Carter Barron Amphitheater in Rock Creek Park. 450 7th St. NW (between D and E sts.). ✆ **202/547-1122.** www.shakespearetheatre.org. Tickets $26–$76, $10 for standing-room tickets sold 1 hr. before sold-out performances; discounts available for students, seniors, and groups. Metro: Archives/Navy Memorial or Verizon Center/Gallery Place.

SMALLER THEATERS

Some of Washington's lesser-known theaters are gaining more recognition all the time. Their productions are consistently professional, and sometimes more contemporary and innovative than those you'll find in the more acclaimed theaters. These more intimate theaters have their own strong followings, which explains the fact that at least two, the Studio Theater and the Woolly Mammoth Theatre Company, have recently revamped and expanded their performance spaces.

Studio Theatre, 1333 P St. NW, at 14th Street (✆ **202/332-3300;** www.studio theatre.org), since its founding in 1978, has grown in leaps and bounds into a four-theater complex, revitalizing this downtown neighborhood in the process. Artistic director Joy Zinoman showcases interesting contemporary plays and nurtures Washington acting talent; the 2007–08 lineup marks the theater's 30th season. The **Woolly Mammoth Theatre Company** (✆ **202/393-3939;** www.woollymammoth.net) offers as many as six productions each year, specializing in new, offbeat, and quirky plays (Sarah Ruhl's *Dead Man's Cell Phone* was one such production staged in summer 2007). In May of 2005, the Woolly took up residence in its new 265-seat, state-of-the-art facility, 641 D St. NW, at 7th St. NW, in the heart of the Penn Quarter.

In addition, I highly recommend productions staged at the **Folger Shakespeare Library,** 201 E. Capitol St. SE (✆ **202/544-7077;** www.folger.edu), which celebrated its 75th anniversary in 2007. Plays take place in the library's Elizabethan Theatre, which is styled after the inn-yard theater of Shakespeare's time. The theater is intimate and charming, the theater company is remarkably good, and an evening spent here guarantees an absolutely marvelous experience. The 2007–08 season brings to the stage Shakespeare's *As You Like It, Macbeth,* and R. B. Sheridan's 18th-century comedy, *A School for Scandal.* The Elizabethan Theatre is also the setting for musical performances, lectures, readings, and other events.

INDOOR ARENAS & OUTDOOR PAVILIONS

When John Mayer, U2, or the Dixie Chicks come to town, they usually play at one of the huge indoor or outdoor arenas. The 20,600-seat **Verizon Center,** 601 F St. NW, where it meets 7th Street (✆ **202/628-3200;** www.verizoncenter.com), in the center of downtown, hosts plenty of concerts and also is Washington's premier indoor sports arena (home to the NBA Wizards, the WNBA Mystics, the NHL Capitals, and Georgetown NCAA basketball). Less convenient and smaller is the 10,000-seat **Patriot Center** at George Mason University, 4500 Patriot Circle, Fairfax, VA (✆ **703/993-3000;** www.patriotcenter.com).

During the summer, there's quality entertainment almost nightly at the **Merriweather Post Pavilion,** 10475 Little Patuxent Pkwy., just off Route 29 in Columbia, Maryland (✆ **410/715-5550** for general information, 800/551-SEAT for tickets;

Fun Fact Baseball Returns to Washington

As of 2005, Washington, D.C., has its own Major League Baseball team again, for the first time since 1971. For the 2005–06 and 2006–07 seasons, the **Washington Nationals** played at **Robert F. Kennedy Memorial Stadium,** 2400 E. Capitol St. SE (✆ **202/547-9077**). If all goes as planned, the Nationals will find themselves playing the field in their newly built **Nationals Ballpark,** come opening day April 2008. Located in southeast Washington, the 41,000-seat stadium is bounded by South Capitol Street, N Street, First Street, and Potomac Avenue. For tickets, go to the website, **www.mlb.com,** and click on "Nationals" in the list of MLB (Major League Baseball) sites; prices are reasonable: $7 to $55. Meanwhile, the 55,000-seat RFK remains the location for D.C. United (men's) and Washington Freedom (women's) soccer games, at least until these teams get their own stadium, which is slated for 2009.

www.merriweathermusic.com), about a 40-minute drive from downtown D.C. There's reserved seating in the open-air pavilion (overhead protection provided in case of rain) and general-admission seating on the lawn (no refunds for rain) to see such performers as Neil Young, Counting Crows, Diana Krall, The Killers, The Cure, or No Doubt. If you choose the lawn seating, bring blankets and picnic fare (beverages must be bought on the premises).

My favorite summer setting for music is also the closest to D.C. and easiest to get to: **Wolf Trap Farm Park for the Performing Arts,** 1551 Trap Rd., Vienna, VA (✆ **703/255-1900** for general information, 703/255-1868 for tickets; www.wolftrap.org). The country's only national park devoted to the performing arts, Wolf Trap, 30 minutes by car from downtown D.C., offers performances by the National Symphony Orchestra (it's their summer home), and has hosted Lucinda Williams, Shawn Colvin, Lyle Lovett, The Temptations, Ani DiFranco, and many others. Performances take place in the 7,000-seat Filene Center, about half of which is under the open sky. You can also buy cheaper lawn seats on the hill, which is sometimes the nicest way to go. If you do, arrive early (the lawn opens 90 min. before the performance) and bring a blanket and a picnic dinner—it's a tradition. Wolf Trap also hosts a number of very popular **festivals,** including a daylong Irish music festival in May; the Louisiana Swamp Romp Cajun Festival and a weekend of jazz and blues in June; and the International Children's Festival each September.

The **Carter Barron Amphitheater,** 16th Street and Colorado Avenue NW (✆ **202/426-0486**), way out 16th Street, is in Rock Creek Park, close to the Maryland border. This is the area's smallest outdoor venue, with 4,250 seats. Summer performances include a range of gospel, blues, and classical entertainment. The shows are usually free, but tickets are required. You can always count on Shakespeare: The **Shakespeare Theatre Free For All** takes place at the Carter Barron usually for 2 weeks in late May/early June, Tuesday through Sunday evenings; the free tickets are available the day of performance only, on a first-come, first-served basis (call ✆ **202/334-4790** for details). The 2007 Free For All featured *Love's Labours Lost.*

SMALLER AUDITORIUMS

A handful of auditoriums in Washington are really fine places to catch a performance.

DAR Constitution Hall, on 18th Street NW, between C and D streets (✆ **202/628-4780;** www.dar.org), is housed within a beautiful turn-of-the-20th-century

Beaux Arts building and seats 3,746. Its excellent acoustics have supported an eclectic group of performers: Sting, the Buena Vista Social Club, John Hiatt, the Count Basie Orchestra, the Los Angeles Philharmonic, Lil' Bow Wow, Ray Charles, Trisha Yearwood, The Strokes, and the "O Brother Where Art Thou?" tour.

In the heart of happening U Street, the **Lincoln Theatre,** 1215 U St. NW (✆ **202/328-6000;** www.lovethelincoln.com), was once a movie theater, vaudeville house, and nightclub featuring black stars like Louis Armstrong and Cab Calloway. The theater closed in the 1970s and reopened in 1994 after a renovation restored it to its former elegance. Today the theater books jazz, R&B, gospel, and comedy acts, and events like the D.C. Film Festival.

The **Warner Theatre,** 513 13th St. NW, between E and F streets (✆ **202/783-4000;** www.warnertheatre.com), opened in 1924 as the Earle Theatre (a movie/vaudeville palace) and was restored to its original, neoclassical-style appearance in 1992 at a cost of $10 million. It's worth coming by just to see its ornately detailed interior. The 2,000-seat auditorium offers year-round entertainment, alternating dance performances, like the Washington Ballet's Christmas performance of *The Nutcracker,* with comedy acts, like those of Steven Wright or Damon Wayans, with headliner entertainment (John Prine, Bob Dylan).

2 Nightclubs

If you're looking for a more interactive, tuneful night on the town, Washington offers hip jazz clubs, gay bars, warehouse ballrooms, places where you sit back and listen, places where you can get up and dance, even a roadhouse or two. If you're looking for comic relief, Washington can take care of that, too (the pickings are few but good).

Many nightspots wear multiple hats. For example, the Black Cat is a bar and a dance club, offering food and sometimes poetry readings. I've listed each nightspot according to the type of music it features. The details are in the description.

The best nightlife districts are Adams-Morgan; U and 14th streets NW between 16th and 9th streets; north and south of Dupont Circle along Connecticut Avenue; the Penn Quarter, notably 7th and 8th streets and from Pennsylvania Avenue north as far as H Street; Georgetown; and D.C.'s newest bar and club scene, H Street NE, between 12th and 14th streets, in the area known as the Atlas District. As a rule, while club-hopping—even in Georgetown—stick to the major thoroughfares and steer clear of deserted side streets.

As stated in the introduction to this chapter, the best sources of information about what's doing at bars and clubs are *The Washington Post*'s "Weekend" edition, online at www.washingtonpost.com, and "Going Out Gurus" blog; the fat weekly, ***City Paper,*** available free at bookstores, movie theaters, drugstores, and other locations, and online at www.washingtoncitypaper.com; and the blog www.dcist.com. Also check out the monthly *On Tap,* another fat freebie found mostly in bars, but whose website, www.ontaponline.com, is essential reading for carefree 20-somethings. By the way, Thursday night is "College Night" at nearly every club.

Washington's clubs and bars tend to keep their own hours; it's best to call ahead to make sure the place you're headed to is open.

COMEDY

In addition to these two comedy venues, the **Warner Theatre** (see "Smaller Auditoriums," above) also features big-name comedians from time to time.

The Capitol Steps *Moments* This musical political satire troupe is made up of former Congressional staffers, equal-opportunity spoofers all, who poke endless fun through song and skits at politicians on both sides of the aisle and at government goings-on in general. Washingtonians have been fans since the Steps got started in 1981. Since then, the troupe has performed more than 5,000 shows and released more than 27 albums, including the latest, "Springtime for Liberals." Shows take place in the Amphitheater, on the concourse level of the Ronald Reagan Building and International Trade Center, at 7:30pm Friday and Saturday. Order tickets from Ticketmaster (✆ 202/397-SEAT) or in person at the Visitor Center of the Ronald Reagan Building. 1300 Pennsylvania Ave. NW (in the Ronald Reagan Building). ✆ **202/312-1555.** www.capsteps.com. Tickets $35. Metro: Federal Triangle.

The Improv The Improv features top performers on the national comedy club circuit as well as comic plays and one-person shows. *Saturday Night Live* performers David Spade, Chris Rock, and Adam Sandler have all played here, as have comedy bigs Ellen DeGeneres, Jerry Seinfeld, and Robin Williams. Shows are about 1½ hours long and include three comics (an emcee, a feature act, and a headliner). Showtimes are 8pm Sunday, 8:30pm Tuesday through Thursday, 8 and 10:30pm on Friday and Saturday. The best way to snag a good seat is to have dinner here (make reservations), which allows you to enter the club as early as 7pm Sunday through Thursday or after 6:30pm Friday and Saturday. The Friday and Saturday 10:30pm show serves drinks and appetizers only. Dinner entrees (nothing higher than $9.95) include sandwiches and Tex-Mex fare. You must be 18 to get in. 1140 Connecticut Ave. NW (between L and M sts.). ✆ **202/296-7008.** www.dcimprov.com. Cover $15–$35, plus a 2-item minimum. Metro: Farragut North.

ROCK/INDIE/ALTERNATIVE/HIP-HOP/DJ

This category is mostly about live music clubs, but also includes a sprinkling of nightclubs known for their DJs and dance floors.

The Birchmere Music Hall and Bandstand Worth the cab fare from downtown, if you're a fan of live music by varied, stellar performers, such as Garth Brooks, Jonatha Brooke, Jerry Jeff Walker, Crash Test Dummies, Shawn Colvin, Joe Sample, and John Hiatt. The Birchmere is unique in the area for providing a comfortable and relatively small (500-seat) setting, where you sit and listen to the music (there's not a bad seat in the house) and order food and drinks. The Birchmere got started 32 years ago, when it booked mostly country singers. The place has expanded over the years and so has its repertoire; there are still many country and bluegrass artists, but also folk, jazz, rock, gospel, and alternative musicians. The menu tends toward American favorites, such as nachos, burgers, and pulled-pork barbecue sandwiches. 3701 Mount Vernon Ave., Alexandria, VA. ✆ **703/549-7500.** www.birchmere.com. Ticket prices range $17–$60. Take a taxi or drive.

Black Cat This comfortable, low-key club draws a black-clad crowd to its concert hall, which features national, international, and local indie and alternative groups. The place is made for dancing, accommodating more than 600 people. Adjoining the hall is the Red Room Bar, a large, funky, red-walled living-roomy lounge with booths, tables, a red-leather sofa, pinball machines, a pool table, and a jukebox stocked with a really eclectic collection. A college crowd collects on weekends, but you can count on seeing a 20- to 30-something bunch here most nights, including members of various bands who like to stop in for a drink. Black Cat also hosts film screenings, poetry readings, and other quiet forms of entertainment in its ground-floor room called "Backstage," and serves vegetarian food in its smoke-free cafe. Say hello to affable

Tips Metro Takes You There

Not only do Metro trains run until 3am on weekends, but special shuttle service runs between Adams-Morgan (home to lots of nightclubs, but no Metro stations) and U Street.

Here's what you do: Take the Metro to the Red Line's Woodley Park–Zoo/Adams-Morgan Station or to the Green Line's U St.–Cardozo Station, and hop on the no. 98 Adams-Morgan–U St. Link Shuttle, which travels through Adams-Morgan, between these two stations, after 6pm daily, except on Saturday, when service starts at 10am. The U Link Shuttle operates every 15 minutes and costs only 25¢.

owner Dante Ferrando while you're here. Black Cat is open until 2am Sunday through Thursday, and until 3am Friday and Saturday. Concerts take place 4 or 5 nights a week, beginning at about 8:30pm (call for details). 1811 14th St. NW (between S and T sts.). ✆ **202/667-7960.** www.blackcatdc.com. Cover $5–$20 for concerts; no cover in the Red Room Bar. Metro: U St.–Cardozo.

DC9 This medium-size venue—which holds 250—debuted in spring 2004, with a commitment to offering both live music and DJ shows. Open nightly, DC9 features both indie rock bands and DJs for dancing, including a popular Liberation Party dance event Friday nights. The two-story club includes a bar downstairs with couches, booths, bar stools, and a digital jukebox of 130,000 tunes, and the hall upstairs reserved for music. 1940 9th St. NW. ✆ **202/483-5000.** www.dcnine.com. No cover downstairs, $5–$10 cover upstairs, depending on show. Metro: U St.–Cardozo.

Eighteenth Street Lounge This place maintains its "hot" status. First you have to find it, and then you have to convince the bouncer to let you in. So here's what you need to know: Look for the mattress shop south of Dupont Circle, then look up. "ESL" (as those in the know call it) sits above the shop. Wear something exotic and sexy, anything but preppy. If you pass inspection, you may be surprised to find yourself in a restored mansion (Teddy Roosevelt once lived here) with fireplaces, high ceilings, and a deck out back. Or maybe you'll just get right out there on the hardwood floors to dance to acid jazz, hip-hop, reggae, or Latin jazz tunes spun by a DJ. Weekends often feature live jazz or bossa nova. 1212 18th St. NW. ✆ **202/466-3922.** Cover $10–$20 Tues–Sat. Metro: Dupont Circle or Farragut North.

5 This small, three-level, DJ-driven dance club aims to capture some of the late-night crowd who are too wired to go home. Those in the know take a break by heading for the hammocks on the rooftop patio. Open Wednesday through Sunday nights, with music starting after 9pm. 1214-B 18th St. NW. ✆ **202/331-7123.** www.fivedc.com. Cover $5–$10. Metro: Dupont Circle or Farragut North.

kstreet Lounge You pay for the privilege of partying here: $300 to $500 will reserve you a table and bottle service. (A full bottle of your favorite liquor is delivered to your table with juices, mixes, limes, and glasses, just to make sure that the alcohol flows steadily throughout the evening.) Exclusivity is the name of the game, and if that appeals, call days ahead to book your table, especially for a Saturday romp. Even with a reservation, you might find yourself standing in line for a time. Decor is white minimalist and high tech, with plasma TVs broadcasting VIP arrivals. Dress code is simply minimal, the tighter and littler the dress the better in this beauty-competitive scene. Since there's no dedicated dance floor, dancers shimmy to the DJ beats wherever they find room. Open Monday to Saturday after 5:30pm and Sunday after 10pm. 1301 K St. NW. ✆ **202/962-3933.** www.kstreetdc.com. Cover $10 women, $20 men. Metro: McPherson Square.

9:30 Club Housed in a converted warehouse, this major live-music venue hosts frequent record-company parties and features a wide range of top performers. You might catch Sheryl Crow, Simple Minds, The Clarks, Luna, The Tragically Hip, Lucinda Williams, or even Tony Bennett. It's open only when there's a show on, which is almost every night (but call ahead), and, obviously, the crowd (as many as 1,200) varies with the performer. Best to buy tickets ($10–$50) in advance, whether at the box office or online. The sound system is state of the art and the sightlines are excellent. There are four bars: two on the main dance-floor level, one in the upstairs VIP room (anyone is welcome here unless the room is being used for a private party), and another in the distressed-looking cellar. The 9:30 Club is a stand-up place, literally—there are few seats. 815 V St. NW (at Vermont Ave.). ✆ **202/393-0930.** www.930.com. Metro: U St.–Cardozo, 10th St. exit.

Play Lounge For all of the Peters and Wendys out there who never wanna grow up, but who are old enough to drink. Arrive at the right time and you'll find everyone jumping up and down on the furniture. Located on the second floor of a town house in the same block of Connecticut Avenue as Dragonfly and 1223 (see listings in "Bars & Lounges"), Play is all about having a good time. Patrons rave about the DJ's choice of tunes, everything from '80s disco to Kanye West and the Black Eyed Peas. Those not bouncing on couches and ottomans are twirling around the stripper pole or go-go dancing on platforms set against the wall. Like all the latest clubs, Play allows you to reserve your own spot, to the tune of a $500 bar tab. Otherwise, the cover is usually $10. Open after 10pm: until 2am Tuesday and Thursday, until 3am Friday and Saturday. 1219 Connecticut Ave. NW. ✆ **202/466-7529.** www.playloungedc.com. Cover $10. Metro: Farragut North.

The Red & The Black Located along D.C.'s newest nightlife avenue, H St. NE, this club aims to offer an intimate setting for singer-songwriter acts, although louder indie rock bands frequently appear. The Red & The Black's owners also own the larger DC9 (see above), and it seems to catch that club's alternative sounds overflow. The two-story R&B features a New Orleans–style bar on its first level, with a tin ceiling and red velvet drape decor, jambalaya on the menu, and Abitas listed among the beers. The music takes the stage nightly upstairs. Drive here or take a taxi. Friday and Saturday nights, 10pm to 2:30am, the H Street bars offer free transportation, via the Atlas Courtesy Shuttle (✆ **202/906-0697**), to Union Station, where you can catch the Metro. 1212 H St. NE. ✆ **202/399-3201.** www.redandblackbar.com. Cover $5–$8.

Rock and Roll Hotel On the same street as The Red & The Black, above, the R&R opened first, attracting devoted music lovers and night crawlers to come shoot pool in its second-floor pool hall, listen to live bands in its 400-person concert hall, or toss back shots in its bar. Washingtonians are loving the punk rock decor of vintage furniture and flying guitars, but most especially the nightly acts, which range from local garage bands to national groups on tour. ***FYI:*** "Hotel" is just part of the name, no sleeping here. Drive here or take a taxi. Friday and Saturday nights, 10pm to 2:30am, the H Street bars offer free transportation, via the Atlas Courtesy Shuttle (✆ **202/906-0697**), to Union Station, where you can catch the Metro. 1353 H St. NE. ✆ **202/388-7625.** www.rockandrollhoteldc.com. Cover $8–$15.

Warehouse Next Door This tiny music venue is part of an art house complex, the Warehouse Theater (www.warehousetheater.com), which puts on plays and art shows, screens films, and offers a bar and cafe, as well as nearly nightly performances in the club. Musicians range widely from R&B to futuristic to hip-hop. It's cheap, funky, and a haven for aspiring artists in every medium. Check website for calendar. 1017 7th St. NW. ✆ **202/783-3933.** www.warehousenextdoor.com. Tickets $6–$10. Metro: Mount Vernon Sq./7th St. NW.

JAZZ & BLUES

A calendar of jazz gigs for these and other clubs is posted at **www.dcjazz.com**, although the website can be notoriously out-of-date. For instance, when last I looked, the website did not mention D.C.'s fabulous **Duke Ellington Jazz Festival.** The 2008 event will be its fourth annual. If you're a jazz fan and planning a trip to D.C. in September, check out the website, www.dejazzfest.org, for exact dates of the weeklong festival, which showcases the talents of at least 100 musicians in various venues around town, leading to a big free concert on the Mall on one of the final days.

Blues Alley Blues Alley, in Georgetown, has been Washington's top jazz club since 1965, featuring such artists as Karrin Allyson, Ahmad Jamal, Sonny Rollins, Wynton Marsalis, Rachelle Ferrell, and Maynard Ferguson. There are usually two shows nightly at 8 and 10pm; some performers also do midnight shows on weekends. Reservations are essential (call after noon); since seating is on a first-come, first-served basis, it's best to arrive no later than 7pm and have dinner. Entrees on the steak and Creole seafood menu are in the $17 to $23 range, snacks and sandwiches are $5.25 to $10, and drinks are $5.35 to $9. The decor is "classic dive": exposed brick walls; beamed ceiling; small, candlelit tables; and a very worn look about it. Sometimes well-known visiting musicians get up and jam with performers. 1073 Wisconsin Ave. NW (in an alley below M St.). ✆ **202/337-4141.** www.bluesalley.com. Cover $16–$75 (most fall in the $20–$40 range), plus $10 food or drink minimum, plus $2.50 surcharge. Metro: Foggy Bottom, then take the Georgetown Metro Connection Shuttle.

Bohemian Caverns Rising from the ashes on the very spot where jazz greats such as Duke Ellington, Billie Holiday, and so many others performed decades ago, Bohemian Caverns hopes to establish that same presence and host today's jazz stars. The club's decor is cavelike, as it was in the '20s. Artists appear on Friday and Saturday nights, at 9pm. The Caverns is also a restaurant, whose entrees are named after jazz legends and range in price from $7 to $19. 2001 11th St. NW (at U St.). ✆ **202/299-0801.** www.bohemiancaverns.com. Cover $5–$15. Metro: U St.–Cardozo.

HR-57 This cool club is named for the House Resolution passed in 1987 that designated jazz "a rare and valuable national American treasure." More than a club, HR-57 is also the Center for the Preservation of Jazz and Blues. Step inside Wednesday through Saturday evenings for a jazz jam session or star performance. 1610 14th St. NW. ✆ **202/667-3700.** www.hr57.org. Cover $6–$10. Metro: U St.–Cardozo or Woodley Park–Zoo/Adams-Morgan and catch the U Link Shuttle.

Madam's Organ Restaurant and Bar *Finds* This beloved Adams-Morgan hangout fulfills owner Bill Duggan's definition of a good bar: great sounds and sweaty people. The great sounds feature live music nightly: a funk/jazz/blues group on Sunday and Monday; Delta bluesman Ben Andrews on Tuesday; bluegrass with Bob Perilla & the Big Hillbilly Bluegrass Band on Wednesday; and the salsa sounds of Patrick Alban or Johnny Artis on Thursday, which is also Ladies' Night. On Friday and Saturday nights, regional blues groups pack the place—hope for Bobby Parker or Cathy Ponton King. The club includes a wide-open bar decorated eclectically with an antique gilded mirror, stuffed fish and animal heads, and paintings of nudes. The second-floor bar is called Big Daddy's Love Lounge & Pick-Up Joint, which tells you everything you need to know. Keep climbing the stairs to the rooftop deck, which is now open all year; you can't hear the music up there, but you'll discover an awesome view. ***Other notes:*** You can play darts here, and redheads pay half-price for drinks. Food is served, but I'd eat elsewhere. 2461 18th St. NW. ✆ **202/667-5370.** www.madamsorgan.com. Cover $3–$7. Metro: U St.–Cardozo or Woodley Park–Zoo/Adams-Morgan and catch the Adams-Morgan/U St. Link Shuttle.

Mr. Henry's Capitol Hill Mr. Henry's features Milan Sweet singing standards on Thursday nights, and the Kevin Cordt Trio Friday nights at 8pm; the musicians perform on the second floor of this cozy restaurant. There's no cover, but it's expected that you'll order something off the menu (perhaps a burger or gumbo). Mr. Henry's has been around for 42 years and has always attracted a gay and lesbian clientele, though it's a comfortable place for everyone. 601 Pennsylvania Ave. SE. ✆ **202/546-8412.** Minimum food/drink charge of $8. Metro: Eastern Market.

Smithsonian Jazz Café *Value* What a treat! The museum that's a must during the day is also a must Friday evenings, 6 to 10pm, when the Atrium Café features performances of local jazz pros. Smaller venues, like Blues Alley and HR-57, strictly enforce the "no talking during performance" policy, but the jazz cafe, which holds upward of 300 people, is too big and laid-back for that. It feels like a supper club, complete with couples dancing in front of the stage, only it's a nightclub with no age requirements, so go on and bring the family, if you like—children 12 and under are admitted free. A cash bar and extensive buffet are available. In the National Museum of Natural History, 10th St. NW and Constitution Ave. NW. ✆ **202/357-2700.** www.mnh.si.edu/jazz. $10 cover, no minimum for food and drink. Metro: Federal Triangle or Smithsonian.

Twins Jazz This intimate jazz club offers live music nearly every night—it's closed on Monday. On weeknights, you'll hear local artists; weekends are reserved for out-of-town acts, such as Bobby Watson, Gil Scott Heron, and James William. Musicians play two shows on Friday and Saturday nights, at 9 and 11pm. Sunday night is a weekly jam session attended by musicians from all over town. The menu features American, Ethiopian, and Caribbean dishes. The age group of the crowd varies. 1344 U St. NW. ✆ **202/234-0072.** www.twinsjazz.com. Cover $10–$30, with a 2-drink-per-person minimum. Metro: U St.–Cardozo.

U-topia Unlike most music bars, the arty New York/SoHo–style U-topia is serious about its restaurant operation. A moderately priced international menu ($12–$21 for entrees) features vegetable couscous curry and shrimp jambalaya, not to mention pastas and filet mignon with béarnaise sauce. There's also an interesting wine list and a large selection of beers and single-malt scotches. The setting is cozy and candlelit, with walls used for a changing art gallery show. The eclectic crowd here varies with the music, ranging from early 20s to about 35, for the most part, including South Americans and Europeans. There's live music Tuesday through Sunday, with Thursday always featuring live Brazilian jazz. 1418 U St. NW (at 14th St.). ✆ **202/483-7669.** www.utopiaindc.com. You must order drink or food. Metro: U St.–Cardozo.

Zoo Bar *Value* During the day, this establishment located across the street from, you guessed it, the zoo, caters to hungry families, but Thursday through Saturday nights after 10pm, it's a blues joint. Expect a divey setting and an eclectic crowd that skews

Late-Night Bites

If your stomach is grumbling after the show is over, the dancing has ended, or the bar has closed, you can always get a meal at one of a growing number of late-night or all-night eateries.

In Georgetown, the **Bistro Francais,** 3128 M St. NW (✆ **202/338-3830**), has been feeding night owls for years; it even draws some of the area's top chefs after their own establishments close. Open until 4am Friday and Saturday, until 3am every other night, the Bistro is thoroughly French, serving steak frites, omelets, and pâtés.

On U Street, **Ben's Chili Bowl** (p. 155), 1213 U St. NW (✆ **202/667-0909**), serves up chili dogs, turkey subs, and cheese fries until 4am on Friday and Saturday nights.

In Adams-Morgan one all-night dining option is the **Diner,** 2453 18th St. NW (✆ **202/232-8800**), which serves some typical (eggs and coffee, grilled cheese) and not-so-typical (a grilled fresh salmon club sandwich) diner grub.

Finally, in Dupont Circle, stop in at **Kramerbooks & Afterwords Café,** 1517 Connecticut Ave. NW (✆ **202/387-1400**), for big servings of everything, from quesadillas to french fries to French toast. The bookstore stays open all night on weekends, and so does its kitchen.

older. The quality of the music varies: Sometimes you'll stop in and find a serious bluesman from New Orleans, the next night it'll be a local boomer band fronted by a 20-something singer who can really belt it out. If you're looking for a hot club scene, this ain't it. But if you're a blues lover, the Zoo Bar's worth checking out. Plus, it's cheap—no cover—and conveniently located, right on Connecticut Avenue, a short walk from the Woodley Park–Zoo Metro stop on the Red Line. 3000 Connecticut Ave. NW (above Cathedral Ave. NW). ✆ **202/232-4225.** www.zoobardc.com. No cover. Metro: Woodley Park–Zoo.

INTERNATIONAL SOUNDS

Chi-Cha Lounge *Finds* You can sit around on couches, eat Andean-inspired tapas, and listen to live Latin music, which is featured Sunday through Wednesday. (DJ plays Fri–Sat.) Or you can sit around on couches and smoke Arabic tobacco through a 3-foot-high arguileh pipe. Or you can just sit around. This is a popular neighborhood place. 1624 U St. NW. ✆ **202/234-8400.** (Call after 5pm.) www.latinconcepts.com/chicha. $20 cover after 8pm. Metro: U St.–Cardozo.

Habana Village This three-story nightclub has a bar/restaurant on the first floor, where a band plays Latin jazz (Fri–Sat); a bar/dance floor with DJ on the second level; and a salsa-playing combo on the third floor (Fri–Sat). Salsa and merengue lessons are given Wednesday through Saturday evenings, $10 per lesson. 1834 Columbia Rd. NW. ✆ **202/462-6310.** www.habanavillage.com. Cover $5 Fri–Sat after 9:30pm (no cover for women). Metro: U St.–Cardozo or Woodley Park–Zoo/Adams-Morgan, and catch the Adams-Morgan/U St. Link Shuttle.

Zanzibar on the Waterfront This area is pretty deserted at night, except for a handful of restaurants and Arena Stage. It really doesn't matter, though, because inside the nightclub you're looking out at the Potomac. Yes, this is a club with actual windows and a covered deck overlooking the marina. In keeping with current trends, Zanzibar has lots of couches and chairs arranged just so. A Caribbean and African menu is available, and you can dine while listening to both live and DJ music. Open nightly, Zanzibar offers something different each night, from jazz and blues to oldies. Wednesday is salsa night, with free lessons from 7 to 8pm, though a cover still applies: $5 to get in before 10pm and $10 after. An international crowd gathers here to dance or just hang out. 700 Water St. SW. ✆ **202/554-9100.** www.zanzibar-otw.com. Cover typically $5–$15 (the club has an elaborate pricing structure). Metro: Waterfront.

GAY CLUBS

Dupont Circle is the gay hub of Washington, D.C., with at least 10 gay bars within easy walking distance of one another. Here are three from that neighborhood; also refer back to **Mr. Henry's Capitol Hill** (p. 274), whose live jazz on Friday night pleases every persuasion, though the restaurant itself has long been a popular spot for gays and lesbians.

Apex Apex (used to be called "Badlands") is an institution and still going strong as a favorite dance club for gay men. In addition to the parquet dance floor in the main room, the club has at least six bars throughout the first level. Upstairs is the Annex bar/lounge/pool hall, and a show room where karaoke performers commandeer the mic Friday night. 1415 22nd St. NW (at P St.). ✆ **202/296-0505.** www.apex-dc.com. Sometimes a cover of $3–$12, depending on the event. Metro: Dupont Circle.

Gazuza Actually, this second-story watering hole with its year-round deck overlooking Connecticut Avenue attracts straights as well as gays, couples as well as singles. Everyone wants to stand up there and survey the scene. The decor is upscale and industrial, but the glass-and-metal look is softened by candlelight and loungey sofas. D.C. doesn't offer lesbians an awful lot of club choices, but Gazuza's a good one. It's nearly right next door to the lesbian bookstore, Lambda Rising (p. 251), so if you meet someone there first, you can treat her to a drink just a few steps away at Gazuza. 1629 Connecticut Ave. NW (at Q St.). ✆ **202/667-5500.** www.latinconcepts.com/gazuza. Metro: Dupont Circle.

J.R.'s Bar and Grill This casual and intimate all-male Dupont Circle club draws a crowd that is friendly, upscale, and very attractive. The interior—not that you'll be able to see much of it, because J.R.'s is always sardine-packed—has a 20-foot-high pressed-tin ceiling and exposed brick walls hung with neon beer signs. The big screen over the bar area is used to air music videos, showbiz singalongs, and favorite TV shows. Every night offers a special something, like the Sunday $2 Skyy Highball all night long or Thursday's Retro night theme with free shots at midnight. The balcony, with pool tables, is a little more laid-back. Food is served daily, until 5pm Sunday and until 7pm all other days. 1519 17th St. NW (between P and Q sts.). ✆ **202/328-0090.** www.jrswdc.com. Metro: Dupont Circle.

3 Bars & Lounges

Washington has a thriving and varied bar scene. But just when you think you know all the hot spots, a spate of new ones pop up. If you want to be sure to visit the latest bunch, travel to U Street NW, between 9th and 18th streets; to H Street NE, between 12th and 14th streets; and to the Penn Quarter—these are the current favorite areas

Tips A Place to Drink In the View

If you visit Washington anytime between April and October, you must take yourself up to the eighth-floor, outdoor Sky Terrace of the Hotel Washington on 15th Street; order a classic gin and tonic or something more exotic; snag a seat on the covered veranda; lean back; take a sip of your cocktail; and admire the view: of the Washington Monument, Jefferson Memorial, White House, and beyond. This is the only place in town with just this vantage point. The atmosphere's a tad touristy, so if you're looking for romance, go later (the terrace is open until 12:30am), when families have retired to their hotels and the landmarks are illuminated.

for revelry in the city. Lounges are all the rage, so be sure to stop in at restaurants such as IndeBleu, Zengo, and Rasika. (See chapter 6 for details and more suggestions.)

If you're in the mood for a sophisticated setting, seek out a bar in one of the nicer hotels, like **the Willard,** the **Sofitel Lafayette Square,** the **Ritz-Carltons** (Degrees in the Georgetown Ritz is hip, the Bar in the West End Ritz is traditionally luxurious), or **the Hay-Adams** (see chapter 5). Otherwise, here is a range of options, from upscale to low-key, but each with its own character.

Big Hunt This casual and comfy Dupont Circle hangout for the 20- to 30-something crowd bills itself as a "happy hunting ground for humans" (read: meat market). It has a kind of *Raiders of the Lost Ark* jungle theme. A downstairs room (where music is the loudest) is adorned with exotic travel posters and animal skins; another area has leopard skin–patterned booths under canvas tenting. Amusing murals grace the balcony level, which adjoins a room with pool tables. The candlelit basement is the spot for quiet conversation. The menu offers typical bar food, and the bar offers close to 30 beers on tap, most of them microbrews. An outdoor patio lies off the back poolroom.

Note: This place and the Lucky Bar might be the perfect antidotes to their exclusive neighbors down the block, the Eighteenth Street Lounge, Dragonfly, and 1223. If you're rejected there, forget about it and come here. 1345 Connecticut Ave. NW (between N St. and Dupont Circle). ✆ **202/785-2333.** www.thebighuntdc.com. Metro: Dupont Circle.

Blue Gin Washingtonians still marvel that this buzz-worthy bar/lounge that attracts the likes of Owen Wilson and Vince Vaughn was once the domain of rowdy jocks and Georgetown students in its life as the sports bar Champions. You find it at the back of an alley off of Wisconsin Avenue, near M Street. Downstairs maintains a party atmosphere, where everyone drinks exotic martinis and ends up dancing on tabletops. Upstairs is a laid-back lounge, where you can spy on those below by looking through the glass-inlaid floor, or sit back and watch a film. Blue Gin's a swanky place, so dress accordingly. 1206 Wisconsin Ave. NW (at M St.). ✆ **202/965-5555.** www.bluegindc.com. $10 cover on weekends. Metro: Foggy Bottom, then take the Georgetown Connection Shuttle, D.C. Circulator, or a cab.

Bourbon *Finds* North of Georgetown, in the homey area known as "Glover Park," is this neighborhood bar that has a comfortable feel to it. The owners have invited their regulars to bring in black and white family photos, which they use to adorn the walls. Downstairs is a narrow room and long bar; upstairs is a dining room with leather booths. Fifty bourbons are on offer, along with 12 wines on draft, 10 beers on tap, and the usual complement of bar beverages. Another plus is the rooftop deck.

Value Cheap Eats: Happy Hours to Write Home About

Good-value promotions are often available at area bars and nightclubs, such as **Whitlow's on Wilson** in Arlington (see the "Electric Avenues for Live-Music Lovers" box on p. 280), where you can chow down on a half-price burger every Monday, good all day. A step above these are certain restaurants around town that set out tasty bites during happy hour, either free or for an astonishingly low price. Here are three that you might like:

In the bar area only, **McCormick & Schmick's,** 1652 K St. NW, at the corner of 17th Street NW (✆ **202/861-2233**), offers a choice of giant burger, fried calamari, quesadillas, fish tacos, and more, for only $1.95 each. The offer is good Monday through Friday from 3:30 to 6:30pm and Monday through Thursday 9:30 to 11pm.

In the Dupont Circle neighborhood, **Heritage India Brasserie,** 1337 Connecticut Ave. NW (✆ **202/331-1414**), serves up small-plate versions of Indian street food, in its rather sophisticated bar setting, Monday through Friday, 5 to 7pm (half-price tapas) and 4:30 to 7:30pm (drink specials). For $2 or $3, you can enjoy grilled chicken rolled in flat bread and cheese, or maybe a samosa or a lentil dumpling.

A few steps from Heritage India, at 1343 Connecticut Ave. NW, **Café Citron** (✆ **202/530-8844**) has sweet deals for those with Latino tastes: a range of items, from fried plantains, to fried cheese patties, to Bolivian potato cakes stuffed with beef and cheese, priced between $3 and $7.50. Café Citron's happy hour runs Monday through Friday, 5 to 7pm, with a second happy hour on Monday nights, 8 to 9pm, when the weekly flamenco show takes place.

Bourbon has a second location at 2321 18th St. NW (✆ **202/332-0800**). 2348 Wisconsin Ave. NW. ✆ **202/625-7770.** www.bourbondc.com. Take a taxi.

Brickskeller *Value* If you like beer and you like choices, head for the Brickskeller, which has been around for about 50 years and offers more than 1,000 beers from around the world. If you can't make up your mind, ask one of the waiters, who tend to be knowledgeable about the brews. The tavern draws students, college professors, embassy types, and people from the neighborhood. Brickskeller is a series of interconnecting rooms filled with gingham tableclothed tables (upstairs rooms are open only weekend nights). The food is generally okay; burgers are your best bet, especially the excellent Brickburger, topped with bacon, salami, onion, and cheese. 1523 22nd St. NW. ✆ **202/293-1885.** Metro: Dupont Circle or Foggy Bottom.

Busboys and Poets Salon, bookstore, restaurant, performance space, lounge, bar, political activist hangout: Busboys and Poets is all these things. The name pays tribute to poet Langston Hughes, who worked as a busboy at the Wardman Park Hotel in the 1920s, writing poems on the side. Busboys has been popular right from the start, and a diverse crowd collects here day and night to peck on their laptops, plan the revolution, and listen to spoken-word performances, pausing only to take a sip of a preferred beverage, whether a Corona or champagne. 2021 14th St. NW (at U St.). ✆ **202/387-POET.** www.busboysandpoets.com. Metro: U St/Cardozo.

Clyde's of Gallery Place This enormous new Clyde's, the latest in the local empire that includes a Georgetown branch (see chapter 6), looks like Las Vegas from the outside. Inside, the two-level, 23,000-square-foot salon is filled with eye-catching oil paintings of sailing and equestrian scenes, Tiffany glass, and burnished cherrywood furnishings. Three bars anchor the place, which is pretty much hopping every night of the week. As big as Clyde's is, it still gets crowded, especially before and after sports events at the Verizon Center, which is in the same block. Late-night prowlers will be happy to know that Clyde's stays open until 2am weekdays, 3am on weekends, with a late-night menu available daily until 1am. 707 7th St. NW (at H St.). ✆ **202/348-3700.** www.clydes.com. Metro: Gallery Place/Chinatown.

Dragonfly Expect to wait in line to get in here and the other hip clubs along this stretch of Connecticut Avenue. Dragonfly is a club, with music playing, white walls glowing, white-leather chairs beckoning, and people in black vogueing. And Dragonfly is a restaurant, with serious aspirations to please sushi lovers. 1215 Connecticut Ave. NW. ✆ **202/331-1775.** www.dragonflysushibar.com. Metro: Dupont Circle or Farragut North.

The Dubliner This is your typical old Irish pub, the port you can blow into in any storm, personal or weather-related. It's got the dark wood paneling and tables, the etched and stained-glass windows, an Irish-accented staff from time to time, and, most importantly, the Auld Dubliner Amber Ale. Most come here to imbibe, but the Dubliner is open daily from breakfast 'til last call; so if you're hungry, consider the burgers, grilled-chicken sandwich, or fish and chips. The Dubliner is frequented by Capitol Hill staffers and journalists who cover the Hill. Irish music groups play nightly. In the Phoenix Park Hotel, 520 N. Capitol St. NW, with its own entrance on F St. NW. ✆ **202/737-3773.** www.dublinerdc.com. Metro: Union Station.

ESPN Zone This is not a date place, unless your date happens to be Anna Kournikova. It's three levels of sports mania, in the form of interactive sports games, a restaurant, 200 televisions throughout the place tuned to sporting events, a bar area, and the most popular attraction, the Screening Room. This last venue offers a giant 16-foot video screen flanked by six 36-inch screens, each showing a different event. Seats with special headphones are arrayed in front of the screen, and you control what you listen to. ESPN Zone is also a sports bar/restaurant serving American staples: burgers, fries, huge salads, chicken tenders, and ribs. 555 12th St. NW. ✆ **202/783-3776.** www.espnzone.com/washingtondc. Metro: Metro Center.

Fadó Another Irish pub, but this one is Ireland as a theme park. The odd thing about it is its location: in the heart of Chinatown. Fadó was designed and built by the Irish Pub Company of Dublin, which shipped everything—the stone for the floors, the etched glass, the milled wood—from Ireland. The pub has separate areas, including an old Irish "bookstore" alcove and a country cottage bar. Authentic Irish food, like potato pancakes, is served with your Guinness. *Fadó,* Gaelic for "long ago," doesn't take reservations, which means that hungry patrons tend to hover over your table waiting for you to finish. The pub occasionally hosts live music performances. 808 7th St. NW. ✆ **202/789-0066.** www.fadoirishpub.com. Metro: Gallery Place/Chinatown.

Lucky Bar Lucky Bar is a good place to kick back and relax. But, in keeping with the times, it also features free salsa dance lessons on Monday night. Sometimes the music is live, but mostly it's courtesy of a DJ. Other times the jukebox plays, but never so loud that you can't carry on a conversation. The bar has a front room overlooking Connecticut Avenue and a back room decorated with good-luck signs, couches, hanging TVs, booths, and a pool table. Lucky Bar is known in the area as a "soccer bar," with its TVs

Electric Avenues for Live-Music Lovers

Live music venues are ever more popular in the capital, and one neighborhood is particularly noteworthy for the sheer number and variety of fabulous music on tap on any given night: U Street NW, between 9th and 18th streets, and its side streets. Whether you're a fan of jazz, hip-hop, indie rock, or blues, you're bound to find something to please you just by strolling along the U and 14th street corridors, especially on a Friday or Saturday evening. Bohemian Caverns, HR-57, Twins Jazz, Chi-Cha Lounge, U-Topia, the 9:30 Club, DC9, and the Black Cat are among the clubs listed in this chapter. In another part of town that's come to be known as the "Atlas District," live music venues also are springing up along H Street NE, between 12th and 14th streets (though it must be said that this locale, especially at night, is pretty iffy). Two Atlas District clubs are reviewed in this chapter: The Red & The Black, p. 272, and the Rock and Roll Hotel, p. 272. For a less urban experience, you might also check out a stretch of suburban street in Arlington, Virginia: a section of Wilson Boulevard in the Clarendon neighborhood, roughly between Highland and Edgewood roads. Arlington Row is a lot tamer and tends to attract a crowd of all ages, usually dressed for comfort. And though it's outside the District, the area is easy to reach by Metro. Streets are safer and clubs front the streets with picture windows and aren't as exclusive.

The music is live, it's outstanding (most of the time), and it's here almost nightly. So take the Metro to the Clarendon stop and walk down Wilson, or drive up Wilson from Key Bridge, turn left on Edgewood Road or another side street, and park on the street. Check out these three spots, all within walking distance of each other; all serve food:

Galaxy Hut, 2711 Wilson Blvd. (✆ **703/525-8646;** www.galaxyhut.com), is a comfortable bar with far-out art on the walls and a patio in the alley. Look for live alternative rock Saturday and Sunday nights; sometimes a $5 cover.

At **IOTA,** 2832 Wilson Blvd. (✆ **703/522-8340;** iotaclubandcafe.com), the best of the area's bands (if either Little Pink or Last Train Home is performing, go), as well as up-and-coming groups, take the stage nightly in a setting with minimal decor (cement floor, exposed brick walls, and a wood-beamed ceiling) and a patio in back. There's live music nightly. When a cover is charged, it's usually $8 to $18.

Whitlow's on Wilson, 2854 Wilson Blvd. (✆ **703/276-9693;** www.whitlows.com), is the biggest spot on the block, spreading throughout four rooms, the first showcasing the music (usually blues, with anything from surfer music to rock thrown in). The place has the appearance of a diner, from Formica table-booths to a soda fountain, and serves retro diner food. (Mon half-price burger nights are a good deal.) The other rooms hold coin-operated pool tables, dart boards, and air hockey. Cover is usually $3 to $5 Thursday through Saturday after 9pm.

turned to soccer matches going on around the world. 1221 Connecticut Ave. NW. ✆ **202/331-3733.** www.luckybardc.com. Metro: Dupont Circle or Farragut North.

Lucky Strike Lanes Drink up and bowl the night away at this bowling alley/lounge in the heart of the Penn Quarter, directly across from the Verizon Center. Here you'll find a rambunctious crowd cheering, drinking, and giving the game their best shots, as a DJ plays loud hip-hop and R&B tunes. If you have to wait for a lane, which is likely if you haven't called ahead to reserve one, you can lounge on a sofa or banquette, play a game of pool, have a drink or a bite to eat at the 50-foot bar, or watch sports on one of the 10-foot projection screens. The alley is open 11am to 2am daily; ages 21 and older after 9pm. 701 7th St. NW. ✆ **202/347-1021.** www.bowllucky strike.com. Metro: Gallery Place/Verizon Center.

The Tombs Housed in a converted 19th-century Federal-style home, The Tombs, which opened in 1962, is a favorite hangout for students and faculty of nearby Georgetown University. (Bill Clinton came here during his college years.) They tend to congregate at the central bar and surrounding tables, while local residents head for "the Sweeps," the room that lies down a few steps and has red-leather banquettes.

Directly below the upscale 1789 restaurant (p. 165), The Tombs benefits from 1789 chef Nathan Beauchamp's supervision. The menu offers burgers, sandwiches, and salads, as well as more serious fare. 1226 36th St. NW. ✆ **202/337-6668.** www.tombs.com. Metro: Foggy Bottom, then take the Georgetown Metro Connection shuttle into Georgetown, with a walk from Wisconsin Ave.

Top of the Hill This is three separate bars in one. The Pour House, on the first floor, plays on a Pittsburgh theme (honoring the owner's roots), displaying Steeler and Penguin paraphernalia, and drawing Iron City drafts from its tap and pirogi from the kitchen. Downstairs is the Scheisse Haus, a faux biergarten. The basement has pool tables, a bar, and a lounge area (behind beaded curtains); the street level has booths and a bar. On the top floor is "Top of the Hill," which is promoted as "hip and upscale," but it's not, really (although you will find leather chairs, art, and chandeliers here). 319 Pennsylvania Ave. SE. ✆ **202/546-7782.** www.politiki-dc.com. Metro: Capitol South.

Tryst This is the most relaxed of Washington's lounge bars. The room is surprisingly large for Adams-Morgan, and it's jampacked with worn armchairs and couches, which are usually occupied, no matter what time of day. People come here to have coffee or a drink, get a bite to eat, read a book, or meet a friend. The place feels almost like a student lounge on a college campus, except alcohol is served. A bonus: Tryst offers free wireless Internet service. 2459 18th St. NW. ✆ **202/232-5500.** www.trystdc.com. Metro: U St.–Cardozo or Woodley Park–Zoo/Adams-Morgan and catch the Adams-Morgan/U St. Link Shuttle.

Tune Inn *Finds* Capitol Hill has a number of bars that qualify as institutions, but the Tune Inn is probably the most popular. Capitol Hill staffers and their bosses, apparently at ease in dive surroundings, have been coming here for cheap beer and greasy burgers since it opened in 1955. (All the longtime Capitol Hillers know that Friday is crab-cake day at the Tune Inn, and they all show up.) 33½ Pennsylvania Ave. SE. ✆ **202/5432725.** Metro: Capitol South.

1223 At swank 1223, hipsters line up at the velvet rope, dressed to catch the eye and convince the doorman to admit them; drinks and food are outrageously high-priced; a soaring ceiling, plush couches, and crystal chandeliers create an opulent interior; and beautiful women servers purr at you, as other beautiful people mill about. Interested? 1223 Connecticut Ave. NW. ✆ **202/822-1800.** www.1223.com. Cover $10 after 10pm. Metro: Dupont Circle or Farragut North.

10

Side Trips from Washington, D.C.

To those of us who live in the Washington area, Old Town Alexandria, a mere 8 miles south of the capital, feels less like a side trip and more like just another neighborhood, or like another room in our house—a fun room. (It's no coincidence that the Alexandria Convention & Visitors Association website address is www.funside.com.) Founded in 1749, this compact, walkable waterfront town contains cobblestone streets, colonial and pre-Revolutionary architecture, of-the-moment eateries, and boutiques catering to everyone from fancy soap lovers to fashion nuts. We tend to take for granted our Old Town and its sister attraction, George Washington's Estate (another 8 miles farther south), but you shouldn't miss them. If you're mainly here to take in the capital but have just enough time for a day excursion, cross the Potomac River to visit Old Town Alexandria and Mount Vernon.

1 Mount Vernon

Only 16 miles south of the capital, George Washington's Southern plantation dates from a 1674 land grant to the president's great-grandfather.

ESSENTIALS

GETTING THERE If you're going by car, take any of the bridges over the Potomac River into Virginia and follow the signs pointing the way to National Airport/Mount Vernon/George Washington Memorial Parkway. Travel south on the George Washington Memorial Parkway, the river always to your left, pass by National Airport on your right, continue through Old Town Alexandria, where the parkway is renamed "Washington Street," and head 8 miles farther, until you reach the large circle that fronts Mount Vernon.

You might also take a bus or boat to Mount Vernon. **These bus and boat tour prices include the price of admission to Mount Vernon.**

Gray Line Buses (© **800/862-1400,** or at Union Station 301/386-8300; www.graylinedc.com) go to Mount Vernon daily (except Christmas, Thanksgiving, and New Year's Day), leaving from the bus's terminal at Union Station at 8am and returning by 1:30pm. The ticket kiosk is on the first level of the parking garage. The cost is $40 per adult and $20 per child. (AAA members can show their membership card to receive a 10% discount.) From mid-June to October, Gray Line operates a second tour to Mount Vernon, leaving Union Station at 2pm. Ticket prices are the same. Gray Line offers several other tours, so call for further information.

The Spirit of Washington Cruises' (© **202/554-8000;** www.spiritcruises.com) ***Spirit of Washington II*** leaves from Pier 4 (6th and Water sts. SW; 3 blocks from the Green Line Metro's Waterfront Station) at 8:30am, returning by 3pm, on the following schedule: Tuesday through Sunday from April to September; Thursday through

Fun Fact The George Washington Memorial Parkway

Though few people realize it, the George Washington Memorial Parkway is actually a national park. The first section was completed in 1932 to honor the bicentennial of George Washington's birth. The parkway follows the Potomac River, running from Mount Vernon, past Old Town and the nation's capital, ending at Great Falls, Virginia. Today, the parkway is a major commuter route leading into and out of the city. Even the most impatient driver, however, can't help but notice the beautiful scenery and views of the Jefferson and Lincoln memorials and the Washington Monument that you pass along the way.

Sunday for the last 2 weeks of March; and Friday and Saturday September through October. The cost is $39 per adult, $32 per child (ages 6–11; younger children free).

The Potomac Riverboat Company's (© **703/684-0580** or 877/511-2628; www.potomacriverboatco.com) ***Miss Christin*** operates Tuesday through Sunday April through August, weekends only in September and October, departing at 11am for Mount Vernon from the pier adjacent to the Torpedo Factory, where Union and Cameron streets intersect, at Old Town Alexandria's waterfront. The weekday fare costs $34 per adult, $17 per child (ages 6–11; free for children under 6); the weekend rate is $36 per adult, $18 per child. Arrive 30 minutes ahead of time at the pier to secure a place on the boat. The narrated trip takes 50 minutes each way. The boat departs Mount Vernon at 4pm to return to Old Town.

If you're in the mood for exercise in a pleasant setting, rent a **bike** (see "Biking to Old Town Alexandria & Mount Vernon," on p. 290, for rental locations and other information).

Finally, it is possible to take **public transportation** to Mount Vernon by riding the Metro to the Yellow Line's Huntington Station and proceeding to the lower level, where you catch the Fairfax Connector bus (no. 101) to Mount Vernon. The connector bus departs hourly on weekends, every 30 minutes weekdays; it's a 25-minute ride and costs $1. Call © **703/339-7200** for schedule information.

TOURING THE ESTATE

Mount Vernon Estate and Gardens If it's beautiful out and you have the time, you could easily spend half a day or more soaking in the life and times of George Washington at Mount Vernon. The centerpiece of a visit to this 500-acre estate is a tour through 14 rooms of the mansion, whose oldest part dates from the 1740s. The plantation was passed down from Washington's great-grandfather, who acquired the land in 1674, to George's half brother, and eventually to George himself in 1754. Washington proceeded over the next 45 years to expand and fashion the home to his liking, though the American Revolution and his years as president kept Washington away from his beloved estate much of the time.

In Fall 2006, the estate opened a fantastic orientation and education complex, just inside the main gate, with much of it built underground so as not to take away from the estate's pastoral setting. A 15-minute film in the orientation center fills you in on the life and character of George Washington. The education center's 25 galleries and theater presentations inform you further about Washington's military and presidential careers, rounding out the whole story of this heroic, larger-than-life man. It's especially

Tips Special Activities at Mount Vernon

Events at Mount Vernon, especially in the summer, include tours on 18th-century gardens, slave life, Colonial crafts, or archaeology; and, for children, hands-on history programs and treasure hunts. Call or check the website for schedule details.

helpful to absorb this information and gain some context for the life and times of Washington before setting off for the mansion, where tours are self-guided. Attendants stationed throughout the house and grounds do provide brief orientations and answer questions; when there's no line, a walk-through takes about 20 minutes. What you see today is a remarkable restoration of the mansion, displaying many original furnishings and objects used by the Washington family. The rooms have been repainted in the original colors favored by George and Martha.

After leaving the house, you can tour the outbuildings: the kitchen, slave quarters, storeroom, smokehouse, overseer's quarters, coach house, and stables. A 4-acre exhibit area called "George Washington, Pioneer Farmer" includes a replica of Washington's 16-sided barn and fields of crops that he grew (corn, wheat, oats, and so forth). Docents in period costumes demonstrate 18th-century farming methods. At its peak, Mount Vernon was an 8,000-acre working farm, reminding us that, more than anything, Washington considered himself first and foremost a farmer.

You'll want to walk around the grounds (especially in nice weather) and see the wharf (and take a 40-min. narrated excursion on the Potomac, offered several times a day, seasonally, Mar–Oct; $9 per adult, $5 per child ages 6–11), the slave burial ground, the greenhouse, the lawns and gardens, and the tomb containing George and Martha Washington's sarcophagi (24 other family members are also interred here). In spring 2007, Mount Vernon opened the restored distillery, located 3 miles south of the estate, next to the gristmill. Costumed staff operate the gristmill and distillery and demonstrate 18th-century techniques; admission is charged: $4 per adult and $2 per child, or, when combined with your Mount Vernon admission, $2 per adult and $1.50 per child. Celebrations are held at the estate every year on the third Monday in February, the date commemorating Washington's birthday; admission is free to anyone who shares Washington's birthday, February 22.

Mount Vernon belongs to the Mount Vernon Ladies' Association, which purchased the estate for $200,000 in 1858 from John Augustine Washington, great-grand-nephew of the first president. Without the group's purchase, the estate might have crumbled and disappeared, for neither the federal government nor the Commonwealth of Virginia had wanted to buy the property when it was earlier offered for sale.

Today more than a million people tour the property annually. The best time to visit is off-season; during the heavy tourist months (especially in spring), avoid weekends and holidays if possible, and arrive early year-round to beat the crowds.

Southern end of the George Washington Memorial Pkwy. (mailing address: P.O. Box 110, Mount Vernon, VA 22121). ✆ **703/780-2000.** www.mountvernon.org. Admission $13 adults, $12 seniors, $6 children 6–11, free for children under 6. Apr–Aug daily 8am–5pm; Mar and Sept–Oct daily 9am–5pm; Nov–Feb daily 9am–4pm.

DINING & SHOPPING

Mount Vernon's comprehensive **gift shop** offers a wide range of books, children's toys, holiday items, Mount Vernon private-labeled food and wine, and Mount Vernon licensed furnishings. A **food court** features indoor and outdoor seating and a menu of baked goods, deli sandwiches, coffee, grilled items, pizza, and Mrs. Fields cookies. Although you can't **picnic** on the grounds of Mount Vernon, you can drive a mile north on the parkway to Riverside Park, where there are tables and a lawn overlooking the Potomac. But the Mount Vernon Inn restaurant is the option I'd recommend.

Mount Vernon Inn AMERICAN TRADITIONAL Lunch or dinner at the inn is an intrinsic part of the Mount Vernon experience. It's a quaint and charming Colonial-style restaurant, complete with period furnishings and three working fireplaces. The waiters are all in 18th-century costumes. Be sure to begin your meal with the homemade peanut and chestnut soup (usually on the lunch menu). Lunch entrees range from Colonial turkey "pye" (a sort of Early American stew served in a crock with garden vegetables and a puffed pastry top) to a pulled-pork barbecue sandwich. There's a full bar, and premium wines are offered by the glass. At dinner, tablecloths and candlelight make this a more elegant setting. Choose from soups (perhaps broccoli cheddar) and salads, entrees such as roasted duck served with George Washington's favorite apricot sauce or roast venison with peppercorn sauce, homemade breads, and dessert (like whiskey cake or English trifle).

Near the entrance to Mount Vernon Estate and Gardens. ✆ **703/780-0011.** www.mountvernon.org. Reservations recommended for dinner. Lunch main courses $5.50–$8.50; dinner main courses $13–$25. AE, DISC, MC, V. Daily 11am–3:30pm (11:30am–2:30pm weekdays in winter) and Mon–Sat 5–9pm.

2 Alexandria

Old Town Alexandria is about 8 miles south of Washington.

The city of Washington may be named for our first president, but he never lived there. No, he called this other side of the Potomac home from the age of 11, when he joined his half brother Lawrence, who owned Mount Vernon. Washington came to Alexandria often, helping to survey its 60 acres when he was a capable lad of 17, training his militia in Market Square, worshiping at Christ Church, and dining and dancing at Gadsby's Tavern.

The town of Alexandria is actually named after John Alexander, the Scot who purchased the land of the present-day town from an English ship captain for "six thousand pounds of Tobacco and Cask." Incorporated in 1749, the town soon grew into a major trading center and port, known for its handsome houses.

Today, many of those handsome houses and the places frequented by George Washington stand at the heart of Old Town, a multimillion-dollar urban renewal historic district. Market Square is the site of the oldest continuously operating farmers' market in the country. (Go there on Sat between 5 and 10am and you'll be participating in a 256-year-old tradition.) Christ Church and Gadsby's Tavern are still open and operating. Many Alexandria streets still bear their original Colonial names (King, Queen, Prince, Princess, Royal—you get the drift), while others, like Jefferson, Franklin, Lee, Patrick, and Henry, are obviously post-Revolutionary.

Twenty-first-century America thrives in Old Town's many shops, boutiques, art galleries, bars, and restaurants. But it's still easy to imagine yourself in Colonial times by listening for the rumbling of horse-drawn vehicles over cobblestone (portions of Prince and Oronoco streets are still paved with cobblestone); dining on Sally Lunn bread and other 18th-century grub in the centuries-old Gadsby's Tavern; and learning about the lives of the nation's forefathers during walking tours that take you in and out of their houses.

ESSENTIALS

GETTING THERE If you're driving from the District, take the Arlington Memorial or the 14th Street Bridge to the George Washington Memorial Parkway south, which becomes Washington Street in Old Town Alexandria. Washington Street intersects with King Street, Alexandria's main thoroughfare. Turn left from Washington Street onto one of the streets before or after King Street (southbound left turns are not permitted from Washington St. onto King St.) and you'll be heading toward the waterfront and the heart of Old Town. If you turn right from Washington Street onto King Street, you'll find an avenue of shops and restaurants. You can obtain a free parking permit from the Visitors Center (see information about parking in the "Visitor Information" paragraph, below), or park at meters or in garages. The town is compact, so you won't need a car.

The easiest way to make the trip may be the Metro's Yellow and Blue lines to the King Street station. From the King Street station, you can catch an eastbound AT2 or AT5 blue-and-gold DASH bus (✆ **703/370-DASH;** www.dashbus.com), marked either OLD TOWN or BRADDOCK METRO, which will take you up King Street. Ask to be dropped at the corner of Fairfax and King streets, which will put you right across the street from Ramsay House, the visitor center. The fare is $1 most of the time, but free from Friday evening to Sunday night, aboard the colorfully painted Dash About buses. Or you can walk into Old Town, although it's about a mile from the station into the center of Old Town.

VISITOR INFORMATION The **Alexandria Convention and Visitors Association**'s Ramsay House Visitors Center, 221 King St., at Fairfax Street (✆ **800/388-9119** or 703/838-5005; www.funside.com), is open daily from 9am to 5pm (closed Jan 1, Thanksgiving, and Dec 25). Here you can obtain a map/self-guided walking tour and brochures about the area; learn about special events that might be scheduled during your visit and get tickets for them; and receive answers to any questions you might have about accommodations, restaurants, sights, or shopping. The center supplies materials in five languages.

If you come by car, get a free 1-day parking permit here for any 2-hour meter for up to 24 hours; when you park at the Visitors Center, be sure to put money in the meter to cover yourself until you get back outside with your permit. The permit can be renewed for a second day.

ORGANIZED TOURS Though it's easy to see Alexandria on your own by putting yourself in the hands of Colonial-attired guides at individual attractions, you might consider taking a comprehensive walking tour. Architectural and history tours leave from the Visitors Center garden, weather permitting, at least once a day, Monday through Saturday, at 10:30am, with additional tours added during busy seasons. The 1½-hour tour costs $15 per person (free for age 6 and under), and you pay the guide when you arrive at the Visitors Center.

Alexandria Colonial Tours (✆ **703/519-1749;** www.alexcolonialtours.com) conducts a number of different tours, including its Ghosts and Graveyard Tour, offered March through November (again, weather permitting) at 7:30 and 9pm Friday and Saturday, 7:30pm only on Sunday, with a 7:30pm tour offered Wednesday and Thursday evenings in the summer. This 1-hour tour departs from Ramsay House and costs $10 for adults, $5 for children ages 7 to 12, free for children under 7. You purchase tickets from the guide, who will be dressed in Colonial attire and standing in front of the Visitors Center.

Old Town Alexandria

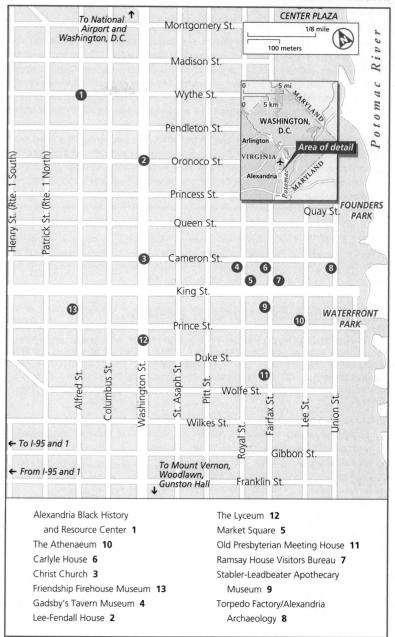

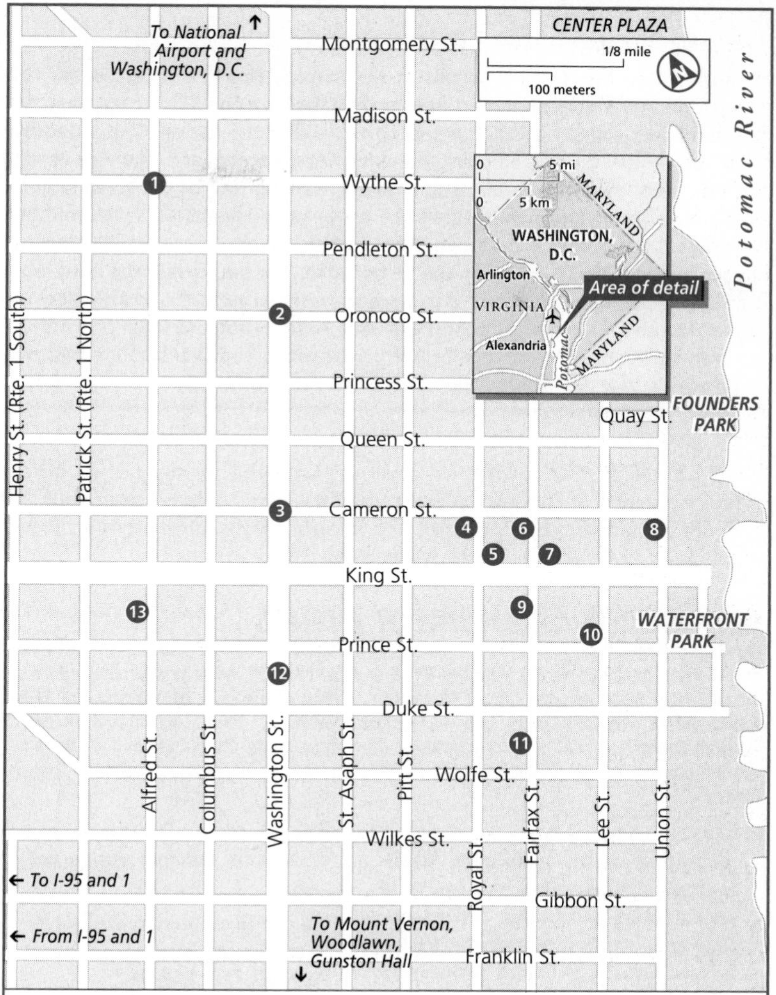

Alexandria Black History and Resource Center **1**
The Athenaeum **10**
Carlyle House **6**
Christ Church **3**
Friendship Firehouse Museum **13**
Gadsby's Tavern Museum **4**
Lee-Fendall House **2**
The Lyceum **12**
Market Square **5**
Old Presbyterian Meeting House **11**
Ramsay House Visitors Bureau **7**
Stabler-Leadbeater Apothecary Museum **9**
Torpedo Factory/Alexandria Archaeology **8**

Value Very Important Patriot (VIP) Pass

Money-saving tickets are on sale at the **Ramsay House Visitors Center.** One example is the **Very Important Patriot (VIP) Pass,** costing $23 for an adult, $11 for children ages 11 to 17. The pass admits you to the Carlyle House, Gadsby's Tavern Museum, the Stabler-Leadbeater Apothecary, and the Lee-Fendall House and reserves your place on a guided walking tour of Old Town (a ghost tour or a history and architecture tour), as well as a ride aboard a riverboat that cruises the Potomac River along the Alexandria waterfront. The VIP Pass can save you at least $7 per adult and $8 per child. The pass makes the most sense if you're staying more than 1 day, since it covers an awful lot of activities. You should also know that the pass is available April through October and only on weekends during the months of April, September, and October; the pass may be used at any time during the season. Ask about other passes.

CITY LAYOUT Old Town is very small and laid out in an easy grid. At the center is the intersection of Washington Street and King Street. Streets change from North to South when they cross King Street. For example, North Alfred Street is the part of Alfred north of King Street. Guess where South Alfred Street is.

ALEXANDRIA CALENDAR OF EVENTS

Two organizations publish helpful calendars of key Alexandria events: the **Alexandria Convention and Visitors Association** (© **800/388-9119** or 703/838-4200; www.funside.com), which covers Alexandria at large; and the City of Alexandria's **Office of Historic Alexandria** (© **703/838-4554;** www.ci.alexandria.va.us: Click on "Historic Alexandria," then "Tourism and History," then "Historic Events Calendar"), which focuses on the historic sights. You can call and ask them to mail you information, or you can access their separate and continually updated websites. Event highlights include:

February

Alexandria celebrates **George Washington's Birthday** over the course of several days, including Presidents' Weekend, which precedes the federal holiday, usually the third Monday in February. Festivities typically include a Colonial costume or black-tie banquet, followed by a ball at Gadsby's Tavern, a 10-kilometer race, special tours, a Revolutionary War encampment at Fort Ward Park (complete with uniformed troops engaging in skirmishes), the nation's largest George Washington Birthday Parade (50,000–75,000 people attend each year), and 18th-century comic opera performances. Most events, such as the parade and historical reenactments, are free. The Birthnight Ball at Gadsby's Tavern requires tickets for both the banquet and the ball.

March

On the first Saturday in March, King Street is the site of a popular **St. Patrick's Day Parade.**

April

Alexandria celebrates **Historic Garden Week in Virginia** with tours of privately owned local historic homes and gardens the third Saturday of the month. Call the Visitors Center (© **703/838-4200**) in early 2008 for more information about tickets and admission prices for the tour.

June

The **Red Cross Waterfront Festival,** the second or third weekend in June, honors Alexandria's historic importance as a seaport and the vitality of its Potomac shoreline today with a display of historic tall ships, ship tours, boat rides and races, nautical art exhibits, waterfront walking tours, fireworks, children's games, an arts-and-crafts show, food booths, and entertainment.

July

Alexandria's birthday (its 259th in 2008) is celebrated with a concert performance by the Alexandria Symphony Orchestra, fireworks, birthday cake, and other festivities. The Saturday following the Fourth of July. All events are free.

September

Alexandria Festival of the Arts features the ceramics, sculpture, photography, and other works of more than 200 juried artists. On a Saturday and Sunday in early September. Free.

This year is the 67th Annual **Tour of Historic Alexandria Homes,** which takes you to some of the city's most beautifully restored and decorated private homes. Third Saturday in September. Tickets and information from the Visitors Center.

October

Halloween Walking Tours take place toward the end of October. A lantern-carrying guide in 18th-century costume describes Alexandria's ghosts, graveyards, legends, myths, and folklore as you tour the town and graveyards. Call the Visitors Center for information.

November

There's a **Christmas Tree Lighting** in Market Square the Friday after Thanksgiving; the ceremony, which includes choir singing, puppet shows, dance performances, and an appearance by Santa and his elves, begins at 7pm. The night the tree is lit, thousands of tiny lights adorning King Street trees also go on.

December

Holiday festivities continue with the **Annual Scottish Christmas Walk** on the first Saturday in December. Activities include kilted bagpipers, Highland dancers, a parade of Scottish clans (with horses and dogs), caroling, fashion shows, storytelling, booths (selling crafts, antiques, food, hot mulled punch, heather, fresh wreaths, and holly), and children's games. Admission is charged for some events.

The **Historic Alexandria Candlelight Tour,** the second week in December, visits seasonally decorated historic Alexandria homes and an 18th-century tavern. There are Colonial dancing, string quartets, madrigal and opera singers, and refreshments. Purchase tickets at the Ramsay House Visitors Center.

There are so many **holiday-season activities** that the Visitors Association issues a special brochure about them each year. Pick one up to learn about decorations, workshops, walking tours, tree lightings, concerts, bazaars, bake sales, craft fairs, and much more.

WHAT TO SEE & DO

Colonial and post-Revolutionary buildings are Old Town Alexandria's main attractions. My favorites are the Carlyle House and Gadsby's Tavern Museum, but they're all worth a visit.

Except for the Alexandria Black History and Resource Center, whose closest Metro stop is the Braddock Street station, and Fort Ward, to which you should drive or take a taxi, these sites are most easily accessible via the King Street Metro station, combined with a ride on the DASH bus to the center of Old Town.

Moments Biking to Old Town Alexandria & Mount Vernon

One of the nicest ways to view the Washington skyline is from across the river while biking in Virginia. Rent a bike at Thompson's Boat Center, across from the Kennedy Center and right on the bike path, or from some other location listed under "Outdoor Activities," in chapter 7; then hop on the pathway that runs along the Potomac River, heading toward the monuments and the Arlington Memorial Bridge. In Washington, this is the Rock Creek Park Trail; when you cross Memorial Bridge (near the Lincoln Memorial) into Virginia, the name changes to the Mount Vernon Trail, which, as it sounds, is a straight shot to Mount Vernon.

As you tool along, you have a breathtaking view of the Potomac and of Washington's grand landmarks: the Kennedy Center, Washington Monument, Lincoln Memorial, Jefferson Memorial, and the National Cathedral off in one direction, and the Capitol off in the other.

Of course, this mode of transportation is also a great way to see Old Town Alexandria and Mount Vernon. The trail carries you past Reagan National Airport via two pedestrian bridges that take you safely through the airport's roadway system. Four miles out of Old Town you'll reach Daingerfield Island and a great new restaurant, Indigo Landing, whose riverside location and delicious menu might beckon you off your bike; if you're not too grubby, surrender. Then continue on to Old Town, where you really should lock your bike to a lamppost, walk around, tour some of the historic properties listed in this chapter, or, if you haven't dined at Indigo Landing, take in some refreshment from one of the many excellent restaurants, before you proceed to Mount Vernon. The section from Memorial Bridge to Mount Vernon is about 19 miles in all.

Old Town is second only to Georgetown for the area's best shopping district. Brand-name stores, charming boutiques, antiques shops, art galleries, and gift shops sell everything you might desire. The Visitors Center offers brochures for specific stores as well as a general guide to shopping. Also see chapter 8, which includes some Alexandria shops.

Alexandria Black History Resource Museum In 1940, African Americans in Alexandria staged a sit-in to protest the segregation of blacks from Alexandria's main library. The community built their own public library and it is this 1940s building that now serves as the Black History Resource Museum. The center exhibits historical objects, photographs, documents, and memorabilia relating to black citizens of Alexandria from the 18th century forward. In addition to the permanent collection, the museum presents rotating exhibits and other activities. If you're interested in further studies, check out the center's Watson Reading Room. A half-hour may be enough time to spend at the center.

The museum is actually on the outskirts of Old Town, and from here, it makes sense to walk, rather than to take the Metro or even a taxi, into Old Town. Have a staff person point you in the direction of Washington Street, east of the center; at

Washington Street, turn right (or south) and walk 2 blocks or so to the Lee-Fendall House (p. 293) at Oronoco and Washington streets.

902 Wythe St. (at N. Alfred St.). ✆ **703/838-4356.** http://oha.ci.Alexandria.va.us/bhrc. Free admission (donations accepted). Tues–Sat 10am–4pm. Metro: Braddock Rd. From the station, walk across the parking lot and bear right until you reach the corner of West and Wythe sts., where you'll proceed 5 blocks east along Wythe until you reach the center.

The Athenaeum This grand building, with its Greek Revival architectural style, stands out among the narrow old town houses on the cobblestone street. Built in 1851, the Athenaeum has been many things: the Bank of the Old Dominion, where Robert E. Lee kept his money prior to the Civil War; a commissary for the Union Army during the Civil War; a church; a triage center where wounded Union soldiers were treated; and a medicine warehouse. Now the hall serves as an art gallery and performance space for the Northern Virginia Fine Arts Association. Pop by to admire the Athenaeum's imposing exterior, including the four soaring Doric columns and its interior hall: 24-foot-high ceilings, enormous windows, and whatever contemporary art is on display. This won't take you more than 20 minutes, tops.

201 Prince St. (at South Lee St.). ✆ **703/548-0035.** www.nvfaa.org. Free admission (donations accepted). Wed–Fri 11am–3pm; Sat 1-3pm, Sun 1–4pm. Closed Nov–Feb.

Carlyle House Historic Park One of Virginia's most architecturally impressive 18th-century homes, Carlyle House also figured prominently in American history. In 1753, Scottish merchant John Carlyle completed the mansion for his bride, Sarah Fairfax of Belvoir, a daughter of one of Virginia's most prominent families. It was designed in the style of a Scottish/English manor house and lavishly furnished. Carlyle, a successful merchant, had the means to import the best furnishings and appointments available abroad for his new Alexandria home.

When it was built, Carlyle House was a waterfront property with its own wharf. A social and political center, the house was visited by the great men of the day, including George Washington. But its most important moment in history occurred in April 1755, when Maj. Gen. Edward Braddock, commander-in-chief of His Majesty's forces in North America, met with five Colonial governors here and asked them to tax colonists to finance a campaign against the French and Indians. Colonial legislatures refused to comply, one of the first instances of serious friction between America and Britain. Nevertheless, Braddock made Carlyle House his headquarters during the campaign, and Carlyle was less than impressed with him. He called the general "a man of weak understanding . . . very indolent . . . a slave to his passions, women and wine . . . as great an Epicure as could be in his eating, tho a brave man." Possibly these were the reasons his unfinanced campaign met with disaster. Braddock received, as Carlyle described it, "a most remarkable drubbing."

Tours are given on the hour and half-hour and take about 45 minutes; allow another 10 or 15 minutes if you plan to tour the tiered garden of brick walks and boxed parterres. Two of the original rooms, the large parlor and the adjacent study, have survived intact; the former, where Braddock met the governors, still retains its original fine woodwork, paneling, and pediments. The house is furnished in period pieces; however, only a few of Carlyle's possessions remain. In an upstairs room, an architecture exhibit depicts 18th-century construction methods with hand-hewn beams and hand-wrought nails.

121 N. Fairfax St. (between Cameron and King sts.). ✆ **703/549-2997.** www.carlylehouse.org. Admission $4 adults, $2 children 11–17, free for children under 11. Tues–Sat 10am–4pm, Sun noon–4pm.

Tips Planning Note

Many Alexandria attractions are closed on Monday.

Christ Church This sturdy redbrick Georgian-style church would be an important national landmark even if its two most distinguished members had not been Washington and Lee. It has been in continuous use since 1773, the town of Alexandria growing up around this building that was once known as the "Church in the Woods."

Over the years, the church has undergone many changes, adding the bell tower, church bell, galleries, and organ by the early 1800s, and the "wine-glass" pulpit in 1891. For the most part, the original structure remains, including the handblown glass in the windows.

Christ Church has had its historic moments. Washington and other early church members fomented revolution in the churchyard, and Robert E. Lee met here with Richmond representatives to discuss Lee's taking command of Virginia's military forces at the beginning of the Civil War. You can sit in the pew where George and Martha sat with her two Custis grandchildren or in the Lee family pew. You might also want to walk through the graveyard and note how old the tombstones are, including the oldest stone, dated March 20, 1791.

It's traditional for U.S. presidents to attend a service here on a Sunday close to Washington's birthday and sit in his pew. One of the most memorable of these visits took place shortly after Pearl Harbor, when Franklin Delano Roosevelt attended services with Winston Churchill on the World Day of Prayer for Peace, January 1, 1942.

Of course, you're invited to attend a service (Sun at 8, 9, and 11:15am and 5pm; Mon–Fri at 7:15am, with an additional Wed service at 12:05pm). There's no admission, but donations are appreciated. A guide gives brief lectures to visitors. A gift shop is open Tuesday through Saturday 10am to 4pm, and Sunday 8:45am to 1pm. Twenty minutes should do it here.

118 N. Washington St. (at Cameron St.). © **703/549-1450.** www.historicchristchurch.org. Donations appreciated. Mon–Sat 9am–4pm; Sun 2–4pm. Closed all federal holidays.

Fort Ward Museum & Historic Site *Kids* A short drive from Old Town is a 45-acre museum and park that transports you to Alexandria during the Civil War. The action here centers, as it did in the early 1860s, on an actual Union fort that Lincoln ordered erected. It was part of a system of Civil War forts called the "Defenses of Washington." About 90% of the fort's earthwork walls are preserved, and the Northwest Bastion has been restored with 6 mounted guns (originally there were 36). A model of 19th-century military engineering, the fort was never attacked by Confederate forces. Self-guided tours begin at the Fort Ward ceremonial gate.

Visitors can explore the fort and replicas of the ceremonial entrance gate and an officer's hut. There's a museum of Civil War artifacts on the premises where changing exhibits focus on subjects such as Union arms and equipment, medical care of the wounded, and local war history.

There are picnic areas with barbecue grills in the park surrounding the fort. Living-history presentations take place throughout the year. This is a good stop if you have young children, in which case you could spend an hour or two here (especially if you bring a picnic).

4301 W. Braddock Rd. (between Rte. 7 and N. Van Dorn St.). ✆ **703/838-4848.** www.fortward.org. Free admission (donations welcome). Park daily 9am–sunset. Museum Tues–Sat 9am–5pm (Nov–Mar 10am–5pm); Sun noon–5pm. Call for information regarding special holiday closings. From Old Town, follow King St. west, go right on Kenwood Ave., then left on West Braddock Rd.; continue for ¾ mile to the entrance on the right.

Friendship Firehouse Alexandria's first firefighting organization, the Friendship Fire Company, was established in 1774. In the early days, the company met in taverns and kept its firefighting equipment in a member's barn. Its present Italianate-style brick building dates from 1855; it was erected after an earlier building was, ironically, destroyed by fire. Local tradition holds that George Washington was involved with the firehouse as a founding member, active firefighter, and purchaser of its first fire engine, although research does not confirm these stories. The museum displays an 1851 fire engine, and old hoses, buckets, and other firefighting apparatus. This is a tiny place, which you can easily visit in 20 minutes.

107 S. Alfred St. (between King and Prince sts.). ✆ **703/838-3891.** http://oha.ci.Alexandria.va.us/friendship. Free admission. Fri–Sat 10am–4pm; Sun 1–4pm.

Gadsby's Tavern Museum ★ Alexandria was once at the crossroads of 18th-century America, and its social center was Gadsby's Tavern, which consisted of two buildings (one Georgian, one Federal) dating from around 1785 and 1792, respectively. Innkeeper John Gadsby combined them to create "a gentleman's tavern," which he operated from 1796 to 1808; it was considered one of the finest in the country. George Washington was a frequent dinner guest; he and Martha danced in the second-floor ballroom, and it was here that Washington celebrated his last birthday. The tavern also welcomed Thomas Jefferson, James Madison, and the Marquis de Lafayette (the French soldier and statesman who served in the American army under Washington during the Revolutionary War and remained close to Washington). It was the scene of lavish parties, theatrical performances, small circuses, government meetings, and concerts. Itinerant merchants used the tavern to display their wares, and traveling doctors and dentists treated a hapless clientele (these were rudimentary professions in the 18th century) on the premises.

The rooms have been restored to their 18th-century appearance. On the 30-minute tour, you'll get a good look at the Tap Room, a small dining room; the Assembly Room, the ballroom; typical bedrooms; and the underground icehouse, which was filled each winter from the icy river. Tours depart 15 minutes before and after the hour. Inquire about lantern tours, offered Friday nights from 7 to 10pm, admission $5, and about special living-history programs. Cap off the experience with a meal at the restored Colonial-style restaurant, **Gadsby's Tavern,** 138 N. Royal St., at Cameron St (✆ **703/548-1288;** www.gadsbystavernrestaurant.com).

134 N. Royal St. (at Cameron St.). ✆ **703/838-4242.** www.gadsbystavern.org. Admission $4 adults, $2 children 11–17, free for children under 11. Tours Apr–Oct Tues–Sat 10am–5pm, Sun–Mon 1–5pm; Nov–Mar Wed–Sat 11am–4pm, Sun 1–4pm. Closed most federal holidays.

Lee-Fendall House Museum This handsome Greek Revival–style house is a veritable Lee family museum of furniture, heirlooms, and documents. "Light Horse Harry" Lee never actually lived here, though he was a frequent visitor, as was his good friend George Washington. He did own the original lot but sold it to Philip Richard Fendall (himself a Lee on his mother's side), who built the house in 1785.

Thirty-seven Lees occupied the house over a period of 118 years (1785–1903), and it was in this house that Harry wrote Alexandria's farewell address to George Washington, delivered when he passed through town on his way to assume the presidency. (Harry also wrote and delivered, but not at this house, the famous funeral oration to Washington that contained the words "First in war, first in peace, and first in the hearts of his countrymen.") During the Civil War, the house was seized and used as a Union hospital.

Thirty-minute guided tours interpret the 1850s era of the home and provide insight into Victorian family life. You'll also see the Colonial garden with its magnolia and chestnut trees, roses, and boxwood-lined paths. Much of the interior woodwork and glass is original.

614 Oronoco St. (at Washington St.). ✆ **703/548-1789**. www.leefendallhouse.org. Admission $4 adults, $2 children 11–17, free for children under 11. Tues–Sat 10am–4pm; Sun 1–4pm. Call ahead to make sure the museum is open, since it often closes for special events. Tours on the hour 10am–3pm. Closed Thanksgiving and mid-Dec to Feb.

The Lyceum This Greek Revival building houses a museum depicting Alexandria's history from the 17th to the 20th century. It features changing exhibits and an ongoing series of lectures, concerts, and educational programs.

You can obtain maps and brochures about Virginia state attractions, especially Alexandria attractions. The knowledgeable staff will be happy to answer questions. But even without its many attractions, the brick and stucco Lyceum merits a visit. Built in 1839, it was designed in the Doric temple style to serve as a lecture, meeting, and concert hall. It was an important center of Alexandria's cultural life until the Civil War, when Union forces appropriated it for use as a hospital. After the war it became a private residence, and still later it was subdivided for office space. In 1969, however, the city council's use of eminent domain prevented the Lyceum from being demolished in favor of a parking lot. Allow about 20 minutes here.

201 S. Washington St. (off Prince St.). ✆ **703/838-4994**. www.alexandriahistory.org. Free admission. Mon–Sat 10am–5pm; Sun 1–5pm. Closed Jan 1, Thanksgiving, and Dec 25.

Old Presbyterian Meeting House Presbyterian congregations have worshiped in Virginia since the Rev. Alexander Whittaker converted Pocahontas in Jamestown in 1614. This brick church was built by Scottish pioneers in 1775. Although it wasn't George Washington's church, the Meeting House bell tolled continuously for 4 days after his death in December 1799, and memorial services were preached from the pulpit here by Presbyterian, Episcopal, and Methodist ministers. According to the Alexandria paper of the day, "The walking being bad to the Episcopal church the funeral sermon of George Washington will be preached at the Presbyterian Meeting House." Two months later, on Washington's birthday, Alexandria citizens marched from Market Square to the church to pay their respects.

Many famous Alexandrians are buried in the church graveyard, including John and Sarah Carlyle; Dr. James Craik (the surgeon who treated—some say killed—Washington, dressed Lafayette's wounds at Brandywine, and ministered to the dying Braddock at Monongahela); and William Hunter, Jr., founder of the St. Andrew's Society of Scottish descendants, to whom bagpipers pay homage on the first Saturday of December. It is also the site of a Tomb of an Unknown Revolutionary War Soldier. Dr. James Muir, minister between 1789 and 1820, lies beneath the sanctuary in his gown and bands.

The original Meeting House was gutted by a lightning fire in 1835, but parishioners restored it in the style of the day a few years later. The present bell, said to be recast from the metal of the old one, was hung in a newly constructed belfry in 1843, and a new organ was installed in 1849. The Meeting House closed its doors in 1889, and for 60 years it was virtually abandoned. But in 1949 it was reborn as a living Presbyterian

U.S.A. church, and today the Old Meeting House looks much as it did following its first restoration. The original parsonage, or manse, is still intact. There's no guided tour. Allow 20 minutes for touring.

321 S. Fairfax St. (between Duke and Wolfe sts.). ✆ **703/549-6670.** www.opmh.org. Free admission, Mon–Fri, 8:30am–4:30pm, but you must obtain a key from the office to tour the church. Sun services at 8:30 and 11am, except in summer, when a service is held at 10am.

Stabler-Leadbeater Apothecary Museum When its doors closed in 1933, this landmark drugstore was the second oldest in continuous operation in America. Run for five generations by the same Quaker family (beginning in 1792), the store counted Robert E. Lee (who purchased the paint for Arlington House here), George Mason, Henry Clay, John C. Calhoun, and George Washington among its famous patrons. Gothic Revival decorative elements and Victorian-style doors were added in the 1840s. Today the apothecary looks much as it did in Colonial times, its shelves lined with original handblown gold leaf–labeled bottles (actually the most valuable collection of antique medicinal bottles in the country), old scales stamped with the royal crown, patent medicines, and equipment for bloodletting. The clock on the rear wall, the porcelain-handled mahogany drawers, and two mortars and pestles all date from about 1790. Among the shop's documentary records is this 1802 order from Mount Vernon: "Mrs. Washington desires Mr. Stabler to send by the bearer a quart bottle of his best Castor Oil and the bill for it."

105–107 S. Fairfax St. (near King St.). ✆ **703/836-3713.** www.apothecarymuseum.org. Admission $4 adults, $2 children 11–17, free for children under 11. Apr–Oct Tues–Sat 10am–5pm, Sun–Mon 1–5pm; Nov–Mar Wed–Sat 11am–4pm, Sun 1–4pm. Closed major holidays.

Torpedo Factory This block-long, three-story building was built in 1918 as a torpedo shell-case factory but now accommodates some 165 professional artists and craftspeople who create and sell their own works on the premises. Here you can see artists at work in their studios: potters, painters, printmakers, photographers, sculptors, and jewelers, as well as those who create stained-glass windows and fiber art.

On permanent display are exhibits on Alexandria history provided by Alexandria Archaeology (✆ **703/838-4399;** www.alexandriaarchaeology.org), which is headquartered here and engages in extensive city research. A volunteer or staff member is on hand to answer questions. Art lovers could end up browsing for an hour or two.

105 N. Union St. (between King and Cameron sts. on the waterfront). ✆ **703/838-4565.** www.torpedofactory.org. Free admission. Daily 10am–5pm; archaeology exhibit area Tues–Fri 10am–3pm, Sat 10am–5pm, Sun 1–5pm. Closed Easter, July 4, Thanksgiving, Dec 25, and Jan 1.

ACCOMMODATIONS

With a total of 4,200 hotel guest rooms throughout Alexandria, the city should have no trouble accommodating you, should you decide to stay overnight here. Two properties lie especially close to the heart of historic Old Town. The **Hotel Monaco Alexandria,** at 480 King St. (✆ **800/KIMPTON;** www.kimptonhotels.com), is a former Holiday Inn, recently converted by the boutique hotel group, Kimpton Hotels, into a luxury property with 241 stylish rooms, a pool, health club, and chef-driven restaurant. The hotel was due to open in the fall of 2007. If the Monaco is not available, consider another Kimpton property and standout, **Morrison House,** 116 S. Alfred St. (✆ **800/367-0800** or 703/838-8000; www.morrisonhouse.com), with only 45 rooms, each appointed in high style with canopied four-poster beds, mahogany armoires, decorative fireplaces, and the like. Rates start at $150 for the smallest room off-season, and at $499 for a suite in season. Morrison House is known for its restaurant, **The Grille,** which presents award-winning contemporary American cuisine.

For other recommendations, check the **Alexandria Convention and Visitors Association** website, **www.funside.com**, where you can book an online reservation and also read about various promotions that hotels are offering.

DINING

There are so many fine restaurants in Alexandria that Washingtonians often drive over just to dine here.

EXPENSIVE

La Bergerie ★ CLASSIC FRENCH This old-school French restaurant has been here forever and is ever popular. Waiters are tuxedoed and entrees are updated traditional: escargots sprinkled with hazelnuts, smoky foie gras, lobster bisque with lobster and its coral, tournedos of beef with wild mushrooms and béarnaise sauce. La Bergerie is known for its dessert soufflés, which you must request when you order your entrees. You'll want to dress up here. And be sure to order an Irish coffee, which is prepared at your table with flourishes and drama—and it tastes great, too.

218 N. Lee St. ✆ **703/683-1007.** www.labergerie.com. Reservations required. Lunch prix-fixe menu only, $20; dinner main courses $22–$49. AE, DC, DISC, MC, V. Mon–Sat 11:30am–2:30pm; Mon–Thurs 5:30–9:30pm; Fri–Sat 5:30–10:30pm; Sun 5–9pm.

Restaurant Eve ★★ MODERN AMERICAN Named for the first child of owners Cathal (the chef) and Meshelle Armstrong, Eve has quickly become everybody's favorite restaurant. It's as hard to book a table here as at CityZen in the District. You choose between dining in the casual bistro and dining in the elegant tasting room, where a five-course menu ($95 per person) and a nine-course menu ($125 per person) are offered. Bistro entrees might include bouillabaisse and sirloin of veal. Tasting-menu items range from butter-poached lobster with heirloom carrots to gnocchi with spring garlic and golden beets. Available at the bar and on the five-course tasting menu is the best dessert: an old-fashioned "birthday cake," which is a mouthwatering slice of white cake layered and iced with pink frosting and sprinkles. Delicious. Really beautiful rooms. Excellent service. And be sure to read over the wine and cocktails list, since sommelier and "liquid savant" Todd Thrasher has gained such renown for his inventive concoctions—"Millions of Peaches" (peach vodka, champagne vinegar pickled peaches), "Jose's Yin and Tonic" (made with house-made tonic)—that he's opened a nearby speak-easy lounge, PX, located just above Eamonn's a Dublin Chipper (see below), where he dispenses more fun drinks and good times.

110 South Pitt St. (near King St.). ✆ **703/706-0450.** www.restauranteve.com. Reservations recommended. Bistro: Lunch items $16–$21; dinner main courses $27–$35. Tasting room fixed-price dinner $95, $125. Lunch menu served at the bar weekdays 11:30am–4pm for $14. AE, DC, MC, V. Bistro Mon–Fri 11:30am–2:30pm and Mon–Sat 5:30–10pm; Tasting Room Mon–Sat 5:30–9:30pm.

MODERATE

Indigo Landing AMERICAN/SOUTHERN Its location, at the marina just outside Old Town, overlooking the Potomac River, is such a winner, it's kind of amazing that other restaurants have never succeeded here. There's really no other place like it in Washington or Alexandria. Indigo has taken off because now you can enjoy an excellent meal as you take in the magnificent view. Chef Bryan Moscatello heads up the kitchen, sending out shrimp and grits, pecan-crusted pork loin, oyster pie, and pecan pie, revealing that he's spent time in Charleston restaurants. Washingtonians love it, and so do the critics: Indigo landed on the *Washingtonian* magazine's list of its top 100 area restaurants before it had celebrated its first birthday. And if you're riding your bike along the path that winds this way, stop in for a bite to catch your breath: There's an all-day menu, a kids' menu, a "low country oyster hour" weeknights 5 to 7pm. It would just be a shame to pass this one by.

1 Marina Dr. (off the George Washington Memorial Pkwy.). ✆ **703/548-0001.** www.indigolanding.com. Reservations recommended at dinner. Lunch main courses $8–$16; dinner main courses $14–$26; brunch $35. AE, DC, DISC, MC, V. Mon–Thurs 11:30am–10pm; Fri–Sat 11:30am–11:30pm; Sun 10am–3pm and 5–9pm.

Majestic Café ★ MODERN/SOUTHERN AMERICAN A lively bar fronts the narrow restaurant, making a dining experience here a little noisy, and that can be either annoying or festive, depending on your mood. I promise, though, that you'll enjoy the grilled calamari salad, soft-shell crabs, artichoke and fontina cheese tart, spoon bread, hush puppies, and, for dessert, German chocolate cake. The Majestic was slated to close in 2006, until that dynamic couple Meshelle and Cathal Armstrong, of Restaurant Eve, rode in to the rescue.

911 King St. (near Alfred St.). ✆ **703/837-9117.** www.majesticcafe.com. Reservations recommended. Lunch $8.50–$13; dinner $17–$25. AE, DC, DISC, MC, V. Sun 11am–3pm; Tues–Sat 11:30am–2:30pm; Sun and Tues–Sat 5:30–10:30pm.

INEXPENSIVE

Eamonn's A Dublin Chipper IRISH/SEAFOOD Fish and chips and a few sides—onion rings, coleslaw—that's what we're talking here. But it's charming. Upstairs is PX, an exclusive lounge, where mixologist Todd Thrasher may be on hand to shake the drinks he's created. This is another in the priceless strand of rare restaurant experiences that Cathal and Meshelle Armstrong are perpetrating on this side of the Potomac. The Chipper is named after their son, Eamonn; Restaurant Eve (above), for their firstborn daughter. The Armstrongs have a following, so expect a crowd.

728 King St. ✆ **703/299-8384.** www.eamonnsdublinchipper.com. Courses $3.50–$8. AE, DISC, MC, V. Sun–Thurs 11:30am–11pm; Fri–Sat 11:30am–1am.

La Madeleine *Kids* FRENCH CAFE It may be part of a self-service chain, but this place is charming nonetheless. Its French-country interior has a beamed ceiling, bare oak floors, a wood-burning stove, and maple hutches displaying crockery and pewter mugs. Also, the range of affordable menu items here makes this a good choice for families with finicky eaters in tow.

La Madeleine opens early—at 6:30am every day but Sunday, when it opens at 7am—so come for breakfast to feast on fresh-baked croissants, Danish, scones, muffins, and brioches, or a heartier bacon-and-eggs plate. Throughout the day, there are delicious salads (such as roasted vegetables and rigatoni), sandwiches (including a traditional croque-monsieur), and hot dishes ranging from quiche and pizza to rotisserie chicken with a Caesar salad. After 5pm, additional choices include pastas and specials such as beef tenders *en merlot* or herb-crusted pork tenderloin, both served with garlic mashed potatoes and green beans almondine. Conclude with a yummy fruit tart, or chocolate, vanilla, and praline triple-layer cheesecake with graham cracker crust. Wine and beer are served.

500 King St. (at S. Pitt St.). ✆ **703/739-2854.** www.lamadeleine.com. Reservations not accepted. Breakfast main courses $2.50–$7; lunch and dinner main courses $5–$13. AE, DISC, MC, V. Sun 7am–10pm; Mon–Thurs 6:30am–10:30pm; Fri–Sat 6:30am–11:30pm.

Index

See also Accommodations and Restaurant indexes, below.

General Index

Accommodations

Restaurants

FROMMER'S® COMPLETE TRAVEL GUIDES

Alaska
Amalfi Coast
American Southwest
Amsterdam
Argentina & Chile
Arizona
Atlanta
Australia
Austria
Bahamas
Barcelona
Beijing
Belgium, Holland & Luxembourg
Belize
Bermuda
Boston
Brazil
British Columbia & the Canadian Rockies
Brussels & Bruges
Budapest & the Best of Hungary
Buenos Aires
Calgary
California
Canada
Cancún, Cozumel & the Yucatán
Cape Cod, Nantucket & Martha's Vineyard
Caribbean
Caribbean Ports of Call
Carolinas & Georgia
Chicago
China
Colorado
Costa Rica
Croatia
Cuba
Denmark
Denver, Boulder & Colorado Springs
Edinburgh & Glasgow
England
Europe
Europe by Rail
Florence, Tuscany & Umbria
Florida
France
Germany
Greece
Greek Islands
Hawaii
Hong Kong
Honolulu, Waikiki & Oahu
India
Ireland
Israel
Italy
Jamaica
Japan
Kauai
Las Vegas
London
Los Angeles
Los Cabos & Baja
Madrid
Maine Coast
Maryland & Delaware
Maui
Mexico
Montana & Wyoming
Montréal & Québec City
Moscow & St. Petersburg
Munich & the Bavarian Alps
Nashville & Memphis
New England
Newfoundland & Labrador
New Mexico
New Orleans
New York City
New York State
New Zealand
Northern Italy
Norway
Nova Scotia, New Brunswick & Prince Edward Island
Oregon
Paris
Peru
Philadelphia & the Amish Country
Portugal
Prague & the Best of the Czech Republic
Provence & the Riviera
Puerto Rico
Rome
San Antonio & Austin
San Diego
San Francisco
Santa Fe, Taos & Albuquerque
Scandinavia
Scotland
Seattle
Seville, Granada & the Best of Andalusia
Shanghai
Sicily
Singapore & Malaysia
South Africa
South America
South Florida
South Pacific
Southeast Asia
Spain
Sweden
Switzerland
Tahiti & French Polynesia
Texas
Thailand
Tokyo
Toronto
Turkey
USA
Utah
Vancouver & Victoria
Vermont, New Hampshire & Maine
Vienna & the Danube Valley
Vietnam
Virgin Islands
Virginia
Walt Disney World® & Orlando
Washington, D.C.
Washington State

FROMMER'S® DAY BY DAY GUIDES

Amsterdam
Chicago
Florence & Tuscany
London
New York City
Paris
Rome
San Francisco
Venice

PAULINE FROMMER'S GUIDES! SEE MORE. SPEND LESS.

Hawaii
Italy
New York City

FROMMER'S® PORTABLE GUIDES

Acapulco, Ixtapa & Zihuatanejo
Amsterdam
Aruba
Australia's Great Barrier Reef
Bahamas
Big Island of Hawaii
Boston
California Wine Country
Cancún
Cayman Islands
Charleston
Chicago
Dominican Republic
Dublin
Florence
Las Vegas
Las Vegas for Non-Gamblers
London
Maui
Nantucket & Martha's Vineyard
New Orleans
New York City
Paris
Portland
Puerto Rico
Puerto Vallarta, Manzanillo & Guadalajara
Rio de Janeiro
San Diego
San Francisco
Savannah
St. Martin, Sint Maarten, Anguila & St. Bart's
Turks & Caicos
Vancouver
Venice
Virgin Islands
Washington, D.C.
Whistler

CLOSED
due to
accidental demolition
WEGEN BISSIGEN
EICHHÖRNCHEN GESCHLOSSEN
CERRADO
CABRAS
Κλειστό
Μετεωρίτες
POOL CLOSED
プールも
閉鎖中
ELECTRIC EELS
FERMÉ POUR
RAISON
DE GRÈVE
DES BONNES
Hotel
closed for
facelifting
FECHADO!
POR CAUSA DE
ATAQUES DOS CROCODILOS

I don't speak
sign language.